DATE DUE

MAR 12 1991 BIRD	MAR 1 1991	
NOV 27 1995	NOV 3 1995	
JAN 3		

Demco, Inc. 38-293

Applied Psychology

APPLIED

J. M. Brown

PROFESSOR OF PSYCHOLOGY
LAFAYETTE COLLEGE

F. K. Berrien

PROFESSOR OF PSYCHOLOGY
RUTGERS—THE STATE UNIVERSITY

D. L. Russell

ASSOCIATE PROFESSOR OF PSYCHOLOGY
OHIO UNIVERSITY

With the collaboration of

W. D. Wells

ASSOCIATE PROFESSOR OF PSYCHOLOGY
RUTGERS—THE STATE UNIVERSITY

PSYCHOLOGY

THE MACMILLAN COMPANY, New York
COLLIER-MACMILLAN LIMITED, London

Preface

IT IS THE PURPOSE of this book to examine man in contact with his milieu and to view the specific ways in which he impresses psychological fact and method on his world. Such a purpose is, of course, a clear reflection of the goal of the book which was seminal to the present survey of applied psychology, Dr. F. Kenneth Berrien's *Practical Psychology*, first published in 1944.

The life of modern man is increasingly influenced by the science of psychology. Information flowing from research in many areas of psychology is regularly adapted and used in gross and subtle ways to amplify contemporary life. In viewing these ways in this book particular attention has been given to experimental procedures and techniques (supported by relevant basic and applied research data) that have been turned by man to his practical advantage in major aspects of his environment.

Because the applications of psychology are so pervasive, we have followed our inclinations and concentrated on selected areas that seem to us to be of first importance. In the discussion of psychology applied to adjustment there have been omitted, by design, details of clinical and abnormal procedures that are thoroughly covered in other sources. The discussion of psychology applied to industry offers a relatively rapid but comprehensive survey of man's relationship to special facets of industrial situations. The role of the psychologist in opinion, advertising, and market research is emphasized in viewing the applications of psychology to consumer problems and political issues. A departure from the usual is the inclusion of important new material that considers the application of psychology to international relations and its use in the negotiation process. Finally we have addressed some of the major problems of crime and the applications of psychology toward the solution of these problems.

Throughout this presentation, it is assumed that the reader has not had the benefit of the standard introductory survey of contemporary psychology.

v

Later chapters are a continuation and extension of earlier chapters. A fairly comprehensive central reference system has been used, culminating in a consolidated list at the end of the textbook. For further study, suggested references are located at the end of each chapter.

As the direct descendant of Berrien's *Practical Psychology*, this book is an attempt to reflect the flavor of applied psychology while rooting its discussions in research findings and techniques. Coverage is broad and somewhat eclectic, but this is the nature of the field. The first stirrings of applied psychology were heard not long after modern experimental psychology emerged from Wundt's laboratory, for in 1908 Walter Dill Scott completed the book *The Psychology of Advertising*. Soon after its publication, he was appointed professor of applied psychology at the Carnegie Institute of Technology. However, Hugo Münsterberg, a professor at Harvard University, has often been called the first applied psychologist. In 1913, his book *Psychology and Industrial Efficiency* was published. Four years later, the first periodical for the dissemination of information concerning applications of psychology (particularly to the business and industrial world) began publication as the *Journal of Applied Psychology*. By 1920, applied psychology was the subject of a small number of college courses and several new books. Topics usually stressed were industrial selection and efficiency, advertising, and psychology and the law. Two decades later the province of applied psychology had burgeoned to the point where Dr. Berrien, in writing *Practical Psychology*, had difficulty in providing adequate coverage without slighting many significant findings and conceptual approaches.

The senior author has taken general responsibility for the entire book and wrote Chapters 1, 6, 7, 8, 9, 10, 11, 15, and 16. Dr. Berrien rewrote Chapter 5, and prepared Chapters 13 and 14, which are entirely new. Dr. Russell contributed Chapters 2, 3, and 4 and Dr. Wells provided Chapter 12. Those familiar with Dr. Berrien's earlier books will find in this one something old, something borrowed, and much that is new.

Many others have helped in the task of preparing this textbook, and there is genuine gratitude to all these individuals. Other expressions of gratitude of special warmth are extended to Mrs. Winifred Brown, Mr. Thomas Skyler, and Mr. Jon Martinsen. Many valuable criticisms of the manuscript were received enroute to its completion, but of particular utility were the views of Dr. Kinsley R. Smith, who read the entire manuscript, and Dr. Philip Ash, Dr. Jack Gibb, and Dr. Bernard P. Indik, who each read various chapters.

J. M. B.
F. K. B.
D. L. R.

Contents

PART TWO

Psychology Applied to Industry

PART THREE
Psychology Applied to Consumers
and Political Issues   407

PART FOUR

Psychology Applied To Crime

PART ONE

PSYCHOLOGY APPLIED

TO ADJUSTMENT

E ACH HUMAN ORGANISM exists in a complex world in which he must continually adjust his behavior. The continuing activity of each person—that is, his behavior—is the result of characteristics within him as well as the multitude of stimulations he has received and is receiving from his environment. How adjustments of each person may be brought about is discussed in the first five chapters of this book.

Behavior can be modified or changed. In Chapter 1 we discuss how behavior can be modified by the processes called learning. We examine general principles and discuss specific applications and techniques for increasing efficiency in learning, particularly in school situations.

In Chapters 2, 3, and 4 mental health is discussed. The importance of mental illness and mental retardation in American society is shown in Chapter 2. There is also an introduction to the concept of several critical stages in the development of mental illness. In Chapter 3 the stages in the development of personality as well as how mental illness develops during the life span from prenatal through adulthood is discussed. By the end of Chapter 3 we have seen how mental illness may be avoided through the life stages or developed during the same periods. We also examine the various types of prevention and treatment facilities usually available in the United States.

Chapter 4 concentrates on treatment and rehabilitation of mentally disturbed people. It is explained that progressive failures in early developmental stages may result in poor functioning or adjustment of an individual. Such a mentally ill person can often be helped by various kinds of therapy so that he may better get along in his society.

1

Techniques for helping a person return to his society and normal functioning make up the topic of rehabilitation.

The special adjustments of people in later life are discussed in Chapter 5. This chapter continues the discussion of the developmental sequence in the forming of personality and behavior begun in Chapters 1, 2, and 3. The processes of aging, the ordinary adjustments made, and the special programs or efforts needed to help individuals in later life are discussed.

Chapter 1
Experience Changes
Behavior

WHEN DRIVING AN AUTOMOBILE, we cruise through a green traffic light confident that opposing traffic will stop for the red light. We expect and generally find little or no noise among theatergoers while the show is in progress. We know that most students arrive for class just before or at the time the bell rings. We therefore recognize and accept the fact that human behavior is *predictable*.

When we come to a crosswalk with a pedestrian traffic light control, we press a button, the light turns red for the automobile traffic, and the drivers obediently halt. Sometimes we stand before a group of talking students and raise our hand or verbally ask for quiet, and the noise subsides. We not only can *predict* but also *control* behavior.

Yet there are exceptions, even for the examples just cited. Some drivers do not stop at red traffic lights, some theatergoers talk during the show, and some students arrive late for class. Even so, there is lawfulness in the differences in behavior as well as in the similarities.

Psychology, as the science of behavior, studies both the background and the prediction and control of behavior. This book discusses general principles or techniques involved in control and prediction of behavior. Although these principles may not seem to work in all cases, an understanding of the basic principles will enhance the possibility of a better understanding of the predicting and controlling of behavior.

Scientists and philosophers have discussed learning throughout the history of mankind. Even so, there is not complete unanimity over a definition of learning. For the purposes of this book, *learning* refers to the modification of behavior due to experience. This definition suggests that changes in behavior are used as estimates of learning. Changes due to the unfolding of inherited characteristics with the passage of time and changes resulting from fatigue, receptor changes, or effector changes[1] are *not* to be considered learning.

Theorists explain how learning takes place according to their own interpretations of experimental evidence. It is not within the scope of this book to explain each of these different views. However, the following sections highlight a group of general principles. These principles are generally compatible with those of such leading learning theorists as W. K. Estes, E. R. Guthrie, D. O. Hebb, O. H. Mowrer, B. F. Skinner, K. W. Spence, and E. C. Tolman. In the final portion of this chapter, several sections are devoted to efficiency in learning.

GENERAL PRINCIPLES OF LEARNING

Before we can discuss adequately how learning takes place, we must be familiar with human behavior in general. We have already suggested that human behavior can be studied with some precision and ultimately predicted and controlled. Behavior is instigated and controlled by stimulation from the external and internal environment of the individual.

Each of us lives in an environment which constantly bombards him with stimulation. From the external environment, physical energy, such as light, heat, and sound, falls upon the entire organism. Internally, movements of joints, contractions of muscles, and so on, produce stimulation. Certain receptors in the organism are adapted to receive and be activated by different kinds and strengths of energy. When such receptors are activated, neural stimulation is propagated through the nervous system of the organism. When the organism is aware of such stimulation or responds to it, we say that the stimulation has been *perceived*. Thus a person is receiving neural stimulation routed from various receptors at all times. He is aware of, or responds to, only some of this stimulation. The *perceived stimulus situation* is that portion of the neural stimulation from receptors of which the organism is aware or responds. As an example, consider a person watching a movie. At a particular moment sound, light, heat, and other physical energies are affecting him. He is probably aware only of the light and sound stimulation from the area of the movie screen. Thus the perceived stimulus situation consists of a photographic image and some sound. The heat of the room, the lighted exit signs, the sounds of movement of people in the back of the theater, and many other stimulations are not noticed by the

---

[1] *Receptors* are specialized organs that receive stimulation and set up signals in the nervous system. *Effectors* are muscles and glands that respond to stimulation from the nervous system to produce behavior.

person. Even though these additional stimulations impinge upon appropriate receptors, they are not part of the perceived stimulus situation.

We must take care to make this discrimination between stimulus situation (all of the stimuli impinging upon receptors) and perceived stimulus situation (stimuli the person is aware of or responds to). The perceived stimulus situation is crucial to our understanding of how learning takes place. The general principles we will discuss are reinforcement, shaping, generalization and discrimination, schedules of reinforcement, and motivation.

When a change of behavior occurs, there is a change in the probability of a response occurring after a given stimulus. Thus any change in behavior due to experience is called learning and may be considered in terms of change in the probability of a response occurring. We are going to discuss learning as any change in the probability that a response will occur. This means that an increased probability of a response occurrence is to be termed learning, *and* a decreased probability of a response occurrence is also to be termed learning.

In everyday usage, we are often interested in controlling for increase *or* decrease in probability of response occurrence. We will use a special term for each of these modifications of behavior. The term *acquisition* will refer to changes of behavior where there is an increased probability of a response occurring. The term *extinction* will refer to changes of behavior where there is a decreased probability of a response occurring. To restate the terms briefly:

Learning is any change (increase or decrease) in the probability of response occurrence.
Acquisition is increase in the probability of response occurrence.
Extinction is decrease in the probability of response occurrence.

This terminology is slightly different from that used by some learning theorists and considerably different from general usage. Here we call increased probability of response *acquisition*. Some people use the term *learning* to refer to such increased probability of response occurrence (even after they have defined learning as *any* change in probability of response). We emphasize the use of *learning* to refer to *any* change in probability of response occurrence.

Learning usually takes place each time a response[2] occurs. If the *perceived* stimulus situation changes a sufficient amount *immediately after a response occurs*, acquisition takes place. If there is no change in the *per-*

---

[2] Response is any muscular, neural, or glandular process or activity following stimulation.

ceived stimulus situation or the change is too little or too great, extinction takes place. If the *perceived* stimulus situation changes just the right amount, there will be no change in the probability of response occurrence.

We must remember that it is change in the *perceived* stimulus situation that is of importance to learning. The stimulus situation (all of the stimuli impinging upon receptors) will change from one instant to another and certainly before and after a response. However, the *perceived* stimulus situation may remain constant for an organism before and after a response. Or vice versa; the *perceived* stimulus may change while the stimulus situation remains constant.

In review, we now know that if a sufficient amount of change in the perceived stimulus situation (any particular amount within a rather broad range) is provided for an organism just after a response occurs, acquisition of that response takes place. Just what the sufficient amount of change should be is open to investigation. At this time there is no set rule as to how much change of any particular stimulus must take place in order to have acquisition. However, if *less* than a certain amount of change in the perceived stimulus situation follows a response, extinction of that response takes place. If *more* than a certain amount of change follows a response, extinction also takes place.

An example here will help us to understand how varying amounts of change in the perceived stimulus situation may produce acquisition or extinction. Let us suppose an organism is placed in a situation where a light source can be applied at controlled levels of intensity. Just after the organism makes a response, light is turned on at a very low intensity. The level of intensity may be so low as to be barely perceived or not perceived by the organism. Thus extinction of the response would take place. (The response would be less likely to occur again in the same situation.) If, just after a response occurs, a light of very strong intensity is turned on, the organism might perceive it as a severe change in the stimulus situation, and extinction of the response would take place. If, after a response occurs, a light of proper intensity is turned on, the organism could perceive the change in stimulus situation, and acquisition of the response would take place. (The response would be more likely to occur again in the same situation.)

Reinforcement.   Many theorists believe that reinforcement is important to learning. They generally apply the term *reinforcement* to a stimulus which, if it follows a response, increases the probability of that response occurring again when the same stimulus situation reoccurs. Thus *reinforcement* refers to any change in the perceived stimulus situation within the limits necessary to result in acquisition (a light of proper intensity, in the previous example). The term *aversive stimulus* is often used for a stimulus that produces a decrease in the probability of a response occurrence. Too much change in the perceived stimulus situation is an aversive stimulus and is followed by extinction (a light of very strong intensity, in the previous example). Too little change in the perceived stimulus situation (a light of very low intensity, in the previous example) is also followed by extinction but is usually not labeled by a specific term. The relation of change in the perceived stimulus situation to commonly used terms and to resulting behavioral modifications is shown in Table 1.1.

TABLE 1.1 Relations of Change in Perceived Stimulus Situation to Commonly Used Terms and Resulting Modifications of Behavior

Change in Perceived Stimulus Situation	Very little	Sufficient amount	Too much
Commonly Used Terminology	Lack of reinforcement	Reinforcement	Aversive stimulus
Behavior Modifications	Decreased probability of response (Extinction)	Increased probability of response (Acquisition)	Decreased probability of response (Extinction)

Table 1.1 shows that zero or small changes in the perceived stimulus situation immediately following a response are commonly referred to as lack of reinforcement and result in a decreased probability of the response occurring (extinction). Severe changes are commonly referred to as aversive stimuli and result in a decreased probability of response (extinction). A wide range of sufficient change in stimulation immediately following a response is commonly called reinforcement and results in an increased probability of the response occurring (acquisition).

As an example of the importance of reinforcement in learning we present a hypothetical case history. A hungry dog is in a room with his master. Light, sounds, and other stimuli make up the stimulus situation. (The dog is aware only of some of these stimuli at any one time—his perceived stimulus situation.) If the dog raises his forepaw and his master immediately gives him food, the stimulus situation has been changed. (Since the dog was hungry, we assume he was aware of the food presented, so that his perceived stimulus situation changed.) If the response (raising forepaw) is followed by reinforcement (sufficient amount of change in stimulation), the probability of the dog's raising his forepaw when the initial preresponse situation is presented again is increased (acquisition). Thus the dog has learned to raise his forepaw.

The stimuli in the original stimulus situation become *controlling stimuli*. If, after several reinforced trials, the original stimulus situation is presented again, the dog will give the same response. Each time a sufficient amount of change in stimulation follows a response, there is an increased probability of that response occurring again on future trials (acquisition).

What if the master does nothing after the dog raises his paw? The perceived stimulus situation just after the response will be almost the same as before the response. The dog will have a lower probability of making the response the next time the original stimulus situation is presented (extinction). It is also possible that the master does very little after the response, but that the dog perceives a change in the stimulus situation. This change in the perceived stimulus situation may be just the right amount to hold constant or even increase the probability of a response occurring. However, such a happening is not too common, so that we can usually expect extinction if little or no change in the stimulus situation follows a response.

To recapitulate, when a response is followed by a sufficient amount of change in the perceived stimulus situation, the probability of that response occurring in the future when the preresponse conditions are presented again is generally increased. This is called acquisition. When a response is followed by a small amount of (or no) change in the perceived stimulus situation, the probability of the response occurring when preresponse conditions are presented again is generally decreased. This is called extinction.

Shaping Behavior.   Once an organism gives a response, the response may be followed by reinforcement. Often, however, the organism does not emit a desired response. Consequently, the organism must be trained to give a desired response by *shaping*.

If a desired response is not emitted by an organism, successive *approximations* of the desired responses may be followed by reinforcement. Such a process is called shaping.

When a particular response is desired, reinforcement should be given after each response that approximates or is a step toward the desired response. Thus the approximate response will tend to occur more frequently. Each time a closer approximation to the desired response is followed by reinforcement, that response will tend to be repeated in the future. As closer and closer approximations are followed by reinforcement and less desired responses are not followed by reinforcement, the less desired responses are extinguished. Finally the desired response will be emitted and can be followed by reinforcement. The desired response will thus be acquired.

As an example, we cite a trainer who wishes to teach his dog to sit with forepaws in the air. Unfortunately, the dog does not emit this response. Thus, the trainer cannot provide reinforcement immediately after the dog sits. Instead, the trainer must shape the desired behavior by providing reinforcement whenever approximations of the desired behavior occur. If the dog stops in front of him, the trainer provides reinforcement; thus the dog will tend to stop in front of his master more often than before. When any movement toward sitting up occurs, the trainer provides reinforcement but does not provide reinforcement when such behavior does not occur. The nonreinforced behavior decreases in frequency of occurrence (extinction) and the approximate desired response becomes more frequent (acquisition). After successive approximations are reinforced, the desired response is eventually given and the trainer provides reinforcement. The desired behavior tends to reoccur when similar preresponse stimuli are presented and all other responses have lessened probabilities of occurrence. The dog has learned to respond to a specific stimulus situation with a specific response.

An organism can be trained to give a desired response even if such a response has never occurred. We also know that the organism responds to a specific stimulus situation. This situation is composed of controlling stimuli. If the dog just mentioned learned to sit in a particular room when commanded to do so by his master, the stimuli controlling this behavior consisted of all those factors in the external and internal environment of the dog that entered his brain via the nervous system. Thus a complete set of stimuli (stimulus situation) was available when the response was given and reinforced. If the same stimulus situation is available to the dog again, he can be expected to give the learned (acquired) response. But sometimes the preresponse stimulus situation is varied. Suppose, for example, that the trainer was with his dog in a different room and still wanted the dog to sit up.

Fortunately, a response acquired in one situation will tend to reoccur in similar situations. The response *generalizes* from one set of controlling stimuli to another.

Generalization and Discrimination. Generalization means that a learned response is given in the presence of a set of stimuli similar to, but not identical with, that present at the time of learning. A person may learn in one situation and *transfer* the learning to a variety of similar situations—he *generalizes*.

To expand the concept of generalization and bring in another term, *discrimination*, we return to the example of the trainer and dog. The dog learned this behavior while hungry and under many other internal stimulus conditions (fatigue, thirst, and so on) as well as in an external environment consisting of verbal commands from his trainer and other stimuli (temperature, light, sounds, and so on). Suppose the trainer and his dog are in a new room with different external stimuli and some changes in internal stimuli (dog has become fatigued or thirstier). If, when the command "sit" is given, enough similar stimuli are available as controlling stimuli, the dog sits up. If he is provided reinforcement, he will continue to sit up on future commands by his trainer. Thus the similar, but different controlling stimuli have been followed by the learned response. The more similar the stimuli, the greater the probability of occurrence of the learned response.

If the trainer desired to teach the dog to discriminate between somewhat similar but different stimulus situations, he could have done so by providing reinforcement in one situation and not in the other. Suppose the trainer desired to have the dog sit up when commanded to sit but only if there were some other control stimulus in the situation. For example, when the trainer commanded "sit" and raised his hand, he wanted the dog to sit up. If the dog were given reinforcement immediately after sitting up when the verbal command and hand signal were given, the dog would learn to sit up for these signals. If not reinforced after sitting up when just the verbal command were given, the dog would extinguish the sitting up response (or learn not to sit up) to just the verbal command. Thus, the dog would discriminate between two rather similar sets of stimuli.

In addition to the effects upon learning previously discussed, we must also consider the persistence of changes in behavior. Reinforcement is important not only in bringing about changes but also in the maintenance of such changes. The relation between responses and schedules of reinforcement is important and is discussed in the next section.

Schedules of Reinforcement.   Reinforcement may be given after every desired response, after every other response, or at variable times. Schedules of reinforcement have been investigated and reported in detail by Skinner, his associates (Ferster and Skinner, 1957), and others interested in understanding learning. The reported work generally described reinforcement schedules as fixed or variable intervals or fixed or variable ratios. When reinforcement is given after each response, it is called *continuous*; when given on an interval or ratio schedule, it is called *intermittent*. Ratio refers to the number of responses between reinforcements. A fixed ratio schedule means that a reinforcement follows each time a certain number of responses are given. A variable ratio schedule means that reinforcement follows after varying numbers of responses. Thus a fixed ratio schedule might call for reinforcement after the third, sixth, ninth, twelfth, fifteenth, and so on, response, whereas a variable ratio schedule may call for reinforcement after the first, third, fifteenth, seventeenth, thirty-second, and so on, response. Interval refers to the time between reinforcements. Interval schedules have the time between reinforcements either fixed or variable regardless of the number of responses occurring.

Broadly speaking, the quickness or facility with which acquisition takes place is dependent upon reinforcement, and therefore it is advantageous to get the largest number of reinforced responses as rapidly as possible. However, we are not concerned only with acquiring new material. How the learned behavior will persist is also of importance.

Although continuous reinforcement brings about the most rapid learning, it is also followed by the most rapid extinction when reinforcement is withheld. Many learned responses will persist for a long period of time without additional reinforcement if they have been learned under intermittent reinforcement schedules. In general, the longer the time or the greater the number of responses between reinforcement during learning trials, the longer the time or the greater the number of responses that will occur when reinforcement is withheld. Thus, an organism given 100 reinforcements will continue to respond without reinforcement longer if he received the original reinforcements spread over 500 responses than if he had received all of the reinforcements consecutively (100 responses).

When learning for longer retention, an intermittent reinforcement schedule is better than a continuous schedule. However, training using only intermittent reinforcement is almost impossible. Early in the training the desired responses may not be reinforced often enough to be repeated. The desired response, when not often repeated, may be extinguished if it is given and not followed by reinforcement. Consider a training situation where a fixed ratio schedule of reinforcement after every fifth trial is to be attempted. If the organism is reinforced after first giving the desired response, the probability of repeating the response is increased. But, extinction will take place if the next four emissions are not followed by reinforcement. Waiting for the response to occur so that the next reinforcement may be given becomes impractical. Thus, training usually begins with continuous reinforcement schedules and progresses through greater and greater ratio or interval schedules. In such a way, schedules as high as one reinforcement per 1,000 responses have proven useful. Once a response is learned using such a schedule it persists through many nonreinforced trials.

So far we have discussed the relation between behavior change and *perceived* stimulus situation change. It is obvious that the amount of stimulus variability in the environment is not always directly reflected in an organism's nervous system. At times, small environment changes will be perceived by a person, and at other times the same variations in the environment will make little or no impression upon the nervous system. For example, the presence of relatively small amounts of food in the environment may be noticed by a dog that has not had food for 24 hours, but may be completely ignored by a dog that is satiated[3] with food.

Motivation.   Motivation has to do with a subjective shifting of the value of stimuli to an organism. *Motivation* is an internal condition of an organism that influences its responses to stimuli. If an animal is deprived of food, introducing a moderate amount of food into the stimulus situation, just after a response, might provide a sufficient change in the perceived stimulus situation to result in acquisition of the response. If the animal is satiated with food and the same amount of food is introduced into the stimulus situation just after a response, only a small change in perceived stimulus situation would occur and extinction of the response should be expected. The amount of perceived change produced by a variation in stimulus situation depends on the motivational condition of the organism.

Reinforcement effects from changes in the environmental stimulus situation of an organism take place only when the changes are perceived. How much of a change in the environmental stimulus situation is perceived by an organism is dependent upon its motivational state. The more highly motivated organism will notice more change when an environmental stimulus situation varies than will a poorly motivated organism.

Now that we have discussed a few general principles of learning, it is appropriate to show how these principles, plus other techniques, may be put to use. Very little knowledge of how to study is gained, and only few attempts at being efficient are made by most students. Most often the techniques used in study were developed accidentally early in school life and have simply been carried on throughout life. For example, it is well known that students vary greatly in the time spent studying. One study at the University of Minnesota (Weinland, 1930) showed that some students studied 10 hours per week and others with equal loads studied 50 hours.

The following sections will discuss how to put forth efforts in an effi-

---

[3] Satiated describes the condition of an organism when it is completely gratified concerning a need or desire (for example, food).

cient manner. Often, people with average ability surpass performance of superior or gifted people simply by using their capacity more efficiently. The material below is not to serve as short cuts to transitory success but rather to show how to gain the greatest returns from the time and effort expended.

INCREASING EFFICIENCY IN LEARNING

Getting the most done for the least amount of time and energy is one way of explaining efficiency. In terms of study efficiency, this means learning the greatest amount of material so that it will be useful in the future, and doing so in the least amount of time. The expenditure of energy studying is frequently measured only in the time used with an assumption that the same amount of energy is expended per unit of time. This assumption will generally hold in the following discussions, but occasionally mention of total energy expended will be made.

Much of this material is based on the general principles of learning explained earlier. We will use these principles in our discussions. Study efficiency will be covered under six major topics—reinforcement, distributed versus undistributed practice, whole versus part learning, getting action in learning, physical factors, and study skills.

Increasing Probability of Reinforcements. Basing acquisition on reinforcement of responses naturally means that opportunities for the occurrence of responses followed by reinforcement must occur. In fact, learning will generally be more efficient if many such occurrences are brought about during the study sessions. Fortunately, the human organism derives reinforcement from the completion of a task itself, giving a response, verbal or written communications from others and a huge array of other possible stimuli changes. It is, therefore, not at all impossible to arrange a learning situation where reinforcements are very likely to occur after responses are given.

A learning situation with immediately available reinforcements for correct responses has been used at one time or another by most students. Learning a foreign language often involves memorizing vocabulary lists. Many students have endeavored to do such memorizing by using a double list with the foreign language, such as French in one column and the English in the next. The student reads the French and tries to think what the proper English translation is, and then immediately checks himself by seeing the English. If he is correct he receives reinforcement (the knowledge of having given the correct response) and if not, he does not get reinforcement. In the former case, acquisition takes place, whereas extinction occurs in the latter. The student thus uses reinforcement to memorize correct translations for a list of foreign words.

Many students have gone beyond the technique just described and have devised a very simple "machine" to help themselves learn. A sheet of paper or a card is held over the translation so that the student must give a response before he can check whether his response is correct or not. This use of a file card or sheet of paper provides some of the same conditions as do teaching machines or autoinstructional devices. Since this relatively new field of learning is receiving so much publicity and may be of great importance in the future, it will be discussed in some detail.

AUTOINSTRUCTIONAL DEVICES. *Teaching machines, programed learning, self-tutoring, automated training* are some of the terms used to describe self-instruction devices. The history of such devices is relatively short and can be found in many publications (Lysaught and Williams, 1963; Galanter, 1959; Lumsdaine and Glaser, 1960; Smith and Moore, 1962). Kopstein and Shillenstad (1962) have described the scientist's view of autoinstruction as ". . . nothing but an application of the principles governing the interaction between the teaching presentation and the learning individual. It is, however, a minutely systematic application of the scientific principles of learning; and the application itself is guided by the general principles of engineering-design logic. It strives to select the optimal values for those parameters of the learning situation that facilitate learning and favor later proficient performance in a criterion (application) situation."

As might well be assumed, autoinstructional devices are dependent upon programs or material prepared for them. In general, the type of information taught most efficiently in autoinstructional devices is that which is relatively simple or must be memorized. There have been attempts to devise programs for more difficult, integrative material and logic, but these are mostly experimental. Programing may be roughly divided into two classes: linear and branching. These terms apply to the sequencing of the subject matter and the possibilities of reinforcement.

The linear approach involves breaking down the subject matter into small segments of information which are presented to the student in sequence. Each small piece of information is given to the student with a question in what is typically called a "frame." After each "frame" the student gives a response, and if the response is correct the student is reinforced. The reinforcement is often just the knowledge of having given the correct response, although some machines also use signal lights as reinforcement. After pretesting with appropriate subjects, programs can be prepared where the number of errors for the average student is very low and reinforcements maximized. The program may be presented in any one of a variety of different machines or pieces of apparatus.

Most of the work in linear programing follows Skinner's (1954) principles and extensions of his and Pressey's (1926) earlier work. Figure 1.1 shows a typical machine for use with a linear program.

Figure 1.1. The Koncept-O-Graph, Kog-7 teaching machine. A program of material is presented in the larger window with a blank roll of paper in the smaller window. After reading the question the learner writes his answer on the paper tape, turns the knob which moves his answer under the glass in the smaller window and also moves the program in the larger window exposing the proper answer. Thus the learner can check his answer immediately. (Photograph courtesy of Graflex, Inc., Rochester, N.Y.)

The machine shown in Figure 1.1 provides an opening or window for presentation of the information and question as well as a separate place for recording an answer. More elaborate machines may provide for multiple choice answers by use of gadgetry and will possibly have a light or other stimulus to give a signal (reinforcement) when a correct response is given.

Linear programs may also be prepared in printed or book form with a statement and question on one page and correct answer on the next page or presented in some other manner. Using a programed book, the student asks himself the question and either records or thinks of the answer and then checks the answer given in the book. If he is correct he is reinforced for his response and then goes to the next frame.

Several programed books are available, and more are entering the market. Figure 1.2 shows an early entry in the field—Holland and Skinner, *The Analysis of Behavior*—that teaches the learning principles generally used in linear programing.

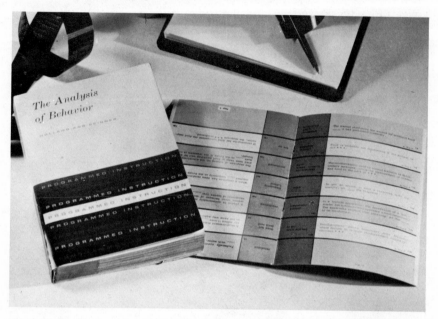

Figure 1.2. Photograph of book *The Analysis of Behavior* showing the cover and page 11 of the text. Each frame of material is printed on a page with an answer to the frame from the preceding page. A learner reads a frame, thinks of the answer or records it, turns the page and checks himself, and then goes on to the next frame. (Photograph courtesy of McGraw-Hill Book Company, Inc., New York, N.Y.)

Branching programs have been emphasized by Crowder (1959) and his associates. Essentially starting from work in trouble-shooting electrical circuits, Crowder developed a technique of teaching by presenting relatively small segments of information to students and then asking them multiple-choice questions about the material. When the student makes his choice of alternative the machine indicates that his choice was correct (reinforcement) and refers him to more information or that he chose an incorrect response and why it is wrong. The program thus branches from the original information. Usually after the incorrect response is given, the student is led back to review the original information and make another choice of alternative. The program may also have other branching devices—that is, a side track from the regular sequence may be followed when a certain alternative is chosen even if it is not a wrong choice.

Several machines have been developed to accommodate branching programs, and more new ones are being designed. As with linear programs, branching programs may also be in book form. Several such books are already on the market and others are being added. Instead of the machine's indicating a correct or incorrect choice of alternative, the student turns to an indicated page for whatever alternative he chooses. The written material on the new page either indicates the choice was correct (reinforcement) and provides new information and another question or indicates the choice was an error, explains why, and routes the student back to the original information for review and another choice.

In addition to the two major autoinstructional techniques just described, there are always other new and exciting experiments in progress. Several reports have indicated that electronic computers may be tied to teaching machines in such a manner that a student may skip material he knows and can have more selective drill on his weak areas or integrate more material in his learning. There are also investigators working on visual presentations through regular moving picture films and slide films with and without audio stimulation. Others are working on straight audio stimulation. In short, fascinating new aids to education are developing. Much information formerly presented in classrooms or traditional books may be more efficiently given to students in the future in programed fashion. Thus teachers may be allowed to concentrate more efforts on materials that cannot be handled by autoinstructional devices.

Distributed Versus Undistributed Practice. A general conclusion concerning studying an assignment all at one sitting or dividing the study time into a number of shorter sessions is that distributed practice is more efficient than massed practice. Many studies under a large variety of conditions support this general finding, but of course there are exceptions.

As early as 1885 one investigator (Ebbinghaus, 1885) reported that it was more efficient to space learning over a period of three days than to mass the practice into one sitting. Since that report numerous investigators have substantiated the value of distributed practice, including most of the more recent studies, such as those reported by Underwood (1961). However, the more recent investigations have thrown additional light on when distributed practice is of value and when it does not serve better than massed practice.

Underwood, working with the acquisition of verbal lists, showed that "distributed practice will enhance learning only when interference occurs in the response-learning phase." This means that some words in the list, previous word lists, or previous learning must cause some interference in the learning of new material before distributed practice will be any better than massed practice. Put another way, a word in the new list or something previously learned must interfere with, make more difficult, or cause more errors in the learning of the new material. Underwood also showed that a certain minimum amount of such interference must occur before distributed practice is better than massed practice and that with too much interference massed practice would be better. Thus there must be a minimum but not over a certain amount of interference for distributed practice to be better than massed.

The length of the interval between practice sessions is also important. The effect of distributed practice is contingent upon an interaction of interference in the response-learning and the time between practice sessions. Although the actual minimum and maximum levels within which interference must be for distributed practice to be effective are not known, Underwood suggested that if interference is high and the time between practice sessions is too long, distributed practice will not facilitate learning. Thus, if interference is high, the interval between practice sessions should be short.

In the practical situation this means that we must make some gross judgments of the amount of interference we can expect while learning new material. If, for example, we have a poem to memorize and it is a fair length and rather similar to one learned before, we might expect a good deal of interference. Thus, we should space the distributed practice sessions fairly close together. On the other hand, if we have to memorize material that is completely different from anything we've had before, and of moderate difficulty, we may expect only moderate interference and should space learning sessions relatively far apart. If we have to memorize new material that apparently has no relation with previous learning and is in segments that will not interfere with each other, massed practice would probably be better.

Several other variables are worthy of consideration, including the length of the material to be learned, meaningfulness of the material, and the rate of going over the material to be learned; but experimental evidence at this time does not establish definite rules. The best hypotheses to be made from available experimental studies seem to be that distributed practice is more valuable for (1) long rather than short lists of material to be learned (maybe because more interference comes in), (2) material of low rather than high meaningfulness, and (3) material presented to the learner rapidly rather than slowly.

There also seem to be a few conditions when massed practice must be considered preferable to distributed practice. Several studies summarized by Erickson (1942) have shown that more variability in responses comes from massed practice, whereas more stilted or fixed responses come from distributed practice. Some connected material simply cannot be broken down into parts (see "Whole Versus Part Learning"), and thus a massed practice session becomes a necessity. Many tasks also require a warm-up or adjustment period. When considerable time or effort is involved in such an activity it naturally means that the time is not available for learning; thus massed practice may be more valuable. Of course, massed practice is essential if the periods between practice must be extremely long, because so much loss of retention may take place that learned material may never accumulate.

Now, how can these general findings be applied to specific assignments? Suppose a list of English vocabulary words and French equivalents must be memorized. Assume that several of the French words have somewhat similar spellings or sounds, exact French words must be associated with the English words, the list of words is relatively long, and the learner has control over the time he uses and the speed at which he works. Distributed practice would probably be of considerably more value than massed practice. The list should be studied by looking at the English word and saying and thinking the French word or writing it on a separate sheet. Immediately after giving the response (French word) the answer should be checked (to maximize the effect of reinforcement). The study session should be a relatively short period of time. If one hour is budgeted as the entire time for the study of French vocabulary, the time should be broken into several short periods or at least two half-hour sessions. Some other activity—studying another subject, a coffee break, sports, or going to dinner —should be engaged in between sessions of studying French vocabulary. The same procedures can be followed advantageously for all material to be memorized, such as chemical formulas, dates, short-hand notations, and even motor skills, like shooting a basketball, playing golf, and so on.

It is also important to recognize the value of distributing practice or study even on difficult nonmemorizing types of problems. Many people have found that reviewing all of the information about a problem, thinking about it for a short time, and then letting things rest for a period of time is more efficient than trying to complete solutions to problems immediately after reviewing the available information. It is known that information stored in the brain is not all lost while not being consciously used. Sometimes information gets "worked over" so that problems may be solved more easily after a day's rest or even after a short coffee break.

Whole Versus Part Learning.   When confronted with a set of instructions or a list of words or dates to memorize, is it better to learn just the beginning, then small segments, until all is learned or to go through the entire material at once? It is apparent that material can be learned as one whole unit, as a series of individual parts, or in some major segments of the whole.

As with studies concerning distributed versus massed practice, there has been a common agreement from 1900 through recent reports (McGuigan, 1960) that in general the larger the practice unit, the better the performance. Although there has been such general agreement in favor of the whole method, there are many other considerations.

Most people who have memorized a set of instructions or a part for a play know that it somehow seems more interesting and more logical or easier to memorize the first few lines or phrases, then the next, and so on. This problem of "ease" in learning must be given cognizance since motivation (see section on motivation) is extremely important in efficient learning. Even if it is ultimately more efficient to learn a poem by the whole method, there may be many trials, particularly at the beginning, when there is little sense of accomplishment. Thus, motivation may be lowered while few reinforcements occur and any positive effects of the whole method may be destroyed.

There seems to be relatively little published information concerning studies about the amount of material that can be best handled by the whole method. The available evidence was summarized by Hovland (1951) and reduced to the following statement: "In a practical situation, factors like fatigue, interest, etc., may play an important part in the relative advantage of whole or part learning. But, if these are held reasonably constant, the best advice seems to be to learn by using the largest units that are meaningful and within the individual's capacity." This is an extension and is in general agreement with Cook (1937), who indicated that when the size of unit to be learned was smaller than the maximum of an individual's capacity, whole learning is best, but when the length of the material is greater than an individual can handle with maximum efficiency, it should be broken into parts for learning.

Using the available information concerning whole versus part learning, how can a person decide which approach to use in memorizing a set of instructions? Should he try the whole method? Will he have motivation to keep at it through the early trials, which will have little if any reinforcement? Is his span of ability greater than the length of the list of instructions? Obviously the answers to these questions can come only from earlier experiences. The solution, if the person has not been using the whole method, is to start with something he is sure he can handle. Reasonably conclusive evidence has shown that the whole method is better for more intelligent learners; or put another way, the higher the intelligence and the greater the experience, the longer the whole may be and still be learned efficiently.

If a person feels that the material at hand is too long to try the whole method, he should consider using the progressive part method. He should pick the length he can easily handle and learn that part, then learn a second segment, as long as the first, and put the two together. After gaining control of the two sections joined as one, he should work on the third part. When part three is well learned, it is added to the first two, and thus one unit is formed from all three parts. By continuing such a procedure through the material but remaining cognizant of the amount he can handle, the learner will memorize the entire list. He should also remember that with experience, capacity increases, so that on the next occasion a longer part or maybe an entire assignment can be handled at once.

Learner Must Be Actively Engaged. To be really efficient in studying, the learner must be "in" the learning task. True, something can be learned merely watching someone else. It is fairly well established that watching or passive studying does slowly change behavior of the observer. However, there is evidence that shows the active person is the one who gets the most from the learning situation. (Perhaps what has usually been called passivity in a learning situation is really only a very small amount of activity. No learning at all can take place if there isn't at least some activity since there must be sufficient reinforcement after a response for acquisition to take place.)

There are many things that can be done to enlarge the activity or to get the learner more deeply engaged in the learning situation. Some of the major considerations are: attitudes and motives, and techniques for getting action in learning.

ATTITUDES AND MOTIVES. To be truly efficient in a learning situation the learner must approach the task with a feeling that he is going to succeed in accomplishing a goal that he has set for himself. He must fully understand in his own thinking what the learning of a particular task means to him. Unless a person can answer for himself the question "What do I expect to learn and how will this contribute to my goal?" learning efficiency will be considerably lower than it should be. In terms of our previous discussion concerning principles of learning, the learner must try to bring about a subjective shift to enhance the reinforcement value of changes in the stimulus situation. This means that a student increases motivation by increasing his awareness of changes in the stimulus situation just after giving a response. (A further discussion of motives may be found in Chapter 2.) Thus the changes in stimulus situation result in enough reinforcement to bring about acquisition of the response. The following paragraphs concern techniques useful to many people in increasing motivation for studying.

Setting Subgoals. The goals a person sets for himself are frequently far in the distance. For example, the typical college student dreams of the day when he will complete his Bachelor's degree and go out into the world. Perhaps the only goal that he has been thinking of is a far distant B.S. or B.A. degree. It would be wise for this student to consider what it takes to accomplish this long-range goal. A series of subgoals or steps on the way to the final achievement will provide a more realistic incentive when he comes to the question of whether to study or to go to the movies.

Finding Interest Areas. It is profitable to look through the material at hand with an eye for finding areas of interest. Especially in liberal arts colleges, the curriculum is not specifically designed to give vocational training, and often students feel that there is little specific applied knowledge to be gained from any particular course. On the other hand, looking deeper than just the superficial subject matter at hand may uncover some additional values. One case history demonstrates this. John visited his advisor about the middle of a college semester with the complaint that he simply couldn't learn French. Although John had the ultimate goal of a Bachelor's degree firmly in mind and had recognized one of his own subgoals as passing this particular language, he simply couldn't get involved in French adequately enough to learn even the minimum amount necessary to pass the course. After several discussions it was apparent that John was looking at French like many other students do, only as a subject that must be memorized in order to fill a requirement for graduation. John was encouraged to discuss his problems concerning the language with some of his fellow students who, although not particularly interested in French for its own sake, did realize some positive value in the subject. One of John's buddies had become very interested in some early work in psychological testing done by Binet. John was also interested in psychological testing and had done some research on his own in one of his courses, but he had never thought seriously of trying to read material that wasn't available in the regular articles and books. His motivation to learn French was increased considerably when some interesting material published in French, but not in English, was made available to him. John became engaged actively in learning the subject matter and eventually passed the course.

Developing Questioning Attitude. Another way to increase motivation in the subject matter at hand is to develop a generally questioning attitude. People should question the thoughts behind the writer's or speaker's statements. Why does an author state a certain point? What evidence or reason does he have for his statements? Can the items previously presented fit with the new information? A general questioning attitude helps a person pay more attention to the material and thus increases study efficiency.

A real interest and an attitude of wanting to learn the material is essential for efficient study.

TECHNIQUES FOR GETTING ACTION IN LEARNING. As was previously pointed out, it is possible to learn a little with almost complete passivity. However, more active learners learn more per unit of study time. Assuming that efficiency is desired, everything possible to increase the amount of learning accomplished in a given amount of time should be tried.

PARTICIPATING IN CLASS. In a classroom situation, participation is a method of being active. In sessions where there are relatively few students and an interaction can take place with the instructor, students should actively engage in such interaction. This does not mean that students should dream up questions in order to impress the teacher. It does mean that they should think of questions about the material being presented, and if they are not clear about the appropriateness of their own answers, they should question the instructor. By actively participating in this manner, students engage in a review and at the same time have a much better chance of learning, following the principles previously discussed.

At times students find themselves in large lecture sections where it is impossible to communicate with the instructor. At such times, it is wise to consider the topics as they are presented by questioning what each point means. Many students list their own questions in the notes as they take them. If the notes are not completely clear, it is wise to speak to the lecturer after the close of the session. If this is impossible, the student should seek the answers at a later date by discussions or checking the references himself.

Sensible note taking during lectures increases activity of the learner. Material should not be written verbatim as presented by the lecturer. Except in rare instances where the instructor is going to ask for verbatim material on an examination (he should notify students if this is his procedure), students will profit from recording the material in their own words. However, the thoughts must be recorded correctly and not confused with the ideas of the recorder.

BEING ACTIVE OUTSIDE CLASS. There are many tricks or techniques that have been used by students. Some are very valuable, others are of questionable value, and some actually detract from the learning. Some students claim to study best by stretching out on the floor in front of the television set and overcoming the picture and sound from the receiver by working harder on the subject matter at hand. This is certainly not a procedure recommended for most students, but it does force us to recognize an important factor. When we concentrate hard enough to overcome other stimulations from our environment, we will increase the amount of energy put into the studying situation. In so doing we get more studying done per unit of time. However, the total amount of energy put into the studying may have increased even though the amount of time has decreased. Thus, there is some question whether efficiency increases, because such an expenditure of energy is used to overcome extraneous stimuli. To repeat, an environment with a great deal of background noise and action is not particularly conducive to study, but some background noise may result in increasing the amount of energy or activity expended by the learner. This seems to activate the nervous system, so that learning is more efficient. If the background stimulation is of a general nature, or noise rather than specific stimulation, it is frequently easier to overcome, yet also has the advantage of forcing the learner to raise his concentration level on the subject matter at hand.

Now, what other techniques will help increase efficiency of studying alone? As has been repeatedly mentioned, allowance must be made for frequent reinforcement. This means that the situation must be such that the learner can frequently obtain something from the material he is studying that will provide reinforcement. An important technique that enhances such possibilities is called *self-recitation*.

SELF-RECITATION. We practice self-recitation when we ask ourselves what a paragraph was about just after having read it. We may use more elaborate self-testing procedures. For example, many students write out questions about the subject matter, underline key words or phrases, or make marginal notes in the book they are reading. Self-recitation, then, consists of thinking out the answers to the questions or recalling the subject matter emphasized by the underlines or marginal notes. Other students simply try to think what the instructor would like them to know and then ask themselves whether they know it or not. When any of these techniques are used, and the student finds that he doesn't know the material, he should go back to the source and reread or investigate further.

Another self-recitation technique consists of putting the subject matter on cards; three-by-five file cards are useful, especially for subject matter that can be put in brief form (for example, learning another language). On one side of the card the question or English word is written, and on the reverse side of the card the answer or the word in the other language is given. (Such study cards are also available commercially.) The student studies by looking at the question side of the card, thinking out the answer, and repeating it to himself. He can turn over the card and immediately see whether he had the correct answer or not. If he did have the correct answer, the reinforcement enhances acquisition. If he gives an incorrect response he receives little or no reinforcement, and the incorrect response would tend to have less probability of reoccurrence (extinction).

Although self-recitation techniques are advantageous, they must also be used with understanding. Self-recitation techniques are similar to auto-instructional techniques (discussed in an earlier section of this chapter). Too much use of a question-card technique or any other self-recitation may lead to memorization of a particular summary sentence or statement. Thus learning may take place without understanding. The proper way to use self-recitation techniques involves trying to answer the questions in a different fashion each time they are reviewed. It is also wise to consider several alternative questions so that a broader understanding will be obtained, which will aid in transferring the material to another situation at a later date.

Physical Factors.   Consider for a moment the surroundings where learning is to take place. If the desk is to be used for studying, is it relatively uncluttered, or is there a good deal of extraneous material on top? Many students find that the top of their desk includes two or three textbooks, perhaps some from past semester's work that are no longer used, a miscellaneous assortment of pencils, a ball-point pen or two, perhaps a dictionary, some scraps of paper, maybe a larger supply of paper that has just been opened, a photograph or two (a theater stub tucked down in the corner of the photograph), a note from the girl friend of the moment, last night's sports page telling about the chances of success in the coming athletic events of their particular school, and a magazine or novel, along with a few scattered notes concerning the subject matter at hand. Of course, this is a rather strong statement about the average sudent's work space, but it should be considered in comparison to a more efficient atmosphere.

For efficient study the desk does not have to be fancy, but the top should be cleared of all materials except those that will enhance the efficiency of studying. It should be arranged in an orderly manner, with textbooks and reference books neatly stacked, perhaps between bookends or against the wall, a small box or tray containing pencils, erasers and pens, and another box containing paper clips and other supplies necessary for academic activity. Current magazines, novels, letters from home or girl friends, photographs, old papers, trinkets, and so on, should be stored in other places. Perhaps the drawers of the desk could hold an additional supply of paper and equipment necessary for efficient studying and even some of the "junk" that cluttered the previously mentioned desk.

It is no doubt obvious that the latter desk is a more efficient work area. As few distractions as possible are provided for the student. The former work space provided many stimuli to catch the eye of the student when he is trying to study. For example, he may glance over some of the papers on his desk and note a letter from his girl. He can very easily rationalize that just a couple of minutes may be used to review the letter, and he remembers she said something about being able to attend a forthcoming party weekend. It is all too easy for the student to spend a few minutes thinking about the upcoming weekend, a few minutes jotting down notes concerning events to attend, a few minutes more dreaming about how much it is going to cost, and where he might get the money. Soon the entire study period is lost in dreaming about other activities. The basic principle is this: make it easy to do the things that should be done. Conversely, arrange the situation so that it is difficult to come in contact with objects that lead away from the main purpose of the moment. As previously stated, study habits that are well entrenched may be more suitable for a particular student than some of the more efficient techniques being suggested. It is entirely possible that one student may concentrate better with a cluttered desk than he would if the desk top were cleared, simply because the cleared top of the desk would become a distraction to him because it was so different. But, in general, concentration will improve as any stimuli which tend to make it easier to digress from studying are eliminated. If a student has been studying with a rather cluttered work situation for a long time, he cannot expect immediate improvement by changing the work situation. A period of adjustment extending over some days or weeks may be necessary before efficiency is increased, but better efficiency can be expected eventually.

Another point concerning the work area is frequently overlooked by students—the placement of the desk or chair used for studying. Not only should all distractions be eliminated from the immediate work area, but the location of the desk should be such that extraneous stimuli will have the least possible effect upon study efficiency. This means that placing the desk against the wall where the visual stimuli is relatively homogeneous to a person seated at the desk is better than placing it in front of a window where stimuli from outside may attract attention. Placing the desk against the wall also has the advantage of forcing the student not to look out the door to see people going by, or for that matter, to have people going by see him and say a word or two. In short, everything possible should be done to provide efficient materials for studying with a minimum amount of distraction.

Three other major characteristics concerning the physical situation are discussed in the following sections. They are lighting, noise, and place habits. (Additional information about working efficiency in various light and noise conditions is covered in Chapter 8.)

LIGHTING.   Probably the most efficient lighting is that provided by sunlight. Naturally, people do a good deal of studying when sunlight is not available. Thus artificial lighting must be considered. The best illumination for reading and other study activities is light that floods the entire working area in sufficient intensity to be comfortable but is well diffused and does not produce marked contrast. Some of the reasons for this statement are given below.

Light-dark contrasts attract the eye. Study lamps that provide a good deal of illumination in one area but leave dark shadows along the edge of the illumination create areas that tend to attract the eyes. When trying to read or do other work while using such illumination, the reader's eyes will tend to be attracted to the contrast area. The eyes will try to make momentary shifts from the work at hand to that contrasting area and back again. In fact, even if there is no actual shifting of the eyes, the competing stimuli of the illuminated and the dark areas set up antagonistic muscle tensions and provide a more rapid fatiguing of the eyes. Lighting should be comfortable and adequate in intensity and fairly well diffused.

How can diffused lighting be provided? It is not the purpose of this book to discuss illumination engineering, but it is wise to consider the kind of lighting that should be available. An opaque shade usually increases the amount of the dark-light contrast. Thus, there is a very dark area away from the work space, and not only is there the fatigue from contrast effect previously mentioned, but there is also the difficulty of readjusting to the light or dark area whenever the eyes are forced to look from one area to another. The pupil of the eye dilates in response to a decrease and contracts to an increase in intensity of light. When part of the visual field is bright and an adjacent section is much darker, contradictory or antagonistic muscular reactions are initiated when the eyes are forced to adjust to the varying light intensities and the eyes become tired more rapidly than they should. This may become obvious when working under such conditions if a pencil is dropped under the desk. Either another source of light has to be used or a period of time has to pass while the eyes adapt to the lower illumination before the pencil can be found. If a lamp with an opaque shade must be used, a ceiling light or other source should supplement the lamp so that diffused light will be available in the surrounding area.

NOISE.   Occasionally, students have decided to beat the problem of noise in the dormitory, fraternity, or other study area by going to bed fairly early and setting the alarm for three or four o'clock in the morning. They have been especially surprised when they found how quiet it really was at that hour of the day. In fact, they were so surprised that they were not as efficient as they had hoped to be.

Previously in this chapter the effect of background noise in forcing the learner to concentrate harder was discussed. In general, it is better to have relative quiet rather than a great deal of competing stimuli. On the other hand, the student who awoke at three o'clock in the morning to study found that he was unable to study under such quiet conditions. A certain minimum amount of background noise forces neural activity on the part of the learner, and apparently increases the efficiency of the learning situation. In a quiet area, such as the dormitory room at three o'clock on a weekday morning, the student's neural activity will be very low, and at the same time small sounds from movements in other parts of the building or even far-distant sounds are magnified in relationship to the general background noise. They thus have more attention-getting value, and the student may find that they detract from his study efficiency as much or more than the general background noise found in most study situations during the regular workday.

PLACE HABITS.   Some students routinely study in the library of their college or university. Other students find it very difficult to study in the same situation. When careful observations are made, it is evident that the students who routinely study in a library situation very rapidly get down to the actual studying. Such students have created a study-place habit. Such a strong association between a physical environment and a particular activity has been developed that efficiency has increased. Little time is lost in getting down to work; the preliminaries are reduced to a minimum, and therefore amount of studying done per unit of time is increased.

When considering the development of a work area, consideration should be given to getting the most efficient surroundings and then associating work with that particular location. For example, most students have some sort of desk or table at which to work. If the arrangement of this area is satisfactory and the lighting and noise conditions are within sensible limits, it would be wise to reserve this area just for study. Studying should not be done at the location used for reading the sports page or comics. If an easy chair is available, it might be wise to devote that to the reading of novels and relaxation activities. The more efficient work area should be devoted to study activity, and the activity–place association should be consciously developed. Many of the characteristics previously discussed about reinforcement come into play in this manner. Studying done in an efficient work situation with no other activity allowed in that situation results in reinforcement of this behavior, because more will be done per unit of time, and the student will receive a sense of accomplishment or reinforcement. Thus the more often a student studies in one place, the greater the acquisition of the activity-place association becomes. Then the student finds it easier and faster to start studying in the place set aside for studying.

Study Skills. This section includes a discussion of techniques or skills that increase efficiency for the typical academic activities engaged in by students and many workers in the world at large. They are considered under the titles "Reading Speed," "Note Taking," "Test Taking," and "Budgeting Time."

READING SPEED. A good deal of the studying involved in higher education and much of the work in the business world requires reading. Many people find that they must read hundreds of pages of material in relatively short periods of time. But how fast do people read? Each person should know how fast he reads and should constantly aim to improve.

It is relatively easy to estimate reading speed. All that is needed is a watch or a clock with a second hand, some reading material, and a little time. It is easier to test reading speed on material that involves relatively few pictures or blank spaces on a page, but reading speed is generally faster for light material or novels than for textbook material. On the other hand, most students are interested in how fast they read for average school activity, so they might well test themselves on material such as this book. The average page of this book contains approximately 500 words. Any one page may be checked by averaging the number of words on a few lines chosen at random and then counting the total number of lines and multiplying to find the number of words on the page. A person working in the business world should check himself on the average type of material he must routinely read. To measure his reading speed, a person should start reading new material when the second hand of his watch passes a certain point. He should read through one page of material as rapidly as possible. At the end of the page a check of the watch provides the information necessary to find total time to read one page. Dividing the total time into the number of words read, results in words read per minute, or reading speed. Reading speed is often not as fast as we think it should be.

Articles in popular magazines sometimes indicate that super high-speed reading may be attained after specialized training in certain schools or special programs. Some stories report people reading 1,000, 1,500, or even 3,000 words per minute. The average college student is far below these levels. On the other hand, a person reading less than 200 words per minute of textbook material, or 400 to 500 words per minute of light material, should seriously consider expending genuine effort on increasing reading speed. Several commercial tests for measurement of reading speeds are available and might be used if a student wants to compare himself against other people of similar age and education. Norms on the adult form of one such test (Nelson–Denny, 1960) show that a reading speed of 240 words per minute might be expected for the above-average college senior on the material used in the test. (The material is storylike but includes infrequently used words.) A distribution of reading speed on this test is shown as Figure 6.10 in this book.

In addition to speed, consideration must also be given to the amount of material that can be remembered or used. Thus comprehension is also of importance. On standardized reading tests, comprehension as well as reading speed is measured. A student can do the same thing for the material read in any reading test by checking himself to see how much of the material is known following the principles previously discussed under self-recitation. Immediately after reading the material, at least 90 percent should be recallable.

Now, what other things must be considered in changing reading speed? First of all, slow readers often find that they are actually trying to read aloud. This should be eliminated from silent reading. A student interested in checking himself can do so by feeling his vocal chord or lips while reading. If there is movement there at the time of reading, the student may be trying to actually talk to himself and is thus slowing himself considerably. Ordinary speech is delivered at the rate of about 100 to 125 words per minute and thus limits reading speed if lip movements must be formed for each word read. Reading should be so rapid that there isn't time to move the lips. Deliberately attempting to read faster will often force the reader to stop moving his lips, and thus aid more rapid reading.

Another important aspect in reading is to read the main ideas of the material rather than all the small words or illustrations. The main idea may be part of a sentence or it may be in several sentences. However, there are always adjectives, adverbs, and examples that may fill pages or paragraphs that are not necessary to remember in the future, but serve only to help make it easier to remember important facts or main topics.

The more familiar the vocabulary, the more rapid the reading. In fact, vocabulary growth is closely related to increased reading speed. A person willing to take the time to learn vocabulary that is unfamiliar will find that the speed with which he reads material including the new vocabulary will be tremendously improved.

Reading speed can be improved through self-training. Although there are schools and special training programs designed to increase reading speed, most people may do a great deal to help themselves. Self-discipline and practice are necessary even if special courses are attended. If a person desires to read faster, he can practice in a determined manner and increase his speed.

At first it is wise to choose easy, storybook material, especially in relatively short selections. With increasing speed and confidence, longer selections and more difficult material may be included. By following these steps a person can conduct his own speed reading training:

1. Pick an article that looks interesting and check reading speed.
2. Keep records of reading speed for each practice day.
3. Practice each day, reading at least one selection specifically for speed-reading training.
4. Every time any material is read, think about reading more rapidly.

Most studies show that comprehension increases with reading speed, so that the reader generally can expect to improve comprehension as he speeds his reading. He must also recognize that he may have several practice sessions without improvements in reading speed, but over a number of sessions, he can expect to increase his reading speed.

Finally, a word must be said about the movements of the eye during reading. Perhaps this particular phase of reading speed is overly emphasized or has received too much publicity. However, some of the time in reading involves eye pauses (fixations), and some of the time is used for eye movement. The more pauses made, and the longer each pause, the more time it is going to take to read a given amount of material.

Human eyes cannot read material when they are moving in relation to the material. During movement the eye simply gets a blur much the same as observing the ground as it is going by a car window. In order to see an object, it must stop in relation to the eye. In terms of reading a page, this means that the eye looks at one spot, then moves along the line to another, to another, and so on, down to the next line of material and through the entire passage. The more rapidly the eye can move over these passages, the more rapid is reading. Also, if the eyes do not have to return or regress to earlier material, a great deal of reading time is saved. Thus, each item should be read as it is first seen, as rapidly as possible, but not so rapidly that regressive movements must be made because the reader is not sure what was stated in an earlier phrase.

The best single way to decrease the number of fixations is to enlarge vocabulary, because words that are familiar are much more rapidly seen and understood than words which are unfamiliar. A large vocabulary allows a person to make fewer stops or pauses and reduces regressive movements and thus increases reading speed.

NOTE TAKING.   As with other suggestions for increasing efficiency, organization is a key to efficient note taking. Notes may be taken from lecture or classroom material presented by the instructor or from written material, such as textbooks. Of course, it is difficult or impossible to organize properly if the remarks of an instructor or a textbook are not organized. However, most instructors are generally organized in their presentations and if the listeners will concentrate adequately, they will end up with good notes.

A loose-leaf notebook has great advantages for organized note taking because various sections of the book can be separated for use in individual subjects and additional sheets of paper may be inserted or irrelevant material deleted by simply adding or taking out a page. Students who take one kind of pad or paper to class one day and another pad on a different day and then try to recopy the material into a well-organized, neat notebook may find they are doing themselves a disservice. Studies indicate that the amount of time and effort involved in rewriting notes can generally be put to far better use in self-recitation if the notes are adequately taken in the first place. The important point is to do an efficient job of taking notes originally.

Notes are not an end in themselves but merely a help to better understanding subject matter. Thus it is advantageous to take notes of the high points that the instructor presents, including the organization that he has used in his notes. Students should record as many of the major topics as possible in their own words, not just copied verbatim from the speech or the notes that the instructor has placed on the blackboard. In so doing, they force themselves to think about the material and to learn it better as they take notes. Many good students find they need to spend only a minimum amount of time studying such notes for examinations because they remember what they recorded at the time of the note taking. This is because they have listened attentively and converted the instructor's comments into their own words while maintaining the important organization and subject matter.

Little tricks or techniques are frequently helpful for organizing notes around the subject matter prepared by the instructor. For example, skilled instructors frequently say, "In contrast, the evidence against this point of view is . . . ," or "Four factors of importance will be discussed. Number one is . . ." The attentive note taker is on the alert for such phrases and uses them as headings and subheadings in his own notes. Also, changes in quality of voice, long pauses, or a shift in posture, or certain phrases such as "Now we will look at another topic" or "Good" are often used to separate major topics. Students should be aware of such comments when attending lectures.

Whether notes should be kept in outline or paragraph form depends pretty much on the lecture and the individual note taker. If the student is able to understand the major points and fill in the minor points from the major headings alone, an outline rather than paragraph form is useful. One study done some years ago (Barton, 1930) indicated that superior students used outline notes more frequently than students who achieved relatively low grades. A student who takes well-organized outlines during classroom work is not as easily diverted from what is being said and is prepared for a quicker review of the material. Of course, the efficient learner must be active, taking notes, and asking questions if the classroom situation permits.

Note taking from textbooks can be done in much the same fashion as for classroom presentations, and it is generally easier to follow the outline of a book. Most textbooks are written from an outline, so that students may very easily follow the major headings and subheadings. Many students find it advantageous to underline or underline and make marginal notes rather than recopy the outline of the book on another sheet of paper.

It must be remembered that note taking is of value because it forces active participation in the learning process. If the student writes in his own words what is going on in the classroom or what he has just read in a textbook, he cannot really fool himself about knowing it. He must figure out what is meant and therefore be actively engaged in the learning process. Of course, this also makes it considerably easier to review or study for any future test.

TEST TAKING. Many authorities disagree in the wisdom of discussing how to take tests; however, it seems only fair that all students should know the same rules or explanations that may make it easier to obtain better test scores. First of all, the student must be prepared for the test by learning the material, according to all the principles previously mentioned.

Now, what of the examinations themselves? In general, there are two types: (1) objective, requiring relatively little writing, perhaps just a check mark, a true-false indication, picking a correct alternative from several multiple choices, or recognizing one of many alternatives, and (2) subjective or essay exams, involving relatively short questions and a good deal of writing and recalling rather than recognizing information. Many students ask how to study for each of these types of examinations.

In general, higher scores may be achieved on one type of exam or the other by special review and study techniques for that particular type. However, a really adequately prepared student should be competent to handle an essay or objective examination equally well. What frequently happens is that students knowing they are going to take objective examinations feel that the test will be easier because they are required to only "guess" or select a correct answer, and consequently they spend less effort in studying. The purposes of examinations are to test knowledge of main ideas and important details and to assign a grade for such knowledge. Assuming the instructors preparing the examinations are doing a conscientious job, both types will measure approximately the same information. It is admittedly more difficult to prepare a good objective examination, and therefore objective exams may sometimes cover material that does not seem to be important and major points of a course may be missed. On the other hand, an essay question often covers only one or two major points that the instructor felt important, whereas others that the students felt were equally important are omitted.

To repeat, the two general forms of a test are (1) objective tests, which usually have complete coverage of a large variety of information, and (2) subjective tests, which emphasize integration and depth of material with considerably less variety of information. If a student does not know which type of exam he is going to have, it is probably advantageous to study for the objective examination. He should learn as much detail as possible while also trying to spend a few additional study periods organizing these details into meaningful packages or overall concepts.

Assuming knowledge of the subject matter, a few general suggestions for taking objective examinations may improve test scores. First, the student should know the rules for taking objective exams. Instructions must be read carefully and followed. Answers must be shown in the way that the instructor has indicated and scoring rules understood. In a true–false test, for example, scoring may be just the number correct, which in general means it is better to guess at items not known than to leave them blank. On the other hand, scoring may be according to a formula taking off one point for each wrong answer and giving one point for each correct answer.

In this case, it doesn't make much difference whether the student guesses at the items he does not know or leaves them blank. Assuming a 50–50 chance of getting correct a particular item not known at all, the same number of items should be guessed correct as incorrect and thus will balance out in the scoring procedure. However, a student seeing material that is even slightly familiar should mark his choice of the correct answer. Even though not sure, his chances are better than 50–50 of getting a true–false item correct if the material seems the least bit familiar.

Now, going through the test itself, what should be done after reading the instructions and understanding the scoring procedure? Remembering again that a large amount of material will be covered in an objective examination, it is wise to start at the beginning of the test and go right through the test answering each item in sequence, but not pausing for a long time worrying about an item that cannot be answered. Items that seem impossible should be skipped and some method used to indicate that they should be reconsidered if there is time later. In so doing, the student can maximize his possibilities for the greatest score according to the knowledge that he has. After completing the entire test in this manner, the student should go back to the items where he felt he needed to spend more time and again try to answer them. Taking the test may help the student remember material that could not be recalled and thus to answer previous "impossible" questions. Thus, the student will do better than if he had insisted on completing each item as he came to it.

There are techniques described in many sources showing how to estimate correct alternatives on multiple-choice questions by the wording or phrasing used and how to tell when an item will be true or false simply by the words used rather than the subject-matter content. Such methods may improve test scores but do so at the expense of the subject matter and in the long run are a disservice to the student.

In taking essay examinations, one of the key things to remember is planning the use of time. More students have difficulty on essay exams due to timing than any other factor. Most instructors indicate the amount that each item on the essay exam is going to count in terms of the total test score. A good student will budget his test taking time accordingly. If some subject that the student knows well has the same value in the total test score as some other material that he is not as familiar with, he should budget his work in such a manner as to allow a little extra time on the item with which he is most familiar. For completing unfamiliar material, he budgets only a very little time after completing all those items with which he is familiar. He thus maximized his possibilities for high scores while reducing his own tensions. He also takes advantages of any knowledge that he may have been reminded of as he answered items he knew.

BUDGETING TIME. Perhaps the most important topic in study efficiency is budgeting time. As a matter of fact, any discussion concerning getting the most done per unit of time must include budgeting. At the same time, one of the biggest problems for college students is using time wisely.

When we suggest scheduling activities, people frequently throw up their hands and say, "Well, I don't want my life managed like that." Perhaps they have the wrong impression of a schedule. Schedules should be flexible, but at the same time allow enough planning so that there can be efficiency. For most students, a weekly time schedule can be established that will hold throughout a college term or semester. The schedule should show approximate times for waking, dressing, eating, attending classes, and studying. It should also include a good deal of time for recreation and, if necessary, time for employment. Now, for some general rules concerning what to do at various times.

It is well established that learned material is lost from available use or "forgotten" most rapidly immediately after learning with a decreasing loss of retention as the time after learning increases. In other words, material that has just been studied is available for use or is remembered best, whereas one hour later a great deal of the material is lost; within one day quite a bit more of the material is gone from available use; within a couple of days, 90 percent of the material may be gone, whereas over another week or two, very little additional loss takes place. A common explanation for this loss of retention is that newly learned material inhibits that previously learned. A technical term for this is *retroactive inhibition*. Some subject matters are influenced more by retroactive inhibition than others.

The general rule concerning retroactive inhibition is that the more similar the material, the more retroactive inhibition takes place. Thus, material learned now will be inhibited more if material similar to it is studied next than if material that is different is studied next. It is also advantageous for the material learned to have the least amount of learning take place afterward. Thus, subject matter learned just before going to sleep will suffer less loss of retention than if it is studied early in the evening before many other subjects are studied. As a general rule, a study period for a particular subject should come as close to that class period as possible. Naturally, this does not mean that study time should be devoted to subject matter just before the class meets and only on the days that tests are going to be given. It does mean that studying should be scheduled so that classes that are mainly recitation have study periods as close before them as possible, whereas classes that are primarily lecture have study periods immediately after them. Thus studying time is scheduled to prepare for recitations and to provide time for reviewing and organizing the notes just taken in lectures.

A schedule dividing time into one-hour chunks should be devised and placed in use for one week at a time. The student should not be disturbed if he cannot maintain his original schedule, but should accept the fact that a period of adjustment is needed before the schedule becomes habitual and that many modifications of the schedule might be necessary. Students who have been following schedules over a period of time frequently find that they are working at an efficient level and that they no longer need a written schedule.

The schedule should be realistic, and the interpretation of the amount of time actually used in activities should be objective. If the schedule indicates study from 7 to 8 P.M. in the evening, the time getting situated in the work place, going across the hall to bum a cigarette, participating in a bull session, searching through drawers for a match, and so on, should not be counted as study. Actually, during such a one-hour "study" period only 10 minutes may actually be used in studying. For many students a great amount of "study" time is wasted time. Scheduling should indicate in advance the amount of time that is really going to be used for various activities, and then the student should stick to his schedule. Two or three hours of study a week for an average three-hour college lecture course is probably a minimum, yet is enough for many students to do an adequate job in. Most instructors expect students to study twice as many hours outside as they attend in classes. However, this often takes into account the fact that what is called studying may not really be studying but much wasted time.

Time must be used efficiently. Students can become more efficient by setting up a schedule, adhering to it, and (if it seems unrealistic) revising it, but then adhering to the revision. It does no good whatever to devise a schedule and then file the schedule under the desk, in the waste basket, or buried in a drawer where it will never be followed.

SUMMARY

Experience changes behavior. Although individuals are different, there are many similarities in behavior, and there are general rules or principles that explain how the behavior of individuals has developed.

When a response is followed by variation in the perceived stimulus situation, the probability of that response reoccurring may be changed. A sufficient amount of change in stimulation is called reinforcement and results in acquisition or increased frequency of response occurrence. Smaller or larger amounts of change in the perceived stimulus situation result in extinction or decreased frequency of response occurrence. Changes in motivational conditions of the organism change the reinforcement value of environmental stimulus situation changes.

In an applied situation, reinforcement must be allowed for. Thus a student must study in a manner that allows for reinforcement after desired responses. Autoinstructional devices, self-recitation, and getting action into learning situations enhance the possibilities for reinforcement. Studying in distributed sessions rather than undistributed periods, as well as learning whole chunks of material rather than parts, influence the efficiency of studying.

Tests are often required as measures of retention of learned material. Objective tests usually cover large amounts of material with relatively short-answer questions, whereas subjective exams cover broader areas in relatively few questions. Performance on both forms of tests is enhanced by proper preparation and by doing the best possible job on each item while remembering to budget time and not to waste time on unknown material.

SUGGESTED REFERENCES FOR FURTHER STUDY

DeCecco, J. P. (1964). *Educational Technology.* New York: Holt, Rinehart & Winston.

A paperback book of readings bringing together research reports and theoretical discussions about automated instruction and learning theory.

Galanter, E. H. (ed.) (1959). *Automatic Teaching: The State of the Art.* New York: John Wiley & Sons.

A summary of information available about programed instruction. This book was the first compilation of material about automated instruction.

Hanson, L. F. (ed.) (1963). *Programs '63. A Guide to Programmed Instructional Materials Available to Educators by September 1963.* Washington, D.C.: The Center for Programmed Instruction, and U.S. Dept. of Health, Education, and Welfare, Office of Education, U.S. Government Printing Office.

A survey of programs available commercially, indexed by topic of the program. Includes a brief description of each program, costs, publisher, methods of use, and field tests completed.

Hilgard, E.R. (1956). *Theories of Learning.* New York: Appleton-Century-Crofts.

A survey of each of the major learning theories. Each chapter of this book provides a complete coverage of one theory.

Holland, J. G., and B. F. Skinner (1961). *The Analysis of Behavior.* New York: McGraw-Hill.

A programed book covering the major points of Skinner's explanation of how and why learning is accomplished.

Lumsdaine, A. A., and R. Glaser (eds.). (1960). *Teaching Machines and Programmed Learning: A Source Book.* Washington, D.C.: N.E.A., Department of Audio-Visual Instruction.

A discussion of automated instruction techniques and devices oriented toward public school teaching.

Lysaught, J. P., and C. M. Williams (1963). *A Guide to Programmed Instruction*. New York: John Wiley & Sons.

A description of the steps to follow and organization needed to develop a programed instructional training unit.

Mednick, S. A. (1964). *Learning*. Englewood Cliffs, N.J.: Prentice-Hall.

A concise, short paperback book covering the salient, basic facts known about the learning process.

Chapter 2

Principles of Mental Health

. . . Mental illness and mental retardation are among our most critical health problems. They occur more frequently, affect more people, require more prolonged treatment, cause more suffering by families of the afflicted, waste more of our human resources, and constitute more financial drain upon both the Public Treasury and the personal finances of the individual families than any other single condition (Kennedy, 1963).

THE LATE PRESIDENT OF THE UNITED STATES, John F. Kennedy, included the above statement in a message to the Congress requesting legislation and appropriations that might provide better facilities, personnel, and research to improve methods of preventing and treating mental illness and mental retardation, and rehabilitating people disabled by these disorders. It has been estimated that at least one person in 10—over 19,000,000 people in the United States alone—has some form of mental or emotional illness, ranging from mild to severe, that needs treatment. It is believed, too, that mental and emotional problems play important roles in many physical illnesses, such as heart disease and tuberculosis. Probably 50 percent of the medical and surgical cases treated by private doctors and hospitals have some mental illness involvement (*National Association for Mental Health*, 1963).

What is mental illness? What causes it? Such questions are easy to ask, yet difficult to answer. Perhaps it would be easier if we could turn the questions around. Let us ask, "What is mental health?" Once we know some of the criteria for mental health, then we can ask, "How does adjustment take place?" If we understand how a person copes with problems in satisfying his motives, how he reacts to frustration, and especially how he functions under stress, we might know better how behavioral maladjustments, such as psychoses and psychoneuroses, occur. We shall then be in a better position to explore the factors that contribute both to normal behavioral adjustment and to mental disorder. Our inquiry into these questions in this chapter will follow this pattern.

We will review briefly how public attitudes and practices regarding the mentally ill have evolved from an era of cruelty to and fear of the insane to a humanitarian mental health viewpoint which stresses prevention, treatment, rehabilitation, and optimum human adjustment.

EMERGENCE OF A MENTAL HEALTH VIEWPOINT

Public attitudes toward the mentally ill have not always been sympathetic, benevolent, or salutary. Indeed, our modern social and medical emphases have evolved slowly and painfully from a dark age of barbarous abuses of those considered "possessed," through successive stages of scientific and humanitarian enlightenment. Certain overlapping phases in this evolution of public attitudes and practices can be sketched: (a) prescientific phase, (b) humanitarian enlightenment and reform, (c) emergence of medical and scientific discoveries that directed concern to treatments and search for cures, (d) mental hygiene and mental health movements, and (e) the present era of attention to "optimal human functioning." Historically, each of these phases has merged into and overlapped the next but has never completely disappeared. Attitudes and practices characteristic of each of these phases exist even today in our society.

Prescientific Phase. In the prescientific era prior to the seventeenth century, mental disturbances were regarded with fear and shame. The mentally disordered were believed to be possessed by evil spirits, such as witches and demons, or to be influenced by the moon (to which we owe the origin of the word *lunatic*, after Luna, the moon goddess), or to be atoning for wickedness. They were chained in dungeons, locked in barns, punished as criminals, or subjected to brutal mutilations and tortures designed to "drive out the devils," to purge the bad humors, and to chastise the wicked. As medicine became a science, the so-called insane were recognized more as being physically sick and were given treatment in hospitals, or asylums, as they were called. Care of the mentally ill in these asylums was little better than treatment accorded prisoners, however. Inmates were caged like dangerous beasts in cells—shackled, ill-fed, and filthy—sometimes exposed to the taunts of amused on-lookers who would pay admission fees to observe their antics.

Enlightenment and Humanitarian Reform. The phase of enlightenment and humanitarian reform in the treatment of the insane and mentally retarded was introduced in both England and France in the 1790's. At the Paris hospital Bicêtre, the physician-in-chief, Phillipe Pinel, experimented with "moral treatment" by showing patients kindness rather than treating them as criminals or wild animals. He discovered that by removing their chains and permitting them freedom in the hospital patients became more tractable, and some even became cured. Pinel also carried out these benevolent practices and instituted many other reforms at Salpetrière Hospital, thus establishing two of the first modern hospitals for the mentally ill. During the same decade in England, William Tuke, a Quaker, developed a hospital known as York Retreat, which featured treatment of the mentally ill in a family environment, with employment, exercise, and treatment of patients as guests. As reports of the successes of Pinel and Tuke became known, mental disorders came to be recognized more widely as illnesses rather than as criminal or satanic defects. Thus, humanitarian improvements in the treatment and care of the insane spread throughout the Western world (Zilboorg and Henry, 1941).

But changes were slow. Half a century after Pinel and Tuke initiated their reforms, Dorothea Dix, a crusading schoolteacher from New England, found conditions in American asylums deplorable. She reported to the Congress of the United States that mental patients were bound to ball and chains and were "scourged with rods and terrified beneath storms of execration and cruel blows; now subject to jibes and scorn and torturing tricks; now abandoned to the most outrageous violations (Zilboorg and Henry, 1941)." Largely through her efforts the public and their legislatures were aroused to provide new mental hospitals with improved care. Between 1841 and 1881, her campaign for reform in the treatment of the mentally ill resulted in the founding or enlarging of at least 30 mental hospitals (Zilboorg and Henry, 1941).

Medical and Scientific Discovery.   In the latter part of the nineteenth century scientific discoveries in medicine shifted the focus from more custodial care to treatment and cure. Large hospitals arose, staffed with medical personnel rather than untrained keepers. Progress in neurology and in understanding biological aspects of disease established a physiological basis for many disorders, such as paresis, which had been formerly thought due to bad character or faulty heredity, and therefore believed untreatable. Spurred by pioneering in understanding unconscious bases for mental phenomena by such men as Sigmund Freud, Pierre Janet, and Jean Charcot, new theories of neurosis and psychotherapies were developed. Many mental disturbances were found to be related to unrecognized psychological conflicts, fears, and tensions originating in childhood. Further explorations of reflex conditioning by Pavlov, a Russian physiologist, and others in the early part of the twentieth century showed how physiological processes, including those regulating emotions, could be influenced by learning. Gradually research in the sciences of medicine and psychology paved the way to understanding how biological and psychological functions interact in a person, now a major concern in the study of psychosomatic disorders.

A new conception of mental illness during this phase of medical and scientific discovery has been called the *holistic* viewpoint. According to this view, it is reasoned that, since the origins of mental disorders are to be found in the combined organic, sociological, and psychological development of the whole person, the treatment of disorders must also include consideration of all of these factors. As a consequence of this holistic approach, modern treatment of mental disorders embraces not only medical treatment with shock, surgery, or drugs, but group and individual psychotherapy, and consideration of the total social milieu of the person in the hospital, the home, and in the community. Modern efforts in prevention and in rehabilitation owe much to this holistic or psychosomatic point of view (Coleman, 1956).

Mental Hygiene and Mental Health. Overlapping and merging into this phase of medical and scientific discovery is what has been termed the "mental hygiene," or more recently, the "mental health," movement. In 1908, Clifford Beers (1948) published an autobiographical account of his experiences as a patient in several mental hospitals in America in a book entitled *A Mind That Found Itself*. In this book he described the cruel treatment he had received, including beatings and being placed in a strait jacket. With the support of a prominent psychiatrist, Adolf Meyer, a famous psychologist, William James, and others, Beers founded the National Committee for Mental Hygiene. The term *mental hygiene* epitomized several objectives, such as prevention of mental disease, education of the public regarding mental problems, promotion of mental health, and the application of a "philosophy of public health to psychiatry" (Lemkau, 1959, p. 1948). Widespread support of the mental hygiene movement was sponsored by this Committee's efforts to improve mental hospital conditions and to promote preventive measures. These resulted in the establishment of many child guidance clinics and a more general public awareness of and interest in the problems of mental illness. As the movement gained impetus, the term *mental hygiene* proved to be too limiting; so the term *mental health* began to supplant it. This new term includes problems of psychiatric disorder in mass populations, such as incidence, epidemiology, and treatment, as well as care and prevention.

A significant outgrowth of this movement was the National Mental Health Act of 1946, which authorized the establishment of the National Institute of Mental Health in Bethesda, Maryland, in 1949. This Institute supports research on mental diseases and mental health facilities and provides funds to assist states to develop mental health clinics and hospitals and to improve and increase personnel staffs and services. Many states benefited from these services by improving, reorganizing, and augmenting their mental health programs.

In 1955, the Joint Commission on Mental Illness and Health, a multi-disciplinary organization representing 36 national agencies concerned with mental health and welfare, was authorized to conduct the first overall study of the mental health of the nation and to make recommendations for strengthening it. A series of studies was initiated that resulted in a final report, *Action for Mental Health* (Joint Commission on Mental Illness and Health, 1961), which recommended many changes in the treatment of the mentally ill and increased financial support for mental health programs.

In 1963 the Mental Retardation Facilities and Community Mental Health Centers Construction Act was passed. This act authorized a three-year $238-million program to aid states in providing mental retardation research centers and facilities, construction of community mental health centers, and grants for training teachers of handicapped children.

Optimal Human Functioning.　Emerging from the mental health era we note another phase in this development of attitudes and practices: concern for positive aspects of human growth and functioning. Studies by the Joint Commission show that mental disorders are quite different from most other types of illnesses in origin, process, and cure. Not only are they related to genetic, maturational, and physiological factors, but they are "inextricably bound up with child rearing practices, education, employment, recreation, health, religion—in sum, with the totality of family and community life" (Hobbs, 1963). It is just as important, therefore, to understand the positive role of these social factors in enabling a person to realize his fullest potential and his greatest happiness and satisfaction as it is to know their detrimental aspects in causing or augmenting mental disorders.

In order to emphasize that mental health should encompass more than mere prevention or alleviation of disease pathology, Jahoda (1958) proposed that positive personal development be promoted in mental health programs. "Positive mental health," so called, would be sought through attainment of favorable self-attitudes, growth and self-actualization, personality integration, autonomy, effective perception of reality, and environmental mastery.

Dissatisfaction with an exclusively medical model for mental health programs led to a search for terms that would avoid the word *health* yet more adequately describe the new emphases. One term that has been proposed epitomizes the enhancement of positive assets in persons regardless of their condition of health: *optimal human functioning* (Smith, 1961).

Together with this new concern has come the conception of the community mental health center (*Mental Retardation Facilities and Community Mental Health Centers Construction Act of 1963*). Such a center would go beyond the traditional preventive, therapeutic, and rehabilitative emphases of the child guidance clinic or mental health clinic. It would provide diagnostic and counseling services to help to identify and to release a person's creative potentialities and assist him to attain more effective personal development in all aspects of his life, even if he were not mentally ill. Thus we can see concern for multiple aspects of social and personal positive forces superseding the protective and restorative medical accent of the mental hygiene and mental health movements. In this new kind of community mental health center various activities and functions often performed inefficiently by many separate agencies of society, such as health, corrections, welfare, education, employment, psychological, financial, and legal services, would coordinate and merge to the end of fostering creative growth and realization of one's potentials for optimal human functioning.

WHAT IS MENTAL HEALTH?

The changes in attitudes toward and treatment of the mentally ill over the years that we have noted—from punishment to humane treatment, from fear to sympathy, from incarceration to rehabilitation, from emphasis upon prevention and then to promotion of creative, positive growth and functioning—are due not only to advances in science and changes in society but are due to new and different ways of defining mental health. Much has depended upon whether social, individual, or functional criteria for mental soundness have been employed. In this section we shall examine what is implied by each of these criteria.

The *social* criteria for mental health include determination of how closely a person resembles others in his behavior, how well he gets along and is liked by others, how much he contributes to and supports his social group, and how much he conforms to the approved codes, laws, or ideals of his society or social group. When applying *individual* criteria, we are concerned with the person himself and his attitudes, such as his happiness, ability to withstand psychological stress, assumption of personal responsibility, the integration of his personality, favorable or realistic self-perceptions, and self-actualization. *Functional* criteria involve the ability of the person to cope with and to master environmental stresses and demands efficiently, productively, and maturely.

From earliest times *mental illness,* as the opposite of *mental health,* has been defined primarily by social criteria. Those who have deviated from prescribed, expected, or typical social behaviors have been considered either insane, criminal, eccentric, or sick. Little concern has been shown for individual criteria, such as their happiness or feelings, or even for their effectiveness in functioning as members of society as long as they were not public nuisances. As a result, treatment has traditionally aimed at restoring desirable social behavior, alleviating symptoms, and protecting the public from bother and danger through custodial care of patients.

Only in relatively recent times have the mental hygiene and holistic viewpoints directed more attention to the individual and his functioning as points of reference in hospital therapy and public programs of prevention. Today, much more concern is felt for how the patient can resolve his torturing inner conflicts, how he can be made happier, and how he can be returned to his family and job to become more effective as a self-respecting, self-supporting, and responsible member of his community.

Each of these criteria of mental health places positive or negative values on different behaviors. The overall condition of one's mental health is usually determined by assessing the degree to which a person displays behaviors typical of the criteria we have mentioned, conceived as having these positive or negative, or desirable versus undesirable characteristics.

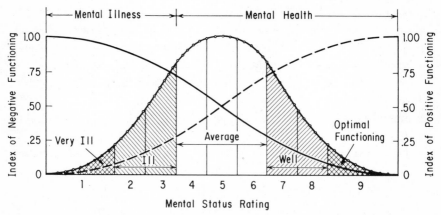

Figure 2.1. Hypothetical distribution of mental health/illness in a "normal" population. Indexes of positive and negative functioning superimposed.

These hypothetical relationships are shown schematically in Figure 2.1. The base line in this diagram describes on a stanine scale (a nine-unit scale, each unit equal to one ninth of the total range of standard scores in a normal distribution) a range of health conditions from Very Ill, at the extreme left, to Very Well, at the extreme right. People who are very ill show the greatest number or magnitude of defects or symptoms of pathology and the least number or magnitude of positive and desirable traits. Those adjudged very well reverse this, showing valued behaviors at a maximum, and undesirable traits at a minimum. A separate diagram could be made for each criterion according to the behaviors and the degree to which they are desirable or undesirable in terms of that criterion. Some representative behaviors are listed in Table 2.1 according to the three criteria that have been suggested.

TABLE 2.1 Criteria for Mental Health

CRITERIA	CHARACTERISTICS
Social	
A. Statistical	Behavior typical of comparison group considered "normal"; general conformity to average with little deviation in frequency or generally accepted judgments of "intensity"; acts in manner "natural" to the species.
B. Social interactional	
1. Interpersonal judgment and choice.	Receives approval and acceptance by social group; regarded as leader, friend, or desirable group member; enjoys satisfactory interpersonal relationships; gives and reciprocates affection; can accept and share dependencies.
2. Social benefit.	Contributes to welfare and benefit of others with altruism, loyalty, support, and democratic social interest; promotes group harmony and objectives; displays interpersonal responsibility.
C. Ethical and ideal	Conforms to or does not violate socially approved or ideal behaviors as defined by custom, law, or code. Absence of defect, deficiency, or pathology.
Individual	
A. Hedonistic	Feelings of enjoyment, pleasure, comfort, or happiness.
B. Stress management	Freedom from, resistance to, tolerance of, or control of psychological stress due to frustration, conflict, guilt, and other disturbing thoughts and emotions; use of appropriate tension-reduction techniques or mechanisms.
C. Personal responsibility	Self-control and self-discipline; autonomy, not overdependent.

TABLE 2.1—continued

CRITERIA	CHARACTERISTICS
D. Self-attitudes	Harmonious, positive self-perceptions; sense of self-confidence and adequacy; self-esteem; feelings of acceptance and belonging; feelings of security.
E. Integration	Coherence or unity of personality; balance of psychic forces, not overdetermined by a few; unifying philosophy of life; sense of meaning in life, a feeling of identity or sense of "being." Self-actualization or feeling fulfillment of one's potential; becoming a "person."
Functional	
A. Coping	Adaptability and effectiveness in adjusting to or in modifying environment; skill in problem solving; mastery of thwarting situations.
B. Efficiency	Performing tasks and coping in smoothly organized, systematic manner with minimum energy; maintenance of organismic functions or homeostatic balance at optimum; high survival potential.
C. Ontogenetic	Learning or practicing behaviors that insure maximum future mental health or functioning.
D. Maturation	Realization of fullest potential of capacities and development for one's particular growth stage.
E. Productivity	Operating as a creative or productive person in connection with work, recreation, family or social group, or community life.

The diagram shown in Figure 2.1 and the chart of behaviors associated with different criteria of mental health shown in Table 2.1 illustrate some important principles of mental health. We might explore some implications of these principles:

1. *There is continuous variation between mental health and mental illness on a single continuum.* It is likely that the distribution of persons with different degrees of mental health in the general population would be normal.

2. *The degree of one's mental health depends upon the magnitude of intensity of positively and negatively valued behaviors, gauged according to various criteria, acting in combination.* Thus all people possess characteristics which if developed or aggravated could signal mental illness, at the negative extreme, or optimum functioning and mental health, at the positive extreme. Causes of mental illness can thus be sought in environmental or individual conditions that either increase negative or faulty behavior or

that reduce or negate positive functioning. This implies that programs to promote mental health should aim, therefore, to foster and to strengthen positive traits for both those who are presently healthy and those who are mentally ill. Applied to the healthy, such efforts are called *primary prevention;* applied to the ill, they are called *secondary prevention* or *rehabilitation,* depending upon the emphasis.

The design of primary prevention is to keep mental illness from occurring at all. Secondary prevention depends upon early detection of difficulties and treatment to ward off more serious developments or to reverse a trend. Rehabilitation is concerned with therapy and training which will build the positive functioning to a maximum for those who have been ill. Programs that focus primarily upon reducing pathology and restoring functions are termed *therapy* or *treatment.* Rehabilitation efforts are often part of a therapy program. Whereas the focus of mental health efforts in the past has been upon providing better care and treatment of the mentally ill, it is now recognized that, to cope effectively with the broader problems of mental health, efforts must include adequate provision for prevention and rehabilitation as well.

Certain technical problems arise when this hypothetical model is examined closely, but it does highlight important facets of the mental health problem. To begin with, this model assumes a rather naive conception of bipolar traits which have simple positive or negative values. There are many ways of conceiving of traits involving different behavioral dimensions and limits, depending upon the broadness of the observations and inclusiveness of their operational definition. Some behaviors range from presence in extreme degree to absence. Hallucinations, for example, are characterized by presence or absence only. Other traits range from one extreme to an opposite extreme, as with pain and pleasure. Also, the positive or negative nature of behavior is relative to the particular criterion employed. Normal food-getting behavior in a prison camp might be quite improper at a formal dinner. All of these technical problems make determination of the magnitude of effect of a particular behavior in most criterion categories quite relative and subjective, hence undependable in empirical studies, unless carefully specified. This, in turn, makes assessment of the relative balance and interaction of positive and negative traits, and how they might augment, compensate for, or suppress each other in an individual, extremely conjectural for purposes of assessment and comparison. We learn to live with such problems in the behavioral sciences, however. We take great care to specify variables in terms of phenomena that can be observed and verified by others, so that there might be no question about what we are describing. Table 2.1 merely illustrates very loosely the kinds of traits that might be involved. For purposes of classification or measurement we would need to be much more exact.

Another source of complexity is in the criterion categories themselves. Some are independent; some overlap and are not mutually exclusive. In part, this confusion is caused by their origins. Several different behavioral science disciplines are represented in these categories, each being concerned with the human being at a different level of organization. As J. P. Scott (1957) has said:

> . . . the different schools of thought appear to be thinking about the same phenomenon at different levels of organization. The organicist views behavior in terms of factors which are at the genic level, the tissue level, and the organic level; the psychologist considers behavior in terms of factors that operate at the organismic level of the whole individual; the psychodynamicist is interested in the smaller units of societal organization as well as in man as a psychological unit; the sociologist or anthropologist is concerned with social and cultural factors in entire human societies.

An example of overlap would be in categorizing a behavior such as "feeling of hostility." This could be considered related to self-conflict or frustration (a supposed cause, and an individual criterion). It could also show as marital maladjustment (social interaction criterion) based upon people's reactions to the hostile behaviors. Both criteria would be correct.

A psychoanalyst, representing a psychodynamic point of view, might object to a statistical criterion of mental health. He could claim that the conformer to the behaviors most typical of his group, who scores at the average on personality inventories, could actually have poor self-attitudes or unresolved conflicts of motives. He might also ask, "Who decides how deviant a person can be in a statistical sense and still be normal?" Would the very unusual person who had no worries or anxieties be considered unhealthy? Certainly not all exceptional behavior is pathological, nor are conforming or typical behaviors necessarily desirable.

Does this mean that a statistical criterion should be abandoned? No, it is a helpful criterion because it does emphasize the continuity of traits, and has encouraged objectivity of measurement, which in turn has facilitated scientific testing of hypotheses. The statistical view also reveals the variability of human traits within the person and the range of individual differences between persons.

There is evidence to indicate that the criteria for mental health (Table 2.1) are sometimes independent. Comparisons of three methods of personality measurement, each representing different criteria of adjustment,

were made by Russell (1953). A personality inventory, representing a statistical criterion, a sociometric questionnaire and group ratings of the individual, representing interpersonal judgment criteria, and self-ratings were intercorrelated. He found that although intricate networks of interrelationships existed between traits and their measures, the correlations were generally low and inconsistent enough to warrant considering these measures of adjustment relatively independent, depending upon the trait considered and its method of measurement. It would thus be possible for a person to be well adjusted in a statistical sense, as revealed by a personality inventory, and yet to be poorly accepted by his associates, an interpersonal choice criterion. A person might enjoy great esteem by his fellows, yet rate terion of mental health we use, we can see that it might conflict with himself as inferior in similar traits, a self-attitude criterion. Whatever criterion.
another criterion.

Does this incompatibility of certain criteria mean that a concept of mental health is meaningless? Not at all. It means just that we must specify with what level of human organization we are concerned, what criterion we are using, and must recognize the validity of that criterion only in that particular context. Many studies of mental illness and adjustment which yield apparently contradictory results have assumed different criteria for mental health. The studies of the effects of psychotherapy are prime examples.

Despite such technical difficulties, these categories of mental health criteria (Table 2.1), together with the diagram (Figure 2.1) do illustrate two further basic principles of mental health:

3. *Multiple criteria are needed to describe one's condition of mental health.* No single concept of adjustment is adequate to identify one's status at all levels of organization. It is for this reason that we must always consider multiple criteria in planning comprehensive mental health programs of prevention, treatment, or rehabilitation.

4. *No mental condition is static or simple; each involves complex, changing, and dynamic relationships between individual and social behaviors in constant interaction with complex and changing environmental situations.* Mental conditions rarely stand still; they are always subject to change, for better or for worse.

In review, our answer to the question "What is mental health?" is not a simple one. We see it involves at least three major criteria: social, individual, and functional. Each of these criteria includes behaviors and characteristics having desirable or undesirable features in varying combinations which determine the degree of mental health or illness. Since these criteria tend to be independent, on the whole, it is quite possible for a person to be considered mentally healthy by one criterion and mentally ill by another criterion.

A comprehensive mental health program must deal with both positive and negative behaviors, and each requires a different approach. In order to remove or to alleviate negative functions, programs of secondary prevention, therapy, and rehabilitation are needed. Programs of primary prevention which include family care, education, and counseling serve to develop and to support maximal positive functioning. Both aspects are considered important in building effective mental health services.

BASIC PROCESSES OF ADJUSTMENT

Adjustment in terms of the mental health criteria depends largely upon how an individual interacts with his environment, his social environment in particular, in satisfying his needs and in meeting demands placed upon him. Typically, the psychologist views the human being as a complex energy system consisting of many subsystems coordinated to maintain the optimum functioning of the organism. As a person participates in his environment, certain changes in the operations of the subsystems are required due to changes in the environment or changes originating within certain subsystems. Such changes require a redistribution of energy among the subsystems. Until the redistribution takes place, uncoordinated energy is released into the system resulting in what may be termed stress or tension. Such a mobilization of energy tends to persist until either the conditions which aroused it have been neutralized or removed, or a reorganization and harmony of the subsystems can be effected that will restore efficient general functioning to the organism. Changes in behavior in response to these demands upon the organism are termed *adjustment* (Miller, 1955).

All living systems tend to maintain steady states of many variables, by negative feedback mechanisms which distribute information to subsystems to keep them in orderly balance with their environments, which have outputs into systems and inputs from them. . . . There is a range of stability for any parameter or variable in any system. . . . Inputs . . . which, by lack or excess, force the variables beyond the range of stability constitute stresses and produce strains within the system. These strains may or may not be capable of being reduced, depending upon the equilibratory resources of the system.

The adjustment sequence, as shown in Figure 2.2, proceeds by the following steps. (1) Inputs of stimuli are selected and organized by processes

Organism

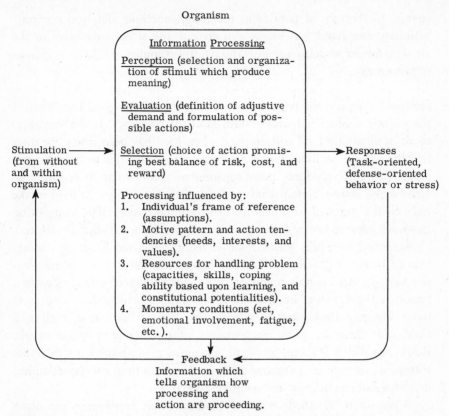

Figure 2.2. Adjustive behavior. (Adapted from *Personality Dynamics and Effective Behavior* by James C. Coleman. Copyright © 1960 by Scott, Foresman and Company.)

of perception. (2) Input information is compared with previous learning and understanding of one's capacities and demands and formulations of actions are evaluated. (3) Responses that provide maximum functioning or satisfaction with a minimum of risk or cost in effort, threat, or pain are selected. (4) The consequences of the responses made are then fed back into the system as further stimuli and are processed in similar fashion.

Should the input stimuli be pleasurable, the individual seeks to maintain or to increase them. Should inputs be noxious or irritating (as with pain or hunger), the individual seeks to reduce, remove, or to avoid them. If they cannot be reduced, removed, or avoided, a condition of stress builds up which is experienced as unpleasant and, if permitted to continue, could threaten or disrupt the smooth and coordinated functioning of the subsystems. This causes a mobilizing or accumulation of energy. Energy thus built up demands release and may result in responses that will either remove the stimuli, reduce the stress, or permit release of the pent-up energy. In the case of pain from touching something hot, you not only withdraw your hand, but might also cry out and shake your hand in the air. The former response removes the painful stimulus; the latter responses release energy.

Motives.   We use the term *motive* to describe an energized condition of the organism associated with certain kinds of responses. If the responses result in obtaining food and decrease when food has been eaten, we infer that the motive was hunger. Deficiency in bodily tissue due to lack of nutriment apparently produces irritating internal stimulations in certain subsystems and arouses certain kinds of food-getting responses. As food intake reduces the internal stimulations, the stimuli cease, the food-getting responses become fewer, and the motive is said to be satisfied or reduced.

Response sequences which remove, reduce, or avoid irritating stimuli, aroused by either deficiencies or disturbances, are said to characterize *aversive motives*. An example might be thirst, due to lack of water. We say a person is thirsty when he seeks to drink water when we know he lacks water. He may drink water to satisfy other motives, of course, such as a child who demands water as a means of prolonging bedtime rituals. Responses which lead to, augment, or prolong pleasurable or desirable stimuli are considered *appetitive motives*. Many motives are very complex, involving both appetitive and aversive aspects.

A motive is "satisfied" when an end situation or stimulus condition originating either within or outside of the organism completes or terminates the response sequence. End conditions which are capable of satisfying motives are called *incentives* or *goals*. In general, satisfaction of a motive of either type—that is, attaining the goal of an aversive or appetitive motive—is pleasurable and reinforcing. Behavior patterns associated with goal attainment or motive satisfaction are thus likely to be learned and repeated under future similar motive arousal conditions. Sometimes satisfaction of only part of a motive, or irregular reinforcement, can also strengthen the learning of certain response patterns.

The topic of motivation is exceedingly complicated and controversial in the behavioral sciences. Some theorists prefer not to consider it at all. Even to name a motive becomes speculative. We do find it helps our understanding, however, to label certain kinds of response sequences of approach or avoidance behavior according to assumed general stimulus categories. Accordingly, a list of commonly accepted motives is presented in Table 2.2, along with examples of their assumed aversive or appetitive stimuli. It is understood that any such list could be extended or reorganized indefinitely, depending upon the nature and complexity of the hypothetical stimuli and the responses being considered.

TABLE 2.2   Selected Motives and Examples of Aversive and Appetitive Stimuli

MOTIVE	AVERSIVE STIMULI	APPETITIVE STIMULI
Food	Lack of food; food aversion.	Savory favorite foods.
Water; liquid	Lack of water; noxious fluids.	Enjoyed beverages.
Air	Asphyxiation; unpleasant humidity.	Fresh air; pleasant humidity.
Rest	Fatigue; physical tension.	Feeling vigorous or relaxed.
Elimination	Unpleasant bowel or bladder tension.	Pleasurable sensations of elimination.
Temperature	Unpleasant extremes of heat or cold.	Pleasing contrasts (sunbathing or brisk winter winds).
Sensory stimulation	Pain; unpleasant sensations.	Pleasing stimulation (sucking, stroking, "contact comfort").
Activity	Immobilization; boredom.	Motion; manipulation; noise making.
"Stress"	"Alarm reaction"; anxiety; strong emotional tension.	"Excitement"; mild emotional arousal or tension.
Sex	Blocked sexual responses; strong arousal.	"The chase," mild arousal.
Safety; security	Fear of pain, danger, or deficit in any of above motives.	Thrill and excitement of possible pain, danger, or deficit with expectation of triumph or success.
Acquisitiveness	Fear of deficiencies or stimulus objects that satisfy motives or their stimulus equivalents.	Joy and self-enhancement of collecting or possessing.
Esteem	Feelings of inferiority or unworthiness.	Feelings of prestige or status.
Achievement	Feelings of inadequacy, incompetence, or failure.	Feelings of mastery, adequacy, and accomplishment.
Love; belonging-ness	Feelings of rejection, or being unloved, or unwanted.	Feelings of affection, affiliation, and acceptance; being sought after and wanted.
Autonomy	Feelings of unwanted dependency, domination, or restriction of freedom.	Sense of freedom and independence.
Aggression	Feelings of frustration of any motive; unpleasant tension.	Pleasure of hurting or injuring others; sadism.
Self-actualization	Lack of self-fullfillment and undeveloped potentialities.	Sense of "becoming" or "being"; feelings of self-fulfillment.

Maslow (1943) has proposed that human motives can be arranged in a hierarchy from stronger and more basic at one end to weaker and more related to self-growth, thus "higher," at the other end. In his scheme, the physiological and safety needs, because they are based upon bodily deficiencies and dangers, would assume priority in goal-seeking responses. Such higher motives as love, esteem, and self-actualization, being growth motives not vital to survival, could emerge as energizers only as the more basic motives had been satisfied to a substantial degree. These motives are often used in industry, as explained in Chapter 11 of this book.

The Self As a Subsystem. Mark Twain said, "Man is the only animal that blushes—or needs to." Obviously man can reflect upon his own behavior and can evaluate it. At least two kinds of responses are indicated in this activity: (1) an inferred cognitive response to his own behavior or person, and (2) an active, observable response to this cognitive response stimulus. Each of these inferences implies a unity of function and a constellation of attitudes and habits in a person that are unique and make him different psychologically, as well as physically, from every other human being. We use the construct *self* to embrace all of these attributes of the person.

The self-concept is that part of the self which is aware of itself—the perceptions one has of his own characteristics, feelings, attitudes, and abilities. These self-attitudes, which are symbolic habits or enduring states of readiness to respond in characteristic ways, form points of reference or anchorage points for interpreting stimuli and acting. Ready-made behavioral reactions are thus provided by this aspect of the self.

The more obvious, active part of the self is represented by the typical coping and expressive behaviors shown in environmental and interpersonal situations. These may involve the self-attitudes mentioned above, but more specifically concern the habitual response patterns that develop over a lifetime. Blending these two aspects, the term *self* becomes a way of describing a coordinated organization of personal subsystems, in effect a subsystem in its own right.

We shall see how this particular subsystem, the self, and the growth, maintenance, and stability of its habit patterns, become pivotal in the adjustment process. To change any of these patterns requires a change in many associated subsystems, hence demands a substantial expenditure of energy. When certain habits, attitudes, self-cognitions seem contradictory or inconsistent to a person, he feels insecure and anxious until subsystem harmony can be obtained. The adequacy of the self—that is, the extent to which a person feels prepared to meet new situations and to cope with changes and perceived threats from his environment—also affects his sense of safety and security. A threat to the self, therefore, may be perceived as a danger to one's very existence. Consequently, a person strives not only to maintain the adequacy and efficiency of his physiological functions but also to develop and to establish his competence and his conception of himself at an optimum. The self in this way becomes involved to some degree in all psychological motivation.

Frustration. In the course of everyday experience, we encounter frequent blocks, interferences and delays in the satisfaction of our motives or in the activities we employ in this process. Some blocks or barriers are more disturbing or more permanent than others. Some are tangible physical limitations that prevent or curtail effective action; some are psychological and intangible, causing the person to restrict his own actions, to question or to fear negative self-attitudes, or to become indecisive.

When the barriers to action are outside of the organism and inherent in practical situations or the social order, we speak of *external* or *impersonal frustration.* Such frustrations might be due to privations, such as social discrimination or poverty, in which a person lacks privileges or advantages enjoyed by others, or they might be due to deprivations, as when a person is denied satisfactions he has previously enjoyed, such as losing his job or property. More obvious external barriers, which are called obstructions, involve blocks or restraints by persons, confinement, or circumstances, such as missing a bus or being refused by a person you have asked to dance.

Internal, or *personal, frustration* involves privation, deprivation, or obstruction in satisfying motives related more directly to the self. If a person has never known love from parents, or might never enjoy gratification of motives for achievement or mastery due to mental handicaps, he might be frustrated by internal privation. If he has been deprived by illness or aging of vigor or physical attractiveness, he might also feel frustrated. Obstructions to action might be found in fears of punishment or failure, feelings of conscience or guilt, or conflicts that cause a person to feel distressed and to inhibit responses that might result in motive satisfaction (Rosenzweig, 1938).

Conflicts that involve arousal of competing responses or motives are especially frustrating, because of the fear a person has of making responses that might have an undesirable or painful outcome. In the typical *approach–approach conflict* (Lewin, 1935), an individual must choose between two positive but incompatible goals. "Which college should I choose?" "Which car should I buy?" An *approach–avoidance conflict*

(Lewin, 1935) occurs when a single-goal object has both attractive and repellent aspects. "If I go to the concert, I cannot complete my work for tomorrow." A person might crave rich desserts but fear these goodies might cause overweight. An *avoidance–avoidance conflict* (Lewin, 1935) occurs when a person must choose between two goals, both of which are undesirable. He would prefer to choose neither. Perhaps the child on the playground must decide whether he will fight or be called "yellow." A *double approach–avoidance conflict* (Lewin, 1935) requires choice between two or more alternatives, each of which involves both appetitive and aversive aspects. Should I take this job or that job? This one offers more money but little prestige; that job offers less money but has many fringe benefits. The frustration in conflicts comes from the suspension of action pending the decision, the loss of satisfaction of one motive if another one is favored, and the fear of the consequences of a choice.

Task-Oriented Reactions to Frustration[1].   When the organism is aroused by motivational stimuli, thus prepared for action, if external or internal frustration occurs, the tension built up is prevented from being discharged in responses that can satisfy the motive. The immediate effect of frustration is to increase the number and strength of the responses, thus facilitating the discovery and success of responses that can satisfy the motives. Mild frustration thus tends to increase the strength of motivation and to improve the efficiency of a person in solving problems and in learning.

In the case of aversive motivation, the task would be to remove or to reduce bodily or psychological deficiencies and disturbing stimuli to the organism, to overcome or to bypass frustrations, or to build up resistance to or toleration of such stimuli (frustration tolerance). With an appetitive motive, such as seeking variety or excitement, the task would be to strengthen or to improve responses that might overcome, bypass, or remove barriers, to locate, increase, and prolong desirable stimuli, or to set attainable and suitable goals.

Two principal methods in task-oriented reactions are typically used: *problem solving* and *persistence*. In *problem-solving behavior*, a person might increase the strength of his responses, produce more of them, or try out new responses until he finds successful ones. Should he find that the goals he has set are not accomplishing his motives, he might substitute more realistic and appropriate ones. In some situations, the problem is solved by abandoning the originally conceived goal and withdrawing from the situation. As an example, suppose you are bored (desire for excitement

---

[1] The terms *task-oriented* and *defense-oriented* were suggested by Coleman (1960).

and change: an appetitive motive) and decide you would like to attend the movies (goal). After searching all pockets and purses (old responses), perhaps you try to borrow some money (new responses). Or maybe you decide to wait until you have the money (abandoning the goal) and decide instead to go for a walk (goal substitution).

Persistent behavior would be shown if you continued to use the same responses over and over (searching all pockets repeatedly). Sometimes persistent behavior is preliminary to problem solving, as revealed by the maxim "If at first you don't succeed, try, try again." More often, however, it reveals emotional blinding of a person to alternatives as a result of strong motivation. In some instances this persistent behavior is more defense-than task-oriented. Extreme stress may produce stereotyped behavior, called a *fixation*, in which the person repeats his responses even when they are ineffective. Perhaps the person fears that changed responses will not work and that the risk of failure is high. Like the inveterate gambler, the person may believe that one more time he might succeed. Sometimes, however, he lacks the skills or knowledge which would enable him to try new responses. Other times, old methods have been so strongly reinforced in the past that he cannot respond in any other way. Although persistence is less often effective in satisfying motives, and may contribute to rather than relieve frustration, it is, like problem solving, a task-oriented reaction, because responses are directed primarily toward satisfying the original motive.

Defense-Oriented Reactions to Frustration. Excessive or continued frustration of motives causes unorganized energy to build up to a level of tension that disturbs the coordination of various subsystems, including the self. When this point is reached, the tension can be called *stress*. Stress is threatening to a person both physically and psychologically. As a result, any responses that can reduce stress and provide outlets for release of tension by means of activity and emotional expression begin to assume dominance over responses associated with the original motive. In this compounding of motive energies, unpleasant emotions and fears arise as threats to the self, such as anticipated loss of security or esteem, punishment, or any of the aversive psychological motives. These disturbing emotions, which are termed *anxiety*, also act as aversive stimuli.

Most aversive motives, if strong enough, could be said to be anxiety-producing; hence response reactions to anxiety are avoidant and defensive in character. The worry of a student before an important examination transcends mere concern for a passing grade. He is anxious about acceptance and approval of parents and friends and worries about what a poor grade might do to his self-image as well. His whole self-system might be threatened, so defenses for this are added to task-oriented reactions, thus multiplying the arousal energy.

What determines the magnitude of anxiety aroused by frustration? One factor is the strength of the original motive (Symonds, 1946). If we are very hungry, our reactions might be stronger to thwarting than if we had eaten recently. If the goals of motivation are very important to a person— we might say he is self-involved—any blocking will be more frustrating. Another factor might be the strength of the barrier (Symonds, 1946). If the frustration can be overcome rather easily, the tension might not build up as much. Frustration close to a goal-object is more disturbing than frustration occurring at a point some distance in space or time from the goal (Kimble and Garmezy, 1963). Also, if a frustration seems unreasonable, the reaction might be more violent than if a person can accept it as reasonable and to be expected (Kimble and Garmezy, 1963). Reactions depend also upon the opportunities one has to respond (Symond, 1946). If one has learned how to handle problems or can satisfy his motives even partially, the frustration might be less. A further factor might be the prevailing level of anxiety (Symonds, 1946). A highly anxious person will react more strongly than one who is not already anxious. A person who has experienced many frustrations might be more upset by additional frustrations than one who has had few previous experiences with thwarting.

FRUSTRATION TOLERANCE. Some people, however, develop attitudes toward repeated thwarting which enable them to endure it and to cope effectively with a minimum of stress. Such capacity to withstand delay, blocking, and conflict without resorting to ineffective, maladaptive responses is termed *frustration tolerance* (Rosenzweig, 1938). A child who has been sheltered or protected from experiencing problems or who has been overindulged in childhood might react strongly to slight thwarting because he has never had an opportunity to learn to cope with it or to accept the anxiety.

Frustration tolerance can be learned. In one study it was found that immature nursery school children could be taught to solve problems, to cry less, and generally to show more mature reactions to frustrations (Keister and Updegraff, 1937). One of the main functions of discipline in childhood is to train the child to accept thwarting and to endure restraints in order to enjoy greater future gains.

AGGRESSION. Perhaps the most obvious defensive reaction to frustration is aggression, shown as hostility toward or attacks upon the perceived source of frustration or some substitute, with the object of removing, hurting, or destroying it. We express this when we say, "The best defense is an offense." Not all aggression is expressed by physical acts of fighting or striking objects or persons, however. Verbal attacks, such as swearing, gossiping about others, or symbolic attacks in fantasy, as in dreaming about the death or injury of others, may occur. One woman repeatedly dreamed her husband was on an operating table about to receive an incision. Just as the knife was about to cut, she would awaken screaming. In the course of counseling it was revealed that the person on the operating table did not represent her present husband but was the man she had previously divorced for having an affair with another woman. Children who continually break rules in school or who quarrel and fight with others are often greatly frustrated in some situation outside of school, perhaps at home.

As we find with other adjustment behavior, aggression is learned. Bandura, Ross, and Ross (1963) have shown that aggression is learned by imitation of models. In their study, preschool children were exposed to aggression shown by three types of models: real-life people, humans in films, and film cartoons. Following this observation, the children were mildly frustrated and tested for the amount of aggression displayed. All three groups showed more imitative aggression than a control group which had not received the exposure to aggression stimuli. Exposure to human subjects portraying aggression in the movie produced the greatest degree of aggression.

In another study Lovaas (1961) found that children who were rewarded for directing verbally aggressive behavior toward dolls showed more physical aggression toward the dolls in later play sessions. Not only do reinforcements shape the aggressive behavior but we find generalization of the behavior to other situations.

When the risk of punishment for aggression is great, a person may discharge his aggression upon a substitute of some kind—a phenomenon called *displacement*. Scapegoating would be an example. One often observes how a boy who has been picked on by older boys, not daring to retaliate, may become a bully himself with younger boys. Minority groups become the butt for discrimination and persecution as outlets for a prejudiced status group that has been frustrated in various ways.

Should no adequate substitute be found, and the risk of punishment or rejection for aggressive acts be great, hostility can be turned inward on the self, resulting in self-injury, inferiority feelings, and depression. Perhaps the person can atone for guilty feelings about his hostility toward those he feels he should love or for aggressive feelings he feels are wrong by hurting himself. He may even find he can muster sympathy or manipulate others by self-deprecation. Certainly the child who deliberately holds his breath until he turns blue or bangs his head learns he can control his worried parents with acts of self-aggression.

Although the main function of aggression is defensive, because it relieves stress and anxiety by permitting release of emotions and substitute responses for those that have been denied their original goal functions, occasionally aggression does satisfy an original motive and is adopted by the person as a task-oriented problem-solving behavior. Parents, employers, and teachers may find that aggressive maneuvers enhance their power and status and thus facilitate their control of others. Whether or not aggression, or any frustration reactions, are task- or defense-oriented will depend upon the primary functions they serve for the individual. What begins as a defense may become a task-oriented response if reinforced.

MECHANISMS OF DEFENSE. We have seen how unresolved frustration results in further stress and anxiety, which in turn become additional threats to the self. When the original frustration is predominantly internal due to unresolved personal conflicts, to feelings of guilt or shame, or to threats to positive self-attitudes, a person is at the mercy of his own reactions, with no easy solution or escape. The only relief he can find in such circumstances is in his ability to modify or to eliminate the reactions that bring him anxiety. He might alter the direction of his thinking. He might apply rigid controls to himself to inhibit chaotic or undesirable emotional reactions. He might avoid places and thoughts that remind him; he might even blot them from his memory.

Some of the greatest contributions of Sigmund Freud were in his analyses of the self-protective maneuvers people employ without awareness. Such *defense mechanisms*, as they are called, relieve or prevent anxiety by disguising or screening the sources of frustration or by redirecting responses.

Only a few of the more common defense mechanisms shall be mentioned here. For a more complete list, the reader is referred to Table 2.3.

TABLE 2.3   Common Adjustment Reactions

Task-Oriented Reactions

Problem solving	Goal-directed behavior involving increased effort, trial-and-error responses, and substitute goals.
Persistence	Goal-directed behavior using repetitive responses.

Defense-Oriented Reactions

Aggression	Attacking persons, objects, or situations with the aim to injure or destroy.

Displacement	Directing hostility or other feelings toward substitute objects or persons.
Repression	Exclusion of specific thoughts, memories, impulses, feelings, and actions from awareness.
Denial	Reaction involving repression; refusal to accept or to recognize situations.
Fantasy	Imagining objects, people, events, or conditions that will satisfy motives.
Regression	Return to behavior typical of an earlier period of learning or development.
Rationalization	Giving plausible reasons or justifications for beliefs, behavior, or motives that might reflect unfavorably upon the self or might be socially disapproved.
Projection	*Disowning:* Imputing one's unacknowledged faults or unacceptable motives to others. *Assimilative:* Assuming others possess the same traits and motives as oneself.
Identification	Assuming the role behaviors, traits, status, values, and accomplishments of another person, group, or institution. May involve imitation and introjection.
Introjection	Process of accepting and incorporating the values and standards of another as one's own; precedes development of identification. Termed *defensive identification* when prompted by aversive motives, such as fear of punishment or loss of love.
Sublimation	Satisfaction of socially unacceptable motives with socially acceptable behavior.
Reaction formation	Expression of behavior opposite to socially unacceptable motives.
Compensation	Development of traits or skills that will substitute or make up for deficiencies in characteristics or behaviors which will satisfy certain motives.
Emotional insulation *	Withdrawal into passivity to protect self from hurt.
Isolation *	Cutting off affective charge from hurtful situations or separating incompatible attitudes by logic-tight compartments.
Undoing *	Atoning for and thus counteracting immoral desires or acts.
Sympathism *	Striving to gain sympathy from others, thus bolstering feelings of self-worth despite failures.
Acting out*	Reduction of the anxiety aroused by forbidden desires by permitting their expression.
Stress Reactions	
Alarm reaction	Physiological reactions involving changes in respiration, pulse, blood pressure, secretion of adrenin, muscular tension, etc., experienced as emotion.
Anxiety	Oscillation behavior; apprehensiveness, uneasiness, dread, worry, diffuse, nonspecific feelings of tension, panic.

*Adapted from Coleman (1956), p. 99.

1. *Repression.* This mental mechanism has been called "motivated forgetting," because of the manner in which motives, impulses, and thoughts that are incompatible with self-needs are excluded from awareness, thus permitting an individual to maintain satisfactory self-attitudes. The following case illustrates how repression might even distort one's perceptions.

Doris, aged 15, was referred by a state family welfare agency to a psychologist for an evaluation of her adjustment problems with her foster parents. For the past 10 years, Doris had lived in three different foster homes, since her natural mother left her to state custody following desertion by her natural father. Though her natural mother had remarried, and had produced another child, she had made no attempt to recover Doris or even to see her, and Doris knew this. In responding to a picture of the projective Blacky Test, which shows a Mama dog nursing her puppy, Doris described some small figures in the background, rather than the central figures. Later she picked this card as the one she liked least of all the cards, but could not say why. It seemed to the examiner that Doris was repressing conflicting feelings about her natural mother: she felt hurt and hostile because of her abandonment, yet basically she craved the loved of her mother. In refusing to recognize the motherly behavior shown in the picture, Doris protected herself from feelings of anxiety.

Repression can benefit a person by blinding him to conflicts and problems that could overwhelm him. This self-shielding gives him time to think things through rationally and to manage his difficulties in more appropriate ways. As a mechanism, repression is risky, however, because repression does nothing to alleviate the original frustration. If allowed to become insidious, such frustration could permit more serious mechanisms, such as denial, fantasy, projection, or regression, to assume mastery. It is for this reason that repression has been called a *master mechanism.*

2. *Escape Mechanisms.* A common by-product of repression is *denial,* a refusal to acknowledge that an intolerable situation or condition exists— a type of psychological escape. One example might be the girl who announced she expected to become a physician despite the fact that she had very low measured ability and was failing every subject in her first college term. She could not accept the limitations that were apparent to anyone who knew her.

Sometimes the escape is physical, such as in the case of the student who finds social obligations much more compelling for his attention than study for an examination, which might mean being dropped from college. In extreme cases, a reluctant bridegroom fails to appear for the wedding ceremony, to be found later living in another community with an assumed name, oblivious of the circumstances or of his former life. Such flight is termed a *fugue*; loss of memory for the event is called *amnesia*.

Daydreaming and *fantasy*, in which a boy imagines himself sinking the winning basket, or a man pictures being applauded for a rousing after-dinner speech, or a person contemplates how people will be at his own funeral, weeping and sad, regretting their nasty ways—all supply escape from feelings of inadequacy or low self-esteem. *Regression*, another mechanism, represents retreat from mature to less mature solutions as an escape from responsibility—a kind of giving up. An older child, jealous of the new baby, may revert to bed-wetting or thumbsucking; a soldier may cry for his mother when wounded or dying; the returning alumnus may attempt to recapture the spirit of a less responsible past, singing ". . . we'll all be boys again together. . . ." Each is showing a variant of regression, an unconscious return to patterns of behavior typical of earlier periods of dependency and security.

Each of these escape reactions represents withdrawal from or avoidance of threat to the self. Although escape might relieve anxiety partially or temporarily, ultimately their use adds to overall maladjustment because they substitute for positive solution behavior that could satisfy the original motivations. When denial, fantasy, and regression take over as solutions to anxiety, a person tends to become increasingly detached from a real world. He may drift into more serious conditions that require even more drastic mobilizations of energy.

3. *Masking Mechanisms.* By controlling the nature of one's responses, sometimes the true source of anxiety can be concealed both from oneself and from others. *Rationalization* is perhaps the most common of the mechanisms employed to disguise motives. It consists of giving plausible reasons that will excuse or justify mistakes, failures, or behavior which we sense will not be approved. This protects the self from loss of esteem or feelings of incompetence. Rationalizations range from harmless statements like "Just one more won't matter . . ." or "The prof had it in for me" to serious psychotic delusions, such as those in which a person believes he is being forced to commit immoral acts by men from outer space. Rationalization combines repression with displacement to shift the blame away from the self and onto circumstances beyond one's control or onto other people.

In *projection*, a person disguises motives, which are unacceptable to the self, by imputing them to others. An adolescent boy who harbors hostile feelings toward his father for imposing restrictions might accuse his father of hating him, in this way disowning his own aggressive feelings for the father. This is called *disowning projection*. By shifting the blame, he can relieve himself of guilt for such feelings. It is a form of displacement. Another type of projection is called *assimilative projection*, in which a person assumes that other people are like himself. If he can be convinced that "they all do it," or that others have the same feelings and motives, he is relieved of feelings of guilt or shame.

Identification is a masking mechanism in which a person assumes certain behaviors or attitudes of another person or adopts the values and behaviors of a group or institution. In doing this, the person cloaks himself vicariously with the benefits or attributes of the model person or group. Not only does this build self-esteem but this mechanism is vital in the socialization of the child. By identification with his father, a child learns to play a masculine role; from his mother he may develop attitudes of tolerance and affection for others; from his teacher he may learn patriotism or perseverance in work. Virtually every meaningful personal relationship for a child provides identifications and influences his subsequent changes in attitudes and social behaviors. Imitation of heroes is a first step in developing motives for achievement and mastery. Political parties, clubs of all kinds, alumni groups, team sports, and military morale would disintegrate were it not for identification processes. The person who identifies with others can feel bigger and stronger. Knowing he belongs to a certain group gives him a feeling of status and belonging. When the identification becomes only basking in reflected glory with little attempt to develop genuine accomplishment, however, then the identification mechanism becomes a hindrance to good adjustment, just as with fantasy.

We sometimes speak of *defensive identification* or *introjection* to describe how one adopts the standards and values of other persons in order to ward off punishment. The expression often cited is "If you can't beat the enemy, join them!" The child who has been severely dominated and punished may develop rigid codes of conscience and strongly punitive attitudes toward others who transgress his rules. The formation of a rigid conscience regarding moral or ethical matters is often traceable to the introjection of social controls enforced with fear and punishment in the toilet-training years. By adopting self-controls, anxieties of guilt and shame are prevented.

4. *Response-Modification Mechanisms.* In its earliest use by psychoanalysts, *sublimation* referred to satisfaction of unacceptable sexual impulses by such substitutes as dancing, art, or musical performance. Today, it refers more generally to socially acceptable substitute behaviors for any motives. We recognize that there are many components to a motive–response sequence and that certain components of the response found in so-called substitute behaviors can partially satisfy the motives. Hence, a person might discharge feelings of aggression in some degree through par-

ticipation in competitive sports or by reading novels of crime and violence. In the same way a woman can satisfy certain sexual motives by reading confession magazines or a man can read man-about-town magazines. A childless woman may become devoted to raising dogs or to causes that benefit children.

When an unacceptable response is blocked by the expression of its opposite, it is called *reaction formation*. Some of the most militant crusaders against smoking or drinking are former addicts. Preachers who rail against sin and corruption often admit they were themselves once sinful. In each of these cases, their present exhortation and preoccupation with a cause suggests they are reacting strongly in opposition to their own inclinations. Some persons attracted to law enforcement or legal vocations similarly seem to be controlling the opposite impulses, to commit crime. When the mechanism fails, we observe police who form crime rings and lawyers who specialize in defending underworld bosses.

Through *compensation* one can make up for deficiencies in one area with excellence in another. The outstanding scholar or athlete is often one who suffered severely in his youth from physical or social handicaps. Sometimes a shy and inarticulate youth perseveres to overcome his handicap and to become outstanding as an actor or orator. Advertisements often appeal to compensation defenses by suggestive promises of instant youth, status, or talent to persons who use their products, whether in booklet or tablet form. By compensation in one area a person neutralizes his weaknesses in other characteristics; this helps him to maintain a strong self-concept.

Stress Reactions. Another class of responses to frustration, called *stress reactions*, is oriented neither to task nor to defense alone but is preliminary and, to some extent, preparatory to both.

The *alarm reaction*, according to Selye (1956, p. 31), is a syndrome or pattern of physiological reactions to a "stressor," which represents "the bodily expression of a generalized call to arms of the defensive forces in the organism."

Cannon (1960) describes the alarm reactions of the body to rage and fear as follows:

Respiration deepens, the heart beats more rapidly, the arterial pressure rises, the blood is shifted away from the stomach and intestines to the heart and central nervous system and the muscles, the processes in the alimentary canal cease, sugar is freed from the reserves in the liver, the spleen contracts and discharges its content of concentrated corpuscles, and adrenin is secreted from the adrenal medulla. The key to these marvelous transformations in the body is found in relating them to the natural accompaniments of fear and rage—running away in order to escape from danger, and attacking in order to be dominant. Whichever the action a life-or-death struggle may ensue.

The emotional responses just listed may reasonably be regarded as preparatory for struggle. They are adjustments which, so far as possible, put the organism in readiness for meeting the demands which will be made upon it. The secreted adrenin cooperates with sympathetic nerve impulses in calling forth stored glycogen from the liver, thus flooding the blood with sugar for the use of laboring muscles; it helps in distributing the blood in abundance to the heart, brain, and the limbs (i.e., to the parts essential for intense physical effort) while taking it away from the inhibited organs in the abdomen; it quickly abolishes the effects of muscular fatigue so that the organism which can muster adrenin in the blood can restore to its tired muscles the same readiness to act which they had when fresh; and it renders the blood more rapidly coagulable. The increased respiration, the redistributed blood running at high pressure, and the more numerous red corpuscles set free from the spleen provide for essential oxygen and for riddance of acid waste, and make a setting for instantaneous and supreme action. In short, all these changes are directly serviceable in rendering the organism more effective in the violent display of energy which fear or rage may involve.

Funkenstein (1955) reports even more distinctive physiological reactions between men who typically express their anger outwards—that is, displace their aggression—and those who express their anger inward, either against themselves or inhibiting it.

A group of 125 college students were subjected to stress-inducing situations in the laboratory. The situations, involving frustration, were contrived to bring out each student's habitual reaction to stresses in real life; that the reactions actually were characteristic of the subjects' usual responses was confirmed by interviews with their college roommates. While the subjects were under stress, observers recorded their emotional reactions and certain physiological changes—in the blood pressure, the pulse and the so-called IJ waves stemming from the action of the heart. This test showed that students who responded to the stress with anger directed outward had physiological reactions similar to those produced by injection of nor-adrenalin, while students who responded with depression or anxiety had physiological reactions like those to adrenalin.

There remained the question: Does the same individual secrete unusual amounts of nor-adrenalin when angry and of adrenalin when frightened? Albert F. Ax, working in another laboratory in our hospital, designed experiments to study this question. He contrived laboratory stressful situations which were successful in producing on one occasion anger and on another occasion fear in the same subjects. His results showed that when a subject was angry at others, the physiological reactions were like those induced by the injection of nor-adrenalin; when the same subject was frightened, the reactions were like those to adrenalin. This indicated that the physiology was specific for the emotion rather than for the person.

ANXIETY REACTIONS. When first confronted by conflict or frustration, a person may be surprised and unable to decide what action to take. He may start to make a response, check it, start another, stop, and perhaps begin over again or try something new, never really completing any response pattern. Such back-and-forth behavior is called *oscillation*. Under even greater stress, a person might "freeze" and make no response at all. Many accidents involving autos that stall at railroad grade crossings before onrushing trains are probably due to temporary "freezing" of the driver in extreme fright.

Doubt, indecision, apprehensiveness, or worries all contribute to such feelings of anxiety. Emotions of stress range from mild general uneasiness or concern, such as stage fright, to stronger feelings of dread, grief, helplessness, or mortal fear. Such nonspecific feelings do not indicate definite responses of a task or defense orientation, hence promote oscillation and disorganized behavior.

We can observe a mild form of oscillation and generalized anxiety when a student panics several days before an important examination. Even though he knows he should study, he cannot get down to work. He frets, worries, distracts himself with trivial activities, begins to read, quits, turns to something else, comes back to the reading, stops, listens to the radio, then returns to his task. Then he may repeat the whole fruitless cycle. He thinks he is studying! Perhaps he experiences dryness in his throat, sweaty palms, and heart pounding. His sleep may be fitful; his stomach does "flip-flops." These oscillation behaviors, coupled with alarm reactions and many other symptoms of behavioral disorganization, are stress reactions typical of "test anxiety."

Effects of Prolonged or Extreme Stress or Frustration. What happens if a stress condition continues or becomes even stronger? Sometimes this will occur if the motivation of a person increases or if he cannot release the energy that has been mobilized during the alarm reaction. Both the frustration and its secondary stress build up. In this situation, a person goes all-out and enters what Selye (1956) has called the *stage of resistance*.

In the face of mounting anxiety the person shifts away from using weaker but more socially approved defense mechanisms like rationalization, identification, or compensation. He turns to more powerful protective unconscious strategies that may be less socially accepted, or even socially criticized, such as denial, regression, or fantasy (Thorpe and Katz,

1948). These mechanisms are more costly to the individual. They require greater expenditure of energy in order to maintain the repression which will preserve positive self-attitudes, for there is more personal risk if they fail. Gradually use of more drastic mechanisms leads the person even further from satisfying his initial motivation. His tolerance for further stress weakens. He fails to meet new problems realistically and maturely. Gradually, what began as an emergency measure in the alarm stage becomes a rigid response characteristic of the stage of resistance. Feelings of anxiety and fear of losing self-control begin to dominate the individual. The siege has begun. Defensive behavior reigns; task-oriented behavior declines.

Defense Mechanisms Can Be Helpful. It should be understood that there is nothing inherently good or bad about the use of defenses. As temporary expedients in meeting small crises of everyday living they are used by everyone without ill effects. The wheels of social machinery often run smoother with occasional "white lies," identification, or by use of rationalizations. Normally such defenses are discarded following the threatening situation with few, if any, residual effects, and the stress is relieved successfully. The neurotic person, however, resorts to defenses almost constantly, rigidly, and in less socially desirable or efficient ways. Although his anxiety might be reduced momentarily, ultimately the stress increases, because his initial motives never become satisfied.

BEHAVIORAL MALADJUSTMENT

At this stage the behaviors become sufficiently deviant to be called symptoms of mental illness. It is beyond the scope of this chapter to deal extensively with the many varieties of psychoneuroses, psychoses, personality disorders, and mental retardation. We shall merely sketch the major types of disorders and outline the subclassifications in Table 2.4.

Psychoneuroses. When the symptoms are characterized by anxiety, directly felt or unconsciously controlled by use of various psychological defense mechanisms, but without gross disorganization of personality or loss of contact with reality, the disorders are called *psychoneuroses*. Ordinarily, persons with such problems are able to make marginal adjustments in everyday living and to carry out social responsibilities without need for hospitalization, although they might benefit from medication and counseling.

Many people have pet aversions which they find difficult to explain, such as uneasiness in crowds, fear of knives, or impulses to jump from high places. Many times we feel "nervous" and upset without knowing why. Sometimes we have convenient "headaches" which get us out of social obligations. Were these mild reactions to play a central role, to be used rigidly, almost as a ritual, or to be associated with lasting anxiety, they might be considered psychoneurotic. Happily, most of us live quite easily with such symptoms and feel little concern. Thus, although hardly symptoms of mental illness, they might signal underlying inferiority feelings and feelings of inadequacy which are common and expected in everyday life.

Psychosomatic Disorders. When the usual channels for expressing emotion are blocked by repression, the energy may be discharged through bodily systems, such as the skin, respiratory, cardiovascular, gastrointestinal, or other systems. We have seen already how the alarm reaction produces visceral changes in the blood, breathing, and stomach. When such arousal in any system is prolonged, a reaction occurs in the system. It has been shown, for example, that peptic ulcers result from oversecretion of digestive juices in the stomach triggered by chronic anxiety, worry, and repressed hostility (Wolf and Wolff, 1946). The author recalls a student who repeatedly had migraine headaches almost invariably on days when he received a letter from home. During counseling he revealed his strong feelings of resentment of his parents and guilt over his weak scholastic performance. As counseling continued he became more able to express his feelings and to come to understand his problems better, to effect a better relationship with his parents, better grades, and his migraine headaches ceased.

Almost any bodily system is vulnerable. Even illnesses involving cancer and cardiac failure have been shown to have psychosomatic complications. Such diverse ailments as skin eruptions, backache, hiccoughs, menstrual disturbances, "heartburn," and various glandular disorders have been found sometimes to be psychosomatic in origin.

Psychotic Disorders. When there is more severe personality disorganization with disorientation for time, place, or person, and the person is frequently out of touch with reality, has delusions, hallucinations, or speech defects, and shows little insight into the nature or degree of his disturbance, the disorders are called *psychoses*. For psychotic persons, hospitalization is ordinarily required not only to receive more extensive medical treatment with drug and shock therapies but also because they could injure themselves or others and require care and supervision. The major psychotic disorders, as described in the *Diagnostic and Statistical Manual for Mental Disorders* of the American Psychiatric Association (1952), are listed in Table 2.4.

TABLE 2.4   Major Mental Disorders *

Psychoneurotic Disorders:
1. *Anxiety reaction*—diffuse acute anxiety not restricted to definite objects or situations.
2. *Dissociative reactions*—amnesia, fugue, dream state, multiple personality, etc.
3. *Conversion reaction*—repressed anxiety converted into symptoms of physical illness in organs or parts of body.
4. *Phobic reaction*—fears attached to ideas or objects, such as fear of germs, high places, elevators, etc.
5. *Obsessive-compulsive reaction*—persistent unwanted ideas or irrational impulses to perform morbid acts.
6. *Depressive reaction*—acute feelings of dejection or self-depreciation following loss or events.

Psychosomatic Disorders (psychophysiologic autonomic and visceral disorders):
1. *Psychophysiologic skin reaction*—dermatitis, for example.
2. *Musculoskeletal reaction*—psychogenic backaches or tension headaches, for example.
3. *Respiratory reaction*—such as psychogenic asthma or hiccoughs.
4. *Cardiovascular reaction*—such as hypertension, migraine.
5. *Hemic and lymphatic reaction*—emotionally caused blood disorders.
6. *Gastrointestinal reaction*—such as chronic gastritis, ulcerative colitis, hyperacidity, nervous vomiting, etc.
7. *Genitourinary reaction*—includes some types of menstrual disturbances and difficulties in urination.
8. *Endocrine reaction*—emotionally caused obesity, for example.
9. *Nervous system reaction*—such as general fatigue or emotionally generated convulsions (other than epilepsy).
10. *Organs of special sense*—such as changes in eyes or ears due to emotional causes, other than conversion reactions.

Organic brain disorders, acute (associated with):
1. *Intracranial infection*—such as encephalitis, meningitis.
2. *Systemic infection*—such as typhoid fever, rheumatic fever.
3. *Drug or poison intoxication*—bromides, opiates, lead, gas, etc.
4. *Alcohol intoxication*—such as delirium tremens (D.T.'s).
5. *Trauma*—gross head injury.
6. *Circulatory disturbance*—due to hypertension and cardiac, etc.
7. *Convulsive disorder*—only idiopathic epilepsy.
8. *Metabolic disturbance*—such as hyperthyroidism, uremia, or diabetes.
9. *Intracranial neoplasm*—brain tumors.
10. *Unknown causes*—such as multiple sclerosis.

Organic brain disorders, chronic (associated with):
1. *Brain conditions associated with mental deficiency*—due to mongolism, prenatal maternal disease, birth injury, etc.

2. *Syphilis*—general paresis, and others.
3. *Intracranial infections*—such as encephalitis.
4. *Intoxication*—due to drugs, alcohol, gas, and poisons.
5. *Brain trauma*—due to head injury or surgery.
6. *Cerebral arterioscleroses.*
7. *Circulatory disturbance*—blood clots and hemorrhages in brain, for example.
8. *Convulsive disorders*—due to epilepsy.
9. *Senile brain disease.*
10. *Metabolism, growth, or nutrition*—endocrine disorders, vitamin deficiencies, when permanent damage is done.
11. *Intracranial neoplasm*—brain tumors and pressures.
12. *Unknown causes*—such as multiple sclerosis, Huntington's chorea, Pick's disease, and others.

Functional psychoses:
1. *Involutional psychotic reaction*—depression or paranoia occurring in the involutional period without previous psychosis.
2. *Affective reactions*—disorders of mood with disturbance of thought and behavior consistent with emotion.
   a. *Manic depressive reactions*—marked mood swings with excited, active, or dejected phases or either alone.
   b. *Depressive reactions*—severe depression, with delusions and hallucinations, with precipitating factors.
3. *Schizophrenic reactions*—a group of psychotic reactions with disturbances in reality relationships and thinking with emotional and behavioral disturbances.
   a. *Simple type*—impoverished social relationships, indifference, and apathy, without apparent delusions or hallucinations.
   b. *Hebephrenic type*—marked disorganization, giggling, silly behavior, delusions, hallucinations, and regression of social behavior.
   c. *Catatonic type*—generalized inhibition of behavior, negativism, even stupor, or hyperactivity and excitement.
   d. *Paranoid type*—fantasy type, unrealistic thinking with poorly systematized delusions of persecution or grandeur, with unpredictable, aggressive, hostile behavior.
   e. *Mixed types*—various combinations of the foregoing types.
4. *Paranoid reactions*—persistent well-systematized delusions, ordinarily persecutory or grandiose, generally without hallucinations. No impairment of intelligence.

Mental Retardation (mental deficiency):
1. *Mild*—IQ = 70–85; can learn academic skills to approximately 6th grade by late teens; capable of self-maintenance in unskilled or semiskilled occupations.
2. *Moderate*—IQ = 50–70; can talk or learn to communicate; cannot learn functional academic skills; profits from systematic habit training; can contribute partially to self-support under complete supervision; needs controlled environment and guidance.
3. *Severe*—IQ = Below 50; functional impairment requiring custodial or complete protective care; some speech and motor development; totally incapable of self-maintenance.

Personality Disorders (developmental defects or pathological trends in person-

TABLE 2.4—continued

ality structure based upon lifelong behavior patterns rather than reactions to stress; show little anxiety):
1. *Personality pattern disturbance*—types similar to major psychoses, which may shift to psychosis under stress.
2. *Personality trait disturbance*—emotionally unstable, immature, passive-dependent or passive-aggressive persons.
3. *Sociopathic personality disturbance*—social nonconformists; show lack of concern for others; irresponsible.
    a. *Antisocial reaction*—always in trouble without profiting from experience or punishment; feel no loyalty to persons or groups.
    b. *Dyssocial reaction*—violate social codes due to poor environmental background; not otherwise deviant.
    c. *Sexual deviation*—may include many pathological sex behaviors.
    d. *Addiction*—drug addiction and alcoholism.
4. *Special symptom reactions*—special symptom prominence, such as stuttering, nail-biting, enuresis, etc.

---

* The major part of this table has been adapted from the *Diagnostic and Statistical Manual for Mental Disorders*, 1952. Parts of the section on mental retardation have been suggested by Sloan and Birch, 1955.

The principal categories of psychotic disorders are:

1. *Organic brain disorders.* Many psychotic disorders are caused by or associated with impairment of brain tissue function. The basic syndrome that characterizes them consists of impairments of orientation, memory, all intellectual functions, judgment, and emotional expression, the amount of brain damage determining the amount of impairment. These symptoms may be associated with other psychotic, psychoneurotic, or behavioral symptoms not necessarily related to the organic disorder, and may have been precipitated by the organic damage. The organic disorders are classified as "acute" if the disorder seems reversible or "chronic" if the disorder seems permanent.

Acute brain disorders (from which one can recover) may be caused by intoxication from drugs, alcohol, or poisons, infections, and fevers, such as encephalitis ("sleeping sickness"), brain injuries, high blood pressure, hyperthyroidism, and so on. Chronic brain disorders result from relatively permanent impairment of tissue functions due to congenital defects, syphilis, toxic poisons (such as lead, arsenic, carbon monoxide, drugs, or alcohol), brain injury, epilepsy, cerebral arteriosclerosis, senility, and other causes.

2. *Functional psychoses* are disorders of psychogenic origin that show no physical changes in the brain. There are three main types: affective (including manic-depressive), schizophrenic, and paranoid reactions. (See Table 2.4.)

Those with *affective disorders* show severe disturbances of mood and emotional expression. In a manic condition the patient may show elation or irritability, overtalkativeness, rapid changes of ideas, with delusions (false beliefs) of grandeur common, and almost constant motion or activity of the body. In a *depressed* condition a patient may be dejected, express feelings of guilt or worthlessness, reduced activity, retarded speech —even stupor. Some patients alternate between manic and depressed phases; others may show but one condition.

Schizophrenic reactions show a wide range of symptoms characterized by withdrawal from social relationships, rejection of reality, bizarre thinking, hallucinations and delusions, emotional dulling, or emotions that have no apparent meaning, and deterioration of personal habits and social control. Several types are sketched in Table 2.4. Often the symptoms shown by a psychotic patient represent acting out of his inner turmoil and conflicts, as portrayed in Figure 2.3.

Figure 2.3. Psychotic patient "acting out" her anxieties and conflicts. Depicted in film *People Who Care*. (Courtesy of National Institute of Mental Health, Bethesda, Maryland.)

Patients with paranoid reactions show well-systematized, persistent delusions, usually of a persecutory or grandiose type, but ordinarily without hallucinations or impairment of intelligence.

Mental Retardation.   Mental retardation refers to those individuals whose limitations in intellectual functioning impair their capacity to meet the demands of their environment or to develop social independence. Their lack of mental ability may be due to heredity, disease, injury, or to impaired maturation of the brain during its developmental period, as revealed by faulty growth of motor and verbal skills, deficient learning, and poor social adjustment.

There are many ways to classify mental retardation disorders: (1) according to measured mental ability, (2) according to assumed causes, (3) according to adaptive-behavior-level classifications, such as "trainable" or "educable," or (4) by omnibus terms that classify patients according to "severity" on the basis of composite social and intellectual criteria, such as mild, moderate, and severe. The last-named classification is employed by the American Psychiatric Association.

Personality Disorders.   Several personality disturbances, sometimes called "character disorders," which do not fit readily under any other categories, fall into this classification. The most general characteristic is behavior which is immature or socially unacceptable with little indication of remorse, concern, or anxiety. Deviations from social mores bordering upon criminal activity, sexual pathology, and addictions to drugs or alcohol not involving psychosis are included. Diagnosis is difficult because many features of these disorders are similar to those found with psychoneuroses and psychoses.

CAUSES OF BEHAVIORAL MALADJUSTMENT
Multiple Causation.   Many factors acting together are responsible for one's mental health or illness. Occasionally one factor or another may predominate, but even then the weakness or activity of other factors affects how one will respond to events or conditions. At any one time our behavior depends upon characteristics we have inherited, the stage of our development as accelerated or retarded by metabolic or nutritional factors, physical potentialities, and patterns of learned behavior all acting and reacting in complex, changing systems of environmental stimuli. Some persons who might have physical or psychological susceptibilities to stress might never encounter the conditions that would trigger illness. Others who may be basically stronger might encounter such stress that they become ill. Each person has a breaking point. For some it is less than for others.

Noyes and Kolb (1963) observe that disturbed communication between and adjustments of various psychological and physiological subsystems, rather than either alone, are the main determinants of breakdown.

Stresses in interpersonal relations and in the sociocultural field are no less to be considered than stresses in the biophysical sphere. Behavior cannot be adequately described in the terms of an impersonal disorganization of cellular structure or physiological processes, nor do there seem to be any psychiatric symptoms—except in some cases of toxic organic syndromes—which can be considered as correlates of brain changes, physiological, biochemical, or electrical.

. . . Any disturbance of the brain or other bodily tissues which influence the capacity of man to receive, perceive, and integrate information from his environment with past information will lead to defective psychosocial functioning and thereby disturb personality functioning. Any physical disturbance which upsets man's capacity to communicate with others again will lead to ineffective communication that produces disturbing feedback. The latter, in turn, induces anxiety, conflict, and personality unrest.

Thus one may recognize as etiologic [causal] factors in disrupting the communicative activity between men the effects of constitutional defects in the perceptual system, such as deafness or blindness, failures of development or acquired defects in the central nervous system (the integrating organ of communication), or the later dysfunction of this organ due to metabolic or toxic agents. Again, failures to learn language, to understand social codes, or to speak effectively, with resultant interference with later ability to recognize and integrate psychosocial or provide guiding signs again may be seen as contributing factors to disturbance in communication or psychosocial illness. Viewed as a disorder in interpersonal communication, the arguments relative to the etiology of psychiatric illness as primarily psychical or psychological become meaningless. One attempts to understand the totality of the personality functioning in a communicative relationship with others.

HEREDITY. Except for a few rare mental deficiencies (infantile and juvenile amaurotic idiocy and phenylketonuria) and the psychosis Huntington's chorea, there is little conclusive evidence for direct single-gene inheritance of mental disorder. Possible genetic involvement in schizophrenia has been demonstrated by studies of concordance in illness of identical and fraternal twins. Studies by Kallman (1959) and Slater (1961) have shown that the identical twin of a schizophrenic was five or six times more likely to become schizophrenic than the fraternal twin of a schizophrenic. The expected incidence of schizophrenia among siblings of schizophrenics ranges from 5 to 10 percent if both parents are normal, from 8 to 18 percent if one parent is schizophrenic, but rises to 45 to 68 percent in children of two schizophrenic parents. Questions have been raised about the statistical treatment or lack of comparability of the twin groups in these studies, however, so that the issue of genetic involvement is debatable (David and Snyder, 1962).

Varying degrees of genetic cause have been claimed for several senile diseases, manic-depressive and involutional psychoses, homosexuality, and myoclonic epilepsy (Shields and Slater, 1961). The complex interweaving of pre- and postnatal influences of disease, nutrition and disturbing early family environment with genetic factors, however, makes conclusions hazardous. We must turn, therefore, to a study of these influences for a more complete understanding of causal factors.

BIOLOGICAL AND PHYSICAL FACTORS. Physical defects, such as deformations of the spine, clubbed feet, cleft palate, and congenital[2] defects of vision or hearing take their psychological toll in feelings of inferiority, social isolation, and negative self-attitudes, thus reducing a handicapped person's resistance to stress. It is known too that several mental deficiencies are caused by maternal prenatal diseases, such as German measles, birth injuries, or endocrine disorders.

Illnesses of any kind sometimes contribute to conflicts and frustrations already present. Much of the disability in both mental and physical illness is traceable to the hospitalization itself as well as to the disease. Separation from family, worry over finances and loss of wages, plus feelings of helplessness and fear of the illness, all contribute to stress. Any weaknesses already present may become exaggerated. Psychosomatic disorders may accompany, augment, or be precipitated by almost any other mental or physical illness and greatly complicate the symptom picture. This is true especially of the biological decline due to aging.

It is true, of course, that many disease conditions influence or cause mental disorder directly. Because they are listed under acute and chronic organic brain disorders in Table 2.4, they will not be elaborated here. It might be added, however, that any of several biological conditions may precipitate psychological stress reactions. The list would include oxygen deprivation, perhaps due to neardrowning or to high altitude, nutritional deficiencies, such as due to starvation or lack of vitamins, sleep or dream deprivation, and sensory deprivation.

SOCIAL LEARNING EXPERIENCES. Perhaps the greatest contributor to maladjustment is in the area of socialization. When a child is born into a family he forms a meaningful relationship first with his mother, then with other members of his family who satisfy his needs and administer rewards and punishments for his behavior. Through these relationships, systems of punishments and reinforcements, and by generalization of attitudes so

---

[2] *Hereditary* refers to characteristics transmitted from parent to offspring genetically; *congenital* refers to characteristics existing at or dating from birth which are acquired during development in the uterus but not due to heredity.

formed to others, the child comes to attach certain values to people, to depend upon them, and to form conceptions about himself from these interactions.

These relationships are the wellspring of the self. If the early family experiences are pleasant and reassuring, the child adjusts and develops well socially, forms wholesome self-attitudes, and is able to accomplish various developmental tasks with a minimum of stress. Should any of numerous unfavorable family conditions or child rearing practices establish fears, conflicts, hostilities, or negative self-reactions, not only will the person experience intrafamily tensions, but he will be handicapped in future social relationships. These, in turn, affect future self- and other-adjustments, and the stresses amass like a rolling snowball. Depriving a child of a close, secure maternal relationship, whether due to deliberate or unintentional separation or rejection, at a critical period can reduce his ability to form close relationships of trust and affection with either parent or with others later in life. Frustrations in toilet training, of inconsistent or severe discipline, rejection, indulgence, domination, jealousy of siblings or of a parent, unreasonable demands for perfection—all prevent a child from developing social skills and favorable self-attitudes and thus reduce his ability to cope with frustration and his resilience to stress. The effects are often cumulative and progressive. Poorly adjusted in his family, the child may lack the skills to adjust well to his peer group, and lacking these skills, he may fail to adjust in his schooling, his work, his marriage, and possibly fail in understanding his own children.

Special social or catastrophic conditions may aggravate these problems. Unemployment, poverty, war or threat of war, natural disasters, such as floods, earthquakes, or tornadoes, may bring weaknesses to the point of illness. Problems of religious, racial, or social class discrimination may affect self-evaluations and social interaction. These have been mentioned as sources of external frustration earlier in this chapter.

Critical Stages in the Development of Mental Health or Mental Illness

STAGE I: PRENATAL CONDITIONS, EARLY FAMILY ENVIRONMENT, AND BEHAVIORAL DEVELOPMENTS OF THE CHILD.   Most children are born healthy, but some are born defective or injured. This is the period when the basic influences of heredity and congenital traumas and diseases are asserted, and the foundations are laid for social learning and personality. Occasionally adjustment problems of childhood signal the deeper disturbances, but too often such symptoms are dismissed as "nervousness" or are treated as misbehaviors or bad habits, and so are left untreated or are met with rejection and discipline. This is sometimes true even for organic difficulties associated with mental deficiency. Needless to say, this is the period of incubation for many mental illnesses which will flower in later years.

STAGE II: CRISES OF EVERYDAY LIVING AND DEVELOPMENT, FROM PREADOLESCENCE THROUGHOUT THE LIFE SPAN. This stage covers from problems of early peer group and school adjustment to difficulties in social relationships and responsibility in family and community living, religion, courtship, marriage, and parenthood, occupational choice and satisfaction, economic stability, physical illness, aging, and various other emotional and environmental stresses. In Selye's (1956) terminology, this stage encompasses the stages of alarm and resistance.

STAGE III: ONSET OF MENTAL ILLNESS. Difficulties developed in the first two stages culminate in symptoms of mental breakdown. There is rapid deterioration of work habits, family and social relationships and responsibilities, and overall personal control in the home and community.

STAGE IV: TREATMENT. The treatment often requires prolonged hospital care and therapy. For milder or earlier cases, outpatient treatment may be given in a psychiatric clinic or general hospital. For some disorders, psychiatrists in private practice may offer outpatient medical treatment or psychotherapy.

STAGE V: REHABILITATION OF THE MENTAL PATIENT. This includes various types of therapy, training, and community services which assist the patient to return to the community, to obtain satisfactory employment, to make adequate social and personal adjustment following treatment, and to prevent recurrence of the disorders.

Prevention, Treatment, and Rehabilitation. As we have seen in this chapter, many mental illnesses have a long history in the individual, beginning in early childhood, and are the result of many interacting factors of a physical and emotional nature resulting in stress. Cloaked by family and friends, many mental illnesses appear only after years of progressive maladaptation to problems of everyday living, plus physiological changes, some of which are believed to be aggravated or caused by crises of growing up or aging, disease, and unresolved frustrations.

For this reason we no longer think of treating disorders only when they appear fully developed, but we search for ways to prevent or to arrest their growth, and seek means to restore to normal, responsible, and productive living in their homes and communities those who have been treated successfully.

The modern emphasis has shifted from concern only for treatment and care of mental illness to more comprehensive attention to ways to develop and to maintain mental health and to promote optimal human functioning.

In the next chapter we shall be concerned with the first line of attack upon the problem of mental illness—prevention—by means of improved care, training, and guidance which will develop optimal human functioning during the first two stages: Stage I, which encompasses prenatal life, early family experiences, and behavioral development, and Stage II, which includes the crises of everyday living from preadolescence throughout the life span. The chapter following will deal with the second line of attack: detection in Stage III (onset of mental illness), treatment in Stage IV, and return of the patient to productive, satisfying living in Stage V (rehabilitation).

SUMMARY

Mental illness and mental retardation together affect about one person in 10 and constitute the greatest health problem in America. In numbers of patients, in cost to every wage earner and his family through medical bills and taxes, in numbers of hours lost from work, mental disorders lead all other illnesses combined.

From earliest times the mentally disordered were chained and tortured because they were feared and believed to be wicked or controlled by demons. It was found that, treated with medical care, kindness, and given more freedom, patients were less disturbed, and some even became well. Bolstered by medical and scientific discoveries, treatment in hospitals and clinics became more prevalent. Public concern for prevention, as well as improved care and treatment, was further stimulated by the mental hygiene and mental health movements. These movements enlisted extensive governmental support for developing and maintaining mental health facilities and training personnel in hospitals, clinics, and community mental health centers.

Mental health is a difficult term to define because it embraces several often contradictory criteria: social, individual, and functional. Mental health and mental illness are seen as extreme ranges of a scale of composite behaviors which are positively or negatively valued according to these criteria. Therefore, multiple criteria are needed to describe one's mental status. Mental conditions are ever-changing and complex, resulting from dynamic interactions between the individual, his many social groups, and shifting environmental conditions.

The human being is seen as a complex energy system consisting of many coordinated subsystems interacting with many other systems. Changes in the person or his behavior which result from changes in inner or outer stimuli are called adjustment. Response patterns aroused by such stimuli acquire labels as aversive or appetitive motives according to the apparent goals of the responses, so we speak of needs for food, activity, achievement, and so on.

The self is a construct denoting a cognitive and action-controlling subsystem which becomes a focal point for stability and resourcefulness in satisfying motives and coping with changes. Maintaining the adequacy and safety of the self thus becomes a major function of the individual. Whatever threatens the self or blocks satisfaction of either appetitive or aversive motives is termed frustration.

Reactions to frustration may be either task-oriented—that is, directed toward initial motive satisfaction—defense-oriented—that is, protective of the self—or a stress reaction. Task-oriented reactions include problem solving and persistence. Should frustration continue or increase, stress may ensue, thus arousing defense-oriented reaction, such as aggression or various self-deceptive maneuvers called defense mechanisms. Such mental mechanisms may serve a person in any of the following ways: (1) by blocking awareness of the frustration with repression; (2) by permitting escape psychologically by denial, fantasy, or regression; (3) by masking the frustration by rationalization, projection or identification; (4) by modifying the responses by sublimation, reaction formation, or compensation. Stress reactions may include emergency physiological alarm responses, emotional release, or indecisive, oscillation behaviors.

Prolonged, extreme stress calls for more drastic defenses, even to the point of behavioral maladjustments, such as those of the psychoneuroses, psychosomatic disorders, psychoses, and various personality disorders. Many factors acting in concert with stress are responsible for mental health or illness. Although certain characteristics of a person are inherited, their significance in adjustment depends also upon early development, social learning, many biological factors, and particular environmental situations.

A person passes through at least five critical stages in developing mental illness: *Stage I*, prenatal conditions, early family experiences and behavioral development; *Stage II*, crises of everyday living, from preadolescence throughout the life span; *Stage III*, onset of mental illness; *Stage IV*, treatment; and *Stage V*, rehabilitation. A two-pronged attack upon problems of mental illness emphasizes prevention through care, counseling, and education to promote optimal human adjustment in the first two stages and early detection, improved treatment, and rehabilitation in the last three stages.

SUGGESTED REFERENCES FOR FURTHER STUDY

Cofer, C. N., and M. H. Appley (1964). *Motivation: Theory and Research* New York: Wiley & Sons.

This book provides an excellent comprehensive review and evaluation of various concepts and studies of motivation. The chapters on homeostatic concepts, frustration, conflict, and stress are particularly relevant to our discussion in this chapter.

Coleman, J. C. (1964). *Abnormal Psychology and Modern Life.* (3d ed.). Chicago: Scott, Foresman and Company.

A fine review of the evolution of modern approaches to mental illness, the adjustment reactions, and the causes of mental illness is presented. Behavioral disorders are described in detail together with evidence and speculations regarding their dynamics and origins.

Joint Commission on Mental Illness and Health. (1961). *Action for Mental Health.* New York: Basic Books.

This final report of the Joint Commission on Mental Illness and Health reviews the problems in various current approaches to identifying, treating, and rehabilitating the mentally ill in America.

Miller, J. G. (1955). "Toward a General Theory for the Behavioral Sciences." *American Psychologist,* **10**:9, 513–531.

An outline and explanation of the common properties of individual and social systems in terms of information theory that would be helpful in understanding the concepts of stress, defense, and energy exchange.

Chapter 3
Promoting Mental Health

DEVELOPING MENTAL HEALTH and maintaining optimal human functioning is a task never completed. Mental health, as we have seen, represents a style or process of living and social interaction that spans a lifetime. It is not a final stage or condition of a person to be sought or achieved by special training or treatment. Rather, mental health is a dynamic function or property of a specialized energy system—the person—that participates in many larger systems. It is important, therefore, to study how an individual develops within and interacts with these larger systems or social groups in order to understand how optimal human functioning can be fostered (Clausen and Williams, 1963).

The child develops within a social matrix. The nature of that matrix influences what he learns and how he feels about it, even though the processes by which learning takes place may be the same in all societies. Each culture and, to a lesser extent, each group to which the individual belongs provides patternings of expectations and relationships which influence the development of the child's behaviors, skills, and attitudes. More generally, it is only by becoming a participant in society that the child becomes fully human, acquiring a sense of self and realizing his potentialities for symbolic thought.

In this chapter we shall review the growth of the individual as a system as he operates in and contributes to other systems. We shall examine how positive and negative functions of both group and individual systems originate, increase or decrease, and how these systems mutually influence each other. Crises typical of particular periods of development and how the individual meets them with adjustive or maladjustive behavior will be reviewed. Such an analysis might reveal some of the factors responsible for mental illness and also might suggest methods for preventing some of these factors from having effects, and thus help us to promote optimal human functioning.

SIGNIFICANT INTERACTIVE SYSTEMS

At one and the same time a person may be a member of many different systems, some of which overlap or include other systems. Let us consider a particular young man named Andy. As a family member, Andy is part of a group system. Andy belongs to a church, but his father and sister attend a different church. Some of his brothers attend the same school as Andy, however. So we see that Andy does share group systems with some members of his family group, but not all of his family participates in the same systems. All of these groups are located in the same town, however, so one system does encompass all of them. Each system varies in its size, members, complexity, rules, and structure.

As a member of multiple groups, Andy plays a role, perhaps a different role, in each system. Each group, therefore, has a special meaning for him. When any group is important to a person, for whatever reason, it is called a *significant interactive system* (Sundberg and Tyler, 1962). All through Andy's life changes will occur in his significant systems. As older systems add or lose members, change leaders or structure of relationships, new or reconstituted systems will become more relevant to Andy. As a child the family group was completely dominant in his life, but as he grew older he participated in other systems—his playmate, school, scout, church, and other groups. Gradually he became less dependent upon his family and related more to these other groups.

MEANINGFUL INTERPERSONAL RELATIONSHIPS

Within each system certain persons often seem to stand out and to play uniquely influential parts in the life of an individual. Such interactions are called *meaningful interpersonal relationships* (abbreviated as *MIRs*). These relationships, or *MIRs*, become vital to the development of the self. As we have seen the self is dynamic, not static or unchanging. It matures and changes just as any other bodily system—physical, intellectual, or emotional. Just as all development depends upon continuous and varying interaction with environment, the self develops in continuous meaningful interaction with people, their models and surrogates, or their roles as played in fantasy, ideals, or wish.

These *MIR* interactions commence very early in infancy and proceed to form the basis for affectional bonds and role identifications, first with parents, then with siblings, peers, teachers, coaches, employers, girl friends or boy friends, work associates, one's children, and many others. Such *MIRs* need not be positive, however. They can involve negative reactions and hostilities, as well. Often the persons whom we dislike and reject can contribute significantly to the self. When such attitudes predominate, the child may appear to be belligerent or aggressive.

Throughout one's life the patterns of one's *MIRs* change and reconstitute themselves, quite like the colors in a kaleidoscope, as one finds new persons, roles, or models that assume importance to him and those of former significance die, move away, or lose relevance. Along with changes in these patterns come changes in the self.

These *MIRs* help to protect, strengthen, and stabilize the self by providing a dependable structure or supporting persons or models. In turn, the strength and security thus afforded allows a person to feel adequate and safe enough to reach out to acquire new *MIRs*, thus permitting further changes in self.

Just as the self system depends upon *MIRs*, so do significant group systems. The patterns of affection and influence within the family group affect not only the functioning of the system as a whole but the functioning of individual members as well. Great shifts in family authority patterns and interdependencies occur when a parent dies or becomes disabled. Divorce or family quarrels may radically alter the *MIRs* between family members, thereby disrupting a family system. There is thus a close association between group systems and their component *MIR* affinities or negative attitudes.

STAGES IN DEVELOPMENT

Although we recognize that there are important *differences* in how and when changes in group and individual systems take place, it is more convenient to analyze these changes in terms of *similarities* among people. Each pattern of behavior seems to have a life cycle of its own in which it begins, grows, flourishes, and then blends into a superseding pattern. We find such patterns in all subsystems of the individual: physical, mental, and social.

When a certain constellation of traits seems to characterize a given age group it is called a *developmental stage*. Piaget and Inhelder (1958) described certain stages of intellectual development, for example. From birth to two years is called the "sensorimotor stage"; from ages two to seven years the child passes through the "preconceptual" and "intuitive

thought" stages. From age seven to 11, he is in the stage of "concrete operations," after which, until age 15, he can master "formal operations." Other
stages in behavioral development have been noted for such diverse traits as
learning moral rules of right and wrong (Piaget, 1932), psychosexual
behavior (Freud, 1905), concept formation (Werner, 1948), and self-
awareness (Nixon, 1962).

Such complex changes in behavior are orderly and continuous, one stage
of development forming the basis for the next, and merging almost imper-
ceptibly into a new pattern. Jenkins, Shacter, and Bauer (1953) have
observed the following:

> All normal children will follow an essentially similar sequence of growth,
> yet because of the great variations in endowment and experience and the
> interplay between them, no two children, even in the same family, will pass
> through this sequence in just the same way. . . . within the range of "normal"
> some children will develop much more rapidly than the average, some much
> more slowly. . . . But in every group of children some will be ahead of the
> others of their age physically, mentally, and emotionally, and some will be
> behind the others in one or all aspects of development. So when we talk about
> "the six-year-old" or "the eight-year-old," we are talking of averages—the
> stage of development *most* children reach at six or eight. Some children will
> reach "six-year-oldness" at five or even four, others not until seven or eight
> or even later.

From this statement we see that all persons do not enter a stage at
the same age, nor are all traits typical of a stage necessarily revealed in a
particular person. The boundaries of the stages are quite fluid. There is
great variation between persons.

Until maturity is reached, most developmental stages are closely associated with age and biological growth. This is true especially of physical
and mental ability. After physical maturity has been attained, however, the
stages are related more closely to events and environmental conditions. The
behavior pattern of the young adult, for example, depends much more upon
his marital status, his employment, and his social group membership than
upon his chronological age.

Developmental Tasks. At each developmental stage, certain skills, behaviors, and roles need to be mastered in order for the individual to adjust
satisfactorily to his several systems. Such needed behavioral patterns are
called *developmental tasks* (Havighurst, 1953). Some developmental tasks
relate to physical maturation, such as learning to walk. Other tasks arise
from cultural expectations of society, as, for example, learning to read. Still
others arise from the personal values and goals of a person that are part of

the self, such as forming a philosophy of life. Mastery of developmental tasks at any stage is vital to adjustment not only at that particular developmental stage but to future stages as well.

In America, for example, one developmental task of early childhood is to learn control of the elimination of bodily wastes. Should a child, due either to immaturity or to emotional stress, not be toilet-trained by the age of two, family pressures to conform will increase. The child who makes such "mistakes" may be punished or rejected by his parents or teased by his brothers and sisters. These treatments could have lasting effects upon his self-image and his MIRs.

Another example might be found in the middle childhood period. Suppose a boy has failed to learn the physical skills needed to play rough-and-tumble games, perhaps due to weak physical development, illness, overprotection, or fear. This might hinder his assuming a masculine role identity. In young adulthood he might shrink from competition or from taking a new job because he lacks self-confidence. It is important in promoting mental health and preventing later maladjustment for a person to master developmental tasks at the time they are required by society and when he is physically and mentally mature enough to perform them.

Critical Formative Periods. For all types of learning, there is a period of readiness when the organism is "ripe"—a time which is most conducive to learning. Learning prior to or after this time is likely to be inferior, perhaps even impossible, depending upon the time intervening prior to or following the formative period and many other factors. Studies of certain kinds of learning, particularly those related to intelligence, language development, and social responsiveness have shown that it is difficult for a person to make up for or to offset deficient or inappropriate learning which has occurred during a formative period.

One study by Goldfarb (1943) compared the later development of children who had been reared in an institution for the first three years of their lives with children who had been raised in foster homes. In adolescence, the children who had been reared in the impersonal environment of the institution showed more problem behavior, lower mental ability, and less social maturity. Even those raised initially in the institution who had later entered foster homes that were more intellectually stimulating and emotionally supportive continued to be retarded in mental development and to be socially callous. Apparently the lack of early stimulation of language skills and the impersonal, emotionally cold social environment during the formative period for learning language and social responsiveness contributed to a lasting impairment of the development of these characteristics.

Many aspects of system growth—mental, social, and emotional—thus have *critical periods* which, if passed without the learning of certain tasks, handicap the mastery of developmental tasks that depend upon it. Should a male child, for example, fail to develop a secure MIR with his mother in infancy and early childhood, he may fail to transfer positive MIR attitudes to his father, such as a sense of trust. Later, because he does not accept his father as a model, the same young boy could experience role identification conflicts during the middle childhood period, with concomitant difficulties related to this in adolescence. In another case, a girl who learns how to get along with playmates—the usual give and take—in the middle childhood period when social skills are forming is more likely to find social relationships in her adolescence and adulthood satisfying and meaningful.

Significant interactive systems, such as the family, also show developmental stages and critical periods of growth. Just as MIRs with family members affect the individual systems of each participant, so do the patterns of MIRs affect the family system as a whole. Families that have close affectional bonds, or positive MIRs, meet crises, such as bereavement, as problems for the group. In families where MIRs are negative, involving hostility or jealousy, for example, such crises precipitate quarrels and separate, rather than group, task-oriented behavior. There are critical periods in family system development which if weathered successfully and the family learns to cooperate as a team respecting the individuality of each member, the family survives and functions well as a system. But if parents cannot accept the increasing demands for independence of their adolescent children, or if young parents cannot agree on how to discipline the children, these may become critical periods, not only for the growing children, but for the family itself. If the critical period for developing family solidarity passes, basic damage is done, no matter how matters are patched up later. The family as a system, the basic linking MIRs, and the participants themselves all become permanently changed.

This can be seen with even larger systems, such as a church. Should a church fail to bring young people actively into the fold at a critical period in their quest for faith, it may never influence them. Then, lacking MIRs with younger people, the older members influence the system to suit their needs, and the whole system gradually undergoes a change which makes it less and less attractive to younger people. This has far-reaching effects, because adolescents who seek a philosophy of life as a developmental task thus become less likely to seek or to find meaning or identification in a religious system.

AIMS OF PREVENTION

Along with advancing years come ·new stages of biological, psychological, and social development, each of which ushers in new tasks to master, new problems to solve, and new demands from new systems. Failure to learn developmental tasks, whether in periods of rapid growth or in the adult years, tends to make a person more vulnerable to traumas, frustrations, and stresses at later stages. What might be an ordinary problem for a person who has been successful in earlier phases could become a serious crisis for one who has not developed competence or resilience.

Primary prevention of mental illness, or its obverse, promoting optimum human functioning, has the following aims:

1. *Equipping a person to cope with the stresses typical of each developmental stage.* The objective is to facilitate the mastery of developmental tasks by providing for training experiences which will permit the person to build a diverse repertoire of responses upon which he can draw when frustrated. This strengthens his resources for dealing with problems of life and averts the establishment of inadequate, inefficient, or inappropriate habits.

2. *Removing, reducing, or obviating unnecessary or avoidable stresses or obstacles that weaken or destroy a person's ability to cope adequately with his environment at critical formative periods and at crucial stages in later development.* An example in the middle childhood period might be the provision for straightening protruding teeth which could be a source of self-devaluation or social handicap. Making emergency loans to persons who are between jobs, shifting a child to a less punitive teacher, or observing special prenatal diet precautions might be ways of avoiding stresses or obstacles to effective coping.

3. *Assisting a person in coping with problems, not only to teach him, but to prevent destructive side reactions to stress and to provide psychological support until the person can cope with the problems successfully himself.* Although it may in some cases be a matter of solving the problems completely for a person it can more often be characterized as "lending a helping hand." The comforting counsel of a clergyman in times of bereavement, the vocational information by a school guidance counselor, the work of a Big Brother with a delinquent boy, the practical nurse who cares for a large family of children when the mother is ill—all represent intervention to relieve debilitating reactions to stress and to assist in coping with problems.

As suggested above, many persons, not only professional workers, may be involved in promoting mental health and adjustment. In Stage I, the prenatal and early childhood phase, which includes many critical formative periods, the emphasis is upon providing the best possible maternal care and child training. In Stage II, preventive functions are performed by schools, community parent–child guidance services, various professional and informal consultants, and advisers on medical, legal, religious, governmental, and economic matters. Prevention may involve person-to-person intervention in dealing with short-term crises, as with vocational counseling, or it may entail general programing for public education and community services to combat chronic forces like delinquency or mental retardation. It may aim at large systems, as in slum clearance or veteran's benefits, or at smaller systems, as with family financial counseling.

Whatever the method, the distinguishing feature of primary prevention is in its goal of increasing the positive functioning of the individual and reducing his negative functionng, thus decreasing the risk of his becoming mentally ill.

Problems of Prevention.   Which of many factors is most significant in contributing to behavioral maladjustment? Which factors are not causes, yet are associated with disorders? Of the factors we know to be important, how can they best be controlled? Is prevention feasible or even possible? These are problems that must be considered before an effective program to promote optimum adjustment can be inaugurated.

Rarely do causal factors occur alone. Interaction and compounding of causes are more frequently the case. This, of course, multiplies problems of prediction of behavioral outcomes and of instituting preventive measures. Consider the matter of maternal deprivation, for example. We know from accumulated evidence that lack of motherly care and attention at a formative period with institutionalized children tends to be associated with adolescent adjustment problems. The evidence is not consistent, however, because not all institutionalized children show these reactions. It is possible that some children who lacked mothering made up for it with other relationships. Possibly those who showed bad effects had been left in the institutions instead of being chosen for placement in foster homes because of poor health, physical unattractiveness, or maladjustment, any of which reasons could contribute to later maladjustment. Problems such as these prevent one from making certain conclusions regarding the effects of maternal deprivation. Even so, enough is known about the dangers of maternal deprivation to warrant having serious concern for its possible dangers and to justify steps to avoid it, despite the fact that all persons might not be equally affected by it. Most behavior problems have multiple causes.

Mere association of a factor with a disorder or a negative function does not mean, necessarily, that this factor has caused the disorder. Carefully controlled investigations are needed to establish the causes. Even when such factors are known, however, other factors could modify or dilute their effects and thus obscure their possible influence.

Because of the large chance of error in predicting individual behavior, some mental health workers suggest that prevention is not only difficult but impossible or impracticable. Others perceive the role of prevention to be one of reducing the risk of mental illness for larger populations. They believe that better control of the known contributing factors, even if they are not exclusive causes, might substantially minimize the risk for a whole population. The tasks of prevention are geared to both ends, actually: (1) reducing overall incidence of disorders, and, hopefully, (2) forestalling individual maladjustments. (These are the same approaches taken in reducing criminal behavior, and are discussed in Chapter 16.) As in all behavioral sciences, the uncertainties are numerous and great.

Tarjan (1961) summarizes the problems as follows:

Mental function is affected by a variety of forces. Some act singly, others in combinations concurrently or at different times; there are infinite possibilities for interaction. Repeated and relatively mild infections, for instance, may have a suppressive effect on adaptive ability and intelligence. The quality of mother-child relationship may influence the clinical manifestations of the sequelae of birth trauma. Socioeconomic status may have an effect on the frequency of perinatal [birth] injuries. . . . Though present knowledge is limited, the utilization of known facts in preventive programs would produce significant results.

With these cautions in mind, we shall explore in the next section those factors that are associated with maladjustments during Stages I and II, the predecessors of mental health or illness. Optimistically these factors might suggest how to minimize hazards to mental health and how to achieve optimum adjustment.

GUIDING MENTAL HEALTH IN STAGE I

At the instant of conception, a new life begins. From this moment until the child enters school around the age of six is perhaps the most important period in his life for building toward optimum adjustment in later years. His heredity, which determines in many important ways what he can become or fail to become, has "set" the course of his structural and functional development. Whether this inherited potential will be realized or thwarted, facilitated or distorted, maximized or curtailed, will depend upon the environments encountered by the growing organism. As one writer put it, "Heredity deals the cards, but environment plays them" (Cronbach, 1963, p. 238). The courses "set" by heredity are altered constantly throughout one's life by positive or negative factors of nutrition, disease, accident, stimuli (or their lack), opportunities, and so on.

Stage I brackets these foundation years during which the fundamental physical structures and coordinating functions are formed. It is a span of time with many critical periods—a time of dawning of basic physical skills, verbal proficiency, social relationships, and attitudes, and a sense of self. These skills and attitudes provide the groundwork for the developmental tasks of later adjustment, thus preparing the child for independent action in a world beyond his home.

Prenatal Influences. The first environmental encounters for the new being are in his mother's uterus. Suspended in a fluid world, the conceptus receives his nourishment and chemical signals via the umbilical cord, by which he is attached to the placenta, a disklike structure attached to the wall of the uterus. He also swallows amniotic fluid in which he is suspended, thus receiving chemical substances present in the fluid. In this relatively stable environment the conceptus develops very rapidly in a regular or orderly sequence from a small egg state, called the ovum, to a responsive fetus with many functioning organs in just two months.

Whatever interferes with his nutrition, oxygen supply, chemical balance, metabolism, or organ functions in the first three months, when the vital nervous system and brain are forming, may result in permanent malformation and subsequent disability, should the child survive. If the mother should contract rubella (German measles) in this first critical three months, for example, permanent damage to the fetus involving gross malformations or neurological deficit is highly probable.

Some representative outcomes of prenatal factors upon the subsequent mental health of offspring are listed in Table 3.1. The mechanisms of action in producing these results in many of the factors listed in Table 3.1, however, are not known. We are often unsure from the evidence whether a factor is directly responsible or whether some related variables could be at fault. For purposes of prevention it may not be necessary to make such distinctions, although we would have to admit that our approaches to prevention would be more direct and efficient, were the basic causes known.

The reader may note that mental retardation and neurological impairments predominate as outcomes listed in Table 3.1. Were fewer years to intervene between birth and onset of mental illness, which is more frequently detected in adult years, perhaps more definite associations of these prenatal factors and mental illness might be found. From present evidence there are too many confounding factors to be sure.

Malnutrition of the mother during pregnancy, passed on to the developing fetus as various deficiencies, is related to poor living conditions and inadequate food supply, often attendant upon war, depression, poverty,

TABLE 3.1 Prenatal Influences Upon Subsequent Mental Health of Offspring

FACTOR	REPORTED OUTCOME OR TENDENCY
Maternal Nutrition	
General malnutrition	Higher incidence of major and minor illnesses, neural defects, and premature birth (Burke, *et al.*, 1943; Ebbs, 1942; Tompkins and Wiehl, 1954); greater risk of anancephaly (absence of brain) and deformities of central nervous system (Anderson, *et al.*, 1958).
Iodine deficiency	Possible endemic cretinism (disorder with physical and mental deficiency).
Vitamin deficiency	Lower intelligence (Harrell, Woodyard, and Gates, 1955).
Maternal Attitudes and Emotions	
Rejection of pregnancy	"Neurotic infants": hyperactive, irritable, squirming, crying, unusually dependent, with feeding and sleeping problems (Sontag, 1944; Wallin and Riley, 1950).
Emotional stress and anxiety during pregnancy	Hyperactive, hyperirritable infants; mental retardation; "impaired motivation" (Sontag, 1944; Stott, 1959).
Maternal Dysfunctions and Diseases	
Diabetes (defective sugar metabolism)	Premature birth (see below).
Hypothyroidism (lack of thyroid)	Cretinism (see "Maternal Nutrition" above).
Toxemia (disturbances in blood circulation and kidney function)	Possible mental retardation (Battle, 1949).
Hydramnios (excessive fluid in fetal sac)	Anancephaly (absence of brain).
Rubella (German measles)	Deafness; microcephaly (small head, with retardation); malformations; high risk of mental retardation if infected during first 3 months of pregnancy.
Measles	Microcephaly.
Influenza	Anancephaly.
Toxoplasmosis (infection of blood plasma)	Hydrocephaly (dropsy of brain with mental deficiency); microcephaly; mental deficiency; brain defects.
Fungus infections	Hydrocephaly; brain defects.
Rh factor (maternal-fetal blood incompatibility)	Brain damage; mental deficiency.
Maternal Age	
Under 20	Greater risk of mental retardation (Pasamanick and Lilienfield, 1955).

TABLE 3.1—continued

FACTOR	REPORTED OUTCOME OR TENDENCY
Over 35	Greater risk of anancephaly (absence of brain), defective spine, hydrocephaly (dropsy of brain with mental retardation), mongolism (a type of mental deficiency with distinctive physical deformities), malformations of central nervous system, mental deficiency, mental illness, and premature birth.
Order of Birth	
First born	More mongoloids in first birth rank at all maternal ages, except at 40 years and over (Smith and Record, 1955).
Fourth born and later	Greater risk of neurosis.
Other Conditions	
Anoxia (asphyxiation due to use of anesthetics, pain relievers, gas, difficult or prolonged delivery, etc.)	Mental retardation; neurological abnormalities; greater risk of cerebral palsy and schizophrenia.
Smoking (excessive)	Premature birth (see below).
Premature birth	Higher incidence of mental retardation, pre-school-age behavior problems, "nervous disturbances," cerebral damage.
X-ray and other irradiation	Microcephaly; mental deficiency; hydrocephaly.
Birth injury	Various neurological and mental impairments.

disaster, and ignorance. In one study of congenital malformations at birth in children of mothers from a very low socioeconomic population, Murphy (1947) found the rate to be 11.3 per 1,000 births, over twice the rate of 4.7 per 1,000 in the general United States population.

It is encouraging to note that improved nutrition may improve mental status. Harrell, Woodyard, and Gates (1955) reported unusual improvements in intelligence of the offspring of women who had received vitamin supplements while pregnant. Children of mothers who had received varying amounts of vitamins prenatally showed an 8-point superiority in IQ over children whose mothers had received placebos containing no vitamins when tested at four years of age. The authors suggest, too, that had the supplements been given early, rather than late, in pregnancy the effects might have been even larger.

Numerous studies have shown that children born to mothers who were emotionally disturbed during pregnancy or who did not want their children produced hyperactive, irritable infants who had feeding and sleeping problems (Sontag, 1944; Wallin and Riley, 1950). Various glandular and blood infections and dysfunctions, such as rubella, are associated with such malformations as hydrocephaly (excessive fluid in the brain area), microcephaly (small head), and other brain defects, with mental retardation.

Many diseases and dysfunctions of the mother have been associated either directly or indirectly with brain defects or mental retardation in her offspring. The list includes diabetes, thyroid deficiency, blood disturbances (such as those due to Rh-factor incompatibility and infections like toxoplasmosis), influenza, measles, and fungus infections. Also, when the mother's age is under 20 or over 35 the risk of bearing defective offspring is greater. Other prenatal conditions found related to mental disorders or defects are excessive smoking (related to prematurity of birth), irradiation by X ray or other means, premature birth, injury in birth, or temporary anoxia caused by anesthesia, pain relievers, gas, difficult, or prolonged delivery.

Certainly an adequate prenatal preventive program should include measures that would seek to minimize the incidence or effects of these factors. Such programs might include improved prenatal medical care, education, and counseling of girls and brides concerning the importance of nutrition and the possible effects of certain prenatal factors upon their future children. Programs of economic and health assistance for the disadvantaged members of society would also be necessary. In order to demonstrate overall effectiveness and improvement resulting from preventive measures a large-scale approach that would reach the bulk of the population would be needed.

Family Influences upon Socialization and Adjustment. Five natural periods for important changes in socialization have been described by Scott (1963). Each constitutes a critical period in the development of adjustment. They are:

1. Neonatal period. (0-40 days of age).
2. Primary socialization (about 5 weeks to about 7 months of age).
3. First transition period (7 to about 15 months).
4. Second transition period (about 15 months to 27 months).
5. Period of verbal socialization and the struggle for autonomy (27 months to 4 years).

We shall add one more period which may be identified in this Stage I:

6. Period of development of identification and role (4 to 6 years).

1. NEONATAL PERIOD. During the first, neonatal, period, which extends from birth until an age of about 40 days, little or no socialization occurs. Physiological processes relating to sleep, feeding, and elimination predominate. The infant displays strong demands to use the few responses at his disposal, consisting of swallowing, sucking, crying, sneezing, yawning, and so on.

Although he does respond vigorously to pain and discomfort, the only distinguishable emotion is that of general excitement (Bridges, 1932). With reasonably prompt satisfaction of demands and release from pain, there are no noticeable after effects. Although it is possible to establish conditioned responses of sucking, winking, and other motor reflexes within this period, it is difficult to do so, and the resulting conditioning is quite unstable. Parents need not fear the emotional results of upsetting experiences at this time. The infant not only is incapable of experiencing intense emotions as adults might feel them, but he has a very short memory. Even social smiling responses are absent in this period.

More important, perhaps, than disturbing experiences of the child are the reactions that parents might have to such experiences. The crying of the child sometimes arouses feelings of empathy, guilt, or resentment in the parents, promotes quarreling, and creates tensions that disturb the nursing routines, and thus sets off a chain of psychological reactions that could persist to affect the marital relationship and the future attitudes of the parents toward the child.

Scott (1963) summarized the neonatal period as follows:

. . . the chief needs of the neonatal infant in the first 2 months are for normal physical care, feeding, and comfort. Since the neonate is not a completely self-regulating organism, he will need adequate handling and stimulation, or "tender loving care." Physiological stress is likely to be more dangerous than emotional distress, and the baby can be passed from hand to hand and carried from place to place with little disturbance if physical care is adequate.

2. PRIMARY SOCIALIZATION. The second period, primary socialization, begins at five to six weeks and extends to about seven months. Within this period, the infant can make associations with visual stimuli and smile in response to any human face, even to a Halloween mask. It is a time when anyone can approach and develop a social relationship with a child. Since the strongest relationships formed are with those he sees most often, reaching a peak at four to five months, the mother becomes the chief agent of socialization, although the father and other siblings may also assume important roles. Throughout this period fear responses to strangers increase, and the primary social relationship with the mother becomes stronger.

It was once believed that the increasing depth of the mother attachment was due to her association with the satisfaction of many of the child's basic motives, such as obtaining food or relief from discomfort. Recent research by Scott (1963) discloses that the attachment does not depend upon food intake, reward, or punishment. Rather, the primary social attachment seems to occur regardless of external conditions of reward and punishment, and is associated only with emotional arousal. For whatever reason, positive or negative, increased emotion accelerates the formation of a primary attachment.

The infant also forms attachments of a similar kind to objects, such as stuffed toys, and places, probably as a result of the same process. Although an adequate physiological or psychological explanation for this process remains unknown, it is quite likely that this period of primary socialization represents the formative period for the basic MIR of the child with its mother.

Erickson (1963) suggested that the *sense of trust* emerges at this time. When there has been maternal deprivation at crucial periods in the six-to-nine-month period, lasting emotional reactions are likely, involving, among other responses, inability to relate to or to trust others and emotional blunting, as revealed in studies of neglected institutionalized children (Ribble, 1943; Spitz, 1945). Whether such results are due to lack of "mothering," sensory deprivation, or other factors, the matter has been debated, because the studies had weaknesses and uncontrolled factors. Some have argued that adverse reactions to separation from the mother by reason of institutionalization prior to seven months of age are due to *sensory*, or perceptual, *deprivation*, whereas psychological damage after this time, when the MIR has become stabilized, is best characterized as *maternal deprivation* (Schaffer, 1958). In either case, long-range studies are needed to determine the extent to which psychological problems considered related to early deprivation persist and the extent to which they could be reversed by environmental improvements.

Prominent among the experiences of the child during this period of primary socialization are the acts associated with feeding. Psychoanalytic theories of personality have stressed the importance of breast feeding, rather than bottle feeding, self-demand, rather than rigid feeding schedules, and gradual and late weaning as being essential for subsequent mental health. After an extensive review of research pertaining to infant feeding practices, Orlansky (1949) concluded, however, that no specific infant nursing discipline had a consistent impact upon the child and that "the effect of a particular discipline can be determined only from knowledge of the parental attitudes associated with it, the value which the culture places upon that discipline, the organic constitution of the infant, and the entire sociocultural situation in which the individual is located."

Many factors are associated with the mother's choice of nursing procedures that might be more important than any specific nursing practice. Watson (1959) suggested that the general attitudes of the mother toward her child and the larger family pattern in which the nursing procedure is embedded are of greatest importance. A cold, rejecting mother may carry out such "approved" practices as breast feeding, self-demand feeding, and gradual weaning merely as a duty, whereas employment or illness may force an acceptant, affectionate mother to use bottle feeding on a schedule with early weaning. Regardless of specific practices, when feeding is accompanied by warm maternal attitudes and close physical contact between mother and infant, thus giving the child feelings of contact comfort and emotional support, the basic mother–child MIR is strengthened. The mother benefits as much as the child. To the extent that breast feeding, demand feeding, and gradual weaning foster this sensory stimulation and feeling of security without arousing conflicting maternal attitudes, they are desirable practices.

It is clear that in this period of primary socialization occurring between six weeks and about seven months the baby forms his most important social relationships with his parents and family members, particularly with his mother. Whatever disturbs the formation of these basic MIRs—separation due to hospitalization or institutionalization, lack of warm, satisfying contacts with a mother or mother substitute, or negative maternal attitudes—may have lasting effects upon the child, thus hindering his mastery of later developmental tasks which depend upon these MIRs and feelings of security and trust.

3. FIRST TRANSITION PERIOD. Two distinct periods of transition are said to occur between the ages of about seven and 27 months, during which the child develops skills that facilitate his assumption of a more responsible family role. The period of primary socialization does not terminate abruptly at this time, however. Close family ties formed in the earlier period continue to deepen, and relationships with strangers become more and more difficult to form. There is considerable overlapping of periods.

During the *first transition period*, initiated by the eruption of teeth and crawling at about seven and a half months, the child becomes weaned from breast or bottle to a more adult style of eating. With greater mobility and increasing capacity to learn, he is able to respond to a wider range of stimuli, thus to become prepared for an adult mode of locomotion, walking, at about 15 months.

4. SECOND TRANSITION PERIOD. Walking marks the beginning of the second transition period, which extends to about 27 months. During this period the child begins to use and to understand words. "Do's" and "don'ts" become attached to many of his actions and form the basis for learning simple concepts of right and wrong—an important developmental task for this age. The active curious child is told to be quiet and to keep away from fascinating objects like electric outlets and china figurines. Even though he enjoys elimination processes, he is punished or scolded for performing when and where he should not. He must spit out interesting objects he finds on the sidewalk and is forced to give up or to avoid many activities that would gratify his motives and to acquire voluntary control over bowel and bladder processes, which are initially involuntary processes. It is a time of great frustration and feelings of conflict for both the child and the parent.

Excessive use of aversive stimuli by parents may spread negative reactions of fear and stress to many of the behaviors and persons in the world of the child. When a parent is angry or punishes a child for acts over which the child lacks control, as in the early stages of toilet training, emotion stemming from frustration in the child may actually interfere with his forming desired habits. Instead of learning to control his sphincters, the child learns to avoid and to fear painful stimuli and the loss of love and approval by his parents. He learns also to associate unpleasant stimuli and emotions with the whole process of elimination. Approach responses to master tasks and to please parents conflict with avoidance responses, thus further promoting stress and defense-oriented behavior. Prominent among these defense reactions are those of hostility and aggression, wherein a child expresses defiance of parental wishes and anger through tantrums and rage. Such behavior often arouses aggressive retaliation by parents by means of punishment and rejection. Anticipating such reactions, the child learns to fear and to inhibit his own anger and aggression, giving rise to what has been called *anger-anxiety conflicts* (Dollard and Miller, 1950).

Dollard and Miller (1950) described the origin and implications of these conflicts as follows:

Anxiety responses . . . become attached not only to the cues produced by the forbidden situation but also to the cues produced by the emotional responses which the child is making at the time. It is this latter connection which created the inner mental or emotional conflict. After this learning has occurred, the first cues produced by angry emotions may set off anxiety responses which "out-compete" the angry emotional responses themselves. The person can thus be made helpless to use his anger even in those situations where culture does permit it. He is viewed as abnormally meek or long-suffering. Robbing a person of his anger completely may be a dangerous thing since some capacity for anger seems to be needed in the affirmative personality.

One can see from the above that severe and strict methods of discipline, especially if initiated before a child is mature enough to comprehend or to master a task, may have lasting consequences. A whole cycle of punishment, fear, conflict, retaliation, punishment may commence which generalizes to the whole parent–child relationship in all areas of socialization, not only the specific cleanliness training.

The whole pattern may be accentuated if a parent who is punishing or rejecting has already acquired other anxiety-arousing characteristics.

If the mother has been nurturant during the first year of life, her positive value might be sufficient to neutralize some of the negative feelings produced by socialization demands without a marked change in the perception of the mother. But if the mother has been cold and rejecting, then use of strict toilet training is much more likely to have a deleterious effect on the child, and lead to negative feelings toward her (Mussen, Conger, and Kagan, 1963).

Furthermore, a child who has received constant disapproval and rejection for his behavior may come to regard himself as dirty, loathesome, worthless, unwanted, and unloved—hardly a feeling conducive to positive efforts to learn and to improve.

Principles of learning stated in Chapter 1 of this book plus the above discussions suggest several points to consider for child training in the transition and later periods of developments.

1. *Training in a socialization task should be begun only when a child is mature enough to master the task.* Although training can be forced before this time, it is often at the expense of the child's feelings of emotional security and the formation of close MIRs.

2. *No disciplinary measures should be employed that weaken or threaten to weaken MIRs.* Parents should avoid making their love contingent upon the behavior of the child. The child should never be made to feel he is unwanted, unworthy, or unloved, no matter what he has done. He needs to understand what he has done wrong and what he should do to be correct. He must learn also to accept aversive stimuli that will assist him to discriminate desirable from undesirable responses. But the aversive stimuli must not be so severe as to produce stress; it should be associated

with the undesirable behavior, not with the person producing it, nor with self-evaluations. Punishment should not interfere with the formation of healthy self-attitudes or block positive strivings to learn.

3. *Appeal by parents to positive, rather than aversive, motives is more effective in the long run.* This prevents generalization of avoidance responses to other areas of behavior. A child scolded for not eating a certain food may come to dislike mealtime, for example. A good rule is to "accentuate the positive!"

4. *The aim of discipline should always be to promote learning.* Prompt, sure, but light discipline insures learning better than delayed, inconsistent, or severe discipline. Discipline is not synonymous with punishment, however. Good discipline is corrective and strengthening, rather than merely punitive.

5. *Many behaviors once regarded as "bad" by parents are now seen as natural and to be expected of children at this age.* Such activities as thumb-sucking, bedwetting, or masturbation, in most cases, will cease to be problems without harmful aftereffects as the child matures, if undue attention is not paid to the behaviors. Severe punishment by parents tends to increase whatever emotional tension may have contributed to the problems, thus delaying the normal abandonment of the practices, sometimes indefinitely. It is better to try to understand the causes of the behavior and to remedy them than to try to suppress or to scare the behaviors away by aversive acts which tend actually to fixate behaviors and to cause fear and hostile reactions that can generalize to the parents and to the whole home environment.

5. PERIOD OF VERBAL SOCIALIZATION AND THE STRUGGLE FOR AUTONOMY. As the child develops language a new type of social control and learning becomes available to the child. The stage of *verbal socialization* commences around the age of 27 months, according to Scott (1963), when the child becomes able to use and to understand sentences. Simple communication is available before this time, of course, but now the child is able to use and to understand more complicated rules and to assume greater responsibility. As he explores his world and experiments with his newfound powers, he expresses his individuality and learns to cope with many new situations, free of parental direction and help. Again, as noted with cleanliness training, the reactions of the parents can shape attitudes either of confidence or of overdependency of the child.

Levy (1943) described how overprotective, clinging mothers, for neurotic reasons of their own, keep their children dependent. Through excessive contact, infantilization (performing activities in the care of a child beyond the time they are needed), and generally preventing independent behavior by overcontrol, an overprotective mother may prevent her growing child from assuming a mature and self-confident social role. Likewise, fearful, overmeticulous mothers may restrict the child's opportunities to explore and to experiment.

Such overshielded and restricted children tend to become socially inhibited, fearful of trying new tasks, and excessively dependent upon mother and others for care and for making decisions. Although no parents want to expose their children to danger, if a child is never permitted freedom to try things on his own or to explore without fear of being punished or hurt, later developmental tasks that require courage, confidence, and spontaneity will be difficult, perhaps even impossible. The child will lack a sense of initiative to tackle new tasks and will remain immature and overdependent. For example, it is important for the young boy in middle childhood to acquire skill in rough-and-tumble games. The boy who has been overprotected may become fearful of such activities and find it difficult to win the social acceptance of his peer group.

Parents need to relinquish controls judiciously and to encourage the child to assume responsibility for his behavior commensurate with his ability to accept it. As soon as he is able, the child should be encouraged (not forced or coerced) to dress, feed, and wash himself, and to manage his own toilet functions. Boundaries of play areas can be relaxed gradually as the child shows he can accept responsibility. Children are usually eager to perform these tasks, to extend boundaries, and to acquire independence in the second and third year of age.

Even before he seems ready, the youngster may refuse help, resist rules, and generally insist upon having his own way. It is the beginning of a sense of self-esteem or pride in accomplishment. These periods of *negativism*, which will recur throughout the child's development, are expressions of his needs for mastery, his growing sense of pride in his skills or need for them—a struggle for "selfhood." Negativism becomes particularly pronounced at certain times when the child is experiencing difficulty in acquiring skills. Sometimes, the *best* help from loving parents as he learns these tasks is the *least* help. Much of the contrariness and pugnacity expressed by the child is due to the natural frustration he experiences before he succeeds in constructive problem solving. For a parent to provide too much help, too strong control, or to punish or to restrict the accompanying negativistic behavior severely may compound the problems, prevent the development of frustration tolerance, and retard the learning of developmental tasks.

Parents need great patience, faith, and perspective to balance between crushing the child's drive for autonomy by forcing their will upon him and permitting the child completely free rein, which can become a "reign" over the household. A tolerant middle course is needed. The exasperated parent needs to reassure himself often: "This too shall pass!" Extremes of either punishment and rejection or permissiveness and indulgence are undesirable for both the family and the child. It is a critical period of socialization for both parents and children which requires wise judgment, emotional control, and forbearance.

6. DEVELOPMENT OF IDENTIFICATION AND ROLE. In the period between ages four and six the child participates more and more vigorously in his environment. It is a period of enterprise and imagination when the child develops a strong sense of possession, becomes competitive, and extends his self to include *"my* house," *"my* tricycle"—everything becomes *"mine."* It is a most egocentric period because the child extends self by absorbing new territory (Allport, 1961). He also includes people in his orbit, so his attachments at this time can involve possessiveness and jealousy of his friends or siblings.

Should a new child be brought into the family about this time, the *sibling rivalry* can be disturbing to the whole family system. Parents need to be especially careful not to ignore the feelings of the older child when the new baby enters the household. Despite all assurances, the older child often perceives the threat of the newcomer to his basic *MIRs.* He finds *MIRs* very difficult to share. Such rivalry is strongest when the age separation is from two to four years, because it is then that the oldest child is developing his self-image and identifications.

One of the chief sources of a favorable self-image at this stage of development is the identification of the child with the role responses of significant others. Identification can be defined as a belief that the characteristics and attributes of a model belong to the self. Not only do parents and others act as direct rewarders or punishers of behaviors and as mirrors or interpreters of the child's behavior, but they also become models for the child.

What determines the adoption of a model? One opinion is that adults command positions of power over their environment, possess competence and skill, autonomy, and have respect from others—all highly desirable goal states for the child. In order to share vicariously in these highly desirable goals possessed by the model, the child adopts beliefs and behaviors that he sees or believes are practiced by the model (Kagan, 1962). Another view (Mowrer, 1950) is that the child will value and imitate those behaviors that are characteristic of the persons he values most. The stronger the *MIR*, the closer the child will identify.

This is the period of male and female role identifications that play so important a part in later peer-group adjustments and the roles played as marital partners and as parents. The boy is expected to be masculine, to prefer the activities and interests of boys. The girl is expected to imitate the mother, to play with dolls, to play house, to enjoy dresses, to be interested in her appearance. When parental absence, illness, or overprotection prevents the formation of appropriate role identifications, the effects upon later role identifications may be extensive. Parental identification has been found important in the later development of vocational interests (Henderson, 1958; Stewart, 1959; Steimel, 1960; Crites, 1962), conscience (Kohlberg, 1963), and aggression (Mowrer, 1950).

Identification in this period contributes also to the acquisition of a conscience and moral standards. Whereas earlier, before his understanding and retention of language were well developed, he might respond to things he knows he has done wrong with fear of rejection or punishment by parents, now he can identify with how his parents might react and feel guilty. Because he is better able to anticipate consequences and to delay satisfactions, he comes to demand of himself the rules of conduct which have previously been set and enforced by his parents. Identification is thus an important step in learning to conform to the rules and expectations of society. In his later years the child will interact with others and experience gradually the role identifications of others and come thus to appreciate the more complex moral concepts of reciprocity, justice, and group welfare (Kohlberg, 1963).

Patterns of Family Influence. Not too long ago people believed that strict discipline was the most important means of controlling the growing child. "Spare the rod, spoil the child" was a maxim that reflected this belief. Another maxim, "As the twig is bent, so inclines the tree," implied that early application of strictness was needed to insure the firm implantation of habits of obedience and "good" behavior.

That strictness and strong discipline might have been successful in keeping children "seen, but not heard" was probably true, but we know today how many undesirable side effects are likely when discipline becomes the tool of a hostile and rejecting parent. We know, also, that children are influenced by many other factors in the home, such as the attitudes that accompany discipline, the patterns of alignment—that is, the connectedness and significance to the child of each other family member, including brothers and sisters, even grandparents. Often the total family situation provides a "theme" that sets boundaries to a child's behavior and goals which is even more effective than the interaction he has with any one person in the family circle.

Such patterns of alignment and "themes" often reveal the *salience*, or particular importance, which a family member might have—the MIR which will determine how great an influence this person will have in shaping the child's behavior. Each of us can recall how an older brother, or perhaps an aunt, was important to us in approving or disapproving, punishing or praising, our actions. Even so, most of our information about family influences has come from studies of parental behavior, particularly their patterns of affection and control.

Effects of Parental Attitudes and Controls.   Most studies of discipline and control within the home have shown that the specific methods used are not as important as the attitudes that accompany the practices. Several dimensions of these attitudes have been studied. Affection or warmth, in contrast to rejection or hostility, has been given much attention. It has been found that when a warm and loving attitude prevails, the parents tend to control mainly by praise and reasoning, as positive actions, or by isolating the child, showing disappointment, or by withdrawing love, as negative actions (Becker, 1964). Providing love contingent upon behavior is a highly questionable procedure. However, manipulation of affection tends to result in forming strongly internalized reactions in children, with guilty feelings when they sense they have done wrong and with acceptance of responsibility for their own actions. When combined with permissiveness, parental warmth tends to develop a child who is socially active, outgoing, creative, independent, and generally responsible. When combined with strictness of control, which is sometimes associated with overprotection, the child may be somewhat inhibited, submissive, dependent, polite, and not outgoing, friendly, or creative.

Power-assertive methods tend to be used by parents who are hostile toward or rejecting of their children (Becker, 1964). Such parents employ more physical punishment, threats, shouting, and coercion. In general, such discipline tends to induce hostility and aggression in children. This is often shown as disobedience and resentment of persons in authority, such as teachers, parents, or camp counselors, fighting and quarrelsomeness with other children, and tendencies to externalize their reactions to wrongdoing by blaming it on others, fearing punishment from others, and displaying hostility toward those who detect them, rather than feeling shame or guilt. Thus the aggressive, hostile parent often "reaps as he has sown" an aggressive, hostile offspring who is likely to experience continual difficulties in his social relations with both children and adults at later developmental stages. Such a pattern can be exaggerated when one parent, usually the father, is extremely hostile and rejecting, and the other parent is very permissive, or lax, about discipline. In such a situation, the hostility in the child, borne of his feelings of helplessness and frustration in the face of his father's brutal aggression, has no inner controls, and the result is often delinquent behavior (McCord, 1959).

Boys and girls tend to respond differently to parental controls. One study has shown that boys who were given moderate but not harsh discipline from fathers and warm nurturance from their mothers showed the most responsibility and leadership. Girls, in the same kinds of situations, tended to overreact emotionally to much discipline, and to become more inhibited, anxious, and dependent. With girls, lighter discipline was needed to achieve the same results (Bronfenbrenner, 1961). On the other hand, lack of discipline from fathers who rejected or neglected their sons tended to produce irresponsibility and poor leadership in boys.

The optimal development of responsibility, leadership, and social outgoing characteristics with sound emotional development in children seems to be associated with parents who are typically warm and permissive, rather than rejecting, hostile, and restrictive. Such parents tend to use praise liberally and to reason with, rather than physically punish, their children. They use more positive measures, rather than using isolation or love withdrawal, or threat. Punitive or "contingent love" methods tend to inhibit behaviors rather than to reinforce and to strengthen the better social responses and acceptance of responsibility. This is not to say that discipline should never include punishment. Perhaps the optimal situation for childrearing and successful socialization is found in families (1) where boys receive light to moderate discipline from fathers and unqualified love from both parents, and where discipline is lighter for girls under the same conditions, (2) in which permissiveness, rather than restrictiveness, prevails, and (3) in which there is agreement rather than conflict between parents regarding discipline.

No rules can apply invariably, however. As Becker (1964) said:

There are probably many routes to being a "good parent" which vary with the personality of both the parents and children and with the pressures in the environment with which one must learn to cope.

GUIDING MENTAL HEALTH IN STAGE II

As the child enters school around the age of six, he moves into Stage II.

His basic, meaningful, interpersonal relationships with family members have been formed, and his role and status within this system have been defined. He has developed routines and habits expected by society concerned with walking, eating, elimination, and modesty. He has learned to communicate with others, to follow directions, and has formed simple concepts of right and wrong, the rudiments of a conscience, and moral character. His concepts of self now include a sense of identity, autonomy, self-esteem, and initiative. The child who has mastered these developmental tasks will not find this transition to Stage II difficult. He will be able to take in stride, without undue stress, his rapid physical changes, the expansion of his social world, and the demands for new skills and achievements in the school and on the playground.

Middle Childhood Period.   In the middle childhood period, which ranges roughly from ages 6 to 12, the most demanding adjustments may be considered under three main headings: social, skills, and self. Speeded by new school relationships, the socialization process begun at home continues. At this point, parents often feel somewhat helpless as they see their children, once their concern alone, being influenced and depending upon other people: teachers, playmates, group leaders, babysitters, and others. The best thing they can do is to try to maintain contact, to keep informed, and to supply the interpretations needed to foster healthy social growth. If there is continuing training in consideration for others, in taking constructive approaches to problems, and in good social and personal habits, the going will be smoother, but naturally we could not expect this period to be completely free of the kinds of stresses that are typical of any processes of change and growth.

At this stage, the principal role of the family is to strengthen the appropriate learnings and attitudes being formed by many experiences. Parents still play a significant role in defining the meaning of experiences for a child and the social roles he will play. Through their interpretations the child will develop basic understandings of competition, money, and social class distinctions based upon economic level, occupation, religion, and nationality. Attitudes and values regarding sympathy, achievement, respect for the opposite sex and for people in authority, alcohol, smoking, sex, honesty, justice, and loyalty originate largely in the family system.

It is during this middle childhood period that parents for the last time will play a dominant role in the education of their children. It is a stage in which parents are being taught the most by their children, too. Because of this, this period is a critical transition zone. With their power and strength to dominate, it is possible for parents not to recognize their roles in contributing to the insidious problems of rejection, overcontrol, or neglect, which may erupt later, full-blown as adolescent rebellion or severe self-devaluation.

Both at home and at school great stress is made upon achievement and skills. This can be a great source of anxiety and frustration for the child. Children differ greatly in their rates of mental, social, and physical maturation, and at any one time a child may be at very different levels of development in each of these areas. This may cause a parent or teacher to regard a child as being a "problem," when all he may need is more time to grow. Although Mary might be tall for her age and faster in reading, she might be emotionally or socially immature. It is often difficult for a parent or teacher to know just how much to expect of a child. It might be too much or too little. The inconsistent demands and punishments of parents sometimes reflect this uncertainty.

Subconsciously, most parents want their children to achieve well in school, if possible to surpass their own degree of success. These desires tend to induce pressures upon the child to excel, which, if combined with rejection or punishment for lack of success, could affect seriously the child's feelings of self-esteem. In the peer group, where his social acceptance hinges more upon physical skills and strength, he may feel such inadequacy even more strongly. Caught in a cross fire of striving to win acceptance from both parents and peers, whose values may be opposed, the child might resolve the conflict by choosing to pursue the anti-intellectual goals of his age mates, much to the distress of his more school-oriented parents.

Parents could minimize such conflicts by reducing the emotional penalties associated with strongly negative controls, such as restriction, punishment, and rejection, which tend to intensify the aversive reactions of the child. Emphasis should be upon positive methods by building up his skills and confidence to meet problems constructively, in the knowledge that he will receive acceptance and approval for trying and for progress, not only for victory and full achievement. Pressures of strong competition tend to reinforce feelings of failure and inadequacy in a child who lacks the skills or maturity to become a winner. The child who feels confident that he will be accepted and will be loved whatever the outcome will be more likely to exert his maximum effort and to develop better frustration tolerance than one who senses that "all will be lost" if he fails. He also will be better oriented toward accepting the values and attitudes of his family. In his peer group he will also win acceptance because he is not a "quitter" and supports the group, rather than showing hostility and aggressiveness when he loses.

Friendships become increasingly important during the middle childhood period. The youngster has begun to make his own choices, and the group becomes a testing ground for his need for achievement, belongingness, and self-esteem. For boys and girls alike it becomes increasingly important to have a pal or best friend. Secret clubs, with special meeting places and secret codes, often make these relationships secure from others by excluding them. It is an important step in the development of those social bonds of loyalty and affection that precede the attractions to the opposite sex during adolescence. The child who has no person or pet upon which to bestow and from which to receive affection is lonely indeed, as he gradually transfers his MIRs away from his nuclear family.

Adolescence. The adolescent years, between the ages of 12 and 21, show very rapid social expansion. It is the era of the peer group. The adolescent spends most of his day, whether in or out of school, with others of his own age, so it is natural to expect this peer society to dominate his thinking and his behavior. At a time when the adolescent is struggling for independence from parental controls, when he feels the greatest pressures of competition, inadequacy, and parental disapproval, the youth can find in his peer group freedom from a demanding adult world, opportunity for acceptance and even status, and secure MIRs. Thus the peer culture becomes both an arena and a forum for self-expression exploring new social roles, learning new standards of behavior, and developing social skills in a group away from the family. Not all such learning is bad. At best the youth is afforded opportunities for status, responsibility, and leadership and for learning how to compete, to cooperate, and to share in group goals. Only when the peer group promotes antisocial attitudes of prejudice, delinquency, or separates the youth from the beneficial influences of his home before he has absorbed them would there be serious social implications. Equally unfortunate is the severe social selection process of the peer group which can leave emotional scars upon the girl who is not accepted into a sorority or the school elections which are basically popularity contests.

Erikson (1963) mentioned important differentiations of self, such as the *sense of identity*, which emerge at adolescence. The young person begins to ask "Who am I?" and "Where am I going?" As he commences to separate himself from parental and home MIRs and to associate more and more with his age mates in new MIRs, he carries with him lingering doubts about his adequacy to stand alone. Once he was sure, but now he is not; he has found neither a sure reason for being nor a tangible goal. He feels a need to be independent of his parents, but he still needs their MIRs. He feels many inner conflicts and anxiety over role confusion.

As the adolescent sexual functions develop, it follows that sexual tensions would contribute to such anxiety, especially if there were lingering uncertainties concerning masculinity or femininity of role. At this point, the adolescent seeks stability through new MIRs which will bridge the gap and stabilize the self. He may seek them symbolically in his religious faith, in new identifications with persons he can respect and admire (perhaps a hero astronaut, athlete, teacher, counselor, or coach), in peer-group pals, in "going steady," or even in early marriage. Where a close person does not gratify these needs the youth may display attachments to objects or symbols, as in fantasy, crushes on teachers or TV celebrities, love for pets, collecting class pictures and autographs, and so on. Many adolescent dating problems center about being "in love with love"—almost like being all dressed up and having nowhere to go. Yet it is from such MIRs as these in the adolescent years that firm loyalties to school, to teams, to clubs, which later develop into more remote allegiances to church and country, are formed.

Perhaps the most serious adjustment demanded of the adolescent is that of choosing and preparing for an occupation. With some 23,000 occupations to choose from, the adolescent needs to know a great deal, not only about jobs, but about himself, and to see these in relation to many variables, such as family expectations, financial limitations, opportunities for training, military obligations, automation changes of the future, going steady, idealistic versus realistic goals, and so on. Many of these conflict with each other, and give rise to many psychological defenses and emotional reactions.

The major tasks and adjustments to be made by adolescents are summarized in Table 3.2.

TABLE 3.2   Tasks and Adjustments of Adolescence *

---

1. *Social maturation:* achieving emotional independence from parents and emancipation from home control; developing new relationships with age mates of both sexes; desiring and achieving socially responsible behavior.
2. *Role development:* accepting one's physique; establishing a masculine or feminine role; forming a sense of identity.
3. *Occupational selection and preparation:* selecting appropriate educational and vocational goals; preparing for entry occupations and training for the future.
4. *Preparing for social and civic responsibilities:* educating oneself broadly; developing intellectual skills and interests; acquainting oneself with social needs and problems.
5. *Preparing for marriage and family life:* developing a close relationship with one person of the opposite sex; forming wholesome attitudes toward marriage and having children; learning home management and child rearing.
6. *Building a philosophy of life and harmonious system of values:* accepting moral values; identifying with a religion; finding meaning in life.

---

*Adapted from Cole (1959), Havighurst (1953), and others.

Early Adulthood. The tasks and adjustments of early adulthood center around marriage, establishing a home, getting set in an occupation, and assuming the obligations of an independent, responsible citizen. Table 3.3 lists some of these tasks.

TABLE 3.3   Tasks and Adjustments of Adulthood

Early Adulthood (ages 21–35)

1. *Courtship and mate selection:* premarital testing of roles and dependencies; compatibility; changing partners.

2. *Marriage:* adjusting emotionally to partner; assuming new roles and dependencies; changing roles with parents; assuming new roles with in-laws.

3. *Nonmarriage:* adjusting to single life; developing new kinds of dependencies.

4. *Family living:* tasks and roles in childrearing; managing finances; housekeeping responsibilities (cooking, chores, maintenance).

5. *Occupational development:* completing training; problems of advancement and relocation; problems of combining work with marriage (women).

6. *Community responsibilities:* assuming roles in civic, public welfare, and charitable groups (PTA, scouts, fund drives, etc.); voting and political activity.

7. *Social and recreational activities:* finding congenial social relationships in church, clubs, and activity groups; developing hobbies and interests; finding enjoyable recreations.

8. *Health:* maintaining health and vigor (weight control, exercise, keeping fit); adjusting to emotional stresses of bereavement, illness, or handicap.

9. *Values:* continued formation of philosophy of life and religious meanings; self-actualization.

Middle Adulthood (ages 36–60)

1. *Marriage:* changing relationship to each other; decline of sex activity; changing roles with parents.

2. *Nonmarriage:* continuation of adjustment problems from earlier adult years.

3. *Family living:* changing roles toward children; continuing financial and housekeeping responsibilities (now paying for children's education); assistance to grown children and their families.

4. *Occupational development:* "Peaking" in work; problems of retraining due to technological changes; reentry into job market (women); continued problems of advancement and relocation; preparing for retirement.

5. *Community responsibilities:* continuation of early adult tasks, but with increasing roles of leadership.

6. *Social and recreational:* continued, with increased importance as family disperses.

7. *Health:* of increasing concern due to aging.

Initially there is great uncertainty about selecting a mate and establishing a secure and intimate relationship. If the young adult has been successful in his earlier relationships with his parents, siblings, peer group, and others, his chances for a happy marriage are good. Children from broken or unhappy homes are less likely to have successful marriages. The young man looks to his wife for the MIR he found with his mother or other significant persons he has known, and the wife looks to her husband to play roles once played by her father or former boyfriends. Marriage involves the blending of whole cultures or families, not just the matching of persons alone. The marriage of two persons represents the interaction of significant systems based upon religion, nationality, and social and economic stratifications. Conflicts between these systems can promote conflicts of MIRs and give a marriage less likelihood of happiness.

Many quarrels, especially in the earlier stages of marriage and courtship, represent tests of the strength of new roles and relationships. It is sometimes difficult for the new couples to relinquish their former dependencies upon parents. Later stresses are more often related to conflicts of roles and role expectations of the wife and husband. The young wife, for example, may be expected to be a good cook, housekeeper, nurse, lover, career diplomat, "mother," partner in sports, scout leader, teacher, and so on. As children are added to the family even further role changes are demanded. Now the husband must share the attention of his wife with others, and is expected to maintain the love and respect of them, at the same time he is expected to be prime disciplinarian.

The early years on the occupational ladder are tense ones for the young husband. How to complete the training he needs and how to meet the round-the-clock competition for advancement, while burdened by home responsibilities and financial obligations at a time when his income is low, puts quite a strain upon him. Added to such frustrations are the military uncertainties.

Somehow, many young couples weather the strains and come to assume contributing roles in their communities. There are others who cannot, and whose lives become torn by divorce, chronic debt, alcoholism, and meaningless drudgery in their work. The early adult years may be more stressful or more enjoyable than any other period of one's life, depending upon how well or how poorly a person has mastered the tasks and adjustments of his earlier years.

Middle Adult Years. As one moves into the middle adult years, many of the self-conflicts and doubts become intensified. Now the brutal facts are known, and hopes are waning for becoming the kind of person one might have been; time begins to run out. Both the man and the woman must live with their mistakes. Automation has increased problems of work dislocation and unemployment for the older workers. Women who reenter the job market after their families are more self-sufficient must accept unchallenging positions unless they have special training. (See Table 3.2.)

The woman who has concluded her childbearing may sense the loss of being needed as a mother as her children leave the "nest." She has come to depend upon their *MIRs,* just as they have come to depend upon hers. Then there are the adjustments required by aging parents. Former roles of dependency become roles of care and protectiveness for the young couple toward their parents. Friction may develop, too, because aging grandparents resent their dependency upon their children, and may try to maintain their roles of authority.

Later Maturity.   Chapter 5 of this book is devoted to the problems of the later years, and so they will not be discussed here.

PREVENTION AND INTERVENTION IN STAGES I AND II

We have seen how each age period has its characteristic tasks and adjustment problems. In Stage I, the foundations for social living are laid. The interpersonal relationships and social learnings are formed that will provide the "launching pad" for the expanding significant social systems to be developed in Stage II. Whatever weaknesses exist in Stage I will handicap the person and will become sources of maladjustment or negative functions in Stage II. Early prevention and intervention, whenever such problems can be detected, may help to overcome, reduce, restrict, or at best keep the problems from affecting the functioning of other persons unduly. Many different persons and agencies perform these services in society.

Services Performed by Mental Health Agencies and Professional Personnel.   A chart showing the amount of working time spent by different mental health services in dealing with adjustment problems of varying severity is shown in Figure 3.1.

COMMUNITY HEALTH AND WELFARE AGENCIES.   At the right of Figure 3.1 are those community services (A) which devote the majority of their efforts to the tasks of prevention and intervention by offering services designed to promote better personal and family adjustment, school efficiency, and overall life success and happiness during Stages I and II. Public education, such as we see in magazines, at PTA meetings, or on TV, helps parents to understand themselves and the needs of their children. Improved prenatal care helps to curb the production of congenital defects that result in mental retardation.

Some families have multiple problems. Some are disabled by the

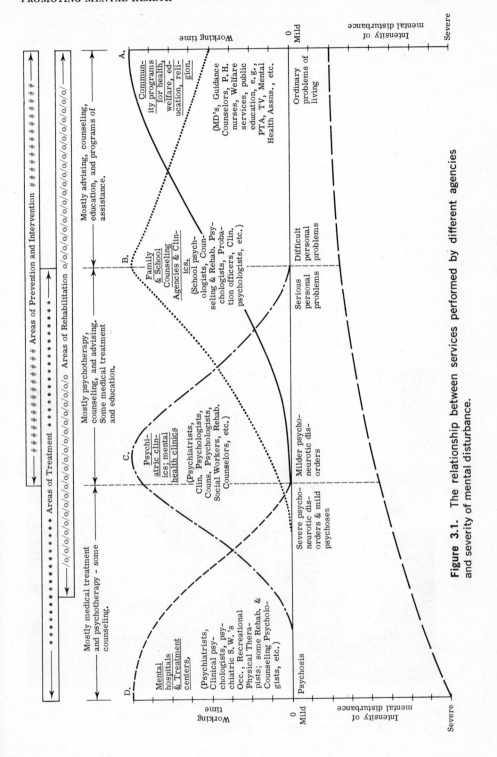

Figure 3.1. The relationship between services performed by different agencies and severity of mental disturbance.

absence of a breadwinner, inadequate income, substandard housing, chronic illness, lack of job skills, lack of education, alcoholism, and so on. Such problems are often met by improved welfare programs such as Aid to Dependent Children, vocational rehabilitation of parents, disability benefits, and so on. Mental health problems both arise from and contribute to problems of social disability. Strengthening the social welfare programs, along with an integrated approach that seeks to rehabilitate such families, as seen in the United States Economic Opportunity Act of 1964, is a crucial step in a broad effort to prevent mental illness.

Counseling by the family physician, the clergyman, the social welfare worker may help young parents to better marital adjustment and higher social standards. The school guidance counselor may assist the adolescent to select and train for a suitable career or to study more effectively. The public health nurse may help a young mother to understand better nutrition and to practice good personal hygiene.

FAMILY AND SCHOOL COUNSELING AGENCIES. Additional resources for help with Stage II problems of a more severe nature can be found in professional counseling services (B), such as those offered by a child and family guid-

Figure 3.2. Family counseling with a professional therapist helps family members to understand and work out their problems as a group. (Courtesy of National Institute of Mental Health, Bethesda, Maryland.)

ance agency, a school psychologist, a school social worker (sometimes called a visiting teacher), a speech and hearing specialist, a juvenile probation officer, a clinical or a counseling psychologist, and so on. Here the problems are more advanced and more deeply involved and should be dealt with by professionally trained persons. Limited psychotherapy, both group and individual, is often offered by such agencies or persons, but they are usually not equipped for working with persons suffering from severe psychoneurosis or psychosis.

PSYCHIATRIC CLINICS. Often directed by a psychiatrist who has medical training, a clinical psychologist, or psychiatric social worker, the psychiatric clinic (C) utilizes the team approach for preventive work with more severe Stage II, or even Stage III, problems, and may provide limited outpatient treatment of a medical or psychotherapeutic kind. Their primary aim is usually to provide early diagnosis and treatment in the hope of forestalling more serious breakdown, arresting the progress of the disorder, and hopefully, restoring persons to more normal living. Since their primary function is prevention, the psychiatric clinic treatment can never substitute for the more intensive treatment that may be found in the mental hospital. Neither by personnel nor by facilities is an outpatient clinic equipped to treat or to deal with the more serious mental disorders. They can assist in their treatment by providing early diagnosis and referral, however, and by playing a supportive role in the rehabilitation of the ex-mental patient. Diagnosed and treated in time, many persons seeking aid from a psychiatric clinic may never need to be hospitalized. The psychiatric clinic thus represents a third line of defense in the battle for the prevention of mental illness and promotion of mental health, or optimal human functioning.

THE COMPREHENSIVE COMMUNITY MENTAL HEALTH CENTER. The comprehensive community mental health center is an establishment that combines many of the diagnostic and treatment functions mentioned above under one roof, so to speak. Although different plans exist, one which has gained considerable favor offers the services of A, B, and C types, encompassing services to those who have relatively ordinary problems of living, now being dealt with by public welfare agencies, remedial school services, ministers, lawyers, loan companies, and public health departments, as well as the more complicated services being performed by counseling agencies and psychiatric clinics. Some plans call for such centers to be attached to hospitals, in which case they would involve the kinds of treatment services mentioned under D. Others feel that only when medical treatment is indicated should the person be treated as if he were "sick." As we have seen, many of the problems of adjustment and mastery of tasks are problems of social learning and of building positive functioning, rather than only physical or mental pathology. Rather than try to stretch the services of one specialty—for example, medicine—to cover all areas of human functioning, the community mental health center is an attempt to bring together many separate specialties to work more harmoniously toward the end of improving human functioning. As separate disciplines pursue their separate, often duplicative services, problems of personnel shortage and inefficiency mount. But not as fast as the problems of mental illness and minimal human functioning.

MENTAL HOSPITALS AND TREATMENT CENTERS. Intensive treatment and long-term care of the most severe mental disturbances is usually carried out in mental hospitals (D). Specialists in psychiatry, psychology, psychiatric social work, occupational, recreational, and physical therapy work together to help cure mentally disturbed patients.

The function of mental hospitals is primarily medical treatment, psychotherapy, and some counseling. Very little, if any, preventive work is done by this level of service. Some more recent concepts do involve the mental hospitals with community programs in prevention, and as suggested in the previous discussion, there are investigations underway concerning the feasibility of tying community mental health centers to mental hospitals.

SUMMARY

Mental health is a process of optimal functioning that characterizes successive stages of development throughout life. Through meaningful interpersonal relationships and participation in significant interactive systems, such as the family, the individual is confronted with tasks of socialization and self-development. To the extent that a person can master these tasks he will adjust to each stage of development and thus be prepared for the tasks of later stages. Should the critical period for such mastery pass without success, later mastery becomes difficult, even unlikely, and may constitute an obstacle to mastering other and later adjustments. It is the aim of prevention to equip a person for mastering these tasks, to remove obstacles to their mastery, and to assist him in their solution and in avoiding detrimental reactions to frustration and stress.

In Stage I prevention is sought through prenatal care and appropriate parental behavior during the early growth stages. Family influences are strongest in this period, transmitted by patterns of alignment and salience of family members, "themes," and the attitudes of and control methods used by important family figures, most often the parents.

In Stage II, which proceeds from school entrance on throughout life, the meaningful interpersonal relationships extend beyond the family to age-mates and significant other persons. Tasks of achievement in social, physical, and scholastic skills predominate in the middle childhood period. These tasks continue into adolescence, augmented by new tasks in establishing relationships with members of the opposite sex, choosing and training for appropriate life goals, in emancipation from family controls and dependencies, and in developing a meaningful system of values. Early adulthood tasks center about marriage and sexual adjustment, family living, occupational development, and assuming community responsibilities. Middle adulthood tasks involve changes in family structure and responsibility due to losses of children's dependencies and assumption of aging-parent dependencies, occupational "plateaus," and the beginnings of physical decline.

Community programs of prevention and intervention typically include family and school counseling services, psychiatric clinics, and community mental health centers. Such programs and services require the harmonious efforts of all of the helping professions and many nonprofessional persons in order to be effective and efficient.

SUGGESTED REFERENCES FOR FURTHER STUDY

Blair, G. M., and R. S. Jones (1964). *Psychology of Adolescence for Teachers.* New York: Macmillan Company.

This small paperback, one of the Psychological Foundations of Education Series, is clear, concise, yet comprehensive. Written for teachers, it provides a wealth of material based upon research important for understanding the tasks and characteristics of adolescents.

Duvall, Evelyn M. (1957). *Family Development.* Chicago: J. M. Lippincott Company.

Various stages of family development from establishment through the aging years are considered in this textbook directed toward understanding the sociological patterns and problems of modern family life.

Havighurst, R. J. (1953). *Human Development and Education.* New York: Longmans, Green & Co.

Although formulated principally for developing educational objectives, this presentation of the various developmental tasks is helpful in understanding all phases of psychological growth. Developmental tasks are presented for the following periods: infancy and early childhood, middle childhood, adolescence, early adulthood, middle age, and later maturity.

Mussen, P. H., Conger, J. J., & Kagan, J. (1963). *Child Development and Personality.* (2nd ed.). New York: Harper & Row.

Adjustments in the preschool, middle childhood, and adolescent years are discussed in greater detail. Many references are made to the Fels Institute follow-up study of 36 men and 35 women who had been studied and observed from birth through adolescence. By comparing their adult adjustment and traits with data obtained in their childhood from observations in the home, nursery school, day camp, public school, and from interviews with their mothers, interesting indicators of formative influences were revealed.

Scott, J. P. (1962). "Critical Periods in Behavioral Development." *Science*, **138**:3544, 949–958.

———— (1963). "The Process of Primary Socialization in Canine and Human Infants." *Monogr. Soc. Res. Child Develpm.*, **28**:1, (Whole No. 85).

Research on critical periods and primary socialization of infants and dogs is reviewed, showing parallels in behavioral growth stages.

Chapter 4

Treatment and Rehabilitation

STAGE III—ONSET OF MENTAL ILLNESS

IN THE LAST CHAPTER we saw how an individual moves from Stage I, his formative years within the nuclear family, to Stage II, the years of interaction within significant interactive systems away from his home and within his own family and community. If prevention and guidance have failed, his mental-status rating could reflect a progressive shift in the balance of positive and negative functioning in the direction of mental illness. Persons who fail to master the developmental tasks typical of certain age periods may display adjustment patterns so inadequate as to require outside help to restore positive functioning and to find constructive solutions to their problems.

We might consider such examples as these:

Duane, aged 14, was referred to the psychologist for mental evaluation by a juvenile court judge. Recently Duane had thrown a carving knife at his grandmother, sworn at his mother, hit her with a broom, and pushed her down the cellar stairs. Duane told the judge he had lost his temper when his grandmother "bawled him out," and he would certainly do it again if she kept it up. His measured mental ability was "dull normal." He stated that he hated his teachers and school and that he was failing several school subjects. He skipped school frequently, even with his mother's knowledge. Duane's mother complained that she could neither control nor discipline him because she feared his temper tantrums. Duane's father was in prison at this time.

Albert, aged 27, a former college senior, was in the midst of slashing his wrist with a razor in his rooming house when he became frightened and telephoned police. In describing the event to a psychologist, Albert said he had been drinking rather steadily for several hours prior to the slashing, when it seemed as if his mind went blank. (Shortly after, he modified his account to say that he had been perfectly aware of what he was doing and that his mind had been perfectly clear at the time.)

Albert had been in and out of the university once before due to marginal scholarship, and was currently "out." Just before enrolling for the last term his wife had obtained a divorce. In the subsequent term he attended few classes, and ended by not taking his final examinations, failing two courses, and receiving "Incompletes" (or "Indefinites," as he called them) in two other courses. He was then dropped again from college. During the semester, he had done little more than write free verse, which was concerned largely with exposing what he perceived was the political and moral decadence of the modern world. His suicide attempt, he explained, was due to his despair over graft and corruption in government and the dishonesty of persons in positions of public trust, especially lawyers, such as the one who "railroaded" his divorce.

As he talked, he seemed almost to flaunt his bandaged arm, as if he were proud of it. He discussed his many problems quite freely, but without feeling, almost as if he were describing another person or a specimen. No emotion was shown, for example, when he talked about his fear of becoming "insane." He did show anger and resentment when he talked about women, especially motherly, dominating women, and expressed many doubts about his mental ability. He did believe, however, that when his poetry was published it would have a profound effect upon the political and social thinking of the modern world.[1]

In both cases described above, failures in Stages I and II to cope successfully with the adjustments demanded resulted progressively in defense-oriented behaviors. As each person matured, his behavior showed less and less positive, and more and more negative, functioning, according to each of the criteria: social, individual, and functional. In each case other persons were drawn into the orbit of these maladjustments and were to become disturbed or troubled by them. In neither case were the basic motives of the individual satisfied by the adjustment behaviors chosen, nor were their self-attitudes and concepts pleasant or comforting. Instead, each felt inadequate and insecure. Their efficiency of living was definitely impaired. Each had entered Stage III, the time of *onset of mental illness.* In terms of the behavioral functioning (mental status rating) shown in Figure 2.1, their behavioral functioning had dropped below into the category 3. If not discovered and treated in time, such persons could regress even further to the most serious levels, categories 1 or 2, as their negative functioning increases and their positive assets reduce proportionately.

STAGE IV—TREATMENT

With early and effective assessment and treatment, such persons as we

---

[1] Taken from personal cases of the author.

have described might be prevented from slipping to more serious levels of functioning and might even be improved. As this is done, the person enters Stage IV, the treatment stage. *Treatment* has been defined as ". . . any measure to ameliorate an undesirable condition; an endeavor to help a person attain better health or better adjustment by whatever means: surgical, psychotherapeutic, counseling, or direct aid" (English and English, 1958). In terms of our description of mental health status, the following definition is suggested:

Treatment: Any procedure or effort which is employed to reduce negative functioning or to develop and restore positive functioning.

Ordinarily, *treatment* refers to efforts with persons who are at the "ill" end of the behavior status continuum (Ratings 1, 2, and 3 in Figure 2.1). When the endeavors, perhaps even the same efforts applied to those in the lower ratings, are applied to persons at essentially "well" status levels, we may use terms like *prevention, counseling,* or *rehabilitation,* depending upon whether a person is on his way down or up the behavior-status scale. If a person is functioning, let us say, at the lower end of Status Rating 4, he might consult a clinic or agency in order to receive advice or counseling that might enable him to solve his problems better or to understand himself, thus to accept a change in self-concept or to reduce troublesome emotions. This could be thought of as *preventing* more serious developments by building up his positive functioning, and perhaps removing some of his negative functions, such as self-doubts and conflicting emotions. If this same person had progressed to Status 4 from a lower level as a result of professional treatment, further counseling and training in skills might continue to increase his positive functioning and further reduce his negative functioning. This would be called rehabilitation. Since these terms are frequently confused, the reader may often find *treatment, prevention,* and *rehabilitation* used synonymously in various sources. It is hoped that the use of these terms as suggested here might better differentiate their meanings and use.

Many different professions and services contribute in the treatment program, and their work is found in many different kinds of settings. Just to name a few, we find both clinical and counseling psychologists, psychiatrists, social workers, occupational and physical therapists, nurses, attendants, recreational and educational specialists all playing significant roles in treating mentally ill persons. They may perform their services in private offices, clinics, camps, schools, general and psychiatric hospitals, special workshops, prisons, special centers and residences called halfway houses, and even on playgrounds. Certainly no profession or discipline can claim to have a monopoly upon treatment of the disturbed.

The treatment stage includes two main activities, each of which supports and depends upon the other: assessment and therapy. The first of these, *assessment*, refers to an evaluation of the status of the positive and negative functioning in the person. It seeks to answer the question "What are his strengths, and what are his weaknesses?" Sundberg and Tyler (1962) define assessment as follows: ". . . the processes used for decision-making and for developing a working image or model of the person-situation." As a result of assessment, appropriate decisions can be made about what outcomes of treatment are desirable and feasible and what kinds of treatment produce such outcomes.

The second activity concerns *therapy*. Once the status of behavioral functioning, both positive and negative, has been assessed, certain measures designed to reduce negative, and to increase positive, functioning can be instituted. Generally they can be classified under three headings: (1) *psychotherapy*, either individual or in groups; (2) *somatic therapy*, which may

Figure 4.1. Staff case conferences including various hospital professional personnel are held at intervals to review the assessments of a patient, to plan for therapy, and generally to review his progress and behavioral functioning status. (Courtesy of National Institute of Mental Health, Bethesda, Maryland.)

include convulsive, surgical, and drug therapies; (3) *environmental,* or *management, therapy.* Each will be considered in greater detail.

Assessment. The process of assessment involves collecting, organizing, and interpreting information about a person and his environment that will result in valid decisions regarding appropriate treatment. Each person presents a very different problem in assessment. In a typical hospital setting, it is expected that after a medical and neurological examination, and a psychological evaluation, including interviews, tests, and other observations, all information will be organized and presented together with a written report as a "case" for review at a staff conference. This report might indicate the psychopathology, the presumed causes, dynamics, or antecedent conditions, predictions, and recommendations for treatment. (See Figure 4.1.)

Sundberg and Tyler (1962) presented the following guide for formulating a case:

A. Present functioning
    1. Functioning in groups and living situations
        What are the important situations in the patient's life? What are the primary groups with which he affiliates?
        How does the patient interact in these groups? What role does he assume? How consistent is he from group to group?
    2. Functioning skills and abilities
        What is the level of the patient's intelligence as he functions now? Is there evidence of changes from earlier periods in his life, of intellectual impairment from brain damage or emotional disorder?
        What strengths and weaknesses does he show in his work or academic performance? What potentialities have not been developed?
        Does he show disorders of thought and distortions of reality? What are his problem-solving skills?
    3. Physiological limitations and effects
        What physical restrictions are placed on his functioning?
        How well does his "body image" correspond with reality?

B. Motives and emotions
    1. Interpersonal purposes
        What is the patient attempting to accomplish by his typical interaction patterns? How does he "teach" others to respond to him?
        What are the interpersonal effects ("gains") from his symptoms?
    2. Emotional characteristics
        What is the patient's characteristic mood? How anxious is he? What are his fluctuations in emotions?
        How does he express his emotions? How controlled or how impulsive is he? Is there a disparity between his self-report and his objective dis-

play of emotions? How appropriate are his emotional expressions to his age and situation?

3. Intrapsychic conflicts and adjustive reactions

How does the patient react to anxiety? What are his typical defense mechanisms and "self-protections" against threat?

What is the intraphysic function of his symptoms? How do they relate to his adjustment to stress?

C. Self-concept and core belief system

1. Identity

Who does the patient believe he is? What are the central assumptions or unquestioned beliefs about his own nature?

Is there evidence of delusions and other distortions about his beliefs about himself?

2. Values and authorities

What are the basic values, interests, and goals implied by his present behavior and his choices throughout his life?

Whom does he accept as an authority? Whose word would be unquestioned?

D. Development and change

1. Choice patterns

What were the "turning points" in the patient's life? What are the kinds of alternatives the patient has chosen at these significant points in his history? How has he gone about making these choices?

What alternatives does he face now?

2. Situational developments

In what kinds of situations has the patient functioned poorly or well?

What changes are going on in his present situation? What shifts in role are expected of him? What are the sources of support or stress from significant others? What developmental tasks is he facing?

3. Capacity for learning and change

How capable is the patient of shifting roles, learning new ways of reacting to stress, reorganizing his self-conceptions?

E. Diagnostic impressions

1. Psychiatric classification (if appropriate)

What category in the official psychiatric diagnostic system (American Psychiatric Association, 1952) does this patient match most closely, and why? What are the second or third alternatives, if any?

2. Disorders of ability and performance (if appropriate)

What are the patient's disorders of speech, reading, academic performance, etc.?

What classes of jobs is he qualified for presently and with training?

F. Recommendations and prognosis

1. Developmental needs

What changes need to occur in the patient in order to meet the demands of present or potential situations?

2. Situational changes
   What kind of home, work, or ward situation would be conducive to the
      patient's development?
   What kind of counseling or psychotherapy should be done with the
      family or other people who are important in his life?
3. Special assignments or training
   Are there any special kinds of treatment, such as occupational therapy,
      industrial therapy, or training courses which would be of help in
      rehabilitating the patient?
4. Psychological effects of somatic treatments
   What benefits or difficulties might accrue from drugs, electroconvulsive
      therapy, etc.?
5. Psychotherapy
   Is psychotherapy likely to be of value? If so, what kind and by whom?
   Is group therapy or counseling indicated?

MEDICAL EXAMINATION. Information regarding the person's physical condition may be determined from a thorough medical examination by a psychiatrist and other medical specialists. The aim is to identify all physical, physiological, and neurological factors that tend to reduce functioning. Typically, an evaluation would be made of blood pressure, heart, lungs, blood, spinal fluid, glands, and so on. The neurological examination might note the person's gait, the size of his pupils, his reflexes, his sensory responses, and perhaps an electroencephalogram (a recording of minute electrical charges taken from different regions of the brain, sometimes called an EEG) to determine irregular "brain wave" rhythms that could be associated with epilepsy and other brain pathologies.

PSYCHOLOGICAL ASSESSMENT. Interviews are important ways of learning about a patient. When he first comes to the clinic or hospital the person may receive an *intake interview* with a social worker or a psychologist. In the intake interview the person explains his problems and the interviewer describes the available services and arranges for the next step. This might be referral to a member of the staff for assessment or treatment, or referral to some other service or person. The intake interviewer might also obtain a case history. The *case history interview* would review the history of the person's problems, the patterns of his development in childhood, his significant interactive systems, including his family, both past and present, his educational and work history, his interests and pastimes, his sexual adjustment, and his medical history.

MENTAL STATUS EXAMINATION INTERVIEW. A mental status examination interview may be conducted by a psychologist or a psychiatrist. Usually this interview is concerned with discovering psychological indicators of pathology, contributing or causal factors, possible psychological reactions to physical illness, or psychological factors that might interfere with treatment, as, for example, denial of illness (Stevenson and Sheppe, 1959). The mental status examination typically covers six main topics: (1) general appearance and behavior; (2) stream of talk and activity; (3) emotional tone or mood; (4) mental content and special preoccupations, such as obsessions, delusions, and hallucinations; (5) sensorium and intellectual resources, such as the person's orientation to time, place, and person (does he know where he is, who he is, what day it is, and so on?) and evidence of his intelligence, memory, judgment; (6) insight (does the person know he is ill and what might be bothering him?) (Strecker, Ebaugh, and Ewalt, 1947; Sundberg and Tyler, 1962).

Used alone, clinical interview methods are not always dependable. They may tend to reflect the personal biases and inaccuracies of the interviewer. Under well-structured conditions, however, a clinical interview may be very valuable. Machir and Russell (1963) reported that ratings on the Wittenborn Psychiatric Rating Scales of incoming patients made by four psychologists, three of whom observed the fourth conduct structured, fact-finding interviews, agreed with later psychiatric classifications of these patients with 75 percent accuracy. In general, however, an interview needs to be supported with plenty of information from medical and psychological tests.

PSYCHOLOGICAL TESTING. A great variety of tests is available to help the clinician make a more complete and accurate assessment. Tests have the advantage of permitting the behaviors observed to be compared systematically with behaviors of many other persons and groups, both normal and pathological. At their best, tests provide reliable and valid procedures for discovering the degrees and kinds of mental ability, motivation, emotional expression, and control of a person. At their worst, they can be misleading, meaningless, and trivial. Used by experienced, and qualified psychologists, good psychological tests can reveal accurately in minutes information that might not be determined for days by other methods, if discovered at all. But, just as medical and interview data should not be used alone, neither should test information be used exclusively. All should be used together.

Typically, the clinical psychologist includes an intelligence test and several measures of personality of an objective or projective kind in making his evaluations. Should organic brain dysfunction be suspected, special tests of intellectual deficit or impairment might also be given. Lack of space precludes a review of the many measures often employed by a clinical psychologist. Additional information about testing may be found in Chapter 6 of this book or in books on testing (Anastasi, 1961; Horrocks, 1964) or clinical references, such as Garfield (1957) and Hadley (1958).

An *intelligence test* requires a subject to perform tasks that demonstrate his "developed ability" to learn. By comparing his scores with others of his age the clinician can estimate the extent to which advanced or retarded mental ability might be an important factor in understanding the disorder, choosing the proper therapy, and planning rehabilitation training.

One test commonly used with children is the Stanford–Binet Intelligence Scale (Terman and Merrill, 1960). Individually administered, this test yields a single deviation IQ, with a mean of 100 and standard deviation of 16 points, which is derived from norm groups of children aged 2 through 18. A child of 8 with an IQ of 116 thus will usually exceed 84 percent of the children of his age in performing certain tasks related to his learning ability.

At the adult level, the Wechsler Adult Intelligence Scale (WAIS) (Wechsler, 1955) is often used. The WAIS, which provides norms for persons from 16 to 64 years of age, yields three deviation IQs (Full Scale, Verbal, and Performance), which have a mean of 100, and a standard deviation of 15 points. The separate Verbal and Performance IQs allow a clinician to measure discrepancies in these abilities which might be diagnostic. A downward extension of this test to children between 5 and 15 years of age, the Wechsler Intelligence Scale for Children (WISC) (Wechsler, 1949) has been used as a substitute for the Stanford–Binet when separate scale IQs or subtest patterns are desired.

As he gives these tests, the psychologist is alert to other cues provided by the testing situation. A subject might display erratic behavior or make unusual responses. Garfield (1957) cited the following example:

> When asked in what way a dog and a lion are alike, this patient replied, "There are lions and tigers and dogs are the little animals. We often see that lions are great big animals and people aren't very close to them." . . . he [the patient] brought forth some type of associational content which was related only peripherally to the questions, and which was a manifestation of his disturbed functioning.

The clinician will notice things such as speech defects, distractibility, nervousness and tension, poor memory for directions, weak vocabulary, and personal reactions to the testing situation. For example, the writer once tested a young man who, though severely retarded intellectually, could add correctly columns of four-digit numbers mentally as fast as they were written. Such information might be important in understanding the nature of one's mental impairment.

Other tests, such as the Bender Visual Motor Gestalt Test (Bender, 1938) or the Goldstein–Scheerer Tests (Goldstein and Scheerer, 1941), can be used to assess losses of brain function.

Personality assessment techniques fall into two main classifications: objective and projective. Objective personality measures may include such instruments as rating scales and personality questionnaires. One example of a *rating scale* is the Wittenborn Psychiatric Rating Scales. (WPRS) (Wittenborn, 1955). In these scales, a rater, who could be a nurse, psychologist, psychiatrist, or some person in close contact with the person, rates his behavior. "The Scales provide for the assignment of numerical values to indicate the presence and degree of pathological symptoms in a patient (Wittenborn, 1955)." The rating categories include such items as the following (Wittenborn, 1955):[2]

Scale 27. Believes others influence him.   *Rating*

No evidence that patient feels that others seek to spy upon or
control his behavior or thought.   0
Wonders if others have a particular interest in his thoughts
or personal behavior.   1
Wonders if others attempt to influence his behavior in some
unknown manner or attempt to control his thoughts.   2
Believes that others influence his behavior in some strange
manner or control his thoughts.   3

On clusters derived from factorial analyses, a person receives a score for such diagnoses as acute anxiety, paranoid condition, phobic compulsive, and so on.

The Minnesota Multiphasic Personality Inventory (MMPI) (Hathaway and McKinley, 1951) consists of 550 questions and statements to which a subject gives one of three replies: Yes, No, or Cannot say. It can be administered individually or in groups. The scores are given in certain psychiatric classifications based upon how closely the subject approximates the scores of patients diagnosed according to these classifications. As the MMPI is used more and more with groups from the general population (for example, juveniles and college students), the psychiatric meaning of the scales has become inappropriate, and reference to code numbers of the scales rather than scale names is more usual. Instead of identifying persons according to such scale elevations as hypochondriasis or depression, a patient may be called a "12 or 21 code." A wealth of research has accumulated that permits a clinician to describe many personality characteristics

---

[2] Reproduced by permission. Copyright © 1955 The Psychological Corporation, New York, N. Y. All rights reserved.

and even typical medical symptoms of persons who show various code types. Over two hundred special scales that purport to distinguish various psychiatric syndromes and personality types have been derived by item analysis of the original 550 items of the MMPI (Dahlstrom and Welsh, 1960).

Projective methods provide the subject with certain stimuli or tasks and give him an opportunity to interpret them in his own way. It is assumed that he will "project" his own feelings and needs in making his responses, thus involuntarily and spontaneously reveal the substructures of his motives, values, and typical adjustment patterns. Many kinds of stimuli and tasks, structured and unstructured, are used for these tests, such as ink blots, pictures, cartoons, incomplete sentences, one's own drawings and words. Often elaborate scoring systems, theoretical assumptions, and interpretations are involved in using these tests.

Perhaps the best known and most widely used projective method is the Rorschach (Rorschach, 1942). For this test subjects are shown 10 cards that have printed inkblots of various shades and color upon them and asked to say what each looks like, what it could be, or what it makes him think of. Responses are recorded and many features of the subject's behavior are noted, such as how he holds the card, how long, and so on. Following the initial presentation there is an *inquiry* to determine what prompted the person to respond as he did and to give him an opportunity to clarify his responses. The scoring and interpretation of the responses is too elaborate to mention here.

The Thematic Apperception Test (TAT) (Murray, 1943) employs pictures as stimuli. The subject is usually shown 20 cards, including a blank card, in two sessions. He is told that it is a test of imagination, and he is asked to make up a story about each picture, indicating how he thinks the scene came about, what is happening, what the characters are feeling, and what the outcome will be. There are no time limits, and the stories are recorded as verbatim as possible. This too might be followed by an inquiry. The stories are then analyzed to determine the "hero" in each story with whom it is believed the subject might have identified, his motives, trends, and feelings, the forces in the hero's environment, the outcomes, happy or sad, successful or unsuccessful, *themas* or dominant need patterns, and the interests and sentiments displayed toward significant figures. A typical testing with the TAT is shown in Figure 4.2.

To a great extent the value of the projective method depends upon the faith of the investigator in their use and his ability as a clinician to use the information they provide. Rather consistently they fail to meet the require-

Figure 4.2. Psychologist administering a Thematic Apperception test to a patient. (Courtesy of National Association for Mental Health, Bethesda, Maryland.)

ments of reliability and validity for psychological measuring instruments as they are typically used in clinical situations. Anastasi (1961) summarized the research on projective methods as follows:

. . . well designed validation studies utilizing blind analyses and adequate experimental controls have demonstrated that even under optimal conditions such techniques have inadequate validity to justify their use as *psychometric tools* in making individual decisions. The utilization of projective techniques as tests thus appears to be on the decline. Nevertheless, certain projective techniques may serve a useful function as *interviewing aids* in the hands of skilled clinicians. . . . qualitative content analysis is proving more fruitful than formal scoring categories.

In many ways these comments could apply to the use of all personality instruments. Although specific predictions for the individual from personality test data tends to be undependable and inaccurate, the experienced psychologist can often use the data he obtains with them to further his understanding of the self-perceptions, dominant motivations, and personality traits of a person. It would be naive to assume that these tests *measured* significant aspects of one's inner life, for there could be no way one could verify this. These tests merely represent rather standardized ways to get a person to make responses with reference to himself and others, and to suggest his typical modes of adjustment. From these responses an experienced and trained clinician gains more information from which he can make inferences about the patient's personal characteristics, significant identifications, and behavioral adjustment status.

Therapy. As we have seen earlier in this chapter, the role of therapy in the treatment program is to reduce or to eliminate negative functioning and to restore and increase positive functioning. Though certain types of therapy have been designated as psychotherapeutically, somatically, or environmentally oriented, it must be kept in mind that a whole person is involved, and that his functioning includes all of these areas. Each type of therapy has unique properties, yet each aims in its sphere of concern to improve the overall behavioral functioning of the individual.

PSYCHOTHERAPY. Treatment that depends mainly upon the psychological methods for producing behavioral change are classed broadly as psychotherapy. There are many variations of approach ranging from simple individual–therapist verbal interactions to the activities of group work, psychodrama, and play therapy. Harper (1959) described 36 systems of psychotherapy, and there are many more. Their differences revolve around theoretical systems, professional identities, procedures, and goals. Whether it be a minister advising a young married couple, a psychologist talking with an emotionally disturbed child, or a psychiatrist engaged in a classical type of psychoanalysis, we are dealing with psychotherapy and its services. Each has its unique way of understanding and working with the person and his problems. Despite such differences, however, there are common features to all types of psychotherapy. Sundberg and Tyler (1962) reviewed these resemblances as follows: Each aims to (1) reduce anxiety in a person enough to enable him to explore the painful areas of his experience; (2) establish a strong interpersonal relationship between the person and the therapist as a "vehicle for constructive change"; (3) facilitate verbal or other types of communication of the person which will permit him to "establish connections with his inner and outer worlds"; and (4) gain some "commitment" of the person to seek to change his behavior.

Ford and Urban (1963) considered only individual verbal psychotherapy in their comparison of 10 systems of psychotherapy. They define this type of psychotherapy as "a procedure wherein two persons engage in a prolonged series of emotion-arousing interactions, mediated primarily by verbal exchanges, the purpose of which is to produce changes in the behaviors of one of the pair." Perhaps the most widely known psychotherapy of this type is *psychoanalysis*, introduced by Sigmund Freud, a Viennese physician.

PSYCHOANALYSIS. Although there are many modifications of the therapeutic techniques originated by Freud, each aims to uncover and to gain insight into repressed motives, impulses, and feelings that are believed to produce symptoms of anxiety and maladaptive behavior. As emotional tensions are removed and insights are gained by means of a close interpersonal relationship with a therapist, gradually the defense-oriented, neurotic behavior becomes more task-oriented; the person develops self-confidence and self-control.

In a typical psychoanalysis, the person may meet with his psychoanalyst three to five times per week for a period of two to five years. Usually the psychoanalyst is a physician who has received extensive training in psychoanalytic methods, including a personal psychoanalysis, although some psychologists also use psychoanalytic methods. Originally the patient relaxed on a couch facing away from the analyst during the session, but modern psychoanalysts permit much more freedom. Most important is the "free association" by the patient of his thoughts, memories, and feelings; he is encouraged to withhold no thoughts or ideas, no matter how trivial, embarrassing, or illogical they might seem. Freud assumed that through such associations long-forgotten but significant events, feelings, and relationships would be revealed which were at the root of one's anxieties. All behavior during the session thus becomes potentially meaningful and relevant. Slips of the tongue, emotional reactions, defensive behaviors, such as hostility toward the analyst, and symbolic associations, such as dreams, are discussed, noted, and interpreted by the therapist. The therapist is especially alert to "resistances" of the patient, in which the patient seems to be avoiding discussion of certain topics or opposing certain suggestions or interpretations by the therapist. He also notes and interprets "transference," a displacement by the patient of positive or negative feelings applicable to another person, perhaps a parent, onto the therapist. Such resistances and transferences often provide clues to key unconscious attitudes and to meaningful early identifications and experiences.

As therapy progresses, the patient gradually gains insight into his motives and feelings, many of which have been repressed because they were socially unacceptable and guilt-arousing, he feels less anxious and better able to make appropriate adjustments in his social and working life.

Many modifications of the Freudian techniques and theory are common today. Some therapists use a face-to-face prescriptive interview technique with little "free association," whereas others may be more permissive and indirect. Some require a complete historical revelation of sexual and developmental traumata; others stress growth of understanding and interpersonal relationships with little "digging" into the past. There is no standard technique.

CLIENT-CENTERED PSYCHOTHERAPY. Partly as a rejection of psychoanalytic emphasis upon sexual causes of behavior and partly as a result of different conceptualizations of personality growth, *client-centered psychotherapy* has become popular today. According to Carl Rogers, who described this type of psychotherapy (Rogers, 1942 and 1951), behavior is governed by one's perception of himself and his world. Psychological maladjustment exists when the individual denies symbolization to certain threatening perceptions of himself. The psychological tensions which result cause him to erect defenses against these threats to the self-concept. Therapy consists of creating an interpersonal situation in which the person will feel free to experience these denied perceptions, to accept them as part of himself, and thereby to reduce discrepancies between his idealized self-image and his perceived self. Rogers sees this as a perceptual growth process of the self necessary for socially mature adjustment.

In the client-centered approach, responsibility for the direction and course of therapy is left to the client. (NOTE: he is not called a "patient.") What he chooses to talk about, what meanings he finds, how fast or slow he proceeds or digresses are decided by the client rather than by the therapist (Harper, 1959). The therapist neither diagnoses nor evaluates the client; he avoids making interpretations; he does not advise, suggest, or inform; he offers no reassurances or solutions. Rather, he creates a genuinely warm, permissive interpersonal relationship and "growth-promoting climate" of acceptance and "unconditional positive regard," which will allow the client to explore his ideas and to experience emotions, even negative self-attitudes, without feeling threatened or defensive. Through his "empathic understanding of the client's feelings and personal meanings" the therapist attempts to clarify and to reflect the essence of what the client is saying about himself (Rogers, 1962). Through this relationship and the security it represents the client develops self-understanding and comes gradually to accept himself for what he really is; the disparity between real and ideal self-concepts reduces, and his anxiety lessens. He becomes more open to experience, at harmony with his own feelings, and more capable of feelings emotionally close to others.

Client-centered theory and therapy has stimulated much research upon the techniques and processes of psychotherapy. Because it seemed simple to perform, did not require medical preparation or years of training, promised shorter-term relationships (which would be less expensive), and explained personality in a less complicated and esoteric way, client-centered therapy quickly won many adherents in a variety of settings: industry, schools and colleges, clinics, counseling agencies, and hospitals. Although rarely practiced strictly in the manner prescribed by Rogers, the concepts and techniques of client-centered therapy have been absorbed into eclectic methods and remain, as have psychoanalytic concepts and methods, major contributions to therapy.

Figure 4.3. A psychodrama session. This patient is acting out some of her previous experiences. (Courtesy of National Institute of Mental Health, Bethesda, Maryland.)

OTHER PSYCHOTHERAPIES. Other commonly used kinds of psychotherapy are group psychotherapy, psychodrama, and play therapy. In *group psychotherapy* several persons are treated together. (See Figure 4.6.) In psychodrama, shown in Figure 4.3, a patient is encouraged to act out earlier experiences or situations that may relate to his problems, as if he were in a play. Other persons, who may be patients or specially trained therapists, may become supporting members of the cast to help him to express such usually inhibited feelings as fear, guilt, or hostility and to find new ways to cope with his anxieties.

In *play therapy*, children are encouraged to act out and to vent their feelings in play activities. (See Figure 4.4.) In pretending that dolls are persons in his family, perhaps a parent or sibling, a child can treat it as he wishes without fear of retaliation. This helps him to release feelings of hostility or to express need for love or esteem, and may also help to identify interpersonal stresses. The child can practice new roles in these play situations which might be transferred to other places, such as school.

Figure 4.4. Play therapy session of child with a psychologist. (Courtesy of National Association for Mental Health, Bethesda, Maryland.)

BEHAVIOR THERAPY.   This therapy breaks from traditional psychoanalytical and client-centered approaches. Instead of assuming that symptoms of neurosis or maladjusted responses originate in underlying conflicts and unconscious motives, behavior therapists assert that all symptoms and neurotic behaviors are maladaptive habits acquired under particular conditions, then generalized to other situations. Treatment, rather than being aimed at relief of inner conflicts and at development of insight, consists of modifying the behavior patterns according to principles of learning.

In the case of an abnormal fear, or phobia, for example, the treatment might be to train a person to relax on signal, perhaps while hypnotized. He is told to visualize a rather mild fear situation, then told to relax. After a few trials, the person can visualize it without fear. Then he is told to visualize a stronger fear, again followed by instructions to relax. Again this is repeated until he does not react with fear. As the trials progress to stronger and stronger fears, the process is repeated. Gradually the fear stimuli become "desensitized"—that is, they lose their power to induce anxiety because they have been conditioned to antagonistic relaxing responses. This has been called "reciprocal inhibition" (Wolpe, 1958) or "counter-conditioning" (Bandura and Walters, 1963).

In another form of behavior therapy, the person is required to practice the unwanted habit until it extinguishes. This kind of "negative practice" has been successful with some kinds of speech defects. In the case of addictions, such as smoking or alcohol, the maladaptive responses are paired with aversive stimuli, such as nauseant drugs, so that the addictive stimulus acquires the same avoidance reactions.

Bandura and Walters (1963) reported a study by Lazarus (1958), who treated an architect, whose compulsiveness interfered with his productivity, by placing him under hypnosis and asking him to imagine he was compulsively and unnecessarily checking his work. It was then suggested that he was becoming anxious. The opposite reaction was hypnotically induced as the person imagined himself relaxed and pleased while completing his work and carrying out necessary steps. "By thus associating anxiety with the performance of compulsive acts, while at the same time encouraging him to feel relaxed when avoiding compulsive behavior, Lazarus was able to eliminate unnecessary rituals and to considerably increase the client's work productivity."

Behavior therapy has been criticized for being superficial and temporary by treating only symptoms rather than the underlying causes of disorders. Such critics maintain that until basic problems are treated, one symptom will merely replace another; the "real" problems will be masked, and will persist, perhaps more dangerously. In answer to these criticisms, Grossberg (1964) made the following observation after an extensive review of studies of behavior therapy outcomes:

The overwhelming evidence of the present review is that therapy directed at elimination of maladaptive behavior ("symptoms") is successful and long-lasting. Substitute symptoms were reported in two cases of all those surveyed. . . . Unfortunately, psychotherapists seem to have stressed the hypothetical dangers of curing only the symptoms, while ignoring the very real dangers of the harm that is done by not curing them.

The general effectiveness of psychotherapy has been severely questioned by Eysenck (1952). He compared the outcomes of over 19 studies covering 7,000 cases in which psychotherapy of many types had been employed with base rates for the improvement of hospitalized neurotics and neurotic disability insurance claimants who had received either custodial or regular medical care. Both groups showed a recovery rate of about two thirds. Eysenck interpreted this to indicate that psychotherapy made no difference. In evaluating later studies Eysenck concluded in 1961 as follows:

With the single exception of the psychotherapeutic methods based on learning theory, results of published research with military and civilian neurotics, and with both adults and children, suggest that the therapeutic effects of psychotherapy are small or non-existent, and do not in a demonstrable way add to the non-specific effects of routine medical treatment, or to such events as occur in the patient's everyday experience.

Many objections have been raised to Eysenck's analyses, mostly concerned with questioning the comparability of his control and therapy groups and with the criteria of improvement he employed (Luborsky, 1954; Rosenzweig, 1954). Certainly the last shot has not been fired in the controversy over the effectiveness of psychotherapy, and psychotherapy retains its preeminence and respect as a method of treatment. Perhaps the most important result of Eysenck's criticisms will be to force psychotherapists to define more carefully just what they intend to accomplish and to show by definitive research that this is in fact being done. Until this is done, the verdict will have to be: "Not proven."

SOMATIC THERAPY. With severely disturbed or psychotic patients, physical or medical treatments with convulsive shock therapy (induced by electricity or insulin), brain surgery, or drugs may be employed. These somatic treatments are administered by psychiatrists who are medically trained, not by psychologists.

SHOCK THERAPY. In *electroconvulsive shock therapy* the patient is given a brief current of electricity in the head. He immediately loses consciousness, and has no memory of the shock. Brief convulsive movements occur, followed by unconsciousnesss lasting from several minutes to an hour. When he awakens, the patient may experience confusion and loss of memory for a period of time, but no permanent intellectual impairment occurs (Noyes and Kolb, 1963). Depending upon the results and the type of disorder, treatments are usually given three times a week, most often in a hospital, although outpatient treatment can be given in a clinic or physician's office. Electroconvulsive shock therapy has been found most effective with depression, either of the involutional type or in the depressed phase of manic-depressive psychosis. It has been used to some extent with certain types of schizophrenia. It is of little value in treating psychoneuroses, however (Noyes and Kolb, 1963).

Another way of inducing shock and coma is by injecting doses of *insulin*. This is less frequently used and treatment is limited to schizophrenia. Since this type of therapy may involve serious complications, a larger staff of medical personnel and more attention are required. Sometimes a combination of insulin and electroshock is employed, to gain the benefits of each, but there is little evidence that it is more effective (Noyes and Kolb, 1963).

The mechanism of action for electroshock or insulin convulsive therapy is not understood. Some argue that it represents extreme punishment; others believe it alters brain activity. As use of tranquillizing and energizing drugs has increased, shock treatments have become less widely used.

PSYCHOSURGERY. A more drastic type of treatment, called *prefrontal lobotomy*, involving severance of connections between parts of the forebrain, the thalamus, and the frontal lobe, is sometimes used after patients have not responded to other types of treatments, such as shock therapy and use of drugs. Patients who show excessive tension and agitation, depression, aggressiveness, or excited, impulsive behavior can sometimes be relieved.

The operation may make a hospital patient much easier to care for, even permit him to go home. If successful, the patient becomes less anxious, more friendly and cheerful, even to the point of being able to work.

Some oppose lobotomy treatment because of the uncertain and irreversible effects of destroying neural tissue. Sharp changes from the preillness personality and social behavior of the patient are common. Often the patient, although becoming less disturbed, seems to lose his "herd sense" and to show lack of responsibility and social feeling for others. He may be tactless, childish, selfish, and demanding, sometimes even vulgar or profane. Reports of effects upon intellectual processes are somewhat inconsistent—some showing significant losses; others showing none.

Most follow-up studies report significant improvement in about two thirds of those treated by brain surgery. Only about one third fail to respond—usually the more deteriorated, chronic schizophrenics. Just as increasing use of drugs has decreased the use of shock therapy, psychosurgery has decreased in many places almost to zero (Noyes and Kolb, 1963).

DRUG THERAPY. The use of energizing and tranquillizing drugs has revolutionized the treatment of mental patients. Many patients who have failed to respond to previous treatments and who have been considered chronic psychotics have improved, often to the point of being permitted to return to their homes and communities under continued medication.

As a result, drug therapy has become the most widely used somatic treatment.

Tranquilizers, such as reserpine or chlorpromazine, tend to calm down excited, overactive, agitated patients, to reduce their destructiveness, and to minimize their hallucinations and delusions. These drugs are particularly effective with schizophrenic patients, and are used to some advantage in speeding recovery with manic-depressive psychosis.

Depressed patients are not helped by tranquilizing drugs; they need energizing rather than tranquilizing. *Antidepressant drugs*, such as phenalzine or malamide, therefore, have been found useful in treating manic-depressive and depressive reactions.

Tranquilizing and energizing drugs have permitted many patients who might otherwise have remained hospitalized indefinitely to return to productive lives in their communities. Within the hospital their use has so

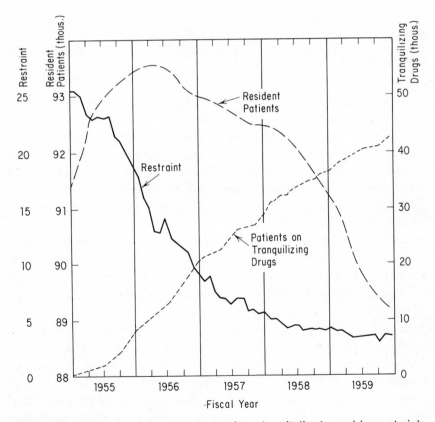

Figure 4.5. Numbers (in thousands) of patients hospitalized, requiring restraints, and on tranquilizing drugs in New York State hospitals 1955–1959. (From Brill and Patton, 1959.)

alleviated symptoms that locked wards and use of restraints are less needed. As their use has increased the convulsive shock and surgical therapies have become almost obsolete. Perhaps the greatest benefit has been in permitting patients who formerly were too excited or depressed to participate in or to profit by psychotherapy and other therapeutic programs to be treated now in the hospital or community. For example, Figure 4.5 shows the trends in percentage of patients requiring seclusion (restraint) and in the total number of patients residing in New York State Hospitals in the four years following the introduction and during the increasing use of tranquilizing drugs.

Just as with other types of therapy, it is not clearly understood how tranquilizing drugs work. They have a quieting effect upon the midbrain, which somehow "permits the nervous system to cope more effectively with . . . [external and internal] stimulation" (Hoch, 1959).

The tranquilizing drugs, as far as we know today, suppress symptoms, but they do not eliminate the basic structure of the psychosis. In many patients the symptoms can return rather quickly, even after successful treatment and when the drugs have been withdrawn.

ENVIRONMENTAL THERAPY. The total environment of a patient can be an important part of his treatment. The mental hospital and its staff can be thought of as a small society (Caudill, 1958) in which all hospital personnel—physicians, nurses, attendants, psychologists, social workers—participate with patients to create a *therapeutic community*. Each member of the treatment team attempts to reach patients as individuals, rather than merely to corral them into huge institutional fortresses that would provide them with little more than custodial care and comfort. In better hospitals patients live in smaller groups, or "cottages." Instead of locked wards, many hospitals now have "open-door" policies that permit patients greater freedom of the buildings and grounds. The object of the "open hospital" is to develop through freedom a sense of responsibility and to provide experiences in social living.

A patient who becomes isolated from home and family and who is excluded from active social experiences outside of the ward tends to "deteriorate" socially. He seems to "give up" trying to make adjustments, sometimes to the point where it is difficult to distinguish the disabilities due to his behavior disorder from the disabilities caused by hospitalization. To overcome this, *tertiary prevention* is instituted. "Tertiary prevention includes all those measures, other than or in addition to treatment of the disease, designed to reduce the frequency and severity of disability associated with mental illness" (Williams, 1962).

Programs of *social therapy* are planned, wherein the hospital staff and the patients participate together in work, activity, and therapy programs that approximate the conditions in the community to which the patient will return. Some hospitals sponsor "patient government" programs that

Figure 4.6. Group psychotherapy in a mental hospital. (Courtesy of National Association for Mental Health, Bethesda, Maryland.)

permit patients to determine democratically with elected officers many of the policies on the ward, to present suggestions and petitions to the hospital administration, and to plan their own group activities and work. Through group psychotherapy (see Figure 4.6), group recreation, and occupational therapy (see Figure 4.7), the patient restores or maintains his social interests and skills and finds the hospital experience more enjoyable. Nurses and psychiatric aides become members of these groups occasionally and may even participate in the group activities, recreation, or psychotherapy (see Figure 4.8). The emphasis is upon providing social and work experiences that are like those the patient will encounter in the community. He thus learns to cope with the kinds of problems he will face when he is discharged.

Figure 4.7. Occupational therapy in the hospital contributes both to treatment and to rehabilitation. From film *People Who Care*. (Courtesy of National Institute of Mental Health, Bethesda, Maryland.)

Close ties with the community are encouraged as another way to reduce the debilitative effects of hospitalization. Patients are permitted to attend community functions, such as movies, concerts, and sports events. Volunteer workers and aides come from the community. "Adopt-A-Patient" programs of community groups have been popular wherein volunteers regularly spend time with certain patients. These programs have been strongly supported by college students and have enabled patients to form more personal relationships. Hospital facilities may be used by members of the community for such functions as night courses, art classes, or mental health programs, also attended by patients. Through liberal parole privileges patients may be permited to attend church, go shopping, or to attend community functions, unattended. Such opportunities as these to become closer to community life help the patient to regain confidence in his ability to cope with life outside of the hospital and to keep him aware of the community and its social values. It also provides him with incentives to improve and gives him retraining in social living.

ALTERNATIVES TO HOSPITALIZATION. No longer is it a simple matter of being either "in" or "out" of a mental hospital. There are varying degrees of care and treatment at both receiving and discharge ends of the treatment program. In general, the aim is to keep the patient in his community

Figure 4.8. Psychiatric aides play important roles in social therapy programs. From film *People Who Care*. (Courtesy of National Institute of Mental Health, Bethesda, Maryland.)

as much and as long as possible. Not only is it more economical, but recovery is facilitated if the patient learns to cope with problems in their natural setting.

In keeping with such aims several alternatives to hospitalization can be employed. Some of these are used mainly for the ex-patient rehabilitation, but they can be used to advantage for early treatment in lieu of full hospitalization. In the *day hospital* program patients come to the hospital in the morning, have an opportunity to talk with a nurse, social worker, or psychologist, then to participate for the rest of the day in prescribed activities, and go home at night. Patients too ill to participate can spend the day on the wards with other patients. Such programs provide for extended opportunities to observe the patient, for temporary respite for weary families, and for special rehabilitation programs. At the same time the patient returning to his home at night receives family support, cooperation, and interest—all of which he could lose if fully hospitalized. Sometimes *night hospitals* provide these services in reverse. The person works during the day, but returns to sleep in the hospital at night.

Outpatient clinics, often associated with either mental or general hospitals, provide still another bridge to the community for patients. In these facilities, patients can be seen regularly by professional personnel and receive various kinds of therapy, including drugs, shock, and psychotherapy, both individual and group. When such clinics deal with ex-patients, they may be called *aftercare clinics.*

STAGE V—REHABILITATION

It would be impossible to say at which point therapy ends and rehabilitation begins. Rehabilitation planning ideally should begin as soon as the patient is admitted. As we have seen in Chapter 2, rehabilitation is concerned with therapy and training which will build positive functioning to a maximum for those who have been ill. This implies "assisting the patient to achieve an optimal social role (in the family, in a job, in the community generally), within his capacities and potentialities" (Williams, 1953).

VOCATIONAL REHABILITATION. While the patient is in the hospital, a vocational rehabilitation counselor may help the patient to plan for his return to work after discharge. The counselor may help the patient to evaluate his abilities and interests to decide upon a suitable vocation, if he is not returning to his former job. This could involve taking psychological tests that would yield information, which, together with data concerning his education, experience, and expressed preferences, would give the patient a clearer picture of his characteristics and potentialities. He might then explore, with the counselor, various possible occupations. He would need to know what aptitudes and skills and training were required, the wage or salary scales, the general job setting, opportunities for advancement, and where employment opportunities exist, both in the local area and elsewhere. Some hospitals provide opportunities for job training right in the hospital. Others may cooperate with state vocational rehabilitation agencies in obtaining training in nearby institutions, workshops, rehabilitation centers, and public schools. Rehabilitation counselors, not necessarily attached to the hospital, may assist patients to get work after discharge or to obtain placements in halfway houses or sheltered workshops, and may provide follow-up services to be sure the patient is adjusting.

Sheltered workshops are small businesses operated on a nonprofit basis to provide paid employment for persons who are handicapped. Some shops operate as training centers to develop the worker's capacity to perform competitive work. *Rehabilitation centers* may provide a variety of services including "vocational evaluation and counseling, vocational training, sheltered employment, competitive placement, psychological counseling, and social casework" (Joint Commission on Mental Illness and Health, 1961).

AFTERCARE PROGRAMS.   Very often the community outside the hospital is threatening to the ex-patient.

The world outside the institution, the world to which they once belonged, has moved along without them. Patients returned into this world are often defenseless against overwhelming social and economic obstacles. Sometimes their families have found means of existing without them, and may be openly hostile. Neighbors and friends are suspicious and distrusting.

The patient frequently returns to the same stress situation which originally contributed to his illness. He is weakened by the knowledge that he had been committed once. Surrounded by discriminations, fear, prejudice, and ignorance, he finds it harder than before to surmount these difficulties, and under pressure frequently relapses. It has been shown that if these patients are offered aftercare services providing psychiatric treatment and social service assistance, the return rate to mental hospital can be reduced (Williams, 1962).

Aftercare clinics, often the same as outpatient clinics, provide another bridge to normal life. *Ex-patient groups* can also be helpful during the first few months after release. Some are social clubs, others are therapy or activity groups, sponsored by the hospital or by mental health organizations or local clinics. Through continuing friendships formed in the hospital and sharing with other ex-patients his problems of readjustment, the ex-patient receives emotional support until he can feel at ease in his community. *Family care* may be used as an alternative to hospitalization or as a transition from the hospital to the community for persons who lack homes or who have undesirable home situations (see Figure 4.9).

In all rehabilitation and aftercare programs, the emphasis is upon building positive functioning. This is done through counseling, educational and work experiences, partially assisted social living experiences, and by continuing the therapeutic removal of disabilities in protected, supportive environments.

NEEDS IN TREATING MENTAL ILLNESS

Lest the reader believe that treatment and rehabilitation programs have solved the problems of mental illness, we will close by listing some recommendations made by the Joint Commission on Mental Illness and Health (1961) for a national mental health program in the United States. After analyzing the needs and resources of the mentally ill in this country, they listed three major areas of concern: need for new knowledge; better use

Figure 4.9. Mental health associations establish fellowship clubs where discharged patients are made welcome in their community and where they find a cheerful setting in which companionship, recreation, and other aids to social rehabilitation help speed their full recovery and the growth of positive functioning. (Courtesy of National Association for Mental Health, Bethesda, Maryland.)

of present knowledge and experience; and increased federal, state, and local expenditures for public mental health services.

1. *Need for new knowledge.* More basic mental health research, more long-term projects, greater support of young scientists, expanding program research in established scientific and educational institutions, establishment of mental health research centers, or research institutes, are needed, especially in states or regions that lack them.

2. *Better use of present knowledge and experience.*

    a) *More and better-trained manpower:* Better use of trained personnel in therapy; increased use of volunteers and nonmedical personnel; extensive recruitment and training for all mental health careers.

    b) *More community services for Stage III: onset of mental illness.*

In the absence of fully trained psychiatrists, clinical psychologists, psychiatric social workers, and psychiatric nurses, counseling should be done by persons with some psychological and mental health training, with access to expert consultation.

c) *Immediate care of acutely disturbed mental patients.* The earlier the treatment, the more likely the recovery.

d) *Intensive treatment of acutely ill mental patients. Community mental health clinics* serving both adults and children, operated as outpatient departments of general or mental hospitals, as part of state or regional systems, or as independent agencies, should be established. At least one clinic per 50,000 of population is recommended. Psychiatrists in private practice should devote a substantial part of their time to community clinic services, both as consultants and as therapists. General hospitals should provide for psychiatric units. More smaller intensive psychiatric treatment centers are needed for patients with major mental illness in the acute stages or with a good prospect for improvement or recovery if the illness is more prolonged.

e) *Convert all large state hospitals with over 1000 beds into treatment centers for long-term and chronic patients,* including the aged, and develop special techniques of socialization, relearning, group living, and gradual rehabilitation or social improvement.

f) *Institute aftercare, intermediate care, and rehabilitation services.*

The objective of modern treatment of persons with major mental illness is to enable the patient to maintain himself in the community in a normal manner. To do so, it is necessary (1) to save the patient from the debilitating effects of institutionalization as much as possible, (2) if the patient requires hospitalization, to return him to home and community life as soon as possible, and (3) thereafter to maintain him in the community as long as possible. Therefore, aftercare and rehabilitation are essential parts of all service to mental patients, and the various methods of achieving rehabilitation should be integrated in all forms of services, among them: day hospitals, night hospitals, aftercare clinics, public health nursing services, foster family care, convalescent nursing homes, rehabilitation centers, work services, and ex-patient groups (Joint Commission on Mental Illness and Health, 1961).

g) *More effective dissemination of information on mental illness to the public is needed* to (1) overcome general difficulty in recognizing and understanding mental disorders, (2) overcome society's manysided pattern of rejection of the mentally ill,

(3) make clear what mentally ill people are like and dispel popular, but erroneous, conceptions, and (4) overcome public attitudes of defeatism or hopelessness regarding mental illness and chances for recovery.

3. *Public expenditures for mental patient services.* Public expenditures for mental patient services should be doubled in five years, tripled in ten years. The federal government should gradually assume a larger share of such costs in matching grants to state and local governments.

SUMMARY

When progressive failures in Stages I and II to cope successfully with tasks and adjustments result in a preponderance of negative functioning according to various criteria, a person reaches Stage III, onset of mental illness. Treatment of persons with such maladaptive behaviors comprises Stage IV and includes both assessment and therapy. Assessment entails collecting, organizing, and interpreting information about a person and his environment so that valid decisions regarding appropriate treatment may be made. Typically, the assessments include thorough medical evaluations, interviews, and psychological testing of intelligence and personality. The latter include rating scales, inventories, and projective methods.

Various kinds of therapy—psychotherapy, somatic, and environmental —are employed to reduce or to eliminate negative functioning and to restore and increase positive functioning. Psychotherapy, either individual or in groups, assists the person to reduce anxiety, to form new interpersonal relationships that facilitate changes of behavior, to gain insight, and to motivate the person to learn better ways of functioning. Psychoanalysis, client-centered psychotherapy, group psychotherapy, play therapy, and behavior therapy are examples of the many kinds of psychotherapy employed. Somatic therapy, including electroshock and insulin-coma shock therapies and psychosurgery are being rapidly supplanted by drug therapies, which employ tranquilizers and energizers. Environmental therapy involves conceiving of the total hospital milieu as a therapeutic community. Programs of social therapy and aftercare may be employed to reduce the debilitating effects of prolonged hospitalization, to foster closer community contacts, and to facilitate the return of the patient to normal living.

As treatment merges into rehabilitation, Stage V, alternatives to hospitalization assist the ex-patient to make the transition to community life. Day and night hospitals, aftercare clinics, and halfway houses, vocational counseling, training, and sheltered work experience, foster family care, and ex-patient groups all assist with the rehabilitation.

The pressing needs for improvement of treatment of the mentally ill are for developing new knowledge, better uses of present knowledge and experience, including more and better manpower, more and better treatment centers, and for increased federal, state, and local expenditures for public mental health services.

SUGGESTED REFERENCES FOR FURTHER STUDY

Ford, D. H., and H. B. Urban (1963). *Systems of Psychotherapy*. New York: John Wiley & Sons.

This comprehensive review of the major systems of psychotherapy provides intercomparisons and evaluations. For a quick introduction to the theories of Freud, Rogers, learning-theory-oriented psychotherapies like those of Wolpe and Dollard and Miller, Sullivan, existentialism, and others, this book would be very helpful.

Joint Commission on Mental Illness and Health (1961). *Action for Mental Health*. New York: Basic Books.

Incorporating the principal findings of the five-year study of the mental health and programs for its improvement in America, this final report of the Joint Commission presents in greater detail its recommendations. Although debatable, many recommendations do indicate areas of need for better resources and more and better uses of manpower.

Sundberg, N. B., and Leona E. Tyler (1962). *Clinical Psychology*. New York: Appleton-Century-Crofts.

The work of the clinical psychologist in assessment, counseling, and psychotherapy is reviewed together with pertinent research and evaluation of research. The reader's attention is drawn especially to the critique and suggestions regarding the role of tests in assessment.

Chapter 5
Adjustments in Later Life

An 80-year-old woman has been stone deaf for almost 40 years. Yet she continues at that age and with that handicap to hold a position in a college alumni office, which she took after the deafness brought a stop to her teaching. There she is of great value because of her half-century acquaintance with the institution and its former students, astonishing numbers of whom she knows and greets by name when she sees them even after many years. When 70, she was asked to write a history of the college. She is jolly and full of stories, travels much, shops, always has a pad and pencil to give anyone with whom she talks, but is quick at lipreading. For years she has had a room in a women's dormitory, and greatly enjoys her associations with young people.

Mrs. D. was an 80-year-old widow who had one of her legs amputated as a result of an accident when she was in her late 60's. Persistent determination kept her struggling to learn the use of an artificial limb; she practiced and practiced until she could get about quite readily. The wooden limb she called Jimmy Joe, and the good leg Suzanne. Apparently all her difficulties had been approached with the same light-hearted touch.

A very well-to-do 86-year-old lawyer had an informal partnership with another also past 80; several younger lawyers shared the practice. To them the 86-year-old turned over the court cases, but he did much consulting for corporations. He was slender, erect, distinguished-looking, and gave the impression of a man in his early sixties. Every morning he exercised for half an hour, and gardened in the summer. Hearing was excellent and he did much of his reading without glasses. Recently as a hobby he picked up French and soon was reading French fiction. He was an active church member, a Mason, and a crossword puzzle fan. Recently his car was struck from behind by a truck whose brakes had failed. Though he was not injured, his car was wrecked. He calmly bought a new car and drove it home that evening.

An 81-year-old physician was still in active practice with his physician son, who had specialized in the same field. The father went to his office regularly six days a week and did much consulting.

An 81-year-old tile-setter who began this work when he was a boy of 16 was still continuing it on a part-time basis, having an understanding with builders and contractors (some of his business associations have carried through three generations) that he was free to stop whenever he tired. (Pressey, 1957)

ALTHOUGH THESE CASES MAY BE EXCEPTIONAL they tend to force one to revise a common stereotype that elderly people are generally decrepit, feeble, useless, "Sans teeth, sans eyes, sans taste, sans everything." These modern oldsters have their counterparts in earlier periods. Plato died (according to Cicero) with pen in hand at 80. Michelangelo worked as chief architect of St. Peter's Basilica up to his death at 89. Isaak Walton completed *The Compleat Angler* at 83. Benjamin Franklin served as president of the University of Pennsylvania at 82. Noah Webster did a new edition of his dictionary at the same age, and Verdi composed *Othello* and *Falstaff* just under 80.

The preceding chapters have been concerned with the problems of adjustment in the early and mid years of life. The cases just mentioned dramatize the importance of adjustments in what has been variously called the golden age, the senior years, or the period of later maturity. In fact, no age is without its distinctive adjustment problems, whether it be adolescence, early maturity, adulthood, or retirement. Successful living, psychologically viewed, is not an achievement attained at some specific age but is constantly reachieved throughout life. Just as childhood and adolescence prepare one for the adult years, so the experiences of maturity influence one's adjustments in successive years.

The systematic study of gerontology (that branch of knowledge concerned with the social and psychological problems of postmaturational years) and geriatrics (medical problems of the aged) has a short history. The first National Advisory Committee on Gerontology was not organized until 1940. Perhaps the first major research effort of a continuing sort in this field was established by Miles in 1928 at Stanford University and was brought to the attention of psychologists in his presidential address to the American Psychological Association in 1932. Consequently, the dependable knowledge about some aspects of aging is young, less well established, and less comprehensive than is true of many other fields.

One of the reasons for the belated study of later life is the fact that until this century so few people lived beyond maturity. In 1900 the life expectancy of the United States male at birth was 49 years, and there were only 374,000 Americans aged 80 or over. Contrast this with a life expectancy of 70 years and 2.5 million Americans over 80 in 1960. By 1975 it is expected that the American population will include about 20.7 million people 65 years or older, and represent about 1 person in 10 of the total population. These figures indicate that as a nation the United States is growing older, and as a result will come significant changes in the political, economic, social, and psychological climate of the country.

It will not be the purpose of this chapter to deal with all the consequences of an aging population. Instead we shall concentrate on the problems of adjustment that arise out of the measured abilities, interests, and capacities of postmature persons as they interact with the environmental limitations and opportunities open to such persons. Toward the end of the chapter we shall examine two alternative theories of aging, proposed to account for and conceptually unify some of the otherwise unrelated facts presented earlier.

CAPACITIES OF LATER MATURITY
Physiological Functions.   Life past 60 years of age has often been called the declining years with some, but not total, justification. Not all capacities follow a declining trend nor do they decline at the same rate. For instance, within certain limits, as speed decreases, endurance increases. All records for sprint running have been held by persons between 18 and 22 years of age, but marathon running is characteristically an older man's sport, with the champions varying between 38 and 45. The record for swimming the English Channel was captured by a 42-year-old Egyptian—next to the oldest in the 1950 race. Furthermore, as age increases, immunities to certain diseases are strengthened. The teeth, for instance, are less subject to cavities, although it is equally true that some diseases, such as arteriosclerosis and similar cardiovascular disorders, are characteristically diseases of old age. Unlike the fictitious one-horse shay of Oliver Wendell Holmes, the body does not wear out at an even rate. Figure 5.1 shows the relative growth and decline in several physical functions. Grasping strength (not shown in Figure 5.1) remains essentially the same between 30 and 60 years of age, whereas the back muscles generally lose strength much more rapidly.

The physiological basis of aging is not well understood. It is deceptively simple to compare the human body with a machine, such as an automobile, whose bearings wear out with use. On the other hand a physiological system has the capacity that a mechanical system has not, of reconstituting itself and regenerating cells that wear out. In the growth stages of life the anabolic (building up) processes overbalance the catabolic (breaking down) processes. In the postmaturity years the reverse is true. But why should the reversal take place? Moreover, where does the reversal begin; in the blood system, in the endocrine balance, in the nervous system? Alexis Carrel kept a portion of chicken's heart alive for more than 25 years

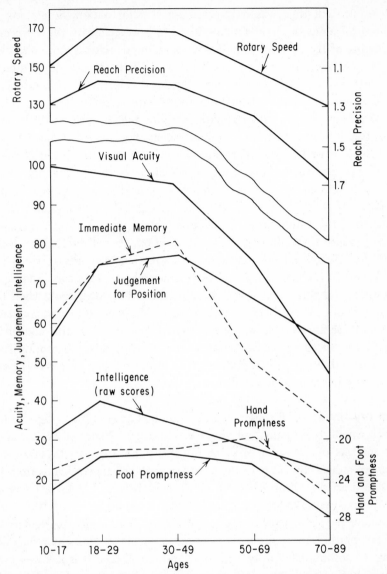

Figure 5.1. Decline in functions with advancing years. Adapted from W. R. Miles, (1933), "Abilities of Older Men," *Personnel J.,* **11,** 352. Reprinted from F. K. Berrien, *Practical Psychology* (2d ed., The Macmillan Company, New York: 1952).

by bathing it with the blood from young chickens. This experiment suggested that somehow the blood system might account for aging in that it failed to maintain the normal healthy balance of hormones, enzymes, nutrients, and wastes that bathe the cells of the body. However, when blood from puppies was repeatedly injected into the veins of an old dog, the result each time was only a temporary rejuvenation. Something lies behind the aging of blood, for this seems to be a secondary effect reflecting the aging of tissues that manufacture compounds released into the blood stream. On the other hand, it has been found that the calcium content of cell membranes increases with age, leading to decreased permeability of the membrane and thus reducing both the rate of cell intake and output.

Whatever the physiological basis for aging may be, there is little doubt that the relatively fast pace of our society has some influence on the process. It is well known that some primitive people have generally lower blood pressure than those living in Western cultures. A group of 100 Africans between the ages of 55 and 59 years had an average systolic pressure of 107, which compared with 136 for equally old Europeans. At the same time the European and African norms at ages 15 to 35 years were almost identical (Donnison, 1943). In addition, several studies have shown that the Chinese have lower blood pressure than Americans, which may be related to the greater calm of the former people. This conclusion gains additional support when we consider the fact that Americans, when they go to live in China, experience a decrease in blood pressure, and conversely the Chinese an increase in pressure when they come to this country. If the process of aging is in any way related to cardiovascular tensions, and in all probability it is, it is clear that one other relevant factor is the kind of social climate in which we live.

Sensory Inputs. All senses manifest some changes with aging—hearing, vision, smell, taste, pain, and vibratory sensations. Many of these changes are matters of common observation, but some are not. In total these changes reduce contact with the environment. The repercussions from this fact as it affects adjustments will be dealt with later. Let us first consider the various sensory changes in some detail.

Older people experience a general loss in visual acuity, particularly for distant objects. In addition the reduced elasticity of the lens reduces the range of accommodation to both near and far objects. It is less well established, but probably true, that the visual field becomes restricted with age (Mann and Sharpley, 1947; Lange, 1952). Color vision seems to have received very little attention as it relates to age. One study of university faculty men revealed that about 20 percent of those above 60 years of age were color blind, whereas among the younger men the percentage was about four or five. The study however is only a straw in the wind because the investigators were able to test only 40 persons 60 or more years old, and these were limited to the university population (Boice, Tinker, and Patterson, 1948). Using a color-matching test another researcher found that the ability to match greens or blues declines with age more rapidly than matching reds or yellows. These results possess some implications for persons working with colors, but there remains the possibility that practice might overcome the slight deficiency that this report indicates (Gilbert, 1957).

Dark adaptation is known to be related to age. That is to say, the amount of light needed to be just perceived when the eye is otherwise unstimulated and has been exposed to no light for upward of 20 minutes must be greater for older than for younger people.

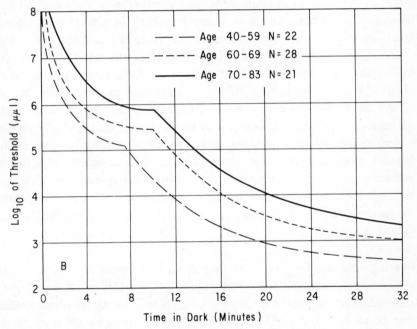

Figure 5.2. Recovery of visual sensitivity. Older people recover more slowly and less completely. From J. E. Birren and N. W. Shock (1950), "Age Changes in Rate and Level of Visual Dark Adaptation," *Applied Physiol.*, **2**, 407–411.

Figure 5.2 shows two things. First, that as one extends the time from zero to 32 minutes in complete darkness the amount of light that is just perceptible declines for all ages. Second, that older people are less sensitive to dim light at each of the time periods tested. Part of the reason for this relative insensitivity to dim light can be found in another fact; after dark adaptation the size of the pupil in eyes of older people is smaller than in younger people (Birren, Casperson, and Botwinick, 1950). This limits the amount of light that can reach the retina by as much as 50 percent.

In practical terms the findings on dark adaptation mean that older people experience increasing difficulty in night vision—in moving about in the home and on the street or highways when the general illumination is very low. Auto driving at night, for instance, is somewhat more hazardous for persons over 70, other things being equal.

Another interesting change has been found in the decline of the critical-flicker fusion time. This refers to the rate at which a light must flicker in order for it to be just seen as flickering rather than steady. It is known that fatigue reduces the critical-flicker fusion time. That is, the light must flash more slowly for the flicker to be apparent. Such a measure gives an indication of the speed of response either in the retina or in the visual projection areas of the brain and is an indirect measure of general neurological functioning. It has been demonstrated that there is a progressive slowing of the flicker rate as people grow older, such that the rate for persons 60 to 70 years old is about 25 percent slower than for persons 20 to 30 years of age (Weekers and Roussel, 1946). Furthermore, in a small number of older men the flicker fusion rate increased after a course of treatment with sex hormones (Simonson, Kearns, and Enzer, 1944). Consequently we are probably justified in concluding that the visual mechanisms generally respond more slowly as age advances. Although no direct adjustment problems appear to flow from this decline in flicker fusion, these findings are important because they suggest a lowering of efficiency in neural mechanisms, which is in tune with other data to be presented in the following sections.

Hearing. As people grow older their hearing is impaired. The principal loss occurs at the upper frequencies, above 1,024 cycles per second (cps), although some decrement is common over all frequencies for persons older than 60 years. One report covering 360 persons varying in age from childhood to the early eighties showed a loss in the older people of about 20 db[1] for the low tones around 128 cps but about 50 db loss for high tones of 5,800 cps or greater (Weiss, 1959). Fortunately, the highest tones are not generally involved in speech. On the other hand, consonants such as *f*, *v*, or *s* are more difficult for older people to distinguish because they contain a high proportion of high tones. The vowels that contain fewer high tones are less often misunderstood.

Hearing aids of miniature size have become available for persons with auditory deficiencies. These can be fitted to the individual so that they

---

[1] *db* is an abbreviation for decibel, a unit for measuring the energy of sound waves as they strike a microphone or other sensing device. In approximate terms, an increment of 10 db represents a doubling in loudness.

amplify selectively those frequencies for which the person is especially deaf. However, it has been a matter of common observation that elderly persons who delay being fitted with hearing aids have considerable difficulty in adjusting to their use. A hearing aid is not a high fidelity amplifier and, in addition, produces a background hum that can be annoying. Users sometimes complain that the sounds are not natural or clear. Space does not permit here an adequate discussion of the adjustment problem, but part of the difficulty may come from the gradual change in sound qualities that the partially deaf person experiences and comes to accept as normal. When the sound quality is suddenly different and all sounds are louder with the use of a hearing device, the user must to some extent relearn what is normal hearing.

Pain. A number of medical observers have reported that often severe thoracic or abdominal disease exists in the aged without pain. Sometimes extensive peritonitis can be entirely unsuspected because the patient does not report any internal pains. Even minor surgical operations can be performed with little discomfort. It is generally impossible to carry out controlled experiments on sensitivity to internal pains, but a number of studies have been completed on tactile or skin sensitivity. However, the results are not in general agreement. Using a thermal stimulus applied to the forehead of subjects ranging in ages from 10 to 80 years, no relation could be found between age and the intensity of the stimulus that produced pain (Hardy, Wolff and Goodell, 1943). On the other hand, there is some evidence that the Meissner corpuscles (presumed to be the sense organs for pain in the skin) become less numerous, certainly in the fingertips, as one grows older. Sensitivity to pressure on the cornea of the eye also decreases with age (Weiss, 1959). Part of the difficulty in arriving at any general conclusion about pain sensitivity lies in the difficulty, as in other studies of aging, in assembling a sufficient number of cases at the various age levels. This is purely a solvable administrative, and not a technical, problem. More serious for studies of pain is the question of the appropriate stimuli to be employed and the area of body surface to be explored. In all probability sensitivity to pain does not decline uniformly over the entire body any more than does muscular strength decline equally in all muscles.

Taste. Extensive anatomical taste bud censuses have been made on humans from birth to 85 years of age (Arey, 1935). The findings indicate a very rapid increase in their number after birth, remaining at about 245 until 20 years of age. From that time onward the number decreases until in maturity and early old age the mean value is about 208. For ages 74 to

85 years the average number of buds is about 88. Although there is no direct information on taste acuity in relation to age, these anatomical studies would lead us to expect some decline in taste discriminations.

In general, the changes in sensory equipment and sensory functioning are inclined to isolate the aging person from contact with his objective world. He does not see, hear, taste, or touch his surroundings with the same acuity he once experienced. His senses are more likely to deceive him. Consequently, unless measures are taken to socialize the individual he is likely to retreat to an inner world of self-absorption and memory. His failing senses play an important part in his adjustments.

Motoric Responses. On the response side a large body of data has indicated that with increasing age, speed of response declines, although somewhat more slowly than is generally believed. As early as 1899 Sir Francis Galton tested visitors to an international health exhibit. With a simple reaction-time apparatus, in which the subject pressed a key as quickly as possible in response to a sound, he discovered average time increased from 0.154 seconds for people in their twenties to 0.174 seconds for persons 70 or more years old. Although more precise apparatus has become available and other kinds of reaction–stimulus situations have been studied, the magnitude of the speed decrement of simple reactions is about the level that Galton found.

Are older people slower in responding in all situations or just in simple reactions? The answer seems to be that older people are generally slower in all kinds of responses, verbal and otherwise. Using 22 different measures from choice reaction time and color naming to word associations and word completions (given the first syllable, complete the word from one of a list of other syllables), older people, 60 to 80 years of age, were compared with young adults, 18 to 33. Not only were the older persons slower in all measures, but a factor analysis showed that the speed of response accounted for more of the variance among the measures in the older than among the younger subjects. "Thus, how quickly the young may make simple movements has little relation to the time they require when the symbolic complexity of the stimuli is increased. Older subjects show by contrast that their response speed tends to be related for both simple and complex stimuli" (Birren, Riegel, and Morrison, 1962).

If we measure decision time by asking persons to sort playing cards into suits or cards of the same number, subjects over 60 require about 20 percent more time than those under 40 years of age (Welford, 1959). The more complex the task becomes, the greater is the decrement in speed with increasing age. That is to say, the more decision elements that enter into the task or the more information the individual must integrate before making a response, the greater will be the difference between the time required of young people compared with oldsters. A careful analysis of these and other data has led to the hypothesis that a major reason for the decline in complex operations does not lie either in the deficiencies of the sense organs (although these contribute to the decline) nor in the muscles, but rather in the integrative processes occurring in the central nervous system. Under circumstances where incoming stimuli from various sources have to be organized into a perception of a total situation before appropriate action can take place, the older person is especially slow. For instance, it is possible that sensations of light, heat, sound, and smell might combine to form a perception of fire. What action is appropriate to this perception would depend upon a large number of other conditions—estimates of danger, memory of preventive measures, sources of help, nearness to alarm systems, and so on. It is the ability to organize or integrate both incoming sensory information and to shape the appropriate response that may account for the major decline of complex actions with age (Welford, 1950).

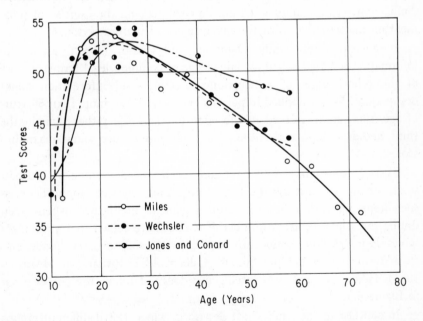

Figure 5.3. The influence of age on intelligence test scores. The curves, comparing results from three different intelligence tests, show that the mental functions measured by the tests increase up to 20 to 25 years and then show a gradual decline. Data from O. J. Kaplan, Jr. (ed.), *Mental Disorder in Later Life*, (Stanford, Calif.: Stanford University Press, 1945), Ch. 4.

INTELLIGENCE

The rise and decline of general intellectual functions over the life span has been plotted by at least three major studies with results that are displayed in Figure 5.3. Although the investigators used different tests of intelligence and geographically different populations, the results are in general agreement in placing the inflection point of the curves in the third decade of life. Beyond that point measured intelligence declines until, according to the Miles data, persons beyond 60 years old appear to be about as intelligent as 10-year-old children. This clearly does *not* seem to be an inference that agrees with common observations. What is wrong?

The tests used as a basis for determining the scores given in Figure 5.3 were primarily designed for, and standardized on, young persons of school age. These place a premium upon speed of response and also contain items that interest young people. We have already seen in the previous portion of this chapter that older people slow up, not only in their simple motoric responses, but also in the speed with which they can integrate incoming stimuli. Hence tests that are scored in terms of speed rather than quality or accuracy of responses place the older person under a special handicap. Furthermore, the content of the test items rarely call for information "indigenous" to the adult years nor do they demand the exercise of judgment on matters that enlist the involvement of mature persons.

In an exploratory study, Demming and Pressey (1957) devised an information test that called for knowledge of common legal terms, the use of the yellow pages of a telephone directory, and information about occupations. When applied to persons between 15 and more than 50 years of age, these items peaked in the 30-to-40-year range rather than in the third decade, where conventional tests of intelligence show maximum scores.

Tests of vocabulary skills have long been considered one of the best single measures of intelligence. High correlations have been found between such items and any other measures of general intelligence, when taken during the school years. A number of studies have shown that vocabulary scores do not decline significantly until after the sixth or later decade, and then the decline is not precipitous (Gilbert, 1952; Birren and Morrison, 1961). Hence this aspect of intelligence does not follow the curves given in Figure 5.3.

In contrast to the studies just described, which tested different groups of persons at different ages, only one study has followed the same individual over a relatively long span of years. In the former design it is necessary to *infer* that differences in test scores between the age groups represent developmental or degenerative changes. A more rigorous design would test the same individuals at two stages of life. In 1949–50, 127 men who had taken the Army Alpha test in 1919 were retested (Owens, 1953). The results of the retesting and original scores were compared. Differences between the means of 1950 performance and 1919 performance for the eight subtests and the total score are shown in Table 5.1.

TABLE 5.1   Changes in Subtest and Total Alpha Scores Between 1919 and 1950 in 127 Men *

SUBTEST	MEAN 1950–MEAN 1919	"t"
1. Following Directions	0.042	0.43
2. Arithmetical Problems	− 0.101	1.53
3. Practical Judgment	0.542	8.22 †
4. Synonym–Antonym	0.549	8.26 †
5. Disarranged Sentences	0.633	7.29 †
6. Number Series	0.001	0.01
7. Analogies	0.143	2.02 ‡
8. Information	0.931	17.44 †
Total Scores	0.550	11.17 †

† = $P < 0.01$.
‡ = $P < 0.05$.

* From W. A. Owens, Jr. (1953), "Age and Mental Abilities: A Longitudinal Study," *Genetic Psychology Monographs*, **48**, 3–54.

The data in Table 5.1 indicate significant *increases* in scores in five of the eight subtests as well as in the total score. A detailed analysis of the data suggested that the more education the individuals had, the greater was the change in total scores. These findings are clearly in disagreement with the cross-sectional studies, but need to be confirmed by additional studies of the same sort before we can reach a clear conclusion concerning the age curve of intelligence. The administrative difficulties in conducting longitudinal studies are so formidable that few can be accomplished.

These findings argue in favor of some reconsideration of our conventional tests of intelligence. It must be remembered that developments in this field grew up in response to the need for measures useful, first, for the early school years and, second, for the early stages of employment. For these purposes the conventional tests of intelligence have been helpful even though some scaling problems developed as tests were applied to persons beyond 15 or 16 years of age. That is to say, the initial scores were in terms of mental age. This scale unit proved useless for young adults. Other kinds of scale units came into use, such as percentiles, that provided a basis for comparing an individual with a standardized population. Most intelligence tests were never devised to trace general mental abilities over a life span. For these reasons it is not legitimate to infer from Figure 5.3 that general mental ability at 60 years is about equal to that of children. At this time we do not have appropriate tests to measure intelligence at the postmaturity stage of life.

In spite of this limitation on our knowledge about measured intelligence in the later years a factor analysis of the Wechsler Adult Intelligence Scale showed that the common element running throughout all items did not decline with age up to 60 years if the effect of different levels of schooling were eliminated (Birren and Morrison, 1961).

In the absence of definitive information the best conclusion we can draw is that some aspects of general intellectual capacity probably maintain a plateau to about the fifth decade and decline slowly thereafter. Other aspects depending primarily upon speed of response reach a peak about the third decade and decline steadily with a very rapid decline in the seventies and later. It is well to remember that such a generalization applies to the average of the general population. The range of individual differences probably increases with age, so that a cross section of the population at age 65, for instance, measured on some tests of intelligence would probably be greater than the range on the same test for persons aged 20. This is an inference based on the knowledge that younger persons have had less time in which to develop their potentialities and are somewhat more homogeneous with respect to their experience.

LEARNING AND MEMORY

Two widespread beliefs have characterized most conceptions of old people. The first is well expressed by the proverb "You can't teach an old dog new tricks." Old people are expected to be slow learners. The second belief is that old people generally have poor memories. The two beliefs are closely related psychologically. But what is the evidence on these issues?

Unfortunately, few studies of adult learning have included persons beyond 45 or 50 years of age. A very well-known report by Thorndike of a group of studies on Teachers College students 20 to 45 years of age gained much attention for the conclusion that "nobody under forty-five should restrain himself from trying to learn anything because of the belief or fear that he is too old to be able to learn it" (Thorndike, 1928). It will be noted that this statement does not imply a complete retention at the maximum level of learning ability throughout the years of maturity. Rather, the data on which the statement is based indicate a slight drop in learning ability from a peak point about 22 or 23 years of age. The decline up to the forty-fifth year in university students, however, is quite insignificant, as Thorndike correctly suggests.

Is the decline recorded in Thorndike's studies inevitable? Can it be slowed or checked? Thorndike suggested that one of the possible reasons for slight decline in learning ability beyond 25 years of age was the onset of unavoidable degenerative biological processes. He was quite convinced that the degenerative processes were not, however, the sole cause of the drop in learning power. It remained for Sorenson (1933) to demonstrate that persons more than 60 years old, when matched with younger persons of equal occupational and educational status, showed no decline in their ability to grasp the meaning of standard test paragraphs. Indeed, these same elders were superior to the younger persons in vocabulary ability. On the other hand, when the subjects of investigation have not recently been in contact with learning situations, they do show a decline in learning ability (Sorenson, 1930). From these and similar data Sorenson concluded that disuse rather than biological degeneration is largely responsible for the recorded decline in learning ability. Consequently, one way to avoid some loss in learning ability is by continued contact with stimulating literature and situations that call for some out-of-the ordinary learning responses.

Dovetailing with the work of Sorenson and Thorndike is the study reported by Ruch (1934), in which both verbal and motor learning at various ages were investigated. The first of two motor skills called for the development of a simple eye–hand coordination habit; the second

---

TABLE 5.2 Showing Average Performance of Two Groups on Several Learning Tasks. Performance Expressed As a Percentage of the Scores Obtained by a Group 12 to 17 Years of Age.*

	PERCENTAGE OF ADOLESCENT PERFORMANCE	
Task	34–59 years	60–83 years
Eye–Hand Coordination	98	84
Mirror Eye–Hand Coordination	96	54
Logical Associates	90	82
Nonsense Equations	80	48
False Multiplications	72	47

*Adapted from F. L. Ruch (1934), "Differentiative Effects of Age Upon Human Learning," *Journal of Genetic Psychology*, **11**, 261–286.

demanded the same action except that the subject observed his move-ments as they were reflected in a mirror. The verbal tasks required the subject to learn (1) a series of logical associations (stem—butt; man—boy); (2) a series of nonsense equations ($a \times b = r$); and (3) a group of false multiplications ($3 \times 6 = 15$). The first, third, and fourth of these tasks involved simple learning, but the second and last required reorganization of earlier learning. In general the results showed that the older persons were less handicapped in simple learning tasks than on those requiring reorgan-ization (nonsense equations and false multiplications).

A restudy of these tasks with a different set of subjects suggested that the principle source of the differences between the ages did not lie in the rate of learning but rather in the *initial* level of performance before learning took place. That is, the *improvement* on each successive trial on these tasks was about the same for each age group, but the older persons started at a lower level. Moreover, an examination of the kinds of errors committed led the subsequent investigators to report that the oldster is more cautious, preferring to withhold an answer rather than take a chance that a response might be correct. The younger subjects were more apt to offer hypotheses or guesses concerning the correct responses. Blending with findings given earlier in this chapter, this study also showed that older people require more time to integrate the available information before giving a response (Korchin and Basowitz, 1957).

Following the description of how learning takes place as stated in Chapter 1 of this book, oldsters and youngsters must both have responses reinforced if acquisition is to occur. Thus they must be able to perceive changes in the stimulus situation. With advancing age, the receptors generally decline in ability to receive stimulation. Thus oldsters might be expected to learn slower or with more difficulty because they will have less possibility of reinforcements.

Another attempt to discover changes in learning and memory asso-ciated with age involved 174 persons 60 to 69 years old who were compared with an equal number of persons in their twenties of equal intellectual level. Memory was tested in a variety of ways, as shown in Table 5.3, which gives the average percentage loss on each task, assuming the perform-ance of the younger group to be standard. In other words, the score obtained on the test of visual memory span for digits was on the average 8.5 percent lower in the older group than in the younger. (Average score for younger group, 8.21; for older group, 7.51. The difference is 0.7. The percentage loss is therefore 0.7/8.21 multiplied by 100, or 8.5.) The same interpretation can be applied to all other entries in this table.

Again it is evident that no single generalization can be made concerning

TABLE 5.3 Percentage Loss in Memory Tests Applied to Old People (60 to 69 Years) As Compared with Performance of Persons 20 to 29 Years Old *

PER CENT LOSS	TEST
8.5	Visual Memory Span for Digits
11.8	Auditory Memory Span for Digits
21.2	Reversed Digit Span
21.3	Sentence Repetitions
26.2	Knox Cubes (Reproduction of Designs with Blocks)
39.7	Retention of Paragraph
41.8	Immediate Memory of Paragraph
45.9	Memory for Designs
54.6	Retention of Paired Associates (Illogical)
58.7	Paired Associates
60.4	Retention of Turkish-English Vocabulary

* From J. G. Gilbert (1941), "Memory Loss in Senescence," *Journal of Abnormal and Social Psychology*, 36, 73–86.

memory loss in old people to cover all types of material. There is least recession on tests calling for simple repetitions devoid of meaning (digit spans). The greatest memory losses are found in those tasks calling for some reorganization of existing patterns of thinking. Of course, the most obvious finding in this study, as well as the others reviewed, is the unevenness of the decline on different tasks.

From time to time various nostrums have been marketed as rejuvenation medicines in the hope that they would bring back the capacities of youth. Although most of these have proven valueless, the search for some elixir on a scientific level continues. One such line of investigation has concentrated on the injection of sex hormones. A collection of 30 women, average age 75, free from significant physical defects, were divided into two groups, one of which received a course of treatment with progesterone plus estrogen while the other group received injections of sesame oil (physiologically inert). All subjects were given a number of psychological tests before and six months after hormone therapy began. Although not all the psychological measures revealed improvement for the therapy group, the changes were marked on measures of associative learning. That is, when given lists of paired words such as metal–iron and cabbage–light and asked to learn them so that presentation of the first would require recalling the second, the treated women improved markedly over their first scores, whereas the untreated women remained about the same (McCaldwell and Watson, 1952). It is of interest that measures of mood changes and general intellectual functioning did not change importantly in the treated as compared with the control women.

This study alone represents only a straw in the wind, but it does suggest that by appropriate medication some modification can be made in memory and learning functions in the aged.

DRIVES AND MOTIVATION

Some of the observed differences between older and younger subjects in the studies already reviewed in this chapter have been attributed to lowered drives and motivation. It is exceedingly difficult to isolate these features in any experimental design with humans, although some work with animals has shown a decline in the hunger and activity drives. The menopause in women, occurring usually during the late forties, definitely marks the end of reproductive powers but not sexuality. This change in bodily functions is accompanied by a number of physical symptoms and often a period of emotional disturbance. The most characteristic manifestation is a series of vasomotor crises (hot flashes) in which the woman abruptly experiences a sense of smothering and a feeling of heat that passes upward from the abdomen or chest to the head. Spells of dizziness and palpitation are also common complaints. From the psychological standpoint the more important symptoms are periods of worry, anxiety, and depression which accompany the physical manifestations. The smothered feelings associated with the vasomotor crises are intense experiences that may cause apprehension of death itself. The degree to which a woman is emotionally disturbed during the menopause is related to her previous mental health. Although some hormone treatment has been found helpful in this transition period, women who have previously been ill adjusted are likely to present exacerbation of previous neurotic disorders (Ripley, Shorr, and Papanicolaou, 1940).

The climacteric period in men occurs much later than in women, and the time of its onset may fall any time within the sixth, seventh, or even eighth decade. The symptoms are less noticeable, but include headache, weakness, vasomotor crises, and tightness about the head. Some evidence exists that suggest that hormone treatment at such a period is beneficial in increasing physical strength and endurance provided the individual has no other physical complications (Simonson, 1947). In both the case of men and women it is unsafe to conclude that modern medicine has now discovered the fountain of youth. The hormone treatments mentioned above are still very much in the experimental stages and do little more than relieve the major physical symptoms of the climacteric. They do not in any sense rejuvenate.

The study reported by Kinsey, Pomeroy, and Martin (1948) indicates that sexual vigor in men declines steadily from its maximum in the late teens and twenties throughout the remainder of life. They found no evidence of a "sexual recrudescence" in their averages, although for certain individuals who marry late or change partners beyond the age of fifty, brief periods of increasing sexual activity may be experienced. Kinsey and his colleagues have suggested that those instances in which older men have been accused of infatuations or improper advances toward young girls can be explained without assuming any increase in sexual drive. Such men, Kinsey suggests, have often been frustrated in their normal social contacts and resort to fondling a defenseless youth merely as a way of gaining some kind of friendship devoid of sexual overtones. Many such older men are actually incapable of overt sexual activity.

The gradual and steady decline in the male's sexual vigor presents some problems in adjustment, although the menopause in women is perhaps more disturbing. Adolescence has often been pictured as the period of storm and stress because of the appearance of new and strange impulses. From one standpoint early senescence, at least in women, is an equally distressing period.

It would be a mistake, however to infer that menopause represents the termination of sexual drives in women. On the contrary, the evidence, although complicated by greater cultural restrictions on female than on male sexuality, indicates that there is little decline in sexual capacities in women until late in life (Kinsey, Pomeroy, Martin, and Gebhard, 1953). They furthermore reach a high point of sexuality in the third decade of life, with some diminution thereafter but without a marked decline until approximately 10 years after menopause.

The drive to search for new insights and new skills or to improve one's bridge or golf game appears to decline. For many old people a change presents a hazard. Their habitual modes of action and thinking have brought them some degree of satisfaction and perhaps success. In later years there is not sufficient time to experiment, to reshuffle one's behavior patterns in the hope of finding a more satisfying combination. In addition, physical vigor and endurance are depleted so that little surplus is left after the normal demands of bodily maintenance are satisfied. Even mental activity requires some physical effort, with the result that old people frequently cannot, if they would, maintain the pace of thinking that characterized their youth.

It has been observed that old people tend to grow careless of their appearance, slovenly in their habits, and often gluttonous in the satisfaction of their more sensual pleasures. These characteristics apparently reflect a growing egocentricity related to depleted drives for social approval on the one hand and, on the other, to the social isolation produced by failing sensory acuity. These features seem to contradict Emerson's statement that the essence of age is intellect. No necessary contradiction exists provided we remember that the principal defects of age are physiological and the gluttonous behavior of the aged is related to their introversion—a common feature of intelligent college professors.

In summary, with the exception of sex urges that follow an erratic downward course, the principal motives of old people appear to decline gradually. Any discussion of motives in old people is handicapped by a regrettable lack of precise studies, and depends heavily in this section on the opinions of unsystematic but penetrating observers.

CREATIVE ABILITY

It has sometimes been claimed that late maturity and early senescence, when the individual has accumulated a rich fund of experience, are the years during which the great, lasting contributions to human knowledge and culture are made. Illustrative cases can be cited by the score to support

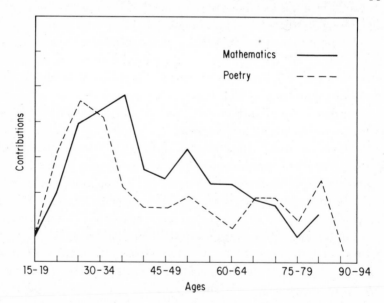

Figure 5.4.   Number of original contributions made at various ages by prominent mathematicians and poets. Adapted from H. C. Lehman (1936 and 1941), "The Creative Years," *Scientific Monthly,* **43,** 151–162, and **52,** 450–461.

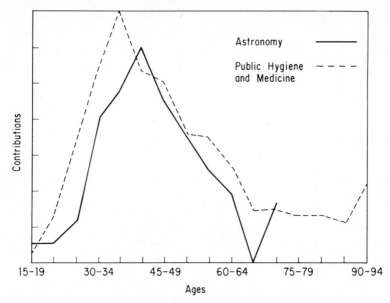

Figure 5.5. Number of original contributions made at various ages in astronomy, public hygiene and medicine. Adapted from H. C. Lehman (1936 and 1941) ,"The Creative Years," *Scientific Monthly*, **43**, 151–162, and **52**, 450–461.

this proposition, as well as the opposed notion that youth is the time of greatest creative production.

Happily, this point need no longer be argued with collected individual cases: Lehman (1936) and his associates have reported a series of illuminating systematic investigations of the ages of the important contributors in medicine, literature, mathematics, astronomy, chemistry, and related fields. The period of maximum productivity in every field so far studied is at some time earlier than the fiftieth year. That is to say, if one collects the outstanding discoveries and contributions in a given field of science or art and then unearths the age of the authors of these contributions when they were announced, one will find the greatest number were made at some age period before fifty. Figures 5.4 and 5.5 show, for four areas, the rapid rise of creative productions in early maturity, followed by a gradual decline, with a secondary peak in some cases occurring in early senescence.

The curves in Figures 5.4 and 5.5 are not necessarily representative of an individual's creative ability, although they may be. These curves are based on group data and may in some respects differ from curves showing the number of contributions made by a single individual during his lifetime. Figure 5.6 shows the number of patents secured by Thomas A. Edison during each year of his life. Even though he was not active during

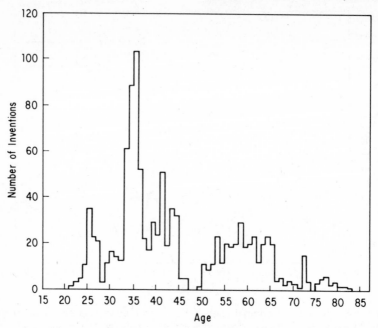

Figure 5.6. Patents obtained by Edison at various ages. Redrawn from H. C. Lehman (1936), "Creative Years in Science and Literature," *Scientific Monthly,* **43,** 151–162.

his early adult years, senescence found him still producing creative work.

The meaning of Lehman's studies for adjustment may not at first be apparent. Old age is not a period when originality and creative ability are at their maximum. On the other hand, it is not a period when the individual who has actively participated in creative work need close his books and lock his laboratory. Important creative work is still possible for men beyond 60 years of age. It may be that during retirement, when much of the necessary routine of a livelihood is set aside, the individual may find sufficient time for the tasks he had to neglect formerly. Perhaps the decline in the number of creative productions noted by Lehman is merely a reflection of declining drives rather than an actual decline in creative ability.

It has been pointed out in this section that intelligence, learning ability, memory, and creative productions decline slowly during maturity and early senescence. The precise extent to which the deterioration of these functions is the necessary consequence of degenerative biological processes is still debatable. However, it is known that the rate of decline is influenced by the strength of drives and motives often subject to control by the individual. Sensory acuity and speed of action appear to be more directly dependent upon physiological degeneration. Decline in these functions often complicates adjustments of the aged, because failing sensory acuity tends to isolate the individual at a time when socialization is important.

LEADERSHIP AND INFLUENCE

We are again indebted to Lehman (1947) for his thorough investigations of the age of prominent leaders in religious and educational institutions, government, and armed services. He has demonstrated that, contrary to the facts with respect to creativity, the political and social leadership of the United States is gradually getting older. This conclusion applies to members of the President's cabinet, members of the House of Representatives and of the Senate, foreign diplomats, college presidents, Popes of the Roman Catholic Church. The only exception was found in the presidents of religious organizations in the United States. In all areas surveyed, the average age of the recent leaders was well beyond 55 years. These facts point to the area in which old age is likely to be of greatest service to society. Lehman is careful to avoid saying that because the age of leaders has advanced in roughly the last 75 years over what it was in an earlier period it is therefore better. He does present evidence that the leaders of both the German Nazis and the Japanese militarists were younger than their predecessors, which carries the suggestion, if not the proof, that our current, highly complex society demands the broadest and most profound wisdom that long-term experience develops.

Two additional factors have probably contributed to the advancing age of leadership. The first is the mere fact that more old people are living today and provide a larger pool of possibilities. The second is the principle of seniority, which operates in a variety of ways to increase the age of elected or appointed leadership. By contrast, the average age of "creators" has decreased, and in this area the seniority principle cannot operate.

In connection with these findings we must revert to a point made earlier that our current society tends to restrict outlook and skills by reason of our technical and managerial specialization. Our knowledge of specific abilities shows an unmistakable but uneven decline that becomes evident in most cases by 60 years of age or earlier. These are the skills that younger people can often perform more easily or more cheaply. On the other hand the distillates from experience, provided the original experience was broad and encompassing, are the special and unique products of age that are needed and useful. Our society should become aware that the supply of such wisdom can be stifled at its roots by overspecialization that rarely permits a man in his prime to vary his operations or become acquainted with matters outside his bailiwick. Among unspecialized societies certainly the old Hebrew axiom holds, "With the ancient is wisdom; and in length of days understanding."

This brief review of the capacities of the aged emphasizes one outstanding fact. The aged in good physical health need not feel condemned to inactivity or sterile mental exercise. One of the chief obstacles in the way of attaining satisfactory adjustment in the late years of one's life is a pessimistic superstition that aged people are decrepit, inactive, worthless. Persons with that attitude justify the belief by acting the part. There may, however, be other attitudes.

THE ATTITUDES OF OLD AGE

The passage from late youth to middle age has many of the same traits as growing old. We suddenly realize, perhaps in a flash, that life is no longer all before us. When youth begins to die it fights and struggles. The panic is not so much that we cannot do handsprings, but we have to compromise with our youthful hopes. We have been out of college perhaps twenty years. Napoleon lost Waterloo at forty-five, Dickens had written all his best at forty, and Pepys finished his diary at thirty-seven. We lose the sense of superfluous time and must hurry. We feel the futility of postponements and accept the philosophy of the second best as not so bad. We become more tolerant toward others and perhaps toward ourselves (Hall, 1922).

In these words Hall described one of the principal changes in attitude that comes with age. When a person approaches retirement, he looks back over the years of his life and tries to evaluate the time and effort spent. He may realize quite suddenly that he has not attained his youthful ambitions. The outstanding people in his profession may have represented the individual's ideal of accomplishment. Now that time is short the old man may recognize he will not be another Justice Hughes, or a Dr. Mayo, or a Marshall Field, or a John D. Rockefeller. Life has been a series of half accomplishments in terms of youthful aims. And then after contemplating the past with a tinge of regret and disappointment one may turn his attention to the very short future, which is likely to be filled with more aches and pains than the past. Little wonder that old age is often a period of pessimism.

The commonly observed interest of old people in death, funerals, and cemeteries is, however, not necessarily part of a morbid pessimistic attitude. A friend of the author's drove his grandmother on an extensive auto trip and noticed her frequent comments about the cemeteries they passed. Another grandmother was observed to make frequent reference over a period of months to the funeral she had attended. Without special inquiries she voluntarily recited at various times a great many of the details that would have escaped the notice of younger people. Such an interest in death is entirely in keeping with a normal attitude. In youth we look forward perhaps to building a home of our own. In traveling about we tend to notice new houses. In visiting our friends we observe details of floor plan, construction, location, new developments in lighting and heating. Such things are at least potentially a part of our near future. For the old person, death holds a similar position, and it is only natural that he should calmly project himself into that future.

The fear of death is sometimes much overrated by persons far removed from it. Sir William Osler made a careful study of some 500 persons on their deathbeds. He stated that about 90 suffered bodily pain, 11 showed mental apprehension, two were positively terrified, one expressed spiritual exaltation, and one suffered bitter remorse. "The great majority gave no sign one way or the other; like their birth, their death was sleep and a forgetting" (quoted by Cowdry, 1940). Death is obviously a mystery for all; but for most it is apparently not a terrifying mystery.

Retirement from active life because of arbitrary age limits frequently brings in its train very rapid deterioration. Men particularly are forced suddenly to break off their business or professional life simply because the clock has caught up with them. The aging woman can continue her sewing, embroidery, some of the housework; but a retired businessman has little he can do but read, listen to the radio, or watch TV and daydream. The inactive, retired individual often grows old dangerously fast. Yet why should inactivity and rest, ordinarily recommended to recoup one's energies, reduce the physical vigor of old people? The answer lies in the attitudes often assumed by the aged toward themselves.

George Washington at the age of 26, having retired from command of the Virginia militia before the close of the French and Indian War, wrote, "I have now too much reason to apprehend an approaching decay." And a year later, "I hope to have more happiness in retirement than I ever experienced amidst a wide and bustling world." After 17 years of this retirement he was recalled, against his will, to command the Continental Army. "I this day declare with utmost sincerity I do not think myself equal to the command I am honored with." Washington's brilliance returned with the strenuous demands of his task. He became a distinguished soldier, but in 1783, at the age of 51, he wrote, "The scene is at length closed. I will move gently down the stream of life until I sleep with my fathers." A little later, "Heavy and painful oppressions of the head, and other disagreeable sensations often trouble me." "[I am] descending the hill

I had been fifty-two years climbing . . . soon expect to be entombed in the mansion of my fathers." In spite of his failing health, more prominent in retirement than in active life, he was again drafted for eight years as President of the United States during the nation's critical early years (Helton, 1939).

The example of Washington is only one that might be cited to show that retirement often brings with it physical ill health. The duties of office, the appetites for the rewards of labor, the competition of work, all direct attention outward away from one's self. When these are removed, without substitutes, attention is directed inward. As Helton (1939) aptly puts it, "The inactive senile fondles his interior arrangements with anxious imagination." His liver, stomach, and kidneys are carefully examined and invariably found disorganized (by himself). There may, of course, be some truly important organic defect, but too much amateur diagnosing and drugstore doctoring, to which the old easily become addicted, might readily be avoided if attention were focused outward rather than inward. Inactivity encourages ill health.

Extreme cases are sometimes reported that illustrate the extent to which inactivity in forced retirement may affect one's health (Kardiner, 1937).

An executive was compelled to resign his position after a very active life because of the age limit. He had up to this time been in perfect health. As soon as his private telephone to the firm was removed from his home, a symbol of his connection with it, he went into a quiet depression. He chafed against the inactivity, but his sufferings took no very articulate form. The problem was not economic because he was retired on three-fourths pay, enough to meet all his obligations. And now the mysterious thing began to happen. First, he acquired meningoencephalitis from overindulgence in alcohol. Two months later he developed a cancer, had a radical operation, and finally died of esophageal varices within six months of retirement.

An aged person's physical health exerts a very important influence on his entire adjustment. Physical handicaps, in addition to impaired sensory acuity, interfere with one's work and recreation. Rheumatic joints not only make it more difficult to maintain one's former pace on the job, but many prevent the individual from participating in many light forms of recreation from which he formerly derived considerable pleasure.

A study of nearly 400 old people 70 years of age in New York showed that health scores for men correlated $+0.43$ with "happiness," but for women the correlation was $+0.29$ (Kutner, Faushel, Togo, and Langner, 1956). These coefficients suggest that health is a more important contributor to contentment in older men than in women. Men who are suddenly short of their responsibilities of making a living and less interested in other matters are apparently more likely to become unhappy when illness overtakes them.

The recently developed political pressure of the older segments of our population probably reflects another attitude—a feeling of rejection. It has been argued, for instance, that a sizable portion of the total tax load is expended on youth. Why should not comparable sums be directed at services for senior citizens? This feeling has probably existed for some time but has remained submerged by the numerical dominance of younger segments of the population.

Few criticisms cut deeper into human pride than the charge that one is useless. Surrounding the aged on all sides are subtle yet pointed implications that they do not fit in this world; that they are worthless parasites incapable of contributing to the common welfare. It is not surprising, therefore, that the aged should turn this widespread yet unwitting suggestion into political capital in demanding liberal cash support. The popularity of such proposals can in part be traced to the fact that they raise the aged to a level of economic and social importance not previously attained, yet do not conflict with the stereotyped conviction that old people are incapable of important productivity. The schemes hold promise, moreover, of reversing the common adage that youth must be served. The political shuffling of old-age groups has called attention to their feelings of insecurity, inferiority, and worthlessness in a world dominated by youth.

Enormous differences, of course, appear in primitive societies, but Simmons has concluded that "most primitive societies insure some respect for old people—often remarkable deference—at least until they become so 'over-aged' that they are obviously powerless and incompetent. But under close analysis, respect for old age is, as a rule, accorded to persons on the basis of some particular asset possessed by them. They may be respected for their extensive knowledge, seasoned experience, expert skill, power to work magic, performance of priestly functions, control of property rights, or manipulation of family prerogatives. They may be highly regarded for their skill in games, dances, songs, and story telling. They may even receive consideration for their faithful performance of camp or household chores" (Simmons, 1946). This description stands in marked contrast with the status accorded old persons in our society, which in part accounts for the response the aged make to their station in life.

The attitudes of old people are profoundly influenced by their physical health, by their decreasing participation in the active affairs of their vocations, by the prospect of a short and uncertain future, and by the ever-present suggestion that they are of little use to society.

PROVISIONS AIDING OLD-AGE ADJUSTMENTS

As a person reaches retirement age he or she can reasonably expect to be called upon to make adjustments in at least four areas. Such people need to adjust to (1) loss of employment or lowered income, (2) depleted physical energy or infirmities, (3) loss of close relatives and friends, or (4) altered living arrangements. How can these problems be met successfully? How can people prepare for their adjustments in the years prior to the time when those adjustments must be made?

A Job.   As has already been pointed out, many of the difficulties of senescence stem from the inactivity of the aged and the suddenness with which boredom settles upon them. The cantankerousness and irritability of many old people is a reflection not only of their more pessimistic attitude but also of their distaste for their seemingly "unnecessary" role in life. The obvious remedy for this condition is some form of activity that does not tax the individual's declining physical vigor.

One sour old man, 70 years of age, of considerable means and energy, was a source of much bitter strife in the home of his son. His wealth consisted chiefly of a block of canning company stock. It was suggested that he might enjoy a visit to some of the orchards, farms, and plants he had never seen and which belonged to the corporation. The first trip altered his entire outlook on life. He was soon making trips to other farms, became interested in farm problems, made intelligent and helpful suggestions on management, and asked innumerable questions about agriculture and the canning processes. One of his tours took him as far as Panama to investigate transportation problems of the industry. The new channel of interests drained off his energies so that he ceased to be a grouch around his home.

The prevalent practice of setting arbitrary age levels for retirement is not always conducive to efficiency in business nor to good adjustment for the individual. A much sounder procedure would take into consideration the actual ability of the candidate for retirement and adjust his duties accordingly, so that the break between having a job and not having one would be less abrupt. (This topic receives additional treatment in Chapter 11 of this book.) Gilbert (1936) has studied the mental efficiency of persons 60 to 69 years of age by means of the Babcock test, which uses vocabulary as the measure of original intellectual level, and a series of other tests involving timed recall of older learning, motor ability, new learning, and various types of memory and retention for the efficiency phase. Gilbert found a highly significant difference in the efficiency index of those who were employed, compared with those unemployed, the difference being in favor of the employed group. Possibly those who have successfully resisted the effects of age have managed to hold their jobs because of this fact. On the other hand, the leisure of unemployment may have accelerated the decline in efficiency

An important series of studies conducted in England has been directed at identifying those industries where jobs suitable for older people may be available. In periods of labor shortage it would be especially important to make maximum use of all available manpower. The English studies have shown that it is possible, and often desirable, to redesign equipment, tools, or tasks so they do not make excessive demands on the perceptual or muscular limitations of older workers. Although wage rates are often tied to speed of production, many jobs requiring judgment and special skills developed on the basis of long experience can best be performed by older workers, if they are not rushed (Murrell, 1962). Furthermore, an examination of 3,660 previous employees in an American company revealed that fewer older than younger workers were discharged as incompetent. The older worker was less often apt to quit because of family needs or personal dissatisfaction, and only about a fourth older than 60 years quit for physical reasons. Their work was generally judged by their supervisors as at least equal to the younger persons. On the other hand, the hiring policies of this company favored applicants under 30 years old. These data strongly suggested that the workers over 60 years of age were being judged by their age rather than in terms of their fundamental contributions to the organization (Smith, 1952). The possibilities of providing work in this company for the workers of advanced years with benefit both to them and the company are obvious.

Most people like to work, or at least do something. As one painter over 70 years old expressed it, "If I was worth a million dollars, I'd still want to get around and do something." More than two thirds of the people from the lower- and middle-income groups receiving old-age assistance and questioned by Morgan (1937), in her study of attitudes, evidenced an enthusiasm for work. The positive attitude, moreover, was more frequent among the well-adjusted than among those who were unhappy and bitter.

One of the best antidotes for the shelved, discarded, burdensome feeling common to persons in their sixties and beyond is some form of useful activity. The pleasures of life come in living it, not in contemplating it from the sidelines. Approximately half of the people interviewed by Morgan reported their happiest years were between 25 and 45 years of age, when they were most actively engaged in the adventures of building a home, earning a living, and rearing a family.

Landis (1942) independently found essentially the same thing among Illinois residents. Understandably enough, the 5 percent in the latter study who found old age to be the happiest period were those who were divorced, widowed, or had experienced very unhappy marriages. The carefree days of youth are not always, in retrospect, the best. Happiness comes in those years of active responsibility, which gives significance to work.

Mere boondoggling is no more satisfying to the aged than to youth. Some imagination must be used to discover, within the range of the older man's ability, a task of importance that will keep his mind directed toward the future and away from himself or the minor irritations that may easily become magnified.

Privacy and Independence.
A degree of privacy is an important contributing factor to good adjustment in the aged. This condition is not always easy to provide in urban communities where a "spare bedroom" means additional rent. The precise degree of privacy is, of course, difficult to define because it varies with the individuals concerned. In some instances even the spare bedroom is not sufficient, particularly when well-intentioned grown children try to "take in" their parents (Fox, 1937).

I have in mind a once charming old lady, who had lived all her life in a small western town, prominent in social and religious circles. After her husband's death she continued to live at home with an old servant rather than move to her only daughter's home in another state. A close and affectionate relationship between Mrs. Smith and her daughter and son-in-law made the usual reunion at holiday times delightful. As the grandchildren arrived, two girls and a boy, there was added joy. The daughter, however, kept trying to persuade her mother to give up her home and live with her for her own peace of mind. The mother resisted until after the servant's death. But finally, although she wanted to live in an apartment hotel with some of her friends, her daughter won her over and she moved away from all her familiar surroundings.

At first, things went smoothly. It was delightful to be with the children and the daughter's friends were most attentive. Mrs. Smith tried to find her place in church work, but the ways here were "different." After the novelty wore off she found it difficult to accustom herself to the children and their friends. She read and did some crocheting, but these did not keep her busy or interested enough. More and more she was left to herself, for her daughter's activities took up most of her time. She began to brood. She developed a critical attitude, scolding her daughter for going out so much, for giving the children so much freedom, and so on. She was curious about everything and gradually developed suspicions, particularly after her hearing began to fail. The old lady changed in appearance too—once a stylish, well-dressed person, she became untidy. Her once happy face acquired a continual expression of bitterness. The happy relationship between mother and daughter vanished. Even the daughter's character has suffered, and she is now the martyr enjoying the commiseration of her friends.

The privacy offered in this home was probably satisfactory enough on the surface, but it is evident there was insufficient privacy of action both for Mrs. Smith and her daughter.

Again referring to Morgan's (1937) investigation, 68 percent of the old people questioned were in favor of living alone, and less than 14 percent of those who had children with whom they might have lived actually had come to live with them *of their own free choice.* Commenting on these figures, Morgan says:

Why do so many people prefer to live alone? In the homes of their children they feel unwanted, neglected and in the way. They resent the direction and "bossing" of their children and even more so that of the "in-laws." They do not want to be treated as if they were old and feeble and helpless, incapable of doing the smallest task properly. In their own homes they are independent, free to run their households in their own fashion. This last is very important. Over and over again the difference in the ways of life of the older and the younger generation was mentioned by the subjects. As it was pointed out, the old people cling to their old ways, while to the young people these methods seem old-fashioned, foolish and irritating. Both men and women emphasized the personal freedom and independence that homes of their own gave them, and in addition to this the women were likely to point out that it was better for the younger people also not to have the generations mixed in the home.

Retirement Homes and Communities. In a society that has grown progressively urban and increasingly compact, older persons have found themselves with less and less living space. This lack of space has contributed to family discord. The conflict between the generations has as many facets as there are families. Repeatedly, one finds disagreements between parents and grandparents over financial matters, methods of disciplining children, political or social issues, meals, the manner in which the housekeeping chores are completed, and a host of other matters. These adjustment problems that become acute in crowded quarters find one solution in moving the grandparents into a retirement home.

An unhappy popular prejudice exists against homes for the aged. Sons and daughters who "send their parents away" are sometimes looked upon as not showing sufficient interest in them or as not discharging their family obligations as they should. Actually, life in homes for the aged is often superior to the unhappy existence forced upon all members of the family in a crowded apartment or a small suburban house. Institutions for the aged are often in a better position to give the proper care than private homes. Efforts are made to provide healthful surroundings and congenial companions. Often there are opportunities to develop interests and useful work under the direction of a trained occupational therapist. Periodical physical examinations are given, and remedial measures are promptly taken.

In addition to homes maintained by various fraternal, religious, and governmental organizations a number of retirement communities have

(a)

(b)

Figure 5.7, (a) and (b). Photographs showing an aerial view of a community designed for active retirement (5-7a) and a group of the inhabitants engaged in a common recreational activity (5-7b). (Photographs courtesy of Del E. Webb Development Co.)

grown up in Florida, Arizona, California, and elsewhere. (See figures 5.7a and 5.7b.) These are limited to families without school-age children and are especially designed for the convenience of financially independent persons capable of caring for themselves. One such community of more than 5,000 homes situated near Phoenix, Arizona, has its own shopping center, golf course, medical center, and several community buildings in which a large number of hobby shops and recreational activities are centered. The absence of schools makes possible a low tax rate and eases the financial burdens.

With the increasing numbers of older people in the population such communities may increase. However, one may raise the question whether this form of isolated living will be satisfying in the long run. Existing evidence suggests that many retired people want and need some social contact with the younger generations on a casual, frequent, and short-term basis. Retirement communities of the size indicated above tend to prevent the usual mixture of ages. Perhaps a better arrangement would involve the development of relatively small enclaves of houses for retired persons within established communities, thus providing for the growth of independence, common interests, and mutual psychological support among the older citizens without the enforced disengagement from other generations.

Related to these measures to assist in the adjustment of elderly persons is the establishment of day centers, more than 30 of which have been opened in New York City alone (Maxwell, 1962). Members with special interests can join groups in music, dramatics, current events, painting, ceramics, nutrition, woodworking, and literature. Low-cost lunches are often available, and a thrift shop serves as an avenue for the sale of hobby-produced objects. Such centers hold promise for meeting the special needs of older persons without isolating them from younger segments of society.

Financial and Psychological Security. Within recent years much attention has been directed toward the problem of financial security for the aged. Organized labor following World War II made a concerted drive for pension plans. The federal government's Social Security Act from 1936 onward provided modest financial allotments to certain classes of workers in the form of old-age assistance and old-age and survivors' insurance. In 1950 and in subsequent years these allowances were extended to cover still other classes of wage earners and were increased in amount. These efforts, amounting to staggering sums in the aggregate, represent a basic but incomplete approach to old-age security. Important as it is, financial security is not enough to guarantee a pleasant and wholesome adjustment in the late years of one's life.

Freedom from worry and anxiety is probably as important as financial security. In Chapter 2 a general discussion of adjustment included points that are applicable to all ages. However, in the early stages of senescence there is apparently greater concern about death than is true of those closer to it or those further from it. Not only is there a fear of death, but old people are likely to be concerned with their children's future; they may regret their own youthful follies, wasted time, and injuries to health caused by unhygienic habits. Family relationships, estrangements, and concern for the financial welfare of one's spouse or family constitute some of the common worries in old age. By and large, most of the psychological insecurity of senescence is not caused by reflection on the past but by the pessimistic anticipation of a short future.

Anxious concern for one's future may be dissipated by developing latent interests and active participation in some job, as already suggested in the preceding pages. A healthy outlook, free from the corroding effects of morbid introspection, may be a by-product of, rather than a necessary condition for, good adjustment. At any rate, mental strain is relieved, and psychological security is bred in those surroundings where the aged are permitted some responsibility and action but where the pace is in keeping with their retarded speed of action.

Recreation in Old Age.   In youth and maturity people look forward to vacations when they can relax from the mad pace of the workaday world and engage in leisure-time activities. In moments of reflection they may look forward to retirement with the expectation that they can then really enjoy living. Regrettably many have found that what promised to be rest and enjoyment proved to be boredom. The recreations of youth are often too strenuous for age. Most games place a premium on speed and motility— factors in which the aged are first handicapped. Few recreations give advantages to those with the kind of experience common to older people. When one has mentioned chess, checkers, and cards he has nearly exhausted the list of games that are suitable. It is evident that one of the needs in the coming years, when the markets for children's games will be shrinking while those for adult games will be expanding, will be for a wider variety of entertaining recreation for the upper-age groups.

The relation between recreational activities and subjective measures of adjustment was tested among the residents of a retirement home (Burgess, 1954). Those persons who had few friends within the home engaged in the fewest recreational activities and also felt least useful and satisfied. At the opposite extreme, persons who had the largest number of friends engaged in about twice as many different recreational activities and felt most useful and satisfied with their current living arrangements. One may raise the question of causality: does a favorable attitude toward one's surroundings and general feelings of usefulness cause him to be outgoing and engage in recreational activities, or does involvement in activities create and contribute to the development of feelings of favorable adjustment? Strictly on the basis of the data the question cannot be answered, but logically the second of the two alternatives appears to be more reasonable. On the other hand, it is possible that a reciprocal relation exists, such that the attitude encourages activities, and engagement in activities reinforces the attitude. The further fact that the number of activities declined with age, as well as feelings of usefulness, gives some credence to the reciprocal relationship.

The previously mentioned study by Morgan (1937) revealed that hobbies were for a number of reasons given up as people grew older: lack of opportunity (no gardening space), poor health (unable to stand the rigors of hunting), or prohibitive cost. These suggest that as one approaches retirement, the selection of a hobby ought to take such considerations into account.

THEORIES OF SUCCESSFUL AGING

This chapter has presented a large number of facts—some trivial, some interesting, some of central importance. How do they fit together? Is there any systematic way that one can view the process of aging that will provide a framework of understanding or a strategy for further investigation? In short, is there a useful theory of aging?

Two theories have been proposed as guides for aging so as to maximize the benefits to the individual and minimize the disadvantages to other segments of the population. These have been labeled the Activity and Disengagement theories (Havighurst, 1961). According to the first, the best adjustments and greatest personal satisfactions come from maintaining as far as possible the activities and attitudes of one's earlier years. One attempts to maintain a youthful outlook and a set of activities that characterize in pattern, if not in amount, the activities of the vigorous years. Retirement may force a man to give up his job, but successful aging according to this theory requires that he continue to be active at a reduced pace or time schedule in some related or preferred endeavor. The club woman, active in committees and community affairs during her maturity, should, according to this approach, continue these activities but on a reduced scale, commensurate with her physical limitations. The notion is that the aging person should, and ordinarily does, attempt to maintain and continue his contacts and activities as a means of ensuring his own well-being and contentment.

The Disengagement theory, on the other hand, proposes that as one passes from middle age toward retirement, there is a natural desire to become less involved in many of the activities of one's earlier years. Like the phenomena of growth to which the adolescent must adjust, the process of disengagement is thought to be both inevitable and necessary. Rather than attempting to continue a pattern of activities comparable to maturity, disengagement implies that the individual deliberately relax his hold on these interests and involvements to reach a new balance between social demands and one's own resources. Growing old is thus a constructive developmental process in its own right with its own special problems and not merely the reluctant dribbling away of activities and contacts at the ragtag end of the prime years.

Cumming and McCaffrey (1960) express the notion this way: ". . . one of the early stages of disengagement occurs when the individual withdraws emotional investment from the environment. We have thought of the inner process as being an ego change in which object cathexis is reduced; this results in an appearance of self-centeredness and an orientation to others which betrays less sense of mutual obligation. This is accompanied by a somewhat freer and more expressive manner." Some support for this view comes from a 74-year-old woman, one of the respondents in a study, who said, when asked what were the best things about her age: "The change—over a period of years—freedom—from petty conventions, children, husband. A sense of relief from petty fears about jobs, finances, social position, new clothes. Freedom to accept or decline invitations and appointments without strain on my husband's business or hurting my children, or the Victorian standards of my parents" (Havighurst, 1961).

Obviously, rational arguments may be marshaled for either of these theories. The crux of the issue depends upon how one measures adjustment in later life. Given some such an agreed-upon criterion, we could go about the task of discovering whether people who strove to maintain and continue the activities engaged in when 50 to 65 years old were more or less well adjusted than those who followed the other path of deliberately disengaging themselves from the whirl of events. Although Havighurst and others have attempted to devise such measures, those measures are far from universally accepted.

One of the best of these is really a combination of five scales that measures (1) zest versus apathy (enthusiastic response to and interest in activities versus boredom, listlessness); (2) fortitude (accepting personal responsibility versus blaming others or self for mistakes); (3) consonance between desired and achieved goals (the extent to which the individual feels he has achieved what he intended of what he considers important); (4) positive self-concept (the extent to which the individual is concerned with grooming, thinks of himself as wise, mellow, and deserving of respect); and (5) mood tone (optimistic, content versus depressed, bitter, lonely, blue). Presumably this *Life Satisfaction Index* could serve as a measure of one's adjustment and then make possible some empirical tests of the two theories briefly sketched above.

It should be noted that the Activity theory of aging essentially assumes that the pattern of living that typifies the person in mid-life is a kind of model to be emulated or approximated. It is generally true that these people make the major contribution to society and carry the main burdens, whereas both early youth and old age represent, to some extent, drains upon their energies and resources. On the other hand the previous pages have pointed out that aging clearly involves some decrements in personal resources that are just as realistic as the deficiencies of early growth. We do not expect children or adolescents to behave like adults to be considered well adjusted. Instead, their adjustments are always evaluated within the framework of their resources. The same logic would seem to hold for the later years of life. However, it remains for the student at this point to decide whether the Disengagement or the Activity theory is more appropriate as a basis for adjustment. It is also a task for empirical research to discover which type of person, the "disengager" or the "activist," in fact makes the better adjustment as measured by some satisfactory criterion of adjustment.

SUMMARY

In this chapter we have surveyed some of the major findings of the aging process; first in terms of the sensory inputs and motoric outputs, then later in terms of the more complex psychological functions. In general, persons past 50 experience both sensory and motor deficiencies compared with their former capacities. General intelligence as measured by conventional tests shows a steady decline beyond the third decade. However, these findings may be an artifact of the particular measuring devices rather than a real decrement. Learning and memory decline in the later years of life but not at the same rate for all kinds of material, suggesting that aging is not a uniform process either at the physiological or psychological levels of description. Drives, motives, and creative productions unquestionably decline but in ways that contradict much of our folklore about aging.

The adjustments of elderly persons to the changes in their own performances and capacities are partly a function of what they expect of themselves and are partly determined by the subtle but often pointed assumptions society makes about the older segments of the population. Arbitrary retirement age limits and the nonproductive status accorded elderly people as a whole tend to complicate their adjustments.

Current efforts to assist older people to face their adjustment problems include the development of retirement communities, day centers, and homes for the aging. Some evaluation of these efforts have been made, but more are needed. A criterion of later adjustment is needed for this task as well as the task of determining whether the Activity or the Disengagement theory of aging is the more valid.

SUGGESTED REFERENCES FOR FURTHER STUDY

Birren, James E. (ed.) (1959). *Handbook of Aging and the Individual.* Chicago: University of Chicago Press.

A basic reference source summarizing the major psychological and physiological findings in the field.

Gilbert, J. G. (1952). *Understanding Old Age.* New York: Ronald Press.

The author has spent a major portion of her life on the task described by the title of this book. She writes without sentimentality, and is research-oriented.

Journal of Gerontology.

Current research pertaining to psychological factors in aging are reported here. For the student who wants the latest information, this is the source.

Kutner, B., D. Faushel, A. M. Togo, and T. S. Langner (1956). *Five Hundred over Sixty.* New York: Russel Sage Foundation.

One of the few extensive field studies of adjustments among the aged.

Lehman, H. C. (1953). *Age and Achievement.* Princeton, N. J.: Princeton University Press.

A monumental collection of biographical data gathered over nearly a lifetime of work pertaining to the age at which persons of eminence made their greatest achievements in various field of endeavor.

Thorndike, E. L. (1958). *Adult Learning.* New York: Macmillan Company.

A classic study by one of the pioneer educational psychologists. This book has historical interest because it provided an early stimulus for the psychological study of later years.

Welford, Alan T. (1950). *Skill and Age.* London: Oxford University Press.

A summary of studies conducted in England pertaining to industrial workers. Detailed results are presented.

PART TWO

PSYCHOLOGY APPLIED

TO INDUSTRY

O F ALL THE APPLICATIONS discussed in this book, the science and methods of psychology have been most widely used in business and industry. The psychologist entered the industrial world when his own science was young. Using scientific methods, the early applied psychologists developed techniques for selection and placement of personnel. As the psychologists gained experience, the industrial world learned more about the new science and psychologists. Then the psychologists were called on in other areas of the business and industrial world where men worked with machines or other men. Present-day psychology is concerned with much broader forces than just proper selection and placement of workers; in fact, it is important in all phases of business and industry.

Briefly stated, the function of industry is to take raw materials and convert them into products desired by consumers. In other parts of this book the desires of consumers are discussed. The description and manipulation of raw materials is not directly the concern of psychology. But the efforts of men working with machines to change raw materials to desirable goods is the realm of industrial psychology and the subject of this section.

First, a discussion of work and descriptions of jobs tells what is expected of the human factor in production. Next, an explanation of the differences in individual abilities to perform certain activities leads to a discussion of techniques of selecting and placing on the job men who are best qualified to do the work. These topics comprise Chapter 6, "Employment Psychology."

After a worker is placed in a job for which he is fitted, the function of the psychologist is to see that the worker produces in the most efficient manner. To achieve maximum efficiency, the worker must know how to do his job in his environment. This training of workers is discussed in Chapter 7.

Four major relationships influence a man in his working world. After proper selection and training, efficiency is still influenced by man's relationship to (1) work environment, (2) machines, (3) other men, and (4) himself. Chapters 8 through 11 each discuss one of these major relationships.

All of the material covered in Chapters 6 through 11 is interrelated. In each chapter there are attempts to coordinate the material from other chapters. The reader should observe the overlap and recognize the importance of adequate competence in all areas.

Chapter 6

Employment Psychology

APPLIED PSYCHOLOGISTS HAVE HAD EXCELLENT OPPORTUNITIES to develop and use scientific methods while working with the problems of selection and placement. This work represents to the business world the oldest application of psychology. The techniques of measuring human characteristics and using them to place men into proper jobs are well validated. However, this was not always so, and it is not unusual to find organizations that still do not use scientific methods of selecting workers.

At one time all the hiring and firing of workers was done by a foreman. He had absolute control over his men; he probably knew each of them before he hired them. Consequently, his selections of employees were often quite good. As industry expanded, jobs were standardized, larger populations accumulated around the factories, and transportation facilities improved, so that workers could commute greater distances. The foremen found that he no longer knew the men that he must hire. Into this situation came scientific selection and placement techniques.

To find a good worker for a job it is necessary to know what functions are performed on the job. It is also essential to find a man that can perform these functions. Thus scientific selection is the matching of the abilities of a man to the functions of a job. This is sometimes referred to as "fitting the square peg in the square hole."

The process of hiring workers is discussed in this chapter under the following major topics: (1) measuring and describing work, (2) individual differences, and (3) selection and placement procedures—tests, interviews, application blanks.

Most of the examples cited are taken from production jobs in industries where large numbers of workers are employed because (1) more information is available from completed studies, (2) measures of successful performance on the job are available, (3) more standardized jobs mean more workers do the same functions and thus valid studies are more readily accomplished, and (4) the functions of selection and placement may be of greater economic consequence where large numbers of workers are involved. Selection procedures for higher-level jobs are being developed but are more difficult to establish and validate.

WORK

Work may be thought of as the use of a man's physical and mental abilities to achieve a goal. Thus work involves activity on the part of the worker. This may require physical activity, such as tightening bolts, running a drill press, or chopping wood. Or it may require mental activity, such as deciding which proposal to follow in plant expansion or what advertising campaign to use. Often it requires a combination of physical and mental activity, such as driving a truck or building a part from blueprints.

Work may be measured in a variety of ways. Some objective estimates of work for production-line employees are number of units produced per hour, number of rejects per hour, total time on the job, and amount of money earned. For many jobs, measures such as these are impossible or extremely difficult to obtain, and so another technique is used. This technique usually involves ratings by other people. For example, a sales manager estimates how well a salesman sells, or an editor evaluates how well a copywriter does his job.

The objective measurements of production are well understood, so they have merely been mentioned here. However, techniques of evaluating performance by other men need further clarification.

Rating Techniques. Even when formalized methods or techniques of evaluation are not used, men often estimate what others do. Rating systems are formalized techniques to improve the objectivity of such ratings. They are by no means perfect, but they are of great help in situations where objective measurements of production cannot be made. In the working world no one technique is used exclusively; all available information is combined to provide a total picture of performance.

Rater bias and "halo effect" are two of the most common problems in rating other men. These two pitfalls and seven techniques of rating are discussed in the following paragraphs.

RATER BIAS AND "HALO EFFECT". Some raters do not like to give low ratings, others do not like to give high ratings, and some raters give only average ratings. Such biases often appear in ratings. Thus precautions must be taken when interpreting ratings.

Halo effect is a term used to describe a rater's tendency to rate a man the same on a variety of characteristics, even if he knows about only a few of them. For example, a rater may know a worker is cooperative, loyal, and trustworthy and thus rates him high on these characteristics. When rating this worker on intelligence, he may also rate him high even though he doesn't know about the worker's intelligence. This effect may also occur in the opposite direction if a rater knows only about bad characteristics of a worker and is forced to give ratings on characteristics he is not familiar with.

Attempts to limit rater bias and "halo effect" are described as they pertain to specific rating techniques.

Seven formalized systems for evaluating what others do are presented in the following pages. All rating techniques have some shortcomings but the last two described are specifically designed to lessen rater bias and "halo effect."

DESCRIPTIVE PHRASES RATING TECHNIQUE. One of the oldest techniques in use consists of a list of phrases or statements seemingly important to a job. The rater indicates the phrases that adequately describe the worker being rated, usually by checking each appropriate phrase. Thus the technique is sometimes referred to as a checklist system.

Although this technique generally does not result in an overall score comparable from one person to another or from one group to another, it does result in a word picture of the characteristics of an individual. There are also methods of preparing scale values so that men can be compared (Richardson and Kuder, 1933).

The descriptive phrases technique is a valuable way to summarize available information about a worker. This may be used to assist the rater in ranking workers or completing one of the other rating techniques.

RANK-ORDER RATING TECHNIQUE. The rank-order technique of evaluating workers consists of a rater considering the group of men he is rating and deciding which one is best, second best, third best, and so on, down to the poorest in the group. A separate ranking must be made for each characteristic of importance in the work situation. For example, a supervisor may rank the workers in his group in terms of supervisory ability, integrity, and knowledge of the job. In this example, three individual rankings would have to be made. Sometimes a composite rating is all that is needed, so the rater just ranks the group in terms of overall ability. The most efficient way to use the ranking technique is to select the best, the poorest, and an average worker in the group. The remaining men are then placed appropriately by comparison with the men already ranked.

The ranking technique has several shortcomings. It is useful only with a relatively small number of men, since the rater must remember all the men in his group while making the rankings. The technique gives only relative standings within the group and does not allow for comparisons from one group to another. Rank-order rating has the advantages of being a relatively fast technique to use, needing few instructions, and is generally accepted by foremen as a "natural thing to do."

PAIRED-COMPARISON RATING TECHNIQUE. The paired-comparison system of rating is similar to the rank-order technique but with more rigorous controls. In this method, the rater systematically compares each individual in his group to each other individual in the same group. Thus, if five workers are involved, the rater must compare each of the five members against each of the other four. The method is often used to rate overall efficiency. If a variety of characteristics are to be evaluated, the comparisons have to be repeated for each particular characteristic rated. A common method of applying this technique is to use a plus each time the man under consideration is rated as better than another and a zero when he is rated as poorer. In such a manner, the total number of pluses and zeroes for each man is obtained, and the man with the highest number of plus scores obtains the highest rating. Figure 6.1 shows an example of a check sheet useful in paired-comparison rating.

The paired-comparison technique has many of the same disadvantages

Workers	Joe	Bill	Dave	Bob	Jim	Score
Joe		0	0	+	0	1
Bill	+		+	+	+	4
Dave	+	0		+	0	2
Bob	0	0	0		0	0
Jim	+	0	+	+		3

Figure 6.1. A possible check sheet for use in paired comparison ratings. This shows an example of five men rated on overall efficiency. A plus mark indicates the man in the row (horizontal) is better than the man in the column (vertical). Bill rates highest in this example.

as the rank-order technique, since it (1) is applicable only to relatively small groups, (2) is useful only in getting relative standings within the group, and (3) does not provide ratings comparable from one group to another. It has the particular advantage of forcing the rater to consider each man in his group against each other man and thus do a more thorough evaluation than with the rank-order technique. If it is completed correctly, it gives a double check on each rating.

FORCED DISTRIBUTION RATING TECHNIQUE. The technique of forced-distribution rating forces the rater to estimate where each of his men should be placed in terms of previously designed quotas. Typically, the rater is instructed that he should expect certain percentages of his men in various categories. For example, 10 percent superior, 20 percent above average, 40 percent average, 20 percent below average, and 10 percent very poor on a particular characteristic or an overall evaluation. The rater must distribute his men according to these previously set percentages.

This technique is more useful in larger groups than the rank-order or paired-comparison techniques. On the other hand, it is a difficult technique to use with extremely large groups because the rater may not be able to consider each man adequately. In very small groups the rater may not be

Characteristics	0	10	20	30	40	50	60	70	80	90	100	Don't Know
Intelligence												_____
General Information												_____
Skill on his Job												_____
Cooperativeness												_____
Leadership Ability												_____
Popularity												_____
Integrity												_____

Figure 6.2. Example of a section of a traditional rating scale. Rater places a check mark along the scale line to indicate amount of each characteristic possessed by ratee. When rater is unfamiliar with a ratee's ability on a particular characteristic, he should check the "Don't Know" column.

able to distribute the few members into the proper percentages. It also produces ratings applicable only to the one group and not comparable to another.

TRADITIONAL AND GRAPHIC RATING SCALE TECHNIQUES. The traditional and graphic rating scales usually involve a printed form on which one man is rated. One form is used for each ratee, with the rater assigning an evaluation for each of the characteristics. The traditional rating scale consists of the names of the characteristics and a scale where the rater indicates the amount of each characteristic possessed by a particular worker. Figure 6.2 provides an example of a section of a traditional rating scale.

Over many years of use, the traditional rating scale evolved into a graphic rating scale. Points along the scale part of the graphic form are indicated by descriptive phrases. Early descriptions used numbers and an indication of high and low ends of each scale. As those preparing rating scales gained more experience, they more thoroughly described the points along the scales. Figure 6.3 shows an example of two items from a graphic rating scale. When evaluations are being made, the rater has a description of the amount of a particular characteristic expected for each point along the scale.

Characteristic

Quality of Work	Always above standard	Often above standard	Usually meets standard	Often below standard	Always below standard	Don't Know

| Leadership Ability | Inspires all men to follow him | Others seek his advice | Minds his own business | Usually follows the leader | Always looks to others for help | Don't Know |

Figure 6.3. Example of two items from a graphic rating scale. Rater places a check mark on the scale line to indicate the level of the characteristic for man being rated. If rater doesn't feel capable of rating a man on any characteristic, he may check the "Don't Know" category.

Graphic and traditional rating scales have particular assets as compared to other rating techniques: (1) they are useful for large groups of workers, (2) ratings are comparable from one group to another, and (3) they are generally understood by foremen and workers. They also have some disadvantages: (1) the traditional rating scale may not be used consistently from one rater to another, and (2) rater bias easily enters the ratings.

To help reduce rater bias and "halo effect" in the use of traditional and graphic rating scales, the ends of the scales are often randomly reversed. For example, the high end of the scale may be on the right for the first, third, fourth, sixth, eighth, and so on, characteristic and on the left end on the other characteristics. Thus the rater must at least read the scale for each characteristic instead of giving a man an overall good or poor rating by just checking down one side of the page. Providing a place to check for "insufficient knowledge" or "don't know" also helps to reduce rater bias and "halo effect." Forcing a rater to rate a man on characteristics for which he has insufficient knowledge only reduces the value of the rating scale as a measure of performance.

FORCED-CHOICE TECHNIQUE OF RATING.   Developed during the 1940's in industry and the armed services, the forced-choice technique "forces" the rater to choose between two descriptive phrases or terms that appear equally acceptable but differ in predictive value. The paired phrases are both desirable or both undesirable. The assumption is made that the rater is not able to differentiate between the two good or the two undesirable phrases on the basis of the phrases alone. Thus he is "forced" to choose a phrase in each pair on the basis of what he knows about the individual being rated. When the pair of phrases are desirable the rater is usually asked to indicate the one that most nearly describes the worker; when the pair of phrases are undesirable the rater is required to pick the one that less adequately describes the worker. Each of the phrases must previously have been evaluated to see how well it relates with a measure of success on the job.

The forced-choice method often uses tetrads of two desirable and two undesirable phrases. The rater indicates the phrase most descriptive and the phrase least descriptive of the worker from the tetrad of phrases. Figure 6.4 shows an example of a tetrad from a forced-choice type rating form.

The forced-choice technique has received a great deal of publicity.

	Most	Least
Compliments each of his subordinates that performs well	___	___
Knows his job and performs it well	___	___
Carries out orders only under protest	___	___
Drives his men rather than leads	___	___

Figure 6.4.   Example of a tetrad from a forced-choice rating form. For each such set of items (tetrad) the rater must check the one item that is most characteristic of the ratee and the one that is least characteristic of the ratee.

Most has been favorable, although several opponents claim that the technique cannot really be applied in an industrial situation. As with other rating techniques, it has certain advantages and disadvantages. A good deal of statistical sophistication and a lot of time and effort are needed to construct and validate the descriptive phrases. Another disadvantage is that it is not easily understood by workers or foremen, and so it is difficult to convince the raters that they should use the technique. Advantages of the technique are (1) it yields ratings comparable from one group to another, (2) it can be used with large groups, and (3) it is specifically designed to control rater bias and "halo effect."

CRITICAL-INCIDENT TECHNIQUE OF RATING. Dr. Flanagan (1949) devised the critical-incident technique as a method of lessening rater biases. This technique places the emphasis on describing rather than evaluating behavior. Items associated with an individual worker's success or failure on a given job are collected. This is done by a rater recording his observations of what he considers "critical incidents" in the behavior of a worker. Examples of "critical incidents" might be completion of an assignment in less time than expected, working through the regular rest period in order to complete a rush job, returning from lunch a half hour late or not properly clearing up the work area. These records are reviewed periodically and are generally available for worker and rater discussion at all times. The rater is thus able to explain his views of a worker's behavior at any time during a rating period.

The greatest advantage of the critical-incident technique is that the rating is a measure of behavior that actually occurred. Other advantages are (1) rater bias is decreased (2) raters have objective evidence to support their ratings, and (3) it is usable with large groups. Several disadvantages are (1) ratings are not comparable from one work group to another, (2) some supervisors notice only "good" behavior, whereas others notice only "bad," and (3) raters can easily forget to record their observations of critical incidents.

Job Descriptions. A job description is a summary of workers' activities in a production situation. It describes the typical duties, machinery involved, and processes used by a worker in doing his job. Job descriptions are important in selection, placement, and training of workers. They are also used by employment agencies as aids in rehabilitating or transferring workers. As more automation forces additional workers to change jobs, adequate descriptions will be of increasing importance in retraining and reevaluation of workers.

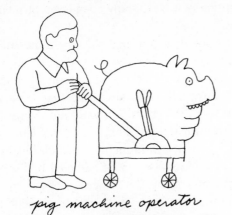

pig machine operator

Operates a conveyor made up of a string of molds into which molten pig iron is poured.

grizzlyman

Manipulates ore and broken rock onto heavy sizing screen directly after ore is blasted out at an underground mine.

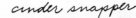

cinder snapper

Takes care of cinder runners or troughs, along which slag and molten pig iron flow from a blast furnace.

oven patcher

Patches coke ovens with a refractory slurry. Uses hand tool, refractory gun, or sandblast machine.

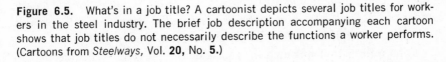

nipper

Handles drilling and other supplies in an ore mine.

Figure 6.5. What's in a job title? A cartoonist depicts several job titles for workers in the steel industry. The brief job description accompanying each cartoon shows that job titles do not necessarily describe the functions a worker performs. (Cartoons from *Steelways,* Vol. **20**, No. **5**.)

Before techniques of obtaining job descriptions are discussed, several terms must be defined. In a particular organization, a group of tasks performed by one person is usually referred to as a *position*. A group of similar positions in an organization is called a *job*. The term *occupation* refers to a group of similar jobs in different organizations or companies. Thus, when discussing a job description, reference is made to similar tasks performed in one organization. A job description may be for only one person or many people doing the same functions.

In order to prepare job descriptions, a job analysis should be completed. The job analysis tells what a worker does, how he does it, why he does it, and the skill that is involved. A typical way of preparing a job analysis is to study one person on a particular job. After collecting as much information as possible by observation and discussion with the worker, a check is made with other men on similar jobs. This is not the same as motion-and-time study in that it does not seek to improve the job but just studies it as it is. The same sort of information can be gathered by use of a job questionnaire sent to individual workers. To be certain of the functions of a particular job, many evaluators use a job questionnaire sent to all workers performing a job and observe at least one of the workers in detail.

After completion of the job analysis, a formal job description may be prepared. In the practical situation of hiring workers, the job description or the job analysis sheet may be useful to the employment manager. Frequently, both are available and although the job description gives technical information about a job, the job analysis sometimes provides additional data.

Job descriptions are often completed by cooperative efforts of representatives of management and workers. Because exact definitions of functions to be performed are liable to be subject to dispute during contract negotiations, it is wise to prepare job descriptions cooperatively. The job description shown in Figure 6.6 is an example of a form to be jointly approved by management and union. The sheet includes a place for job title, functions involved, materials handled, equipment used, supervision given, and working procedures.

Although job descriptions are usually prepared for jobs within a particular organization, descriptions for most jobs in the United States are available in the *Dictionary of Occupational Titles* (United States Department of Labor, 1939). This material is somewhat dated but still contains adequate descriptions prepared after thorough job analyses.

The information provided by a job description is also valuable for job classification and job evaluation. Chapter 8 of this book discusses techniques of job evaluation.

INDIVIDUAL DIFFERENCES

The opening chapter of this book stated that the differences between the abilities and the performances of individuals would not be emphasized.

<u>XYZ Steel Corporation</u>
NAME OF COMPANY

_____Main_____ Plant   PLANT CODE ___XYZ___

DATE _August 10, 1963_

JOB DESCRIPTION

Department ___Bar Mill___   Sub-division _Materials Handling Unit_

Present Title ___Brownhoist Crewman___   Proposed Title _Brownhoist Crewman_

Primary Function
    Conducts the movement of the Brownhoist crane.

Tools and Equipment
    Chains, bars, scrap pans, blocks, etc.

Materials
    Scale, scrap, grease, oil, etc.

Source of Supervision
    Master Mechanic.
    Directed by Foreman in department in which working.

Direction Exercised
    Directs Brownhoist Follower.

Working Procedure
    Relays orders for supervision to Brownhoist crew for movement of
        cars or the loading or unloading of cars.
    Hooks up materials to be loaded or unloaded from cars.
    Signals Brownhoist Crane Operator when lifting with crane or
        moving Brownhoist crane.
    Couples and uncouples cars.
    Throws switches.
    Weighs railway cars of material.

    The job description which appears above is intended to be sufficient merely to identify the
position and should not be interpreted to describe all of the duties performance of which may be
required of employees holding such position.

Approved:

For the Union   For the Company

by _____ Date: _____   by _____ Date: _____

Figure 6.6. An example of a job description form completed for a brownhoist crewman in the bar mill division of a steel plant.

However, it is necessary to be aware of individual differences. Some men are tall, some are short, some are very intelligent, some are less intelligent, and they all have different personalities. Many individual characteristics of humans can be assessed and recorded. Since these characteristics relate to success in fulfilling job functions, it is within the province of psychology as applied to industry to measure them.

Psychological differences can be measured only by measuring differences in performance. Physical differences, such as height, weight, color of eyes, and so on, can be measured directly. However, measures of ability, motivation, training, or experience must be estimated from the performance of an individual. In a formula,

$$\text{Performance} = \text{Ability} \times \text{Training} \times \text{Motivation.}$$

To evaluate any of the three factors in performance, it is necessary to hold the other two constant while varying the third and measuring changes in performance.

When interested in measuring the effects of training, performance is measured before training and after training, whereas ability and motivation effects are held constant. Any variation in performance in the two measures is then interpreted as the result of training. If interested in measuring ability, training and motivation effects must be held constant while measuring performance. Holding constant the effects of any of the factors is an extremely difficult task. Thus the data available for selection and placement functions is not always as clear and concrete as might be desired.

Before going further it is important to understand what is known about the distribution of psychological characteristics among the population at large. Many psychological and physiological characteristics of humans are distributed in the general population in a so-called normal fashion (normal curve). What does the normal curve represent? It represents a line connecting all of the points on a graph showing the proportion of the total population at certain scores along the base line. For example, Figure 6.7 shows the distribution of IQ's obtained from measurement of a large sample of the general population. It can be noted that very few persons have IQ's as low as 55 or as high as 145. On the other hand, a great many people have IQ's between 85 and 115. This distribution shows that a job necessitating a worker having an IQ of 130 or higher has only a few possible applicants even in a large population. Selection would be a difficult problem even if this were the only characteristic needed. On the other hand, if an IQ of 100 or higher is adequate, there would be a great many applicants available in the population, and selection on this characteristic would be easier.

Not all psychological and physiological characteristics are distributed

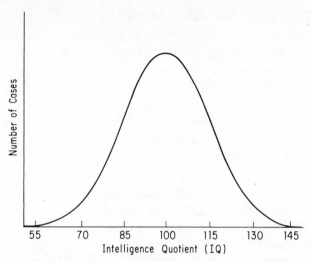

Figure 6.7. The "normal curve." This curve shows a line connecting all the points of a graph indicating the number of persons obtaining each of various IQ scores. Although this is a hypothetical presentation, most psychological and physiological measurements distribute in this fashion when large groups of people are measured.

in a normal fashion in every group of people. Many of the characteristics important to industry are not distributed normally in a group of applicants. For example, some occupations require college training. This eliminates a great deal of the curve shown in Figure 6.7, because college itself was a selection device in terms of IQ. Prospective students with IQ's below 100 or 110 were generally not permitted to start college training. Although one characteristic may not be normally distributed among one group, most human characteristics are distributed in a normal fashion in general populations.

One person will not necessarily have the same relative position in the normal distribution curve for all characteristics. A person may have an IQ of 120, which would place him considerably above the center of the normal distribution shown in Figure 6.7. However, he may have manual dexterity equal to about 50 percent of the population and would thus fall in the middle of a curve drawn for manual dexterity. On the other hand, a person may have an exceptional ability in mathematics and only average IQ.

Individuals vary on psychological and physiological characteristics, and these differences can be adequately measured. How to measure the psychological differences in people is the general topic for the remainder of this chapter.

SELECTION AND PLACEMENT OF WORKERS

Selection and placement are interrelated processes. Ordinarily, selection is the process of finding the proper man to fill an opening in an organization. Placement is the technique of finding the proper opening to use most effectively the capacities and abilities of a man. In small organizations there is little attempt at placement because a man is usually hired to fill a particular opening. In larger organizations, men may be hired because they apparently have potential for future work. They are then placed in jobs where their abilities can be used. Placement techniques are also used by employment agencies in assigning men to suitable jobs.

The procedures for assessing the capacities and abilities of a man are the same for selection and placement. Job descriptions and measures of work provide information about the functions of a job. Selection, then, is the process of matching man's abilities to the requirements of the job.

Different organizations use various sequences in their selection procedures. A typical program includes a variety of events or hurdles that must be passed, such as application blanks, psychological tests, and reference or credit checks. The order in which these events take place varies according to the dictates of the particular organization. It is frequently determined by the cost involved in each of the several steps. If interviewing requires an expensive representative of the organization, some other step in the procedure might first be used. Since an application blank can usually be completed at a relatively small expense to the company, it is often the first step in the selection process. Other companies use interviews more than once in the sequence. The first interview may be very short—a brief contact between the prospective employee and a representative of the company. The applicant may talk to a secretary or a receptionist indicating his interest in working for the organization. He may then be given an application blank or instructed to follow another step in the hiring procedure. A common sequence of successive hurdles is interview, application blank, tests, comprehensive interview, and credit or personal references checks.

All steps in the selection process are designed to improve the matching of a man's abilities with the abilities needed to do a job. The measurements of successful completion of work are called *criteria*. Thus production records and ratings are frequently criteria of success in an industrial organization. Those factors that can be measured before a man starts on a job and are found to be related to success are called *predictors*. Tests, interviews, and application blanks are examples of predictors. Credit or personal reference checks are usually not considered predictors even though they are "hurdles" in the selection process. Little objective evidence of methods of using such checks is available; thus they are not discussed here.

Industrial selection is the choosing of employees from applicants in such a manner that only men who are likely to succeed on the job are hired. Scores on predictors that are well related to criteria are used to select applicants so that men hired can be expected to perform well on the job.

To discuss predictors we must understand three terms: *correlation coefficient, reliability,* and *validity.* After covering these concepts the remainder of this chapter will discuss three predictors: application blanks, interviews, and tests.

The Correlation Coefficient. A correlation coefficient is a number indicating the extent to which two measures of a given group of individuals vary in accord with each other. The coefficient is expressed as a number from 0.00 to plus or minus 1.00. The number indicates the amount of relationship between the two measures. The sign indicates the direction of the relationship. Thus a correlation coefficient of +1.00 indicates a perfect constant relationship and means that as one measure increases by a given amount, the other measure increases in the same direction in a constant proportion. If a correlation coefficient of +1.00 is found between scores from two halves of one test, it means that a person would get a high score on one half of the test if he obtained a high score on the other half, or if obtaining a low score on one half, he would obtain a low score on the other half. A correlation coefficient of −1.00 also indicates a perfect constant relationship, but in an inverse direction. If two halves of a test correlate at −1.00, a person scoring high on one half of the test would score low on the other half of the test; and a person scoring low on one half would score high on the other. In practical situations correlation coefficients of plus or minus 1.00 are rarely found. Instead, correlation coefficients of less than 1.00 are usually the case. The coefficient may be as low as 0.00, which indicates no relationship between the two measurements. Correlation coefficients near 0.00, such as those between +.20 and −.20, indicate essentially no relationship between the two measures. Thus, if two halves of a test correlate +.19 or −.15 or +.08, a person might obtain a very high score on one half of the test and a low score, middle score, or high score on the other half. Here are several examples of commonly obtained correlation coefficients and what they mean. The correlation between intelligence test scores and grades in secondary school is about +.60. This shows a high positive relationship between intelligence and high school scholarship. The correlation between two administrations of an intelligence test to the same group is +.94. This indicates a very high relationship and a good deal of consistency of the test and the performance of the people taking the test. The correlation between height and intelligence of persons of a given age group is about $+.11$. This means that there essentially is no relationship between height and intelligence of persons in that given age group.

Correlation coefficients indicate the amount of average relationship between two measures. They do not indicate cause and effect. Thus a high correlation between intelligence test scores and high school scholarship does not mean that high intelligence causes good scholarship or that good grades in high school cause high intelligence. High correlation coefficients show only high relationship. This may be due to an entirely different third factor or because one factor causes the other. Additional investigation is necessary to point out cause-and-effect relationships after correlation coefficients are computed.

Reliability.   Reliability may generally be thought of as consistency. When a measuring instrument is reliable, it measures the same thing time after time in the same manner. Thus a ruler is reliable if it indicates that the page of this book is the same length on repeated measurements. A psychological test is reliable when a person scores about the same on different administrations.

As used in testing, *reliability* is a generic term referring to a variety of different measures or evidence of consistency. The American Psychological Association, the American Educational Research Association, and the National Council on Measurements Used in Education have prepared a joint statement concerning psychological tests and diagnostic techniques. This report (American Psychological Association, 1954) suggested that the concept of reliability should be differentiated into three separate estimates, each expressed in terms of a correlation coefficient: (1) coefficient of internal consistency, (2) coefficient of equivalence, and (3) coefficient of stability.

COEFFICIENT OF CONSISTENCY.   The coefficient of consistency is obtained by an analysis of data from one administration of a test to a group. Scores from two halves of the test are compared. Often scores on the odd-numbered items are compared with scores on the even-numbered items. A correlation coefficient is computed to show the average relationship between the scores on the two halves of the test. Thus the technique is often referred to as the split-half reliability measure.

There are more advanced techniques for computing the coefficient of consistency. The most widely used is Kuder–Richardson Formula 20

(Richardson and Kuder, 1939). We will not describe such calculation here since the method is described in most testing and statistics books.

COEFFICIENT OF EQUIVALENCE. Two equivalent forms of a test are administered at the same time to one group of subjects. A correlation coefficient is computed to show the average amount of relationship between the scores obtained on each form. This is referred to as the coefficient of equivalence.

COEFFICIENT OF STABILITY. A third estimate of reliability may be obtained by administering a test to the same group at two different times. The correlation coefficient between the scores on the two administrations is called the coefficient of stability. This is also referred to as test–retest reliability.

Sometimes two forms of the same test are administered at different times. A correlation coefficient computed from such scores is called a coefficient of stability and equivalence.

It is obvious that each of the three different measures to estimate the reliability of a particular test may result in different coefficients. Each technique has certain advantages. The correlation between retests with the same form administered on different occasions (coefficient of stability) is valuable in estimating the endurance of an individual's responses. However, temporary variations in conditions between the first and second administration of the test may also influence the test performance and bring error into the coefficient of stability. When two parallel forms of the test are used (coefficient of equivalence), item variability or specificity of items introduces an error into the situation, because it is not possible to write exactly the same items for both forms of the test. When the two halves of the test are scored against each other (coefficient of consistency), item specificity may again introduce possible errors in the estimate of reliability. In general, the best estimate of reliability is the Kuder–Richardson estimate.

RELIABILITY IN USE. In specific situations some reliability techniques just discussed are not applicable. Some tests, for example, are speeded tests (scores depend upon speed), and the Kuder–Richardson or other split-half techniques are inapplicable as estimates of reliability. For speeded tests, equivalent form or test–retest reliability coefficients are appropriate.

The reliability of a measuring instrument must be high for satisfactory usage. A yardstick that changes its length markedly from day to day or from measurement to measurement would simply not be usable. By the same token, a test that is not reliable is not dependable for use. Evaluations of one individual cannot be compared to another, nor can measurements of one person on different occasions be compared if the measuring device is unreliable. Good psychological tests usually have reliability coefficients of +.90 or higher. The information concerning reliability for most psychological tests is included in the test manuals and should be checked before administration of the tests.

Validity. The validity of a measuring instrument is the extent to which it measures what it says it measures. Validity is also expressed as a correlation coefficient. In order to obtain such a correlation coefficient, a score and a measure of success must be obtained for a group of individuals. In the case of employment tests, measures of production (criteria) and test scores (predictors) are needed. A test may be very reliable but not correlate well with any measure of success on the job and, consequently, have low validity. The correlation of test performance with job performance is the measure of the test validity.

Validity coefficients for an individual test are always lower than reliability coefficients. A test may have high reliability and low validity, but it can never be more valid than reliable. A high relationship between the test and success on the job cannot be obtained if the measurement of success on the job or the test is not reliable.

Again referring to the technical recommendations of the American Psychological Association, et al (American Psychological Association, 1954), validity indicates to the test user the degree to which the test achieves certain aims. Four estimates of validity are suggested: (1) content validity, (2) predictive validity, (3) concurrent validity, and (4) construct validity.

CONTENT VALIDITY. Content validity involves a systematic examination of the test material to see if it is really a representative sample of the behavior domain to be measured. This is not a mere inspection, but involves a thorough evaluation of the content in relation to the behavior that is to be measured. Quantitative evidence of content validity is often not obtainable, so content validity is usually subjectively estimated. It is especially important to have good content validity in achievement and proficiency measures, but it is not as important in estimates of aptitude or attitude.

PREDICTIVE VALIDITY. Predictive validity indicates the effectiveness of a test in estimating a future performance. This is the measure usually considered "validity" by personnel managers, because they use tests to estimate how well a person will perform in the future. The validation procedure consists of collecting test scores and criterion scores for a group placed on the job regardless of their test scores. The group must perform on the job in order to obtain criterion scores. Since test scores were obtained at the time of hiring, there is a period of time between collection of predictor and criterion scores. After these scores are available, they are used to compute the correlation coefficient called predictive validity.

Unfortunately, validation of most predictive devices must be accomplished in a more rapid manner and with less expense than that involved in measuring predictive validity. Thus concurrent validity is computed as an estimate of predictive validity.

CONCURRENT VALIDITY.   Concurrent validity is similar to predictive validity except that measurements of performance and test scores are obtained at the same time. In an industrial situation, workers presently on the job are given the selection test. The correlation coefficient between the test scores and criterion measure of the people currently performing the job is the measure of concurrent validity. This is the validity measure most often computed in industrial situations, but it is vital to realize that a test may have higher concurrent validity than predictive validity. In the long run, predictive validity would be more useful for industry, but from a practical standpoint it often cannot be obtained.

CONSTRUCT VALIDITY.   When a test measures a theoretical construct or trait, it is said to have construct validity. The validation procedure involves two steps: (1) the investigator estimates from a theory the scores and variations of scores that should be expected from person to person, and (2) he gathers data to confirm these predictions. Construct validity is generally of less importance than predictive or concurrent validity in the employment situation. It is of value for tests that estimate personality characteristics, and so on, for diagnostic purposes.

VALIDITY IN USE.   Validity coefficients for standardized employment tests typically range +.30 through +.60. Such validity coefficients are not weak or impossible to use. However, each selection situation must be evaluated to determine whether tests are doing what is expected of them. A test may be of value for one particular situation and be of no value at all for another. A coefficient of +.50 might be obtained between a test score and criterion in factory A, while the same test may correlate with performance in factory B at +.70 and in factory C at +.30. It is also possible to find tests that have high concurrent validity while predictive validity may be lower or higher.

Typical correlation coefficients of +.30 through +.60 have led many people to misinterpret the value of tests for selection purposes. It is true that a correlation coefficient of +.50 is almost useless for predicting what a particular individual will do, criterionwise, on the job. However, a higher correlation coefficient will be of value for predicting in an individual case. And a +.50 is of value when working with a group of employees. In industry, rarely must the employment manager predict exactly what specific production should be expected for a particular individual. His job is to find employees who will be successful at a minimum standard on the job, those who will perform at above average, and those who should be rejected. This is much less exacting than predicting a particular individual's performance and allows for usage of tests that are correlated with success at +.50 or slightly lower.

Instead of using just one test, the employment manager often uses a battery of tests as a predictor. When using several tests, each of which has a correlation of +.50 with the criterion, the overall predictive validity may be considerably above +.50.

PREDICTORS OF JOB SUCCESS

As discussed earlier in this chapter, the usual function of the personnel effort is to predict who will or will not succeed on the job after hiring placement. Most prediction is based on the assumption that presen measurements of behavior are fair indicators of future behavior. The previous discussions of validity have concerned the estimation of how good a predictor is in estimating future performance. In the following pages we discuss commonly used predictors of job success: application blanks, interviewing, and psychological tests.

Application Blanks.   Although the particular hiring procedures used by industrial organizations vary, practically all use an application blank. One study (NICB, 1960) showed that over 99% of the companies polled use application blanks in their employment procedure. In fact, many organizations use only an application blank in conjunction with interviewing as the entire basis for selecting personnel.

Application blanks need to be thought of as more than adjuncts to interviews. The application blank is extremely valuable to interviewing because it provides leads for possible probing during the interviews. At the same time application blanks are valuable selectors in their own right.

An application blank can provide a very useful step in the "successive hurdle" technique of selection. In this technique an employee must pass successive checks on his suitability for employment. Proper information or scores on interviews, tests, and application blanks are the hurdles.

After an initial contact via letter or personal contact, an application blank becomes an early hurdle in the hiring procedure. (One hurdle is passed if the man is given the application blank, since the original contact may result in a rejection.) Information gathered by an application blank usually includes age, sex, education, experience, and other factors thought to be important to the company. Answers to the questions on an application blank can be compared to job success for those applicants hired. Thus, an estimate of validity may be computed.

"Critical scores" on education, experience, age, and so on, may be set for application blank information. A rapid appraisal of completed application blanks then provides a rough screening of applicants.

Application blanks usually contain considerably more information than is used in selection or preparing for an interview. For many organizations they are the first formal contact with a future employee. Thus they are partially designed to "sell" the organization to the applicant. In addition, they are often used as the beginning of a permanent file of men hired. Thus, the blanks require information that is irrelevant to the selection process.

Many personnel men believe that collecting excess information is a real mistake; the application blank should contain only the information needed for selecting employees. Applicants resent completing long forms or items which seem irrelevant. They may become careless and not complete the items conscientiously even though highly motivated to work for an organization. Even the employment manager may find so much information that he is not sure what is useful and what is not. The best approach is to provide the shortest application blank that provides all of the information valuable in selecting employees. An example of an application blank is shown in Figure 6.8.

SCORING OR EVALUATING APPLICATION BLANKS. The basic assumption behind predictors of job success is that past performance can be used as an indicator of future performance. With this in mind, application blanks should seek information related to success on the job.

An application blank should be designed for the use of a company or industry. A form useful in selecting for one organization is not necessarily of value in another. On the other hand, it is not feasible for all organizations to provide a separate application blank for each department. Special scoring techniques for the information provided by a general application blank can be developed. One such technique described by Wood (1947)

G-4036

Ingersoll-Rand Company

APPLICATION FOR EMPLOYMENT
Ingersoll-Rand Company is an Equal
Employment Opportunity Employer.

DO NOT WRITE IN THIS SPACE | FOR INTERVIEWER'S USE ONLY

ANSWER ALL QUESTIONS.   PLEASE PRINT OR TYPE.   INFORMATION GIVEN IN THIS APPLICATION IS SUBJECT TO VERIFICATION BY US.

PERSONAL

NAME _____
LAST   FIRST   MIDDLE   (MAIDEN)
PRESENT ADDRESS _____
NO.   STREET   CITY   ZONE   STATE   PHONE
PERMANENT ADDRESS _____
NO.   STREET   CITY   ZONE   STATE   PHONE

SOC. SEC. NO. _____ HEIGHT _____ WEIGHT _____
BIRTHDATE _____ { The laws of various states in which Ingersoll-Rand operates prohibit discrimination because of age. This question is asked for record purposes only. }

CHECK ALL THAT APPLY
MALE ☐   MARRIED ☐   DIVORCED ☐
FEMALE ☐   SINGLE ☐   SEPARATED ☐
           WIDOWED ☐   REMARRIED ☐
U.S. CITIZEN?   YES ☐   NO ☐
If not a citizen when and on what basis did you enter the U.S.A.?

LIST SPOUSE & DEPENDENT CHILDREN

NAME	AGE	RELATIONSHIP	NAME	AGE	RELATIONSHIP

IF SINGLE GIVE PARENT'S NAMES

NOTIFY IN EMERGENCY: NAME _____ ADDRESS _____ PHONE _____

DO YOU HAVE ANY LIMITATIONS PHYSICAL, MENTAL or OTHER?
YES ☐   NO ☐
IF YES, EXPLAIN FULLY

HAVE YOU EVER BEEN ARRESTED EXCEPT FOR MINOR TRAFFIC VIOLATIONS?
YES ☐   NO ☐
IF YES, EXPLAIN FULLY

POSITION

POSITION DESIRED? _____ WAGE or SALARY DESIRED $ _____ per _____

OTHER POSITIONS FOR WHICH YOU ARE QUALIFIED? _____

WHO REFERRED YOU TO I-R? _____

LIST NAMES & POSITIONS OF RELATIVES EMPLOYED BY I-R _____

HAVE YOU EVER APPLIED FOR WORK AT I-R? IF SO, WHEN & WHERE? _____ DATE AVAILABLE FOR WORK _____

EDUCATION

CIRCLE HIGHEST GRADE COMPLETED IN EACH SCHOOL CATEGORY

	GRADE SCHOOL 1 2 3 4 5 6 7 8	HIGH SCHOOL 9 10 11 12	COLLEGE 1 2 3 4	GRAD. SCHOOL 1 2 3 4	BUS. or VOC. SCHOOL 1 2 3 4
	NAME	LOCATION	COURSE or DEGREE	YEAR GRAD.	CLASS STANDING
HIGH SCHOOL					
COLLEGE					
GRADUATE SCHOOL					
APPRENTICE, BUSINESS OR VOCATIONAL SCHOOL					
OTHER TRAINING OR SPECIAL SKILLS					

CAN YOU TYPE? _____ Words/Min. _____ CAN YOU TAKE DICTATION? _____ Words/Min. _____

OUTSIDE INTERESTS _____

Figure 6.8. An example of an application blank used by a large industrial organization. (Courtesy of Ingersoll-Rand Company.)

involved the use of a template so that only certain items were scored for each department.

Application blanks have generally been shown to be reliable and valid. However, research completed in the practical situation often produces results that are contrary to published reports. One such study (Brown and Weiser, 1958) is reported here.

Women production workers in a single department of a large industrial

LIST ALL EMPLOYMENT BEGINNING WITH PRESENT OR MOST RECENT EMPLOYER.
ACCOUNT FOR ALL PERIODS, INCLUDING UNEMPLOYMENT & MILITARY SERVICE.   USE ADDITIONAL SHEET IF NECESSARY.

EMPLOYMENT HISTORY

DATES	NAME & ADDRESS OF EMPLOYER	1. JOB TITLE 2. DEPARTMENT	DESCRIBE MAJOR DUTIES	WAGES	REASON FOR LEAVING
FROM MONTH YEAR		1.		START $ per	
TO MONTH YEAR		2.		FINAL $ per	
FROM MONTH YEAR		1.		START $ per	
TO MONTH YEAR		2.		FINAL $ per	
FROM MONTH YEAR		1.		START $ per	
TO MONTH YEAR		2.		FINAL $ per	
FROM MONTH YEAR		1.		START $ per	
TO MONTH YEAR		2.		FINAL $ per	
FROM MONTH YEAR		1.		START $ per	
TO MONTH YEAR		2.		FINAL $ per	

MILITARY

BRANCH OF U.S. SERVICE	DATE ENTERED	DATE DISCHARGED	FINAL RANK	TYPE OF DISCHARGE	SERVICE NO.

SERVICE SCHOOLS _____

SPECIAL EXPERIENCE _____

RESERVE OR NATIONAL GUARD STATUS _____

NAME & ADDRESS OF UNIT _____

SELECTIVE SERVICE NO., CLASSIFICATION & DATE _____

REFERENCES

LIST THREE PERSONAL REFERENCES WHO ARE NOT RELATIVES OR FORMER SUPERVISORS

NAME_____ ADDRESS_____ OCCUPATION_____ YEARS KNOWN_____

NAME_____ ADDRESS_____ OCCUPATION_____ YEARS KNOWN_____

NAME_____ ADDRESS_____ OCCUPATION_____ YEARS KNOWN_____

PRE-EMPLOYMENT STATEMENT————————READ CAREFULLY

I affirm that the information given by me in this application is accurate and complete; I understand that any falsification will be considered ground for dismissal.
I authorize Ingersoll-Rand Company to investigate my record, including any information contained in this application for employment, except where my written statement specifically requests that no reference be made.   I agree not to hold any persons or organizations liable with respect to any information that they may give.
I authorize the examining physician to give a complete report concerning my pre-employment examination.
I agree to wear or use protective clothing or devices as required by the Company and to comply with all rules and regulations of the Company.

DATE_____   APPLICANT'S SIGNATURE_____

Figure 6.8.   *(Continued)*

organization were studied to measure the relationship between factors collected on the application blank and efficiency on the job. Eight variables (residential area, age, weight, height, education, number of dependents, marital status, and whether or not the person was a former employee) from the application blanks were correlated with efficiency ratings for a specified four-week period. None of the resulting correlations were found to be significantly different than zero. Multiple correlation coefficients were also insignificant. The general conclusion was that none of the studied predictors correlated well enough with efficiency rating to be used for selecting workers.

Another study completed by the author showed no significant relationships between currently used predictors and level of job success for salesmen. Studies showing such negative results rarely appear in print. However, men working in the practical selection situation know that there are times and places where popular selection devices will not work.

It is entirely possible for industrial organizations to provide such attractive personnel policies and employment standards within their community that they attract all the desirable productive and efficient workers they can possibly use. With good working conditions, security, good wages, and attractive physical appearance of the plant, workers are attracted who have more than the minimum basic qualities for success on the job. The usual predictors that might be important for selection then show no statistical relationship to job success.

WEIGHTED APPLICATION BLANK. Several organizations have had particular success in using the application blank for selection. They usually score the application blank in a weighted fashion.

The scoring techniques require an analysis of the application blank information compared to some criterion of success on the job. Efficiency ratings, dollar volume of sales, or other criteria mentioned earlier in this chapter are useful for comparison against application blank information.

The percentages of very successful workers of those answering application blank questions in various categories are computed and converted into weights for each of the categories. For example, of the employees living in the city where the plant is located, 70 percent are rated as high-level producers, whereas of those living in outlying areas, 40 percent are rated high level. A weight of 7 is assigned to an answer of living in the city and a 4 for living in outlying areas. Other items related to job success are assigned weights in the same manner. In this way, a total "score" for answers by an applicant can be obtained.

Application blanks, when used properly and checked against criterion of success on the job, may be just as valuable as some psychological tests and may be interpreted in the same manner. Thus total scores may be obtained by adding up the weights for various answers to questions on the application blank. Cut-off scores or "critical scores" for selection may be set.

Again, we must remember that the same application blank cannot always be used in all organizations. Each selection program presents a unique situation where a particular set of informational items must be used.

Consequently, to be most effective, application blanks need to be tailored and evaluated for each particular organization.

Weighted application blanks have been reported as successful selectors by many researchers (for example: Ohmann, 1941; Scollay, 1957; Fleishman and Berniger, 1960). However, we again remark that any selection technique may not be of value in a particular situation even though generally found useful.

Interviews. There are many definitions of an interview, but all include the general concept of purposeful conversation and a face-to-face relationship between two people. In the case of employment interviews, this means a representative of the organization and an applicant for employment carry on conversation for a purpose. The interview is useful for gaining and giving information by both parties. Specific points to be covered in the typical interview are obtaining information by means of specific answers to questions, gaining general subjective evaluations of a person, giving information, providing motivations for employment, and assessing behavior under standardized conditions.

Interviewing is a special technique that can be learned. Although there are interviewers with a special knack or ability that seems to have developed without special training, most good interviewers have worked hard to learn a good technique. Knowledge of how an interview takes place may help both the interviewer and the interviewee. Interviewing can be very valuable for the potential employer as well as for the applicant if handled appropriately.

Generally, there are two broad classes or types of interviews—the standardized and the informal, or "traditional." The traditional or informal interview is the type that most people are familiar with. In fact, most of us have participated in many informal interviews, such as discussing vocational plans with a teacher or discussing symptoms or diagnoses with a physician. Many people have also had experience with employment interviews of an informal or traditional type.

The informal interview has certain assets: (1) it is likely to place the applicant completely at ease, especially if the interviewer is sophisticated in his job, (2) it allows the interviewer to make an overall evaluation of the applicant and to form some general opinions, (3) it allows the applicants to evaluate the representative of management, and (4) it allows the interviewer to gather some very specific information concerning the applicant. A common complaint about the informal interview is that specific information comes as a by-product rather than as the major function of the interview. It is possible to miss the specific information that should be derived

```
                    INGERSOLL-RAND COMPANY              INTERVIEW RECORD      S
                    Phillipsburg, New Jersey            SHOP

    Name                        Soc. Sec. No.           Date
```

WORK HISTORY

Primary Ability_____

Secondary Abilities_____

Previous I-R Experience? Position? Type of Work? Location?_____

What machines can he operate? Set up? Years of experience? Type of work?_____

Can he read & use drawings?_____Micrometers?_____Scales?_____(Check Test Results)_____

Can he sharpen Tools? Which ones?_____

What kind of experience does he have with I-R or similar Products? Which ones?_____

Name of Present or Last Employer? Why left? Why looking for job at I-R?_____

Check of previous employers---

TRAINING

Formal Schooling--- 1 2 3 4 5 6 7 8 9 10 11 12   Location?_____

Trade School? Apprenticeship? Service Schools? When? Where? How long?_____

IMPRESSIONS

Appearance	- Neat & Clean	Fair	Sloppy or Dirty
Attitude	- Enthusiastic	Mildly interested	Bored or Antagonistic
Alertness	- Alert & Attentive	Fairly Alert	Daydreaming
Expression	- Easily expresses self	Average	Difficulty expressing self

Seemed most interested in--- Kind of job?_____Promotional Opportunities?_____Wages?_____

Working Hours?_____ Insurance & Fringes?_____ Vacations?_____

Figure 6.9. An example of a standardized interview form used by a large industrial organization. (Courtesy of Ingersoll-Rand Company.)

from an interview or to obtain different amounts of or types of information from various applicants.

The standardized or "patterned" interview has come into more popularity since the 1940's. This increased popularity is due to new knowledge of what goes on and what can be obtained in interviews. Many men such as McMurry (1947) have reevaluated earlier studies and conducted new research showing the value of patterned interviews. Personnel men have emphasized the importance of covering the same topics and gathering the

TEST RESULTS

State Employment Service _____

_____

_____

INGERSOLL-RAND TESTS   Purdue Mech. Adapt. _____Purdue Print Read. _____

                              Purdue Micro. Read._____Purdue Scale Read. _____

_____

_____

OTHER TESTS _____

_____

JOB SUITABILITY

TYPE OF WORK PREFERRED _____

WORK DISLIKED _____

SUITABLE FOR: 1._____   EXISTING OPENING?_____

                   2._____   EXISTING OPENING?_____

                   3._____   EXISTING OPENING?_____

COMMENTS

INTERVIEWER   DATE   SUPERVISOR   DATE

DISPOSITION

HIRED_____ DATE _____ DEPARTMENT _____

REJECTED _____ REFUSED OFFER _____ REASON _____

Figure 6.9.   *(Continued)*

same information in all interviews, especially when interviewing for one position in an organization.

In the standardized interview, a series of questions is used as a framework. These items are frequently printed on a form and available for the interviewer during the interview. Even so, a skillful interviewer makes such an interview seem completely informal. However, all questions concerning specific information are asked of every applicant, although not necessarily in the same order, so that a comparison of applicants can be made. Such standardized interview forms are sometimes coordinated with the application blank. In such a manner one aspect of the application blank—procuring clues for probing during the interview—is maximized. An example of such an interview form is shown in Figure 6.9. This interview form is used in conjunction with the application blank shown in Figure 6.8.

Thus the standardized interview has the same advantages as the informal interview plus providing more specific information comparable from one applicant to another. In addition, interviewer bias will generally not enter a standardized interview to as great an extent as an informal interview.

Interviewer bias is a tendency on the part of the interviewer to see or to respond to a particular applicant in a certain manner due to preconceived notions. For example, the interviewer may "know" that short, dark-haired workers are generally not as aggressive as tall, blond-haired workers. Consequently, the interviewer looks for signs of submission during interviews with short, dark-haired men. If he searches hard enough, he will find them and then record them in his notes. Standardized interviewing helps keep such bias in check by providing the questions to ask and subject matter to discuss.

Many interviews are carried on by representatives of management who have a number of other functions to cover. For example, a sales manager primarily responsible for production of sales, may also be responsible for interviewing applicants for new sales positions. It is difficult for such a person to be a good selector of men as well as a sales manager, but it is not impossible. Several specific points will help anyone do a better job of interviewing.

Rapport is essential for a thorough interview. Rapport refers to a comfortable relationship of mutual confidence between two people. In an employment situation, this generally means that the applicant feels he can say and act as he wishes and that there will be understanding and willingness to listen on the part of the interviewer. The interviewer must do everything he can to gain real information and not just superficial answers. As a first step in this direction he usually tries to put the applicant at ease. A typical method is to discuss things with which the applicant is very familiar. For example, interviewers begin by talking about a recent event, the weather, or even the applicant's home town and early schooling. This helps establish rapport and gets the applicant relaxed.

After creating a feeling of ease on the part of the applicant, the interviewer must continue to show real frankness and sincerity. He must be attentive and express interest when the applicant is talking. The interviewer does this by looking at the applicant, actively answering questions with sincerity and frankness, and asking relevant questions. A complete interviewing procedure cannot be given here, but may be found in many sources, including the United States Civil Service Commission reports (Mandell, 1956).

The primary function of an interview is to gain information that cannot be as rapidly or as adequately collected by any other method. This fact must remain uppermost in the thinking of the interviewer. He must remember never to get involved in arguments with the applicant. Arguing will not gain information and may create bad feelings that will carry over to the company represented by the interviewer. The interviewer must "turn the other cheek" if necessary and refrain from violently disagreeing with the applicant.

By the same token the interviewer should be careful not to provide answers for the applicant. Leading questions, such as "Don't you feel that our products are the best on the market?" should not be used. Such questions provide an answer for the applicant. Instead of stating his own feelings, he may try to anticipate the feelings of the interviewer and give an answer that is apparently desired.

Finally, an interview should end with a definite understanding by both parties as to what is going to happen next. Time should be allowed to close the interview with appropriate remarks. Usually the interviewer indicates when the applicant will hear from the organization and his appreciation for the applicant's applying to his organization for employment. Good rapport must be maintained through the end of the interview, and the interviewee should leave with a good feeling toward the organization represented by the interviewer.

Interviewing is the most used of all selection techniques. It seems "natural" and appeals to most management men. Although personnel departments, particularly in large organizations, have taken over many of the selection functions, executives usually have a chance for final approval or rejection of an applicant. Since this takes considerable time from busy executive schedules, some organizations have tried group interviewing.

A procedure called round-table interviewing has been tried in some companies (Willing, 1962). This procedure allows executives to see more applicants and at the same time reduces some variables in assessment of the applicants. Six to eight candidates are brought together around a table, introduced to each other, and given a list of discussion topics. A discussion leader is provided by the personnel department. Five executives involved in making the final hiring decisions are then brought into the room and introduced as executives of the company. They are not identified by name or title so that applicants will not "play up" to one executive. The executives do not sit together, they move after completion of each discussion topic, and they do not express approval or disapproval. The discussion leader starts the discussion and changes the topics when it seems appropriate. The executives observe, take notes, and then meet together to form a group opinion based on notes and short rating forms they have completed. This method has several advantages: (1) executives can make good comparisons of one applicant to others, because each applicant is observed at the same time in the same environment, (2) variations in executive interviewing skill are not as important, (3) applicants do not have to repeat the same information to several interviewers, and (4) the procedure takes less of everyone's time. Round-table interviewing may not be interviewing in the usual sense, but it is a practical approach to one step in most selection processes.

The information gathered during interviewing is usually combined in some form of report or scale. These evaluation reports can be compared from one interviewer to another to provide a reliability measure. Comparison of these protocols to job success measures provide an estimate of validity. Thus interviewing can be checked for reliability and validity.

Unfortunately, such checks are not as frequently carried out for interviews as for tests. However, many standardized interviews show good reliability and validity as selection devices for certain jobs.

Employment Tests. Two widely used techniques for estimating a job applicant's likelihood of future success as an employee, the personal interview and the application blank, are subjective. Both techniques may be unduly influenced by personal biases or prejudices. On the other hand, a psychological test is an objective, standardized procedure that measures in a relatively short period of time some characteristics of humans. By standardization we mean that uniform methods of administering and scoring the test are followed. Objectivity refers to freedom from subjective judgment of the examiner when tests are scored and interpreted. A good psychological test measures a small sample of behavior in a manner that indicates a score for an individual regardless of who happens to be his examiner. Generally, the characteristics could also be assessed by long-term acquaintance or extended interviewing. The major value of tests lies in the time-saving and in the more objective assessment.

A large variety of standardized tests is available. The reference publication, *Tests in Print* (Buros, 1961), indicated that in 1961 there were at least 2,126 tests in print. In this book, Dr. Buros briefly reviewed each of these tests and referred to other sources of information concerning psychological measurement. He also included a listing of previously available tests that were no longer in print. It is interesting to note that of the 2,126 entries included, about 88 percent were tests published in the United States.

This substantiates the opinion that as a nation, the United States believes in the value of psychological evaluation by the use of tests, in spite of the ridiculing of tests by some authors (Gross, 1962; Hoffman, 1962).

In this book we emphasize the following characteristics of testing: standardization, norms, test scores in use, and classification.

STANDARDIZATION. Standardization refers to uniformity in administering and scoring tests. If test scores of one individual are compared to another, they must both have been obtained under the same conditions. Most standardized tests provide uniform administration procedures. It is essential that these procedures be followed exactly as stated. Just presenting instructions in a different manner, or smiling or pausing at a crucial word, may influence the behavior of the testee during the testing. Physical surroundings should be standardized, and at very least should provide adequate lighting, proper ventilation, and freedom from discomfort. Finally, standard scoring procedures should be followed precisely.

NORMS. Norms are standards of performance of large groups useful in comparing an individual's test score with the scores of others. Psychological tests have no predetermined standards such as a 70, 80, or even a 100 as a passing or failing score. Instead, an individual's score is compared to other people's scores. Norms are available for most psychological tests.

Two types of norms are generally useful for employment tests, percentile scores and standard scores. A percentile norm is usually in the form of a table. It shows the percentages of a previously tested group that obtained each of the different raw scores on the test. Data is usually shown as a cumulative percentage—the percentage of people scoring equal to or better than a particular raw score. One such cumulative frequency distribution (norm) is shown in Figure 6.10.

Some tests make use of "standard" score norms. A "standard" score represents an individual's distance from the mean score of the group in terms of the standard deviation of the distribution. Technically, "standard" scores are the best type of scores in that they are directly comparable.

"Standard" scores are obtained by either linear or nonlinear transformations from the original raw scores. It is not in the province of this text to describe how to compute these scores. However, it is important to know that such test scores can be calculated. They are valuable in comparing performance of one individual against another or one individual's performance on a variety of tests. Raw scores are not directly comparable, but standard scores are.

Norms, no matter how expressed, are specific to a particular popula-

The Nelson-Denny Reading Test

%-ile Rank	Form B
99	573-615
96-98	488-551
93-95	438-475
90-92	391-425
87-89	368-379
84-86	356
81-83	344
78-80	327-333
75-77	319
72-74	309
69-71	299
66-68	290
63-65	279
60-62	269
57-59	
54-56	257
51-53	245
48-50	——Av
45-47	235
42-44	
39-41	226
36-38	
33-35	214
30-32	
27-29	203
24-26	195
21-23	
18-20	188
15-17	177
12-14	
9-11	165
6-8	153
3-5	117-141
0-2	106

Figure 6.10. An example of a norm for a standardized test. This norm is based on 961 adult students registered in efficient reading classes. The average student in this group reads better than the average college or university senior. To obtain a percentile rank, obtained score (reading speed in words per minute in this case) is located in the right-hand column. Percentile in matching lefthand column indicates the percentage of the norm group who read at that rate or slower. M. J. Nelson, E. C. Denny, and revised by J. I. Brown. "Nelson-Denny Reading Test," *Self-Interpreting Reading Profile*. Copyright 1960. Houghton Mifflin Company. Used by permission.

tion from which they were formed. In other words, it is not possible to evaluate performances of a high school freshman by comparison to a norm set up on college students. Most standard psychological tests have several sets of norms. In an employment situation, a suitable norm must be used to determine what an obtained raw score means. A specific set of norms for one company can be constructed after a suitable number of applicants have been tested. Such a specific norm is frequently of more value than any published with the test. It reflects the organization and their typical applicants. Thus, an applicant's score can be compared with the applicants usually tested. If the norms provided with the test are to be used, the sample group used must be investigated. A population with a great deal of variability in performance will yield a different set of norms than a relatively homogeneous population. The employment manager must not expect the same variability in performance from his applicants as the norm group if he is testing only applicants who have survived previous steps in the selection procedure while the norms are based on the general population.

TEST SCORES IN USE. After studying validity, reliability, and norms, it may appear that psychological tests are impractical for industrial selection. Low-validity correlation coefficients are frequently reported, and norms for a particular situation may be difficult or expensive to prepare. Fortunately, the employment manager does not need the same level of precision as does a clinician when working with an individual patient. We must also recognize that tests may not show significant relationship with productivity in a particular company and yet may provide a valuable function. The mere fact that a testing program is in effect may eliminate some very poorly qualified applicants who will not attempt to take the tests. At the same time some potentially good employees may be "scared off" by a testing program.

The employment manager must predict performance for a group. If he can increase the percentage of successful workers among the applicants hired over the percentage of successful workers hired before the use of tests, he can show that the tests are of value. Thus the employment manager is not especially interested in tests that would differentiate between people who are very poor or poor, nor between those who are good and very good. Instead, he must strive to improve the overall selection program. Both the validity of the tests and the available manpower are important to the success of a selection program.

Manpower may be difficult to obtain. In the extreme situation, there may be only one applicant for each job opening. In such a case, testing is of little value, since the man must be hired regardless of the test. On the other hand, if there are 30 applicants for one opening, hiring may be very selective. The ratio of the number of men that can be hired to the number evaluated is called the selection ratio. When the selection ratio is low (one man out of 30 can be hired), even a test with low validity may be useful. When the selection ratio is high, tests must have high-validity coefficients to be useful.

A test with low validity is not as efficient for selecting potentially successful workers as is a test with high validity. But if a low-validity test can be used in a low-selection ratio situation, only very high-scoring applicants would have to be accepted. In such a situation the test can be very useful.

In the employment situation, a critical score is often used as one of the "hurdles" in the hiring procedure. A critical score is one selected so that the probabilities of job success are greater for those who score above than those who score below. The use of a critical score simplifies the hiring procedure. After an applicant's test is scored, he can immediately be rejected or accepted for further analysis in the selection procedure.

A critical score is raised or lowered according to the practical situation. When the selection ratio is low, the critical score may be raised. Where the selection ratio is high, it must be lowered. Where a selection ratio is such that the critical score is forced low, the test is not providing as much value in the selection procedure as when the critical score is higher.

Testing is probably more valuable as a method of selection than any other technique. Even so, tests must be used appropriately, and refinements must be made. Personnel men with the responsibility for using tests or other devices must use them for the proper purposes. One manager of personnel research (Gillerman, 1963), in a reply to test critics, emphasized just such points when he stated, ". . . tests are a considerably more effective procedure, when used in appropriate circumstances, than their detractors would have us believe, despite all their criticism."

CLASSIFICATION OF TESTS.   Standardized psychological tests may be classified according to any one of several different characteristics. The most common test classifications are speed versus power, group versus individual, language versus nonlanguage, performance versus paper and pencil, and subject matter measured. Any one test may be classified into all of the above-mentioned categories. For example, the Stanford–Binet Intelligence Scale was primarily a power test, an individual test, a verbal or language test, a performance test, and a measure of intelligence.

Speed tests are administered with a fixed time limit beyond which the applicant is not permitted to work, even though he has not completed all of the questions. Power tests are administered with unlimited time. A great many aptitude tests, including intelligence tests, are timed, whereas some performance tests are power measures.

As the name implies, individual tests are administered to one person at a time. A group test is more economical to administer and is most frequently used in industry because many individuals can be tested at one time with one proctor. Individual tests are of greater value for clinical and guidance work, in that an appraisal of the testee may be made during the testing situation.

Paper-and-pencil tests have applicants write or check answers to written questions. Performance tests require manipulation of apparatus or equipment. The apparatus involved may be bulky and can usually be handled by only one person at a time. However, some psychological measures cannot be obtained by paper-and-pencil tests, so that performance tests must be used. Such tests are more difficult to create and score objectively and usually must be individual measures. Thus they are expensive. Paper-and-pencil tests require little apparatus and are less expensive.

Almost all tests are language or verbal tests. There have been attempts to create nonlanguage or nonverbal tests, but in general, these have not been very satisfactory, because some language is needed. Nonlanguage measures are used when there is a language difficulty, as, for example, in testing immigrants.

Tests are also classified according to the function they measure. Such a general classification may be (1) achievement, (2) aptitude, (3) intelligence, (4) personality, and (5) sensory-motor skills. Examples of each of the five classes will be discussed in the following sections. Complete references and descriptions of the tests are available in several sources, including the *Mental Measurements Yearbooks* (Buros, 1959) and the previously mentioned *Tests in Print* (Buros, 1961).

ACHIEVEMENT OR PROFICIENCY TESTS. When the employment manager is interested in seeking employees with a certain ability or knowledge, he uses an achievement test. An achievement test measures a specific skill or proficiency. Such tests are standardized and are commercially available, but are frequently constructed for individual situations. A series of achievement tests has been prepared by California Test Bureau and is available under the title California Achievement Tests. These tests are for academic achievement. Also well known are the Graduate Record Examinations, achievement tests in social sciences, humanities, and natural sciences for testees with at least undergraduate college education. For employment purposes, standardized achievement tests in bookkeeping, stenography, typewriting, and so on, are available.

APTITUDE TESTS. Aptitude tests are designed to measure capacity to acquire a particular knowledge or skill. Although an achievement test measures the knowledge or ability already possessed by an individual, an aptitude test estimates how well or rapidly a person will be able to acquire knowledge or skill. Aptitude tests are generally of value in industrial situations where there is an insufficient pool of skilled personnel. For newly created jobs, aptitude tests are essential, because no skilled labor pool is available.

Aptitude tests measure capacity to attain information, not the desire to do so. Aptitude test scores for specific abilities are frequently used in employment situations. There are also general aptitude tests to estimate ability to learn in a variety of fields. One such test is the Differential Aptitude Test published by the Psychological Corporation. Scores are obtained in seven areas: verbal reasoning, numerical ability, abstract reasoning, space relations, mechanical reasoning, clerical speed and accuracy, and language usage. Other multiple aptitudes tests are also available. Some measure different characteristics, but all estimate ability to learn in a variety of areas.

One commonly used specific aptitude test is the S.R.A. Mechanical Aptitudes Test. This test estimates the ability of a person to learn mechanical functions. It may be useful for selecting machine operators when achievement tests are not practical.

INTELLIGENCE TESTS.   Although there is not unanimity of opinion on the part of psychologists as to what intelligence is, most agree that it has something to do with mental alertness. Many psychologists agree that it has to do with the ability to learn in general and to solve unusual problems. Intelligence also is involved in manipulating concepts, taking in information through the senses, and controlling behavior.

One of the earliest applications of psychology to the industrial world was the use of general intelligence tests for selection of personnel. During World War I, the United States Army adopted the Army Alpha and the Army Beta Examinations for measurement of general intelligence. In fact, the early history of applied psychology is closely tied to the development of the measurement of intelligence.

Intelligence tests measure a general aptitude to learn. Thus, an applicant who receives a high score on an intelligence test may be assumed to have the ability to learn most subjects relatively rapidly. When coupled with scores from aptitude tests, a pattern or profile of the special ability and general ability to learn is formed. For most employers, a general level of intelligence is all that is needed. This can be estimated by the use of quick screening intelligence tests.

Some commonly used intelligence tests in industrial situations are (1) Wonderlic Personnel Test, (2) Otis Higher Mental Examination, and (3) Civilian form of the Army General Classification Tests. These tests are all group tests. However, individual tests such as the Wechsler Adult Intelligence Scale or the Revised Stanford–Binet Intelligence Scale may be used for special situations. (These tests are discussed in some detail in Chapter 4 of this book.)

A large number of intelligence tests is available. Most of them have been well standardized. On the other hand, the validity of an intelligence test must be checked for each particular job. Published reports tend to question even the relationship of intelligence and college grades (Amrine, 1963). A minimum critical score is of importance, but there seems to be little relationship between intelligence test scores and grades for people scoring higher than the critical score.

PERSONALITY TESTS. For many occupations, personality is the major variable of importance. It is also the most difficult characteristic to assess and one where coefficients with job success are frequently low. The more objective measurements and techniques available for estimating intelligence, aptitude, and specific skills have been well substantiated in years of testing. Estimates of personality are still frequently in the experimental stage. Two types of measurements are used at this time: (1) paper-and-pencil inventories, and (2) projective techniques. (A more detailed discussion of personality tests is continued in Chapter 4 of this book.)

Paper-and-pencil inventories, as the name implies, are techniques of obtaining information about an individual on a paper form. They ask the person to indicate his interests, likes, dislikes, and so on. They are often transparent in that an applicant can estimate what might be the best answer for a particular job. Consequently, they can be "thrown" or biased. For this and other reasons there are often low-validity coefficients between personality inventories and success on the job.

Interest in personality assessment has been directed toward projective techniques that are not as transparent. An individual testee does not know the correct answer and cannot bias the results as easily. Unfortunately, evidence of the value of such devices for industrial selection is not too conclusive. The entire area of personality assessment is one of great interest and importance, but there are many questions not answered by available assessment techniques. One author (Ingenohl, 1957), stated in an article for management personnel: "What personality tests, in fact, are saying to you is this: If you know what you are looking for, we will help you to describe 'it' so that others, too, can look for the same thing. We will also help you to know when you have found 'it.' What you then do with 'it' is for you to THINK about, because this is the one thing that we cannot do for you, Mr. Personnel Manager!"

The Bernreuter Personality Inventory is an example of a paper-and-pencil personality assessment that has been used in industry for many years. Unfortunately, correlations between the test and success on the job have varied considerably, and the inventory is subject to the possibility of bias or being "thrown." A newer test, the Edwards Personal Preference Schedule, is designed as an estimate of personality of more or less normal people. This test has been shown to be useful in some organizations, whereas in others validity-correlation coefficients have been low.

SENSORY-MOTOR SKILLS. This general classification of tests includes tests for specific dexterities frequently mentioned in psychological literature as specialized tests. For example, manual dexterity eye–hand coordination, tweezer dexterity, all have shown positive relationship to success in various jobs.

Figure 6.11. A photograph of a job applicant being tested on the O'Connor Tweezer Dexterity Test. (Courtesy of Weller Electric Corp.)

Two old but well-known estimates of motor skill are the O'Connor Finger Dexterity Test and the O'Connor Tweezer Dexterity Test (see Figure 6.11). The Purdue Peg Board has been in use for many years as an estimate of ability that may be useful for mechanical operations.

In general, sensory-motor tests are not as frequently used in industry now as they were in the 1930's and 1940's, although they often have great value for specific situations. The relationships between job success and scores obtained on these tests vary, but are generally lower than desired.

RESULTS OBTAINED WITH PSYCHOLOGICAL SELECTION TOOLS

Do psychological tools help in the selection process? Of course they must or business and industry would not use them. The question then is how much value is there in a program using psychological tools for selecting workers.

There must be thousands of studies reporting the validities and reliabilities of single psychological tools and complete selection batteries. Most standardized tests have manuals that include reliability and validity data. The list of suggested references for further study at the end of this chapter includes many excellent sources of information about the usefulness of selection techniques. However, most of the studies must be read with the knowledge that the reliabilities and validities reported in one situation will not necessarily apply in all situations. Thus we will not report case histories here.

The general conclusion that we must draw is that adequately used psychological tools can increase the accuracy of selection programs. Most studies report such effective use of psychological tools. When they are used appropriately, the psychological tools save money and effort for the organizations and help the potential workers enter jobs where they are likely to succeed and to be happy.

SUMMARY

Employment psychology represents one of the oldest applications of psychology to problems of the business world. Early attempts at measuring individual differences in humans were soon applied to selecting men for jobs.

In order to do a good job of selecting and placing workers an understanding of the functions involved in work is necessary. Job descriptions are developed to describe specific activities involved in work. Selection then is the process of finding a man who can perform the activities of a certain job. Since men are hired before we know how well they perform on the job, predictors of their performance are used.

The major predictors are application blanks, interviews, and psychological tests. Each of these predictors provides a "hurdle" that must be passed by an applicant when going through a typical selection process. The consistency of the predictor in measuring some aspects of human ability or capacity is called reliability. The degree to which the predictor is related to success on the job is called validity. Each predictor must be reliable and valid to be of use in the selection system. Specific examples of many predictors have been discussed. Many studies show predictors to be reliable and valid for employment usage. In the practical situation, an evaluation of all predictors combined is most often used to aid in selecting employees. Even so, predictive devices cannot be expected to do the work of the personnel manager. They are aids and must be interpreted for each particular situation.

As a final word of caution, it is pertinent to cite an industrial psychologist (Bassett, 1962) who wrote that although most personnel managers believe they are selecting the best candidates for employment, they are in effect systematically rejecting applicants until there are just the right number of survivors. By the use of "cut-off" scores in "successive hurdle" selection programs, unfit applicants are properly rejected. However, such a system generally ignores the positive qualifications of men, and these must be remembered. Bassett reminds us that once suitable rejection standards are set, the personnel function should shift strongly to the evaluation of accepted applicants' success on the job. A low score on a test may be related with failure on a job, but a high score may be associated only with moderate success. Measurable behavior and personality patterns of successful employees and top-notch employees should be sought and eventually worked into selection requirements. A major function of a psychologist or other behavioral scientist is to design and carry out the appropriate research to gain maximum value from the selection and placement programs.

The job of the behavior scientist in the selection and placement procedures is in designing studies and evaluating programs. As more work is completed, better selection devices will become available for use.

SUGGESTED REFERENCES FOR FURTHER STUDY

Educational and Psychological Measurement.
    This journal carries the results of validation studies of tests in various uses.

Personnel and Guidance Journal.
    This journal regularly includes a test review section called "Testing the Test" which presents up-to-date reviews of new tests.

Personnel Psychology.
    This journal provides current studies and information concerning personnel procedures. Each issue also contains a section called "Validity Information Exchange," which provides current validation studies of specific tests in use in various situations.

Anastasi, A. (1961). *Psychological Testing.* New York: Macmillan Company.
    A book covering principles of psychological testing, tests, and comprehensive references and sources for information about tests.

Buros, O. K. (1961). *Tests in Print.* Highland Park, N.J.: The Gryphon Press.
    A book presenting a comprehensive bibliography of tests available as well as previously in print in English-speaking countries. This is a useful index for the reviews contained in the *Mental Measurements Yearbook.*

———— (1959). *The Fifth Mental Measurements Yearbook.* Highland Park, N.J.: The Gryphon Press.

The fifth of a series of books including reviews of most tests published in the United States and Great Britain. Each yearbook presents one or more reviews of each new test published since the last yearbook. Factual descriptions and a bibliography for each test are included.

Dorcus, R. M., and M. H. Jones (1950). *Handbook of Personnel Selection.* New York: McGraw-Hill Book Company.

A book bringing together a variety of validation studies, cross-indexed by title of test and type of work performed by workers.

Murphy, J. M. (1963). *Handbook of Job Facts.* Chicago, Ill.: Science Research Associates.

This third edition contains concise summaries of basic facts about 237 major occupations. This includes descriptions of the functions performed, educational and training requirements, normal working hours, pay and so on.

Chapter 7

Training in Industry

and Business

AFTER THE BEST MAN has been selected for a job he must learn to handle the work at optimum efficiency. To help the man improve his output, industrial organizations have long used a variety of training techniques. In fact, written records from the early 1600's show indentures of men to businesses for the purpose of apprenticeship training. Today, perhaps more than ever before, training is essential and is being given even more careful consideration. Maximum efficiency on a job can be obtained only when a worker performs in an efficient manner. Such a performance is rarely discovered without guidance. Thus training is essential for high-level, efficient production.

In the second half of the twentieth century, industrial production is undergoing rapid change. New methods of using machinery and rapid strides in the development of automated production methods are being developed. Not so many years ago another rapid change in the industrial scene took place when individual handicraft gave way to production lines and mass production. The change from handicraft, or complete construction from raw materials to the finished product by one individual, to newer mass production methods forced business to do more training. Standardized procedures and techniques were essential for uniformity of production. This was essential for construction of finished items from subassemblies. In the twentieth century the revolution is being brought into industry as the result of new technological advances, particularly in the use of machines that can complete all production of goods with relatively little human work. Large, new enterprises are run by relatively few men aided by electronic computers. Complete oil refining distilleries are handled by only a few men with control panels and electronic gear. Many production facilities are now using programmed machines that produce the desired products on a particular schedule with only relatively high skilled technicians available to maintain the equipment. Retraining of men is being emphasized. Special governmental commissions and committees are forming to set up emergency training programs aimed at increasing the capabilities of displaced workers.

In addition to these considerations, skills in supervisory functions are also of increasing importance and are increasingly recognized as essential techniques. As industries grow, the number of supervisory personnel involved increases. This also increases the number of supervisory levels, and it becomes more and more important that the supervisor know how to manipulate men rather than machinery. The primary function of most supervisors involves human relationships. They must encourage and coordinate the work of others. Thus the training of supervisory personnel is increasingly essential.

In many companies training is considered only for indoctrination. As a matter of fact, a study by Mellenbruch (1961) showed that many industries use little or no training. Such organizations involve a little training during a worker's indoctrination period and believe that training can be forgotten after the employee attains his "rate" or production level. This concept of training is indeed shortsighted. Training is a process of development that ideally continues as long as the individual has not reached his full capacity. This is especially important for the new emphasis on higher levels of skill or capacity of the individual employee, with machines doing more and more of the lower-level tasks.

This chapter will cover methods of determining training needs, setting of objectives, organizing training, and training for special groups such as supervisors. Frequently, the reader will note topics concerning learning or areas that were covered thoroughly in the first chapter of this book.

DETERMINING TRAINING NEEDS

Naturally every training program should be based on a company need. Although this is rather obvious, it is also important to recognize that the need for training is not always completely understood. In fact, there are some organizations that occasionally train workers simply because they have a training department or feel that it is desirable, because it is the popular way in modern-day industry. Such occurrences are relatively rare, but a great deal of training is done on a "put-out supplier" basis. In such cases, the only study of need for training is an urgency study. A particular job is not being handled correctly and management insists on improvement, so training is begun; or a new job is established and it is "obvious" that training is needed. Thus, long-term, well-understood general programs of training may not be carried out.

The determination of training needs is difficult, and thus specific training needs are frequently ill-conceived or nonexistent. Automation, rapid expansion, new procedures for material handling, or even a high accident rate frequently stir an organization to emergency training methods. Thus objective measures of production are frequently used as estimates of needs for training. Another approach, rarely used, is to ask employees what kind of training they think they need. This technique is becoming more popular, especially at supervisory level training.

Probably a better way is to have an overall analysis of the entire situation in an organization by a training analyst or other person specializing in this field. The importance of such an analysis of training needs was discussed by Mahler and Monroe (1952). After asking the training directors of 150 companies their preferences for various methods of estimating training needs for production, clerical, supervisory, and technical employees, a summary record was produced. Table 7.1 shows the results of the study. Observation of Table 7.1 shows that training directors preferred informal observation, requests from management, talks with supervisors, group discussions, and analysis of work as methods of determining training needs.

The general questions needing answers concerning training needs are these: What areas of company production need training? Which workers need training? What do the workers need to know that they do not know at this time? Previously mentioned sections on job analysis and job description are extremely useful in determining training needs. Comparisons of job descriptions with performance of individuals provide data for an analysis that can be useful in estimating training needs.

After a thorough analysis of training needs it may appear that everyone needs training. This may be impractical, and most training directors agree that if you cannot train everyone, you must give consideration to economic conditions when starting a training program. Although it might seem advisable to train top-level management first, because their salaries are the highest and their decisions are most influential from an economic standpoint, they are the most difficult personnel to train and the ones for whom the least knowledge is available. On the other hand, training of workers who deal with relatively expensive materials and machinery at a relatively low skill level can be accomplished at a fairly low cost per employee. Such training may result in marked changes in workers' behavior and therefore be of great economic value to the company.

TABLE 7.1 Percentages of 150 Training Directors Prefering Various Methods of Determining Training Needs for Three Different Types of Employees *

METHOD OF DETERMINING TRAINING NEEDS	TYPE OF EMPLOYEES		
	PRODUCTIVE %	CLERICAL %	TECHNICAL-SUPERVISORY %
Informal observation	12	12	11
Requests from management	17	16	15
Talks with supervisors	16	17	14
Talks with non-supervisors	4	6	3
Group discussions	10	10	13
Training advisory committees	5	5	6
Questionnaires to supervisors	2	2	2
Questionnaires to trainees	1	2	4
Supervisory morale survey	1	1	4
Employee morale survey	4	4	2
Tests	3	4	2
Merit ratings	4	6	4
Intensive interview with supervisors	2	4	4
Interview with union officials	2	1	4
Analysis of reports (costs, turnover, grievances, etc.)	12	7	7
Other	4	3	3
Total	100**	100	100**

* W. R. Mahler and W. H. Monroe (1952), *How Industry Determines the Need and Effectiveness of Training*. Contract report to Personnel Research Section, Adjutant General's Office, The Psychological Corporation, New York, New York.
** Columns total less than 100% due to rounding errors.

Naturally, the decision as to whom to train first must be made after a review of the situation in the individual organization. The role of a trainer is often as an advisor to the management personnel in the company. When the supervisors feel that training is needed for their workers, the training department should attempt to provide adequate training with the co-operation of the supervisors. Of course, there are occasions when supervisors are not qualified to act as trainers or even to estimate the training needs. In such situations the training department should be available to provide these functions.

After determining training needs, a program to accomplish these needs must be designed. This involves setting up objectives to fill each of the training needs.

Setting Objectives. To be effective training programs must have well-defined goals and objectives. They must be specific. One should not state that truck drivers need to be skillful in handling trucks, but rather that they should be able to do certain very specific functions, as for example, parking in a space no longer than the truck plus seven feet, or backing through an alley 15 feet long with 10 inches clearance on each side of the truck, and so on. When properly written, training objectives prepared in advance provide bench marks for evaluation of the training program so that subsequently even more effective training programs can be devised. Training objectives generally fall into one of the various categories suggested below.

One of the most obvious needs, and therefore an objective of training, is to increase production. This may mean the increasing of production for workers who have had experience on the job, or it may mean bringing new people into the job and therefore training relatively naive workers. Job analysis reports discussed earlier in this book are essential in setting objectives for production training. The job criterion is frequently useful as a measure of skill acquired. In fact, a minimum level of performance to be attained before release from the training program is often stated in the job analysis. It is particularly important that the training objectives be clearly stated and that the effectiveness of training in meeting these objectives be measured.

Another obvious area related to suitable production is reduction of waste. Training aimed at increasing production may result in relatively low-quality products with a good deal of waste. Thus specific emphasis on waste reduction is frequently an objective of training.

The reduction of accidents or the increase of safety is a prominent objective of training. This is such an important topic that an entire section will be related to accidents and safety in Chapter 8 of this book. However, it is important that it be recognized as a training objective when designing the training program.

An area receiving increasing publicity is sometimes referred to as "job enlargement." This is particularly valuable in organizations subject to changes in production. Job enlargement means training individual workers to handle a variety of different jobs. Thus workers may be switched from one type of activity to another when different orders are obtained by the company or when obsolescence decreases the usefulness of certain production facilities. Job enlargement has received a good deal of publicity, not only from the training standpoint, but also as it affects the psychological environment of workers who feel that they have more value in life in general and more security on their job when they know how to handle a variety of different occupations. Job enlargement also has an influence on the supervisory personnel. Lagemann (1954) stated, "In giving the employee more responsibility, job enlargement changes his relationship with the boss. Perhaps it's more accurate to say it changes the boss. Instead of policing his employees to see that they turn in 'a fair day's work for a fair day's pay,' his job is rather to coordinate their efforts, consult them on decisions involving their jobs, and generally act as a team leader rather than as a taskmaster." Lagemann was emphasizing job enlargement as training workers to carry out many aspects of production on one product, such as setting up the machinery, running the machine, and inspecting the finished production. Training for job enlargement needs more attention as new techniques in automation become more important in industry.

Another area of training deserving emphasis is that of broadening the background of workers. This training most frequently takes place when organizations are doing well financially rather than in poor economic times. But many organizations are beginning to recognize the value of always providing their employees skills and knowledge outside of the functions necessary for the specific work situation. For example, the International Harvester Company encourages educational programs designed primarily to raise the cultural level of their workers. They support courses in high schools and colleges in areas that are of interest to the employees and not specifically related to the work situation. The company thus hopes to raise the morale of the workers in general and to allow them to appreciate the values of the American system of government. This is a relatively new area of training receiving some interest, but it is not popular with many organizations at this time. It will become of more importance with the trend to shorter work weeks and more leisure time.

Another area of training of great importance is in the field of human relations. This, of course, receives most emphasis in training of supervisory personnel. There is agreement that the primary objective of supervisory training programs is to get supervisors to understand interaction among humans. This usually means breaking down misunderstandings about employee–supervisory relationships and learning about individual differences, attitudes, influences, motivations, and frustrations; thus the supervisor achieves a greater tolerance and acceptability from the workers.

In recent years human behavioral engineering has been developed in an attempt to bring learning theory as discussed in Chapter 1 to bear upon work situations. Control of workers by supervisors can be accomplished by applying information now known to behavioral science. Thus the supervisors must understand how individual behavior can be changed in response to stimulation from the environment. An important objective of a supervisory training program should be an understanding of behavioral engineering.

METHODS OF TRAINING

After evaluating the needs and studying the objectives of training, a company wishing to establish a training program must decide on the kind of teaching or the presentation technique to be utilized. In Chapter 1 of this book we discussed principles of learning, methods of increasing efficiency of learning, and programed instruction. This material should be reviewed, for it is vital to industrial training, but it will not be repeated here. Although programed instruction is gaining wide favor in industry four traditional techniques account for most of the training of workers. These techniques are apprenticeship training, vestibule school, on-the-job training, and outside training.

Apprenticeship Training.   Perhaps the oldest of all techniques used for training skilled workers is the apprenticeship technique. Characteristically, it involves a relatively prolonged preparation, the period lasting anywhere from one to seven years, although a typical period at the present time is approximately four years in length. During this time the apprentice works with the skilled journeyman and learns by observing and assisting.

Although apprenticeship training today is different in some respects from apprenticeship programs of many years ago, there are still many similarities. In some organizations, apprenticeship programs are simply a form of inexpensive labor. Little or no instruction is actually given the apprentice. Instead, he merely serves his time under a craftsman, picking up information as best he can. In some industries, it is virtually impossible to obtain a position without serving a period of "indenture," almost as in the eighteenth century, when an apprentice was legally "bound" to a skilled craftsman.

There has been a good deal of interest in stimulating wider adoption of the apprenticeship program, especially with good standards for training. In 1934 the Federal Committee on Apprenticeship Training was established, and standards were drawn up and recommended to all those who assumed responsibility for apprentices. Studies by the National Industrial Conference Board (NICB) revealed that in 1939, 57.5 percent of the 453 companies questioned had some regular form of apprenticeship training. By 1948 only 38.6 percent of the 360 companies surveyed had apprenticeship training programs. Of 500 companies surveyed in 1954, 38.5 percent still had some apprenticeship programs for hourly workers (NICB, 1954).

Assuming the NICB used a representative cross section of industry on both surveys, the difference in percentage indicates a real drop in use of apprenticeship programs from 1939 to 1948. This is in spite of the efforts to improve the training in apprentice types of programs. In 1943 the War

Manpower Commission Bureau of Training specified that the training period for apprentices should not be less than 4,000 hours and that shop instructions should be accompanied by not less than 144 hours of instructions under a public authority. This forced apprenticeship programs to seek qualified instructors as well as tradesmen or craftsmen and may have had an influence in forcing industry to look further outside of the craftsmen for training other apprentices. With increases in mass production, there has generally been a reduction in the proportion of employees who must be skilled tradesmen. In fact it is estimated that less than 1 percent of the total working force in the United States are at this time apprentices in training for skilled tradesmen jobs. Rapid changes in mechanization and modernization of organizations have brought about situations where skilled tradesmen cannot afford to spend the time necessary for a typical apprenticeship program. Consequently, other methods of training grew in importance for several years. Apparently apprenticeship training has maintained the same level of importance since 1948.

Apprenticeship training is still frequently tied to acceptability for admission to a trade union. Thus the apprenticeship training program becomes a joint effort on the part of management and union to create well-qualified workers, competent to handle a high level of production in skilled trades. A well-executed program has some distinct advantages for the employee and the company operating the program.

For the company, the apprenticeship program insures a steady flow of new skilled men to replace those who are leaving through retirement, upgrading, and so on. The indenture agreement of apprenticeship sometimes binds the apprentice to his company for a stated period of time after completion of the apprenticeship program. In addition, the graduate apprentice is trained in a variety of functions and thus can adapt readily to change in methods of production with a minimum of retraining. During their apprenticeship, workers' pay is generally lower than average, but the incentive of guaranteed higher pay as a craftsman is apparent to help encourage them to complete the training program. Finally, of course, the apprenticeship program combines working with learning on the job so that there is little need to worry about transfer of training from the learning situation to the actual work situation.

Most of the same points listed as advantages for management are advantages for the apprentices. They are trained in broad areas and thus are relatively less susceptible to technological unemployment. Apprentices are usually guaranteed a fairly substantial pay raise upon completion of the training program and usually a good bargaining position from then on as skilled workers.

Apprenticeship programs with special training for the craftsman involved can be extremely valuable to industry. As more advances in automation raise the level of skill needed by the men employed in industry, reevaluation of apprenticeship programs should be considered.

On-the-Job Training. Even though apprenticeship training is a very old technique, it is probably not as old as on-the-job training. This is by far the most common technique of training in American industry. According to a survey of over 500 establishments, over 50 percent use this technique (NICB, 1954). Essentially, it is the placing of the new employee as a learner with a skilled workman. It is similar to the apprenticeship program in this respect, but it does not bind a new worker to a set period of time in a subservient position, nor guarantee him a higher-level job after training, but rather allows him to learn while working.

The biggest advantages of this system are the simplicity and the alleged economy. Unfortunately, adequate statistics concerning the latter are not available, but the aspects of simplicity have been verified in terms of the amount of effort needed by management to establish such a program and the number of special technicians needed to carry out the program. Obviously, using the available production manpower to do the training of new workers may be a detriment to production, but at the same time, it does not show up in terms of additional training costs, because no special personnel are hired to do the instruction.

Even though the on-the-job training technique seems to involve no outside expense for special instructors or equipment, there very likely are considerable hidden costs and disadvantages. Workmen and foremen must take time from their regular functions to instruct the trainees. This means that regular production line equipment is tied up for periods of time when highly skilled employees would ordinarily maintain regular production. There is also the danger that the emphasis on production line speed and accuracy is so great that a learner has a much harder time learning than he would have in a pure training situation. Furthermore, although he may want to do the best job possible and be extremely conscientious in his activities, the average working man or foreman is not especially skilled as a trainer.

Naturally there are real advantages in on-the-job training as well as the apparent economy of no special training facilities. An often cited advantage to management and workers is that learning is done on the machines where production will take place (see Figure 7.1). Thus there is no transfer-of-training problem. It is also an advantage to have superior production workers teach their techniques to new employees, if they have the ability to train others. (Some organizations are training key workers to be trainers so that the experience of the skilled workers will be passed on to the new workers.)

On-the-job training is a term widely used and misused. In some organizations it is an excuse for no formal training at all. Where a real effort

Figure 7.1. A photograph of on-the-job training with the worker learning on a regular production machine. (Courtesy of Weller Electric Corp.)

at training is carried out, a systematic and organized program of on-the-job training is followed. Such programs can be very valuable and economical. The worker acting as a trainer must be secure in his job, perhaps even compensated specially for his training functions and not penalized for decreases in his own production. He must realize the importance of the training function as well as the importance of production on the job. At the same time it is crucial that workers be trained in proper methods of performing a job before they have an opportunity to learn to do it the wrong way. If on-the-job training allows a worker to pick out techniques of work by himself and incorrect procedures are learned, they must later be corrected, often with extreme difficulty and high expense.

In many organizations, trainers work in production unless there is training to be accomplished. Thus they have "on the spot" experience and know the situation adequately. If these trainers have suitable knowledge of training techniques and individual differences and capacities of individuals, they can provide valuable instruction.

Vestibule Training. The word *vestibule* is really a misnomer today, but is a carryover from early days when training was done in the separate entry room to the main production facilities. Now a separate room or building equipped with production equipment, staffed with instructors and designed primarily for training of workers, is often called a vestibule school. This is really a miniature production facility where the new workers learn their jobs under conditions similar to those that will be found in the working environment, but under skilled instructors and without the pressures of regular production. Very few companies currently use this technique for training production workers. The previously mentioned survey done in 1954 showed fewer than 5 percent of over 500 companies used vestibule training (NICB, 1954).

Ordinarily, the aim of a vestibule school is to teach the new workers how to operate a particular machine and not to develop all-around crafts-men. It is especially useful in developing large numbers of workers for expansion or specialized workers for production line jobs. The big pro-duction increases necessitated by World War I and World War II forced many companies into vestibule training. Large numbers of workers were needed in a very short period of time, and industry could not risk the available production facilities with on-the-job trainees. Consequently vesti-bule schools were established.

A vestibule school has several advantages. It is specially designed to train workers and thus provide a relatively unhurried atmosphere conducive to learning. The regular production workers and supervisory staff are freed from training functions, and specialists skilled in handling learners are employed in training. Regular production is not impeded by the delays of the spoiled work of the novice, and the psychological impact of the learner's being afraid of hurting regular production is gone. Thus the learner has a more desirable atmosphere in which to establish his new skills. Since the function of the vestibule school is training and not production, a greater amount of individualized attention can be given to the learning of the function by the new workers. In slack time, workers from sections that may be modified by the introduction of new techniques can be brought into vestibule schools for training.

Primary among the disadvantages is the expense involved. A separate school must be established, and if there are not a sufficient number of workers steadily being trained, facilities may be dormant for a good deal of the time. There is also a feeling that the vestibule school provides training in a situation that is not normal, because once the worker completes his training in the vestibule school, he is placed in a production room that is different. Often too, the vestibule school does not contain production line machinery but receives the old machines from the production facilities. Thus workers are trained on one kind of machine and in one situation, whereas later they are asked to perform in a different environment. Moreover, it is difficult in the working world to find instructors who constantly keep abreast of the changes in manufacturing processes and skills, and who also understand humans well enough to be good teachers.

Outside Training. Without formal attempts on the part of industry, a good deal of the training that is of value to business and industry is accomplished outside of the individual company. Most people being hired have had several years of formal education, and many have completed high school. Thus a certain amount of outside training is provided for almost any industrial job.

More and more, there is emphasis in the training programs of high schools and some colleges and universities or specialty schools to prepare individuals for industry. Some secondary schools offer special courses in their vocational and trade programs to prepare graduates to handle specific jobs within industry. By cooperating with the school authorities, industries have been able to set up functions in the public schools similar to those that are carried out in vestibule schools. Industrial organizations have contributed machines and technical manuals as well as expert advice to the schools in their area. Thus graduated students are able to enter industry at a fairly skilled level.

Many business organizations now look to colleges and universities as well as secondary schools for special courses for their workers. In cooperation with industry, courses in supervision, management, human relations, sales training and production line techniques have been established in secondary schools and colleges. These courses are available to the public at large, but are primarily supported by the industries in the area. Such courses constitute a real value in the training for the industrial organization and at the same time enhance the offerings of the individual schools to the public at large.

The disadvantages of such outside training are similar to those found in vestibule training. Particularly, it is possible to find industries contributing machines and technical knowhow concerning production that is almost obsolete even in their own plant. Consequently the learner does not get experience on machines that will be of real value to him when he enters industry. Another disadvantage is that minimum standards and techniques in the secondary schools, universities, and colleges are not necessarily applicable to the working situation in a particular industry or company.

Relatively little research upon the effectiveness of outside training programs is available. However, a study by Judy (1958) of aircraft mechanic trainees seemed to indicate that trainees that were trained "in the field" were just as good at the end of the training period as trainees that spent their entire training time in special schools away from the on-the-job situation. Judy recommended that field training, rather than technical school training, is advantageous. In this particular study, the field group not only were trained in the field but also participated in production for part of the time during their training, whereas the group in residence in an Air Force technical school were involved in no production at all. Yet both groups performed at the same level at the end of the training program.

In conclusion, each individual business or industry must analyze its own problems involving training. A technique or combination of techniques that works for one organization may not work for another.

SUPERVISORY AND MANAGEMENT TRAINING

Specialized training for foremen and other supervisors has gained increasing recognition in the last 20 years. Beginning just before and during World War II, industry realized that managers needed special abilities to cope with their problems in the same way that workers needed special techniques to handle machinery. Thus there was a flurry of interest in specialized training for supervisory personnel.

For many years top-level management recognized that supervisors and front-line foremen have a particularly difficult task. These men are in the unique position of representing management to the workers. Front-line supervisors are part of a management group, and at the same time they communicate with and control workers that are not part of a management group. At no other level in industry is this relationship found. It is one of the most important interpersonal relationships in the industrial world.

As increasing awareness of the importance of this relationship between workers and management emphasized the need for special training of supervisors, many programs were established. Most of the training has been and still is on the topic of human relations. Can workers be treated as parts of machines? Can their efforts be considered as just another step in the production cycle? Can you simply explain the pension plan, hospitalization provisions, recreational programs, and then treat the workers as another part of a machine and expect high-level production?

Foremen must interpret suggestions, rules, and regulations devised by management in such a manner that they will be able to obtain high-level production from the workers and at the same time keep high morale. Training in human relations has helped supervisors to understand individual differences in people, what makes some men want to do some things more than others (motivation), and many other topics. Table 7.2 shows the general topics considered in a typical human relations program.

TABLE 7.2   Some General Topics and Subtopics Often Covered in Human Relations Training Programs

---

A.   Individual differences:
   Understanding the general similarities and differences in humans.
   Becoming aware of differences in human abilities.
B.   Leadership techniques:
   Qualities of good leaders.
   Leading versus directing.
C.   Learning:
   How to modify behavior of workers.
   Teaching workers to train others.
D.   Understanding others:
   Recognizing different methods of approaching problems and the value
      of each technique.
   Motivation.
   Emotion.
E.   Communication:
   The typical systems available.
   Methods of improving.
F.   Labor relations:
   Understanding organized workers views.
   Handling grievances.

There have been many studies showing that human relations programs are of value, and there have been several suggesting that human relations courses as typically offered are relatively ineffective in developing skills. Maier (1960), for example, has shown that the typical human relations course is neither long enough nor includes enough skill training to help trainees really change their behavior significantly. Scheer (1959) indicated that supervisory programs by and large do not accomplish as much when they are set up in the usual fashion by an outside expert as they do when they are set up with the assistance of the men who are going to be trained. Joint planning of the supervisory training program with trainers and potential supervisors succeeds in creating considerably better programs. In another study, Harris and Fleishman (1955) also reported that initial training or refresher training of supervisors had no effect on a supervisory-behavior description scale used before and after the training period.

On the positive side, there have been several studies indicating lasting changes in behavior as a result of supervisory courses. In many instances, human relations programs have concluded with an evaluation session where supervisors were asked to evaluate their training and also suggest ways of improving the program. By and large, these assessments have shown the programs to be of value. However, specific articles generally indicate the value of a particular type of training program or technique used in the training program rather than the overall evaluation of human relations programs.

Use of Supervisory Training.   There is a good deal of evidence that supervisory training is carried out in many, many industries. One survey indicated that 43 percent of the factories in their study provided formal courses in supervisory training for supervisors of hourly employees; 17 percent indicated presupervisory formal training. For supervisors of nonexempt, salaried employees, 41 percent of the companies offered supervisory training, and 15 percent offered presupervisory training (NICB, 1958).

Because it is generally accepted that supervisory training programs are needed and most organizations now involve at least some such training, it is wise to consider the activities involved in such programs. Usually industries are far beyond a "canned" approach. They frequently use their own program devised within their organization or a modification of a program purchased from some consulting organization or provided in a trade journal. In general, there is a differentiation between supervisory training and executive developments. Executive development will be discussed in another section in this chapter.

As with all training, planning for supervisory training must precede the development of such a program. Industries commonly agree that improved supervision helps company relationships between workers and management and often improves production. It also improves turnover and helps to attract good prospective employees. Mostly, the advantages just mentioned are the ones derived from good supervisory practices and, of course, are secondary rather than primary results because immediate changes in production are rarely noticed as the result of supervisory training. When the National Industrial Conference Board (1958) analyzed company executives' ratings of the importance of supervisory training programs, three main objectives were mentioned: (1) training for the immediate supervisory job, (2) dissemination of general information, and (3) personal development from a long-range point of view. Training for the immediate jobs involves learning the skills in areas of knowledge that are essential to good supervision.

As a means of estimating the many varied demands placed on a supervisor, one author reviewed check lists of supervisors' day-to-day activities from large and small industries, office and plant situations, closely confined work places and transportation industries (Gilmer, 1961). This list is shown in Table 7.3.

TABLE 7.3   A Check List of Day-to-Day Activities of Supervisors (each question is phrased for a positive answer; the list demonstrates the demands usually made on supervisors' time)

1. Do you know each of your men well enough to tell where he lives, where he came from, and what his interests are?
2. Do you know the general aims of the company?
3. Can you list in order your men who are ready for promotion?
4. Do your men work together well?
5. Do you know how to give an order?
6. Have you obtained better working conditions for your men?
7. Have you corrected the sources of grievances before they come up?
8. Do you listen to complaints?
9. Do you reprimand without building up ill feelings?
10. Do you avoid talking behind a man's head?
11. Do you reprimand in private rather than in public?
12. Do you have a check sheet for introducing a new man to his job?
13. Do you guide the new employee over rough spots?
14. Do you keep a progress chart on the new man?
15. Do you have a good criteria for judging performance?
16. Are you a good listener?
17. Are your records useful?
18. Do you know how to get a man to talk in an interview?
19. Do you keep up to date on company policies?
20. Do you keep up to date on union activities?
21. Do you plan work schedules in advance?
22. Do you have adequate inspection procedures?
23. Are you familiar with the technical side of the men's jobs?
24. Does work go on efficiently in your absence?
25. Do you keep your superiors informed of your department's activities?
26. Do you avoid taking up bothersome details with your boss?
27. Do you answer correspondence on time?
28. Do you see where your job fits into the overall organization?
29. Do you have a man who could take your job?
30. Do you know what the accident hazards are in your department?
31. Do you train for safety?
32. Do you give recognition to the man who does good work?
33. Do you ask workers for suggestions before attacking a new job?
34. Do you spread overtime work fairly?
35. Do you allow conversation at work on routine jobs?
36. Do you ever ask a worker to criticize his own work?
37. Do you admit your mistakes?
38. Do you believe that ability to handle workers is learned?
39. Do you know what goes on in departments other than your own?
40. Do you use conferences in getting ideas over to workers?

TABLE 7.3—continued

41. Do you keep cash and production records for your department?
42. Do you ever explain company policies to your men?
43. Do you keep your people informed on business conditions of the company?
44. Do you spend part of your time listening to worker complaints?
45. Do you believe the worker wants more from his job than just pay?
46. Do you believe most workers will cooperate in helping solve problems?
47. Do you believe that a worker who does not get promoted should be told why?
48. Do you believe in giving workers rest periods?
49. Do you believe people want to know where they stand on a job?
50. Do you believe in trying to sense how the worker feels?

From *Industrial Psychology*, by B. H. Gilmer. Copyright © 1961. Mc-Graw Hill Book Company. Used by permission.

It will be noted that contacts with other humans are the most common activities of supervisors; thus the emphasis on human relations in most supervisory training programs.

Methods of Training. Methods used for supervisory training vary from one organization to another. The previously mentioned techniques most often used for production workers are also used for supervisory personnel. On-the-job training assumes that the prospective foreman picks up what he needs to know by observation and pertinent questioning. However, it is not so much a training method for supervisors as it is a lack of a planned program.

In recent years, on-the-job supervisory training has been more or less formalized. In 1913 the Goodyear Tire and Rubber Company was probably the first to formalize this method when it inaugurated its "Flying Squad." The company systematically switched a number of promising young men from job to job throughout the organization in the attempt to familiarize potential leaders with the whole plant. Thus they would understand a wide variety of operations and the importance of integrated efforts in all departments. An important side benefit from this system was the availability of individuals trained in a variety of different departments to be used in case of illness, replacement, or other reasons. Modifications of the "Flying Squad" system have been used for training foremen and supervisors by many organizations since the initiation by Goodyear Tire and Rubber. Other more formalized training programs have been developed and have grown in importance in the past 25 years. These are generally formal programs during working hours, and they frequently involve classroom situations.

LECTURE-CONFERENCES. Some companies use a regular lecture and conference type of training very similar to typical secondary-school or college teaching. Because of their past experience in the usual school situation trainees expect the kind of training that they get and thus learn appropriately. On the other hand, adults sometimes resent being treated like students and may rebel and, therefore, not learn as much as might be expected in the formalized training program. It is also possible that because the trainers are mostly college graduates, they tend to lean in the direction of college level materials, with the result that more theoretical rather than practical material is presented. As in all learning, the topics presented must be relevant to the learners' experience, and there must be some reinforcement for the students to learn. Problems or issues of interest to the trainee can be taught by the regular lecture technique. When material is to be taught that is not as obviously important to the trainee, other techniques are often of more value.

THE CASE METHODS. The case-conference techniques continue to receive increasing interest as training methods. These techniques seem to be especially valuable for meeting the objectives of training supervisors to develop understanding of human relations. The case method is frequently thought of as one particular way of presenting material to trainees. However, the case method properly refers to three different techniques or methods (NICB, 1957).

The most common variety of case methods is frequently referred to as the case method. This method started at the Harvard University Advanced Management Course. In this technique a case problem with a good deal of detail is prepared in advance and presented to the students. Usually, the students are allowed to see the case in advance of their conference or class period and are expected to gather additional information from available sources. At the time of the class meeting or discussion period, the individual trainees bring in all the facts and information they have and weigh this information in light of the case presented to see if they can derive a proper solution to the problem. Emphasis is placed upon developing the ability of the trainees to analyze their own assumptions and interpret the processes by which conclusions are derived. Each individual trainee comes to understand that others have the same difficulties that he has in interpreting case information and facts. He may realize that there may be several usable solutions to each problem. Although his solution may not be agreeable to everyone else, it may have certain merit. The problem-solving process and the unspoken initial assumptions are the important considerations of the method rather than the solution obtained.

Dr. Paul Pigors of Massachusetts Institute of Technology has offered another technique using the case method of studying. In his technique, an incident calling for some discussion is presented in very brief form (perhaps only one or two sentences). Before the class or discussion session, each student is to think through his own analysis of the problem. At the time of the class or discussion, the members of the group question the leader to gain additional information that they think is important in coming to a suitable solution. As they gain the information they feel is important, they may progress toward several solutions. One of the virtues of this incident method is the revelation of what kinds of information the trainers believe are important and relevant. Some place an emphasis on regulation, rules, and policies, whereas others ask for additional information concerning the participants' feelings, background, work, and personal history. Some wish to know available means of disciplining a subordinate who is "out of line," and others want information to help them understand *why* the subordinate is "out of line." This technique emphasizes not only the process of arriving at the solution but the solution itself.

A third variation of the case method involves the presentation of a case fitting the particular subject matter under consideration. The case presented is generally a rather clean-cut one and is used as an example to illustrate some of the specific topics under discussion. The case is usually presented in such a manner that there is a fairly obvious correct answer on which most of the class can agree.

ROLE PLAYING. A fairly new technique of training particularly used at the supervisory level is role playing. This technique has the special advantage of allowing the supervisor to practice his skills when they do not really influence production. The major characteristics is the setting up of a problem situation and allowing two or more people to act out the way in which they would handle the problem. Frequently, the role playing is carried out in front of a group of fellow supervisors. One supervisor plays the part of a supervisor and another plays the part of a worker. After each trial trainees' performances are evaluated by the observing group with the help of the leader. Role playing requires a good deal of tact on the part of the leader and the other supervisors or members in attendance. The members playing the roles are at first uncomfortable, ill at ease, and do not really "get into" the situation. However, they generally warm to the situation and become more involved. Then a truly important learning function occurs, for the person playing the role "feels" the part. Role playing is somewhat like an extension of the case conference technique in that it allows the participants to work out solutions that might have been suggested after discussions or thought concerning a particular case. It has the added advantage of actually allowing an individual to experience the feeling involved in the situation. In most cases, supervisors obtain a particularly strong feeling for the workman's view after they have participated as a workman in a role-playing situation. Thus they temper their supervision appropriately when they are back at work as supervisors.

There has been some question about the efficacy of role playing in industries, because usually only two or three people are involved in the role playing. However, several studies indicate extreme value; for example, Barry (1959) indicated that buyers for a business establishment trained by regular techniques could not successfully accomplish what the merchandise managers desired, but when trained by role playing gained the abilities properly. Role playing has also been extended to include a larger group in what may be called multiple-role playing. Maier and Zerfoss (1952) have reported using an entire training class split into small groups, each given the same problem. Every member of the group is then assigned a role to play within his own group. Hence the self-consciousness of the role-playing supervisor is reduced, everyone has an opportunity to participate, and the discussion groups reveal a larger variety of possible solutions to problems than can be done when only two supervisors are involved in the role playing.

GAMING. Recently interest has been shown in a new technique of training supervisors called gaming. This involves the use of management games to help develop decision-making ability. Management gaming is gaining interest for general training of managerial functions, one of which is decision making. Dill (1961) has explained the management-games technique as used at Carnegie Institute of Technology Graduate School of Industrial Administration. In this technique groups of trainees act as teams, each representing a particular company and making decisions governing the operations of that particular company. The decisions that the team come to are fed into a computer for comparison against a "model" of the industry. An evaluation of their decisions then comes back to the teams at the end of each period of "play," and new decisions are made.

The emphasis of management gaming is on decision making with an eye toward production, marketing, and financing decisions. It is also of value for teaching supervisory principles to the extent that it simulates industrial conditions and thus brings the situation into the training area, where individuals may try solutions without disastrous effects on regular production schedules.

SENSITIVITY TRAINING. Another new and increasingly popular method has been labeled sensitivity training. This originated in the summer of 1947, when a small group of psychologists and educators met in Bethel, Maine, under the guidance of what has come to be known as the National Training Laboratories. Their purpose was to study the processes whereby strangers formed themselves into effective, productive groups. In the subsequent years a large and growing body of data has accumulated about these methods, which have as their central core the feedback of each individual's effectiveness and influence in the group by other group members. This is accomplished in an atmosphere of permissiveness and mutual support which enables the individual to see how his own behavior is perceived by others. In turn, he becomes more sensitive not only to the effect that his words and manner have on others but also develops ways by which he may assist the group to accomplish its mission.

Typically, sensitivity training occurs within a context of other procedures built into a concentrated period lasting two or three weeks at some site removed from the usual work location. The group sessions are supplemented by a few lectures on such topics as the group processes, learning theory, or growth within social organizations. Other activities often include role playing and experimental situations requiring groups to compete or cooperate in the achievement of some task. In these latter activities the effective, as well as the ineffective, ways of approaching and dealing with conflict or other feelings are reflected back to the participants for their own analysis and relearning.

In these methods one can see the basic principle that individuals learn to adjust and modify their behavior in the light of the consequences of that behavior. This is less easily accomplished when one is dealing with social interactions than when learning to drive an automobile or operate a machine tool. In the latter situations the results of unskillful behavior are obvious: the car does not stop at the expected spot, or the work produced with the tool fails to meet specifications. (In terms used in Chapter 1, the proper amount of change in the perceived stimulus situation does not follow the action to bring about acquisition.) In group interactions the resentment, pleasure, disgust, opposition, or agreement following one's remarks are often masked or suppressed in ordinary situations, or perhaps the expression of the effect is delayed, so that one does not get an immediate "knowledge of results." Sensitivity training is therefore a special kind of situation in which such feedback can be obtained under circumstances that are maximally reinforcing.

The relevance of such training for persons at supervisory and managerial levels, who deal with people more than materials, is obvious. The roster of companies and public agencies that have sent representatives to these laboratories rolls out like a red carpet. A few major companies have incorporated programs of this kind in their regular training departments. Generally, however, the laboratories are university-based.

The evaluation of sensitivity training is perhaps more difficult than the evaluation of most other kinds of training, because the criteria of improvement in one's social or interpersonal relations are subtle. One of the most recent efforts in this direction involved the rating of laboratory participants and a control sample of nonparticipants in the same organizations eight to 10 months *after* sensitivity training (Bunker 1963). The results showed that the participants, as seen by their associates, changed more than their counterpart nonparticipants in better understanding and attentive listening; being more cooperative, tactful, less irritating, easier to deal with; being more interdependent, less dominating, encouraging to others; showing greater self-control, less often angered; being more analytic of others' actions, more aware of subcurrents in groups, more accepting and tolerant of shortcomings in others, more open to new information, less dogmatic, arbitrary; showing greater understanding of their own behavior, role, and job requirements. This list is such a paragon of virtues that it is well to remember that there was no difference between the participants and nonparticipants in self-confidence and risk taking. In fact, one of the unsubstantiated objections to sensitivity training is that it contributes to the organizational-man syndrome—the willingness to submerge one's individuality to the demands of the organization. The Bunker report does not indicate that participants were *less* self-confident or *less* willing to assume risks, but only that in these respects the participants and nonparticipants were not different.

Comparable information comes from a study evaluating five years experience within an industrial plant numbering 2,400 people (Blake and Mouton, 1964). Although during this time many influences came to bear on this plant while the training department conducted sensitivity programs, there were good reasons to believe that the training contributed to the decision-making process that permitted the plant to move from a deficit operation to a profitable one. In addition, the training helped to improve relations between the plant and the headquarters organization to which it reported.

Although these are only two of many efforts to evaluate sensitivity training they are representative. One needs, however, to be cautious in claiming too much, for it is also true that some individuals do not benefit and some are in fact hostile to the method. What personality or other factors account for such differences is one of the unanswered researchable issues being examined.

EXECUTIVE DEVELOPMENT

In many industrial organizations, supervisory training and executive training or development are considered as one parcel. This may not be appropriate, because although it is difficult to differentiate between supervisory and executive functions, most authorities agree that supervision usually refers to the first-line foremanship relationships of workers to a management representative, whereas executives usually deal only with other supervisors or executives and not with the actual workers or production equipment. The techniques used by executives and supervisors are similar, but there is some reason to believe that the specialized functions carried out by executives may be learned or appreciated more after specialized training of a slightly different nature than the usual supervisory training courses.

The great bulk of business organizations in the United States use programs within the organization for the development of executives. This has been the traditional technique and seems to be the obvious and easy way to develop executives. In order to broaden a man's view, he is given an opportunity to work in a variety of different segments of the organization as he progressively moves to more and more responsible positions. In so doing, he is being developed and is learning about each section of the organization. However, when an interest in overall executive functions is desired, business concerns are more and more often turning to specialized executive development courses offered in colleges and universities or special training sessions.

The National Industrial Conference Board (1957) reported that executive development courses in universities began their rapid growth sometime just after 1950. In 1954 there were 17 such courses in operation in 15 different universities in the United States, and by 1957 there were over 30 courses offered. The only courses included in this poll by the Board were those over two weeks and less than one year in duration. Of course, there are specialized development programs in many universities that run for a few days or on a special occasion concerning a particular topic, but they are not continuously offered on a routine schedule.

The typical college or university course is an example of one special kind of training technique previously mentioned, that of outside the organization training. The on-campus courses vary greatly in the total amount of time devoted to classes per day, number of days involved, number of students allowed to participate, outside activity encouraged, and so on. They all aim at the same function of broadening the outlook of the executives that attend. The subject matter plus the interaction of the executives with men of similar positions from other companies in both intellectual and recreational activities broadens executives' views. By and large, organizations that have had experience with such courses agree that the executives function better upon return to work. However, there is no specific evidence available indicating that increased production or profits are to be expected in an organization immediately upon the return of an executive from a development course.

Perhaps it may be questionable as to whether to send an executive through such a course. Undoubtedly, many organizations are sending them simply because of a band wagon appeal. They have heard of XYZ Corporation sending its executives to such a course, and they feel they must keep up by sending their own executives. On the other hand, the pressure of competition means that they are keeping up with the Joneses not only for the sake of keeping up but because they are afraid that the Joneses may ultimately use some of the learned material to develop better techniques and thus make decisions that will be better than they can make without the specialized courses. Within the last 10 to 15 years it has been recognized that leadership quality in an executive is extremely valuable. Anything that an organization can do to enhance the leadership capacity of their executives is grasped.

In the typical executive development programs in universities and colleges, case method, role playing, discussions, lectures, and seminars are all used. The NICB (1957) report showed that the case method was the most popular technique. The content of the courses is generally the same in all schools and may be classified under five major headings: (1) being an executive—policy formation, organization and control, and so on, (2) business functions—marketing, management of operations, statistical planning and control, and so on, (3) human relations—communication, employee selection, labor relations, and so on, (4) public relations—community and government relations to business, and (5) personal development—leadership, reading and public speaking, investments, and so on. As can be noticed, many of these topics are discussed in supervisory training programs, but there are additional topics and more depth brought into executive development courses.

As mentioned previously, there is little concrete evidence of the value of these programs in immediately increasing the profits of an organization. However, the executives that have attended the courses report satisfaction and a general feeling of having learned something of ultimate value to them. They even feel that it may take several years before they can appraise adequately what they have learned and put it into use, but they are convinced that it has been valuable. Perhaps one of the most important values is the close and intimate relationship of a variety of different executives living and studying together for a period of two or more weeks in an atmosphere of equality and interest without the pressures of the regular business world.

EVALUATION OF INDUSTRIAL TRAINING

Does it work? How many times has the average person stopped to ask whether the public education system is effective or not? Most people take a positive answer for granted. There are relatively few studies to validate most of the teaching techniques used on millions of children. However, in industry it is important that the cost of the training be justified; thus there are frequent evaluations of the effectiveness of training. As a matter of fact, whenever new information or new techniques are tried, evaluation procedures are often involved. New ideas, such as programed instruction, whether they be in business or in the school situation, are commonly tested before they are applied full scale.

In industry, as in any other situation, techniques and programs may produce the desired ends in one situation and not in another. The specific technique that may work in one organization at one time may not even work again in a subsequent situation. Of all the various training techniques mentioned during the preceding pages, the more recent ones, such as role playing and case study techniques, have received more evaluation. The lecture technique is more or less assumed to work on the same basis it has been assumed to work for many years in the public education systems. When specialized or new ways of presenting materials in lectures, seminars, or the other techniques are tried, they are usually evaluated. Role playing, for example, has been shown to work for some kinds of training where other techniques did not work (Barry, 1959). As for specialized techniques that are useful in industry, a few studies concerning efficiency of particular techniques are cited here.

A study reported by Blain (1959) showed what many people already questioned, that because a task is learned in one situation, it may not be the same in a work situation. As a matter of fact, even when a task is learned in the work situation, the mere aspect of learning makes the task different than when it is part of a production or work schedule. Blain suggested that arrangements that reduce the variation in the possible responses during the learning will help to have the learner recognize the proper proprioceptive cues (those cues sent to him by the specialized receptor cells located in his body around muscles and joints that indicate that a person is moving parts of his body in a certain manner) and thus improve transfer of learning to the work situation. In another study,

Seymour (1959) indicated that the environmental cues are often more important in learning than the actual movements involved. He stated that the cues should be the same. By cues he meant the stimuli or the aspects of the environment that are going to be involved in the actual work situation. Clegg (1959) indicated that training done off the job on simulated equipment might well be done with relatively simple apparatus and simple tasks, rather than trying to set up complex simulations of operational tasks. His evidence seemed to indicate that the transfer from simple tasks or training to a complex operational task is just as good as the transfer of training from complex simulations to the work situation. Another example of a study concerning the effectiveness of different techniques of presenting information to the learners was done by Silverman (1959). He presented the same information with slides showing movable parts in static position or animated. There were no differences in learning effectiveness as measured on paper-and-pencil tests, but on performance tests learners who were presented the animated slides did better than the learners shown the static slides.

Considering these various studies as a group, it may be noted that effectiveness of training in industry is being investigated and that many specialized aspects are being evaluated. For some situations, training that emphasizes the environmental setup that is most similar to the actual job seems to be important. Other studies indicate that there is no sense in trying to make the situation as much like the real working situation as possible. Perhaps the general conclusion might be drawn that when performance on a job is of importance, the working situation and training situation should be as closely similar as possible. When measurement of ability to perform is done on a paper-and-pencil test (which probably involves a great deal of verbal ability) it may not be as important to have conditions during training that are identical to the actual work situation. Instead a situation should be designed where the general principles can be understood.

As a final point concerning evaluation of training, two studies are cited that show that training cannot adequately accomplish things that should be done in other ways. For example, Taylor and Garvey (1959) studied training as a technique for overcoming what they considered design deficiencies in equipment. They also tried human engineering for improving the equipment. On a controlled study they showed that training can compensate for design deficiencies, but not nearly as efficiently as can a redesign of equipment making it more compatible with human capabilities. Pickering (1959) studied naval personnel reading Sonar-like equipment. He came to the conclusion that there is a great deal of individual ability in the potential trainees for this particular activity. Those with very poor abilities simply could not be trained to an adequate level of performance with any techniques available. He stressed that it is far better in some situations to select people with ability than it is to try to train them. Training usually increases individual differences in ability. Those with the most ability get the most from the training, and those with the least ability get the least from training.

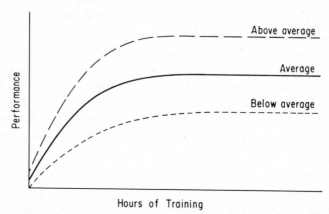

Figure 7.2. The effect of training on performance of workers with below-average, average, and above-average abilities. Training usually increases individual differences in ability to perform.

All in all, industrial training might be said to be efficient if it is well planned, organized, and set up to accomplish certain specific objectives. Evidence for the effectiveness of industrial training is at least as good as evidence for the effectiveness of regular education in the public school systems.

SUMMARY

Maximum efficiency on a job is obtained by selecting the best man for it and having him perform the work in the most efficient manner. Such performance is rarely discovered without guidance. Thus industrial training is provided to maximize the efficiency of the man selected to fill the job.

In order to train efficiently, an organization must determine its needs. Often measures of production or opinions of workers point up the need for training. A better way to determine training needs is to have a complete study of the organization by a skilled training analyst. He will determine the areas of company production that need training, which workers are involved, and what the workers need to know that they do not currently know. Generally, all workers could benefit from some additional training.

However, it may be economically unsound to train everyone. Thus training programs usually begin with relatively low-skilled workers involved in high-level productivity on relatively expensive materials and machinery. Improved performance will provide economic gain most rapidly with this group.

The objectives of training must be well defined. Raising production, reducing waste, reducing accidents, and job enlargement are common objectives of training. For efficient training these objectives must be prepared in specific rather than generalized statements. More recently, broadening the background of workers has become a concern of industry. Management feels that raising the cultural level of their workers and providing them with an understanding of their community and the world in which they live will ultimately help in the productivity of their organization. Human relations training is also a common training topic, although mostly for supervisory personnel rather than production workers. Very recently human behavioral engineering training has begun in an attempt to bring learning theory, as discussed in Chapter 1 of this book, into practical work situations.

After establishing needs for and objectives of training, one of four training techniques is commonly used with production workers. Apprenticeship training consists of a worker assigned as an apprentice or trainee with a skilled craftsman. On-the-job training is probably the most common of all training techniques in use in industry today. In this method a worker is assigned a job and instructed by fellow workers or his supervisor. Vestibule training is a rather rarely used technique. A separate room or building equipped with production equipment and staffed with instructors is provided specifically for the training of workers. Some organizations rely heavily upon outside training where special courses or programs in secondary or technical schools train potential workers for industry.

Supervisory and management training deserve special mention. The interest in such training particularly increased just before and during World War II. The primary emphasis in supervisory training programs is on human relations. Such topics as motivation, communications, handling grievances, individual differences, understanding human behavior, training workers, and learning theory are common topics.

The methods used for training supervisors are the same as those used for production workers plus some specialized techniques. On-the-job training programs are often better organized, and there is more frequent use of lecture and conference type of training. The case methods have been used and have received a great deal of favorable publicity. The most often used variety is patterned after the Harvard University Advanced Management Course technique. A problem situation with a good deal of detail is presented to students in advance of class, and the case is discussed in the group meeting. A second case method involves the presentation of a very brief summary of a situation, perhaps only one or two sentences, to the students before they meet as a group. At the time of the class, members discuss the problem and solutions. In a third variation, a case history is presented to the class to illustrate the subject matter under discussion. Another fairly new technique is role playing. In this technique a problem situation is defined, and two or more people act out how they would handle the problem. Often, the role playing is performed by supervisors in front of other supervisors. In this technique the role player "feels" the part of other persons. Gaming is a relatively new technique, where groups of trainees act as teams representing different companies and make decisions governing the operations of their company. Decisions are fed into a computer and are analyzed so that the business world is simulated and efficiency of decisions can be "scored," thus providing competition between the teams. A new technique called sensitivity training aims at improving supervisory behavior by making people more aware of others. Usually a campus conference or laboratory is established, and participants discuss supervisory problems in a free and open situation where each member tries to emphasize the feelings of others.

Executive development is very similar to supervisory training except for more depth in coverage and some additional topics. Executive development programs in colleges and universities are set up for two weeks to a year in duration. Topics such as organization and control, business functions, personal planning, general public relations, and leadership techniques are considered.

Many people question whether training is worth while. Most industries frequently evaluate their training programs, and there is good reason to believe that the programs are valuable. New techniques, such as role playing and programed instruction (mentioned in Chapter 1), have been more thoroughly tested and do seem to have value in changing behavior. Training is generally efficient when it is well planned and organized to accomplish certain specific objectives.

SUGGESTED REFERENCES FOR FURTHER STUDY

Refer to "Suggested References for Further Study" at the end of Chapter 1 of this book for additional references about learning.

Berrien, F. K. (1951). *Comments and Cases on Human Relations.* New York: Harper & Row.

A book describing several aspects of human behavior, how it can be changed, and a set of case histories useful in human relations training.

Bradford, L. P., J. R. Gebb, and K. D. Benne (eds.) (1964). *T-Group Theory and Laboratory Method*. New York: John Wiley & Sons.
    A description of sensitivity training and facilities for such training.

Cruickshank, H. M., and K. Davis (1958). *Cases in Management*. Homewood, Ill.: Richard D. Irwin.
    A series of cases useful in supervisory training.

Gilmer, B. von H. (1961). *Industrial Psychology*. New York: McGraw-Hill Book Company.
    Chapter 7 of this book concerns training objectives, principles, aids, organization, and new techniques.

Klaw, S. (1961). "Two Weeks in a T-Group." *Fortune*, August.
    A popular description of a laboratory for sensitivity training.

McGehee, W., and D. W. Thayer (1961). *Training in Business and Industry*. New York: John Wiley & Sons.
    A book devoted to determining needs for, methods of, theory, and evaluation of training in business and industry.

Siegel, L. (1962). *Industrial Psychology*. Homewood, Ill.: Richard D. Irwin.
    This book includes setting of objectives, techniques, evaluating, and other aspects of training in Chapter 7.

Chapter 8

Man Related to His

Work Environment

Assuming that an employee has been properly selected, placed, and trained, there are still many factors that influence his efficiency. Efficiency may be noted by a variety of criteria, including rejects, production per unit of time, fatigue, worker turnover, absenteeism, and so on. Getting the greatest amount of production per unit of time with the smallest number of rejects or errors is the desire of all industrial organizations. Thus efficiency is a prime requisite for a good industrial organization.

Worker efficiency is the result of selection, placement, training, and the interaction of the employee with his working conditions, his machinery, his fellow workers, and his own feelings about himself. In this chapter, the worker's relationships with his physical environment or his working conditions will be discussed. Before looking into the factors that might be considered a part of working conditions, we must understand how efficiency may be estimated. One very common technique is to plot a graph of production per unit of time against hours of work or days of work.

THE WORK CURVE

A typical graphic representation of work is shown in Figure 8.1. Production ordinarily starts below the maximum level, increases rather rapidly up to a maximum output, remains fairly stable for a comparatively short period of time, and then decreases slowly throughout the remaining part of the work period until a break occurs. Where the day is broken into two like-timed segments such as 3½ or 4 hours each, the production curve shows an increase during warm-up in the first segment, a relatively stable production for a short time, and then a drop off. The second segment begins with production a little below that of the maximum level achieved during the first segment, but above the level of production in effect just before the end of the first work segment. There is a shorter warm-up period, a more rapid approach to the maximum or leveling-off point (which is probably a little below the maximum production of the first segment), and a decline throughout the remaining part of the work segment. The decrease in production near the end of the second work segment is generally more severe than it was at the end of the first segment. In some organizations there may be an increase in production near the end of the second work segment (shown as the dotted line in Figure 8.1). This is ordinarily interpreted as a production increase (end spurt) due to the workers recognizing that they are almost finished for the day and thus trying a bit harder to achieve a certain level of production that they had set for themselves.

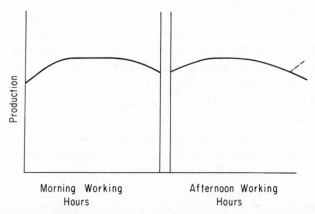

Figure 8.1. Relationship of hours of work and production level for hourly workers on a typical workday. These curves show a lunch break in the middle of the work period and a dotted line near the end of the afternoon work period to indicate the "end spurt" typical of some jobs.

Thus the daily work curve shows a warm-up period, a general level of production, and then a drop-off before a break occurs. The schedule for a week is approximately the same general shape. Considering a working week starting on Monday, the maximum output on Monday is usually not quite as high as on Tuesday or Wednesday, and then there is a gradual tapering off of production through Thursday and Friday. The day-to-day production changes during the week are not as distinct as the hour-to-hour changes during one day.

Of course, the work curve discussed so far is hypothetical, but it can be generated from production records of a group of workers. Naturally, there are many special situations where the work curve would not be as shown in Figure 8.1. For example, many organizations have controlled production rates or assembly lines, so that the work curve would simply show the control factor in the organization. In some organizations this means that the work curve would be a straight horizontal line, because their assembly line is run at a constant speed throughout the work periods. Some organizations have geared their assembly lines to what is known to be the typical work cycle of workers. For such organizations the work curve would be similar to that shown in Figure 8.1.

FACTORS AFFECTING PRODUCTION

The next eight major sections of this chapter discuss factors that may affect the work curve. These factors are naturally interrelated with the worker, with the material discussed in previous chapters, and with material to be covered in later chapters. However, each factor is discussed separately for clarity. At the end of this chapter we emphasize the importance of understanding the worker as a complex being interacting with all these factors and with the material presented in the preceding and following chapters. Of all the factors in the working environment that may affect the worker, the following eight are of prime importance and are discussed here: illumination, noise, atmospheric conditions, music, hours of work, rest pauses, nature of the work task, and pay. The final portion of this chapter contains a discussion of accidents and safety related to the eight factors influencing production.

Illumination. Practically everyone with normal or near-normal eyesight is aware of the fact that a great many of the things that he or she does is dependent upon vision. Experts have estimated that from 85–90 percent of all knowledge is gained visually and that up to 90 percent of bodily motion is controlled by our eyes. Much of this control is accomplished as the result of many past experiences or habit, but our eyes continually bring in new information to check upon motion.

For the eyes to function, at least some illumination must be available in the environment. Fortunately, many human activities take place during daylight hours, when the light from the sun provides enough illumination for the eyes to function adequately. However, there are many times when humans are involved in activity where sunlight cannot be adequate. Thus the major emphasis of this section is upon artificial illumination. However, we must always remember that adequate lighting can often be accomplished by adequately controlled daylight. In newer factories, daylight is sometimes completely eliminated. Factories, and even schools, are constructed with few or no windows. Temperature, humidity, and light conditions can thus be absolutely controlled.

Studies conducted many years ago emphasized that illumination per se is not the only factor involved in efficiency of workers even under varying amounts of illumination. One of the most famous studies, also referred to at other times in this book, was the so-called Hawthorne study. This work was carried out in the Hawthorne branch of the Western Electric Company. The earliest experiments of the series were designed as illumination studies. These studies, carried out in advance of the bulk of the major Hawthorne studies, were under way between 1924 and 1927. In collaboration with the National Research Council, a series of three experiments was conducted. The first involved three different departments where illumination was progressively increased. Despite the similarity in the experimental treatment, production rates did not react the same way in each of three different departments. In one of the departments production fluctuated randomly; in the other two departments, production increased with increase in illumination, but erratically so, perhaps independent of the increase in illumination. The second experiment was conducted in one department. Two groups of employees, chosen to be comparable in terms of age and experience, were established. One group continued to work under the original conditions of illumination, and the other group worked under varying lighting intensities. The production of both groups increased to an appreciable and identical degree. The third experiment essentially repeated the experimental design of the second experiment, but employing only artificial light at decreasing intensities. Production in both the control and the test group rose steadily. Finally, when the illumination for the test group became extremely low, production fell off. The major finding of this series of experiments stressed the point that the experimental groups working under varying levels of illumination varied production due to something other than just illumination changes. This was the take-off point for the Hawthorne studies and the beginning of the realization that a psychological variable might influence production and that the psychological variable might be influenced by physical conditions. Since these early studies, many others have shown that the psychological condition of workers may influence production in various ways. However, many studies have also shown how very specific factors concerning illumination are related to production changes.

Before we discuss the value of different kinds and levels of illumination, it is necessary to be aware of some commonly used terminology. Much of this terminology is provided by illumination engineers, psychologists and other specialists interested in production efficiency. Generally, there is agreement upon the following terms: *candle power* denotes the force of light and is not a measure of the amount of light. Thus one candle power is the force of light coming from a candle of a certain size and composition in a particular direction. *Lumen* is the total quantity of light. Specifically, one lumen is the amount of light falling upon one square foot of surface where every point on that surface is one foot away from the source producing one candle power. In other words, if a candle is placed in the center of a sphere of one foot radius, one lumen of light would fall on each square foot of the sphere. Since lumens are measures of the total amount of light, most light sources are now rated in lumens rather than candle power. A *foot-candle* is the measure of the amount of light falling on a surface. One foot-candle is the illumination on a surface every part of which is one foot from a standard candle. One lumen of light on one square foot of surface produces one foot-candle of illumination. This is a fundamental in lighting design, because once an area is known and the foot-candles desired is established, the total number of lumens that must fall on the total area can be found by multiplying foot-candles by area. Finally, *foot-lambert* is the measure of the brightness of a source or of any surface that we see. One foot-lambert is the average brightness of a surface emitting or reflecting one lumen per square foot. All surfaces absorb some light. Thus the foot-lamberts of a reflecting surface is the foot-candles of illumination times the percent reflected. For example, a white surface might reflect 80 percent of the light that falls upon it. If such a surface receives enough quantity of light (lumens) to have the equivalent of one foot-candle then 0.8 foot-candles are reflected, so that the foot-lambert is 0.8.

CONTROL OF LIGHT. In general it is not necessary to memorize a lot of terminology, but the above-stated terminology plus an understanding of some of the things that happen with light make it easier to understand how illumination affects production. Light comes not only from a source but is also reflected off all objects upon which it falls. Air transmits light with little loss due to reflection, except for dust particles. However, when light hits a solid surface it is reflected. Most surfaces produce a variety of different kinds of reflection.

If a light hits a perfectly smooth surface, that light would be reflected *specularly*—that is, the light coming in at one angle would be reflected in the identical angle in the opposite direction. This kind of reflecting surface is used occasionally for light transmission and is frequently found in the working situation in the form of highly polished pieces of machinery. In such cases, it is often a disadvantage because a bright light source reflecting specularly may enter the eye and cause a great deal of distraction. Other surfaces do not give specular reflection but instead give *spread* reflections. Such surfaces are moderately smooth but have small imperfections that allow light to be spread slightly after bouncing or reflecting from the surface. Most paper used in textbooks has rather high specular reflection but is somewhat spread. (If you hold this page in the proper relationship to a light source you can almost see the light source on the paper. Still, this paper does have a good deal of spread reflection, so that instead of seeing an image of the light bulb, you probably see a bright area.) Other material that has a matte finish or one made up of minute crystals or particles, *diffuses* light, so that when light reflects off such a surface it diffuses in all directions. Some paper creates a nearly diffuse reflection. Such paper is of a soft quality, does not take print as well as the semigloss or gloss papers (especially line drawings or photographs), and is consequently not used in this particular book. Most common materials—for example, the paper in this textbook—produce diffuse, spread, and specular reflection. Reflected light is of importance because a great deal of the light in our environment is reflected to certain areas for our use.

Light may also be controlled by *refractions*, which means the bending of light waves or beams. Ordinarily light beams would be expected to travel in a straight line, but when they move from one medium to another they may be refracted or bent. Light is bent toward the perpendicular to the surface it enters when it goes from a less dense medium to a more dense medium and is bent away from the perpendicular when going from a more to less dense material. For example, when a light beam strikes glass going from air, it is bent toward the perpendicular to the surface, and then when it comes from the glass into the air again, it would be bent away from the perpendicular. This characteristic is important, for it allows bending light into certain areas. For example, light can be introduced into hard-to-get places by refraction from denser material, such as glass or plastic.

Finally, light can be controlled by the process of absorption or polarization. *Absorption* refers to the collecting or absorbing of certain wavelengths of light. Colored light is usually created in this manner. A white light source is filtered by the use of a piece of red or blue glass which allows only the red or the blue light to pass through. Another method of light control is the use of a polarized filter, which allows lightwaves traveling in only one plane to pass through. Polarized light has limited application in industrial installations.

CHARACTERISTICS FOR EFFICIENT LIGHTING. As already suggested, illumination has a variety of variables and just to talk about intensity or reflection is telling only part of the story. The effects of illumination on production or efficiency are here discussed under four major characteristics: intensity of light, distribution of light, quality of the light, and glare.

INTENSITY. In spite of many studies reported in the literature since the early work at Hawthorne in the 1920's there is practically no agreement on just exactly how much light is needed for general working efficiency. Illumination intensity requirements change as the task changes. Attempts to formulate generally useful sets of intensity values have generally ended in controversy. One investigator, for example, concluded that 40 or 50 foot-candles is sufficient illumination for even the most severe industrial task (Tinker, 1947). Other recommendations have ranged into the thousands of foot-candles for a specific occupation. Although exact standards are probably still questionable, the Illumination Engineering Society, through various technical committees, has produced a tabulation of recommended minimum values for a large variety of different industrial situa-

TABLE 8.1 Recommended Minimum Foot-candles of Illumination for Some Industrial Areas (such intensity levels are often obtained by a combination of general and specialized lighting)

JOB	MINIMUM FOOT-CANDLES
Supplementary light for aircraft welding	2,000
Most difficult, fine-discrimination inspections	1,000
Hat-manufacturing sewing	500
Cutting cloth products	300
Color inspection in printing plants	200
Grading and sorting tobacco	200
Rewinder in paper manufacturing	150
Machine pressing in dry cleaners	150
Hand-decorating candy	100
Repair areas of automobile garages	100
Etching photoengravings	50
Rough bench work in machine shops	50
Blooming, slabbing in rolling mills	30
Washing areas of laundries	30
Stairways, corridors, and service areas	20
Loading and unloading platforms	20
Storage areas in parking garages	10
Inactive storage areas (interior)	10
Shipyards—general	5
Active pedestrian entrances	5
Inactive storage areas (exterior)	1
Exterior building surroundings	1

Technical Publication LS–119 (1960), *Foot-candles in Modern Lighting*, General Electric Company, Nela Park, Cleveland, Ohio.

tions. Table 8.1 shows some of the recommended levels of illumination In the complete tables, the various levels of intensity range from one foot-candle for exterior building surroundings, inactive storage areas, and inactive or normally locked entrance ways to as high as 2,000 foot-candles for cloth inspection or supplementary illumination in welding of airplane parts (*Technical Publication LS–119, 1960*).

Figure 8.2. Welding in an industrial plant. A special face mask with eye shield is worn by the worker while welding. In order to see when the welding arc is out, high-intensity supplementary light must be provided. (Courtesy of S. I. Handling Systems, Inc.)

In general, the amount of light, although varying considerably with the task to be performed, should be more intense for manipulation of small objects than when work involves manipulation of large objects or where precision is not critical. When consideration is given to the factors that affect vision and the use of vision, characteristics other than intensity of illumination are obviously of importance. Contrast is one of these. If an object is very similar to its background (for example, inspection of cloth where small imperfections in dark cloth must be noticed by inspectors) then high-intensity illumination is needed. When there is a marked contrast between the background and the object to be seen, less illumination is needed. At the same time if the object is of a larger size in relationship to its background, less intensity is needed. If more time is available to make decisions, less intensity is needed. If the object itself has high reflecting power, then less intensity is needed. Thus it is almost impossible to generalize about intensity requirements.

DISTRIBUTION OF LIGHT. Light may get to a surface in a variety of ways. The entire area of a room may be saturated with a certain intensity of light, or only one small portion may be illuminated to the same intensity by a spotlight. Generally distribution of light may be designated in five types: (1) direct light, when the light is directed at the area of interest, (2) semidirect light, where most of the intensity of the light source falls directly on the surface of interest and some is released in another direction, (3) general diffuse or direct–indirect lighting, where about half of the light is directed at the work area, and half goes to another area (that is, the ceiling) for reflection, (4) semi-indirect light, where most of the light goes to the reflecting surfaces and some goes directly to the work area, and (5) totally indirect light, where all the light is reflected to the work area by a reflecting surface. Figure 8.3 shows examples of each of these types of illumination.

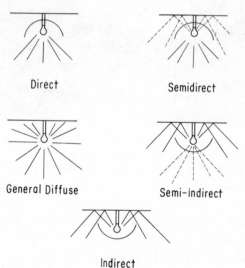

Figure 8.3.   Five types of distribution of light.

Indirect lighting in general offers the best approach from the standpoint of worker efficiency in that bright contrasts, shadows, and glare are reduced; on the other hand, completely indirect lighting requires considerably more lumens at the light source to obtain the same foot-candles on the working area as could be done with direct light producing fewer lumens.

Woodson (1954) showed that visual efficiency is lessened over prolonged periods of time of continuous reading but that indirect lighting causes less fatigue and permits greater reading efficiency than does direct lighting, at least over a three-hour period, as shown in his test.

QUALITY OF LIGHT. The source of light providing the illumination under artificial conditions is generally of one of three natures: the common incandescent bulb, the fluorescent bulb, or the mercury bulb. Each gives a particular type of light, and each has certain advantages.

Incandescent bulbs provide light by a very hot filament inside a closed-glass area. Most of the bulbs, particularly those over 40 watts in size, are filled with a mixture of nitrogen and argon, which has little to do with the actual lighting. The gas does not produce the light. The hotter the filament in the incandescent bulb, the more light is produced for the amount of electricity consumed. On the other hand, the hotter the bulb burns, the faster the tungsten, of which the filament is created, boils away and thus shortens the life of the bulb. A long-life bulb, which might seem at first to have great advantages, will produce less candle power with the same amount of wattage. For example, it has been estimated that using bulbs that could burn for 100 years instead of the normally accepted 1,000 hours would require approximately three times as many bulbs of the same size as does our present bulb of 1,000-hour life expectancy. Some bulbs are designed to burn only a few hours in order to obtain much more candle power (for example, photo-flood bulbs). For most purposes a happy medium has to be hit between cost of the bulb, the electricity, and the labor for installation, and so on.

The fluorescent bulb is generally a glass tube with an electrode in each end through which current is passed. Current conducted by vaporized mercury creates a large amount of ultraviolet radiation, which excites the phosphor placed on the inside of the tube and thus produces usable light. A variety of different fluorescent bulbs are available, but in general, they operate at much cooler temperatures than do incandescent bulbs yielding the same amount of light. On the other hand, the original installation cost and the cost of the lamp replacement is generally higher. There is also a slightly different color created by the fluorescent lights, and when color is important in the work situation, this must be considered. Some deluxe fluorescent tubes are less efficient than standard ones, but produce light that is very near daylight in composition. Another type produces light that is very similar to incandescent light.

The mercury bulb uses a shorter tube and a higher pressure than the fluorescent lamp and does not use phosphor. Instead, the arc created in the lamp creates the light. In general, a mercury lamp creates a blue-green color and lacks all red. Mercury lamps are frequently used for lighting large areas or outside lighting, such as highways and parking areas. They generally provide a given amount of candle power for less electricity than that needed for incandescent bulbs and have a longer life expectancy. However, they have a disadvantage compared to incandescent and fluorescent bulbs in that if they once are extinguished they will not relight until they have cooled and the internal pressure has reduced, which may take five to ten minutes. Thus incandescent lamps are usually provided where a blackout may be hazardous.

Color of light source seems to have little influence on factors involved in ordinary manufacturing or office work. However, specialized functions in modern industry and armed forces activities need special lighting. For example, pilots flying at night need the increased sensitivity of their eyes that follows prolonged periods in the dark. This dark-adaptation time varies according to the color of the light falling upon the eyes. A given level of sensitivity to low-level illumination is obtained more rapidly if the pre-exposure light is of longer wavelengths. Thus ready rooms for pilots who may have to fly at night with little preparation time are illuminated with red (long wavelengths) lights.

GLARE. A source of light of relatively greater intensity than that to which the eye is accustomed results in a glare. Glare reduces visibility of the object in the visual field, causes discomfort, and may disturb vision in the entire visual field. Glare comes from the light source itself or from specular reflection.

Glare generally can be reduced by keeping bright light sources out of the field of vision. The use of shields or hoods on the source or visors above the workers' eyes helps to reduce glare. Having several sources of light or an indirect light source often lessens glare. Another aid to reducing glare is to avoid the use of specular finishes. In theory it might be advantageous to have all objects in the visual field of approximately equal brightness. However, to keep psychological orientation it appears that at least some objects must contrast with the rest of the objects in the visual field. But too great a contrast will bring about decreased efficiency. Thus there must be some contrast but not too much. Some studies suggested that the maximum ratio of the brightness of the task of immediate importance to its adjacent surroundings should be three to one.

Despite the fact that most studies indicate that varying illumination has an effect upon production, many of the studies are probably influenced by the so-called Hawthorne effect, or the psychological impact of doing something for the workers, rather than just the changes in illumination. For example, a 100-percent improvement in quality took place in the Hickock Electrical Instrument Company in Cleveland, Ohio, when they installed a luminous ceiling in their "White Room," where meters are assembled. Hickock also had an increase of 50 percent in productivity. The suggestion made was that this improvement in electrical illumination increased efficiency so much that it more than paid for the cost of the installation and the additional electricity used for lighting (General Electric Company, 1961). However, this study, as many other such studies, does not indicate what control was used for the changes in production that would result from the psychological impact of providing new working conditions.

It seems essential to point out here that illumination engineers are expected to find weaknesses when they investigate the illumination of a work area. Whether it is practical to add the illumination suggested to meet the minimum standards proposed by a variety of different organizations, such as the Illuminating Engineering Society, depends upon a variety of factors. As illumination increases, other factors in the work environment may change. For example, really high-level illumination creates heat. Either specialized techniques must be devised to take care of the heat, or production may suffer as a result of increased heat. At the same time we must recognize that the productivity change that takes place may be the result of change in morale of the workers when they know the entire area is being air-conditioned, rewired for brighter lights, and modernized. Thus the actual effects of varying illumination are not precisely known.

Noise. The truck driver apparently becomes irritated while moving through the business district and, with open-road driving just behind him, he inadvertently presses the button for his air horn even though he is within the city limits. Noise? Certainly, it's noise. It also attracts a great deal of attention, because it seems to be so loud in comparison to anything else, even the other automobile horns and the normal sounds of engines, talk, and shuffling of feet. What is it that causes noise?

All sound is made up of three characteristics: loudness, quality, and pitch.[1] Sometimes we hear sound that is very loud, a desirable pitch, and

---

[1] *Loudness* is the psychological or heard condition corresponding to the physical attribute of intensity. *Quality* is the aspect of experience depending on the kind of stimulus, in the case of sound corresponding to the overtones or complexity of the sound source. *Pitch* is the psychological condition of high or low tone corresponding to the vibration frequency of the sound source.

a quality that we appreciate. Thus, even though it is loud, we do not call it noise. On the other hand, we may hear sounds of relatively low-level loudness but of a quality and a pitch that we find undesirable. The criterion for differentiating noise from sound is undesirability. If the sound disrupts our train of thought or our activity, or causes injury to hearing or reduced skill, we call it noise. In this section we will consider some of the aspects about noise that are most important in the industrial situation.

Although the effects of noise on industrial production are difficult to study, it seems that the effect of noise is of little importance. In general, there is a decrease in performance right after the introduction of noise, but this is generally momentary, and overall decline in production is negligible. However, it must be pointed out that laboratory experiments show different results than do experiments in the field, and that some characteristics of noise are worth noting. For example, laboratory experimentation indicates that increased energy or input is necessary to maintain the same level of performance in a noisy environment as in a quieter environment. On the other hand, a small amount of noise seems to be important in order to maintain maximum efficiency. (See Chapter 1 of this book.)

To review some of the most important factors concerning noise, this section is divided into five sections: adaptation, habituation, hearing loss, performance decrement, and protection against noise.

ADAPTATION.   Most studies have shown that a sound that may be unbearable when first administered may soon be almost unnoticed. We experience this phenomenon in everyday life. When driving on a highway with car windows open, the sound level is considerably higher than when at rest in the same general environment. We may thus notice that we have the volume of the radio extremely loud if we stop the car along the highway, where the environmental background noises are relatively low. Fortunately the human body handles noise just as many other stimuli entering through the nervous system. A sound that may be irritating, cause disruption in performance, or attract attention when it is first introduced soon becomes only a part of the rest of the environment through the process of adaptation.[2] This is especially true of sound that is nearly continuous, but it also holds for regular intermittent sound. (A person can get used to a telephone ringing and ignore it.)

HABITUATION.   Experimental evidence concerning production changes

---

[2] *Adaptation* is the reduced responsiveness of sensory functioning with continuous stimulation.

related to exposure to or familiarity with noise are rather inconclusive. Relatively few studies were reported in the literature discussing habituation[3] per se until 1960. However, two studies deserve mention here.

Culbert and Posner (1960) specifically discussed the habituation effects of noise on performance. They tested the hypothesis that persons not accustomed to the sound of jet aircraft noises may find them more annoying than propellor aircraft noises only because they are more accustomed to the latter. They used taped noises of jet aircraft and propellor-driven aircraft. A group of subjects showed a significant increase in tolerance to the jet engine noise after two series of explosive trials a week for three consecutive weeks. Results of this experiment indicate that unfamiliar noise of equivalent level to familiar noise was far more of a distraction. Certainly there was considerably less tolerance for unfamiliar noise than for familiar noise, and subjects learned to get along with the unfamiliar noise (jet aircraft sound) during the experimental period.

Earlier in this section, noise was described as undesirable sound. This very frequently means sound that is variable. Thus it is interesting to note the report of McBain (1961), which suggested that the effect of noise on monotonous work can be explained by the "arousal hypothesis." Earlier work by Hebb (1955) stated that changes in stimulation activate or arouse areas of the brain that are involved in the effective use of environmental cues. Thus McBain created the hypothesis that lowered efficiency should follow reduction of environmental stimulation to low levels. Such would be the normal expectancy in a monotonous work situation, whereas the introduction of variable noise should increase variability, hence arousal, and subsequently improve performance. This hypothesis is almost in opposition to the usual finding that noise brings about a work decrement immediately upon installation, but with the passage of time has little or no effect on performance. McBain found that there were fewer errors in his work situation under conditions of noise than under quiet conditions.

PERFORMANCE DECREMENT.   A field study of the effects of noise done in 1935 is frequently cited (Weston and Adams, 1935). This study examined the output of weavers over a 26-week period during which the workers wore ear defenders on alternate weeks, thereby reducing noise level from 96 to 87 decibels.[4] Operations requiring five minutes in the normal work situation involved only 4½ minutes when wearing the ear defenders. Since this

---

[3] *Habituation* is the reduction of waste movement after repeated reaction to a given situation.
[4] *Decibel* is a measurement of perceived intensity of a sound.

study, many additional studies have indicated approximately the same results, but often the "Hawthorne effect" was not completely controlled. Thus the change in intensity of noise may have brought about a psychological change in the person and consequently changes in performance.

Most studies indicate that work decrement does not take place as a result of noise, but there are some interesting studies to the contrary. Jerison (1959) reported that with relatively long "work" periods under laboratory conditions, performance at the end of the work condition with noise was poorer than performance at the end of the same length of time under quiet conditions. Broadbent and Little (1960) showed that although noise reduction did not improve rate of work, it significantly reduced shutdowns due to operator error or maintenance calls. This led the investigators to hypothesize an interaction between noise and other aspects of the job that might have magnified the effects of noise reduction beyond what might be observed under other conditions.

An interesting study by Kidd (1959) showed that noise in a communication network of an air-traffic control center had little effect on the success of the control center in handling air traffic. It seems that with increasing noise level, control tower messages were repeated more often or there was a greater attempt on the part of the operator to provide intelligible communications so that air traffic was successfully controlled.

Performance in other than auditory activities suffers from noisy environments only to the extent that noise provides a distraction. Noise was previously described as less-desirable sound. This means it must be of a great enough intensity to create an annoyance for the individual. In general, activity that is most susceptible to decrement by distraction of any sort is most influenced by noise. As previously indicated, the relationship seems to be that noise creates a psychological condition of distraction in the individual which then affects the performance of that individual. A minimum amount of noise may create a condition within the individual that provides greater concentration on the work and thus a slight increase in production, but, of course, with a greater increase in input.

Thus, as with other information from the working situation, it seems impossible to be sure about the effects of noise upon production. In general, it looks as though adaptation is important and that the effect of noise is rather momentary. Perhaps additional studies will prove that there is a decrease in efficiency even though it may not show up in production records but only in excess fatigue.

PROTECTION AGAINST NOISE.   Although noise has not proven to be as great a detriment to production as it was previously considered, it still seems to be important. A great deal of time and expense has been used for noise abatement in the world at large and particularly in industrial and business settings. Most of this effort has been expended in seeking an engineering solution. Other methods for handling the deleterious effects of noise have received little publicity.

Figure 8.4. A worker using a grinding wheel to smooth a cut in a sheet metal part. This operation necessarily creates a loud high-pitched noise and is typical of industrial noise that is difficult to control. (Courtesy of S. I. Handling Systems, Inc.)

Reduction of noise output at the source is an obvious way of decreasing the bad effects of noise. In addition, engineers have approached the problem by revamping the schedules of activities, placing noisy activities in geographical areas away from the more commonly used work areas, or by the use of baffled-insulation or ear-protective devices. Placement of sound-absorbing materials, movement of the noise-generating equipment, and appropriate scheduling are obvious methods of handling the noise. Here we will discuss only some ear-protective devices.

Four major categories of ear protectors available and in use may be classified as (1) earplugs, (2) ear muffs, (3) semi-inserts, and (4) overall helmets. In industrial situations, the use of earplugs has not received much attention. Properly designed, they provide a cheap and simple way of preventing hearing loss that may accumulate during prolonged exposure to intense noise. To be effective, any ear-protective device must make an airtight seal in the ear canal. It is difficult to do this with other than specially designed earplugs, but cotton impregnated with paraffin and properly inserted in the ear canal provides a good reduction in noise transmission. The apparent disadvantage of earplugs is that they are relatively new items to most employees and, of course, they are not quite as comfortable as ear muffs or nothing at all. Ear muffs of sound-absorbing material as well as complete helmets provide completely external barriers to sound, but are not as effective as earplugs. Semi-inserts fit partially into the ear canal and are supported with a headset type of band. They are not quite as effective as earplugs.

It is not within the province of this chapter to discuss hearing loss in detail, but it is wise to recognize that hearing loss can take place as the result of intense stimulation. The human ear can stand very loud noises for a short period of time without lasting effects, but long exposure to high-intensity sounds can cause damage that results in a permanent hearing loss. Most evidence indicates that hearing loss occurs in a cumulative manner. Sounds that may produce a hearing loss generally bring about a temporary decrease in ability to hear. When a person stays away from the sound for a short period of time, his hearing will apparently return to normal. Repeated exposure to the intense sound may ultimately result in a permanent detriment. In general, a hearing loss that is recovered in a relatively short period of time, such as between the ordinary work sessions, is not too dangerous, and a cumulative permanent loss will probably not occur. When it seems as though hearing losses are going to be cumulative and therefore may result in a permanent loss, it is obvious that some sort of ear protection must be provided, or the sound source must be lowered in intensity.

An experiment by Chisman and Simon (1961) provided information concerning another way of handling some high-intensity noises in an industrial situation. Continuous noise has been fairly well controlled in industry; still, large impulse types of noises as produced by punch presses, explosions, and so on, occur. Normally, muscles involved in the hearing apparatus contract (the acoustic reflex) to protect the ear against loud sound as the sound increases. However, impulse noise, as, for example, an explosion, a drop hammer, or punch press, creates an increase in intensity that is so short in duration that the acoustic reflex does not provide muscle contraction prior to the full intensity of the sound. Thus damage to the hearing apparatus may occur. Chisman and Simon ran a series of experiments that showed 'hat the acoustic reflex can be externally elicited. They then suggested and 'ested apparatus that would call forth the acoustic reflex before a high-intensity sound entered the hearing apparatus. They stated that "eliciting 'he acoustic reflex prior to an impact may be an effective means of protecting the ear against industrial impulse noises." Machinery should be devised to create a sound of a relatively low intensity to get the acoustic reflex started before the loud-intensity sound reaches the eardrum. Such a device can be created relatively easily and connected to machines that create loud-intensity impulse types of sound. The authors concluded that this method is psychologically more acceptable to workers than the use of earplugs and cannot be "forgotten" when needed.

The relationship between noise and performance is definitely not clear-cut. Apparently a small amount of general noise in the environment helps provide an increased tension state in the human that may increase performance at the cost of additional input. On the other hand, available evidence is certainly contradictory. There seems to be no definite information about the general relationship between performance and sound level.

Atmospheric Conditions.   Everyone is well aware that we live in an atmosphere that varies. At times, we feel hot and other times cold. This subjective feeling seems to vary according to the temperature of the atmosphere. But it also varies with many other factors. Production seems to be best when atmospheric conditions are at desirable levels for the workers involved. Still, there is conflicting evidence about the direct relationships between production and atmospheric conditions.

The human body is constructed to maintain a constant temperature of about 98.6 degrees F. To maintain this temperature, the body normally loses heat through various regulatory systems. When the body creates more heat by burning of energy, the excess heat must be dissipated into the environment. The regulatory mechanisms of the body are rather complex but automatic. Most of us are very familiar with the events that follow when the body creates too much heat. We automatically start to perspire, to bring more blood near the surface of the skin, and by evaporation of perspiration, to help cool the blood and so reduce the body temperature. Conversely, when we become too cool, we increase bodily activity and thus create heat that raises the blood temperature.

Now, what are the characteristics of the environment that will affect the ability of the normal regulatory system of the human body? Three major aspects of the atmospheric conditions are of importance: (1) temperature, (2) humidity, and (3) air movement.

We are all familiar with temperature as a reading from a thermometer that records in degrees Fahrenheit. *Temperature, air temperature,* and *ambient temperature* are all synonomous terms referring to the amount of heat in the air.

Humidity refers to the amount of moisture content in the air. Relative humidity is much more commonly measured. It indicates the ratio between the absolute amount of moisture in the air and the saturation level of the air. It is therefore a percentage of the amount of water vapor that a given amount of air can hold.

Air movement, of course, refers to the transmission of air past a certain spot. We most often notice air movement when we use fans or other pumping devices.

When we speak of the atmosphere as being more or less comfortable, we are ordinarily referring to a combination of temperature, humidity, and amount of air movement. All are important to the efficiency of the body in eliminating excess heat. Most of us believe that a temperature of about 70 degrees F. is normal. When the temperature goes much higher, we begin to feel uncomfortable in normal clothing. We also know that we feel more uncomfortable on warm, humid days than on warm, dry days. *Effective temperature* or *temperature–humidity index* are terms applied to the combination of humidity and temperature. This combination has a great deal to do with a feeling of comfort in a particular atmosphere. An effective temperature consisting of 90 degrees F. and 10 percent humidity provides about the same comfort range as 75 degrees F. and 100 percent humidity. However, individuals have different tolerance levels for temperature and humidity. The optimum temperature–humidity index for one individual may be quite different than for another.

Air movement over the skin is important. One of the ways in which bodily heat is precipitated is by having the air immediately in contact with the surface of the body moved away, so that cooler air may contact this surface or so that evaporation of perspiration may take place. Very still air of 80 degrees F. and 60 percent humidity will be far less comfortable than moving air of the same temperature and humidity, because bodily heat loss will be restricted to the air immediately adjacent to the body. Of course, movement of air is relative to the body, and thus movement of the body in still air will produce the same effect as moving the air.

Apparently a rather wide range of temperature and humidity are acceptable to the human body. Clark (1961) told of a series of experiments under very cool conditions. Studying armed forces personnel in a standard, not-timed task, he found that performance was not lowered when the temperature of the skin of the hand was lowered from 70 degrees F. to 60 degrees F. while the rest of the body was maintained at 70 degrees F.

and relative humidity at 50 percent. On the other hand, when the temperature of the skin of the hand was reduced to 55 degrees, there were marked performance decrements. These decrements increased with increased exposure to the 55 degrees F. temperature and became stable after about 40 minutes exposure.

Another series of studies (Clark and Jones, 1962) indicated that working under poor environmental conditions had an effect upon performance, but that this effect on performance was lessened considerably by training. The authors found reliable differences between task performances under cold conditions for subjects trained under cold conditions or under warm conditions. They suggest that cold experience during the training becomes part of the stimulus complex that elicits the correct manual response, and thus when a condition of cold is expected in the performance situation, the individual should be trained under cold conditions.

Experimental evidence reported in past years (Viteles, 1932) has shown that rather adverse temperature and humidity situations can be tolerated for extensive periods of time if there is sufficient ventilation or air movement. For example, forced ventilation in mines and factories was followed by increases in production and reduction in discomfort.

It appears that mental activity is relatively unaffected by atmospheric conditions. Fine, Cohen, and Crist (1960) reported on a study involving anagram solutions and auditory discriminations before and after exposure to high-humidity and high- and moderate-temperature situations. They found no changes in performance before and after exposure to the adverse conditions.

The influence on worker productivity of temperature and humidity seems to be a matter of the psychological impact on the workers. Atmospheric changes do have an effect upon production if they go beyond rather wide minimum and maximum temperature and humidity ranges. Whether or not the effect is a psychological one is not certain. One experiment (Berry, 1961) showed some interesting information on this topic. Investigating the tendency of most people to speak of green or blue as cool colors and red or orange as warm, he tested subjects in a special chamber where he had complete control and accurate measurement of temperature and humidity. The subjects were involved in a rather irrelevant task. They were told that the experiment was being conducted for an automobile company concerning the effect of colored lighting on some skills relating to driving. During the experiment various colored filters were used to change the colors of the ceiling, which was the most obviously illuminated area of the room. Each subject was presented different colors during the experiment and asked to rank the five colors according to the amount of heat they transmitted to him. The temperature in the test room was varied over the same range for each of the colors. The subjects reported the onset of discomfort as the temperature was raised in the room under each of the five different colors. They showed no change in the levels of heat they would tolerate as a function of the colors of illumination. Nevertheless, they persisted in the conventional belief that green and blue were cool colors when they were asked to rank what they had experienced. It seems therefore that variation in the color, although psychologically of value to the individual, has nothing to do with the effect upon their feeling of discomfort when temperature does vary.

WORKING UNDER ADVERSE CONDITIONS. Fortunately the human body adapts rather rapidly to excessive temperature conditions. The more severe the heat condition, the slower the adaptation, but with continued exposure, a highly developed adaptation is accomplished in four to seven days. It also seems that adaptation to severe conditions of heat serves equally to increase the ability to work in hot and wet environments. After adaptation to heat, there is a period of time in which a high level of activity can be maintained under adverse conditions even though normally working in cooler environments, but adaptation decreases slowly and the ability to work under extreme conditions is lost. Thus, if it is necessary to be adapted to high-heat work areas, the adaptation must be maintained by repeated exposures to the hot conditions.

It is remarkable that so little specific research data is available concerning the use of temperature and humidity control systems, particularly because so many industrial organizations have installed expensive equipment to maintain fairly constant temperature and humidity under winter and summer conditions which would ordinarily create large temperature variations. In general, the American Society of Heating, Refrigerating, and Air-Conditioning Engineers indicated that people are comfortable when the air temperature is between 73 and 77 degrees F., humidity about 25 to 50 percent, and air velocity about 25 feet per minute, regardless of the season of the year, (ASHRAE, 1960). Thus air-conditioning and heating systems would supposedly attempt to maintain these levels. In spite of the standards provided by the heating and ventilating engineers, it is interesting to note that most people feel comfortable in the summertime with a range of 69 to 73 degrees F., whereas in the winter, they are generally comfortable with 65 to 70 degrees F. Of course, humidity as well as air movements are involved, plus the adaptation effect as suggested in the previous paragraphs.

It is obvious that industry can control atmospheric conditions by suitable air-conditioning and heating systems so as to maintain fairly uniform atmospheric situations throughout the working year. Consideration also needs to be given to selecting men for jobs on the basis of temperature tolerance because it is known that some people have greater tolerance for temperature variation than others. Thought must also be given to adaptation level, because once a person is adapted to a temperature, he can maintain performance for relatively long periods of time. If workers must continue to work under adverse atmospheric conditions, the physiological functions of the human body must be helped by providing liquids, salt, or proper clothing.

Music. The use of music in industrial organizations rapidly increased after the Second World War, but had been used by many workers for years before its large-scale introduction into factories and offices. With little scientific evidence, music has been thought to alleviate fatigue and boredom and to generally improve workers' feelings. References to the use of music as an aid in healing can be found in the Bible, and the chants of workers and sailors have been used for centuries to help "lighten" heavy work.

Although there were several studies published earlier, the impetus for rapid growth in the use of music in United States industries came from experiments carried out during the Second World War. The vital need for goods encouraged a closer appraisal of all possible aspects of production. Thus 100 plants throughout the nation were surveyed. The bulk of the plants indicated that employees and management desired music and thought that it helped them feel better and produce more with fewer errors. Still, the few well-controlled studies available seem to question the value of music in influencing production.

A series of studies reported through the 1940's indicated that special work situations necessitated particular types of music or rhythms. In general, they agreed that employees would have better morale and thus produce more with music than without. The effect of music seems to be as a distractor, so that productivity and morale increase on repetitive jobs, which are ordinarily influenced by boredom and inefficiency.

Examples of specific reports follow. One article (Flack, 1949) showed that 86.1 percent of the listening employees believed that music helped to relieve their fatigue and 93.3 percent said it tended to break the monotony of their work. Some 95.2 percent said it made the work more enjoyable, 94.3 percent said it gave the employees a lift, 91.4 percent said that it kept them from getting nervous, and only 1 percent stated that it created a condition of nervousness or that they would like to see the music stopped. The same study indicated that supervisors estimated workers' efficiency up 10 percent and that work quality and workers' attitudes toward the organization improved during the six-year experience with music in the plant.

A report by H. C. Smith (1947) told of a study involving radio assembly workers during day and night shifts. The effect of music was greater at night than during the day in terms of average performance of workers. However, there was some increase in production during the day, and only 2 percent of all workers indicated that they did not care for the music.

A study by Roberts (1959) cited a general increase in efficiency on routine jobs of 5 to 20 percent when properly programed background music was provided.

Although background music is commonly supplied in many business and industrial concerns and workers seem to like it, evidence concerning effects on production is questionable. Uhrbrock (1961) in a thorough review of the field of music in industry stated that the effects are quite questionable. Most evidence, he pointed out, is of the most value for advertising purposes. Only a few studies were scientific, and they generally lacked critical controls. From the few studies that he felt were worth while, Uhrbrock concluded that most workers prefer to have music, but there is little proof that the music increases production. As in many other aspects of applied psychology, experimentation and research in the field has been extremely difficult and more good research is needed.

Hours of Work. The length of the typical workday and work week in the United States has shown a general decline since the beginning of industrialization. Most of the decline has taken place as machinery has increased in efficiency and total production of goods has risen, even with shorter work weeks. The generally acceptable standard in industry is about 40 hours per week, consisting of five eight-hour days. Unfortunately the evidence supporting a specific length for a workday or work week is not as clear as it might be. A general conclusion from available evidence indicates that workers expect to put in approximately 40 hours per week. Therefore they are more proficient at that length work week. As more information concerning a shorter work week is publicized there is reason to believe that efficiency of workers will be better at the newly established expected norm.

The expectation of workers is perhaps of more importance than is normally cited in the research concerning productivity and working hours. The erroneous assumption that increasing the length of the working day will add in a direct manner to the production is no worse than the erroneous assumption that decreasing the length of workday or the number of hours per week will create more production per hour and thus balance out total production. Fifty years ago a work week of 48 hours consisting of six days of eight hours each was quite acceptable. Thus the average workers produced adequately at 48 rather than at 40 hours per week. However, by the First World War a series of studies showed that the 40-hour week was already the accepted mode.

A series of studies showed that as the numbers of hours of work were increased, the amount of production per hour decreased until a maximum amount of total production could be obtained by maintaining hours of work rather than increasing total work week. Typical of such studies was one reported by Vernon (1926). He showed a 20-percent increase of hourly output for men sizing fuse bodies when a work week in a munitions plant was changed from 58.2 hours to 51.2. With a further reduction to 50.4 hours, production increased 17 percent per hour, so that a total increase of production per hour of 37 percent was accomplished while reducing the work week from 57.2 to 50.4 hours. Similar results have been cited by other researchers. Figure 8.5 shows the effect on total production for varying lengths of work week for four different jobs.

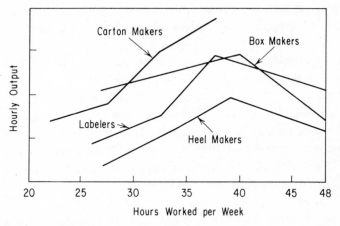

Figure 8.5. The effect of the length of the work week on hourly output in four jobs. Adapted from H. M. Vernon and T. Bedford, Jr. (1925) *Nat. Instit. Indus. Psychol.*, **2**, 157, and G. H. Miles and A. Angler (1925), **ibid.**, 300.

A study often cited was done during the Second World War by Kossoris (1944). He found that a 7½-hour workday led to higher productivity and lower absenteeism than did a 9½-hour workday. He also showed that in one plant that had worked extensively under an 8-hour, 7-day weekly schedule increased production per hour took place when the Sunday workday was dropped. He found that the 7-day work week yielded about the same amount of production as 6 days' output. We must conclude that increasing the length of the work week is not necessarily going to increase production.

We must also consider nominal versus actual hours worked. It is a well-known fact that the number of hours for which an employee checks in and out (nominal hours) is not actual production time. There are always breaks, authorized and unauthorized, times when machinery does not function adequately, times when a man must leave his work for a physical reason, and other times when he is just psychologically not feeling up to working at full capacity. It must also be recognized that in many industries, production is geared to the machinery or the production line speed. Workers must then perform at a rate to keep up with the machine. Even on production lines, total productivity will not increase in direct proportion to increased number of hours worked, because more breakdowns of machinery and rejected production will occur with increasing length of work periods.

In most societies at this time, the 40-hour work week is normal. As more and more evidence is accumulated to show that production per unit of time increases with decreased hourly rate, more and more workers will accept this concept as fact, and consequently a lower number of hours per week will become the norm. As representatives of labor seek and obtain shorter work weeks, additional hours beyond a new norm of 35 or 37½ hours per week will probably result in less production per unit of time. There are at least some studies that seem to indicate that such is the case in offices that are now on 35- or 37½-hour work weeks. When additional business requires more work hours per week, production per unit of time does not seem to be at the same level as during the regular 35- or 37½-hour work week. The optimum work week will of course vary with different situations, depending upon a large variety of factors. Research of a particular situation is necessary before specific recommendations can be made.

The consensus of research data is that a work week that is longer than a normally accepted level brings about more absenteeism and less actual work. A shorter than normal work week runs into the problem of warm-up and skill-loss between work sessions. In many industrial and business activities the first few minutes or even hours of each working period involve a warm-up to get production to the normal level. (Figure 8.1 shows the typical work curve.) As the total work period is shortened, the amount of time for warm-up remains constant, but represents a larger proportion of the total working period. Consequently overall production is lowered.

Time of Day. Most research indicates that it makes little difference whether a person works from 8 A.M. to 3 P.M., 3 P.M to 11 P.M., or 11 P.M. to 3 A.M. On the other hand, Bloom (1961) presented a good case for differences in performance at various times of the day. He cited many studies that show generally that there is a definite rhythm involved in the human body and that disruption of this normal diurnal body rhythm disrupts natural production. Loss of sleep and fatigue occur when this diurnal activity is changed and cumulative effects may seriously impair a worker. Bloom suggested that activities of man must be scheduled around these definite rhythmic functions of the body in order to produce maximum efficiency. He stated that at nighttime the body is best prepared for sleep and least prepared for production. Therefore we must expect lower productivity on night shifts. He also suggested that individuals have different physiological characteristics, and therefore working on rotating shifts or night-hour shifts should be restricted to those who are physiologically best able to work nights. By the same reasoning, fixed shifts are better than rotating shifts. If rotating shifts are unavoidable, he suggested that changes be made as infrequently as possible.

Adequate research concerning applications of Bloom's suggestions has not been completed. More evidence concerning exactly what man can be expected to do at various hours of the day and under various work-hour schedules is needed.

Rest Pauses. "Breaks" or pauses in the working day are so common in industrial and business organizations now that an average worker would probably find it difficult to accept the concept that this was not part of the working day. As a matter of fact, for years before authorized rest pauses or coffee breaks were common, unauthorized breaks, and pauses certainly occurred. In many organizations, the introduction of authorized pauses has reduced unauthorized breaks, but has usually not completely eliminated them. Without apparent focusing of attention on the problem, workers recognize that they cannot maintain efficiency while working constantly at any particular task. We are all involved in this same phenomenon, including the writer while producing material for this book. Occasionally, one simply has to get away from the task at hand for a period of time. The activity engaged in during the break period depends upon the activities during work. Generally a different activity during the break provides more rest than doing the same kind of activity as during the work period.

Unauthorized rest periods are disguised in many ways. Most common are short breaks for a smoke, a trip to the wash room, or complaints that the machine isn't working properly, that it needs a little adjustment, that the worker feels he must check to see whether there is something wrong. In addition to actual time away from production machinery there are also unauthorized breaks by workers who are apparently on the job. They may be daydreaming about the work or about something entirely away from the work situation. Unauthorized rest periods do occur and will probably continue to occur as long as people continue to work. Authorized rest periods have been introduced in an attempt to increase production and create better morale, less fatigue, and boredom. The effectiveness of authorized rest periods in doing these is somewhat questionable, although the bulk of research data indicates that production increases and fatigue and boredom decreases with the introduction of rest pauses.

A study by McGehee and Owen (1940) dealt with the topic of authorized and unauthorized rest pauses in an office situation. Observing comptometer operators in a North Carolina office of the Agricultural Adjustment Administration, the authors kept precise records of rest pauses during an experimental period. They also had the employees complete questionnaires and tabulated the responses. Their investigation indicated that both unauthorized and authorized rest periods can increase production, but the introduction of authorized rest periods reduces unauthorized rest time, and so results in more time worked as well as increasing production per unit of time. In another study (Anonymous, 1938) a similar change was made from no authorized rest periods to allowing authorized rest periods. Working time was reduced by 6 percent per week, but production increased 3 percent per week, and volume of errors was reduced 50 percent.

Smith (1953) reported a good deal of work concerning the curve of output as a criterion of boredom and concluded that contrary to much of the rather classic work reported in the 1920's, she found that output curves were not necessarily related to boredom or other subjective feelings of the worker. Smith reported that there were no consistent relationships between the reports of the workers concerning their feelings of boredom and monotony and their fairly stable individual differences in speed of working, variability of production, and frequency of rest pauses and talking. She concluded that "boredom is not necessarily accompanied by a depression in the curve of output nor is a sag necessarily accompanied by a feeling of boredom."

Some studies have been concerned with more sophisticated measures of tension and production. For example, Kling, Williams, and Schlosberg (1959), while studying skin conductance during a rotary pursuit task, found that they had a measure of tension. They also investigated such variables as introduction of rest pauses and came to the conclusion that there was no reduction in tension necessary for the increase in performance that results from rest pauses. The classical Hawthorne studies (Landsberger, 1958), reported elsewhere in this book, studied length of working day and rest pauses along with other variables. The results have usually been interpreted to indicate that the influence of rest pauses was not to increase production per se but that the rest pause created in the workers a feeling that management was interested in doing something for them. Thus there was increased morale or better general attitude of the workers, which ultimately resulted in production increases. This is especially borne out in two phases of the studies: (1) phase 12 involved no rest pauses, yet followed after an experimental time period where rest pauses had been involved—production still increased in phase 12 after rest pauses were eliminated, and (2) in phase 13 rest pauses were reinstated and production increased again.

The basic concept of the introduction of rest pauses as a means of increasing production is probably the result of the early studies by Taylor (1911). Taylor is well known for his work in scientific management and early motion-and-time study. Studying laborers loading pig iron manually into wheelbarrows and from the wheelbarrows into freight cars, he noted the average production per man per day. Under a piece-rate incentive system, the workers worked hard and rapidly during the earlier part of the day, but by the end of the day were working so slowly that their total production averaged 12½ tons per day. Taylor devised a series of schedules of work and rest periods. After experimenting with a variety of ratios of time of work and rest, he found that an optimum schedule involved 42 percent of the time at work and 58 percent for rest. Under the new schedule production records showed an output of 47½ tons per day by the same man who previously had been able to produce only 12½ tons per day.

As previously stated, many studies have shown increases in production related to reduction in fatigue. Many laboratory studies have shown that the continuous use of a muscle group will result in inability to use that muscle group after a period of time. A rest pause is essential to bring the muscle back into use if it is physiologically fatigued. Scores of jobs involve enough energy use and muscle effort that fatigue must be controlled. In such situations the period of time for rest must be long enough to allow regeneration of the muscle group, but not so long as to force a new warm-up period in the work situation.

Although there are few recent studies reporting changes in production as the result of rest pauses, Colquhoun (1959) reported one study in a controlled situation. A simulated industrial inspection task was performed with the benefit of a rest period after a 30-minute work period or without the rest period. He found fewer failures to detect faults in the inspection program among the group of "workers" that had the rest period.

What is the universal principle to be derived from classical and more current studies concerning rest pauses? Of course, rest pauses are acceptable. They are so ingrained in the thinking of the average American worker that to eliminate rest pauses and coffee breaks would probably cause drastic changes in production. Whether the rest pause or the coffee break is essential from a physiological, fatigue, or boredom standpoint also remains questionable, as does the concept of actual changes in production. (Fatigue, boredom, and monotony are treated in detail in Chapter 11 of this book.) However, the rest pause is accepted in our American society, and it is there-fore needed. When and how long rest pauses should be, and what activity should take place during rest pauses, depends upon the particular industrial or business situation. Each rest pause or break period must be tailored to fit a particular organization. Analysis of the production curve can provide information, so that the rest pause can be inserted just before maximum production starts to drop off. Thus the rest pause will ordinarily provide maximum value in terms of production.

Nature of the Work Task. About the beginning of the twentieth century mass production moved into high gear in the United States and later throughout the rest of the world. Men such as Henry Ford began to realize that producing relatively expensive items for the mass population necessi-tated techniques that were not previously practicable. More uniformity of production came into being, and smaller and smaller amounts of a par-ticular product were produced by one worker. Fractionization of the total manpower effort involved in a product was natural for mass production. With the advent of scientific management and motion-and-time studies by men such as Taylor and Gilbreth, industrial managers moved even more toward dividing work into the smallest segment that could practicably be done by one person. The net result was the creation of a great deal of highly repetitious work involving relatively low skill and often little under-standing of the real value of the particular function in the overall product. Thus there was not very much job satisfaction in terms of completing an important product.

It seems inevitable that one of the by-products of fractionization of work and highly repetitive jobs was the production of monotony and boredom on the part of the workers. (In Chapter 11 of this book, there is a more thorough discussion of these topics.) The nature of the task a man performs may produce within him a feeling of tiredness caused not just by physical activity but by the psychological overtones of a highly repetitive job with little apparent value. This boredom usually has an adverse effect upon production. In the early studies of this effect, the shape of the production curve was used as an indicator of boredom.

As shown earlier (Figure 8.1), the typical production curve in an industrial job shows a trend in an upward direction at the beginning of the work period in what is typically called a warm-up. After the warm-up is completed, there is a relatively level stage in the production curve and then a drop-off toward the end of the work period. For years, investigators stated that irregularity during the working period and an upswing near the end of the work period were characteristic of bored workers. As a matter of fact, when production curves showed such characteristics, an assumption was made that boredom was involved and that this had adversely influenced production. More recently a variety of experiments and research reports have questioned this concept.

We will examine some of the earlier studies that influenced observers for the first half of the twentieth century and then examine some recent findings. A series of studies carried out in England during the early 1930's were reported by Wyatt, Langdon, and Stock (1937). By and large, boredom was equated with a decrement in production. It was also strongly established that boredom was the result of monotonous work. Characteristics of the employees involved in repetitive work who became bored were noted. Thus an attempt was made to study personality and other characteristics of employees to improve selection so that repetitive jobs would not be filled with people who would become bored.

Wyatt (1929–30) published a summary of what he had learned about specialization and subdivision of labor and its effect upon production. He stated that boredom was common but by no means always experienced by workers involved in repetitive activity. He seemed to believe that an activity accompanied by interest or attention goes smoothly and continuously and that time, therefore, seems to pass more rapidly and boredom does not develop. Wyatt suggested that the experience of boredom is largely dependent upon personal characteristics as related to the occupational activity. He wrote that in addition to the personality, temperament, and intelligence of the worker, short rest periods, pauses for conversations, daydreaming, and attempts to make the work more interesting and the working area more conducive to production were all things that needed study. He also indicated that the effects of repetitive work are not confined to the industrial environment, but also extended outside of the working situation into thought and behavior in general. He suggested this might have an influence on human relations outside of the working situation.

Because many other people throughout the world were interested in the detriments in production as a result of repetitive work, it was not strange to find that studies were done to estimate the effects of monotonous work while trying to hold constant the effect of fatigue. It was fairly well established that a few muscles may be exhausted rapidly and that rest pauses will allow the rehabilitation of the muscles so that further work can be accomplished. Another type of experiment, often repeated, involves a monotonous task of relatively little physical effort. As subjects work through the task, more and more variability is noted in their functions. For example, subjects are required to draw vertical lines alternately grouped in two's and three's. With increasing trials the grouping varies and the lines become longer or shorter, heavier or lighter. Later on the entire quality of the production deteriorates and the lines are drawn as curved lines, crosses, and so on. Finally the movements involved become difficult to make, and eventually there is an inability to complete the task. If at this stage the subjects are allowed to involve themselves in a different task using the same muscles—for example, writing something entirely new— they are quite able to go on writing. It seems as though the functional decrement was not muscular fatigue but rather psychological. There is little doubt that a psychological condition may have an effect on production. Just what the effect is or how the effect comes into being needs more study.

Other studies indicate that men like to work on jobs that have variety. In one study (Watson, 1939) of unemployed people, variety was of more importance than money and hours to them in terms of obtaining new jobs. Of 159 obtaining vocational guidance, only 14 said that they could meet competition of others better in routine or standardized work rather than in new and different condition. Of the very few that felt they preferred doing the same thing rather than a wide variety of work, there seemed to be more cases of abnormal lack of self-confidence than in the general population.

In an interesting series of articles, Patricia Cane Smith has examined the topic of boredom and stated a new concept concerning the effects of repetition on production. In one article (Smith, 1953) she told of the relationship between the experience of boredom and the shape of production curves for industrial workers. After thoroughly reviewing the literature, Smith decided to evaluate the feelings of the workers by both interview and questionnaire and then collected output records for the workers. Many of the findings of this study conflict with the earlier studies. This may be due to the attitude of the workers in that they felt they should maintain a certain pace no matter what. Thus, if they worked rapidly during the day and felt that they were ahead, they slowed down or stopped entirely, whereas if they were behind in production, they worked more rapidly near the end of the day. Smith concluded that the pacing of work occurs much more frequently in industrial situations than does spontaneous variation in rate. She suggested that it is quite normal for any worker to decide in advance how much he is going to produce or earn each day and then go ahead to produce that amount.

In another article Smith (1955) again wrote about repetitive work and productivity. She took exception to the rather common notion that variable work does not create boredom, as repetitious work does. She reasoned that repetition, as externally observed, could not be a cause of boredom. It could, however, be a characteristic of a task as perceived by the worker that may bring about the experience of boredom. Smith then conducted a study to investigate the factors in the individual that might predispose him to feelings of boredom. The results of the study showed that the worker more susceptible to boredom was likely to be young, restless in his regular living habits, and less satisfied with his home and plant situations in general. The research did not support the hypotheses that the worker susceptible to boredom is more ambitious, does not daydream, is more intelligent or extraverted.

Since many people working in the field of productivity and boredom have felt that being able to see the completion of a task will tend to reduce boredom, it is important to cite an experiment by Smith and Lem (1955). The authors studied a relatively light repetitive work task. The traditional size lot of material to be handled consisted of approximately enough work to consume four hours of the operator's time. Operators obtained their own work in trays and dropped finished items through a drop shoot. Three sizes of lots of work load were used in the experiment. The large lot was the normal tray of approximately four hours' work, a smaller lot consisted of trays that held one tenth of the normal amount, and a medium sized lot was one fifth of the normal load. Thus the operators were exposed under controlled conditions to three different sizes of lots. They were able to complete a batch of work approximately once every four hours, once every 48 minutes, or once every 24 minutes. During the entire period of the experiment the workers were observed and exact records were kept of their stops for unauthorized rest periods. Included in these stops were recording time, rest room time, and so on, but they were nonproductive periods of time. The workers did not know that this was being observed but assumed that a study of fatigue was being done. No changes in production occurred for any individual under any of the conditions of the experiment as indicated by production records. However, there were significant differences in the number and placing of the stops or the unauthorized rest periods. The most frequent stops occurred for large lots; the least frequent, for the small lots. The average amount of time between stops was the greatest for the small lots and shortest for the large.

It is most interesting to note from Smith and Lem's experiment that production does not vary significantly because of an ability to see the end of a work unit. On the other hand, although production didn't vary, the amount of time spent in unauthorized rest periods varied, so that when larger lots of work were handled, the workers actually had to produce more per unit of working time in order to end up with the same amount of work as when they handled small lots of work. The workers were interviewed after the experiment and commonly indicated that they did not understand what was going on, were very interested in cooperating, but didn't know what results were expected and therefore could not bias the results. They did indicate that they lacked an interest in the small-sized lots, but preferred to have the traditional large segments of work that took approximately half a day each. The authors suggested that the dislike for small lots was probably the result of past experience and indicated that additional experiments needed to be completed in this direction.

What does all this information mean? At the present time, most management men believe that productivity is decreased when workers are bored. Management also frequently assumes that boredom results from nonvariability of work. Consequently attempts at control of this production loss due to boredom follow six major paths: (1) Workers are selected who would seem to be less influenced by boredom. This usually means choosing people with personalities that are not as prone to be bothered by repetitive work and often has meant selecting people of average or less-than-average intelligence. (2) There has been an attempt to vary jobs. Workers have been switched from one activity to another, and some research indicates that this has improved production. However, other studies show no relationship between productivity and job changes, whereas still other studies show a loss in production with variation of work. (3) Attempts have been made to increase the motivation of the workers. This has involved showing the workers how the job that they are doing is important to the overall production of the item and that what they are doing creates a very valuable product. Several studies done during the Second World War showed that workers in highly repetitive jobs didn't decrease production as long as they understood that they were working on something that was important for the war effort. (4) Workers have been encouraged to think of subgoals. The previously mentioned study by Smith and Lem casts considerable question upon this technique, but the setting of subgoals encourages some people to work at a higher rate in order to finish a job. (5) More participation of workers in management of the work situation has been encouraged. Workers have been allowed to cooperate in planning their schedules and carrying them through. They are then more inclined to take fewer unauthorized rest periods and to keep at repetitive work, because they feel they are part of their own goals. (6) The environ-mental atmosphere has been modified. Characteristics mentioned earlier in this chapter are involved, such as the use of music, pleasant colors, temperature and humidity control, and so on, to provide an atmosphere that is more conducive to productivity regardless of repetitive work.

Pay. Joe came to his foreman complaining that he was making less money per hour than Bill, who was doing almost the same kind of work in another section of the same plant. Joe was running a machine involving relatively little physical energy but requiring a knowledge of the machinery and some skill in placing of parts and handling the finished product. Bill was doing almost the same kind of work on a different kind of machine, but producing approximately the same amount of material. Obviously total pay earned is important to workers. How to decide what pay should be earned for particular jobs as well as the value of pay in general will be discussed in this section.

Pay is often described as a motivator for work. (We cannot thoroughly discuss motivation or reinforcement here. If the reader will refer to sections of Chapter 1 and Chapter 11 of this book, dealing with learning and performance, he may review the topics.) Pay, when it is received, is re-inforcement. The difficulty is that it usually is not available after each particular act is performed, but instead comes after a delay of time, per-haps the end of the week or the end of a month. However, pay is a universal reinforcer in that it will provide satisfaction for almost all motivational states. Thus it is of great value in our society and is used almost exclusively by many organizations as a means of increasing productivity. It is also interesting to note, however, that many organizations recognize that pay has value for psychological reasons beyond ordinary reinforcement value.

Workers produce not only to fulfill basic physiological needs but also for psychological needs. To the workers pay represents a reinforcer that will fulfill motivations, and at the same time, it also creates a psychological feeling about their employer. If workers feel their wage scales are adequate or above for their particular kind of work, they have a more favorable attitude toward management. On the other hand, workers feeling stinginess on the part of management may have attitudes that are detrimental to productivity. To be more specific concerning pay, techniques of pay rates will be discussed.

Traditionally, payment for accomplished work was done by means of the amount of time involved. Payment for hours of work is still a very common procedure, but in the early 1900's, when Frederick W. Taylor delved into the possibility of using pay as a method of advancing production, an entirely new emphasis was placed on pay. Taylor assumed that men would be motivated to put forth maximum effort on a job when they were rewarded in proportion to the work accomplished. Thus he suggested a plan whereby a man would be paid for the number of pieces he produced, but with a different payment per unit for workers who produced over and above a standard amount (sometimes called a bogey) compared to those who produced below-standard production. Taylor reasoned that such a plan would encourage workers to raise their production rapidly to standard levels and to expend maximum energy to earn maximum income by getting into the highest piece rate and staying there as much of the time as possible. He also felt that it would eventually cause workers who could not meet the bogey to resign and seek work elsewhere. Such a plan has certain merit, but the setting of the bogey becomes a crucial point. Taylor, of course, suggested motion-and-time study as the means for setting the bogey. Difficulties in this aspect still plague piece-rate payment systems.

More recently a series of different plans have been used for establishing pay for a particular worker. Most of these plans estimate how much value a particular worker's activity is to the organization.

JOB EVALUATION.   In Chapter 6 the technique of studying jobs and preparing job descriptions and merit-rating systems were discussed. Job descriptions are essential for good job evaluations and job-evaluation systems tie in with merit pay plans. *Job evaluation* involves appraising jobs in terms of their total value to the organizational activities. The procedures are particularly valuable in providing management with information to help establish equitable pay rates. Two phases are involved: (1) job evaluation, and (2) translating the evaluation into wage scales, or a dollar value. In some systems, the two phases are tied together, whereas in others the job evaluation is completely separated from the monetary evaluation. It is generally wise to use a committee composed of management and labor representatives to prepare job evaluations. Sometimes evaluating committees also contain membership from outside the industry, particularly a person skilled in rating or evaluation systems.

Four basic methods of job evaluations are commonly used. The oldest of the methods, the classification technique, has been in use in some form or another at least since 1871, when the United States Civil Service Commission established a rough classification scheme. The ranking method is a fairly simple technique, whereas the factor-comparison and the points methods are the more sophisticated or refined techniques. Each will be discussed in the following sections.

CLASSIFICATION METHOD. In the classification method the evaluating committee first sets up a series of labor grades. A description of the various functions, duties, and types of activities is prepared for each labor grade. A maximum and minimum wage scale is then assigned to each of these grades. Finally each job in an organization is assigned to one of the grades by matching the job description with an appropriate labor-grade description. Very typical of the classification method is the current civil service system established by The Classification Act of 1949. This system has 18 levels or grades, for professional, scientific, clerical, and administrative positions. Labor-grade descriptions for three of the 18 Federal Civil Service General Schedule levels are shown in Table 8.2.

TABLE 8.2 Examples of Three Levels or Classes of Jobs as Used in Classification Method of Job Evaluation (labor-grade descriptions from the Federal Civil Service General Schedule)

Grade GS–1 includes all classes of positions the duties of which are to perform, under immediate supervision, with little or no latitude for the exercise of independent judgment, (1) the simplest routine work in office, business, or fiscal operations, or (2) elementary work of a subordinate technical character in a professional, scientific, or technical field.

Grade GS–8 includes all classes of positions the duties of which are (1) to perform, under general supervision, very difficult and responsible work along special technical or supervisor lines in office, business, or fiscal administration, requiring (a) considerable specialized or supervisory training and experience, (b) comprehensive and thorough working knowledge of a specialized and complex subject matter, procedure, or practice, or of the principles of the profession, art, or science involved, and (c) to a considerable extent the exercise of independent judgment; or (2) to perform other work of equal importance, difficulty, and responsibility, and requiring comparable qualifications.

Grade GS–18 includes all classes of positions the duties of which are (1) to serve as the head of a bureau where the position, considering the kind and extent of the authorities and responsibilities vested in it, and the scope, complexity, and degree of difficulty of the activities carried on, is exceptional and outstanding among the whole group of positions of heads of bureaus; (2) to plan and direct or to plan and execute frontier or unprecedented professional, scientific, technical, administrative, fiscal, or other specialized programs of outstanding difficulty, responsibility, and national significance, requiring extended training and experience which has demonstrated outstanding leadership and attainments in professional, scientific, or technical research, practice, or administration, or in administrative, fiscal, or other specialized activities; or (3) to perform consulting or other professional, scientific, technical, administrative, fiscal, or other specialized work of equal importance, difficulty, and responsibility, and requiring comparable qualifications.

The evaluating committee matches each job in the organization against the classification description. For example, in government service, a high-level activity, such as director of a governmental agency, would be evaluated in terms of its job description and would probably be placed in grade GS–18. The method is simple and evaluates job class in terms of overall activity rather than the specific factors that make up the overall work.

THE RANKING METHOD. Perhaps the simplest of all techniques is the ranking method. This requires the committee members to rank all jobs being evaluated in order in terms of relative importance to the organization. Often, each job title is placed on a card or slip of paper so that the committee members simply must pile the cards in order from most to least importance. Sometimes each card also carries a brief job description. Cards may be sorted into order individually by members of the committee and then discrepancies among members ironed out in discussions, or the group may make up the rank order in one long group discussion. This method is difficult to use wherever there are many different jobs to be ranked. It is simple and easy to use for situations where relatively few jobs are involved. Pay for each job is finally assigned by the evaluating committee.

THE FACTOR-COMPARISON METHOD. In the factor-comparison technique there is an assumption that all the jobs included in the evaluation contain some common factors and that jobs may vary in the degree to which any factor is needed. The list of factors involved may deviate according to the company or the committee setting up the job evaluation system. Most lists contain such characteristics as mental demands, physical demands, responsibility, working conditions, and skill requirements. The number of factors used is kept small, allowing for very broad categories so that they can be adapted to a variety of different industrial situations. The first step for the evaluating committee is to describe clearly each of the job factors that might be used. Next, a series of key jobs, usually 15 to 20, are selected. There must be agreement among evaluating committee members that the key jobs are representative of the range of jobs included in the evaluation program and that the pay for these jobs is fair at the time of the beginning of the evaluation. Working independently, the members of the committee then rank the key jobs in two manners. First, each job is ranked with respect to each of the factors. Often these rankings are repeated after two or three weeks, and discrepancies are cleared by discussions with other committee members.

After the individual committee members complete their rankings of the key jobs, an average rank is computed. Table 8.3 shows an example of average rankings for critical factors.

TABLE 8.3 Example of Average Job Rankings of Four Key Jobs on Each of Five Common Factors, using the Factor-Comparison Method of Job Evaluation

			Factors		
Key Jobs	MENTAL DEMANDS	PHYSICAL DEMANDS	RESPONSI- BILITY	SKILL REQUIRE- MENTS	WORKING CONDITIONS
A	2.5	1	1	2	3.5
B	1	2	2	1	3.5
C	2.5	3.5	3	3	2
D	4	3.5	4	4	1

Secondly, individual committee members decide how much of each key job's hourly pay rate is to be paid for each critical factor. These pay rates are combined to produce a committee average pay rate, and these are ranked for each factor in terms of current pay. Discrepancies in the rankings by critical factors versus pay for critical factors are ironed out within the committee, or the job is dropped from consideration as a key job. Table 8.4 shows both kinds of rankings and several discrepancies.

The key jobs with the ranks and pay rates assigned to critical factors constitute the evaluation scale against which all other jobs are rated. When pay is to be set for a job, the job is compared factor by factor to the key jobs in the evaluation scale. Thus, if Job X has mental demands about the same as Key Job A, it would be valued at $0.85 for that critical factor. Job X might have physical demands about midway between Key Jobs C and D (thus $0.75), Responsibility equal to Key Job B ($0.50), skill about midway between Key Jobs A and B ($0.92), and working conditions like Key Job A ($0.15). Thus Job X would be paid $3.17 hourly rate.

This system is somewhat like the ranking method, except that each of several factors is ranked twice. The major difficulties are in picking the key jobs and keeping the evaluation current as economic conditions change.

POINT SYSTEM. The point system is the most common of all evaluation systems in use. Each job is assigned a point value that is the summation of the committee's estimation of ratings on several commonly agreed-upon factors that go into any job.

The general procedure is to establish a series of factors that are thought to be common to all jobs being evaluated. Ten to 15 factors are usually used, but some organizations are reducing this number to four or even fewer. Some frequently used factors are pre-employment training, employment training, mental skill, manual skill, responsibility for material,

TABLE 8.4 Example of Average Pay, Pay Rankings, and Job Rankings by Evaluating Committee for Four Key Jobs on Five Common Factors, Using Factor-Comparison Method of Job Evaluation

Key Jobs	Hourly Pay	Factors														
		Mental Demands			Physical Demands			Responsibility			Skill Requirements			Working Conditions		
		$	$ Rank	Job Rank	$	$ Rank	Job Rank	$	$ Rank	Job Rank	$	$ Rank	Job Rank	$	$ Rank	Job Rank
A	3.15	.85	2	2.5	.65	3	3.5	.60	1	1	.90	2	2	.15	4	3.5
B	3.20	.90	1	1	.60	4	3.5	.50	2	2	.95	1	1	.25	2*	3.5*
C	2.70	.75	3	2.5	.70	2	2	.40	3	3	.65	3	3	.20	3*	2*
D	1.80	.40	4	4	.80	1	1	.10	4	4	.20	4	4	.50	1	1

* Discrepancies that must be adjusted.

responsibility for tools and equipment, responsibility for safety of others, mental effort, physical effort, working conditions, and hazards. After the committee agrees upon factors that are important in all jobs, they must set up a number of levels for each factor with the number of points for each level.

Often the various levels within each factor are described rather thoroughly. Table 8.5 shows an example of five different levels of responsibility for the safety of others and points assigned for each level.

TABLE 8.5 Example of Five Different Levels of Responsibility for Safety of Others and Points Assigned for Each Level for Use in Point System of Job Evaluation

JOB FUNCTIONS	POINTS
Little care required to prevent injury to others:	
Works in area or on machine where others are seldom exposed to hazards of the job.	10
Performs work exposing one other person, such as Helper, where likelihood and probable seriousness of accident is small.	
Ordinary care and attention required to prevent injury to others:	
Coordinated gang or crew work where individual acts may injure others.	14
Operate equipment where others are occasionally exposed.	
Considerable care and attention required to prevent injury to others:	
Operate power-driven mobile equipment where others are exposed but probability of accident is low.	18
Handle inflammable liquids or gases where safeguards minimize the probability of fire or explosion.	
A sustained high degree of attention and care required to prevent injury to others:	
Operate power-driven mobile equipment in congested area.	
Responsible for flow of electric power or steam or the operation of high-pressure vessels where others are exposed to accidents.	22
Control units or equipment handling or processing molten or explosive materials where other persons are exposed but probability of accident is low.	
Extreme care and judgment required to prevent injury to others:	
Handle, control, or transport highly inflammable explosive or molten material exposing other persons to serious injury.	30

Each job can then be compared to a table of points for each of the factors evaluated. As an example, The Brownhoist Crewman job (described in Figure 6.6) is evaluated by the points method in Figure 8.6. The values from Table 8.5 were used for the determination of points for responsibility for safety of others, and points for other factors were assigned by consultation to similar tables not shown here.

	Date _____ Nov. 15, 1964 _____

JOB EVALUATION

Job Title _____ Brownhoist Crewman _____

Factor	Points
Pre-employment Training: Carry out simple instructions necessary for conducting movement of Brownhoist crane and for hooking up.	10
Employment Training and Experience: From 3 to 6 months of continuous progress to became proficient.	14
Mental Skill: Make minor changes in routine where tolerances are liberal.	20
Manual Skill: Use chain or cable slings for simple crane hooking.	10
Responsibility for Material: Handles scale, scrap, etc., where damage is not likely.	10
Responsibility for Tools and Equipment: Some attention and care required to prevent damage to equipment.	12
Responsibility for Operations: Work as a member of a crew performing routine work requiring some coordination with other members of the crew.	15
Responsibility for Safety of Others: Considerable care and attention required to prevent injury to others in ordinary crane hooking.	18
Mental Effort: Light mental or visual application required for crane hooking and for conducting movement of Brownhoist crane.	15
Physical Effort: Moderate physical exertion required in hooking up material and in climbing on railroad cars.	18
Physical Environment: All weather conditions.	18
Hazard: Exposed to injury from climbing on moving cars, hooking up, coupling and uncoupling cars.	18
TOTAL POINTS	178

Figure 8.6. Example of job evaluation by point system for brownhoist crewman job.

Points are assigned to each job by comparing the job description against the point table.

The total points for each job are tabulated, and the value of the job within the organization is determined. Wage rates are then assigned by setting a dollar value for points. For example, each point might be assigned a dollar value of .015 per hour so that if the total points for a job equals 100 the base wage scale for the job would be $1.50 per hour. (The example of The Brownhoist Crewman job would rate $2.67 per hour.) The establishment of dollar values for the points is usually negotiated by the various members of the committee representing management and labor and is established according to going wage rates in the community.

As with other systems, job evaluations are a means to an end. These techniques help an organization to pay properly for the work of a particular function within the organization. The intent is to provide wage ranges rather than specific pay. Consequently a base rate or a range of pay is usually established. An individual working within a particular job classification (a job having a certain number of points) may be paid a different rate than another person on the same job because of greater tenure or more efficiency on his job. Merit systems, piece-rate systems, and other incentive systems may be superimposed on the job evaluation and classification program.

Job evaluation has not been as well accepted as some people might hope. The overall concept is sound, and some of the systems are not too complicated to be explained to workers. But there are several drawbacks: (1) many organizations must set their pay rates to be competitive with their particular community regardless of the value of a job to the company, (2) when job evaluation is introduced some workers will be shown to be receiving too high a rate and thus will be unhappy with the system, and (3) introduction of a plan will probably increase labor costs initially, because "overpaid" workers will be continued at their same rate, whereas "underpaid" workers will be brought up to their proper pay scale. Thus the evaluation committees frequently have "tough sledding" in establishing job evaluation programs for industries where they seem appropriate. As with other industrial relations situations, absolute faith and understanding on the part of management and labor is essential for the job-evaluation team.

Numerous studies, notably those by Lawshe and his associates (1944, 1945, 1946, 1946A), have reported investigations of various functions and aspects of evaluation schemes. Apparently there is no best plan for any one particular organization, but rather all plans work fairly well; it depends more on the people doing the evaluation than on the system itself. Studies of the factors involved in the point technique and factor-comparison technique indicate that very few factors need to be evaluated. In fact, some evidence shows that 95 percent or more of the total variability of point allocations is the result of skill demands, so that the use of other factors is of little value. Other studies have shown that almost all of the variance in terms of point allocation is the result of only two or three factors.

Job-evaluation systems are not designed to handle all the problems of pay and motivation. They cannot be introduced rapidly, they must be understood and accepted by unions and management, and they must be designed so that other characteristics, such as length of service, may also influence a worker's pay rate. In such understanding situations, job evaluation may be very important in maintaining high morale of workers.

PROFIT SHARING.   Another way to help employees feel a sense of belongingness is to have them share in company profits. There are a variety of methods for estimating profit and the relative amount that should be shared with workers, but there are very few general rules useful to all companies.

Profit sharing has been felt to reduce industrial tension whereas wage incentives or piece-rate systems do not. Profit sharing is a method by which employees gain most identification with management and thus seems on the surface to be extremely valuable as a motivating technique.

Unfortunately research data is not at all complete, but a good deal of research indicates that profit sharing has been dropped in as many organizations as ones in which it has lasted. Profit sharing is usually best in an organization that is increasing its profits each year. When a bad year results in lower profits or none to share, there is often unhappiness with the system. The biggest value of profit sharing seems to be the psychological impact on the workers. They are more likely to feel that they are truly participating in an organization and thus may be more efficient in their work.

FRINGE BENEFITS.   In closing the section discussing pay, we emphasize that dollar value in terms of take-home pay is so different than earned income that most workers are hardly aware of earned income. With present tax laws and withholding techniques, a worker receives only an amount of pay that represents a net after deductions for a variety of things, including pension, withholding tax, hospitalization, and so on. These withheld items frequently represent a large segment of a worker's earned income. On the other hand, there are usually many fringe benefits provided by management and not even recorded on statements routinely received by the workers. For example, supplemental payments for vacation pay, holiday pay, pensions, insurance, unemployment benefits, and social security create a large drain on the cost of operation in most organizations today. Reported in *Steelways* (1963), the total hourly cost of pay to steel workers in 1963 averaged $3.99 per hour. Of this, 79¢ per hour was for fringe benefit costs. Thus a worker would show a gross income for 40 hours work of $128.00. After taxes, union dues, and other withheld items are deducted he might get a check for $102.40. Of course, the cost to his company was $159.60. The importance of the fringe benefits available with a job must be clearly understood, because these benefits represent a large cost to the organization and yet are not immediately apparent to workers.

ACCIDENTS AND SAFETY

In 1961, the cities of Bethlehem, Pennsylvania; Greenwich, Connecticut; Kalamazoo, Michigan; Saginaw, Michigan; Roanoke, Virginia; Sioux Falls, South Dakota; and Stanford, Connecticut were all between 50,000 and 100,000 population, many bordering near the latter figure. In that same year, accidental deaths in the United States totaled approximately 96,500 people. In other words, the entire population of any one of those cities could be thought of as lost as a result of accidental deaths (National Safety Council, 1963).

Statistics are merely numbers and as most of us know can be made to show almost anything if interpreted in a particular manner. Perhaps it is not wise to state such startling statistics since almost all accident prevention programs seem to work with the same kind of information. However, the plain fact of the matter is that a tremendous amount of human misery and economic loss occur because of so-called accidents. In this book, accidents and safety are discussed in three different chapters. This first time, a consideration will be given of the factors in the work environment having to do with accidents and accident prevention. In Chapter 9, accidents will be discussed in terms of man as related to his machinery, and in Chapter 11, in terms of man within himself. The emphasis on the discussion of accidents and safety will thus be placed on the psychological characteristics rather than the physical environment or the working situation. This does not mean to deemphasize the importance of the physical environment. However, most estimates of the reasons for accidents indicate that human factors are to blame more than any other factor. The discussions about accidents will include industrial and nonindustrial information, because many of the principles and characteristics discussed are equally important in both situations.

Before discussing specific characteristics of the physical work situation, a few additional statistics are essential. The estimated total cost of accidents in the United States during 1962 totaled the staggering sum of $15,300,000, which included wage loss of $4,400,000, medical expenses of $1,550,000, overhead cost of insurance, and so on, $3,150,000 and property damage of $3,780,000 plus so-called indirect cost of work accidents of approximately $2,400,000. There was approximately a 5-percent increase in accidental deaths and a general increase in accidents of nonfatal nature over the previous year. Accidents as a cause of death in the United States were exceeded only by heart disease, cancer, and vascular lesions of the central nervous system. In the age group of 1 to 36 years, accidents were the leading cause of death.

All is not bleak. Even the statistics show some improvement in accidents. For example, the death rate in 1962 per 100,000 population was 51.9, which is lower than any year on record except 1961, which was 50.4. Furthermore, although the motor vehicle accident rate is up to 5.3 per 100 million vehicle-miles, the death rate in nonmotor vehicle accidents is down. For the five years 1908 to 1912 the accidental death rate for non-automotive accidents was 81 per 100,000 population. By 1962 the nonmotor vehicle rate had dropped to 30 per 100,000 population, which shows that a special emphasis on safety or accident prevention has accomplished a reduction in accident rate. Unfortunately, the successful accident prevention work in industry and nonmotor vehicle activity has been partly overcome by an increase in the death rate by motor vehicle accidents from 2 per 100,000 population to 22 during the same period. Now, let's look at some of the causes of accidents related to the environment.

Although most accidents are not caused by a single factor but rather a multiple series of causes, it is a well-accepted fact that some particular environments are more hazardous than others. Work in some industry by the very nature of the task involves an individual in an environment where he is more likely to be injured or killed. By the same token some organizations, due to the attitudes and relationships between employees and management, have a higher accident rate. There may even be a connotation that accidental injuries and deaths are not too important.

Examination of the National Safety Council Reports (National Safety Council, 1962) showed that some occupations involve considerably more hazards. For example, disabling injuries per 1 million man-hours of employment for communications industries was 0.93. The average for all industries was 5.99, and for mining underground coal it was 35.86. Some other industries between the extreme of communication and mining underground coal show meat packing at 14.06, lumbering at 22.13, steel at 3.25, and aircraft manufacturing at 1.62 per 1 million man-hours of work. The communications injury rates between 1951 and 1961 decreased 48 percent, aircraft manufacturing decreased 70 percent, and average for all industries reporting decreased 34 percent. The better-performing industries are more rapidly reducing their accident rates, which shows that a greater effort on accident prevention pays off. What are some of the specific factors in the environment that can bring about this reduction in injury and death?

In a series of studies concerning ventilation done in the 1920's and 1930's by Vernon (1937) and his fellow workers, evidence showed that increasing temperature above 70 degrees F. greatly increased accident rates. However, the results were compounded by sex differences in accident rate and by the severity of the accidents. The more severe accidents did not increase with the increased temperatures, whereas the minor accidents did. This might mean that unpleasant working conditions are more likely to cause a person to take time off and a minor injury would be reported more readily or even slightly encouraged in order to have a relief from the adverse environmental conditions. More recently Sherman, Kerr, and Kosinar (1957) studied the relationship between 75 variables and accident records in a large number of separate factories. They found a correlation between frequency of accidents and percentage of employees exposed to extreme temperatures to be only 0.06, whereas the severity of accidents correlated 0.55 with extreme temperatures. Thus it seems that the abnormal temperature condition does not bring about a great many more accidents, but does have an effect upon the severity of accidents. Most of the other factors studied by Sherman, Kerr, and Kosinar had no significant correlation with frequency or severity of accidents. Accident frequency was positively correlated with smaller-sized plants, plants having personnel handling heavy materials, and plants in an area surrounded by many other industrial plants. In terms of accident severity, the only other factor positively correlated was plants with a high proportion of personnel needing showers after work. This research seemed to indicate dirty and above-average-temperature working conditions are related to severe accidents.

Accidents related to illumination are not often studied. Recent studies are relatively rare, because studies performed by Vernon and others in the 1920's and 30's are accepted. Vernon showed that about 25 percent more accidents occurred during hours of artificial light than in daylight in a number of English industries, such as dockwork, textile, shipbuilding, and so forth. As discussed earlier, varying levels of illumination or wide contrasts in light intensities bring about temporary blindness or difficulty in seeing and can result in accidents. In terms of highway lighting, there are many reports showing that highway lighting does decrease accidents as compared with unlighted areas. The previously reported National Safety Council Report showed that in 1961 there was a much higher death rate per thousand during the night than during the day. On a national basis, the death rate during the daytime is 3 per 100 million vehicle-miles, whereas at night it is 9 per 100 million vehicle-miles. This difference is even greater in unlighted rural areas, where 5 deaths per 100 million vehicle-miles occur in the day and 12 per 100 million at night.

In terms of physical environment, one study by Kerr (1950) showed that high noise level is associated with more accidents. Additional factors in the environment that are related to accidents include the environmental organization provided by management, a matter that will be discussed in a later chapter. For example, low intracompany transfer mobility, low probability of promotion, large amount of dissatisfaction with management, and so on, seem to be related to high accident rates. Unfortunately most of the evidence available does not partial out or hold constant the psychological variables, so that the pure influence of physical characteristics in the working environment can be made known. It is quite likely that the physical factors have a psychological impact, which in turn may have a great effect upon accident and safety records.

SUMMARY

Production of workers is the result of man interacting with his environment and the tools of production. A typical way of measuring production is by use of a work curve. The work curve shows production per unit of time for one workday or work week. Ordinarily production starts slow, increases to a working level, and then drops off near the end of each work period.

Factors in the work environment that affect the work curve were discussed in this chapter. Characteristics of illumination and their influence on productivity were presented in some detail. Light must be of sufficient intensity and adequately distributed for the particular job at hand. Noise may influence production by distracting workers or with prolonged exposure may cause hearing losses. Apparently the detrimental effects on production are less when workers become adapted to noise.

The humidity, temperature, and air movement in the work area have a combined effect upon productivity. Workers can maintain high-level productivity under adverse temperature conditions if humidity and air movement are adequately controlled.

Music as a special component in the working environment has some psychological effect upon workers. At present there is little good evidence indicating what effect music has upon production. The number of hours of work required per week has an influence on productivity per unit of time. Workers expect to work a certain number of hours per week, generally

35 to 40, and when required to put in more hours, produce less per hour. Rest pauses have become common practice in the United States. Because they are expected by workers, any change in such procedures will have an effect upon productivity.

Many jobs in modern-day industry are highly repetitive and relatively simple. Most management personnel believe that such situations create a bored condition in workers that results in decreases in productivity. Thus steps are undertaken to reduce boredom.

Pay has been traditionally accorded in terms of the amount of time put in or the material produced. Several systems of evaluating jobs in relation to their overall value to an organization were discussed. Profit sharing and other fringe benefits are also important aspects of payment now provided workers.

A final section emphasized the relationship of the working environment to man in the creation of accident situations. Some environments are more hazardous than others, but improvements are being made in most industries.

SUGGESTED REFERENCES FOR FURTHER STUDY

Morgan, C. T., J. S. Cook, A. Chapanis, and M. W. Lund (1963). *Human Engineering Guide to Equipment Design*. New York: McGraw-Hill Book Company.

A comprehensive source of human engineering information, including a thorough coverage of many aspects of the working environment.

Journal of Applied Psychology.

Contains many articles of recent research concerning working conditions and effects upon productivity.

Siegel, L. (1962). *Industrial Psychology*. Homewood, Ill.: Richard D. Irwin.

Chapters 8, 9, and 10 concern the topics of man as related to his work environment.

Chapter 9
Man Related to Machines

FOR MOST OF THE LAST CENTURY the standard of living in the United States has been far above that of most of the other nations of the world. This standard has not been accomplished by slave labor or at the expense of the large multitude of the population. It has been the result of man multiplying his efforts with machinery. American industry has produced more goods per man-hour than any other society known to man.

Although there are many odious overtones involved in the use of machine power, it cannot be denied that fantastic advancements in standards of living have been accomplished by the use of machinery. In a publication by the Center for the Study of Democratic Institutions, Dr. Robert M. Hutchins (1963), former Chancellor of the University of Chicago, stated that in 1959 Americans consumed the equivalent of 8,000 killograms of coal per capita as compared to only 8 in Ethiopia and about 3,800 in Russia. In terms of the energy put forth by slaves in previous days, Dr. Hutchins estimated that each man, woman, and child in the United States has the equivalent power of 85 slaves. It is valuable to know that great amounts of energy are available and are put to use to help man, but it is essential to understand how man can best work with machinery to multiply his efforts efficiently. The purpose of this chapter is to discuss how man and machines can be used together to achieve maximum production with the minimum amount of effort. In case there is any doubt about the necessity of increasing efficiency of man's efforts, let us examine some additional information.

It has been estimated by reliable authorities that the population of the United States will increase rapidly during the next quarter of a century and by A.D. 2,000 will reach 300 million. All of these people will want to maintain standards of living as high or higher than now attained. Chances are good that medical progress will extend life expectancy of all the population and that average hours of work per week will be shortened while retirement begins earlier rather than later. All of these factors must be taken into account when considering how to maintain or raise standards of living of an expanding population. At present, a 2,000-hour work year is about normal. This is based on 40 hours a week for 50 weeks, with 2 weeks vacation. An average worker spends about 45 years in gainful employment, depending upon amount of education before commencing and age of retirement. The present average life expectancy at birth is approximately 70 years. Obviously, an average person must produce enough goods to support himself for an average of 70 years of life. Thus, 45 years, 2,000 hours per year results in a total of 90,000 hours of work in which a man must produce enough to live for 70 years. As life expectancy is increased, the total production for the average person must be greater than 70 years' worth. As the total working time is decreased by early retirement, later starting as a result of more education, or shorter hours per week, it is quite obvious that man must increase his efficiency even more to produce enough to exist for his normal life span. Thus, even though all workers in the United States now greatly multiply their efforts by the use of power and machinery, it is imperative to produce even greater efficiency in man–machine systems in the future.

The standard of living of any group can be raised by increasing the productivity per member of the group. Thus increasing efficiency is important in all countries of the world. Some of the techniques in use in the United States will help provide relatively rapid increases in productivity in other countries. The factors discussed in this book are generally applicable throughout the world, although some are particularly useful by industries in the United States.

This chapter will discuss factors concerned in man–machine systems, motion-and-time study, methods of presenting information to man, man controlling machines, and accidents and safety in man–machine systems.

MAN–MACHINE SYSTEMS

Whenever we observe the control area of modern-day aircraft, ships, submarines, or other sophisticated mechanical apparatus, we recognize that there are many complicated activities or links between man and the machine. All the equipment and the man working with the equipment go together to make up a system. The cockpit of a multijet aircraft with the pilot, copilot, engineers, and so on, makes up a system. Such a system uses

Figures 9.1a, b, c, and d. This series of photographs shows man-machine systems in the oil production industry. Upper left shows a control room from which a huge oil refining plant (background) is operated. An operator assisted by two or more plant men run the refining plant. Lower left shows the interior of a control room. Each unit of a plant is diagramed on control room walls, and appropriate instruments and controls are located within the diagrams so that men can control the production. Upper right shows a conveyor dispatch room. The operator sets up orders for each type of product and distributes them to proper destinations by punching buttons on the control panel. Each barrel then ends up at the proper freight or truck dock. Lower right shows barrels coming off the end of a mile-long conveyor system, with the operator controlling the final destination of each barrel at a loading position on the freight dock. (Courtesy of Standard Oil Company of California, 225 Bush Street, San Francisco, Calif.)

a large group of components to accomplish a given set of purposes. In the case of the aircraft, some purposes are taking off, flying to a destination, and landing. Other systems are more or less complicated, but all serve a set of purposes.

When you are converting your thinking into writing, several components of a man–machine system are involved. Simple machines, the pencil and paper, interact with the human to accomplish a particular purpose. The design of a system so that it serves efficiently to accomplish the purposes set for it is called system design. In the armed forces, a set of purposes is called a mission, and therefore system design is the design of a set of components to serve a particular mission or missions.

In recent years more and more complicated machinery has been developed. Computerized systems seem to involve only machines; however, men are needed in almost all systems. Thus a system analysis must be of a man–machine system. Whenever a man or a series of men is involved with machinery we have a man–machine system. Most simple man–machine systems are components of larger man–machine systems. For example, many man–machine systems function within a modern warship, whereas an overall system is involved in the total functioning of the ship.

The machine components of a system are generally well thought-out and designed for efficient production of the machinery and even for maintenance of that machinery. On the other hand, the human factors that enter into the system are often ignored, particularly during the initial stages of design of the system. This is unfortunate, because the human factor is frequently more variable than any of the machine components and, often, the most difficult to change. If machinery is designed to serve a particular function without adequate understanding of the human factors, expensive redesign is sometimes necessitated when the human is introduced into the system. At times, selection and training of the human operator have been used to overcome shortcomings in the design of the machine components of a system. This is usually an inadequate and, at best, a very expensive and temporary method of handling the basic problem. For a proper man–machine system to work efficiently, it must be designed about the human with understanding of the capacities of the human component of the system.

Open-Loop and Closed-Loop Systems. Man–machine systems, as well as the simplest mechanical systems, are generally of two types, open-loop or closed-loop. In the open-loop system, information enters the system at one point, goes through a controlling mechanism, and results in activity of some sort. Commonly, the word *input* refers to the information entering the system, *output* for the result or action taken by the system, and *control* for the information-processing phase of the system. An example of a simple mechanical open-loop system is an automatic sprinkler system for fire protection. Input is temperature change, which causes the melting of a fuse or control plug in the water line, which releases a flow of water (the output). In such a mechanical open-loop system, there is no self-regulation. Once the water is released by the melting of the plug, water continues to flow until an outside force turns the system off.

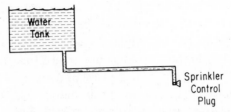

Figure 9.2. An example of a simple mechanical open-loop system (automatic fire sprinkler). When the temperature at the sprinkler control reaches a certain level, the control plug melts and water flows out of the pipe until the supply is exhausted or is turned off by an outside force.

In a closed-loop system, information enters at one point in the system, and the control mechanism creates a certain action, just as in the open-loop system. However, the regulation or change in the situation is also fed back into the system, and so the system reacts to its own activity. One example frequently encountered is an automatic home-heating system. In such a system, a thermostat is activated by changes in the temperature in the room. As the temperature goes down, an electrical circuit is completed and a furnace is turned on. The furnace creates heat, which is fed into the room. As the temperature rises, the electrical circuit is opened by the

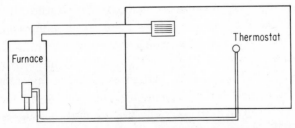

Figure 9.3. An example of a simple mechanical closed-loop system (automatic heat control). When the room temperature decreases, electrical contacts in the thermostat close and turn on the furnace. When heat from the furnace raises the room temperature sufficiently, the electrical contacts in the thermostat open and turn off the furnace.

thermostat, and the system is turned off. Thus a self-regulating, or closed-loop, system is in operation.

In Figures 9.2 and 9.3 simple closed-loop and open-loop systems involve only machines. Man may enter either system by providing a control function, such as opening the control plug or adjusting the thermostat. Completely open-looped man-machine systems are relatively rare. This is understandable since closed-loop systems are generally more efficient.

The input phase of a system involving a man is usually a visual or auditory display, so that receptor organs of the man may pick up the information. Once the information is received by receptor organs, the organism responds to this stimulus by integrating the information and creating activity to adjust controlling mechanisms. This usually is pushing a button, turning a wheel, or manipulating some other mechanical control device. Man, then, is the controlling phase of most man–machine systems. An everyday example is the driving of an automobile. While driving on the highway a person adjusts to many visual and auditory displays. One is the visual stimulus of the car ahead. When approaching an intersection, the driver in the man–machine system observes the red taillight go on in the car in front. The man integrates the input information and creates a series of responses. He takes his foot off the gas and places it on the brake pedal. If the automobile in front actually stops, additional appropriate responses are given. This example is a closed-loop system, because the responses of the man affect the stimulation he is receiving from his environment. As his car slows he integrates that information with the red taillight and speed of the car in front to modify his responses, either pressing harder or easier on the brake pedal, and so on.

As might be expected, closed-loop systems have been most effective when engineering principles have been applied. Taylor (1960) suggested that human engineering in closed-loop systems has been most valuable because a useful mathematical theory based on automatic systems was available before the engineering psychologists started work. In closed-loop systems where feedback to the man is rapid, great improvements in efficiency have taken place as a result of human engineering. In fact, five to six times better performance by adjustment of mechanism dynamics have been reported. (Sweeney, Bailey, and Dowd, 1957.) Taylor further indicated that, as models for understanding and reducing to mathematical logic the function of man in a complicated system where he does not get feedback are developed, human engineering will also make great strides in improving efficiency of open-loop systems.

Since it is not the function of this text to go into great detail on any particular phase of psychology applied in specialized fields, we will present only a brief discussion of some of the information available regarding man–machine systems.

MAN IN A MAN–MACHINE SYSTEM

Men vary far more than machines. As mentioned previously, this must be taken into account in the very earliest stages when designing man–machine systems. We briefly discuss here some of the variability of man as related to man–machine systems. We will cover some aspects of the sensory and response systems of man. There are many variations from man to man on all physiological and psychological measurements. Thus a normal distribution curve, such as shown in Figure 6.6, for IQ can also be expected for most input and output capacities of men.

A great deal about man's sensory abilities is now known. For example, Mowbray and Gebhard (1961) compiled a comprehensive summary of man's senses and the physical energies that stimulate them. They indicated the minimum amount of stimulation intensity necessary to be detectable and the largest practical amount that the man could stand. Such data is available for most of the sensory receptors and must be considered when designing a system in which a human is going to be presented with information.

Let us examine a study concerning the input capacities of man in a man–machine system. For example, Sleight (1948) reported a study in which he compared efficiency of reading five different dial faces. Each of the dials presented the same information with the same size pointers and same distances between numbers, but they were of different shapes. Figure 9.4 shows sketches of the different dial shapes. These dials were presented in a viewing box and exposed for twelve hundredths of a second. In all trials the pointer was set exactly at one of the numbers or on one of the small marks between two numbers. The subjects knew this and were told to read the dial to the nearest half unit. Sleight recorded his information in terms of a percentage of incorrect readings by 60 subjects. The open-window dial gave the fewest errors (only 5 out of 1,020 trials) whereas the vertical dial was poorest.

Naturally, we cannot interpret Sleight's experiment to say that the open-window dial should be used in all situations, because there are other drawbacks: (1) rapid changes cannot be noted as they are taking place, nor can the dial be read accurately, because several numbers may be changing so fast as to be only a blur; (2) direction of change is not easily noted; and (3) when a variety of information dials are needed, open windows with different numbering systems on them might be confusing.

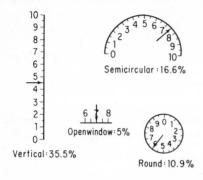

Figure 9.4. Five different-shaped dial faces and percentages of errors in reading each dial face. After R. B. Sleight (1947) "The Effect of Instrument Dial Shape on Legibility," *J. Appl. Psychol.,* **32,** 177.

Man also has to respond after integrating the input information. The capabilities of man as a response mechanism have also been extensively investigated. We cite here two studies to show how knowledge concerning man can be useful in the earliest design stages of man–machine systems. Brown and Slater-Hammel (1949) showed that righthanded men can make right-to-left movements slightly faster than left-to-right movements. Short horizontal movements have been shown to be faster than vertical movements (Woodson, 1954). Thus since most men are righthanded, short control movements such as moving a lever or control stick should be designed to go horizontally from right to left if speed of control is important.

There are many other studies concerning both the input and output phases of man in man–machine systems. However, there are relatively few reports that deal with the function of the man as a controlling mechanism in the system. In many systems, man performs a function that might be handled by machinery if such machines were available. For example, computers can handle information gathering, interpretation, and output. A few studies have reported the release of man from the system by insertion of a computer. But most reports show how the function of man can be eased rather than eliminated. For example, a study by Birmingham, Kahn, and Taylor was reported by Taylor (1960) and showed the complex learning curves of six subjects trying to learn to handle a system somewhat similar to that used to maneuver a submarine. Figure 9.5a shows the variability during the learning phase and difficulty in learning for the six subjects. Training eventually got some of the subjects to efficient operating levels; however, Figure 9.5b shows the same subjects' performances on a

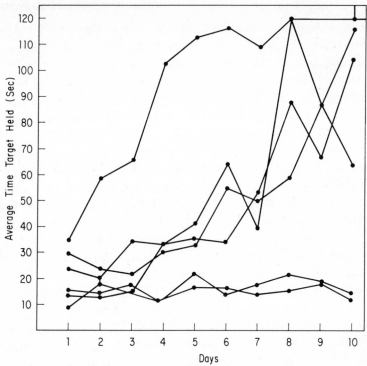

Figure 9.5a. Learning curves of six subjects for complex tracking behavior task.

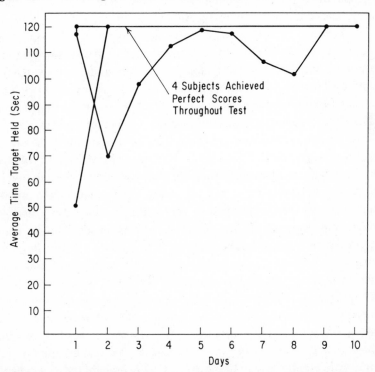

4 Subjects Achieved
Perfect Scores
Throughout Test

Figure 9.5b. Learning curves of six subjects for simple tracking behavior task.

Both figures 9.5a and 9.5b are after E. V. Taylor (1960), "Four Basic Ideas in Engineering Psychology" *Amer. Psychol.*, **15,** 645.

task that accomplished the same mission or performance with slightly modified machines. By modifying the control functions of the apparatus without changing the basic system, four of the six subjects had perfect performance from the first day, and all subjects eventually learned the task. By slight modification of the machine parts, high-level performance of the total man–machine system could be obtained with the use of almost any man with very little or no training.

The book titled *Human Engineering Guide to Equipment Design* by Morgan *et al.* (1963) summarized the values of man and machine in man–machine systems. Suggesting that man and machines have different capabilities and limitations, the authors showed that man as a sensing organism has a relatively narrow range of physical energies to which he may respond, but that he is usually superior to machines in perceiving and interpreting some sensory information. Man is particularly better than machines for tasks requiring discrimination of signals mixed with noise such as echoes, outside or background static, and so on. Man can also identify similar patterns in a different situation. Man can often pick out information from incomplete or partially completed signals, and man is selective in his perception and therefore can shut out certain signals and respond only to others. As a data processor, man has the advantages of not needing extensive preprogramming, is generally more flexible, exercises judgment, and does not require special coding of information. On the other hand, many data-processing devices are superior in that they can store data, can compute answers with much greater speed, can sort and screen information faster, are less subject to fatigue and are more reliable for routine decisions. As controller, man has the ability to work only within certain limited force ranges and is relatively slow compared to machines. Man can make only certain limited types of movements and with only a minimum amount of control over a certain time period. In general, machines can do a good deal more in terms of control, whereas man is frequently overloaded. Finally, in terms of working environment, machines can be designed to operate within very wide environmental extremes, whereas man is required to stay within a much more uniform enivronment to work at his best, or even to work at all. Morgan *et al.* summarized man versus machines in systems as follows: "1. Use machines for routine tasks involving calculations and storage of large numbers of concrete facts or details. 2. Use machines when large forces need to be applied quickly and smoothly. 3. Use machines when large amounts of data need to be sorted and screened and all data not in a desired class rejected. 4. Use machines for making routine decisions, i.e., decisions that are always made in the same way according to specifiable rules. 5. Use machines where anticipated stresses have a high probability of producing failure in human performance. 6. Use machines where controls should be operated with very little delay and with great speed. 7. Use machines if the force to be applied to a control requires precision or where the force must be applied over a long period of time. 8. Use man for tasks requiring discrimination of signals in noise. 9. Use man where the task requires pattern discrimination in a changing field. 10. Use man where discrimination must be made between multiple input. 11. Use man where his flexibility will be required in unforeseen situations. 12. Use man for tasks requiring problem solving. 13. Use man as a monitor with override capabilities, in automatic and semi-automatic systems. 14. Use man where the sensing and recording of incidental intelligence is expected in the course of a mission having other objectives. 15. Use man where alternate modes of operation are likely to be required."

Jordan (1963) has seriously questioned the basic concepts of how to decide whether to use man or machine in automated systems. He stated that for many years, human factor engineers recommended that man be compared with machines and then be chosen for those functions he does better. Jordan argued that this concept is faulty and that man and machines are not comparable. He went on to suggest that the comparability concept results in designing the function of man in the system as simple as possible so he has the least to do. "The conclusion is inescapable—design the man out of the system. If he does the least, the least he can do is zero." Jordan thus suggested that "Men are flexible but cannot be depended upon to perform in a consistent manner whereas machines can be depended upon to perform consistently but they have no flexibility whatsoever. This can be summarized simply and seemingly tritely by saying that men are good at doing that which machines are not good at doing and machines are good at doing that which men are not good at doing. Men and machines are not comparable, they are *complementary*. Gentlemen, I suggest that complementary is probably the correct concept to use in discussing the allocation of tasks to men and to machines. Rather than compare men and machines as to which is better for getting a task done let us think about how we complement men by machines and vice versa to get a task done."

The article by Jordan emphasized the use of man's particular capacities in man–machine systems. As designers further realize the great advantages of man by designing machines to use man's capabilities complemented by the abilities of machines, more efficient systems will be built.

MOTION-AND-TIME STUDY

Although it may seem a little picayune, it is essential that a student recognize the sequence motion-and-time study rather than the often stated time-and-motion study. Truly, motion study must precede time study. Motion study involves the analysis of the functions involved in doing a job. Motion study is done to improve working techniques, to eliminate unnecessary movements, and to expedite performance. Time study is the measurement of the time involved in the various segments of a particular job or function. A job must be analyzed for motion first and time second.

Motion-and-time study has received a great deal of publicity and criticism during the past half-century. Motion-and-time study gained its greatest impetus with the systematic analysis of routine work begun by Frederick W. Taylor in the early 1900's. In one series of controlled observations at the Bethlehem Steel Works, he found that if shovels designed to hold about 21 pounds rather than a larger amount were used, more tonnage of coal could be shoveled per day. Consequently he inaugurated the practice of using special shovels for each type of work, and introduced an incentive wage or bonus system. Taylor was able to show that 140 men in the Bethlehem Yard could do the same work as formerly completed by 500 men (Copley, 1923).

In another early study a gang of 75 laborers was studied by Taylor. One man was observed intensively and trained after Taylor's observations. The laborer was originally able to carry about 12½ tons of pig iron per day from a stock pile to a railroad car. By the use of a bonus incentive and by movement analysis and training, including when to rest, Taylor had the man increase his average output to 47½ tons per day.

It is also important to note the work of Frank D. Gilbreth and his wife Lillian, who worked about the same time but independent of Taylor. They were mostly interested in the elimination of unnecessary motions and did early investigations of brick laying. After development of an easily adjusted scaffold and special tools, Gilbreth showed that with proper handling of tools and bricks the number of motions involved in laying the bricks could be reduced from 18 to 4½. This series of studies also showed that great increases in production per day could be effected by the use of Gilbreth's suggested economies. (Perhaps it is also of interest to know that present union rules set outputs of brick layers at less than half as many bricks per day as could be placed following Gilbreth's suggestions.)

Let us now consider a few examples of the use of some of the motion-economy rules. First, we show an example of some of the rules related to use of the body.

Many people have tried the amusement park task of driving a weight to the top of a scale to ring a bell. The task is performed by striking a lever at the bottom of the scale with a sledge hammer. Perhaps you have been frustrated by not being able to ring the bell and then watched a relatively small "barker" use the sledge hammer with apparent ease to tap the lever and so ring the gong. The barker probably used continuous, curved, flowing motions to produce maximum force with a minimum amount of effort. Instead of lifting the sledge hammer straight up and bringing it down in a jerking movement, he used a smooth flow, swinging the hammer around in a complete arc before landing on the lever.

The control area of a typical automobile fulfills some of the rules concerning motion economy related to the work place. Controls are located within easy reach and positioned in a manner that is readily usable by the driver. Such items as cigarette lighters are prepositioned, ready for use and within the easy reach of the driver. (Of course some manufacturers have designed automobiles for aesthetic purposes or for ease of manufacture and have missed the concept of human engineering.)

Dvorak, Merrick, Dealey, and Ford (1936) suggested an efficient keyboard for typewriters. The arrangement of the keyboard was in terms of the ability of the fingers to perform the work. This work points up some of the rules concerning design of tools and equipment.

Motion-and-time studies have produced the most dramatic results in relatively routine tasks. Attention has been given to highly repetitive work where large numbers of employees were involved. Thus work standardization through the findings of motion-and-time studies reduced effort and time per unit of production. Work standardization also frequently reduced worker satisfaction and helped create boredom and monotony, as discussed previously.

By means of photographs, observations, and motion-picture films, motions have been studied extensively. Careful observation and systematic study have allowed observers to suggest ways of eliminating needless or wasteful motions. Different jobs involve different speeds and finesse in motion, and consequently precision of time measured has to vary from one function to another. Motion-and-time study engineers may frequently be found with a clip board and a stop watch ready to measure a hundredth of a minute or some other fractional part of minutes or seconds. The information that the engineer collects is analyzed and results in suggested improvements for more efficient job performance.

Motion-Economy Rules. Gilbreth recorded a series of rules of motion economy in the early 1920's. Since that time, additional information has been gathered, so that the original rules have been modified and supplemented. A set of motion economy rules grouped under three major categories is shown in Table 9.1. Many of these rules can be applied in most work situations and will add to a worker's efficiency. Figure 9.6 shows the work load for the universal typewriter and Dvorak Keyboard. It is interesting to note that although studies done during the Second World War showed that the Dvorak keyboard was far superior to the universal typewriter keyboard, the latter is still very much in use and being manufactured in thousands of typewriters each year. Of course the universal keyboard is continued in use because of the large supply of trained typists who would have to relearn a new keyboard and the large number of machines that would be immediately obsolete if the new keyboard replaced the old. However, presently used typewriters should be constant reminders to us of the value of good design if only it could be used.

TABLE 9.1 Several Motion-Economy Rules

A. Related to the Use of the Body:
  1. In general two hands perform most economically when they begin and complete movements at the same time and when movements are made simultaneously in opposite and symmetrical directions.
  2. Hands should not be idle at the same time except during rest periods.
  3. Motions should involve the least amount of bodily anatomy necessary for performance of the activity.
  4. Momentum should be used whenever possible unless it must be counteracted by muscular effort.
  5. Continuous curved and flowing motions should be used rather than sharp changes of directions.
B. Related to the Work Place:
  1. Tools, controls, and materials to be used should be located at fixed spots near the place of use and in a position ready for use.
  2. Materials that are completed should be released with the minimum amount of effort into drop shoots or other moving devices that take the materials from the work place.
  3. Working levels should be adjusted to the height of the individual employee with appropriate lighting and atmospheric conditions.
C. Related to the Design of Tools and Equipment:
  1. Other parts of the body are often more economical to use than the hands (for example, the feet).
  2. Work load should be distributed by the use of tools according to the ability of the anatomy to do the job.
  3. More than one function may be served by one tool.

Criticisms of Motion-and-Time Studies. Organized labor has frequently protested motion-and-time study. They specifically state that such studies increase monotony, produce boredom, eliminate jobs, and reduce the effect of worker's own initiative. There is no doubt that some workers are adversely effected by motion-and-time studies. There is also no doubt that insisting that one best way of work must be followed by all the workers simply cannot be tolerated when we recognize that there are individual

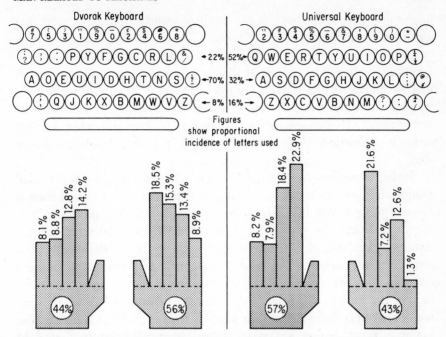

Figure 9.6. Dvorak and universal typewriter keyboards and percentage of use for each finger of typist using the two different keyboards for typing general office letters. The length of the fingers on each represents the percentage of work performed by that finger. Courtesy of A. Dvorak.

differences in workers. However, increased automation and specialization of work have intensified the need and the value of motion-and-time study.

As additional automated production is achieved, the systematic, routine functions in industry may become less and less important in terms of manpower. More work will be performed by machines, and it is conceivable that the importance of motion-and-time study will decrease. However, the semiskilled and skilled groups of workers that do a fair job but don't work to the maximum of their capacity can probably be helped by motion-and-time studies. These men must be trained to more efficient methods or placed in other functions. As better selection and placement of workers takes place and adequate training is accomplished, changes as the result of motion-and-time study will not be necessary and one of the major criticisms will drop from importance.

Some of the other criticisms of motion-and-time study do not bear up under scrutiny. For example, the cost of doing motion-and-time study has been called a detriment. True, it costs something to do motion-and-time study, but invariably the savings brought about by increased efficiency of workers far offsets the cost of the original survey. The complaint that monotony is brought about as the result of standardization of work was dismissed by studies reported in Chapter 8. It may be that different classification and placement of workers is necessary but not that motion study is necessarily wrong. The complaint that piece rates of pay are lowered after motion studies so that workers are forced to speed up is unfortunate, but it is due not to the motion-and-time studies but rather to the philosophy of management. If management is inclined to reduce pay when workers increase production, they may do so with or without motion-and-time study.

Perhaps more important are the criticisms of some psychologists toward motion-and-time studies. A major criticism is based on the fact that there is no such thing as one best way to do a particular job, because individuals vary in abilities. The second major complaint is that the sampling procedures and techniques of observing used to create the standard method are sometimes not adequate. For example, one, two, or perhaps three workers doing a similar job are studied. After an analysis of the job and the time for each of the functions, averages for the three workers are derived. Extreme scores are often eliminated on the basis of the observer's comments. (For example, a rest period was taken or an abnormally fast time may be thought to have been a misjudgment on the part of the observer pressing the stop watch, and so on.) Finally a specific time for the job is derived, and it too is usually given a "fudge" factor to allow for variances in humans. This process has been questioned by many psychologists since precise measurements in terms of a hundredth of a minute have been recorded and then "fudge" factors, eliminations of extremes, and so on, have given results that seem to have precision but have too many estimates mixed with observations. A third seemingly justifiable complaint is based on workers' reports. They state that they know when motion study is being done and perform accordingly. Consequently, motion-and-time studies may not be true indications of the functions of any worker.

Some studies of motion economy involve the use of standardized segments of work. From many previous studies of various working situations, common motions involved in work can be assigned specific times. Then an analysis of motion is all that is needed. The total time for a job can be estimated by using the standard time for the various functions involved.

Finally, a series of statements by Farmer (1923) regarding the conduct of motion-and-time studies might well be remembered. "1. All time and motion study must be undertaken solely in the interest of lessened fatigue and never in the interest of increased production. 2. The underlying principle of motion study is rhythm and not speed. We must look upon the best set of motions as the easiest and not the quickest. 3. The proper use of time study is for the analysis of an operation in order to suggest lines of improvement or to determine the relation between processes rather than for standardization (that is, forcing all men to use the same motion)."

There are specialists trained to do motion-and-time studies. This most frequently is work of an engineer, and the psychologist simply needs to know about it rather than to actually be involved in performing the measurements himself.

PRESENTING INFORMATION TO MAN

Man as a controller and integrator of information in a man-machine system has many advantages and limitations. Before man can control a modern machine he must gain information by which to make decisions. Man fortunately has a large variety of sense organs to allow him to take information from his environment. However, many kinds of information relevant to machinery and action within machines cannot be directly sensed by man's organs. Thus the information is transformed into inputs that can be perceived by humans. The devices that convert information within the machine into inputs for humans are called *displays*.

The most obvious displays are visual, although auditory displays are sometimes used. In a visual display, such as the speedometer of an automobile, mechanical functioning of a particular piece of machinery is translated into a display that can be perceived and interpreted through the use of man's visual senses.

Symbolic and Pictorial Visual Displays. Visual displays are generally of two particular types: symbolic displays, where the information presented bears little or no resemblance to the actual conditions, and pictorial displays, where reproductions of conditions are presented. Words, letters, numbers, symbols, and so on, are symbolic displays that can be interpreted by humans, and photographs, sketches, and television are pictorial displays. In general, pictorial displays can be interpreted more easily, with less training, and more rapidly than purely symbolic displays. On the other hand, a great deal of the information created by machines cannot be adequately displayed pictorially, and consequently a symbolic display is used.

Displays present information of three major types: quantitative, qualitative, or check reading. All three types of displays are in common use in everyday machinery. For example, modern-day automobiles frequently have check-reading instruments for generator and oil pressure activity. A signal light flashes on if the oil pressure is inadequate or if the generator is not functioning properly. Qualitative readings are also included in many automobiles for such things as temperature of the engine-cooling system. No actual numbers are included on the dial, but markers indicate high, medium, or low temperature or an average range where the temperature is adequate. Finally, quantitative readings are usually given for speed of the automobile. The speedometer displays numbers usually with tens of miles per hour marked and with line markers for individual units of miles per hour of speed.

During the past quarter of a century a tremendous amount of information has been gathered and published concerning man–machine systems in general and specifically the sensory capabilities of man and the relationship of these capabilities to the input of information for man-machine systems. Much of the information gathered has been of interest and value; however, many of the studies in engineering psychology were not as carefully controlled as is desirable. Chapanis (1963) summarized the state of engineering psychology by stating: "If one reads the recent literature in engineering psychology carefully, one is forced to conclude reluctantly that a distressing amount of it is not very good. Moreover, the flaws in the work are not minor technical faults, but are serious methodological ones which often invalidate the author's conclusions. Studies of this kind should never have been published in the first place." After citing several examples, Chapanis concluded that there are several explanations for poor quality of reported research, such as, "Inadequate training of people in the field, pressures for getting results quickly, and loose editorial standards." Chapanis also suggested that because so much apparatus and equipment is available some of the people involved forget simple old-fashioned rules about experimentation. He pleaded strongly for more adequately controlled research in the human engineering field. With Chapanis' remarks in mind we will cite a few studies concerning visual displays.

Many of the studies conducted in human engineering and especially in display design have been done for military application. Thus the examples given here primarily involve aircraft or military machinery. In one fairly well-controlled laboratory experiment, Grether (1949) tested the reactions of two groups of subjects to nine different altimeter designs to determine differences in accuracy of reading. He found that the conventional altimeter was difficult to read and recommended a more suitable instrument. He also determined that speed and accuracy of reading are positively related and that instrument reading difficulties are not necessarily eliminated by experience in reading, since air force pilots didn't do a lot better than university or college students. Although Grether's experiments showed that the conventional altimeter was not the most efficient, we must remember that many pilots now flying have had a great deal of experience with this conventional instrument and that many such instruments are in use. As has been stated before, new instrumentation simply cannot be installed even though it may be more efficient because there is such a backlog of qualified personnel using the present instruments, and there is a large investment already made in such instruments.

In another experiment, Grether (1948) experimented with a 24-hour clock dial. Although many people have experience reading clocks, most have not read a 24-hour clock until entering military service. The military services and many international businesses work on this system, whereby hours run from midnight to midnight, rather than starting over at noon. Thus 2 P.M. is 1400 hours. Grether's experiment showed that if the 24-hour system is in use, a 24-hour clock face is much better than a 12-hour clock face, with the subject trying to interpret the additional 12-hour period. He showed that there were two clock dials that were most efficient in terms of reading speed and accuracy. Although there was little difference in the two dials as shown in Figure 9.7, the top dial face was suggested as the preferred since the darkened area shows the hours of darkness—that is 1800 hours to 0600 hours, and 12 o'clock (1200 hours) shows as noon at the top of the dial, as in an ordinary 12-hour clock.

An example of applied research for the business world is a study done for the Bell Telephone system (Karlin, 1961). Laboratory experimentation had shown that all number dialing had certain definite advantages over letter–numeral dialing as far as instrumentation was concerned. Additional telephone numbers can be made available by such a system, and the face of the all-numeral dial can be simpler and easier to read than the more cluttered face involving letters and numerals. On the other hand, there was no previous evidence to suggest that all-numeral dialing was any better in terms of speed or accuracy. The report by Karlin included a series of experiments to test the hypothesis.

The first experiment simulated dialing aspects of letter–numeral and all-numeral dialing. Subjects were tested in a special test room once each day for 22 days. While in the test room they placed a list of calls, which consisted of names of people and places to call rather than numbers. For the first ten of the 22 days, each person used the regular Manhattan New York Telephone Directory to look up letter–numeral numbers and placed the calls. During the other 12 days the Manhattan Directory was modified so that the numbers appeared on the page in its all-numeral form, and the person placing the call had a telephone with an all-numeral dial. All calls actually terminated in a nearby room and were answered by the experimenter. Busy signals and "don't answers" were introduced with appropriate frequencies according to evidence previously gathered by the telephone

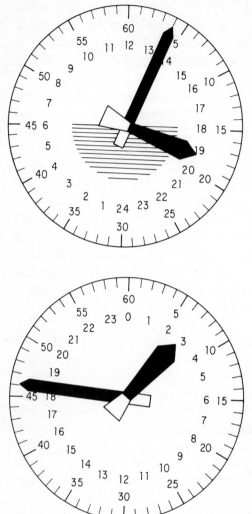

Figure 9.7. The two best 24-hour clock dials according to research by Grether. The top dial is recommended over the bottom dial. After W. F. Grether (1948), "Factors in the Design of Clock Dials Which Affect Speed and Accuracy of Reading in the 2400-Hour Time System," *J. Appl. Psychol.*, **32**, 159.

system. The results of the experiment showed that the all-numeral dialing was about 10 percent faster and slightly more accurate than the letter–numeral dialing. Subsequent experiments showed equal retention by users of the all-numeral dialing or letter–numeral dialing and eventually some advantages in memorization of all numerals. The conclusions were that all-numeral dialing should increase speed and that error rate should be about the same or slightly lower than the letter–numeral dialing. Subsequently the switchover from letter–numeral dialing to all-numeral dialing has been taking place throughout the United States.

The experiments just cited primarily concern quantitative readings.

Some displays are designed to provide information from a large number of machines or multiple characteristics of one machine. Thus the primary function is check reading. Chapanis, Garner, and Morgan (1949) showed the value of a patterned display versus unpatterned display when a variety of information must be presented by somewhat similar dials. Figure 9.8 shows the unpatterned and the patterned display. Each dial indicates by use of a needle a reading of a certain instrument for a certain function of a machine. The darkened area of the instrument dial indicates the range of normal readings. It takes a good deal of examination to notice in the unpatterned display that two of the dials are showing readings out of the safe range, whereas in the patterned display it is immediately apparent. Thus, for check reading, quantitative instruments may be grouped in a manner that allows a rapid scanning to notice anything out of the ordinary.

A tremendous amount of research has been completed, including studies of legibility of the printing, numbering systems, symbolic versus pictorial display systems, checking systems, tables versus graphs for presentation of information, and a host of experiments on auditory presentation of information and even tactual stimulation. Although these experiments are all interesting, we cannot include them all. Thus we leave the topic of putting information into man with one final report concerning a new dimension of communication.

After analysis of many experiments and investigations, Gilmer (1961) concluded that a system of cutaneous electropulse communication is possible since "one can obtain painless pulses under appropriate stimulating conditions suitable for alpha-numeric coding." The possible use of such a newly used input phase for humans opens up a host of possibilities, including at least the use of this system as warning systems when other normal communication channels are completely crowded with regular activities. For example, an aircraft pilot, while landing or flying under instrument conditions, might be "wired" for cutaneous electropulse communication to provide special or emergency information.

MAN CONTROLLING MACHINES

Man, as part of a man–machine system, functions both as a receiver of input information through his sense organs and as a response mechanism or output part of a machine–man system. Man also functions as a control mechanism, but he cannot function exclusively in the control output or input phase.

In this section, man as a controlling mechanism will be discussed, and some experiments concerning controlling equipment will be cited.

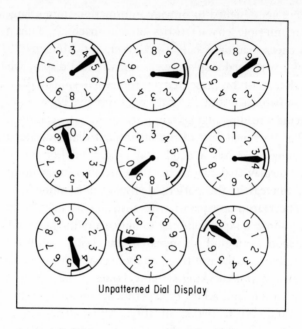

Unpatterned Dial Display

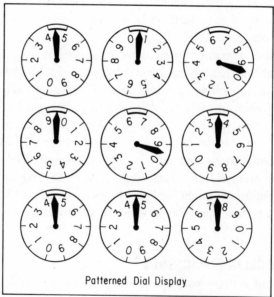

Patterned Dial Display

Figure 9.8. Patterned and unpatterned displays of 9 instrument dials. Dials not reading in the "normal" range (darkened areas) are more easily noticed in the patterned than the unpatterned display. After A. Chapanis, W. R. Garner and C. T. Morgan, *Applied Experimental Psychology* (New York; John Wiley & Sons, Inc., 1949).

As briefly mentioned in the discussion on motion-and-time study, man can perform certain movement or motions. Control systems must be designed to recognize these limitations of man. Essentially the motions of man are positioning motions, where part of the body moves from one particular space or spot to another. This is done by the use of muscles acting on bones, moving the parts of the body about joints. Hinge joints, pivot joints, and ball and socket joints are arranged throughout the body in such a manner that the extremities, the feet and the hands, can move to any angle or position in space within the range governed by the length of the arm and leg. This extreme range of joint motion is of great value and should be taken into consideration when man is used as a controlling mechanism.

Ballistic, Tense, or Static Movements. Muscles are used to move the body in space in a simple positioning movement. Antagonistic muscles or opposing muscles stop the movement or control the speed of the movement. The movements possible are generally classified as *ballistic, tense,* or *static.*

A ballistic movement is a very efficient type of movement. Essentially, the ballistic movement is one in which little or no subsequent forces are exerted after the original energy is used in starting the movement. A sudden well-defined muscle contraction begins the movement which continues until an opposition movement stops it.

Other movements similar to ballistic movements have been classified as tense movements. These are similar to ballistic movements in that a muscle contraction starts the movement, but throughout the movement antagonistic muscles are in play, so that a rigid or more active state of the organism is involved throughout the moving.

A static movement is not truly movement at all, but rather very, very small movements or variations in force while movement is minimal. A common example of static response is the variation of pressure on the brake pedal of a car. Increasing pressure results in increasing braking of the car with practically no movement of the brake pedal. This is especially noticeable with power brakes.

When a group of movements are put together into a chain of events it is called a sequential movement. Many highly repetitive tasks in industry involve the same sequential movements time after time.

The types of movement of which man is capable must be considered in the design of control systems. The foregoing descriptions are indicative of the human output and not the man–machine system. Man may use his output simply to move a lever, press a button, turn a crank, or push a pedal and cause considerably different reactions of the man–machine system.

Now what of the human factors in the control of systems? Orlansky (1949) reported an interesting series of experiments concerning physiological characteristics of man involved in handling aircraft controls. He stated that a study completed in 1936 by the National Advisory Committee for Aeronautics indicated that the maximum amount of force that should be needed to handle aircraft controls was 35 pounds on the elevator, 30 pounds for aileron, and 180 pounds for rudder. Orlansky studied actual push-and-pull force maximums that could be exerted by pilots under normal conditions. He found that the ability to push and pull varies with the distance from the back of the seat to the controls. The ability also varies below the NACA specified maximum levels in several instances. When the seat is too close to the stick, elevator controls conceivably could meet NACA specifications and still need greater human strength than possessed by the average pilot.

Orlansky also measured the psychological aspects of the handling qualities of the control stick and rudders in a fighter aircraft. His analysis of the stick deflections needed for increments in stick force at varying speeds led him to the conclusion that control systems must involve not only the measurement of the forces involved but also methods of providing information back through the system to the pilot as to how much deflection he is achieving with the amount of movement that he exerts. He showed that a small amount of stick position movement should result in a large force or pressure on the stick at the beginning of movement. Then over a relatively large amount of stick movement there should be only a little increase in force on the stick. At the maximum amount of stick movement a great deal of pressure should be presented through the stick. This would mean that the stick would be giving back to the pilot a feeling of pressure as soon as he moved away from the normal or center position, but that during most maneuvering relatively little increase in pressure would result as movement of the stick took place. As the pilot approached maximum movement of the stick, great force should be fed back through the stick to the pilot so that he would not overextend his aircraft.

Controls should be designed to use the body with maximum efficiency. When maximum strength is needed, control position is a vital factor. Hunsicker (1955) showed that strength in the arm movement upward is only 44 percent as great when the elbow is in its weakest position compared to its strongest position. When the elbow is bent at 30 degrees or 150 degrees it is in its weakest position. Thus controls that need muscle strength should be placed so that the elbow will be bent at another angle when operating the controls. With advancing age, there is a detriment in general muscle strength, but particularly more so in nonhand strength. Simonson (1947) reported that hand grip, which generally is recognized to be stronger for the preferred hand than for the nonpreferred hand, also deteriorates less with advancing age than the strength of the back muscles or other muscles of the body. Thus, although general strength of the body at age 60 is probably only 75 or 80 percent of the maximum strength of a particular individual in his late 20's, hand grip has not deteriorated as much, whereas the other muscles have deteriorated to a greater extent.

Most man–machine systems are of the closed-loop type. Thus it is interesting to note the effects of humans responding to relatively rapid inputs of information. In one study, reaction time was recorded of operators who made simple corrective movements when they observed a movement of a spot of light on a screen (Searle and Taylor, 1948). This function is somewhat similar to responding to a radar screen. Reaction time was about the same no matter how large the displacement on the radar screen or how large the correction needed by the subject. Even more surprising, the time required to make the correcting response was about the same no matter how much movement was shown on the screen. Apparently, the subjects changed their acceleration and speed of movement to accommodate different lengths of travel. This data seems to indicate that correcting to a given level as indicated by a display takes approximately the same amount of time no matter how large the correction must be. It also means that when a larger correction must be made, the subject is more likely to move more rapidly during the correction and thus overshoot or pass the correction.

One final study to be mentioned concerning controls is the work of Jenkins and Connor (1949). Using a laboratory piece of apparatus they studied control ratios (the ratio between control movement and movement of the machine system). The subject's task was to move a pointer back and forth by means of a knob. The ratio of the distance the pointer moved in relationship to one revolution of the knob could be varied from 1/10th of an inch to 33 inches. The diameter of the knob could be varied from ½ to 4 inches, and the accuracy criterion could be changed from 2/1000 to 2/100 of an inch tolerance. For a trial, a subject was presented with the apparatus set with the pointer off the target. At the signal to start, the subject turned the control knob to try to get the pointer lined up with the target. When he achieved the accuracy desired, he was given a signal that he had correctly completed the task. A recording system measured the subject's movements and the time required for them. In general, there was an initial lag after the starting signal before the operator began moving the control. This time is frequently called reaction time or starting time. The experimenters then described the next time, which was a rapid movement time, as travel time. After that there was a series of small adjustments as the pointer moved close to the target and fine adjustments were made. This was called adjusting time. Thus the total function of setting a pointer to a given location within a certain degree of accuracy involved three separate times, reaction or starting time, travel time or primary movement time, and adjusting time.

The experimenters found that starting time (reaction time) was about the same regardless of the gear ratio used. Also the travel time was long when a very small ratio was used and decreased rapidly as the ratio was increased. Finally, as the ratio was increased, adjustment time increased. Thus increasing the ratio cut down travel time, did not affect starting time, and greatly increased adjusting time. The experimenters decided that an optimum ratio is about 1:2. At this ratio, travel time is approximately at a minimum, and the adjusting time is fairly low. Further analysis of the results led Jenkins and Connor to indicate that a small size control knob takes longer to get the pointer on the mark than using a larger one; however, varying the ratio of knob turning to pointer movement has an effect upon this, so that the difference is much more marked for the high ratio than for the optimum ratio knob. They concluded that it is a good idea to use a control knob with a diameter of about two inches or more.

The results of Jenkins and Connor's experiments must be considered in light of the previously mentioned study showing that there wasn't much difference in movement time whether a large or a small correction had to be made. When movement speed can be controlled relatively easily by the subject, the subject apparently makes up for travel time by moving more rapidly if he has to make a larger adjustment and moving slower when a smaller adjustment is needed. Both of these situations are likely to result in less fine control or more time in adjusting.

Mechanical systems have been designed more recently to help the human adjust to the problem of overreacting. Such a technique is called *quickening*. Quickening does not affect the output of the machine system after the operator has introduced his control, but it does reduce the difficulty of the task for the human by providing him with information ahead of the time that the system really responds. For example, a human in a man–machine system may note from a display that a speed indicator shows a machine running below the optimum level. Whatever the technique of adjustment may be it usually allows the operator to introduce additional power into the machine so that it speeds up. If it is a very heavy machine, it may overshoot the desired speed mark because too much power is put on in order to pick up speed. In a quickened response system, the speed indicator would be rigged in such a manner that the display would show the speed of the mechanism before it was actually attained. Thus, when power was increased, the speed indicator would show increased speed beyond the actual machine speed, whereas the machine slowly builds up to the indicated level of the display. This type of system helps reduce or eliminate overcontrolling.

ACCIDENTS AND SAFETY

In this text accidents and safety are discussed in three specific places and on various occasions throughout the book. In this particular instance, accidents and safety as related to the design of equipment and the inter-action of man with equipment will be especially emphasized.

To demonstrate the accident problem related to equipment design we cite a brief case history. After driving the same car for many years, Jim finally traded it for a newer model of the same brand of automobile. The earlier automobile was equipped with automatic transmission, with a quadrant mounted on the steering column indicating the gear selected. The quadrant read from left to right: P for Park, N for Neutral, D for Drive, L for Low, and R for Reverse. After just purchasing the newer model, Jim drove to an unfamiliar city one night. He found it was neces-sary to pull out onto a heavily traveled highway. Many years of experience with the old automobile had left Jim with the impression that he needed low gear for a rapid pick up. Thus he carefully placed the newer car in low and entered the highway. When the automobile had attained suf-ficient speed he shoved the shift lever against the stop to the left which had been the drive position on his old car. The back wheels squealed and the car abruptly slowed. The manufacturer of the automobile had changed the quadrant settings of the gear shift so that the positions on the newer model read from left to right: P for Park, R for Reverse, N for Neutral, D for Drive, L for Low. Thus Jim had started in low and shifted his car into reverse at about 30 miles per hour. Fortunately, Jim immediately analyzed the situation and took the car out of reverse. On the other hand, if Jim had not had sufficient space in the traffic, or had not responded so fast, another accident might have occurred. It would probably have been recorded in accident records as due to driver error.

What is an accident, and when do we properly call it due to driver error, or operator error?

Another example of poor human engineering design has been brought to our attention. One brand of automobile has a series of control knobs, all the same size and shape clustered in the middle of the dashboard. Six knobs are located, three in a vertical line just to the left center and three others in a vertical line just to the right center of the dashboard. The three to the left center from top to bottom read: "Defroster Air Control," "Lights," and "Cigarette Lighter." The light switch is pulled out to turn on the headlights. Such controls generally cause no problems. However, when driving at night the control knobs just mentioned are not completely visible. When the driver is watching the road he may be quite shocked to press the button he thinks is the cigarette lighter and find that he has turned off his headlights. In so doing, he also turns off the dashboard lights so he must fumble in the dark until he finds the switch necessary to turn the lights back on. If an accident occurs in such a situation, again it would most likely be called a human error. Is this really an accident, or it is a design problem?

We have emphasized that accidents are not always the result of just the humans involved in the operation of equipment. Many of the so-called human errors have taken place in the design and construction of the equipment. All too many commonly used pieces of apparatus are simply not designed to achieve maximum security, safety, and production when they are in use. Man–machine systems should be designed to be safe systems. When proper human engineering is completed in advance of building equipment, there is less likelihood of accidents when the man–machine system is put into use.

Accidents don't just happen. They are caused. It may be that human behavior involved is inappropriate, that the operator was not as aware as he should have been, or it may be that the combination of the design and the operator is incompatible. Any man–machine combination must be thought of as a system. When the behavior of the system is not appropriate, it is the result not just of the human operator but of the man and the machine. Humans fortunately have the ability to integrate large amounts of information and respond to it in a relatively short period of time. They also have the capacity to learn from past experiences. This combination means that the human part of a man–machine system can frequently overcome difficulties that could result in accidents or improper responses. Even so, it is appropriate for designers to create machines so that the minimum amount of such integration and past experience is needed by the human operator.

As a final point concerning accidents and human engineering, it seems apropos to discuss briefly the training of individuals to avoid accidents. Rarely does the average person get training in how to avoid accidents. Some driver training courses provide such information, and the National

Safety Council has been providing information for industry and the home concerning where accidents occur and what can be done to prevent them. Even so, most people don't prepare for accident situations. In an informal poll we asked 15 adults what they would do if a particular emergency developed when driving their automobile. Only three out of the 15 responded that they routinely think of what to do in case certain emergency situations arise. For example, when passing an automobile on a divided highway they estimate whether they could pull onto the dividing area if necessary because the cars they were passing suddenly swerved into their lane. Pilots, while flying, constantly observe the ground for minimum spaces where they might land in case of an emergency. More training needs to be done concerning the everyday activities in our world so that man can more adequately perform his outstanding function in a man–machine system—meeting new situations in a flexible and appropriate manner.

USING KNOWLEDGE ABOUT MAN RELATED TO MACHINES

We have given some information concerning the interrelationship of man with machine in man–machine systems. A huge amount of experimentally derived information is available. As has been shown at various points in this chapter, much of the available knowledge is not properly put to use.

The lethargy of man in changing to newer and better ways of doing things is well known. We need not only to know how man can function best in man–machine systems but also how to get man to do so. Manufacturers, designers, users, and the public at large ultimately gain from minimizing man's efforts. We must all help overcome the resistance to change and the concern over short-term losses in equipment or previous training in order to raise all man–machine systems to a higher level of efficiency.

To maintain or improve the standard of living of any group of people, more efficient use of man's efforts must be achieved. Many of the principles discussed in this chapter can be of great value in raising every man's work efficiency.

SUMMARY

The population of the United States is expanding at a rapid rate. A high living standard is desired for all of the population, yet we wish to shorten the total number of work hours man must put in during his increasingly longer life span. Multiplying man's effort with machines seems to be the only hope for our goals.

Man–machine systems have been designed to accomplish many purposes. Systems may be as simple as a pencil and paper handled by a man or as complicated as huge automated oil refineries or military weapons systems. Systems are open-loop where information entering the system results in an activity that continues until acted upon by an outside agency. They are closed-loop where the response of the system is fed back into the system to modify the response.

Man most often serves in man–machine systems in a controlling function. He takes in information (input), integrates it, and responds (output). Man has specific capacities and limitations as an input and output mechanism. He seems most valuable at present as a control mechanism in man–machine systems, but current thought still compares man to machines. It seems that the concept of comparability is erroneous and that man and machine are complementary and must be used accordingly.

Specific rules of motion economy were stated as well as the common criticisms of motion-and-time study. Man's capacities for taking in information were discussed, with emphasis on the concept that knowledge of these capacities is essential when designing man–machine systems. The same thing was done concerning man's capacities as a response mechanism.

The topic of accidents and safety was discussed as related to a human working in a man–machine system. Many of the "accidents" blamed on humans may be the result of poor human engineering of the system. Finally, we suggested that man must be trained to handle more adequately emergencies or possible accident situations when he functions as part of a man–machine system.

SUGGESTED REFERENCES FOR FURTHER STUDY

Chapanis, A., W. R. Garner, and C. T. Morgan (1949). *Applied Experimental Psychology*. New York: John Wiley & Sons.

A survey of literature plus interpretation and integration of the material available in the late 1940's.

Journal of Applied Psychology.

Current research on man–machine systems and applications of the science of psychology are published in this bi-monthly journal.

Morgan, C. T., A. Chapanis, J. S. Cook, and N. W. Lund (1965). *Human Engineering Guide to Equipment Design*. New York: McGraw-Hill Book Co.

A comprehensive coverage of human engineering data available through the early 1960's. Information that has appeared in publications with restricted or limited distribution is given good coverage.

Woodson, W. E. (1954). *Human Engineering Guide for Equipment Designers*. Berkeley: University of California Press.

A summary of data available concerning design of equipment for use by humans.

Chapter 10
Man Related to Other Men

EXCEPT FOR AN EXTREMELY FEW HUMAN BEINGS who manage to live almost exclusively as hermits, our world is composed of men and women in daily contact with each other. The purpose of this chapter is to discuss the extremely important relationships of one person with another, particularly as they influence production in a work situation. In other chapters the relationship between man and the machine, man and the work environment, and man within himself have been discussed. The single most important relationship of all remains the relationship between man and his fellow men. In the work situation, this relationship is very frequently between the man on the job and his supervisor.

An entirely new approach to industrial psychology grew out of research completed during the period 1927 through 1932 at the Hawthorne Plant of Western Electric Company. In a book entitled *Management and the Worker*, Roethlisberger (1939) described the five years of research completed by a large number of investigators. The so-called experiments have been universally accepted as the beginning of the human relations approach in industry. In this chapter, human relations will be discussed with an emphasis on the trends since the publication of Roethlisberger's book. Man-to-man relationships, man-to-supervisor relationships, organized-workers-to-management relationships, and communications as a prime function in human relations will be the key topics. There are no simple, clean-cut answers for many of the problems discussed here, but many practical suggestions are included and some available research reports, case studies, and experiences from the world of industry are reviewed.

STRUCTURE OF ORGANIZATIONS

Although the concept of formal organizations and man's place within them has been fluctuating a great deal, most men must work in business enterprises that are highly structured. It is therefore essential for us to know something about typical organizations.

William Whyte (1956) in his controversial book *The Organization Man* began with the following statement: "This book is about the organization man. If the term is vague, it is because I can think of no other way to describe the people I am talking about. They are not the workers, nor are they the white-collar people in the usual, clerk sense of the word. These people only work for the organization. The ones I am talking about *belong* to it as well. . . ." Although Mr. Whyte was generally poking fun at a society that is so highly organized, it is true that men must join together to create the goods and produce necessary to maintain the standard of living to which we have become accustomed. It is physically impossible to attain as much productive efficiency as we are now used to, by having each man produce all the materials for himself or to complete each and every project that he begins. Thus we are in an era of specialization, with large numbers of men performing similar functions and with essential interrelations between men and whole groups of men. Consequently we have organizational structures.

Although it may not be apparent in the General Motors of today, most organizations grew into their current structures as the result of normal increases in their production work load. Typically one man started some activity. Perhaps he repaired buggies and constructed some parts for buggies. As time went on, he hired a young fellow to help him with his work. As his reputation grew, he added more and more helpers, while he continued working. Eventually it became apparent that he could not spend time showing the men what to do and seeing that they did it while performing many of the actual work functions himself. Consequently he moved from the actual work into more or less management capacity, telling the men what to do and perhaps obtaining orders and completing other functions. With additional expansion he could no longer find time to talk to customers as well as manage his workers. Consequently he added a sales force and someone to keep records. Finally a small organization developed into an organization, such as shown in typical organization charts. General Motors Corporation is a far cry from the simple buggie repair shop of 1900; however, as specialties are needed and changes bring about advancement in design in the production of the products, more and more people must be added to an organization. The typical organi-

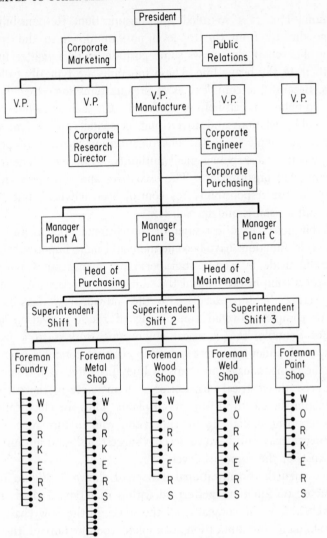

Figure 10.1. Part of a typical organization chart, showing some line and staff positions in the manufacturing section of a corporation. The line chart for other functions would be similar.

zational chart, shown in Figure 10.1, is a display of part of such a complex organization.

The Organization Chart in Figure 10.1 is a simplified schematic diagram of only a few of the functions that might be found in a large industry. There is a heavy line connecting various functions within the organization. This heavy line indicates control or line of authority in the organization. This is a so-called line organization. Responsibility and control go directly from the top-level position down to the front-line supervisor. The chart also shows some positions with a lighter line connecting them to the heavy line. These functions are typically called staff functions. Because the complexities of organizations force executives and managers to obtain special help or advice in areas such as engineering and research, public relations and advertising, personnel, and so on, staff organizations are coupled into the line organization chart. Staff personnel ordinarily do not have management authority. Most larger organizations are line and staff organizations. The executives and supervisors have the authority and the responsibility for control over activities, but they are aided by staff assistants and specialists.

Many businesses have lost some of the clear-cut lines of authority as staff managers' functions have become more and more important. Changes are generally made by giving staff personnel management power over workers specializing in the field of the staff man's specialty. Although the line connecting the top executive to the individual workers is not as straight or complete, overall functioning of the organization may be better. For example, the electrical engineering workers in a particular plant may work under the direct supervision of their foreman, who in turn is under the plant manager in terms of line authority. At the same time, there may be an electrical engineering staff manager in the corporation responsible for the electrical work in all plants. Thus the electrical worker, although reporting directly to his supervisor, who in turn reports to the plant manager, may also have to accept "suggestions" and authority from the specialists at the corporate level.

Even though the organizational flow chart shown in Figure 10.1 and the characteristic functions performed within that typical chart may not be followed in any one company, all the stages in the flow chart involve human-to-human communication. Complete coordination of the overall structure is difficult at best and often impossible. Thus a great deal of study is being done to automate or mathematically program system controls of industrial organizations. We insist that the biggest single problem in any organization is that of humans and primarily one of communication from one human to another. This is the area where most study is needed.

The formal charts discussed so far represent top management and outsiders' views of an organization. Anyone who has worked for an organization knows the outsiders' picture is not the same as the "insiders" concept. John Jones may be assistant vice-president in charge of production in a plant. In a flow chart, he may be second in command to vice-president in charge of production. However, John Jones may not be consulted by

very many people at all. Perhaps the supervisors turn to their plant manager and the plant manager goes directly to the vice-president in charge.
The formal organizational chart is not necessarily followed. Supervisory
power, a way of perceiving things in a manner that seems suitable, and
ability to get things done, all go to create an informal organization chart
that often has much more to do with the functioning of an organization
than does the formalized structure.

Recently there has been a feeling on the part of many specialists
involved in the field of organization that formalized organizational structures are not the most efficient ways of obtaining production. Carzo (1961)
suggested that specialization is known to influence employees attitudes
and perhaps ultimately restrict performance. Formal organization with
emphasis on task specialization utilizes such a narrow range of abilities
and skills that workers are not as efficient as they might be if utilized in
a different manner. Instead of grouping workers by task similarity, he suggested that grouping persons according to normal human sentiments,
social customs, codes of behavior, status, friendships, and so on, will create
more cooperation and perhaps greater efficiency in the long run.

Span of Control. Carzo (1961) also argued that the simplicity and
rationale of formal structuring doesn't adequately accommodate the concept of "span of control." Span of control has been emphasized by many
specialists in administration who have specified the exact number of
subordinates who can be effectively managed. For example, some say that
the maximum number of workers that can be adequately supervised is
six. Obviously when one is restricted in the number of employees that can
be supervised, one also gets involved in many more levels of supervision.
As an industry grows in size, the organizational chart becomes more and
more complex and crowded.

Many companies are very much interested in maximizing span of control. One of the more compelling desires is the monetary savings of having
fewer supervisory personnel. For example, Lockheed Missile Division is
using the term *span of management* instead of *span of control.* Lockheed
span of management excludes assistants, assistants to, and personal staff
assigned to the supervisors and counts only the actual workers who perform under the supervision in a line capacity. They are also analyzing the
supervisory function more thoroughly and assigning supervisory responsibility according to the amount of load the man carries, not just the
number of men that he has to supervise. For example, some men supervise
workers that are controlled indirectly by someone else for a great deal of
the time, and consequently they exert only 70 percent control. Other

supervisors may have complete control over a worker. This takes a great deal more of their time and consequently should receive more credit for supervision (Stieglitz, 1962). No matter how it is looked upon, the problem of supervising employees is still crucial and deserves additional study. Particularly during periods of increased competition, management has been interested in every possible method of reducing production costs. Thus, in the early months of 1963, several companies released large numbers of middle management employees as span of control for each supervisor was increased. Greater competition, more efficient use of personnel, and more understanding of how much a man can do in terms of supervising others will probably continually influence the optimum span of control.

COMMUNICATIONS

The term *communications* refers both to the transmitting of information from one individual to another and the channels for transferring this information. Two most obvious types of communication of importance in the business world are verbal and written. In this section we will discuss each of these, but the major emphasis will be upon verbal communication.

Have you ever listened to a young child communicate with one of its parents or brothers or sisters? For example: "Me go store with Mommie. Buy pretty dress. Wear party next day.' This was an example of a relatively low level of communication as compared with the sophistication that we usually use in our language. On the other hand, we must notice that information was conveyed. If the father were to receive such a message from his daughter, he probably would make the accurate diagnosis that his daughter had gone to the store with his wife and purchased a new dress so that the daughter was ready to go to a party in the near future.

All too often, communication between two individuals is cluttered by extra material that is superfluous and yet commonly used and expected in our society. The key to communication seems to be enough verbal or written information so that the two individuals involved can transfer thoughts or concepts. However, it is often argued in articles concerning communication that simple communicating, such as suggested above, cannot take place in the business world.

For example, Sayles (1962), in an article concerning communication, suggested that two old friends talking to each other have very little difficulty in communicating; even a single word or a raised eyebrow conveys all the meaning necessary. However, he said such communication doesn't work in an industrial situation because subordinates and superiors simply do not know each other well enough. There are many barriers to communications, and generally Sayles is correct, but there are many exceptions.

Recently the author watched a bulldozer and two laborers clear an area of trees preparatory to constructing a road. The bulldozer operator, remaining on his machine, directed the men in connecting a cable to trees that were to be pulled. He was able to make a loud noise to attract their attention and then, by a pointing and a rotating motion with his finger, indicate that the cable was to be placed through the draw bar on the bulldozer and looped over a connecting pin. This was rudimentary behavior and an often-repeated sequence, so that relatively little communication was needed. Nevertheless, the important fact is that a supervisor working with a subordinate was able to transmit information quite adequately with very little verbal or written communication. Many such examples can be cited from industrial situations as well as interpersonal relations in the home or play and school activities. There are also experiments such as that reported by Mellinger (1956), who studied communications patterns in a large organization. He found that increased communication didn't make people more accurate about others' opinions unless they initially trusted one another and were already in considerable agreement. Increasing communication does not necessarily lead to greater understanding. A knowledge of the other person involved in communication is crucial in increasing effectiveness of communication.

Communications between individuals in an industrial situation are complex and a great many barriers exist. In the next two segmnets of this section we will discuss some of the barriers or problems involved and how to improve communications.

Problems in Communication.   Communication from top management to worker is relatively easy, whereas communication from worker to the top level is difficult, if not impossible. On the other hand, communication does not always flow easily down through the supervisory ranks. The larger the organization, the further top management is from the working force. Consequently the greater the number of steps in between, the more difficult becomes communication. It is also true that there is much greater difficulty in getting communication from the working people to the top levels in large organizations. A later section of this chapter discusses unions and their value in improving upward communication. Here we discuss problems of downward communication.

What are some of the basic difficulties in a flow of communication through the organizational hierachy? Each supervisor wants to please the man above him more than the person under him, but we cannot conclude that communication flows downward easily. Jackson (1959) declared that there are three major factors determining whether people communicate or fail to communicate. First, people, while accomplishing their work, have forces acting upon them to communicate with those who will help them achieve their aims and forces against those who will not assist or may retard the accomplishment of their aims. People generally communicate with others of higher status in the organization or people who have some abilities that are felt to be valuable to the communicator. Second, people have powerful forces acting upon them to direct their communications toward those people who make them feel secure and away from those who threaten them. Personal needs are of great importance in determining which way a person will turn in terms of communication. Subordinates are usually reluctant to ask superiors for help because it might indicate a certain inadequacy on their part. Superiors tend to delete from their communication with subordinates anything that indicates they have made a mistake or an error themselves. Third, people in an organization are always communicating as if they were trying to improve their position. Jackson suggested that people tend to communicate toward the direction in which they wish to move. This may be upward, or it may be toward another department. If they are frequently frustrated in their attempts to move upward or into another department, they may communicate even more often as a substitute for actually moving in the desired direction. People communicate to try to improve their relative position in their organization.

In a pair of articles, Rogers and Roethlisberger (1952) discussed some difficulties of communication in industry. Rogers maintained that the major problem in communication from one person to another is the tendency on the part of the listener to evaluate the information that he receives. Thus, instead of simply receiving information from another person, he takes that information and judges it, either approving or disapproving of the statement in some manner. For example, Rogers wrote: "Suppose I say with some feeling 'I think the Republicans are behaving in ways that show a lot of good sound sense these days.' What is the response that arises in your mind? The overwhelming likelihood is that it will be evaluated. In other words, you will find yourself agreeing or disagreeing or making some judgment about me such as, 'He must be a Conservative or, he seems solid in his thinking.' " Thus Rogers concluded that the major barrier to interpersonal communication is the tendency to react emotionally by evaluating from your own point of view. Roethlisberger argued that, "In thinking about the many barriers of personal communication, particularly those that are due to differences of background, experience and motivation, it seems to me extraordinary that any two persons can ever understand each other." He suggested that the biggest problem in communication is man's inability to listen intelligently. He suggested similarly to Rogers that a person must listen understandingly and skillfully to another person in order to achieve good communication. Fortunately both Rogers and Roethlisberger suggested some methods of improving communication, which will be discussed later in this chapter.

Another characteristic of communication is the selective perceptual process of the listener or reader. It is a well-founded fact that people perceive things as they wish to perceive them. Many such occurrences are routine and may have been noted by the reader. For example, college students tell us that sports cars are owned by 15 or 20 percent of the college population. On the other hand, an actual count shows far fewer available. The observers have perceived in a manner that was selective. They noted what they were interested in seeing and consequently thought they saw more sports cars than were actually available. The owner of a particular brand of automobile may notice ads for that automobile much more frequently than for competing models.

In the business world, executives are known to perceive selectively. Dearborn and Simon (1961) reported an experiment done with 23 executives employed by a large manufacturing concern. All were drawn from middle-management positions. These executives were brought into a group session and studied a standard case history. The case history of about 10,000 words contained descriptive material concerning a hypothetical company and the recent history of the industry and the company, but very little evaluation. Interpretation was left to the reader. Then the executives appeared at the class session to discuss the case. Before they discussed it, they were asked to write a brief statement about what they considered to be the most important problem facing the company in the case history. They were reminded that they were to assume the role of a top executive of the company in considering this problem. Analysis of the statements prepared by the individual executives showed conclusively that they perceived the problem in terms of their own background. About 83 percent of the sales executives mentioned sales as the most important problem, whereas only 29 percent of the other executives mentioned sales as the most important problem. Organizational problems were mentioned as the most important by 80 percent of production executives and only by 22 percent of the other executives. Industrial executives exposed to case material perceive that information in relationship to their own activities and goals. They do this in spite of the suggestion that they are to take into account the situation of an organization. Apparently they have internalized aspects of their own job to the point where they perceive other information only in terms of their specific function.

Communication in industry is often inefficient due to style, format and vocabulary. For example, employee handbooks of 11 major companies in the United States were analyzed using the Flesch formula for reading ease and estimating human interest, attractiveness, and so on (Carlucci and Crissy, 1961). Many of the handbooks in the study were not comprehensible to the lowest level of employees in the respective companies. In general, the books lacked human interest, and most covered far fewer topics than might be expected according to standards set by organizations such as the American Management Association. In Flesch Reading Ease score, several of the handbooks were written in such a manner that at least some high school education would be needed to understand the material adequately, whereas the median education level of the nonsupervisory employees in the organiation was often below eighth grade. The authors concluded that written communications to employees are frequently set at a level designed by the person doing the writing and not for the level of the reader.

In both written and verbal communication, redundancy is very common in our language. Most instructors use redundancy to make sure the students understand their information. (This book contains a considerable amount of redundancy with the hope that after repeated readings students may understand the major concepts.) Redundancy has become so common in our communication that we expect it. Consequently we listen or read with the idea that we can pick up the concepts the next time they are repeated if we miss them at first. This increases poor listening or reading habits and ineffectual communications.

In spite of all the difficulties communicating verbally and in writing, the major factor in poor industrial communication is lack on the part of management to give information to workers and allow them to feel that they are participating in the activities of their company. Later in this chapter, the studies done at the Hawthorne plant of Western Electric will be described. These studies resulted in a series of consultations between supervisory personnel and workers. Allowing the workers to talk out their problems with management representatives was shown to be extremely valuable in creating a better attitude among the workers. Good communication systems help workers feel that they are participating and are receiving recognition from their organization. In the next section, we will discuss some techniques that might help to improve communication.

Improving Communications—Verbal.   Answers to the problems of communication cover a variety of suggestions. Roger and Roethlisberger (1952) suggested that the way to solve the barrier in communications is to listen with understanding. Rogers suggested that evaluating during listening is a difficulty that creates poor communication and that the simple solution is for the listener to get the expressed idea and attitude from the other person's point of view, to sense how it feels to him, and to achieve his frame of reference. He suggested that if each person would restate what he thinks the other person has said, including ideas and feelings of the previous speaker, that a much more clear understanding can be accomplished. This technique is valuable, but when feelings and emotions are on edge during a discussion, it is difficult for one person to clearly understand or to parrot back what the other person says. Sometimes an additional person in the situation can help provide cooperation between the two communicators so that communication may be more understandable.

Roethlisberger suggested that a person must be aware that there is an interaction of sentiments with another person during a conversation. The object of this is to get the other person to express himself freely. In so doing, better communication will take place. Listening intelligently, understandingly, and skillfully are the key characteristics of good communication. The listener must accept the views presented by the other person, even if they are opposite to his own, if he sincerely wants to understand the communication.

Even though the above suggestions seem difficult, some of them can be put into effect by training oneself to be a good listener. On the other side, if you are going to be the speaker, consideration should be given as to how to present information most effectively. An administrator for training and development for the Polaroid Corporation, (Arnold, 1961) suggested six points to consider when you are giving information or trying to communicate. (1) Think before you talk. You must make sure you know why you want to say a thing, what you want to say, and what objective you hope to accomplish by saying it. You must consider the person that you are going to converse with before you start your conversation. (2) Remember that people hear what they want to hear. Thus you converse in a manner that will touch at least some of the things that you know are of interest to the listener. (3) Test-run important messages on a trusted friend or qualified person to see how they interpret what you say. (4) Emphasize a key point within the message. (5) Communications should work two ways so that there is an opportunity for the individual receiving your information to feed back to you what he thought you said. (6) Follow up all communications to see if action is following what you thought you told the person. As a final point, Arnold indicated that he recognized these six points are not panaceas, that communication techniques do not improve overnight, and that the secret behind good communication is really an interest in people. No set of rules can substitute for such an interest, but they can supplement it.

Another way of improving worker–supervisor communication is to use regular appraisal interviews as communications tools. As brought out by the early Hawthorne studies, interviewing of any sort gives an employee a chance to build up rapport with supervision. A formalized appraisal system, if carried out adequately, not only creates good rating of employees but good rapport and a better communication system in general.

Communication among executives has caused a great deal of concern among top management. A study done in one company (Davis, 1953) especially emphasized the value of the grapevine as a method of communication within the top-management personnel. The regular formal systems of conferences, reports, memoranda, and so on, provide a basic core of information, but the grapevine adds real value. Davis traced a given piece of information from each communication recipient back to the source of the information. By so doing, he created chains of sequences of information passing through the informal grapevine. He showed the following four major characteristics of the grapevine as a transmittal system. (1) The grapevine is traditionally a fast method of transmitting information. For example, in his study news transmitted by the grapevine by face-to-face conversation and occasional interoffice telephone calls moved throughout the management group in less than half a day. (2) The grapevine system, although frequently referred to as without consciousness or conscience, does have selectivity. In one specific case, when the president of the observed company decided to invite 36 executives to a company picnic, the information was carried by the grapevine to only two of the 31 executives not invited. This, in spite of the fact that the executives didn't definitely know who was going to be invited. (3) The grapevine works mostly at the place of work and not in the home environment. Even though the company studied was in a small community where there was a good deal of contact between employees after hours, the actual transmission of company information took place during working hours, primarily during coffee hours, lunch hours, and before work in the morning. (4) The grapevine system of communication does not fill a communication gap when the formal system is inefficient. The informal and formal communication systems supplemented each other with formal communication frequently confirming or expanding what had already been communicated by the grapevine; however, when there were voids in information being passed through the formal system, the grapevine system did not fill the void.

Davis also observed how information was passed through the grapevine. A particular piece of information was told by one individual to two or three others, and this was passed on by one or two of them to another two or three, and so on, in a clustering sort of arrangement that could be predicted. The information was not passed to the same individuals in all cases, and in almost all cases some individuals simply did not transmit the information any further. Several rules suggested by Davis concerning what information was passed on and by whom were summarized as follows: "1. Tell people about what will affect them (job interest). 2. Tell people what they want to know rather than simply what you want them to know (job and social interest). 3. Tell people soon (timing)." These three points will improve the informal communication system so that it will provide a faster and more efficient means of spreading information through the organization. Davis found that staff men were generally more in the know than line executives. He attributed this to the fact that staff men move from one department to another and get involved in a variety of different functions more than do line executives. Also, he reported that certain functional groups were consistently isolated from the communication chain as a result of (1) geographical separation in terms of being in a separate building away from the main group, (2) work association in terms of being involved in a completely different kind of function, and (3) social isolation, where the level of the foreman group is such that they did not fit in with the rest of the executives. Davis concluded his article by suggesting that if management needs better communication among executives and supervisors, they must remember that the chain of command is not the only communication system. Indeed, it often does not function as adequately as nonofficial systems. Management should use the grapevine system by increasing the number and effectiveness of liaison individuals who pass information on to others, they should count on the staff executives to be more active than the line executives, and they should take steps to keep the isolated groups in communication.

Since early in 1947, the Laboratory of Social Relations, at Harvard University, has been studying various aspects of human relations. In one phase of their studies the successfulness of a conference as a method of communicating ideas and affecting behavior was reported (Bales, 1954). Working in a specially designed room for the purpose of observing the operation of committees and small groups, observers recorded the remarks made by individuals in groups of two to seven members discussing various problems. Experimental groups took part in four sessions of 40 minutes each. The way that they operated as a group was recorded. Action took place in a committee by a series of questions and answers and positive and negative reactions to these. There were three major types of questions—those asking for information, opinion, and suggestion—and three types of answers—giving information, opinion, and suggestion. This research found that 50 percent of all remarks made in the meetings are answers, whereas the remaining 50 percent consists of questions and reactions. One of the more interesting findings was that the men judged by the group members to have the best ideas were not generally the best liked. In other words, there are two separate roles, that of task leader and that of social leader. Very rarely can a man serve both functions. These findings, of course, challenge some of the basic concepts of leadership, because it appears that whatever qualities a man may have as a leader he may still have to have a co-leader of complementary qualities.

Further analysis of the data by Bales indicated that the difficult problem in communicating in a group is not just with the leader but rather among the membership of the entire group. Committees should not be larger than seven members unless absolutely necessary to get all representation of views. Committees should never be smaller than three, and members should be chosen who fall naturally into a moderate gradient of participation rather than all-low- or all-high-level participators. A good committee is not made up of a good leader plus several followers.

In Chapter 9 feedback in a closed-loop system was discussed. In such a system information from one part of the system feeds back to the other and influences the output of the system. Some sort of feedback from one person to another also aids the original communicator in his communicating to a second person. Leavitt and Mueller (1951) conducted a series of experiments concerned with the transmission of information from person A to person or persons B, noticing particularly the effects of feedback.

Although their work is somewhat circumscribed by the limited type of problem in which they completed their experiments, Leavitt and Mueller concluded that the inclusion of feedback increased the accuracy with which information is transmitted and increased receiver and sender confidence in what they accomplished. However, feedback takes additional time. A sender and receiver can also improve communication without feedback.

Leavitt and Mueller used four levels of feedback: (1) zero feedback, in which the communicator sat behind a movable blackboard and described his patterns to a group of students, allowing no questions or noises from them; (2) a visible audience condition, in which students and instructor could see one another, but no speaking by students was allowed; (3) a yes–no condition, in which the students were allowed to say only yes or no in response to a question from the instructor; and (4) a free feedback situation, in which students were permitted to ask questions, interrupt, and so on. Students were given information, asked to reproduce it, and then scored on accuracy. The scores showed increasing performance through the four conditions just mentioned. (Free feedback gave the best performance.) The time involved in giving instructions also varied in the same order, so that the free feedback took the greatest amount of time. The experimenters found that sender experience contributes considerably more to improving accuracy in communications than does receiver experience. They also stated that zero feedback engenders hostility in the receivers, but this hostility is short-lived, lasting through only one or two free feedback trials. Accuracy in interpersonal communication is aided, participants learn considerably more from it, and there is a greater degree of confidence built up between sender and receiver under free feedback conditions.

Improving Communications—Written. Many articles have been published indicating difficulties in business letter writing and the cost of such errors in terms of time, effort, and materials. The work of Morton (1955) is an example of a typical article considering problems in written communication. He suggested, "A 'business-ese' was coined and perpetuated that made it easier for employers to write without thinking, to write without saying anything and to blunder ahead, oblivious to the impact of what they wrote." Businessmen, like others, use the materials that they are familiar with, and unfortunately these materials are often poor for communication.

Morton suggested several principles that should aid in more clearly stating concepts in writing: (1) Get rid of clichés and doublets, such as *full and complete, first and foremost,* and so on. (2) Redundant phrases like *the situation as it actually exists* can be shortened to the single word— *actually.* (3) Use active verbs; for example, write *compete* rather than *are in competition with.* (4) Develop good habits in thinking. What does the reader want to know? What can you as a writer tell him? How can you do this? These questions must be considered before words are put on paper. Finally, he suggested that writing, just like anything else in the business world, needs to be managed. It costs too much money to be inefficient in verbal and written communication. Techniques to reduce the cost can be designed and should be included under a properly managed system. Continued and wholehearted support of top management is as essential as in any other phase of the business world.

The reader is again reminded that our discussion of communications is part of a segment concerning man related to other men, or human relations. One of the biggest difficulties in human relations is the lack of understanding of the other person. Humans perceive what they want to perceive. They try to communicate with others, and although they think they clearly state their attitudes, feelings, and facts, they are surprised to learn that the statements turn out to be "misinterpreted" by the listener. Naturally the problem is not just with the listener but is frequently with the sender of the information. Communications must be clearly sent and received. It takes real effort to listen or to read attentively and to gain what is being said in terms of fact as well as opinions and attitudes. But better communications mean better relationships of man to man.

HUMAN RELATIONS EMPHASIS

It is important to recognize the emphasis on human relations in industry that has occurred since World War II. This entire chapter concerns the topics of human relations or the adjustment of one individual with another and with the work situation. However, the history of industrial development during the last half of the nineteenth century and the first half of the twentieth century must be recalled in order to place the emphasis of human relations in its proper prospective.

Mass production techniques, modern technology, larger and larger work forces, shorter hours, plus a host of other factors brought about great changes in the relationship between managers and workers during the late 1800's and early 1900's. In the early 1900's, scientific management gained a great deal of favor and with the increasing efficiencies brought about by motion-and-time study, productivity increased. Many managers began to think of man as part of a manufacturing process and treated him almost as a machine. Psychologists didn't oppose the concept when they emphasized selection, placement, and training of workers to fill the functions desired by the manufacturers. By the middle 1920's, many specialists were wondering if this was the best approach to the efficient use of humans.

At the Hawthorne plant of the Western Electric Company, a series of studies was conducted from 1927 through 1932 as a cooperative venture between the company and Harvard University. Two authors, F. J. Roethlisberger and W. J. Dickson prepared a book, *Management and the Worker* (1939), which reported the many years of the studies. This book aroused a great deal of interest and led to an entirely new school of thought concerning workers in an industrial situation. More than any other one factor, these studies brought about the current emphasis on human relations. A condensation of the Hawthorne studies is included here.

The Hawthorne Studies.   In the 1920's the Hawthorne plant of Western

Electric was well known for its extensive welfare programs. Before the beginning of the so-called Hawthorne studies in 1927, a series of studies concerning illumination had been carried out for three years. These studies involved three phases, as briefly mentioned earlier. In the first phase, illumination was progressively increased in three different departments. Despite identical treatment, production didn't react the same way in each of the departments. In one department, production fluctuated randomly, relative to the increased illumination. In the other two departments, production increased erratically with increased illumination. A second phase of the illumination study used two groups of workers matched in age and experience. Lighting was held constant for one group and varied for the other. Production increased the same amount for both groups. Finally a third phase repeated the second phase but in a room where natural illumination was eliminated. Production of both groups rose steadily. In fact, when the illumination for the test group was lowered production increased until the illumination got as low as the equivalent of moonlight and then production dropped.

The results of the illumination studies convinced the investigators that there was something involved other than changes in illumination. Thus a study was started in the relay assembly room to investigate other possible factors influencing production. This series is often referred to as the Hawthorne studies and deserves emphasis as the beginning of an awareness of the importance of human relations in industry.

Six female workers from the relay assembly department were selected for the study. Actually two girls, known to be friends, were chosen and were allowed to choose four others to work with them in a test room. They were told to work "as they felt" and not to try to produce any more than normal. They were also told that a series of characteristics of the work situation would be changed but that any changes would be explained to them in advance of the change.

An observer stayed in the test room with the workers and helped maintain the friendly atmosphere while taking notes. Automatic production records were obtained, and a daily log of the physical well-being of the girls, records of temperature, humidity, and so on, of the room were kept.

The study continued for 13 test periods. The conditions of the phases were these:

1. On the regular jobs in relay assembly room (establishing a bench mark).

2. Test room with all hours, and so on, the same as in the relay assembly room.

3. Same as condition 2, but with pay based on test group productivity rather than the entire relay assembly department productivity.

4. A rest period of five minutes was inserted in the morning and another in the afternoon work session.

5. Each rest pause was lengthened to 10 minutes.

6. Six five-minute rest periods were inserted throughout the day.

7. Two rest periods were reinstated, but the morning one was made 15 minutes long, with free snacks, and the afternoon was made 10 minutes long.

8. The work day was shortened a half hour, and everything else was similar to condition 7.

9. Period 8 was repeated, but with another half-hour cut from the work day.

10. Period 7 was duplicated.

11. Period 7 was repeated, except that Saturday work was eliminated.

12. Period 3 was duplicated.

13. Period 7 was again duplicated.

Throughout the phases, there was an almost relentless increase in production per hour and per week. This occurred in spite of the fact that conditions sometimes duplicated earlier conditions. It was apparent that hours of work did not necessarily directly influence production.

Subsequent investigations checked the wage-incentive systems and found that this factor alone could not explain changes in output.

The investigators concluded that attitude and preoccupations of the workers had a lot to do with productivity. Thus an extensive employee interview program was begun. An analysis of over 10,000 interviews indicated a need for still another study.

Systems of interviewing were investigated and an interviewing technique was devised to draw out the deep-seated or latent attitudes of workers. Supervisors were trained to help their workers in feeling better toward their jobs and the company. The human relation aspect of supervision was beginning to gain importance.

Additional studies showed the importance of groups working together. Subgroups within regular working groups were noted, and supervisors were taught to notice that there are different kinds of workers in their groups and that different management techniques are needed for one person as compared with another.

The Hawthorne studies were comprehensive at the time they were done. The lack of conclusive results in each series of experiments led the investigators to further studies. Finally it was understood that the interaction of one person with another and the psychological atmosphere between management and employees can and do influence production.

A large number of industries in the United States have since instituted training techniques to improve human relations. In more recent years, some people have questioned the value of human relations training, per se, but by and large the effects of the Hawthorne studies persist. Selection, placement, and training of workers is essential, but having men well adjusted to the work situation, to their fellow workers, and to their supervisors is essential for efficient productivity.

EMPLOYEE PARTICIPATION

As shown in the Hawthorne studies, employees who felt that they belonged to an organization and had an influence over their lives in the production situation tended to produce more per unit of time. Much additional research since the Hawthorne studies has reinforced these conclusions. Employees who are allowed to participate in decisions concerning their livelihood are more likely to produce at a high level than are employees who have little opportunity for participation. However, this is not necessarily so.

A study by French, Israel, and As (1960) indicated that employee participation varies in effectiveness according to the legitimacy of such participation as perceived by the workers. When workers feel that they have a right to engage in the decision-making process, their attitudes are positively influenced by participating. There are situations in which the workers regard their participation as inappropriate, and they expect the supervisor to take action on his own. This effect is supported by Mann and Hoffman (1960), who indicated that workers may express satisfaction with a supervisor who does not encourage much participation if they perceive him as a considerate supervisor. On the other hand, there are large individual differences in workers' desires for participation in decision making. Persons with strong needs for independence react more favorably when they are allowed to participate than do workers with less need for independence (Vroom, 1959). Thus employee participation is not always desirable. In general, workers like to feel that they have an opportunity to participate in decisions concerning their own activities, but not all workers want such an opportunity.

French et al. (1958) told of the value of employee participation for one company. When the management of a well-known men's apparel firm decided to modernize their production methods, they encouraged participation of the workers in discussions of the changes. On previous occasions trouble had developed as a result of introducing new work methods. Since hoped-for savings were sometimes offset by the cost of conflict, management was very aware of the importance of attitudes and feelings of their workers. As a means of obtaining employee cooperation, a series of interactive discussions between management and workers was held. In these discussions, the workers were assured that no reprisals were to be taken against frank discussions. Operators performing the same function met together with representatives of local plant management. In the course of the program, approximately 80 such meetings were held, with the number of workers varying from one to eight. When there were only a few workers on a particular operation, they were accompanied to the meeting by their shop steward. At the first meeting, the proposed changes in methods were announced. Workers were told about the new setup, and a discussion was encouraged. Immediately after this initial meeting, changes were made on the production floor. Machines were moved, new devices, and small pieces of apparatus were brought in, and experts gave demonstrations and instructions to individual workers in the new procedures. Only a few workers at a time were given the revised task, and it took several weeks before the entire production was changed over to the new techniques. Whenever problems arose, informal discussions were held with workers suggesting possible changes. A new rate schedule was introduced with the new techniques. One year after the change, workers doing the same type of function with new methods had increased production about 10 per cent, whereas there was generally a direct labor cost reduction of approximately 10 per cent. Turnover and absenteeism reduced during the period of the change, which indicated to the researchers that morale was not seriously affected by the new techniques. Only one characteristic measured showed an indication of poor employee–employer relationships. The number of grievances filed increased after the introduction of the new work methods. Most of the complaints concerning rates were handled by discussions with the company and union engineers. Generally the newly established rates were upheld, although in a few cases where the union study did not confirm the management figures, the average increase suggested by the union was 8 per cent. Management felt that the number of grievances was not excessive in view of the number of new rates that had been set. Apparently the workers recognized the honest intentions of management to improve the situation and thus helped achieve a smooth changeover to the new methods.

Employee participation is not the ultimate means of improving production. In fact, one author (Quinn, 1963) suggested that the interaction of boss and subordinate may frequently stunt the subordinate's growth. Some supervisors fail to realize that subordinates do not necessarily follow exactly in their footsteps. Some supervisors retard the growth of subordinates from lack of their own security. Some supervisors just don't want to listen to questions or to hear workers' views. In other words, there are many reasons why supervisors do not want employee participation. This, understandably, results in a poor feeling on the part of the workers, which may adversely affect production.

Although present evidence indicates that employee participation generally influences production, participation isn't always advantageous. As with other stock answers to problems of human relations in industry, employee participation is only one technique. Some workers respond well, others respond poorly. The situation and the interaction of the employee and employer combine in a manner that is often unpredictable.

SUPERVISION—WHAT AND HOW

Napoleon has often been quoted as saying, "There are no poor regiments, there are only poor colonels." For many years, men have been aware that production of a group depends upon the cooperation of the members within the group. Leadership or supervision of the group is needed to assure cooperation and efficient functioning. The type of supervision provided in the armed forces in Napoleon's day was considerably different than what might be expected in modern industry. However, the value of supervision in the management of men is important to production today.

Three aspects of supervision will be discussed in this section: (1) What are the functions of the supervisors? (2) How can supervision be accomplished? and (3) Who can be a good supervisor? Often there is a distinction made between supervisors and executives. Supervisor implies first-line management versus executives who are top-level supervisors. We will combine the discussion of supervision to include all levels of management, although most examples will concern front-line supervisors.

Functions of Supervisors. The function of an industrial organization is to create finished products from raw materials. It is further agreed that business must do this in a manner that enhances the value of the materials. Thus something of value is created by the activities of the workers involved in the process of converting raw materials to finished products. The function of supervision is to get this work accomplished. At the top levels, management is most interested in understanding the overall activity of the organization. At the lower supervisory levels, there is direct responsibility for and activity in the work process itself.

Not so many years ago, workers were supervised by foremen who had been promoted on the basis of experience with the organization. Little or no training of the supervisor took place, and foremen were frequently directors rather than leaders. By the 1920's, interest in human relations was developing, and supervisors started to use techniques of leadership rather than directorship. At one time the foreman in an industry had the responsibility and the authority to run his own section of an industrial organization. He could hire, fire, pay, and control by his own methods. As this changed with the increasing complexity and size of industry and the growth of the organized labor movement, foremen's jobs became more similar to higher levels of management in some respects. In other respects, the foreman's job became more ambiguous with less authority and still the same amount of responsibility. With all the changes throughout the history of supervision, the trend has been from directing to leading.

During the past 20 years, there has been such an awareness of the difference between directing and leading that many writers have created a distinction between "headship" and "leadership." Krech and Crutchfield (1948) particularly distinguished between these two terms. They said that headship is an assigned position imposed upon a group and that the person occupying this position, although he has been appointed the position by his superordinates and has a title and salary, is not necessarily effective as a leader. If such a person has ability and power, he can command obedience. Sometimes such people also have ability as leaders. Leadership implies followers—workers who voluntarily accept a person as a leader and work with him to follow out his suggestions.

In an industrial situation, headship is often required, because management must appoint someone with the title of supervisor and must frequently do this in terms of what they think is best for the organization. Such an appointment may not be the best person in the eyes of the workers. More and more often, management tries to select as supervisors men who have leadership ability and who can also fulfill management's requirements for headship.

Leadership has certain values over headship in the matter of efficiency in a working situation. We will examine several studies concerning techniques of leadership in an industrial situation.

How To Get Work Done. An extensive study concerning the relative effectiveness of different kinds of leadership resulted in an article (Lewin, Lippitt, and White, 1939) that has been cited many times to show the value of one leadership technique over another. The experimental design involved an adult leadership directing a group of five boys, ten years of age, in each of three different manners, authoritarian, democratic, and laissez-faire. Democratic leadership was superior in producing creative and cooperative behavior. Productivity and satisfaction on the part of the members of the group was poorest in the laissez-faire situation. These results have since been generalized to industrial situations and perhaps without complete justification. Even in the original study, the authors suggested that not all the members of the group receiving democratic leadership were happy or had the highest overall morale, and that some of the individuals were more content with authoritarian type leadership. Preference for a leadership technique seemed dependent upon the environment from which the boy had come. Boys who had grown up in an authoritarian type of environment responded better in an authoritarian type situation. Aside from these statements, which were part of the original article, it must also be remembered that these studies were completed with five ten-year-old boys in each of three groups. The interaction of a supervisor with a working man of mature age depends on a variety of factors, not just the type of supervision applied at a particular time.

Since hundreds of articles concerning supervisory techniques have appeared in the last 20 years, we will mention only a few representative reports.

Jennings (1954) studied democratic, autocratic, and laissez-faire leadership in an actual work situation. He found that modern leadership is not the laissez-faire type, in which the workers are left alone to decide what their problems are and recommend solutions, nor the autocratic type, which dictates to the workers what their problems are and how they should be solved. Modern, democratic supervision is dependable and definite, and can be counted on to follow a steady plan of action worked out with the workers. Democratic leadership provides strength and control while at the same time allowing cooperation and suggestions from the workers. Jennings also suggested that many of the characteristics of good democratic leadership can be learned. Democratic supervision implies guidance and suggestion as well as socializing and harmonizing. Democratic leaders encourage informal social leaders among the workers rather than opposing them, and they try to help the group rather than direct the group.

Sometimes the concepts of leadership as presented in textbooks does not work in the real-life situation. Stryker (1959) wrote that a good executive is not necessarily a leader, and sometimes a great industrial leader may be a poor manager. He suggested that the history of American business is replete with many legends of personal success that has been mistaken for industrial leadership, such as the success Andrew Carnegie and John D. Rockefeller, Sr. Both of these men used capital and power to increase production profits in a way that can hardly be considered acceptable modern human relations. There are also men who are successful in the business world while practicing other unconventional beliefs about executive development. For example, Franklin J. Lunding, Chairman of the Jewel Tea Company, insisted that his managers refrain from giving orders and concentrate on serving as first assistants to their subordinates. Stryker suggested that such behavior is an extreme use of the implications of the Hawthorne studies. The real value of such an executive is that he wins the cooperation of his workers by working on a level with them. Placating, humoring, and helping employees makes sure that they find satisfaction in their jobs.

On the other hand, Scott (1963) reported on a series of studies that show conclusively that the characteristics and behavior of men in one organization result in dismissal or lack of promotion, whereas the same kind of behavior and traits would result in promotion to vice-presidency in another organization. As has been repeatedly mentioned in this book, the interaction of the man with the other men and the psychological climate of the organization are of vital importance. Specifying a set of rules or regulations as to how to manage workers cannot be done except in generalities. Workers change according to their physical and psychological environments as well as in reaction to their supervisors. The behavior of a worker in one organization may be drastically different if he moves to another.

What general management principles can be given? Odiorne (1962) feels that management style is changing in the 1960's. He suggested that there have been at least three distinct patterns in the past half-century, "The hard nosed manager of the 1920's and 30's, the human relater of the 1940's and early 50's the management-by-pressure type of the mid and late 50's, the new 'manager of situations' which is emerging with the 60's and will become (I predict) the model of manager of this decade." Each of the first three has been mentioned previously in this chapter. Odiorne's description of the new manager of situations rates additional space here.

There are six things about the manager of the situation that distinguish him from the human relator or the other managers of the past: (1) He is judged by what his followers do, because he is a leader and has followers. (2) He possesses no particular executive personality. (3) He makes things happen by providing the leadership, motivation and drive to see that they take place. (4) He is more of a generalist than in the past and can handle a larger variety of different activities. (5) He will work more through organization than personal effort, particularly delegating more and studying the general situation rather than analyzing the specific facets of the job himself. (6) He will be responsibility- and results-oriented. Odiorne said that the managers of situations will be selected by evaluating what has been done in the past and taking an educated guess concerning the future. This, of course, is similar to normal selection procedures followed for many years. On the other hand, he suggested that instead of evaluating the normal characteristics, such as personality, drive, ingenuity, and so on, appraisals in the future will stress what the man did and how he did it. Training will be in terms of situational thinking to help the man develop decision-making and problem-solving leadership ability. More emphasis will be placed on the behavioral sciences than human relations. The new manager will be more sophisticated in understanding people as individuals and in learning about the behavioral sciences which will help him to control individual and group behavior.

It is interesting to note that many authors are looking forward to the day when managers will be able to use behavioral science. Some of the techniques suggested in the first chapter of this book are the means for controlling human beings in working situations. As more knowledge of behavior develops, better managerial performance can be expected.

Who Can Supervise?   As already suggested there doesn't seem to be one specific method of good supervision. A very adequate supervisory technique in one situation may be inadequate in another. However, there are some characteristics more frequently found in successful businessmen than in nonsuccessful men. Ten such characteristics or attributes are suggested by Argyris (1953): (1) an exhibited high frustration tolerance; (2) an ability to encourage and permit full participation of others without feeling their personal work has been threatened; (3) a continually questioning attitude about their own decisions; (4) they understand the rules of a competitive industrial world; (5) they express hostility tactfully and gracefully; (6) they accept victory with rather controlled emotions and do not become overexcited; (7) they accept defeat without being washed up or shattered; (8) they understand the necessity for limits and that at times certain unfavorable decisions might be handed down to them that they would have to live with; (9) they identify themselves with a group of fellow workers or managers; and (10) they have an ability to set realistic goals and then devote their energies toward successful fulfillment of these goals. No one individual is expected to possess all of these characteristics to a high degree. But Argyris felt that men possessing more of these characteristics than others were the most successful executives.

Others working in evaluation of executives have found that successful men are motivated by achievement, accept authority of their superiors, and have organizational ability, firmness of conviction, realism, a mature attitude, a thorough understanding of the interrelations between the specific business and economic environment, an imagination and ability to change, and other specific traits. Because there is very little experimental evidence concerning just what characteristics are important for good executives, it seems superfluous to list all characteristics that have been suggested by different writers. Thus we include only one other list of characteristics purportedly important to successful managing. Fox (1957), the president of Minute Maid Corporation at the time he wrote the article, stated the qualifications of a successful commander of a business enterprise as (1) creative ability; (2) ability to judge justly or wisely—in other words, be a sound thinker; (3) administrative skill, which includes going over the multitude of details involved in running an organization; (4) a positive attitude that can inspire his fellow workers as subordinates; (5) courage and a willingness to gamble or take a risk well calculated in advance; (6) high integrity or character, sincerity, and morality. Such a list of characteristics shows us what some successful businessmen think is important. Because promotion to high-level jobs often depends upon top-level executives' approval, it is appropriate to know what they think are important characteristics of successful executives.

Apparently there are so many ways to succeed in the business world and such heterogeneous measures of what success is that it is all but impossible to prepare a complete list of characteristics associated with success. An attempt to measure more objective factors involved in effective leadership and correlate them with productivity was reported by Carp, Vitola, and McLanathan (1963). These researchers studied two characteristics of supervisors as related to productivity of their work groups. As a criterion measure of the work of subordinates, a productivity index routinely used by the United States Postal Department for each supervisor's work group was averaged over the period of one year. Each supervisor was given a Human Relations Knowledge Test, and a perceptual set (a predisposition to respond in a certain manner) of the supervisors was measured by means of psychological tests. Comparison of criteria and predictors showed that the supervisors who had high knowledge of human relations principles, and perceived others in a manner that allowed them to have an optimal psychological distance between themselves and their subordinates, supervised workers having the highest productivity. The authors suggested that both knowledge of human relations and the psychological distance measuring scale would be valuable methods of selecting potentially good supervisors.

Predicting leadership ability by means of the usual paper-and-pencil tests or other predictors used for selection of workers seems difficult, if not impossible. However, an approach using a situational test has been shown to have value. Glaser, Schwarz, and Flanagan (1958) studied the unique contribution of interview and situational performance procedures when paper-and-pencil tests and other identifiable predictor variables were controlled. Using two groups of 40 supervisors, they obtained a supervisor's performance report as a criterion of supervisory skill. Five predictor instruments, two interview procedures, and three situational performance tests were studied. These five instruments were (1) A standardized panel interview. A panel of three interviewers informally discussed various topics with the candidates, and at the end of the interview, each interviewer independently completed ratings on the candidate's personal characteristics and attitudes. (2) A standardized individual interview similar to the panel interview but completed by just one interviewer. (3) A group discussion problem in which four candidates discussed recommendations for a particular aspect of plant management while an observer evaluated the performance of each candidate in terms of specific discussion behavior and ratings of the candidates' contributions during the discussions. (4) A role-playing situation, where each candidate was required to deal with a staged personnel problem while the examiner recorded specific aspects of the candidates performance on a check list of effective and ineffective behaviors. (5) A small job-management problem where the candidate was required to train subordinates, organize work flow, and monitor job activities in a miniature work situation. He was scored by an observer using a check list of effective and ineffective supervisory actions and in terms of his actual work output.

The results of the study showed that the group discussion problem was the most reliable of the predictors and the most promising in terms of indicating effective leadership as defined in the study. The panel interview showed no superiority over the individual interview, and the interview procedure and the role-playing situations were about equally successful. The small job-management problems showed little promise for predictive effectiveness. It is unfortunate that the study had to use ratings as a criterion of successful leadership rather than proficiency of the workers under the supervisor, but the evidence is more nearly objective than much of the other available literature.

There is little concrete evidence available for use in selecting good supervisors. Past experience and judgment on the part of the executives in an organization seem to be the best techniques now available for evaluating potential managers.

Although we have discussed all levels of management as a group, we recognize that the motivational needs of various levels of management might well vary. For instance, Porter (1963) recorded the results of a questionnaire administered to 1,916 managers of various levels. Five need areas were studied: (1) Security—the feelings of security. (2) Social—the opportunity to give help to other people and develop close friendships. (3) Esteem—feeling of self-esteem from being in a management position or the prestige of the position. (4) Autonomy—opportunity for independent thought and for participating in the setting of goals in the organization. (5) Self-actualization—the opportunity for personal growth and development in the management position as well as a feeling of self-fulfillment and worthy accomplishment. The results of the study showed that higher-level managers placed relatively more emphasis on self-actualization and autonomy needs than did the lower-level managers. There were no differences between higher- and lower-level managers on the other three needs. Additional discussion of internal motivation or need fulfillment is covered in Chapters 2 and 11 of this book.

LABOR UNIONS

To the average person not connected with unions or organized labor, the term *labor unions* may evoke unpleasant feelings. It is unfortunate that the usual activities sponsored by organized labor that come to the attention of the general population carry negative connotations. Often labor unions are forced to use strikes or other power tactics to gain better working conditions or compensation for their members. Labor unions serve many other purposes and are as integral a part of many industries as are many of the major corporate departments.

One of the most valuable functions provided for workers by unions is the communications activity. In Figure 10.1 a typical industrial organizational chart was shown. The organization of large unions is not much different in a schematic diagram. However, there is a major communications difference within the same structural hierarchy in a management versus a union organization. In the management situation, each man in the hierarchy is the boss of the man below him. The subordinate looks to his superordinate for the possibility of promotion. In a union, the worker or member decides who will serve in the level next above him.

The first level of management in the union, generally referred to as the shop steward or committeeman, is elected by the members. The executive board, the executive officers, the top-ranking management men of the union, and the various levels of supervision within the union are all elected by the membership. Thus there is not the natural reticence toward communication upward through the union that there is in the management organization. The shop steward was elected to his job in the union by the men under him. Thus the men feel free to transmit their gripes and grievances to their shop steward. At the same time the shop steward feels he must please the workers who elected him so he handles the grievances. He is under pressure to pass the grievances up higher in the union organization or to carry it to management's representative to get satisfaction. If low-level management men cannot or will not give satisfaction, the union organization can easily carry the grievance to a higher level in its own organization and then to a high-level management representative. Thus workers can communicate with the high-level management men if it is essential. In the management organization, workers do not want to gripe repeatedly to their foreman for fear of reprisals.

A second major function of the union for workers is to provide a power structure that allows worker's representation to be somewhat equivalent to management's representation. When the feelings of workers are brought up through the union communication system, they can then be taken to higher levels of management by a person representing a large group of individuals who can materially affect the company concerned. An individual worker can gripe to his foreman on the job, but the individual worker always knows that the factory can keep on operating without him. When a top union representative talks to top levels of management, he represents a large number of workers and can greatly affect the industry.

In addition to providing a communication system and the power structure for workers, at least three other personal needs are fulfilled by unions. (1) The worker is made to feel he is important. Instead of a worker, he is a member and a really first-class citizen. He is vital to the organization, and the organization treats him and makes him feel this way. (2) The worker is made to feel that he belongs to a very powerful group. The power of the group is not only within the employing company, but is recognized throughout the United States, especially in terms of social and political power. Unions are well known for their power to influence legislation and legislators toward activities of value to workmen. (3) The union frequently provides members with facilities for meetings, athletic activities, and group get-togethers of a social nature. These needs are often not filled in the workers' society by his community nor by his employer.

Often the actions of unions and the techniques used are not understood. A very brief review of the early labor situation may help us understand some of the reasons for actions of labor unions in the modern world. In the middle and late 1800's, industrialization meant consolidation and cutbacks of skilled workers and increases of low-level, repetitive jobs. Although skilled workers had the best bargaining position, even in the 1800's they recognized the importance of grouping together. By 1850, there were some trade groups organized, mostly along skill lines. Many individual unions at the local, state, and national levels were organized between 1850 and 1950, but essentially only five major federations of unions developed. In 1866 the National Labor Union appealed to both organized and unorganized workers to join a national federation. By 1869, the Knights of Labor, attempting to emancipate workers from slavery, agreed on a policy of no conflict with legitimate enterprise and, in effect, was against strikes and radical agitation in an attempt to bring about a condition where every worker could some day become a capitalist. In 1886, the American Federation of Labor was formed, recognizing the permanence of the working class as a group and aiming for pure and simple unionism with the improvement of wages, hours, and working conditions. They were willing to employ strikes and to enforce collective bargaining for the betterment of their own membership. The AFL, guided by the great leader Samuel Gompers, was essentially a trade union organized along skill groups. It, of course, was one of the major unions that has persisted to the present day.

In 1905 the Industrial Workers of the World (IWW) was organized, and became a small but very strong local group. The IWW, principally appealing to labor classes in the Western sections of the United States, refuted capitalism, and during its relatively short existence it succeeded in considerable violent action, introducing such new strike tactics as sit-ins and mass picketing. It pressed unsuccessfully for a fundamental transformation of the economic order of the United States. It did accomplish the organization of unorganized workers, which led some of the other organizations, such as AFL, to recognize that the ignored unskilled industrial workers needed to be recognized. The Congress of Industrial Organizations was organized in 1936 to bring into organized labor workers from such mass production industries as automobiles, steel, and rubber. A good deal of industrial strife was involved in the eventually successful organization. The CIO, even though more radical than the AFL, did not press for overthrow of the prevailing economic system, but instead endorsed the New Deal of the 1930's and the liberal wing of the Democratic party. Only the AFL and CIO amalgamated unions have persisted. The AFL and CIO were brought together in 1955, showing the basic similarity of interest in each in producing the best possible conditions for all workers.

When much of the organization of workers took place, social conditions in the United States were far different from what they are today. Excerpts from the testimony of Charles L. Harding, President of the Merchants and Woolen Company of Dedham, Massachusetts, to a United States Congress Senate committee in 1883 is abstracted: "When they [the workers] get starved down to it, then they will go to work at just what you can afford to pay. I remember going through 1840, 1841 and 1842. We had very hard times all through that period and the manufacturers were losing money...." Mr. Harding suggested that although he was losing money, his was a small bill, and he felt that he would be all right if he could introduce lower wages, but that when he asked his workers if they were willing to take less money, they said no. Consequently he closed his factory down for the winter. In the spring, he went back to the factory and started to open, and as he did, some of the workers came to him and asked when he was going to start the factory again. Some of the men who had said they would not work for lower wages came to him and begged for any kind of work, because during the winter they had not even enough food for their families. Mr. Harding concluded with, "When help find that they cannot do any better and learn that they have to go to work for a certain price or get nothing, they will have to go to work." He went on to tell the Congressional committee how, in 1873, his mill had a strike. The men were striking for 10 hours of work and he "couldn't afford to reduce their time" to that length each day, so there was a strike. The workers were out for about six weeks, during which time they ran out of funds and could not get credit at his store. Thus they had to come back to work under his conditions with no change in employment conditions (Litwack, 1962). In additional testimony to the same Senate committee, Mr. Livermore said, "The hours of labor in the mills here for those who work the longest are from 6:30 A.M. to 12 and from 1 to 6:45 P.M. and on Saturday until 4 P.M.; making an average of about 10¾ per day for each of the six working days of the week." Mr. Livermore went on to say, "I am informed and have no doubt from my investigation that it is true, that 40 years ago the hours of labor averaged 14½ per day in the mills, that they were gradually reduced by the voluntary act of the mill managers until they reached the limit which I have given as that of today." When asked if there were any unions in the city of Manchester, New Hampshire, Mr. Livermore said emphatically *no*, that there were some attempts to form unions by agitators from the outside, but that generally the working people were not discontented with their pay or their conditions (Litwack, 1962).

Against such a background some of the earlier unions came into being to obtain better working conditions and hours for the workers. The situation was not at all favorable. Mass opinion was much stronger against unions or organized labor than it is today. As typical of the ideology of the country and the attitude toward organized labor's strike as a means of pressuring management into reforms, we mention the railroad strikes of 1877. The strikes, which interrupted railroad traffic in a large part of the country, erupted almost spontaneously, in that there was no well-organized group among all railroads. Militiamen were called out in major cities to restore service and "law and order." In some places—for example, Phila- delphia—the militiamen were actually besieged in a roundhouse by a Pittsburgh crowd that had been infuriated at the killing of 22 of its citizens. President Rutherford B. Hayes then ordered federal troops into action. In Baltimore, Pittsburgh, St. Louis, and Chicago fighting took place, resulting in the death of over a hundred workers. The most fascinating aspect is that the citizens of the United States forgot all about the issues at stake, involv- ing reduction of wages, long hours, poor working conditions, and hostility to effective union organization. The strikes were broken, the workers' demands spurned, and railroad service restored. The strikes did have a delayed effect upon the people of the United States. As a consequence, public opinion changed over the next half-century.

Many difficulties were overcome as labor was organized and became a dominant force in highly industrialized organizations. Even so, organized labor still represented a small percentage of the working force. Probably not more than 10 percent of the working force belonged to organized groups by 1914 and perhaps no more than 30 percent even in 1960.

Thus, although most management and society at large recognized organ- ized labor by the 1920's and 1930's, the trade union movement never really became strong in many areas. For example, of the construction workers in the United States, approximately 80 percent were organized by 1960. On the other hand, only 10 percent of government and wholesale workers were organized by 1960. In certain industries, then, organization has progressed rather strongly and rapidly, perhaps as a result of the poorer working conditions.

Many people in the organized labor movement feel that unionism in the United States is actually decreasing. "The AFL–CIO Department of Organization acknowledges a modest drop in the percentage of organized workers from 40 to 39 percent of the eligible wage and salaried work force from 1953 to 1958. Union membership in 1958 stood at 18,100,000. Both the ratio and absolute number of union members had dropped further by 1961" (Barkin, 1961). With the advent of more automation and newer methods of production that employ relatively fewer unskilled or lower- skilled workers, the labor movement is at an increasing disadvantage.

There is no doubt that there are many things wrong in some of the unions in the United States. Abuses of their offices by union leaders have been well publicized. Racketeers in charge of organized groups have re- ceived a great deal of publicity. But many of the good points of unionism have received little publicity. In many situations, management people have had excellent rapport with unions and recognized their value. Mr. J. Irwin

Miller (1962), chairman of the board of Cummings Engine Company stated, "In the complex industrial society in which we live and in which we are grouped together in very large units, I believe that the presence of strong responsible labor unions is essential to society, to the worker, and to management." When questioned if he meant that industry is more efficient with labor unions than without them, Mr. Miller went on to say: "In a large corporation where the line of communication from the head of the business to all the employees gets too long, you have got to short-circuit it. Otherwise, by the time policies from the head reach the working men they become, through nobody's fault, grossly distorted. With a labor union, what you are really restoring is direct communication both ways, from the head to the workers and back from the working level to the top."

In the next section we will examine some of the interaction of union and management, trying to remember that a healthy atmosphere is advantageous to both management and workers.

UNION–MANAGEMENT RELATIONS

A news item of December 1962 indicated that the members of the Amalgamated Meat Cutters Union at Swift and Company's Moultrie, Georgia, plant ratified a pay cut. The key provision of the newly negotiated contract was a drop of 5 cents in basic hourly rates, which the company had asked for in an attempt to make its plant more competitive in the area.

In October 1962 an unusual request was forwarded by the employees of Rutherford Dairy, Scaroboro Ontario, Canada. They requested that a negotiated $4-a-week raise in their union contract be cut because they feared that an increase of 1 cent a quart in the milk prices resulting from the raise would price them out of their customers.

Of course, the two items just cited were purposely chosen to show cooperativeness of organized workers. It takes little searching to find the opposite kind of items. Requests—in fact, demands—by labor for additional compensation are common. However, many organized groups are recognizing the value of a realistic appraisal of a company's ability to pay wages. With maturing leaders and employees within many organized groups, an understanding of what corporations can pay and can be expected to provide as fringe benefits and working conditions is helping to bring about better union–management relations. Many unions are far better educated concerning the profits of the organization in which they are involved than is the nation at large. For example, an Opinion Research Corporation news release in January 1963 showed that in a nationwide study of 1,000 adults, the estimated net profits of corporations was assumed to be 20 percent after business expenses, including taxes. At the same time, such authorities as the First National City Bank of New York estimated the average net profit of the leading manufacturers was 5.4 percent and for all manufacturers 4.2 percent. The public's perception of the profits made by industry is simply not realistic compared to the actual situation. Unions more and more recognize that the company in which their members are employed must maintain a competitive position and provide a decent return on investment.

As a means toward providing the security desired by workers, several unions have been asking for guaranteed annual wages. For example, in 1961 Walter Reuther proposed to the General Motors, Ford, and Chrysler Corporations that the United Auto Workers membership of 500,000 be given salary status. Such demands force management to consider aspects of their situation that may not have been given adequate thought previously. The guaranteed annual wage may well become common for organized workers.

In the early days of unions, strikes were the generally accepted technique of gaining organized status. Strike activity decreases as unions become more mature, employers' policies change, and the union membership becomes relatively stable. More and more unions are serving their functions without the use of strikes but by other techniques. Currently unions are involved in two big services in labor–management relation: (1) negotiating contracts with management providing for the compensation and working conditions of the employees, and (2) handling questions or disputes concerning interpretations or settlements of the terms written in the contracts. The strike as a method of handling problems is not nearly as important as it is in the contract negotiation. Ordinarily once a contract is negotiated there are three ways in which disputes can be handled without renegotiating a contract. These are labor–management committees, mediation, and arbitration.

It is usually the function of the local or company union official to carry on the daily activities between management and workers. Carrying out negotiated contracts is usually accomplished by a fairly simple union organizational structure consisting of a chairman, executive board, and committeemen or stewards. All of these men are generally workers in the company involved. Thus they serve a dual function working on a job for management and working for their fellow members as representatives. In a labor–management committee, discussions can take place and a joint solution can be derived. Typical of the problems handled at this level are lighting problems, heating problems, arguments between foremen and workers, and other relatively minor difficulties. As long as the prevailing atmosphere is one of good faith, the frequent contacts between management and the workers are advantageous. When the difficulties must be taken to a higher level for solution, arbitration or mediation can be used. (Additional information concerning negotiations is discussed in Chapter 14 of this book.)

Some labor contracts are written with an arbitration clause that calls for arbitration in the case of certain grievances. Some contracts have a very broad arbitration clause that says everything can be taken to arbitration. Some contracts do not allow for arbitration. *Arbitration* refers to the use of a third party, an outsider, who makes decisions after hearing both sides of a grievance or an argument. Typically representatives of management and workers present their views and evidence concerning a particular grievance before a person or a panel of persons acting as arbitrators. The arbitrators then act as judges, ruling in the context of the information presented. In most instances, the arbitration is binding and has been so agreed upon in advance by a vote of management and labor.

Mediation refers to the use of an outside party to help both sides but without the power to make a decision. It is the function of the mediator to come into the situation and help the two sides to understand each other and to get cooperation between the two groups, but the mediator does not have power to make a decision.

In recent years, arbitration has become increasingly popular as a means of handling grievances that cannot be handled by labor–management committees. However, labor and management each have hesitations about using arbitration. It is thus interesting to review a report by Stessin (1959). After analyzing 900 arbitration awards, he concluded that the arbitrator in general upholds the rights of management when it can be shown that a worker has disobeyed rules, when an employee is absent so much, even for the best of reasons, that his services are of little or no value to the company, when the worker does not respect managerial status, when there is proven incompetence, when there are fights or altercations, and when there are strikes or walkouts. Arbitrators in general have found that it is the responsibility of shop stewards or union officials to take action measures to keep their men from walking out if they want any sympathy from the arbitrators. They have generally ruled that time properly used is vital to the success of a business enterprise and that disruption of plant operations is absolutely improper.

More and more evidence is accumulating that grievances sent to arbitration become fewer as managers are better trained in the handling of grievances. Supervisors who understand grievances can handle them before they go to arbitration or mediation, in fact, before they become formal grievances.

Union–management relationships are group interpersonal relationships. The better the skill of representatives of each group, the more successful the interaction. More knowledge of human behavior will aid understanding of interpersonal relations, both group and individual.

SUMMARY

Man is in constant contact with other men. The interpersonal relationship of man to other men in the industrial world is exemplified by the supervisor–worker relationship.

As big business grew, formalized structures developed to aid those in charge in effectively using man and machines. Most organizational charts show line and staff positions. The line functions concern the authority or control responsibilities, whereas staff men are special helpers for the line supervisors. Just how many men should be supervised by each line manager is under consideration. Newer views question the span of control concepts in use, suggesting that the evaluation of how much supervision a manager must do is not determined just by the number of men he controls.

Supervisors control workers by communicating with them. Many barriers to effective communication were discussed with some suggestions for improving both verbal and written communication.

Since the 1920's human relations have been stressed as vital to production. The famous Hawthorne studies were summarized. They showed that workers produce more when they are accepted as humans and given a chance to participate in planning their own destinies on their jobs. The influence of the Hawthorne studies has been great. But recently some authorities have questioned the principle of general participation for all workers.

The questions "What is supervision?" "What do supervisors do?" and "Who can be a good supervisor?" were discussed. There are many variations of supervisory techniques that may be successful. The activities involved in supervision can be learned. Finding a man with the capacity and ability to perform adequately as a supervisor is extremely difficult, for no predictors seem to be adequately correlated with successful job performance.

Many of the man-to-man relations in industry are between representatives of workers and management. A brief review of the labor movement in the United States was presented to help us understand the background for current unions. Negotiation and handling of workers' grievances were discussed as relationships between union and management representatives.

As more understanding of human behavior is accomplished, more efficient use of man's abilities and better human-to-human relations will develop.

SUGGESTED REFERENCES FOR FURTHER STUDY

Landsberger, H. A. (1958). *Hawthorne Revisited*. Ithaca, N.Y.: Cornell University Press.

An interesting additional look at the famous Hawthorne studies.

Leavitt, H. J. (1964). *Managerial Psychology*. Chicago, Ill.: University of Chicago Press.

A book about the human relationships in a working situation. The emphasis is more on management personnel than on hourly workers. A book of readings edited by H. S. Leavitt and L. R. Posdy parallels *Managerial Psychology* and is available from the same publisher.

Likert, R. (1961). *New Patterns of Management*. New York: McGraw-Hill Book Company.

This book discusses organizational structures and management principles as used by successful managers. It is based on research completed at the Institute for Social Research at the University of Michigan.

Litwack, L. (1962). *The American Labor Movement*. Englewood Cliffs, N.J.: Prentice-Hall.

This book traces the history of the labor movement in the United States and indicates some of the qualities, shortcomings, and potential values of the movement.

Roethlisberger, F. J., and W. J. Dickson (1939). *Management and the Worker—An Account of a Research Program Conducted by the Western Electric Company, Hawthorne Works, Chicago*. Cambridge, Mass.: Harvard University Press.

The complete story of the famous Hawthorne studies.

Rubenstein, A. H., and C. J. Haberstrok (1960). *Some Theories of Organization*. Homewood, Ill.: The Dorsey Press, and Richard D. Irwin.

A textbook edited by industrial engineers but providing material concerning organizational theory by many authors from a wide range of disciplines.

Smith, H. C. (1964). *Psychology of Industrial Behavior*. New York: McGraw-Hill Book Company.

This book discusses most of the usual topics concerning industrial psychology and stresses particularly the management of people, supervisor–subordinate relationships, and other social aspects of the industrial situation. Chapters 1, 2, 8, 9, and 12 are especially applicable to man's relationship to other men.

Sutermeister, R. A. (1963). *People and Productivity*. New York: McGraw-Hill Book Company.

The author of this book teaches business administration. He provides a conceptual scheme covering the most important factors affecting performance of employees, and briefly explains the scheme in his writings. The bulk of the book is made up of articles by authors from various disciplines, keyed to Sutermeister's writings and conceptual scheme.

Whyte, W. H. J. (1956). *The Organization Man.* New York: Simon & Shuster.

One author's view of modern American society, emphasizing particularly the influence of industrial organizations in directing man's behavior.

Chapter 11

Man Within Himself

BEHAVIOR IS CAUSED; it is not just a free-wheeling or chance occurrence. In an industrial situation, man is a human organism just as in any other environment. The special functioning of man in a working situation is the result of the interaction of environment and man.

Behavior of humans is so complex and the causal factors so many that the precise relationship between cause and effect is often not known. However, in our daily lives we recognize the importance of causation. Most of us agree with the example from Chapter 1; when riding in an automobile we approach a green traffic light with assurance that traffic at the cross streets will not move into our line of motion. In other words, we believe in causation and control of behavior. We recognize that people become mentally ill or poorly adjusted due to factors that are not completely under their control, and consequently we feel that they need help or treatment rather than whippings or exorcism.

A fascinating aspect of human nature is that the causation principle is acceptable for some behavior, as the examples just mentioned, but not for many aspects of behavior. The principle of causation means that a person must do in a given situation what he does. He may experience feelings of pleasantness or unpleasantness as a result of his action, but blaming or punishing incorrect action will not change the past behavior. The principles discussed in Chapter 1 of this book are obviously of importance at this point. If you are not familiar with general principles of learning, you should review the first section of that chapter.

Behavior is brought about as a result of some stimulation. All action in an organism's repertoire of behavior is the result of some stimulation. Figure 11.1 shows a diagrammatic representation of the relationship between stimulus and response.

The formula in Figure 11.1 is an oversimplification of the principle of causation of behavior. A stimulus leads to some sort of interaction with an organism, which is followed by behavior that we call a response. This response is also fed back to the organism as a stimulus. Thus the $S \longleftrightarrow O \longrightarrow R$ formula indicates Stimulus interacting with Organism fol-

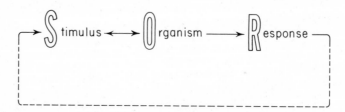

Figure 11.1. A diagrammatic representation of the principle of causation of behavior. A stimulus interacts with an organism and a response follows. The response is fed back into the organism as a stimulus.

lowed by Response. For example, a person touches a hot radiator. Special receptor cells in the organism are activated by the temperature. The neural network of the organism transmits the stimulus from the receptors through various connections to effector cells, which respond. The hand is thus withdrawn. The response is fed back to the organism so withdrawal response stops appropriately. In a very short period of time the organism took information provided by the stimulus, interacted with it, and sent stimuli to certain parts of the body, resulting in a withdrawal response of the part of the body that had contacted the hot surface. Of course, the experience of pain was recorded and persisted for some time after the immediate action. (As described in Chapter 2, the pain sensation may also arouse behavior.) In future situations, the hand will withdraw before a burn takes place, since the human organism has the capacity to interact with the stimulus information and to use experience to modify its behavior. This process was discussed in Chapter 1 of this book.

In this chapter we will discuss adaptations within an organism while interacting with its environment, particularly in a work situation.

DEVELOPMENT OF BEHAVIOR

The enormously complex human organism contains thousands of unsolved mysteries, many in the realm of behavior. Responses are emitted by the organism without known cause or direct relationships between cause and effect. On the other hand, there are many relationships that are fairly well established and can help in an understanding of behavior. Although it may not seem particularly appropriate for an understanding of man in an industrial setting, for a moment we will diverge to a discussion of behavior in the very earliest stages of life. Thus we may more fully understand some of the aspects of behavior seen in adulthood.

Immediately after birth the human organism no longer lives in a completely satisfying environment as just before birth. The baby must breathe, take in food, and eliminate waste products for himself. Although some responses are innate, relatively few complex behavioral patterns exist at birth. Most behavior is acquired through experience. However, some response patterns are emitted without any previous experience. For example, very soon after birth a baby can be expected to give a sucking response when a nipple or other object is placed in its mouth or on its lips. There are also other inborn responses—for example, the grasping reflex of the hands when an object is touched in the palm.

Let us examine the act of responding to the nipple being placed in the mouth or brushing the lips. As soon as the infant makes the first response of sucking and food is taken into the mouth, another inherited response follows—swallowing of the food. This response seems to be satisfying to the organism, and additional responses of the same sort continue. Thus conditions necessary for learning are evidenced, and the organism tends to repeat the action whenever a nipple is placed in its mouth again. Following the S–O–R paradigm, stimulation (in this case a nipple or a material with sweetened substance, such as mother's milk or formula) is provided to a sense organ so that stimulation can enter the organism. As discussed in Chapter 1 the basic need of an organism for food was satisfied by a particular response. Thus the organism perceived the change in his environment so that the response tends to reoccur more often in the future. Any stimuli that also impinge upon receptor organs at the time that the response is reinforced tend to become important in controlling or bringing about the particular response. Thus if the baby was held by its mother at the time of feeding, the stimulations provided in tactual and visual stimulation were also important. Soon behavior is modified so that the baby that might have cried until it was fed learned to stop crying when it was picked up previous to being fed.

Let's back up for a moment to see what conditions were important in the organism in order to bring about crying. The organism that is completely fed and has no need for additional food could not be expected to take in food. However, even just after birth, the organism uses energy and consequently is no longer satiated in terms of food. In fact, he becomes more and more imbalanced as the cells of the body burn up the food. Thus a need is created in the organism.

The relationship between physiological changes in the organism, need, and motivational state can be described by means of diagrams, as shown in Figure 11.2.

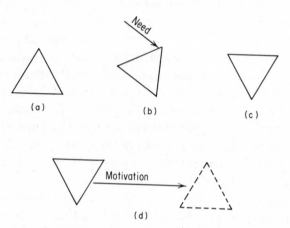

Figure 11.2, a, b, c, d. Diagrammatic representations of an organism in terms of one physiological characteristic. In (a) the organism is in a state of complete balance on this characteristic. As needs create pressure on the organism it moves into a less balanced position, as shown in (b) or extreme imbalance as shown in (c). In (d) the motivation to get back to a state of balance is shown.

In these diagrams a triangle has been used to represent the human organism in terms of one particular physiological characteristic—for example, hunger. Immediately after ingesting all of the food that the organism can hold we can say that the body is in a state of balance or homeostasis on this one particular characteristic. Diagrammatically, we represent this by a triangle, with the base horizontal or flat to the surface upon which it is resting (Figure 11.2a). Immediately upon completion of feeding, in fact even while eating, the cells of the body are burning food, and thus the blood supply is depleting the energy provided by the ingestion of food. As time goes by, more of the available food supply is used, and a greater and greater need is created in the body. Diagrammatically we show this by an arrow forcing one point of the triangle into movement away from balance (Figure 11.2b). Thus, with the passage of time, additional use of the food leads to a greater imbalanced position, as represented by the triangle with a point toward the surface upon which it is resting (Figure 11.2c). In this position, the triangle tends to move to a state of balance again. We have a state of the organism that is frequently called a highly motivated condition. The organism has been forced into this state of imbalance by needs built up within the organism and is now motivated to fulfill these needs (Figure

11.2d). The needs behind the motivated condition may be labeled or completely ignored.

Some theorists feel that a generalized activated condition of the organism is created by innumerable stimuli and that there is no reason to try to name even the more common stimuli that seem to be involved. As explained in Chapter 2, we find it helpful to label certain response sequences of behavior according to general stimulus categories. Table 2.2 presents such a list of commonly accepted motives, with examples of their assumed stimuli. If you are not familiar with Chapter 2 it would be well to review it at this point, because we will not repeat the material here.

If the needs are fulfilled, the organism will essentially revert to a state of balance on this particular characteristic. In most cases in our environment the basic physiological motivations are fulfilled quite easily and the human organism stays relatively in a state of balance. If we go back to the example of the newborn baby, at the time that the baby completely ingests all the food that he can, his motivational condition concerning food could be diagrammatically shown as in Figure 11.2a. Very soon the use of the food creates the condition shown in Figure 11.2b, then Figure 11.2c, and a striving to get back to the balance of all types shown in Figure 11.2d. When the organism is highly motivated (Figure 11.2c or d), behavior of all types increases. If one of these activities results in helping the organism get back into the state of balance again, thus changing the perceived stimulus situation, it will be repeated in the future under similar conditions. One of the most common instances of all random behavior of babies is crying. When a baby is hungry, he expresses the hunger in random movement, including crying. When his mother provides food, the random behavior and the crying both cease as the food is ingested and the baby gets nearer a state of balance on the characteristic of food. In the future, because of learning, the mere presence of the mother or the picking up of the baby by the mother will stop the crying. This then is a very simple explanation of a rudimentary level of behavior.

We have explained simple behavior in quite a naive fashion. Naturally workers don't function as simply as the way we have just described. The work environment is not a situation where just one characteristic, such as food deprivation, works upon an organism at a time. However, let us continue at the elementary level a bit further. Suppose that an organism is in a motivated state, as shown in Figure 11.2d. At that time, the organism is attempting to get back into a state of balance. If this can be readily accomplished, the organism can be satisfied and a fairly normal balance reobtained. However, a variety of factors may be introduced to keep the organism from returning to the state of balance, and the organism might be described as frustrated. Chapter 2 of this book presents a range of possible blockings that result in frustration.

In Figure 11.3 we show a frustrated condition diagrammatically.

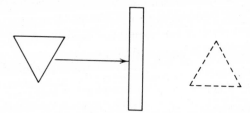

Figure 11.3. A diagrammatic representation of an organism in a frustrating condition. An obstacle blocks the fulfillment of a motivated condition of the organism.

It will be noticed that an obstacle keeps the motivational state from being relieved by the organism's returning to a state of balance. When the motivational state of the organism is not allowed to reorient itself in a balanced position, the organism becomes frustrated or dissatisfied. The result of this dissatisfaction is increased behavior. General responses become more and more frequent as motivation is thwarted. Often a variety of responses that are not particularly conducive to solving the situation take place. For example, when the baby previously mentioned gets hungrier, kicking, squirming, crying, gurgling, wiggling occur, and only a few of these responses have any possible value in reducing the motivational state. Chapters 2, 3, and 4 discuss many of the typical reactions of adults and what might be done to help lessen such situations and reactions. In this chapter we will deal briefly with a few typical responses in an industrial situation.

Behavior is affected by stimuli from within and outside an organism. In previous chapters we discussed some of the stimuli that may enter the organism from his environment. We will now discuss some of the characteristics of the organism that may have an effect upon the responses he gives. It must be remembered that any time stimuli are changed, the organism is changed too, and when the organism is changed, stimulation entering the organism is changed, because the organism interacts with the information from his environment before responding to it himself. In other words, stimulus and organism are inextricably intertwined and cannot be treated separately even though they are often discussed separately for purposes of clarity.

The major characteristics that will be discussed in the next few sections concern motivation, pay, attitudes and morale, fatigue, and accidents and safety. These may all be subsumed under the general topic of reactions to a need situation or motivational state in the organism.

MOTIVES

In his book *Zest for Work* Hersey (1955) stated: "In reality each department or small plant is like a small town. The people in a small town are gossipy, mean, jealous, and narrow. They are also courageous, industrious, kindly, cheerful and helpful in times of trouble. Turning the spotlight on one side of the picture you see the avarice and wickedness of men. Turn it on the other and you see just as clearly their courage and their helpfulness to one another.

"So it was with the workers in these studies. With want and poverty just around the corner they still laughed and joked. They gave part of their last dollar to the fellow worker who was sick or who had suffered an accident. . . On the surface they were callous and rough. . . The worker, however, gives people a false impression of himself. Unless warped by nature or circumstances, he carries beneath that hard exterior a warm heart, ready to respond generously to kindly and considerate treatment, to justice and fair play, with all the finer feelings that distinguish commonship." It is obviously the problem in industry to find the motivators to bring into play the warm heart, generous and considerate treatment, and fair play of the workers in an industrial setting. Hersey was correct when he suggested that these qualities are still in the human, but from years of experience, much of the working force in our society has learned that work is distasteful and that they should do as little as possible to obtain the maximum return.

Historical Perspective.   Brown (1954) emphasized the historical perspective in explaining present attitudes toward work in the first few chapters of his book *The Social Psychology of Industry*. He pointed out three major phases of machine utilization in the past thousand years: (1) The medieval stage lasted from about A.D. 1000 to 1750, when the main material was wood with wind, water, and some animals as the power source. Very little industrialization took place during the period, and the ideas or ideology prevalent at the time was that each member had his own function in the society and that each person was to stay within his own situation. Workers were relatively content because they were secure and knew what their situation was and never really had an understanding of how to move from one position in society to another. The society was certainly not ideal, but in some respects, most members of the different levels of society felt loved and protected even though they were subjected to a relatively low standard of living compared to others.

(2) The industrial revolution brought a new stage of capitalism with much higher standards of living. However, with increasing wealth came the idea of a "just price" (payment for the value of the product produced).

Social justice, which was formerly the important method of estimating value, disappeared, and the capitalistic economy put the individual entirely on his own feet. What he did, how he did it, and whether he succeeded or failed were determined by his own performancs. Thus the individual gained more freedom. At the same time larger amounts of capital were needed for production facilities, more people were involved, less craftsmanship was demanded, and more specialization came into being. The ideology of the period made it appear almost antisocial to help the weak or the poor. The fit were more likely to persist in the environment, and the poor or unsuited were liable to disappear according to Darwinian theory. It was acceptable to be self-interested in human actions, and basic motivations became the avoidance of pain and the obtaining of pleasure. Workers felt less secure and started to feel that their hours at work were just time taken from their real life, in return for the privilege of being able to live the rest of their time as they desired. "Work was, as he had been taught, the antithesis of all pleasure and happiness; it was no longer performed for the greater glory of God, for the master craftsman in whose house he lived, for the honor of the craft, or even out of purely personal pride, but was merely for the sake of earning money to do other things" (Brown, 1954).

(3) About the beginning of the present century, the modern phase began. Mass production brought about efficiency in engineering, and Taylor and Gilbreith brought about the use of man as a function of the man–machine system. Since the original motion-and-time-study work, the concept of "one best way" of work has been questioned. Emphasis has been returned to finding how to get the man motivated to do what he really wants to do, cooperate with other men, be kind to others, gain a feeling of achievement, and not simply earn an income in the working situation.

Brown suggested that it is important to recognize that any society, whether at the national, community, or single factory level, is of the nature of an organism and therefore cannot easily be changed. In other words, a society can be changed only in relationship to how it exists at this moment and in terms of its own needs. It is necessary to keep a healthy skepticism in respect to what can be done in the way of social change.

Primary and Secondary Motivation. With this background in mind, let us look again at the topic of motivation. We will sometimes oversimplify in order to clarify our discussion. Motivation may be divided into primary motivation, based on those physiological changes or imbalances in the human organism, and secondary motivation, which is learned as a result of experience. Both motivations are important in our society, but secondary motivation is generally of more importance in the modern world. For most societies, the basic physiological motivations are fulfilled as a natural consequence of living in organized societies.

Referring to Chapters 1 and 2 of this book, it will be recalled that motivation is construed as an intervening variable resulting from the passage of time or by deprivation of some sort. The organism in its daily functioning creates primary motivation by simply existing. Physiologically, food, liquid, oxygen, and so on, are consumed, and a need for these materials is created. Experience and interactions with others in society create secondary motivation. In the modern world, money will purchase materials needed to satisfy all of the primary and many of the secondary motivations. Thus money has become an important source of satisfaction for work. We will discuss pay more fully in a later section, but now we must examine another method of explaining motivation.

Need Hierarchy. Maslow (1943) essentially suggested that what man really wants is more of everything. Man desires a better and better situation for himself. He wants only what he does not already have, and thus satisfied needs do not motivate behavior. Maslow said that needs or wants can be arranged in a hierarchy of importance. Thus, when needs on the lower level are filled, those on a higher level emerge and demand satisfaction. The hierarchy of needs he suggested placed physiological needs as lowest or basic, then safety needs, social needs, esteem needs, and finally self-realization needs. (This material is included in Chapter 2, and Maslow's hierarchy of needs are combined with others in Table 2.2.)

As already stated, physiological needs are basically filled by living in modern society. The average wage earner quite adequately fulfills the basic physiological needs for food, drink, temperature regulation, rest, and so on, for himself and his family. As adults, there is little safety need, because the need for protection from physical danger is rather remote in civilized society. Children or neurotic or mentally disturbed adults are sometimes more motivated by the needs for safety. However, there is some need for safety expressed in the desire for a guaranteed annual wage, sickness and accident protection, and so on, demanded by labor.

After the physiological and safety needs are fulfilled, the social needs for togetherness and a feeling of belonging are of importance. These needs are difficult to satisfy in our society and have become increasingly important as more urbanization takes place and less group behavior outside of the work situation is expected. Loyalties to groups of fellow workers, bowling clubs, athletic teams, and gangs are expressions of this need for togetherness and belonging. Much of the motivation in industry can be attributed to this need, as shown by the Hawthorne studies and the emphasis on human relations training.

The next higher level in Maslow's hierarchy of needs is becoming increasingly important. A person wants to feel worth while, to feel that he has achieved the goals he has set for himself, and to feel that he has attained status and prestige in the eyes of others. These are very real needs and result in "keeping up with the Joneses" at home as well as performing at least among the average standards of the group at work. Superior performance is acceptable in some work groups, but in others it results in loss of esteem. Thus the worker may be motivated to produce less than he can actually do in order to maintain goodwill among his fellow workers. At the same time he may desire to improve his performance because of his own feeling of self-worth. This results in a conflict or frustrating situation, which may be difficult for the worker to handle. Such blocking of motivation has received considerable attention in Chapter 2 of this book.

The highest need level suggested by Maslow was for self-realization, which refers to doing or being what one really can do or be. This means putting forth to one's fullest potential. A person who attains the activity that he feels that he can do has achieved satisfaction of the highest level of motivation. Relatively few humans are capable of self-realization. Maslow suggested only outstanding men such as Abraham Lincoln and William James have come close to self-realization. As more and more of the lower needs are fulfilled, the higher needs in the hierarchy become more important and the standards of our entire society may be raised. More people will be able to fulfill their esteem needs and thus concentrate on self-realization needs.

McDermid (1960) summarized the practical aspects of Maslow's theory of motivation by suggesting that money can be of value, because it produces purchasing power for the physiological motivation and security or safety needs. Properly handled, money can also be of value at the social need level, since incentive awards can show the participant that he belongs or participates in the group welfare. Money can also be used to confirm a person's sense of achievement in terms of feeling that he adequately completed the job or he would not have received the compensation. It also shows that others esteem a person's performance. Incentive awards may encourage the recipients to fulfill their own potential and thus partially solve self-realization needs, but these needs are the most difficult of all for monetary compensation to fulfill.

PAY

Money is important in rewarding men and must still be considered even
though it has been overemphasized in the past. Payroll represents the major
cost of doing business for many industrial concerns. Even so, McDermid
(1960) emphasized that the studies that have been made concerning
compensation generally discuss what is being done, not why it is being
done or what should be done to get the most out of compensation programs. He explained that compensation programs were traditionally based
on the classical economic theory that man as a rational organism was
motivated by the desire to maximize his economic gain. He argued that
the psychological theory of motivation advanced by Maslow provides a
better method of understanding human behavior.

Many writers have discussed the value of money or pay in terms of
productivity. For example, Rothe (1960) summarized some of the classic
studies and evidence for surveys concerning pay. He showed that a variety
of studies showed that money improved production. On the other hand,
other studies, including the famous Hawthorne studies, indicated that
different factors are more important in production. Surveys of workers have
shown time and again that pay is not the number-one factor when seeking
employment or in providing happiness in the work situation. Monetary
compensation per se is of value, but most likely achieves its value following
the lines of Maslow's theory.

Rothe (1960) argued that learning (and therefore production) is
affected by monetary compensation. As we suggest in this book, Rothe
believes that pay increases may be of value ". . . if they are given soon after
an outstanding accomplishment, if the employee is told the reason for
the increase, and if, on the other hand, his undesirable actions are immediately pointed out to him as grounds for the withholding of a raise."
Rothe thus argued for individually negotiated increases rather than the
general raises that are given to the employees regardless of their particular
productivity. In fact, he suggested that of all the common methods of
increasing pay, including cost of living, length of service, profit sharing,
and bonuses and commissions, the only systems that are really worth while
in terms of fulfilling motivation are individual- and group-incentive plans.
He suggested that the individual-incentive plans are of most value in immediately fulfilling needs and that group incentives are of value when the
groups are such that the individual may recognize his contribution to the
achievement and the relationship between his groups' achievement and
increased compensation. Although Rothe was summarizing many studies,
his conclusions must be tempered. In earlier chapters we have pointed out
many shortcomings of individual- and group-incentive pay plans. These

must also be considered when evaluating possible wage-increase methods.

As another consideration about pay, we again emphasize the need for security and its relationship to compensation programs. The standard of living in the United States is at such a level that the basic physiological needs of most people are provided. As these needs are even more adequately fulfilled, security becomes more important. Organized labor has been emphasizing the importance of payment plans that provide security for their members. Payment plans have involved pensions and fringe benefits, and in the future a salary status for workers will become more common. Some large organizations already have experience with such a payment system. Brooks (1962) suggested that as automation spreads through industry there is going to be a narrowing of the distinction between the white- and the blue-collar worker in terms of compensation plans and other fringe benefits such that there will be a salaried working class. International Business Machines, for example, has eliminated the hourly wage and has all employees on salaries. He cited several business executives who have had experience with automated industry. They suggested that incentive plans and hourly rate systems are not effective. As organizations become more and more automated, workers, in order to gain security, will be seeking and obtaining salaried status.

Kaponya (1962), by means of a case history, told of some of the problems of placing blue-collar workers on salary. He suggested that the first thing that must be considered is the human relations aspects of the worker–management relationship. If there is a basic philosophy of employer relations carefully conceived to increase management's awareness of the relationship of people with each other, then the groundwork has been completed for a transition of blue-collar workers to a salary status. He presented a list of conditions that need to exist in a firm's business climate before it takes the crucial step of putting all workers on salary: "1. The basic objective of an all-on-salary plan cannot be to 'keep unions out.' 2. If management feels that its hourly employees are more conscious of their rights and wishes than they are of their responsibilities, any plans to place such workers on salary should be dropped." (He felt that there should be an effort to understand people, their drives, motivations, needs and interests, rather than consider what they should be.) "3. The firm must have developed meticulously kept records on absenteeism." (If absenteeism is high, it should be reduced before the program is introduced.) "4. A sound personnel department is important."

Many studies have shown that pay is important as a source of satisfaction in a work situation. However, workers are involved not only in earning an income but in deriving satisfaction from a variety of other functions. Many of the secondary motivations or socially important needs can be satisfied by the work situation. Satisfaction on the job has been shown not only to increase performance on the job, as reported by Baxter, Taaffe, and Hughes (1953), but also to improve the general adjustment of the worker in his life and to be especially so for men more than for women (Brayfield, Wells, and Strate, 1957).

Evaluation of Motivation in Industry. Now that we have investigated pay as a possibility for motivating men, let's consult some evaluations of how well motivation is accomplished in the actual work situation. At a conference of the New York State School of Industrial Relations concerning the impact of psychiatry on American management, Dr. Herzberg indicated that the jobs that most people hold are "mental health hazards." He suggested that such satisfaction as achievement, recognition, responsibility, and advancement that are often important to workers are frequently ignored by management. Instead management emphasizes supervision, salary, interpersonal relationships, and working conditions. Dr. McLean at the same conference indicated that trying to satisfy employees by material benefits is essentially impossible. He felt that employees need psychological need fulfillment and that unfulfilled emotions are frequently transferred to drives for higher wages or greater fringe benefits and shorter hours. The psychological needs previously pointed out by Herzberg are not being filled and are causing the unrest. Herzberg concluded that management must help workers obtain a feeling of accomplishment, from creativity and from meaningful jobs so that an employee can have some control over the way his job is done and realize a sense of personal growth and achievement.

Argyris (1961) argued that the present and future of personnel administration must be more closely governed by behavioral science research. He emphasized that human relations policies in the future must be shifted as follows: "FROM policies (1) that emphasize satisfaction, morale, happiness; (2) that individuals are conceived as the most important part of an organization; (3) that require sub-ordinates to be developed by their superiors; (4) that define the objectives of executive development programs the changing of executive's behavior, TO policies (1) that emphasize internal committment, self-responsibility, productiveness; (2) that assume individuals are but one part of the organization and their importance varies under different conditions; (3) that assure no one can develop anyone else except himself. The door to development is locked from the inside; (4) that assume the objective is to help the executive become more aware and accepting of himself and therefore of others.' He summarized that "healthy individuals probably prefer to give of themselves so long as they are not required to give up themselves."

Motivation is a topic that has received a great deal of attention. Still there is little concrete evidence concerning motivation. The hierarchical-need approach suggested by Maslow and expanded by others seems to have merit. For the industrial situation, needs for self-esteem and self-actualization seem to be of importance as motivators. Men entering industry must conceive methods by which these needs can be used to increase productivity in the working situation. Man may fulfill the self-actualization need in his work situation. Great enjoyment as well as satisfaction can be obtained while at work. However, some research indicated that men achieve satisfaction in the work situation but that occupational satisfaction is not necessarily a function of the degree to which needs are satisfied in the occupation. In other words, some people obtain satisfaction of needs by work to a much greater degree than do others. (Kuhlen, 1963; Brayfield and Crockett, 1955).

INCENTIVE

An incentive is a condition or object perceived as capable of satisfying motivation. Incentives tend to arouse dormant motivational conditions within an organism. Incentives apparently cause an organism to become aware of motivational conditions. Thus a deprivation of some sort, created as described earlier, may be overlooked by an organism until an incentive directs the attention of the organism so that he will perceive the motivational condition.

For example, a person who has not eaten for some time may not be hungry. He may be carrying on routine behavior. If a special effort is needed he may exert the necessary energy with little additional incentive except his own desire to do the extra work. If, however, he is shown a juicy steak and told that it will be his upon completion of the extra work, he may work harder and faster. The incentive may make him aware of his hunger, and thus the motivation will increase his activity.

There is probably no one ideal incentive. As Brown (1954) pointed out, "incentives vary from one culture to another, from one firm to another, and from one individual to another (one man may value money where another may find greater leisure or opportunities for promotion a more powerful stimulant)." In the United States, money has become extremely valuable as a satisfier of motivation. However, an incentive is a reward held out in front of an organism to encourage performance. Thus the organism must be motivated so that the incentive may have value as a potential reinforcer. Motivation can be fulfilled by the attainment of the incentive.

In the previous section we discussed motives and pay. Although we concluded that money is generally not the complete solution for workers' motivations, economic incentives are of some value. Men are interested in money and they are interested in good human relations. As Whyte (1952) stated: "The issue then is not: economic incentives *or* human relations. The problem is to fit economic incentives and human relations effectively together, to *integrate* them. In other words, the pulling power of money reward will be strongly affected by the pattern of human relations into which it is introduced." Whyte went on to argue that "Systems of financial incentives in industry today probably yield a net gain in productivity, but most of them fail to release more than a small fraction of the energy and intelligence workers have to give to their jobs. Even when the financial incentive yields higher productivity, it may also generate such conflicts within the organization that we must wonder whether the gains are worth the costs." As Whyte suggested, management must recognize the value of incentives and the human relations problems in industry. A planned program using financial incentives and a good human relations approach will achieve the greatest productivity of workers.

Many studies have shown that workers have different needs. A general list of needs includes steady work, good working conditions, high pay, and other factors. High pay is usually not the top priority for workers. Most studies show that pay generally ranks after conditions of the working environment, the people in the work situation, steadiness of work, opportunities for advancement, and so on. Since this is the case, it would seem that these factors could be of value as incentives. As a matter of fact, they are very valuable as incentives in the hiring situation if they can be shown to be available to perspective employees.

The need hierarchy presented by Maslow and discussed earlier in this book contains a variety of suggestions that might be used as incentives. Often management must point out to the workers how these needs can be fulfilled by work. Thus incentives can be put to practical use.

Gibbs and Brown (1955) presented results of a study using knowledge of performance as an incentive. It has been generally accepted that knowledge of results is important in learning. Generally such knowledge acts as reinforcement. It is possible too that such knowledge of results may also motivate behavior. Gibbs and Brown conducted research in which subjects could see a counter on one half of their trials but not on the other half. The experiment was arranged so that each subject should be motivated only by self-competition and his own satisfaction in doing the work. The results showed that when the subjects could see the counters they produced about 25 percent more than when they couldn't see the count of their own production.

These results have been extrapolated to industry. Generally they have been interpreted to mean that increased awareness of motivation is created. Thus increased production should follow when workers are aware of their production.

Chapanis (1964) essentially repeated Gibbs' and Brown's work. He used four groups of subjects in four simulated work situations: (1) no knowledge of performance was given; (2, 3) a counter showed each worker a continuous record of his production; and (4) a counter showed output, and the worker was required to record his output every 15 minutes. No significant differences occurred in the performance of the groups.

Chapanis concluded that the substantial difference in results between Gibbs' and Brown's study and his own might be due to some differences in methodology. He also suggested that it is possible that Gibbs and Brown attained a positive effect "due to some additional factors present in their experiment which were not present in mine." In the Gibbs and Brown experiment there were no learning effects whereas in the Chapanis experiment there were definite improvements in performance during the experimental sessions. In the Chapanis experiment, the subjects were more nearly under a work situation than were those in the Gibbs and Brown study who probably realized they were in an experiment. We must certainly be careful in applying the results of either study to an industrial situation. Knowledge of results may or may not work as an incentive.

At the present time there seems to be little knowledge as to exactly what incentives are of value. The needs suggested earlier in this book under the discussion of motivation are important to productivity. When a means of fulfillment of these needs can be held out in front of a worker, there is good reason to believe that incentive has been provided.

ATTITUDE, MORALE, AND JOB SATISFACTION

Practically every writer has his own definition for many key words necessary in a discussion of human motivation in an industrial setting. We use fairly common definitions for *attitude, morale,* and *job satisfaction.* The general concept of attitude and morale is similar and the terms are used interchangeably by many. *Job satisfaction* is also used by many to indicate the same general concept as morale or attitude. Thus we have combined all three, although we show that there are some reasons to differentiate at least the term *job satisfaction* from the first two terms.

Attitude refers to a predisposition on the part of a person to respond to situations, persons, or places in a particular manner. The term is very similar in definition and usage to the word *set*, which frequently appears in general psychological literature. The term *morale* refers to an attitude of an individual toward a group situation. It thus becomes more of the perception of an individual toward the probability of satisfying his own motivation through working with a group.

Attitude and morale are almost synonymous and are closely associated with job satisfaction. *Job satisfaction* is a favorable feeling or psychological condition of a person toward his job situation. Blum (1956) argued that "an 'attitude' is not job satisfaction." However, we agree with Blum's argument and additional remarks that job satisfaction is brought about by many factors including attitudes. Thus attitudes are of prime importance in job satisfaction. Since much of the reporting concerning these topics interchanges these terms and since job satisfaction and morale are so closely related to workers' attitudes, we combine our discussion concerning all three terms.

For years there has been an assumption by businessmen, the general population, and specialists that attitudes of workers are related to productivity. This belief has been held in spite of little validating evidence. Thus articles like the one by Brayfield and Crockett (1955) are somewhat shattering. After reviewing the literature they found no correlation or little significant correlation between employee attitude and such performance measures as productivity, absenteeism, accident rate, and job tenure. Brayfield and Crockett showed that there is little evidence to support the concept of predictive or concurrent validity for attitude or morale surveys.

However, Campbell and Tyler (1957) contended that although Brayfield's and Crockett's proof of no predictive or concurrent validity is correct, construct validity can occur. By construct validity, they refer to the relationship between two different measures of attitude or morale. They cite two specific studies, one conducted with office personnel who were given a job opinion questionnaire and at the end were asked in which sections in their departments they would like best to work. The second study involved a group of enlisted men from a squadron of 10 submarines. The men were given a 30-item morale ballot and at the end were asked to name three ships and to indicate which ship in the squadron they would most like to serve on for peacetime duty. The rankings of the ships from the morale ballot correlated .75 with the ranking of the ships in terms of the number of mentions they received from other ships. The correlation between the two measures of the office personnel was .65. Thus there was construct validity indicated by the Campbell and Tyler study. It should be pointed out, however, that there was no significant relationship between either of the measures of attitude or morale and absenteeism or, in the case of the naval study, with reenlistment rate or naval records of ship efficiency.

By and large, it seems that attitude as measured by questionnaires has little to do with productivity on the job. However, when workers' attitudes are more favorable, they are happier whether it shows up in terms of production or not. Most management personnel want their workers to be satisfied as well as productive. Thus we must recognize some factors concerning attitudes and how to assess them.

The regular communication system within the formal organization is one useful method of assessing attitudes. In addition, specialized measurement techniques are available. We do not discuss these in detail, because many of the same techniques are usable in advertising and market research and are covered in Chapter 12 of this book.

The regular communication channels supplemented by the "grapevine" can provide information about the attitudes of workers. It must be remembered, however, that the ordinary hierarchical structure of the typical business is such that communication up through the system is limited. Only extreme views or favorable attitudes can usually be expected to pass up through the formal organization. Davis (1953) emphasized the value of the grapevine as a communication technique in industry and showed that information can often travel more readily than in the formal communication system.

Observation of the behavior of workers is sometimes used to gain an indication of attitude. Although studies question the relationship between workers' attitudes and productivity, management often infers poor attitudes when production goes down or when there are increased union complaints or grievances. We caution against such interpretations, because experimental evidence does not substantiate the concept.

Surveys are formalized or more precise methods of estimating attitudes of workers. Surveys as methods of assessing attitudes may be classified into three categories: (1) *Regular interviewing.* In the interview situation, as discussed in Chapter 6, the worker discusses with his supervisor or an interviewer his feelings and desires concerning the working situation. This technique can provide valuable information, although it is a somewhat expensive method. (2) *The questionnaire technique.* A series of questions in printed form are distributed to workers and returned by mail, special deposit box, or other technique. This method is relatively less expensive in terms of administration, but there is no way of knowing exactly who has returned the questionnaire and what the returns mean. In general, people who complete a questionnaire have stronger feelings than those who do

Some jobs are more interesting and satisfying than others. We want to know how people feel about different jobs. This blank contains eighteen statements about jobs. You are to cross out the phrase below each statement which best describes how you feel about your present job. There are no right or wrong answers. We should like your honest opinion on each one of the statements. Work out the sample item numbered (0).

0. There are some conditions concerning my job that could be improved.
    STRONGLY AGREE   AGREE   UNDECIDED   DISAGREE   STRONGLY DISAGREE

1. My job is like a hobby to me.
    STRONGLY AGREE   AGREE   UNDECIDED   DISAGREE   STRONGLY DISAGREE

2. My job is usually interesting enough to keep me from getting bored.
    STRONGLY AGREE   AGREE   UNDECIDED   DISAGREE   STRONGLY DISAGREE

3. It seems that my friends are more interested in their jobs.
    STRONGLY AGREE   AGREE   UNDECIDED   DISAGREE   STRONGLY DISAGREE

4. I consider my job rather unpleasant.
    STRONGLY AGREE   AGREE   UNDECIDED   DISAGREE   STRONGLY DISAGREE

5. I enjoy my work more than my leisure time.
    STRONGLY AGREE   AGREE   UNDECIDED   DISAGREE   STRONGLY DISAGREE

6. I am often bored with my job.
    STRONGLY AGREE   AGREE   UNDECIDED   DISAGREE   STRONGLY DISAGREE

7. I feel fairly well satisfied with my present job.
    STRONGLY AGREE   AGREE   UNDECIDED   DISAGREE   STRONGLY DISAGREE

8. Most of the time I have to force myself to go to work.
    STRONGLY AGREE   AGREE   UNDECIDED   DISAGREE   STRONGLY DISAGREE

9. I am satisfied with my job for the time being.
    STRONGLY AGREE   AGREE   UNDECIDED   DISAGREE   STRONGLY DISAGREE

10. I feel that my job is no more interesting than others I could get.
    STRONGLY AGREE   AGREE   UNDECIDED   DISAGREE   STRONGLY DISAGREE

11. I definitely dislike my work.
    STRONGLY AGREE   AGREE   UNDECIDED   DISAGREE   STRONGLY DISAGREE

12. I feel that I am happier in my work than most other people.
    STRONGLY AGREE   AGREE   UNDECIDED   DISAGREE   STRONGLY DISAGREE

13. Most days I am enthusiastic about my work.
    STRONGLY AGREE   AGREE   UNDECIDED   DISAGREE   STRONGLY DISAGREE

14. Each day of work seems like it will never end.
    STRONGLY AGREE   AGREE   UNDECIDED   DISAGREE   STRONGLY DISAGREE

15. I like my job better than the average worker does.
    STRONGLY AGREE   AGREE   UNDECIDED   DISAGREE   STRONGLY DISAGREE

16. My job is pretty uninteresting.
    STRONGLY AGREE   AGREE   UNDECIDED   DISAGREE   STRONGLY DISAGREE

17. I find real enjoyment in my work.
    STRONGLY AGREE   AGREE   UNDECIDED   DISAGREE   STRONGLY DISAGREE

18. I am disappointed that I ever took this job.
    STRONGLY AGREE   AGREE   UNDECIDED   DISAGREE   STRONGLY DISAGREE

Figure 11.4. An attitude scale developed by Brayfield and Rothe to measure job satisfaction. From A. H. Brayfield and H. F. Rothe (1951), "An Index to Job Satisfaction," *J. Appl. Psychol.*, **35**, No. 5.

not. Consequently estimating the attitudes of a group from returned questionnaires is a debatable procedure when anonymous questionnaires are used. (3) *Sealed questionnaires.* These attitude scales are designed to elicit the feeling or attitude of an individual toward a particular subject.

Brayfield and Rothe (1951) found after careful investigation that relatively few or no attitude scales were available concerning job satisfaction. Thus they constructed an attitude scale using the techniques of Thurstone and Likert. The scale they constructed and checked for reliability is shown in Figure 11.4.

After testing, revising, and retesting, their scale had a reliability of .87. A check of whether students entered a course or did not enter a course in personnel psychology, after indicating interest or noninterest via the blank, showed a significant difference in the performance of the two groups. The authors felt this indicated validity for the blank.

An indication of the value and sensitivity of attitude questionnaires was reported by Berrien and Angoff (1960). They conducted a study in the field that fairly well duplicated ordinary laboratory controls. A questionnaire was administered to two comparable groups on two occasions. During the interval between the two surveys, subjects in one of the groups were significantly disturbed by a surprise announcement that their plant was going to be moved 75 miles to a new, semirural location. The announcement posed problems for all employees and would seem to affect their attitudes negatively. Berrien and Angoff concluded that the questionnaires were deficient in sensitivity in measuring change in attitude. "The questionnaire showed 14 significant item changes in the disturbed plant against five in the control plant. . . . On the other hand, the questionnaire contained 79 items on which the employees could have expressed a difference in attitude. . . . Therefore, it is evident that a large part of this questionnaire was insensitive to a disturbance of major proportions." They suggested that instead of employing questionnaire data as the only indicator of attitudes, interviews should be considered as supplemental because they provide additional information.

It is extremely difficult to decide just what the advantages, effects, or causes of good or high or low morale are. Brown (1954), for example, stated that "the morale of the worker (i.e. whether or not he works willingly) has no *direct* relationship whatsoever to the material conditions of the job. Investigations into temperature, lighting, time and motion study, noise and humidity have not the slightest bearing on morale, although they may have a bearing on physical health and comfort." There have been many examples cited of extremely adverse conditions, where morale was high and production was low. For example, the armed forces have been known to perform under extremely unsatisfactory conditions, keeping high morale among the troops and efficient production of their function. At the same time, excellent conditions have been accompanied by poor morale on the part of the workers and poor production. There are also reports of high morale, good working conditions, and poor production, as well as low morale, poor working conditions, and high production. Each individual situation must be judged in the light of the available evidence. When morale is high, one can assume that workers might be happier. Whether a happy worker produces more than an unhappy worker is certainly subject to question.

BOREDOM, FATIGUE, AND MONOTONY

The effects of boredom, fatigue, and monotony are of great importance to industry. All three have an effect upon production, usually detrimental. In fact, decreased productivity of workers is often the first symptom of boredom, fatigue, or monotony.

The definitions of the terms *boredom, fatigue,* and *monotony* vary from author to author, but there is a common concept involved by most authors. We use a generally accepted definition of *fatigue* as a condition of a person brought about by work and resulting in a work decrement. Fatigue also includes a tired feeling and physiological changes in the person. *Boredom* refers to a psychological condition or feeling of a person as a result of performing activities considered uninteresting. Boredom is usually followed by an adversion to continue efforts in the same activity. Thus a decrement in work results from boredom or fatigue. *Monotony* is a psychological condition resulting from repetitive activity. It is not necessarily a condition that is undesirable or results in work decrement, although frequently this is the case. Thus work decrement is closely associated with fatigue and boredom and very often associated with monotony.

In Chapter 8 of this book several characteristics of the work situation that have an effect upon production were discussed in detail. Most of these characteristics have an effect upon boredom or fatigue as well as an effect upon production. We will not repeat these points here but refer the reader to the material concerning the effects of illumination, noise, atmospheric conditions, music, hours of work, rest pauses, nature of the work task, and pay.

Physiological Aspects of Fatigue.   Dr. Brouha (1954) emphasized the difficulty of discussing fatigue when he stated "we know that physiological, psychological, and sociological influences are involved in the production of fatigue but, from a scientific point of view, there is no single precise definition of fatigue." Dr. Brouha then discussed some aspects of physiological fatigue. He pointed out particularly that as a person goes from resting to a working condition certain physiological functions change. Heart rate was shown to be related to activity. He suggested that the heavier the physiological load, the higher the heart rate and the more slowly it returns to a resting level upon the completion of work. He also found that the better the physical condition of the worker, the slower was the increase in heart rate for a standard work load and the more rapid was the return of the heart rate to its resting rate. Conditions in the environment, such as temperature, also influenced heart rate recovery. Dr. Brouha reported that "for the same amount of work the heart rate becomes progressively higher as the temperature increases, the load on the cardiovascular system becomes heavier, fatigue appears sooner and exhaustion is reached faster." He also stated that "sex, age, the state of nutrition and exposure to certain chemicals are also factors influencing the fatigue level and their action can be measured by changes in heart rate and body temperature." There seems to be little doubt that with advancing age work stress is greater and fatigue appears sooner. Dr. Brouha suggested several methods of reducing fatigue: (1) Improved motions and timing of operations involving hard manual labor might be supplemented by a partial mechanization. (2) Work area temperatures, when high, should be reduced to nearer 70 degrees F. (3) Adequately organized rest periods should be provided. (4) When workers must work in high-heat areas, a cooled water supply will encourage drinking enough to keep up water metabolism and reduce fatigue. (5) Some workers are better adapted in terms of physiological build to handle heavier work, so adequate selection procedures are essential.

Other studies provide complimentary information concerning physiological fatigue. A muscle group can be used to such an extent that waste products build up more rapidly than they can be eliminated and physiological fatigue sets in.

The physiological component of fatigue was considered early in the study of work efficiency. A device called an ergograph was designed for the conduct of fatigue experiments involving relatively small muscle groups. A weight attached by a cord to an extremity of the body (for example, a finger) was moved up and down by contraction of the muscle. A recording device measured the height of each lift. The resulting chart or ergogram of the movements of the muscles showed the work decrement of the muscle group studied. Early ergograph studies clearly demonstrated that there are large individual differences in human ability to work and to continue working. They also showed that muscle groups may rapidly become fatigued to the point where they can no longer perform at all. Consequently rest pauses were introduced to counteract the effects of fatigue. Early work in reducing fatigue emphasized the spacing of work, lightening the work, or instituting rest pauses in the work sequence to reduce the effect of fatigue.

These characteristics were discussed in detail in Chapter 8 of this book.

Some authors (for example, Brown, 1954) have pointed out that the accumulation of waste products and consequent physiological fatigue is rare in modern industry. In heavy muscular work physiological fatigue is important, but in most modern industry industrial fatigue is not the result of the accumulation of toxic products from the muscles. Thus fatigue in modern industry is mostly the psychological condition or feeling of the worker. Consequently industrial fatigue and boredom are very similar.

When a person considers an activity as uninteresting or psychologically bad, boredom may result. A bored person has a general unhappy and tired feeling that causes a decrement in his work. However, change from one activity to another will often reduce boredom so that an individual may be able to get to a high level of efficiency by simply changing activities.

We may become bored reading a book or an article, listening to a lecture, or watching a television program. We may become bored at one time watching a television program and at another time find the same program interesting. There is an interaction between the psychological condition of the person and the experience which at times may result in boredom. It is very difficult to state exactly what will be boring for a group of workers or when a situation or activity will be boring for one particular worker. Even so, there are work situations where we can expect workers to be bored and other situations when they should not be bored. In Chapter 8 we discussed some of the situations that generally might be expected to bring about boredom and the detrimental effects upon production.

Highly repetitive work may result in monotony and in boredom for some workers. This condition may be followed by a decrement in work. In some instances workers in highly repetitive tasks have maintained production for long periods of time. Conversely some workers in relatively complex, nonrepetitive tasks have experienced monotony and/or boredom and decreased their productivity.

The topic of motivation must certainly be considered along with boredom, fatigue, and monotony. The highly motivated person will not be bored as easily as a person who is less motivated. Thus a highly repetitive job may be boring for one individual, whereas another may be highly motivated to produce an ever-increasing quantity and will find highly repetitive work satisfying. The attitudes and the motivations of the individual influence the physiological and psychological effects of the activity engaged in by a person. Psychological fatigue does not always follow from activity that produces physiological fatigue. The effect of true physiological fatigue is most often a decrement in work, because muscle groups cannot function adequately after the accumulation of too much waste material. Psychological fatigue often results in decreases in productivity but may not always be produced by the activity that produces physiological fatigue. Thus a person may have a physiologically fatiguing job that will result in · a productivity decrease, whereas the worker still does not "feel" bad toward the job. Or, a person may have a psychologically fatiguing job resulting in productivity decrease, but with very little physiological fatigue. Naturally it is also possible to have a job that brings about both types of fatigue.

ACCIDENTS AND SAFETY

Bill had an argument with his girl friend. The argument lasted longer than either person involved would have liked, and finally Bill dropped his girl friend in front of her dormitory and started to drive back to his room. Several witnesses remarked that Bill really "laid on the rubber" when he took off from his parking space, and at least one person saw Bill drive directly into the intersection of the main highway without even slowing for the stop sign. A large truck moving down the highway crashed broadside into Bill's car. Bill died before he entered the hospital and without giving any indication about what had happened.

For the records another accident was recorded. The truck driver was not blamed because witnesses agreed that the car driven by Bill moved right onto the highway in front of the truck, and the truck driver could do nothing to prevent the accident. The accident was probably not caused by mechanical failure. According to records and observation, there were no indications that the brakes had been applied on Bill's car before it moved onto the main highway. Apparently Bill had driven to his own death. We are not suggesting that he tried to commit suicide, but it is entirely possible that Bill was so upset by the emotional strains of the evening that he simply forgot to observe or react to the stop sign and the main artery of traffic.

Of course, reports such as the story of Bill concern relatively few people. But in the United States approximately 40,000 Americans are killed each year in automobile accidents, and over 3 million are injured. Approximately one third of the persons killed in automobile accidents each year are involved in accidents where their automobile was exceeding the speed limit. Over one sixth involve accidents where the automobile was on the wrong side of the road. Almost another sixth involved accidents where the automobile drove off the road. In 1960 approximately 47,600 vehicles were involved in the approximately 38,000 deaths. Of these 47,600 vehicles about 45,000 were apparently in good condition, with no mechanical defects at the time of the accident.

In previous chapters we emphasized that the driver, although often given blame on records, may not be the only cause of accidents. In this chapter we examine the human element in accident causation. Obviously cases such as the one cited above may happen more frequently than we can determine. At the same time, we must recognize that human organisms often do not function adequately under stress to handle the complex machinery under their control. There is no available data that shows conclusively which person will be involved in an accident and under what conditions. However, we must continually remember that great stress on a person is likely to result in lack of ability of the person to handle emergency situations properly. Thus it is appropriate for an individual to prepare himself adequately to handle emergencies. Although an emotional condition may facilitate behavior in terms of increasing strength and activity it often inhibits behavior and may result in inappropriate activity. Increased training in proper procedures to follow in normal and emergency conditions should help reduce accidents brought about by the emotional condition of the person.

Accident Proneness. For many years analyses of accident records have brought many researchers to the conclusion that some people are accident-prone. Analyses of accident records by Greenwood and Woods (1919) convinced the authors that some people have fewer accidents than should be expected by chance, whereas others had considerably more accidents than should be expected by chance. They showed that accident records differed significantly from chance expectancy and agreed with theoretically computed distributions based on the idea that some people are more likely to have accidents than others. Since this early work, numerous reports have shown that a large proportion of accidents in one plant or set of records are caused by a small proportion of people. Additional investigators have then searched for characteristics that would differentiate the accident-prone from the nonaccident-prone individual. Even recent authors have stated that some individuals are so constituted that they are more likely than others to have accidents.

On the other hand, researchers such as Mintz and Blum (1949) have pointed out that a study that showed that 30 percent of workers account for 85 percent of the accidents in a company doesn't necessarily prove that 30 percent of the workers are accident-prone. They suggested that it was incorrect to make the assumption that all people in a population should have the same number of accidents. They argued: "for example, if a group of 100 factory workers had 50 accidents in one year, then a maximum of 50 people could have contributed to the accident record and accordingly about 50 percent of the population would have contributed to 100 percent of the accidents. Obviously a small percentage of the population in this case did not establish the principle of accident proneness."

Another author (Crawford, 1960) suggested that accident-prone individuals ". . . may be identified in terms of chance expectations as compared with others who are exposed to essentially the same occupational hazards. . . ." This was suggested in spite of the fact that his research did not identify any accident-prone individuals by the traditional statistical analysis of accident records. The results of his study indicated "that groups should be matched on the basis of hazard exposure before an attempt is made to analyze data for presence of accident-proneness."

Whether accident proneness is a legitimate concept may be open to question. Certainly some individuals have more accidents over a period of time than others. It seems that a better estimate on accident-proneness is that suggested by Maritz (1950). He proposed that the variation in industrial accident rate as the result of accident proneness is the correlation between numbers of accidents experienced in two different exposure periods—for example, the period 1960–62 and 1963–65. Such correlations usually range between .20 and .40. Thus some 4 to 16 percent of the variance in accident rates would seem to be due to accident-proneness. These correlations may be highly contaminated, because workers exposed to hazardous conditions at one period may be exposed to such conditions at another period, so the correlations may be reflecting the effect of environmental conditions rather than accident-proneness. At any rate, it seems that accident-proneness, as so measured, is of minor importance in industry.

Kerr (1957) suggested two complimentary theories concerning accident proneness. Following approximately the same logic stated in the preceding paragraph, he suggested that about 15 percent or less of variance in accidents is accounted for by accident-proneness. He suggested a goals-freedom-alertness theory and an adjustment-stress theory. He then showed that 30–40 percent of variance in accident rates was due to the former and 45–60 percent to the latter. Adding these to the accident-proneness theory accounting for 1–15 percent, he accounts for 100 percent of the variance in accident rates.

Kerr's (1957) goals-freedom-alertness theory maintained "that great freedom to set reasonably attainable goals is accompanied typically by high quality work performance." Thus accidents were regarded as low-quality work, and Kerr suggested that it is necessary to raise the standard of the psychological climate so that high-quality work will be rewarded. His adjustment stress theory "holds that unusual, negative, distracting stress upon the organism increases its liability to accident or to other low quality behavior." Thus excessive physical or psychological stresses bring about increases in accidents.

The best system for preventing accidents is to improve general working conditions, attitudes, and skill of workers. When proper selection, placement, and training of workers is accompanied by good working environments, proper machinery for the worker, and a situation where the worker feels he is of value and can interact with others, industrial accidents should be at a minimum level. The general psychological condition of the worker will carry over to the work place but is generally not under the control of the employer. Thus the worker must provide the same factors in the nonwork situation as the employer provides in the work environment.

SUMMARY

The functioning of man in a working situation is the result of man interacting with his environment. Stimuli from the environment interact with an organism, which in turn responds. This paradigm is briefly stated as $S \longleftrightarrow O \longrightarrow R$.

Behavior of an organism develops via the $S \longleftrightarrow O \longrightarrow R$ route from conception through its life span. Needs are created by the physiological and psychological demands of the organism. These needs create an imbalance or a striving in the organism to fulfill the needs. This striving for fulfillment is termed *motivation*.

In the work situation motivation becomes a crucial topic. Workers are expected to produce goods in return for fulfillment of their motivated conditions. Motivation may be generally categorized as primary, due to physiological changes in the organism, or secondary, due to learned, or psychological, needs. Some theorists have proposed hierarchies of motives, but the motives generally fit within the two basic categories. In most civilized societies money can be used to fulfill all of the primary motivations and many of the secondary motivations.

Nevertheless, pay is not of most importance to workers. In most advanced societies primary motives that can be fulfilled with pay, such as hunger and thirst, are generally provided by society. Thus the secondary motives become more important, and workers must be shown how their jobs can fulfill these motivations. The psychological needs that cannot be fulfilled in the work situation may be fulfilled elsewhere. Workers may demand more pay, higher fringe benefits, or shorter hours so that they can fulfill their secondary motives in some other way than at work.

Incentives are often used in industry as a means of stimulating workers. An incentive is a condition or objective that an organism believes may fulfill some motivation. In most modern societies money has some value as an incentive, because it may fulfill many motivations.

Attitude, morale, and job satisfaction refer to the same general concept. Most studies have not shown conclusive evidence that production is related to the attitude, morale, or feelings of job satisfaction of workers. Boredom, monotony, and fatigue generally have deleterious effects on workers' production. Proper selection, placement, and training procedures, along with an understanding management and good working conditions, can often reduce boredom, monotony, and fatigue while raising morale and production of workers.

Accidents and safety are discussed from the standpoint of the human organism. Apparently there are some individuals who have more than their share of accidents. It is controversial whether these people are accident-prone or are exposed to more hazardous situations, and so on. Available data indicates that very little of the total accident rate in industrial situations is due to accident-proneness.

SUGGESTED REFERENCES FOR FURTHER STUDY

Blum, M. L. (1956). *Industrial Psychology and Its Social Foundations*. New York: Harper & Row.

This book emphasizes the social meaning of work. In addition it covers the traditional topics of selection, training, and work environments.

Brown, J. A. C. (1954). *The Social Psychology of Industry*. Baltimore, Md.: Penguin Books.

An interesting paperback book by an English author, emphasizing the human relations approach in industry. The author discusses human nature, morale, motivation, attitudes, and the influence of work on the mental health of the worker.

Hersey, R. (1955). *Zest for Work*. New York: Harper & Row.

A coverage of many topics concerning motivation and productivity of workers. Chapter 13, "The Individual Approach—Cornerstone of Satisfactory Group Relations," emphasizes the individual and importance of what he thinks of his working environment.

Maslow, A. H. (1943). "A Theory of Motivation." *Psychological Review*, **50**, 370–396.

This article and subsequent articles by Maslow and his co-workers point out the hierarchy of needs that are important in understanding man's behavior. Thus need-hierarchy has been adapted to the industrial situation by many people working in the field of industrial morale, motivation, and so on.

PART THREE

PSYCHOLOGY APPLIED

TO CONSUMERS AND

POLITICAL ISSUES

O NE OF THE EARLY applications of the young science of psychology
was in the field of advertising and selling. Chapter 12 traces the
development of psychology as applied to problems of consumer behavior from early 1900 through today. Some early psychologists tended
to generalize too much from a few studies, but the development of
survey research techniques and modern laboratory methods has improved the efficacy of modern-day psychologists. Advertising, attitude,
and marketing research techniques are now of great value to business
and political leaders in helping them make decisions of great importance to the general population.

In a world intimidated by large military capabilities in various
countries, the topics of international relations and negotiations are
extremely pertinent. In Chapter 13 areas where psychology may contribute some understanding to international relations are discussed.
Particular emphasis is placed on sources of perceptual distortion,
conditions giving rise to aggressive tendencies, and some suggestions
for methods of reducing tensions.

A general model of the negotiation process conceptualizing the
forces involved is provided in Chapter 14. It is shown that hostile
negotiators approach their task with pessimistic expectations of the
outcome, which hinder negotiations. Negotiations between allies, on
the other hand, are more fruitful because of more initial hopefulness

407

and cooperation. Moving negotiators from initial hostility to collaboration is a difficult task. Very few principles of how to move
negotiators to more cooperation have been developed and tested;
more are needed and are being developed.

Chapter 12

Consumer Psychology

IN THE HOME OF MRS. JOHN THOMPSON of Fort Worth, Texas, eight women sit discussing their reactions to air travel. None of these women has actually taken a trip in a plane, but they all have a lively interest in the discussion, partly because they themselves might take a plane trip someday and partly because several of them have husbands who fly regularly.

Mrs. Thompson, the hostess for the occasion, has called these friends together for coffee and cake and "an interesting discussion with an interviewer from New York." The interviewer from New York is a psychologist employed by a major airline. His job is to gain some insight into women's ideas, attitudes and opinions about air travel and to assess the possibility that air travel might become a popular mode of transportation for family vacations.

The psychologist begins the discussions by talking with each woman individually about her attitudes toward flying, both for herself and for other members of the family. He finds that all the members of this group are intrigued but made somewhat nervous by the prospect. He finds that some favor flying, but some have very definite prejudices against it.

After talking to the women individually for a while, the psychologist begins to encourage a more general discussion. In this discussion, which lasts about two hours, he finds that—among this group at least—the most attractive thing about air travel is its speed, so it is likely to be thought of in connection with long distances and in connection with emergencies. He also finds that several of the women in the group are afraid to fly even though they understand and believe the statistics that show that an airplane trip is actually much safer than a trip of similar length by automobile. He is especially interested by this inconsistency, and he spends a sizable portion of the interview time asking questions and provoking discussions about air travel safety.

With respect to travel for vacations, the women tell him that the airplane is a poor competitor with the automobile when it comes to vacations for the whole family. They remind him of the obvious fact that a family of four must pay four separate fares to travel by plane, whereas they can travel as a group for one "fare" in one automobile. They also point out that an automobile trip permits sightseeing along the way, and that, in their opinion, sightseeing is a very important part of any vacation.

These ideas and many others are explored in detail by the interviewer as he guides the group discussion. He encourages the women to talk at length about the assets and liabilities of air travel, and he keeps them conversing until he feels that he has a clear understanding of the way each of them thinks and feels about air travel's possibilities. He attempts to cover every detail that might shed some light on why some women would, and why some would not, be likely to choose this mode of transportation for themselves or for their families.

When interviews like this one have been collected from various parts of the country, from other groups of women, from groups of men, from husbands and wives interviewed together, from groups with different average incomes and different average ages, the psychologist will begin the long process of summarizing and analyzing. He will relisten with great care to the tape recordings made at the interview sessions. He will pay close attention to what the respondents actually said, and he will make some guesses about what their comments and reactions imply. In making these interpretations he will be guided by the view of human nature provided by his psychological training. No less importantly, he will also be guided by his knowledge of the airline industry, gained from discussions with company officials and from reading other research studies.

Out of all this will come a report which summarizes his understanding of why some people fly whenever and wherever they can, and others never even give flying serious consideration. Much of the report will not be news to company officials, who have spent a major portion of their business lives working with the airline industry. But even the findings that were previously known, or previously suspected, may be confirmed by the research information. Findings that were not previously known will be tested against all available other evidence. New findings that pass this test will influence much of the company's future planning.

What kind of planning can come out of such research? The opinion on the part of potential air travelers that flying is too expensive for family trips may suggest special family-fare reductions. If fare reductions are impossible, it may suggest that advertising for air travel vacations should be directed to single persons and to older two-person households. The idea that sightseeing along the way is an important advantage of automobile vacations may suggest special advertising emphasis on attractions at the destination or a special provision for car rental to take advantage of the air vacationer's added time. The fact that people are afraid to fly even though they "know" air travel is safer than automobile travel might suggest that it would be pointless to give strong and direct emphasis to safety in air travel advertising.

No one of the findings of a study of this kind would have sufficient weight to dictate any of these decisions. But combined with other information company officials have at their disposal, each finding would in some sense be influential.

In a laboratory in Chicago, a man is staring intently at a small dark box. Little by little, the illumination in the box increases, and he begins to see the outlines of an outdoor poster. As the poster brightens, the man begins to make out the largest letters. As soon as he can make out any of the wording or can make sense out of the illustration, he gives a signal and writes a quick description of what he sees. The illumination keeps increasing. Rapidly now the other elements of the poster become visible. Each time something new appears, the subject in the experiment signals the experimenter and records his impressions. Finally the whole poster becomes visible under full illumination.

Later, this same man, and others, will see posters, signs, and packages exposed at full illumination for very brief time periods. The exposure times will be so brief that only the clearest and most prominent aspects of each stimulus will be apparent, and the viewer will again write down descriptions of what he sees. Still later, the subject will see each of the posters, signs and packages again—this time looking at them down a long tunnel. By turning a dial, he will indicate how near or how far away each appears to be.

In laboratory tests like these, psychologists measure the visibility and legibility of complex visual stimuli. By exposing different designs under carefully controlled conditions, they attempt to find out which are most easily read under various exposure times and at various levels of illumination; and they attempt to find which appear largest and easiest to read when seen from a distance.

When the laboratory testing is completed, the psychologist will meet with executives responsible for marketing the products featured in the posters, signs, or packages and will present his analysis of the designs' visual advantages. In presenting this analysis he may have an unusual problem—he may have to work hard to be sure that his findings are not taken too seriously. He may have to emphasize that even though his findings are the results of a "scientific experiment" they show only that one design is more visible or more legible than another, not that it is necessarily the best. He may find it necessary to point out that the "image" or impression conveyed by the design can be as important as its visibility and that both information on visibility and information on image should be given full consideration in the final decision.

In New York, a high-speed electronic computer prints out the results of a long series of computations. The results, which occupy 58 printed pages, represent less than an hour of computer time. If the same computations had been done by hand with the aid of a desk calculator, they would have taken an expert operator many months. Before computers were available, an analysis like this one would seldom even have been considered.

The computer is printing the outcome of a large-scale consumer survey intended to collect and bring together facts concerning consumers' use of instant coffee. Among the facts collected and now stored in the computer's memory are such simple descriptive items as the age, marital status, family income, and geographical location of each survey respondent, as well as the information on each respondent's use of instant coffee, use of ground coffee, and preferences for a dozen different coffee brands.

In addition to questions concerning these more or less factual items, each survey respondent also answered questions designed to uncover attitudes toward instant coffee and its use. Each respondent was asked when, where, and why she used one form of coffee instead of the other. She was asked whether she herself or any of her friends felt that using instant coffee made a bad impression on other people. And she was asked her opinions about the assets and liabilities of various major instant coffee brands.

Each respondent also answered a large number of questions that apparently had nothing to do with instant coffee at all. For example, each respondent was asked to rate herself on a number of personality characteristics to show what kind of person she thought she was and what kind of person she would ideally like to be. She was also asked what magazines she reads, how frequently she reads each of them, and what television programs she watches regularly.

The computer's job was to organize and tabulate the answers to all these questions in such a way that they shed light on the why, when, and where of instant coffee use. The tables it is printing show whether and to what extent the use of instant coffee is different among different age groups, different income groups, and different sections of the country. They show the same information for ground coffee and for each of the major coffee brands. In other tables the "heavy users" of instant coffee are separated from the "light users," and the two groups are compared on objective characteristics, such as age and income, on subjective characteristics, such as the way they think about themselves, and their habits with respect to magazines and television.

When these relationships have been analyzed and understood, they will be used by the sponsor of the survey to design instant coffee advertising and to direct his advertising and marketing plans. Knowing the important differences between "heavy users" and "light users" will help the survey sponsor design ads that speak directly to the segments of the population that are most important to him. Knowing what magazines the "heavy users" read and what TV programs they watch will help him get his messages to these important segments of the population most efficiently.

As was the case with the results of the group interviews and the results of the laboratory experiment on visibility, the results of this study will not be used alone. The company that sponsored the survey has many research studies in its files and has many years of varied experience marketing its products. The information obtained from this study, massive as it is, will form but one part of the total body of information needed to form marketing and advertising policy.

Psychologists contributed to this survey in several ways. Using their training and experience in questionnaire design, they helped insure that the survey respondents would understand and be willing to answer the interviewers' questions. Using their training and experience in data analysis, they helped tell the computer which calculations to perform, and they helped design the statistical tests that tell how much confidence can be placed in the results.

When the computer has completed its part of the job, psychologists will help construct the report that will summarize the millions of calculations, and they will help interpret the meaning of the findings. Even more than in the previous illustrations, the psychologists engaged in this study have worked and will work as part of an interdisciplinary team. Statisticians, economists, marketing experts, and advertising experts have all played important roles in the study from the time it was initiated, and they will continue to play important roles until the time it is put to final use. In fact, the teamwork in a study of this kind is so close that it is hard to tell where one role leaves off and another role begins.

THE ROLES OF CONSUMER PSYCHOLOGISTS

The brief "case histories" given here show some of the ways psychologists participate in the study of consumer behavior. These three examples do not by any means cover all of consumer psychology, but they are reasonably typical instances of the way consumer psychologists work. They also illustrate some important points about the field.

The first point is that psychologists engaged in the analysis of consumer behavior almost never work on their own. As in other applied fields, the research problems consumer psychologists confront are usually originated by someone else, and the research is designed to fill some sponsor's immediate needs. This means that the consumer psychologist must work very closely with the sponsor from the beginning of the project until he has made his final report and that he must be sure he is supplying the answers the sponsor needs to know. Answers to other questions, however interesting they may be to the researcher, are likely to be regarded by the sponsor as of little value for his immediate purposes.

In addition to working closely with the sponsor of the research, consumer psychologists often work closely with behavioral scientists whose primary training is in other fields. This means that the consumer psychologist must develop the ability to communicate psychological concepts without depending on the special jargon psychologists often use among themselves. The consumer psychologist must talk and write in terms his coworkers understand.

The second point these three examples illustrate is that the information produced by the consumer psychologist is almost never used by itself. Decisions about the design of a package, the execution of an advertising campaign, or the selection of an advertising medium are generally made after the decision maker, or the decision-making group, has considered everything they know about the product and the brand. The psychologist's contribution to this fund of information may well be important, but it may also be relatively small.

The third point illustrated by these three examples is that academic training in psychology does not provide all the background necessary for the study of consumer behavior. Although psychology is frequently defined as the "scientific study of human behavior," and the study of the behavior of consumers therefore falls within this field, the academic psychologist who studies consumers quickly finds that methods and concepts from other behavioral sciences have much to add. He must therefore be ready to learn ideas and methods which at first seem strange. He cannot afford the luxury of depending entirely upon what he already knows.

THE SCOPE OF CONSUMER PSYCHOLOGY

It is difficult to get an accurate measure of a number of psychologists engaged in the study of consumer behavior. Of the 23,000 members of the American Psychological Association only about 200 are members of Division 23, the division of Consumer Psychology. However, not all APA members who study consumers are members of Division 23, and many social scientists with professional level psychological training are not members of the APA. An accurate count is therefore next to impossible.

But it is quite clear that consumer psychology is a fast-growing field. Industry is expanding to meet the demands of an increasing population. Within industry, more and more emphasis is being placed upon advertising and marketing. And within advertising and marketing psychologists are in strong demand (Thumin, 1962).

THE DEVELOPMENT OF CONSUMER PSYCHOLOGY

From the beginning of modern advertising, advertisers have been interested in psychology. A good illustration of this interest is a forecast that appeared in 1901 in *Publicity,* an advertising publication. "The time is not far away when the advertising writer will find out the inestimable benefits of a knowledge of psychology. The preparation of copy has usually followed the instincts rather than the analytical functions. An advertisement has been written to describe the article which it was wished to place before the reader; a bit of cleverness, and attractive cut, or some other catchy device has been used, with the hope that the hit to miss ratio could be made as favorable as possible. But the future needs to be full of better methods than these to make advertising advance with the same rapidity as during the latter part of the last century. And this will come through a close knowledge of the psychological composition of the mind. The so-called 'students of human nature' will then be called successful psychologists, and the successful advertisers will be likewise termed psychological advertisers. The mere mention of psychological terms—habit, self, conception, discrimination, association, memory, imagination and perception, reason, emotion, instinct and will—should create a flow of new thought that should appeal to every advanced consumer of advertising space" (quoted in Presbrey, 1929).

When these words were written the first American psychological laboratories were being founded, and psychology, "the scientific study of human behavior," was just beginning to become an important part of the curriculum of American universities.

Although businessmen expressed keen interest in the new science of psychology, most early psychologists paid little or no attention to business problems. Instead they focused their attention on laboratory studies which employed very simple stimuli—discs of light, pure tones, short words or syllables—because they felt that work with complex stimuli should be postponed until reactions to simple stimuli were better understood. Also, most early American psychologists stayed within the confines of universities. They thus had little contact with problems that might be of interest to the business community.

Some Early Studies.   But some early psychologists were interested in business problems. Many of their ideas sound quite modern today, and many of the problems and issues they encountered are still very much alive.

The first psychologist to experiment with advertising was Harlow Gale, a professor at the University of Minnesota. He published a pamphlet *On the Psychology of Advertising* in 1900. By 1913 Walter Dill Scott had published the first book on this subject, and other books and research reports by other psychologists soon followed.

The following quotation from *Advertising and Its Mental Laws*, published in 1916, is a good illustration of the way psychologists interested in advertising were thinking at that time: "Psychology should be able to help the advertising man in two ways. In the first place, it should aid him to understand himself, his strong points and his limitations. The advertising man is a mental worker. His mind is the instrument which he uses in his work. He would have little use for a carpenter who planed boards with his saw, pried out nails with a chisel, and drove them with a mallet. He insists that the workmen he employs shall be able to use the tools of their trade, and use them not only correctly, but to the best advantage. Since the advertiser is a mental worker, he should thoroughly understand his mental tool, knowing what it can do and what it is incapable of doing. A thorough acquaintance with the tool will make him much more efficient.

"In the second place, psychology should help him by giving him the various laws of mental processes: how to get and hold the attention of the reader, how to arrange the advertisement so that it may be easily read; how to make the commodity remembered by those who read the advertisement; under what circumstances to use 'reason why' copy and the kind of argument which is most likely to appeal; what are the desirable emotions to arouse and how to arouse them; and finally, most important of all, how to bring about the desired action on the part of the reader" (Adams, 1916).

THE APPLICATION OF "MENTAL LAWS".   The product of this point of view was work along two quite different lines. One of these was an attempt to apply the "laws of human nature" to advertising and selling in much the same way an engineer applies the laws of physics to the building of a bridge. A standard approach was to summarize what was then known about attention, perception, learning, memory, and emotion and to make inferences about what these "laws" implied for advertising and marketing practice.

For example, in the *Psychology of Advertising*, Walter Dill Scott gave some "laws of symmetry and proportion" ("A line is divided most artistically if the lower section is 1.618 times as great as the upper" (Scott, 1913) and applied these laws to the design of printed advertisements. Much later but still in the same tradition, another psychologist interested in advertising described an experiment that showed that people tend to believe what they want to be true and commented: "This close relationship between belief and desire, which has long been suspected and now has been experimentally demonstrated . . . gives one more argument for the great importance of a knowledge, on the part of the advertiser, of human desires and motives. They form the basis of all our wants, they guarantee that attention will be attracted and held, and, finally, they induce belief" (Poffenberger, 1932).

The trouble with applying psychological "laws" to advertising practice was that the results which emerged from the early psychological laboratories, and from the early experiments like the one cited in the quotation above, did not have the degree of precision and generality necessary for the leap from research to direct application. Laboratory conditions are by their very nature quite different from conditions in the market place. Often these differences are so important that laboratory findings need extensive amendment and elaboration before they can be used to draw valid conclusions about the way consumers behave.

The second reason the results of early psychological experiments proved difficult to apply to consumer behavior is that early psychologists tended to assume that all people are pretty much alike. They therefore used just anybody who happened to be around as subjects in their experiments. Possible differences in reaction on the part of different segments of the population were virtually ignored.

We now know that reaction to advertisements, reactions to various advertising media, and reactions to various products and brands are very much influenced by characteristics such as age, education, and economic class. It is therefore quite important that the effect of such variables be taken into account. Psychologists, accustomed to the use of college sophomores and white rats as experimental subjects, are still sometimes guilty of ignoring this important limitation on the generality of their results.

Finally, the early "laws of human nature" proved hard to use in practice because many of them were based on notions now known to be incorrect.

For instance, in *The Psychology of Advertising*, Scott (1913) devoted a chapter to how advertisements could be tailored to "human instincts" like "the instinct to preserve and further material possessions," "food instincts," "clothing instincts," and "hoarding and proprietary instincts." It is now generally agreed that instincts of this kind do not exist.

These shortcomings of early consumer psychology—the tendency to jump heedlessly from laboratory findings based on a handful of highly selected individuals to conclusions about the behavior of all consumers, and the tendency to base conclusions on unproved "laws"—would be merely historical curiosities if they had then disappeared. But as later sections of this chapter will show, they have reappeared in one form or another throughout the development of consumer psychology, and they are not entirely extinct today.

Development of Research Techniques. Although direct application of psychological "laws" to advertising and marketing problems seldom had the hoped-for effect, early psychologists also adopted another approach to the analysis of consumer behavior, an approach that was to achieve much more enduring results. Very early, psychologists began to apply the techniques and methods of scientific research to problems that originated in the advertising and marketing field.

The problem-centered approach to the analysis of consumer behavior produced the first use of many methods employed today. Ranking and rating methods were used to evaluate the attractiveness, persuasiveness, and believability of advertisements as early as 1911. Laboratory devices were used to evaluate the visibility and legibility of pictures and print about the same time. Recognition tests and recall tests were used to evaluate the memorability of advertising messages by 1915. Systematic field experiments, in which different areas of the country were used to test the effectiveness of advertising campaigns, were in use by 1920. By 1917, psychologists were using questionnaires to evaluate consumers' opinions, attitudes, and ideas.

CONSUMER PSYCHOLOGY AT THE
BEGINNING OF THE SECOND WORLD WAR

Advances in Survey Research. By the time the Second World War began, a number of important advances in the study of consumer behavior had already been made. Perhaps the most important of these was the development and use of survey research techniques that made it possible to obtain information from large and representative samples of consumers. Instead of assuming that consumers are so similar that the findings from almost any group would be typical, scientists engaged in the analysis of consumer behavior began to examine the reactions of large cross sections of the consumer population. These cross sections represented the various segments of the population in their correct proportions, so there was no danger that reactions of consumers in general would be falsely identified with the reactions of a special group. Furthermore, because the number of persons covered in such studies was usually large, and because survey respondents could easily be classified by age, income, education, and other important characteristics, it was possible to examine differences in reaction among these different groups.

Surveys were used to get consumers' reactions to advertisements before the advertisements were run, to measure the size and the character of the audiences of newspapers, magazines, and radio programs, to get consumers' reactions to new products before the products were put on the market, and to measure the number and characteristics of the users of various brands.

Something of the spirit of these times can be seen from the following quote. It comes from the introduction to Henry Link's, *The New Psychology of Selling and Advertising* (1938), and it was written by John B. Watson, a very well-known academic psychologist who later took up a business career. "Not only in theory, but in fact, the consumer today is king. Businessmen are realizing as never before that the sale of their products depends on the accuracy with which they have gauged the requirements of the buying public. Just because a manufacturer has a mouse-trap that he has been building for years is no sign that he is ready to tell the public about his product through advertising. Today before seeking national markets he must find out what kind of a mouse-trap the consumer wants and then he must either modify the one he has been building or, if that can't be done, he must build a new one. The consumer is becoming more and more discriminating, and his needs and his wants change from year to year. Motor car manufacturers have had to learn this at very great cost. Today their ear is always to the ground to find out what people want, and each year's changes in models represent a closer and closer approach to what the man and woman in the home want to buy. The consumer never stands still in his wants. The face creams women want today may not be the creams they will want tomorrow. The car we wanted when traffic was light and roads were bad will not serve for times when traffic is heavy and roads are paved from Maine to Mexico. Consequently this business of manufacturing and advertising has to tag the footsteps of the consumer" (Watson, in Link, 1938).

The surveys that helped manufacturers "tag the footsteps of the consumer" were commissioned by individual manufacturers for their own internal use, and were executed by the manufacturers' research departments, by the research departments of their advertising agencies, or by one of a number of research companies that sprang up to meet the rapidly growing demand for more information about consumers.

Findings with respect to specific products were generally considered private business information and were therefore rarely published. But as research practitioners accumulated experience with survey research methods, they began to publish articles and books as a means of exchanging information on how surveys should be done. In this way a body of scientific knowledge of the greatest importance to present-day consumer psychology began to emerge.

Figure 12.1. A photograph of an interviewer and respondent completing a typical doorstep interview such as often carried out for public opinion or market research.

In addition to these developments in the commercial field, several noncommercial centers were established for the study of survey research methods and techniques. Among the most important of these were the Office of Radio Research at Columbia University, which later became the Bureau of Applied Social Research, and the National Opinion Research Center, established at the University of Denver, and now at the University of Chicago. The purpose of these new centers was to analyze the then current practices in the survey research field and to conduct basic research aimed at the improvement of survey research methods. These centers, and others like them, have made many important contributions to the scientific study of consumer behavior, particularly in the areas of sampling and questionnaire design. They too contributed greatly to the survey methods upon which modern consumer psychologists depend.

Further Applications of Laboratory Methods.   While survey research methods were developing, psychologists continued to develop laboratory methods for studying reactions to stimuli under controlled conditions. Some of these methods were used to test products, some were used to evaluate packages, and some were used to test ads.

AN ILLUSTRATIVE STUDY.   An interesting example of product testing under laboratory control is a study reported in 1941 by Harold Schlosberg, a psychologist at Brown University. The product being tested was shaving cream, and the object of the investigation was to determine whether any of five very similar shaving cream formulas performed better or worse than any of the others.

Carefully measured samples of the shaving creams were applied to the faces of 10 experimental subjects. Each subject was shaved four times at regular intervals, and for each shave, one of the creams was applied to the right side of the subject's face while another was applied to the left. A barber shaved each subject in a prescribed manner—right cheek, left cheek, right neck, left neck. After the shave, the subject rated its quality on a rating scale to describe the amount of "pull and pain" he had experienced on each side. Each subject also rated his "general satisfaction with the shave" and "cool feeling."

The experiment was so arranged that each cream was used on the right side and the left side equally, and the order in which the creams were used was predetermined in such a way that all five creams appeared evenly throughout the series.

The purpose of all these precautions was to be sure that nothing other than the quality of the shave would affect the ratings. Without such precautions, some other factor—such as the side of the face on which the cream was used or the fact that one cream was used early or late in the series—might have influenced the results.

According to the author of the study, "chemists of the sponsoring company laughed at any real differences between the shaving creams, for they knew the formulae from which they were made" (Schlosberg, 1941). But because of the extreme care with which the experiment was conducted, it was possible to show that subjects' reactions to one cream were in fact somewhat different from their reactions to the others.

This experiment provides a good illustration of both the advantages and disadvantages of laboratory experiments in consumer psychology. The great care and precision with which it was conducted made a very small product difference detectable—clearly an advantage for the laboratory. But the same conditions that permitted such precise control make the generalizability of the conclusions questionable. Under home-use conditions, when the consumer does his own lathering and his own shaving, shaving cream qualities undetected in this experiment might be important to the consumer. On the other hand, under home-use conditions, the very small difference detected in the experiment might disappear entirely. If so, the difference would have no influence on consumer choice.

Another disadvantage of laboratory tests is the character of the experimental subjects. Only certain kinds of persons are readily available for experiments of this kind, and it is usually quite difficult to be sure that the available subjects are representative of the consumer population. In this study, for example, the subjects were 10 graduate students and staff members at Brown University. It is probably safe to assume that their beards and skins were much like the beards and skins of men in general. But it is not safe to assume that their reactions to other aspects of the shaving process—the odors of the shaving creams or the "coolness" of the shave— would be typical of all consumers. Reactions to product characteristics of this kind are often different in different segments of the population. The problem of getting reactions from representative subjects under representative conditions will never disappear.

THE EYE CAMERA.   Another laboratory device of some importance was a camera that records eye movements. It shows what portions of an advertisement a viewer looks at first, how long he looks at any part, and what parts he ignores. Although it was first used to study eye movements in readings, it was used extensively in research on advertising for quite a long time.

The eye camera had the great advantage of being completely objective. The researcher using the eye camera was not forced to rely on the viewer's report of where he had looked; instead he had a complete record of where the viewer's eyes had focused and how long they had stayed at any place. Studies with the eye camera confirmed what had been long suspected— that verbal reports of reactions to advertisements are not entirely trustworthy, particularly when the ad contains material the viewer finds embarrassing or unpleasant.

Although the eye camera had the great advantage of objectivity, it had a number of disadvantages that kept it from becoming a standard device for evaluating advertisements. Operation of the camera required the services of a skilled technician, and analysis of eye-camera records required much skilled time, so eye-camera data were expensive to collect. Even more important, viewing an advertisement in the laboratory was so different from viewing an advertisement under normal circumstances that there was good reason to question whether viewing behavior was the same in both cases. For these reasons, in spite of the advantage provided by its objectivity, the eye camera has gradually faded from the advertising research scene. Its permanent contribution has been the lesson it taught about the difference between what people say about their reactions to advertisements and what they actually do.

RADIO RESEARCH. In the years before the Second World War, social scientists were also much interested in research on radio. In the absence of television, radio was a very important entertainment and information medium, and large portions of major advertising budgets were allotted to it. In studying radio, psychologists employed both survey research techniques and techniques borrowed from the psychological laboratory. They were interested in measuring the sales effectiveness of radio advertising, in measuring listeners' attitudes toward radio as a communication and entertainment medium, and in assessing the most liked and least liked portions of specific radio programs. Techniques and methods developed in these studies were all to become important later in research on television.

THE PROGRAM ANALYZER. One development of this time was the "program analyzer." This was a mechanical device that produced a continuous record of listeners' reactions to radio programs. Each person participating in a program analyzer test had a green button and a red button at his chair. When he liked what he was hearing he pushed the green button, when he disliked what he was hearing he pushed the red button, and when he was uncertain he pushed neither. The buttons were connected electrically to a pen that traced a line on a continuously moving piece of paper. (See Figure 12.2.) When all the green buttons were being pushed, the line reached its highest point, and when all the red buttons were being pushed, it reached its lowest. Since the paper moved at a constant predetermined speed, it was possible to match the peaks and valleys thus formed with specific events during the program. Less-liked portions of the program could therefore be corrected, and more-liked portions could be given increased emphasis. This kind of minute-by-minute analysis supplied much more information to the program analyst than would an overall evaluation of the program as a whole.

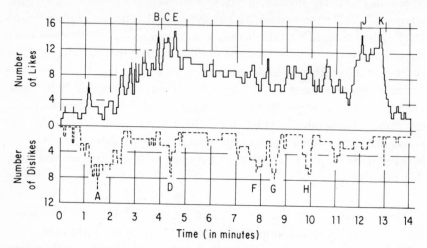

Figure 12.2. Example of a record sheet from a program analyzer. This record shows that parts B, C, E, J, and K of the program were most liked, whereas parts A, D, F, G, and H were most disliked. From J. N. Peterman (1940), "The Program Analyzer": A New Technique in Studying Liked nnd Disliked Items in Radio Programs," *J. Appl. Psychol.*, **24**, 728–741.

A MARKET STUDY OF THE EFFECTIVENESS OF RADIO ADVERTISING.   Psychologists were also interested in evaluating the effectiveness of radio advertising. A study sponsored by the Columbia Broadcasting System provides a good example of work on this problem, and also illustrates an important development in consumer research.

The study employed two marketing areas that were closely matched in population, in retail sales of the product involved in the study, and in a number of retail outlets for the product. One of these marketing areas received radio advertising for the product, and the other did not.

The effect of the radio advertising was measured in several ways. Investigators checked retail sales by counting stock on hand at the beginning of the study, keeping track of how much stock was ordered as the study progressed and counting stock on the shelf at the study's conclusion. This procedure showed an 88-percent greater sale of the product in the area where radio advertising had been used than in the area where it had been withheld.

The effect of the advertising was also checked by means of interviews with consumers. While the programs that carried the advertising were on the air, interviewers called consumers on the telephone to ascertain which consumers were listening to the program and which were not. As part of these interviews, the investigators also found out whether those who were listening at the time of the call were "regular" or only "occasional" listeners to the program.

These same respondents were later interviewed in person, and a count was taken of the amount of the product on the pantry shelf. This procedure showed that sale of the brand was 81 percent higher than sale of the next most popular brand among families that listened to the program, but was only 7 percent higher than sale of the next most popular brand among families that did not listen to the program. Further, sale of the brand was 263 percent higher than sale of the next most popular brand among families that listened "regularly"; but among families that listened "occasionally," sale of the brand was only 59 percent higher than sale of the next competitor.

This study illustrates an important development in consumer psychology. Early psychologists had attempted to generalize the results of their laboratory experiments to the behavior of all consumers. The major problem with this approach, as noted earlier, was that they could never be sure that the laboratory findings were representative. The laboratory conditions may or may not have represented conditions in the market place adequately; the subjects used in the laboratory experiments may or may not have been sufficiently representative of the consumer population.

The CBS study approached the problem differently. Instead of generalizing from laboratory findings to the market place, the scientists who conducted this study treated the market place itself as an experimental laboratory. They controlled the stimuli (the radio advertisements) and measured the responses (purchases) in the best experimental tradition. But since both stimulus and response occurred in their natural environments, and since the subjects in this experiment were consumers, the problem of generalizing the results was much less acute.

DEVELOPMENTS DURING AND AFTER
THE SECOND WORLD WAR

War Activities.   When the United States entered the Second World War a number of social scientists interested in the analysis of consumer behavior turned their attention to problems created by the war effort. Government officials were quite concerned about Americans' attitudes toward such wartime measures as relocation of aliens, conscription, and rationing. They knew that these measures would not be fully effective without strong public support, yet they couldn't adequately estimate degree of public approval. Survey research methods proved ideally suited for yielding this kind of information, and a number of surveys were conducted that proved to be a valuable guide to policy makers.

The sale of war bonds was another important government activity. Psychologists participated in studies of why people did and why people did not buy bonds, and the results of their work had an important influence on how bonds were marketed. One of their findings was that personal solicitation was a powerful force motivating bond purchases. Plans for later war bond drives were altered accordingly. Another finding was that the public had great difficulty understanding the government's interest in war bond sales as a means of controlling inflation. Most people thought the government "needed the money" from war bonds to buy guns, tanks, and ships. As a result of this finding, the themes of later war bond drives emphasized the contribution bonds made to military victory, not the contribution they made to economic stability, which people found difficult to understand (Likert, 1954).

Among the groups of psychologists who served the government during the war, one of the most important from the standpoint of later developments in consumer research was a group of psychologists who worked together in the Department of Agriculture. Because of its interest in the sale of farm commodities, the Department of Agriculture had for some time been conducting consumer surveys to aid in the marketing of farm products. Now, under the leadership of Rensis Likert and George Katona, this group also turned its attention to questions of broader economic policy.

The First Survey of Consumer Finance.   Toward the end of the war economists and others were much concerned over the problems associated with converting from a wartime to a peacetime economy. Because American industry had been almost wholly devoted to the production of war material, civilians were much in need of new refrigerators, new washing machines, and new automobiles. Because it would take some time to convert from military to civilian production, and because many Americans had invested in war bonds and savings accounts that could be cashed readily, some economists feared that the combination of cash reserves and pent-up demands for consumer goods would result in runaway inflation. To help meet this potential problem, government officials needed information on consumers' postwar plans. They needed to know what Americans were going to do with their war bonds and other savings, and what they were planning to buy immediately.

To supply this information, and to supply other data on consumers' attitudes and expectations, the group of social scientists who had been working together at the Department of Agriculture conducted a large-scale, nationwide survey of consumer finances. Although the results of this survey were important enough—they indicated that a great many Americans regarded their bond holdings and savings accounts as long-term investments and were not planning to cash them immediately—the execution of the survey led to two very important developments in the study of consumer behavior.

The first of these was a sharp increase in demand for large-scale studies of consumer attitudes. Most previous attitude surveys had been conducted by business concerns for private use, so their audiences had been quite limited. Now, for the first time, the results of a large-scale consumer attitude study were generally available. These results, plus the results of similar surveys that followed it, led to much wider recognition of the importance of attitude survey data.

The other important outcome of the first survey of consumer finances was the founding at the University of Michigan of the Michigan Survey Research Center. This center was founded by the social scientists who had worked in the Department of Agriculture during the war, and who left government service as the war ended. Since its founding, this Center has been responsible for a whole series of studies of consumer behavior, and it has also been one of the most important forces behind development of survey research methods. From the Center has come a steady stream of reports, articles, and books which have not only added to our substantive knowledge of consumer behavior but also have contributed much to our knowledge of how surveys should be conducted. Improvements in sampling procedures, improvements in questionnaire design, new ways of asking questions—all have been direct outcomes of the Center's studies.

The Michigan Survey Research Center and other organizations engaged in essentially nonprofit research encouraged students and scientists to further investigate methods and procedures for conducting surveys. Questionnaire design and sampling procedures have received particular attention.

QUESTIONNAIRE CONSTRUCTION. A well-worded series of questions is essential for adequate surveying. There are many general rules such as don't ask leading questions and don't use prestigious names in the questions. These are discussed in detail in several of the suggested references for further study at the end of this chapter. However, the usual procedure in questionnaire construction still involves the formulating of questions in the best possible manner and testing the questionnaire with a sample of the respondents. Perhaps a questionnaire can be revised adequately after one pretest. Often, several pretests and revisions are needed before the researcher is convinced that his questionnaire will provide valuable information.

. **SAMPLING PROCEDURE.** Sampling procedures are even more complex than questionnaire construction methods. Again, the references at the end of this chapter provide valuable information about this topic. We suggest only that there are many different sampling methods. However, the reason for all methods is to obtain representative data from fewer than an entire population. Thus there are advantages and disadvantages of all techniques. The most commonly used methods are called quota control, area, and convenience sampling.

In quota-control sampling, characteristics of the population thought to be of importance to the questionnaire data are controlled in the sample in the same proportions as in the populations. For example, sex of the respondents might influence the answers to some questions. Thus a sample of a population would be chosen so that there were the same proportion of males and females in the sample as in the population. The same procedure would be followed for the other characteristics of respondents that might be of importance to the questions.

Area sampling involves dividing a city or area into subsections. We can picture such a procedure by imagining an entire area we wish to survey as being covered with a screen. Instead of questioning every person in the entire area, we would question only people in some of the blocks or areas in the screen.

Many surveys are completed using convenience samples. These are groups of respondents chosen because of their convenience to the researcher. Of course, the researcher believes the respondents are representative of the population and that the information obtained is such that it applies to people in general. Thus the researcher hopes that a good indication of people in general can be obtained from a convenient sample.

There is a great deal of information concerning sampling, but we have not attempted to cover details here. It is important to realize that entire populations can rarely be polled, so that subgroups or samples must be used. Results from relatively few people might be accurate indications of the opinions of large populations. However, we must be continually aware that poor samples can provide biased information that should not be considered indicative of an entire population.

AN ILLUSTRATION OF THE USE OF SURVEY RESEARCH INFORMATION. An interesting application of some data developed by the Survey Research Center can be seen in Table 12.1. Students of consumer behavior have long known that consumption patterns differ by the age of the consumer: young children consume vast quantities of prepared baby foods and cold breakfast cereal; adolescents are the best consumers of Coca-Cola and phonograph records; adults in their 30's and 40's are the buyers of homes and cars.

TABLE 12.1 Ownership of Houses, Cars, and Television Sets in Early 1954 by Spending Units at Different Stages of the Life Cycle

| | | Proportion of Spending Units Owning: | | | | |
		THEIR OWN HOME %	ONE OR MORE CARS %	TWO OR MORE CARS %	A CAR LESS THAN FOUR YEARS OLD %	A TELE-VISION SET %
	Young, Single	8	38	2	19	18
	Young Married, Childless	38	82	6	51	49
	Young Married, Youngest Child Under 6	46	81	9	38	62
Stages	Young Married, Youngest Child 6 or over	66	91	12	52	65
of	Older Married (Over 45), with Children	69	73	16	39	56
Life	Older Married, No Children Under 18	71	72	8	40	51
	Older, Single	46	30	2	12	27
	All Spending Units*	50	66	8	35	48

* For ownership of homes, the proportions shown are based on nonfarm spending unit only.

John B. Lansing and James N. Morgan. "Consumer Finances over the Life Cycle" in Lincoln H. Clark. *Consumer Behavior* Vol. II. New York University Press, 1955, pp. 36–51.

One way of conceptualizing these phenomena is in terms of the "life cycle," a series of stages through which the individual progresses from birth to death.

For example, life cycle stages could be set forth as follows:

Infancy
Childhood
Adolescence
Young, Single
Young, Married, no children
Young, Married, with children:
   Youngest child under 6
   Youngest child 6 or over
Older, Married, with children
Older, Married, no children under 18
Older, Single

The data in Table 12.1, taken from one of the Michigan Surveys of Consumer Finances, show how positions in the adult stages of the life cycle relate to ownership of homes, cars, and television sets. Ownership of all three of these items is at a higher level today than it was in 1954, when these data were collected, but it seems safe to assume that the relation between ownership of these items and stage in the life cycle is not much different now. Notice how home ownership reaches its peak among the older married group, whereas ownership of television reaches its peak among the younger married. (Nowadays it would be ownership of two television sets, not just one.) Notice also how ownership of one or more cars, ownership of two or more cars, and ownership of a car less than four years old is differently distributed among the various life cycle stages.

Motivation Research.   Although the scientists at the Michigan Survey Research Center, the Columbia Bureau of Applied Social Research, the National Opinion Research Center, and various commercial polling organizations were developing the art and science of asking and analyzing survey research questions, Ernest Dichter, a pschologist trained in Austria, began to study consumer behavior by means of the techniques of clinical psychology.

Compared with the methods then being developed and used by the survey research specialists, Dichter's approach to the study of consumer psychology was a radical departure from tradition. Survey research, Dichter asserted, is all right for studying certain superficial aspects of consumer behavior, such as *what* people buy, but it can never get at the "real" reasons for the things consumers do. To get at the "real" reasons, he said, it is necessary to study each consumer's motivations by special methods and in great detail.

An English writer on motivation research described the situation this way: "[The] need to know not only *what* people do but also *why* they do it has been manifested only over the last few years. And at one stage in the development of market research it was thought that this second question could be answered as easily as the first, simply by asking. Faced with the question, 'What brands of cigarette do people smoke?' the market research expert could justifiably answer, 'Easy enough—we will go out and ask them,' and when handed the second question, 'Why?' he was inclined to return the same answer.

"The procedures this led to were very simple. They involved ascertaining the brand currently in use, and then asking a simple question in the form of 'Why do you use this brand?' The answers thus obtained were then tabulated in some convenient way and presented as a reasoned account of the motives which actuated purchasers of the different brands.

"There are advantages in this method, of course. It requires no skill, no technical knowledge, no special training: it occupies very little time in an interview, and is moreover so simple that there is no need to trouble to train or supervise investigators (they can even be briefed by post); the analytical procedures are simple and quick, and such that anybody, however senior, can understand.

"There is only one disadvantage—it produces a picture which is usually false, and frequently dangerously misleading.

"People's reasons for their actions, in fact, cannot normally be ascertained by asking point-blank questions. They usually do not know what their real reasons are, and frequently, even if they do know, they are not prepared to give them in answer to a formal question. Even when they do know something of their own motives, and are prepared to confess them, they are for the most part quite incapable of assessing the relative importance of the various interlocking motives which normally go to make up a particular behaviour pattern.

"The number of women who are prepared to admit, even to themselves, that they use Lux Toilet Soap because they feel it will, in some magical way, perform its implied advertising promise and make them as beautiful as film-stars, is relatively small: the number who are prepared to admit it to anybody else is even smaller. In consequence, they fall back, when asked the direct question as to why they use this brand, on the 'conventional' or 'expected' answer—they praise its colour, its perfume, its lathering qualities" (Henry, 1958).

To get at the "real" reasons for consumer behavior, the motivation researchers asserted, it is necessary to probe beneath the reasonable and logical surface of what people say about themselves. It is necessary to penetrate to the unconscious levels of consumers' minds to study their secret urges, hopes, and fears.

MOTIVATION RESEARCH TECHNIQUES—"DEPTH" INTERVIEWS. The methods used to get at the "real" reasons for consumer behavior were the methods developed by psychiatrists and clinical psychologists for the study of personality. For example, instead of the carefully structured short-answer questionnaires employed by the survey researchers, motivation researchers employed unstructured question sequences patterned after the clinical interview. Respondents were asked broad, general questions about their attitudes toward and use of the product being investigated, and whenever their replies seemed evasive or superficial, they were encouraged to talk more about the subject under investigation. "Depth" interviewers employed whatever strategies they could to penetrate the surface level of rationalization—challenging respondents to support opinions with examples from personal experience, approaching the same subject from several different directions, probing answers that seemed inconsistent, always asking for more detail and more elaboration.

In analyzing the results of such interviews, the motivation researcher, like the psychiatrist or clinical psychologist, generally avoided a literal interpretation of the material in favor of a search for some deeper meaning. Often the basic reasons for such seemingly trivial bits of behavior as a choice of a certain brand of soup or a certain brand of shortening turned out in motivation research reports to be buried deep within the subconscious recesses of the consumer's personality.

MOTIVATION RESEARCH TECHNIQUES—THE RORSCHACH. The Rorschach Test was also used in attempts to uncover the deeper meaning of the behavior of consumers. Responses to the Rorschach Inkblots, which in clinical practice are used to indicate how the individual relates to certain aspects of his environment, were used to provide hypotheses about the personality characteristics of consumers·who made certain kinds of marketing decisions. For example, one study that employed the Rorschach found that obese women, who presumably form an important potential market for diet foods, have a character structure different from that of women of normal weight: "Repression is deeper in the obese women and hence the unconscious content is less available. There is an increase in pain and decrease in worldly pleasure. There is a higher degree of energy poured into defense and hence more internalization and depressive trends. . . . Energies appear to be directed more to the area of internal difficulties, repressed drives and memories . . . than relationship to external objects. The obese women have less flexible ego boundaries. Their reservoir of energy is more tightly bound and not as readily available for constructive use. . . . Hence, obese women may be expected to react more strongly to traumatic experiences.

Their powers of ego integration are less adequate. The obese women are less constructively self-assertive. They resort more to a passive type of mastery and show less operating capacity for achieving active constructive goals. The pattern of the Rorschach variables approximates most nearly the psychic-economic structure of the compulsive neurotic" (Kotkov and Murawski, 1952).

A finding like this, if valid, can be of great value to an advertiser attempting to communicate with a special consumer group. Like any other communicator, the advertiser is two steps ahead when he knows the characteristics of his audience.

But as a market research tool, the Rorschach test had many drawbacks. Because administration and interpretation of the Rorschach test required the services of a highly trained expert, collecting Rorschach protocols from a sufficiently large sample was extremely expensive; and because the Rorschach could not be administered to representative samples of the consumer population, the generality of Rorschach results was always questionable. In addition the Rorschach has questionable validity even as a clinical or diagnostic tool. For these reasons, although the Rorschach Inkblots were almost always discussed in speeches and articles on motivation research, they saw little actual use in motivation research investigations.

Figure 12.3. An example of a picture used in motivation research of attitudes toward cigar smoking. In the course of an interview, women were asked to fill in the balloon to show what the woman was thinking. From G. H. Smith, *Motivation Research in Advertising and Marketing* (New York: McGraw-Hill Book Company, 1954).

MOTIVATION RESEARCH TECHNIQUES—THE THEMATIC APPERCEPTION TEST. A projective test used quite extensively by motivation researchers was the Thematic Apperception Test in one or another of its variations. In its clinical form the Thematic Apperception Test consists of a standard set of pictures about which the person being studied makes up stories. These stories, which are assumed to be at least partly autobiographical, are then searched for clues to how the storyteller thinks about himself, about other people, and about his problems.

When used in the analysis of consumer behavior, this technique frequently required the creation of new pictures to make the stories more relevant to the product under investigation. Sometimes respondents were asked only to tell stories about events shown in the pictures. Sometimes respondents were asked to imagine what the people in the pictures must be saying or must be thinking. Whatever the instructions, the stories were searched for clues to the consumer's motivations.

Figure 12.3 provides a good example of a picture created for a specific investigation. In the course of an interview on attitudes toward cigar smoking, women were asked to fill in the balloon to show what the woman in the picture was thinking. They gave replies like these (Smith, 1954):

"O.K. So will I!"

"Don't smoke around me because I don't like the aroma. I think it will look sloppy, but if you must, don't mess up the house."

"Oh, no! Who's going to clean up after you?"

"It's perfectly all right, as you are the boss."

REACTIONS TO MOTIVATION RESEARCH. Motivation research created a great deal of interest due to the conditions in research at the time it was introduced. Executives interested in consumer behavior had become accustomed to survey research, and were ready and eager to learn what new contributions to understanding could come from these interesting sounding methods.

If motivation research needed any more impetus, it got it when Vance Packard published *The Hidden Persuaders* in 1957. This book intended, said the author, to reveal "The way many of us are being influenced and manipulated—far more than we realize—in the patterns of our everyday lives." Packard (1957) had a strong influence on many advertising and marketing executives. Those who were unconvinced that motivation research would "work" found in *The Hidden Persuaders* page after page of sensational case histories, all of which made motivation research seem magically powerful. This made motivation research all the more enticing to those who had hesitated to try it out.

But even before *The Hidden Persuaders* suggested that motivation research was all-powerful, those who had tried it had begun to discover some of its limitations. In the early 1950's articles on motivation research in the advertising trade press usually had declarative and optimistic titles: "How the Depth Interview Reveals Attitudes Toward New Products," "Depth Interviewing Measures Belief in Advertising—and Reaction to It," "Base Your Advertising on the True Buying Motive," "How Psychiatric Methods Can Be Applied to Market Research," and "Perhaps Research Is Heading for a New Advance." However, by 1955 *Printers Ink*, the journal that printed the articles just cited, began printing articles like "Four Hazards of Motivation Research: How to Avoid Them," "Old Research Technique . . . Turns Out To Be Motivation Study," "What Is New About Motivation Research?" and "Can Advertisers Trust the Psychologists?"

Some of these somewhat disenchanted articles came from businessmen who had made use of motivation research and found that it would not automatically solve all their problems. More importantly, however, criticism of motivation research came from practitioners of more traditional research methods. They were merciless in pointing out its shortcomings:

"The depth interview represents the type of probing used by the clinical psychologists. It does have several advantages. It does give the researcher an opportunity to uncover new motivations. It does permit the development of a motivational pattern with respect to the selection of a given product or brand. It does provide stimulating new ideas to the researcher.

"But it also has a lot of weaknesses and dangers. The first is that, even with a two- or three-hour interview with each individual, the researcher is attempting to do what the clinical psychologist may take weeks or months to accomplish. A second weakness is that most of the people who practice depth interviewing are not trained psychologists and therefore do not have a systematic approach in conducting the interview. An even greater weakness is that no quantifiable data are obtained in the depth interview procedure; therefore, when it comes to drawing conclusions from depth interviews, the conclusion is likely to be simply the judgment of the researcher. Thus, different conclusions will often be found by two different researchers in the same situation . . . There is no possibility of verification" (Scriven, in Ferber and Wales, 1958).

"The semi-directive or 'depth' interview is frequently considered a projective technique but, in reality, is not. It may utilize projective techniques to glean information from the respondents but in and of itself it is nothing more than an informal, semi-directive interview procedure. Use of the word 'depth' implies that the unconscious is tapped and hidden motives identified. However, the unconscious postulated by Sigmund Freud could not possibly be the unconscious alluded to by 'motivation research.' Any similarity between semi-directive interviews and a psychoanalytic session is superficial . . .

"The fact that projective techniques in psychological terminology with constant references to clinical situations are used in so-called motivation research has given it an aura of scientific glamour. Psychologists are, however, well aware of the low validity of these techniques. Many experiments indicate that these techniques have severe limitations even for diagnostic purposes . . .

". . . With or without the activities subsumed under the term 'motivation research' one can develop ideas and hunches. Without ideas there could be no research, for in research we must have ideas (hypotheses) to put to test. 'Motivation research,' as presented to advertisers, is hypotheses hunting, not hypotheses testing; it is pre-research, not research. The dramatic proclamations that accompanied its arrival on the marketing scene stimulated considerable interest in 'motivation research.' If an equivalent amount of interest could be stimulated in the role of experimental design in consumer research, advertisers would benefit from the guidance of

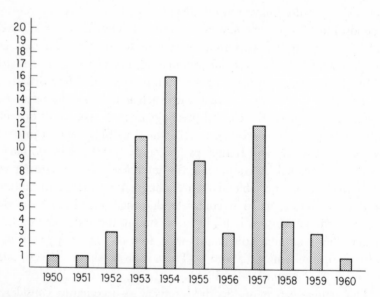

Figure 12.4. Number of articles on motivation research appearing in *Printers Ink*, 1950–1960. The articles that peak in 1954 were mainly articles that described motivation research and its application to advertising and marketing. Many of the articles in the secondary peak in 1957 were evaluative and critical.

genuine research, and from proof instead of possibly unresearched opinions" (Politz, 1956-57).

As Figure 12.4 shows, interest in motivation research reached its peak in the middle 1950's. Thereafter, as judged by the number of articles about it in the trade press, it became less interesting, and at present almost no one talks or writes about it.

Who killed motivation research? It was certainly not Vance Packard, for *The Hidden Persuaders* did at least as much as any other publication to convince businessmen that motivation research is useful. It was probably not the criticisms leveled by the survey researchers. While pointing out the weaknesses of motivation research, they had to acknowledge its strengths. What seems to have happened is that motivation research, like many new schools of thought, died of success. As a result of experience with it, techniques, methods, and ideas that have proved useful have been incorporated into the main body of consumer psychology, whereas those which have not proved useful have gradually been eliminated.

Among the ideas motivation research has contributed to consumer psychology perhaps the most generally useful is the idea that much can be gained from an examination of the motivations and perceptions of the individual consumer. In the days before motivation research, consumers were all too often regarded as ciphers in statistical tables. Differences among individuals were ignored unless they could be measured by some convenient index, like age or education. The complexities of consumers' decision processes were often conveniently forgotten. Today even the most committed statistical researchers recognize and sometimes even attempt to measure the more subtle forces that influence the behavior of individuals.

Among the methods and techniques motivation research has contributed to consumer psychology, perhaps the most generally useful has been the depth interview. Searching examinations of consumers' opinions, attitudes, and ideas—either conducted with individual consumers or with groups of consumers—are now in common use as first steps in large-scale investigations. At times, as exemplified by the airline study with which this chapter started, they also play important roles as parts of a larger pattern of information.

A final observation about the motivation research movement: its shortcomings were similar in many ways to the shortcomings of early consumer psychology. Like the early psychologists, motivation researchers often jumped from findings based on a handful of respondents to conclusions about the behavior of the entire consumer population. And like the early psychologists, they tended to jump from currently fashionable but unsubstantiated psychological "laws"—this time the "laws" of psychoanalytic theory—to conclusions about the structure of effective advertising. These two tendencies keep reappearing.

CONSUMER PSYCHOLOGY TODAY

Current activity in the study of consumer behavior can be seen as an outgrowth of the trends and developments described in the preceding sections of this chapter. Today's consumer psychologists participate in studies of many kinds.

Images and Attitudes.   The major brands of most products are so nearly equal in quality that they are almost indistinguishable. Most consumers would find it quite difficult to tell one major brand of coffee or ice cream from another if they could not see the label with the brand name. Even automobiles, as different as they are in appearance, are basically very much alike. There may well be greater differences in satisfaction from one Ford owner to another than from the owner of an average Ford to the owner of an average Chevrolet.

With such parity in quality among brands, one might think that consumers would pay little attention to brand differences. Yet consumers have their favorites in almost every product category. Sometimes, as in the case of cigarettes, for example, loyalties are very strong. Smokers speak of "my brand" and may refuse a brand which is not their "own."

These loyalties exist because brands have "images"—cohesive sets of opinions, attitudes, and ideas about brands and about the people who use them. The Cadillac is thought of as an expensive car driven by affluent people. Pepsi Cola is thought of as a "lighter" beverage, consumed by "those who think young." Marlboro cigarettes are thought of as masculine.

Some aspects of some images are based on fact. Cadillacs are expensive, and Pepsi Cola is marginally different in taste from other cola beverages. But other aspects of images are manufactured by advertising. Cars that cost just as much as the Cadillac do not have quite the Cadillac aura. The advertising, not the product, makes Pepsi the beverage for young sociables. One paper-enclosed cylinder of tobacco is no more masculine than any other.

Consumer psychologists study brand and product images in a number of ways. Often hypotheses concerning images emerge from qualitative research—group interviews like those used in the airline illustration, or individual depth interviews that explore in great detail consumers' perceptions of the entries in a product field. Often these hypotheses are then tested in large-scale quantitative surveys that show how well defined the images are and how they vary from one segment of the population to another.

Emphasis on the psychological meaning of products and brands is a direct descendant of a similar emphasis in motivation research. The practice of putting hypotheses to quantitative test by means of interviews with representative cross sections of the consumer population is a product of the survey tradition. Image research as it is practiced today is a blend of both.

Product Testing. Most manufacturers maintain expensive facilities for testing their current products against possible improvements and against the products produced by their competitors. The availability of these facilities and their constant use are principal reasons for the parity in product quality that makes images so important in determining consumers' choices.

Many of the methods used in product testing originated in the first psychological laboratories, where the basic techniques for assessing human reaction to sensory stimuli were developed. The shaving cream study described earlier in this chapter is one example of the use of such techniques; the laboratory evaluation of posters and packages is another. Today consumer psychologists participate in evaluations of products of many kinds—watches and washing machines, coffee, candy, and cars.

Evaluating Advertisements. A major task of any advertising agency is that of evaluating the effectiveness of the print ads and television commercials it produces for its clients. Because print space and TV time are so costly, the effectiveness of each individual ad is a matter of great importance to the advertiser. None of the methods presently used for evaluating an ad's effectiveness is entirely satisfactory, and developing a valid and practical measure of advertising effectiveness is one of the greatest challenges facing consumer psychology today.

AD TESTING METHODS: DIRECT SUBJECTIVE RATING BY CONSUMERS. The methods now used to test ads go back quite a long time. One of them—direct subjective evaluation of ads by consumers—was tried by Harlow Gale, the first psychologist to concern himself with advertising.

When this method is used today, print advertisements or television commercials are exposed to cross sections of consumers, and the respondents are asked to give their personal reactions to what they have seen. Sometimes they are asked to restate the ad's message in their own words;

sometimes they are asked whether the ad makes them want to buy the product the ad features.

When testimony of this kind is interpreted judiciously, it can be quite helpful. Misinterpretations of intended messages are not uncommon; and when they occur, it is important that they be detected before the advertisement is put in print or on the air.

Consumers' ratings of an ad's persuasiveness are also used in evaluating an ad's effectiveness, but they are always suspect. It seems reasonable to assume that consumers can tell whether information about price or information about specific product characteristics increases their interest in trying a brand. But if the ad is part of a long-term campaign designed to build a brand image, or if it deals with a subject consumers find unpleasant, consumers' ratings of its persuasiveness may be either irrelevant or wrong. As noted earlier, the work with the eye camera showed conclusively that consumers' reports of their own reactions cannot always be believed.

AD TESTING METHODS: AIDED RECALL.   Another   much-used   copy-testing method is the method of aided recall. This method is based on the assumption that an effective advertisement will make a stronger impression on consumers' memories than an ineffective advertisement will. If this assumption is accepted, a valid measure of effectiveness requires only that memorability be measured in a standard way.

When used to evaluate the memorability of television commercials, the aided recall method follows a definite sequence of steps. The day after the commercial being tested has been shown, a cross section of consumers are called on the telephone. They are asked whether they were watching television the night before, and whether they were watching the program that carried the commercial. Those respondents who were watching the program are then asked a series of questions about the program content to find out whether they were at the television set at the time the commercial was shown, and those who were at the set at the right time are asked what they remember about the advertising.

Respondents who can remember something specific about the commercial they saw, after having been prompted by mention of the brand name if necessary, are counted as having remembered the commercial. The number of viewers who remembered the commercial, divided by the number who saw it, is the commercial's "aided recall" score. Very memorable commercials get recall scores as high as 50—50 percent of those who saw the commercial remembered something specific about it. Very unmemorable commercials get scores as low as 4 or 5.

The great advantage of the aided recall method is that it produces reliable results—that is, repeated tests of the same commercial usually yield approximately the same score. Because the scores attained by different commercials are quite different, it is clear that the method measures some quality of the commercial with considerable success.

The question always raised about this method is, Is the quality it measures effectiveness? Can a commercial be highly memorable and still not promote sales? Can a commercial be hard to recall and still produce an impression on the public that makes it worth its cost? Critics of the recall method maintain that the answer to both these questions is "Yes." At present the evidence is limited and far from clear, but the method is much-used because it has been so difficult to develop a method that is clearly better.

AD TESTING METHODS: SALES TESTS. The CBS study of the effectiveness of radio advertising cited earlier in this chapter is an example of a third method of testing ads. When this method is used, ads are placed in a test market area or a group of test market areas, and withheld from others. If the test market areas and the control market areas are similar in all other respects, the advertising in the test market area must be the cause of any change in sales.

The great advantage of this method is that, when executed correctly, it produces absolutely conclusive results. There is no need to assume that consumers' subjective reactions or the strength of consumers' memory traces are good indicators of future purchasing behavior. Purchasing behavior itself is what is measured.

The difficulty with this method is that it is very expensive to execute correctly. Correct execution demands precise control over the advertising stimuli received by large numbers of consumers, and it requires precise audit of exactly what they do and do not buy. Furthermore, withholding of advertising in major markets can mean a substantial drop in sales, with consequent disruption of relations with retailers and loss of profit to the company.

In spite of their high costs, well-designed advertising and marketing experiments are being undertaken with increasing frequency. They offer the only known way to get sure answers to many of the most important questions about the causes of the behavior of consumers. As more and more of them are conducted, and as findings from them are disseminated, they offer the prospect of an unprecedented build-up of fundamental knowledge about consumer behavior.

Television Research. Consumer psychologists may also participate in research on television programs. Among the most important questions in this field are these: What programs are likely to be successful? What can be done to improve a potentially popular program when the ratings are not high?

TELEVISION RESEARCH: GUESSWORK. A new television series usually starts as a pilot film—a sample episode. The pilot film is loaned to potential purchasers so they can decide whether to buy it for the coming season. If the film shows exceptional promise, a sale is quickly made.

Evaluation of a pilot film seldom leaves much time for research. The film may be in the potential purchaser's possession for only a few hours. At most the film will be available for only a few days.

When research time is available, group interviews with television viewers may be used to provide some indication of public response. Outstanding success or outstanding failure can often be forecast in this way.

When no research time is available the decision must be based on an educated guess. The guess will ultimately be made by executives responsible for making decisions of this kind. Sometimes, before making the decision, they seek social scientists' advice.

Social scientists who give advice under these circumstances are in much the same position as the early psychologists who formulated rules for effective advertising based on the then current psychological "laws." They must apply their knowledge of current theory and research on human behavior to a specific practical problem, and their answers will be exactly as valid as the theories on which they are based. We have already seen how wrong theory led to wrong answers in the past, and there is every reason to believe that the same verdict will be rendered against many of the answers being made today.

There is, however, an important difference in outlook between the consumer psychologist of today and the consumer psychologist of 40 years ago. Today scientists who study consumer behavior are much more aware of the complexities of their field. They know that their current fund of information has its limitations, and that these limitations will not be overcome by experiments on college sophomores.

The truly exciting prospect for consumer psychology is that a new kind of laboratory is becoming increasingly accessible. As advertisers and marketers become more and more aware of the limitations of what they already know, and as the value of deliberate systematic use of well-designed consumer behavior experiments becomes increasingly obvious, consumer psychologists and other scientists interested in studying consumer behavior will be able to participate in experiments that involve large segments of the consumer population. Such experiments are sure to yield a fund of valid information never available before. With this fund to draw on, future consumer psychologists will be able to participate in such business decisions as choice of television programs with greatly increased assurance that they are right.

TELEVISION RESEARCH: THEATER TESTS. When time is available for testing a television program, theater tests are sometimes used. Such tests may be used when a pilot film is available longer than the usual brief period of time or when a show has been purchased and several episodes have been filmed but not yet put on the air.

One system for theater-testing TV programs employs the same principles as the "program analyzer" described earlier in this chapter. Members of the audience, who have been invited to the theater to preview new television programs, hold small dials in their hands. When they like what they are seeing on the screen, they turn the dial indicator up; when they dislike what they are seeing they turn it down. The dials are connected electrically to a device that averages the ratings and prints the average on a paper as a moving line. Since the line is timed precisely, the analyst can tell exactly what the audience liked about the show and what it did not. With this knowledge, parts of the show that get the best reaction from the audience can be emphasized and less-liked parts dropped out.

Users of any laboratory device must be able to show that the subjects they employ in their experiments are representative of the consumer population as a whole, and not just one special group. In the best theater tests of TV shows, great pains are taken to be sure that the audience includes the various age, sex, and income groups in their correct proportions. Samples of this kind are not necessarily perfectly representative, but they are immeasurably better than samples assembled from whatever subjects happen to be convenient. Well-conducted theater tests of TV programs represent good use of laboratory techniques in opinion research.

TELEVISION RESEARCH: TVQ. Each month during the TV season, members of the Home Testing Institute's consumer mail panel receive a lengthy questionnaire in which they are asked to rate all network TV programs on the following scale:

1. One of my favorites.
2. Very good.
3. Good.

4. Fair.
5. Poor.
6. Never seen.

On the basis of these ratings, each program receives a "TVQ" score—the number of respondents who rate it "one of my favorites" divided by the number of respondents who report having "seen" it. Because the TVQ sample is large, and is proportionately distributed among the various important segments of the viewing population, separate TVQ scores can be calculated for any program from men or from women, from members of different age groups, from residents of different areas of the country, from TV viewers with different incomes and different occupations.

Information of this kind has two major uses. Because the TVQ score is related to viewing behavior, TVQ can help locate shows with special kinds of audiences—housewives with at least two children, upper-income males, children between 6 and 11, and so on. Although the correlation between TVQ score and viewing behavior is not perfect, it is fairly close. It is usually safe to assume that if two shows have very different TVQ scores within a given segment of the population, the show with the higher TVQ also has the higher proportion of viewers. Information of this kind is very useful to advertisers who are especially interested in communicating with certain specific population segments.

The other use of TVQ depends on the fact that TVQ is a measure of attitude not behavior, so TVQ score and viewing behavior are not perfectly correlated. Sometimes a show that many people like will get relatively few viewers because it is competing with a show that many people like even better. When this is true the show is apt to pick up viewers if it is moved to another time period.

Before TVQ scores became available, it was impossible to tell whether a disappointing audience rating was attributable to the show itself or to unusually tough competition. Now when proportion of respondents calling the show "one of my favorites" is markedly higher than the proportion actually viewing it, the inference is that the poor viewing rating is due to competition. A change in time is therefore indicated.

TVQ is a valuable and influential application of survey research technique to the study of consumers' reactions to television.

SUMMARY

This chapter has explored some, but not all, of the applications of psychology to the study of consumer behavior. It opened with three brief case histories, which show some of the environments in which consumer psychologists operate. In comments on these case histories it was pointed out that consumer psychologists almost always work in close contact with executives responsible for making advertising and marketing decisions and in close cooperation with social scientists from other disciplines. It was also pointed out that the information the consumer psychologist produces is almost always used in conjunction with other information as part of a much larger pattern. Finally it was pointed out that the consumer psychologist's academic training in psychology is seldom enough—that he must be prepared to learn and use concepts and ideas from other disciplines in his work.

The discussion then turned to some highlights from the development of consumer psychology. Descriptions of some early studies showed the first appearance of two problems that have been with consumer psychology since its earliest days. Early psychologists, like some psychologists today, tended to ignore the fact that results obtained by testing anyone who happened to be available were not necessarily generalizable to people in general. And early psychologists, like some today, were ready to jump from unconfirmed "laws" to pronouncements about the probable outcome of advertising and marketing decisions.

This section of the chapter then turned to the progress consumer psychology had made by the time of the Second World War. It described the development of survey research, and it noted the progress made in experiments with laboratory methods used to measure consumers' reactions to products, to advertising, and to radio programs. It described some of the contributions consumer psychologists made to the war effort, and it made special note of the founding and contributions of the Michigan Survey Research Center after the war.

The next major topic was the rise and fall of "motivation research." This discussion emphasized the differences between motivation research methods and previous methods for analyzing the behavior of consumers, and presented testimony both from advocates of motivation research and from its critics. It suggested that the shortcomings of motivation research resembled the shortcomings of early consumer psychology—too ready generalization from small samples to all consumers, and too much faith in unproved theories. This section also emphasized that, in directing attention to the motivations, perceptions and decision processes of the individual consumer, and in developing methods for studying these functions, the motivation research movement made major contributions to present-day consumer psychology.

Finally the discussion turned to three problem areas that engage the attention of consumer psychologists today. One of these, research on brand and product images, was shown to be a blend of the survey research and motivation research traditions. Product testing was given as a good example of the use of laboratory methods in the analysis of consumer behavior.

Research on advertising effectiveness provided examples of the use of subjective ratings, the use of aided recall, and the use of controlled experiments to measure the effectiveness of ads. The advantages of the latter technique and the promise it holds for the future were stressed.

Research on television was shown to combine educated guesswork based on current theory, inferences made from reactions obtained under controlled conditions, and inferences about behavior made from measurements of attitudes. Whether they are applied to television viewing or to some other aspect of consumer behavior, these three research methods represent the practice and the promise of consumer psychology as it exists today. Faced with the necessity of making a decision that will not wait, executives who purchase television programs or make other strategic advertising and marketing decisions sometimes call on social scientists for advice. In giving such advice, the social scientist must rely on an understanding of human behavior that he knows is at best incomplete. This is the situation today, but there is every reason to believe that understanding of human behavior will be more complete and more accurate in the future.

One of the ways this understanding will grow is through systematic application of controlled experiments to analysis of consumer behavior. One way this is done is represented by theater tests of television programs. Here the stimulus, the program, is deliberately varied, and the response degree of favorable reaction, is measured. Although this general procedure has been in use since the first psychologists became interested in consumer research, the best of today's theater tests represent an important conceptual advance. Instead of assuming that the reactions of just any group of testers will be typical, the scientists who conduct the best theater tests today make every effort to make sure that important segments of the population are represented as adequately as possible. This sensitivity to sampling problems is a lesson that psychologists who do research in other areas will some day have to learn.

The other way controlled experimentation is making increased contributions to the understanding of consumer behavior is by means of market tests, which treat a large geographical area, sometimes the entire United States, as an experimental laboratory. Here the stimulus, an advertising campaign or a media plan, for instance, is controlled by exposing it in selected market areas but withholding it from others, and the effect of the stimulus is measured in terms of purchasing behavior or change in attitude.

In the past both laboratory tests and market tests have been used almost entirely to evaluate specific shows, specific products, or specific campaigns or media plans. For this reason the kind of general knowledge that can lead to the formulation of principles or laws has not accumulated. In the future, however, as the possibility of formulating general principles becomes more apparent to those who must provide the funds for large-scale studies, and as the need for such principles becomes more and more urgent, large-scale studies aimed at deriving general principles are certain to be made.

Finally TVQ was used as an example of the application of attitude measurement to research on television. This example showed that attitude measurements are useful because they are related to behavior (in this case, viewing) and can substitute for behavior measures in certain circumstances when behavior measures are not available. It also showed that attitude measurements can be useful when attitude and behavior do not correspond, as when TVQ data that show that a program is well liked can be used to indicate that it would probably attract a larger audience in a different time period.

Both these applications of attitude measurement are to be found in other areas of consumer research. Attitudes are used as substitutes for measures of purchasing behavior when such measures are unavailable, and they provide useful information when attitudes and behavior do not correspond. When attitudes and behavior do not correspond, an analysis of the marketing situation will often reveal the reasons why consumers are not behaving in accordance with their preferences. When the reasons are known, a change in the situation may be highly beneficial.

SUGGESTED REFERENCES FOR FURTHER STUDY

Anastasi, A. (1964). *Fields of Applied Psychology*. New York: McGraw-Hill Book Company.

Chapters 10, 11, and 12 of this book cover much the same material as the present chapter but in greater depth and detail.

Britt, S. W. (1960). *The Spenders*. New York: McGraw-Hill Book Company.

An interesting treatment of consumers as consumers. Discusses the major motivations for purchasing various products. Describes brand and store "images," and the influence of prices and packages.

Crisp, R. D. (1957). *Marketing Research*. New York: McGraw-Hill Book Company.

A basic and comprehensive description of the major methods used in market research.

Lucas, D. B., and S. H. Britt (1963). *Measuring Advertising Effectiveness*. New York: McGraw-Hill Book Company.

Describes the major research methods used in evaluating the effectiveness of advertisements and in the selection of advertising media.

Packard, V. (1957). *The Hidden Persuaders*. New York: David McKay.

A sensationalistic presentation of the use of psychological theory and psychological research methods in advertising and marketing research.

Smith, G. H. (1954). *Motivation Research in Advertising and Marketing*. New York: McGraw-Hill Book Company.

A description of the application of clinical methods to advertising and marketing research.

Chapter 13
Psychology and
International Relations

THE MOST PRESSING PROBLEMS of our age center on our relations with other nations. Unless we make significant progress in improving our knowledge and skills in this field, our total Western civilization stands in the gravest jeopardy. The enormous destructive capacity of military weapons has not only outstripped our military defenses, but has challenged our capacity for control and constructive relations with other nations. The imperatives for personal as well as national survival lend an unparalleled urgency to the search for rational relations across international boundaries.

Until recently, psychology, or more broadly, the behavioral sciences, had little to offer, and less to say, about international relations. Heretofore, policy makers of our government consulted historians, political experts, economists, lawyers, and military men for advice. Even at this writing, no person educated primarily as a sociologist, psychologist, anthropologist, or political scientist has reached high office in our federal government at a point where international policy is formed and executed. Indeed among our national legislators one may seek almost in vain to find a person who has ever worked in any science—natural or behavioral. C. P. Snow has expressed the situation eloquently, "One of the most bizarre features of any advanced industrial society in our time is that the cardinal choices have to be made by a handful of men: in secret: and at least in legal form, by men who cannot have a first hand knowledge of what those choices depend upon or what their results will be" (Snow, 1961). However, the behaviorial sciences are gradually being consulted, and behavioral research is being done that bears upon issues of international relations.

If one were to place a date on the official recognition of behavioral science as a contributor to international relations it would probably be in

449

1962, when the White House released a report signed by Jerome B. Wiesner, President's Special Assistant for Science and Technology. This report in part said: "Some of the most difficult, complex and vital problems confronting our country are in the area of international relations. Behavioral science is relevant to various aspects of these problems. . . . The general issues studied by behavioral scientists are critically important to our national welfare and security. Ways must be found to strengthen these disciplines and improve their use. . . . We suggest that a particular effort be made to support basic-research ideas for behavioral science on a scale consistent with their importance and without regard to previous levels of funding" (Wiesner, 1962).

Contributions of Behavioral Science.   It is the thesis of this chapter that behavioral science, and especially psychological studies, can provide valuable insights and useful guides to action in the conduct of international relations. These are not offered as substitutes for the insights or guides provided by historians, political experts, or military officers. Instead, they are conceived as important supplements that add significant new dimensions to policy formation and decision making. The psychological contributions to this area are, in a sense, not new, but draw upon established principles verified by empirical and sometimes experimental data derived from small groups and individuals. The application of these principles at the level of nations is new. In this respect the advent of attention to psychological knowledge at the international policy level represents a major step in the extension of psychological information and usefulness.

Basic research in any area proceeds by a reciprocal process. Practical issues demanding answers suggest researchable problems that lead the scientist back to his laboratory or to systematic analysis of past events. These research results then provide guides for new actions that, hopefully, are more effective but still subject to improvement. The cycle then repeats itself. Hence the encouragement of behavioral research in international transactions will provide a new domain of inquiry and application.

A psychological understanding of international relations draws upon our understanding in many fields of inquiry: perception, and the effects of emotion, group identification, and threat on perceptions; the stimulation of aggressive behavior; the development of attitudes and stereotypes; the processes of bargaining and negotiation; some principles of mental health; the effectiveness of mass media communications. It is probably true that no area of study presents more challenging, complex issues than this one, nor is there an area in which so much is at stake. We shall obviously not debate in this chapter the historical, political, economic, military, or moral problems of international relations except as they impinge on the psychological mechanisms. International relations may legitimately be approached from any of these other vantage points, but an understanding of the relevant psychological processes may illuminate and enrich these other approaches, as well as directly provide some guide lines for action or policy.

The objective we have in mind is to develop an understanding of the psychological causes and conditions that lead to international tensions, with the hope that we may also find some means of reducing tensions leading to war and destructive conflict. We are not interested in sharpening those tools, devices, and manipulations that have become associated with Machiavelli, the sixteenth-century political philosopher who was interested in formulating methods of outwitting opponents. Moreover, we reject the Clausewitz notion, which seems to have guided many international experts, that war is merely diplomacy carried on in a different form. In a real sense we are here facing squarely the statement in the UNESCO constitution that "since wars begin in the minds of men, it is in the minds of men that the defenses of peace must be constructed."

THE DELEGATION OF INTERNATIONAL TRANSACTIONS

We need to remind ourselves at the outset that our intercourse with other nations is carried on by a relatively small number of persons who develop policies, carry on negotiations, make decisions, and conclude agreements. These persons are the agents of their respective countries, and cannot, by the nature of things, take a referendum on every decision or policy change. They operate within a framework of public opinion—oftentimes vaguely defined.

Secondly, in our own State Department our stance on particular issues is formulated by teams of officers who prepare "position papers" that spell out the boundaries of permissible flexibility within some broader framework of national policy. The area of freedom left to a chief negotiator at an international conference is therefore closely circumscribed. Nevertheless, an area of freedom is available, and it is within that area that personal perceptions and personal predispositions of the agent can express themselves. Of course, in negotiations and interchanges between the so-called principals (Summit Conferences) the area of freedom is somewhat enlarged. It is therefore well to bear in mind throughout the subsequent discussion that our international relationships are circumscribed by group pressures stemming at their base from public opinion broadly and vaguely articulated.[1]

---

[1] We shall have more to say on this point in the next chapter.

However, more specific group constraints emanate from within the government itself. Consequently one of the psychological problems to be understood is the manner in which group decisions evolve and how group pressures exert themselves on individuals acting as agents for others with only limited freedom to express their private opinions and judgments.

AGGRESSION IN INTERNATIONAL RELATIONS

There was a time when it was widely believed that war was a biological necessity—an expression on a national scale of innate impulses to dominate, excel, and compete that had to be released. War, so some held, was merely a social evolutionary mechanism to assure the survival of the fittest; not necessarily the fittest individuals, but the fittest nation. This notion is happily no longer acceptable. However, this does not mean that aggression does not exist or is not "natural." Our task is to understand the conditions giving rise to aggression between groups and, if possible, to discover ways by which unavoidable aggressions can be channeled into constructive, rather than destructive action.

Four minimal conditions are necessary for the appearance of intergroup conflict: (a) identification or visibility of groups, (b) contact between the groups, (c) competition between the groups, and (d) differences between the groups in values and behavior patterns (Williams, 1947).

The first two of these conditions are obvious and need little elaboration. Conflict is only one form of contact between groups; hence some initial type of contact is a prerequisite for conflict to develop. The contact need not necessarily be physical but may involve only long-range communications. Furthermore, since we are dealing with *intergroup* conflict, we must be able to distinguish from other populations those groups that are parties to the conflict. These two conditions can be considered as defining the phenomenon to be considered.

Competition and Aggression. However, does competition necessarily promote aggressive conflict? The answer seems to be a limited yes, provided no controls are placed on the unfolding of the relationship. First of all, we have to define competition as striving for scarce goals in which one group has the possibility of "winning" and the other of "losing." There is another kind of competition in which nations compete, to raise, for instance, the standard of living within their own boundaries but not at the expense of other nations. Or, there may be competition in scientific discovery, the exploration of space, or the conquering of disease in which the achievements are shared among the competitors. This kind of competition will not necessarily lead to aggressive conflict, although if the competition is for prestige in the eyes of the spectators, even this competition may become aggressive conflict. In uncontrolled win–lose competitions aggressions nearly always develop.

The development of aggression in win–lose competitions between groups starts with the mobilization of forces within each group to outstrip the other. Internal differences become subjugated in the interest of focusing efforts on the group's common task to outrun, outmaneuver, outproduce the opposition. This is such a common observation at the national level in times of crisis that it may be pointless to undergird the statement with systematic observations in small groups. However, Sherif (1953) showed that adolescent boys in a summer camp formed into two groups showed no hostility toward each other until *after* a few days of direct competition between the groups in a planned series of athletic contests. Again, with adult groups engaged in sensitivity training where a strong group spirit develops, a fairly mild win–lose contest between the groups is nearly always accompanied by invective, hostile, and aggressive remarks directed at the opponents. This happens in spite of the fact that the members of the competing groups, prior to the competition, are friendly and often roommates. In the heat of competition the individual becomes closely identified with his own group, seeing it in more favorable terms while simultaneously denigrating members of the opposition.

This phenomenon has been noted with respect to American views of the British, the Russians, and Germans over the past several years. During the Second World War Americans generally expressed positive attitudes toward the British and the Russians; somewhat more favorable toward the British for their defense and fortitude in the Battle of Britain than toward the Russians for their stand at Stalingrad. Americans temporarily "forgot" the rout of the British at Dunkirk and the various defeats of Russian armies in Finland and Western Russia. Simultaneously they viewed the Germans as barbaric, ruthless, and cunning, especially in victory. It was not that defeats were associated with bravery and victories with brutality. It depended on who was defeated and who was victorious. Both in victory and defeat American allies, British or Russian, were honorable, just, wise, courageous. The enemy regardless of winning or losing a battle was foolhardy, reckless, savage, ruthless. Subsequent to the war American allies have shifted. The features once attributed to the Germans were seen in the Russians. This evidence confirms a generalization that has had wide currency among psychologists for many years: we generally perceive favorably those who are *with* us and attribute ill motives and base features to those who are competing against us—irrespective of the "facts." [2]

AGGRESSION FROM FRUSTRATION. Another consequence of win–lose competition is the creation of frustration. The repercussions of frustration have engaged the attention of psychologists for many years. One of the consequences of being blocked in the attainment of one's goals is the stimulation of aggressive impulses; although this is not the only possible, or necessarily the most probable, consequence (Dollard, Doob, Miller, Mower, and Sears, 1939). It is, however, frequent. This can be shown at the individual level, where two persons are both striving for a single goal. One cannot achieve the goal because of the other's victory, and consequently is thwarted. In a classroom situation it has been shown that pitting one individual of the class against the others results in lower liking for the members of the group and interferes with the total class functioning (Deutsch, 1949). The competition disrupted communications, friendliness, and coordination. But beneath these external and fairly obvious manifestations, this competition stimulated some subtle reactions. The competing students generally *expected* hostile behavior from their rivals—even before any was manifested. In all probability a student's expectation of hostility *from* an opponent arises out of his own feelings of hostility *toward* the opponent. "If I feel hostile to him, he must feel hostile toward me." With this starting point, regardless of whether the opponent has expressed any aggressive behavior, hostility may spiral upward. The person with the feelings quoted above acts in a manner revealing his hostility, and that in turn generates aggressive behavior, which confirms in the first person his initial expectation, and the spiral has begun. Hence, not only is the outcome of a competitive situation aggression-provoking, the very beginning of such contests may set the stage for aggression.

Although all this has been developed by careful analysis of students in a very mild competitive situation, the findings may have some relevance to international relations of a much more critical sort. On December 16, 1962, President Kennedy conversed for an hour before the TV cameras with three reporters. Interspersed throughout this conversation were references to *he*, *him*, and *his*, referring to Mr. Khrushchev. For example, "Once *he* fires *his* missiles, it is all over anyway, because we are going to have sufficient resources to fire back at *him* to destroy the Soviet Union." Or "I don't think that we expected that *he* would put the missiles in Cuba, because it would have seemed such an impudent action for *him* to take, as

---

[2] For additional evidence see Hastorf and Cantril (1954).

it was later proved. Now *he* obviously must have thought that *he* could do it in secret and that the United States would accept it. So that *he* did not judge our intentions accurately." (Italics are added.) Evidently Mr. Kennedy thought of the competition between the USA and the USSR in highly personal terms. The opposition was focused in one man. The spontaneity of these remarks and the impromptu nature of the phrasing lends credence to this interpretation. It is curious that Mr. Kennedy did not use *I, me,* or *my* in direct opposition to his references to Mr. Khrushchev. Evidently in the President's mind, *we* were in opposition to *him.* The implication that we draw from these quotations is that pinpointing the opposition in highly personal terms gives some support to the notion that the dynamics of interpersonal conflict are not irrelevant to understanding international conflict. The ebb and flow of international events are not just the result of impersonal complicated political and economic forces, although they play their part. There are equally complicated highly personal forces of a noncognitive sort.

The chief agents of the respective nations may see each other partly as agents constrained by their respective constituents but also as individual decision makers. Of course it is true that in a totalitarian country the chief decision maker has more power than in a democratic country, such as the United States. However, in the same TV conversation, President Kennedy emphasized that final responsibility for the decision to take action at the international level rests with the President, and is a highly personal responsibility. This fact reemphasizes the relevance of individual dynamics and psychological processes to the conduct of international affairs.

Strategic Aggression.   Quite apart from aggression stimulated by frustration, some aggression may be a deliberate policy for strategic purposes. Hostile actions may be directed at another group not because they have been thwarting but because aggression itself has a unifying effect on the aggressing group. According to one interpretation, Hitler's anti-Semitic program was initiated as a means of bringing together segments of the German population who were at odds on a number of ideological issues. In spite of the fact that the Jews represented a considerable proportion of the German population, they were still a minority against which latent hostility was already directed. Hitler no doubt believed many of the accusations, but his deliberately planned and systematic persecution of the Jews was largely a strategic aggression designed to reduce dissonant views within the remaining majority (Needler, 1960).

Such strategic aggressions obviously cannot be mounted unless there exists at least the seeds of discontent with respect to the intended victims.

Some of the aggression directed against the Negro in the United States can be understood in these terms. The Negro may not be directly frustrating, but Negro churches may be bombed, mysterious shots are fired into Negro homes at night, or even an occasional lynching may occur "to keep them in their places." Even in these situations there exists a background of competition for jobs, living space, privileges, which may not be intense but is not absent. Consequently, even though some aggression is not provoked by solid barriers to the aspirations of a group, these strategic aggressions, primarily designed to serve other purposes, are nevertheless directed at convenient scapegoats for whom some animosity already exists.

Aggression from Differences in Belief. "One of the paradoxes in the history of many religions is the frequent disparity between their emphasis upon peace and love on one hand, and their aggressiveness toward nonbelievers on the other. Christianity has been divided by schisms, but its branches have not always lived together in peace and brotherhood. Heretics have been burned at the stake, followers of dissident sects have been slaughtered, Protestants and Catholics have murdered each other—all in the name of the Prince of Peace" (Berkowitz, 1962).[3] Although differences in belief may be associated with intergroup conflict, as this quotation so well emphasizes, it is possible that lying beneath the belief differences is a substrata of win–lose competition, which is the essential causal condition. The adherents of one point of view come in conflict with their opponents in "the battle for men's minds." Each is competing for additional supporters. In this sense, differences in belief as a cause or condition of aggression is a variant of our basic theme of competition.

The matter, however, cannot be dismissed quite so easily. A belief system or ideology is a far-reaching matter that embraces not only a set of abstract ideals but a form of organization or a way of life. When belief systems come in conflict, the issues at bed rock turn out to be differences in the accepted ways of doing business, carrying on community affairs, controlling social behavior, legitimatizing certain goals, and outlawing other goals. In the course of interacting across the boundaries of belief systems people find it difficult to deal with each other. Thus Americans are very time-conscious and punctual, but certain American Indians place very little value on time in our terms. The Sioux, for instance, had no words in their language for *waiting* or *late*. They did not know what was meant by either term. Ceremonial dances even today occur at certain seasons of the year,

---

[3] *Aggression: A Social Psychological Analysis*, Berkowitz, L. 1962. McGraw-Hill Book Company, Inc. Used by permission.

but the day or the hour are not fixed. They occur "when things are ready" (Hall, 1961). One can easily imagine the problems of trying to hire a tribe to put on a program of such dances in New York City theaters. But beyond this, we tend to see the Sioux as lazy, irresponsible, undependable. His belief system about time is different from ours, and within his framework these derogatory characterizations are untrue! Nevertheless our civilization has engulfed the Sioux and has gradually imposed our standards of time on them.

Or take another example: "Despite a host of favorable auspices an American mission in Greece was having great difficulty working out an agreement with Greek officials. Efforts to negotiate met with resistance and suspicion on the part of the Greeks. The Americans were unable to conclude the agreements needed to start new projects. Upon later examination of this exasperating situation two unsuspected reasons were found for the stalemate: First, Americans pride themselves on being outspoken and forthright. These qualities are regarded as a liability by the Greeks. They are taken to indicate a lack of finesse which the Greeks deplore. The American directness immediately prejudiced the Greeks. Second, when Americans arranged meetings with the Greeks they tried to limit the length of the meetings and to reach agreements on general principles first, delegating the drafting of details to subcommittees. The Greeks regarded this practice as a device to pull the wool over their eyes (imputation of ill motives). The Greek practice is to work out details in front of all concerned and continue meetings for as long as is necessary. The result of this misunderstanding was a series of unproductive meetings with each side deploring the other's behavior" (Hall, 1961).[4] Such differences in expected behavior provoke strains that could be eliminated if "everybody were required to do it my way." If our own customs and values were more widespread we could deal with others more easily. This logic leads directly to efforts, often of an aggressive sort, to impose these patterns on others.

Aggression To Reduce Doubts About Self.   In some situations, the adherent to one belief system when confronted with an opposing view may begin to doubt his own beliefs. Up to this point he has been comfortable in holding these beliefs, partly because others around him were of the same conviction, thus giving him support, and partly because no alternatives were ever suggested. The confrontation of another point of view is threatening in two ways. First, he may wonder whether he was correct in

---

4 From *The Silent Language* by E. T. Hall. Copyright © 1959 by Edward T. Hall. Reprinted by permission of Doubleday & Company, Inc.

his beliefs, and this may shake his concept of himself as a sensible person. Second, if he should be persuaded that the opposition has some merit, he runs the risk of being alienated from his friends. This is a very uncomfortable position in which to find oneself. To give up or modify one's view of himself built up over a lifetime requires a great deal of courage and a considerable amount of help. In simplified terms this is often the objective of deep psychoanalysis, requiring a year or more of therapy. Compound this threat with the possibility of cutting off one's friends, and a challenge to one's belief system becomes a terrifying decision point. Most of us react to these uncertainties in ourselves by attacking the external source of those uncertainties—the opposing belief system. The more completely we can destroy that belief system, the more comfortable we can become. Hence threats, both to one's self-concept and to one's acceptance by others, often results in an aggressive response toward the opposition. These are threats that are rarely verbalized or explicitly conscious. Nevertheless, they form the basis for the uneasiness we feel, and the hostility we express in the face of an opposing belief system. We must point out further that this mechanism is in addition to the difficulty of dealing with the behaviors exemplified in the previous paragraph.

It is possible to interpret a portion of the relations between the USSR and USA within this latter framework. At this writing the USA has been repeatedly accused of being imperialistic and war-mongering by the opposition—an accusation that Americans vehemently reject. Americans think of themselves as interested only in maintaining world peace. In turn they charge the USSR with imperialistic intentions and point to their endorsement of wars of liberation. Russia's announced desire for "coexistence" is interpreted as a ruse to deceive others. The Americans' national self-concept does not permit them to see the significance (to others) of the fact that they are the most formidable military power the world has ever known, with bases circling the globe. Moreover, in the years since the Second World War America has given tanks, planes, missiles, guns, and military training to other nations in prodigious quantities. The USA has not only built an invincible military establishment, it has encouraged its allies, both large and small, to do likewise. In doing all this Americans reject any modification in their historic self-concept as a peace-loving, altruistic champion of freedom and democracy while developing simultaneously an increasingly hostile view of the USSR. No doubt the Russians are subject to the same cyclical mechanism with respect to the U.S.A. In summary, aggressive impulses grow when an opposing belief system challenges tenaciously held self-concepts.

Constructive Consequences of Aggression. Aggression under certain limited circumstances may be turned to constructive ends. (We are here following Bach, 1963.) The most easily understood is the emotional release of tensions that prepares the ground for more realistic appraisal of the situation. It is a widely respected principle that emotional tensions created out of frustrations need to be released or dissipated before one may perceive the situation before him accurately. After a particularly explosive emotional outburst on the interpersonal level, one often has the feeling, "Well I may not have changed his view, but *I* feel better." In international disputes we need to provide for opportunities of this sort short of armed outbursts. In all probability the diatribe of Mr. Khrushchev in May 1960 at the Paris summit meeting following the U-2 incident was such a cathartic release, though hardly diplomatic, temporarily disrupting relations between the major powers. In the longer view it was probably beneficial, resulting in a clarification of permissible behaviors.[4] There is little doubt that Mr. Khrushchev expressed not just his personal aggressions but the views of at least a segment of the population he represented.

An aggressive encounter may also result in the discovery of new resources in both parties to the conflict. One does not know the limits of his own capabilities unless forced to extend himself to these limits. In looking back on the Second World War the USA was somewhat surprised to discover that American social economy was capable of producing both "guns and butter" in prodigious amounts previously thought impossible. This is not suggesting that the cost was commensurate with the obtained information—only that new information was discovered. And the same may be said of other parties to the conflict.

Finally an aggressive encounter may provoke either or both parties to examine positions other than the one they assumed at the beginning of the struggle. This is a very unlikely possibility for the undisputed victor although more likely in the defeated party. Japan is an illustration of this possibility. Subsequent to the Second World War there was in Japan a wave of rejection among college students of much that was superficially traditional, and a realization in the early 1960's by many intellectual leaders that the unquestioned allegiance to militaristic controls had led to national disaster. They have thus been willing to search for a different,

---

[4] From the American standpoint this conference was viewed as a success because it was called to negotiate the Berlin issue on which the USA wished to maintain the status quo. The Soviets refused to negotiate, and by this default USA managed to achieve its objective. This further illustrates the possible immediate boomerang effect on the party giving uninhibited expression to his own tensions.

presumably more democratic, way of organizing themselves (cf. Berrien, 1963).

By way of summary, we have been able to identify six sources of aggression in intergroup conflict: (1) win–lose competition for scarce goals, (2) the imputation of hostile feelings to one's competitor, (3) a highly probable response to frustration, (4) a strategic policy to develop internal cohesion or to nullify an incipient threat, (5) a means of enlarging the scope of our own customs, and (6) a way of reducing doubts about self-concepts and threats to one's allegiances. Surely the dynamics of aggression are complicated and the elimination of one or another of the sources of aggression will not be a panacea. Aggressive encounters may result in constructive consequences by reason of the emotional release they provide, the discovery of new capabilities, or the forced reevaluation of one's earlier position that led to the conflict. We said at the outset of this section that aggression is "natural," meaning that understandable conditions provoke aggressive actions. Having identified some of these conditions we shall return later to the problem of reducing the destructive character of aggression at the international level.

PERCEPTION OF OTHERS

It is a fundamental principle that the way we act toward another person or nation is largely dependent upon the way we perceive that other person or nation. In the previous section it was pointed out that if we perceive a competitor as hostile, we are likely to react by becoming hostile too. Perceptions are the beginning of action. What we "see" in a situation, and the way in which we interpret it, form the basis for our behavior.

It is a fundamental principle also that our perceptions of the outside world are not precise copies of that world. The "trickle of messages from the outside is affected by the stored up images, the preconceptions, and the prejudices which interpret, fill them out, and in their turn powerfully direct the play of our attention, and our vision itself" (Lippmann, 1922). In another place it was said: "Each looks at, and looks for, the facts and reasons to which his attention points, perceiving little, if at all, those to which his mind is not directed. As a rule men see what they look for, and observe the things they expect to see" (Lowell, 1923). Perhaps the distortion of perceptions is overstated in these remarks, for we know that the more structured and compelling are the external stimuli, the more our perceptions are controlled by these matters rather than the biases, memories, and transitory interests of the individual. However, every perception of events transpiring around us is a complex product both of what we bring to that situation and what is veridical (true in an objective sense) about the situation (Kilpatrick, 1961).

The task presented to an individual in perceiving the intentions of others, their position on social or political issues, their trustworthiness, sincerity, or integrity is far more difficult than perceiving the length of lines or the size of circles. In the former tasks the input stimuli are ambiguous, poorly structured, confusing, and at times actually contradictory. However, even in the latter case with geometric forms, perceptions are distorted or affected by conditions that the perceiver brings in himself to the perceiving task. For instance, children from slum areas tend to over-estimate the size of common coins—quarters, dimes, nickels—and children from prosperous executive and professional families do not. The *needs* of children affect their perceptions in such simple uncomplicated matters (Bruner and Goodman, 1947).

Political Perceptions. When we come to political issues the possibilities of distortion are enhanced. A political campaign for public office provides a social stimulus situation of considerable complexity in which the voter is offered the opportunity to make a choice, to act. In a detailed and careful study of the 1948 presidential campaign between Truman and Dewey, the way in which voters perceived the stands taken by the candidates on the major issues was analyzed (Berelson, Lazarsfeld, and McPhee, 1954). Although there was some deliberate ambiguity for propagandistic reasons on some issues by both candidates, they differed sharply in their speeches on price controls (Truman was for), Taft–Hartley Law (Truman was against), and public housing (Truman was for). Confining their analysis to these three issues on which the candidates could be distinguished, the investigators discovered that a voter was likely to assign his *own* stand on these issues to the candidate of his choice. That is, if a voter expected to vote for Dewey but was for price controls (Dewey was against) and was against Taft–Hartley (Dewey was for), the voter tended to perceive Dewey as in agreement with himself. The actual statements by the respective candidates were misperceived by their supporters and opponents alike. This distortion did not happen in every such case, but does represent the major trend of the data. If one is for a particular candidate because of political affiliation, personality, or other reasons but disagrees with him on an issue, the voter is placed in a strained situation. One way of reducing this strain is to erect a "perceptual defense" and reinterpret the candidate's statements to fit his own views or even to filter out the statements that are the source of his strain, denying that they were made. To quote from the report:[5] "The voter tends to oversee or to invent what is favorable to himself and to distort or to deny much of what is unfavorable. This must leave him fewer internal conflicts to resolve—with so to speak a favorable balance of perception . . . Second, [the misperception] must make the voter's political judgment *seem* more rational to him because it maximizes agreement with his own side and maximizes disagreement with the opposition. In other words, perception often operates to make differences between parties appear greater than they actually may be—and thus to make the voter's decision appear more rational (in one sense) than it actually is" (Berelson, Lazarsfeld, and McPhee, 1954). The perceptual dynamics of a national partisan election and campaign also apply at the international level such that the similarities between contestants are minimized and the differences are magnified.

The mechanism of perceptual defense introduced in the previous paragraph merits some elaboration. It has been shown that if one exposes for very short periods a series of words within which are some that are tabooed—indecent, obscene, lurid—the perceivers require longer periods of exposure to see such words. It is as if the individual erects a barrier to some incoming stimuli, not because they are unfamiliar, but because they do not fit into his general concept of what is acceptable, legitimate, and approved.

Perhaps these findings fit with another condition that the individual brings to the situation—his expectations of what goes together. By the learning processes discussed in Chapter 1 we have developed the concept that the whine of a siren is often followed by an ambulance or police car, or the façade of a road side tavern signals a bar inside. We would be surprised if the sound of the siren were followed by a lumbering 20-ton trailer truck or the tavern lights advertised a place of worship. In much the same way, we expect hostility from an unfriendly-*looking* person and even more from a person who has previously been hostile. We assume with varying degrees of justification as a starting point that they are hostile; hence their actions are interpreted as direct or veiled hostilities. Any deviation from such a pattern is viewed with at least some suspicion.

It may be remembered that in 1955, during a period of relative concord, the Soviets announced a reduction in the size of their standing army. This was in contrast to the previous behavior of the USSR. A few days after the announcement John Foster Dulles (United States Secretary of State) held a news conference in which he essentially discounted the move as contributing to the easing of tensions. In part he said: "The number of men

---

[5] Copyright (1954) by the University of Chicago.

under arms is only one element of a military strength. The Soviet Union also maintains very large organized reserves of men and equipment capable of being mobilized rapidly. The capacity to utilize modern weapons greatly affects the value of mere numbers in the armed forces" (*The New York Times*, 1955). All of this was obviously true, but the implication of the remarks was to play down any retrenchment or mellowing in the Soviet position. The action was interpreted within the frame of assumptions about the Soviets that they are in every instance bent upon strengthening their military position. A reduction in the standing army was therefore seen as no reduction in strength (Holsti, 1962).

Group Pressures on Perception.   Earlier in this chapter, a brief mention was made of the effect of group identification on the development of hostility and aggression. One's attachment to a group also influences the way in which he perceives his colleagues versus his opponents. By and large, "our" group, town, state, or nation is seen as a whole to be better than some other group, town, state, or nation. Each nationality has its own image of itself that rarely corresponds with the image held by outsiders. Yet each thinks of his own image as the "correct" one while discounting the perceptions of others as being in some respect distorted.

Our national self images are in part maintained by the histories we read. The accounts of the American Revolution as given in English history books may be read with a certain condescension by an American, but if he reads further and probes more deeply into the English view toward the American Colonies he may become exasperated at what are for him the obvious errors of interpretation. One writer put the issue eloquently as follows (Reves, 1946):

> The dramatic and strange events between the two world war could be just as well described from the point of view of any other nation, large or small. From Tokyo or Warsaw, from Riga or Rome, from Prague or Budapest, each picture will be entirely different, and from the fixed national point of observation, it will always be indisputably and unchallengeably correct. And the citizens of every country will be at all times convinced—and rightly so—of the infallibility of their views and the objectivity of their conclusions.

Written histories are partly the consequence of limited information about the perceptions of other peoples on the events being described. However, there is also a social psychology of the historian. If he wishes to write something that will be read and accepted by his audience he must respect the predispositions of that audience. "It is no exaggeration to say that the function of the historian is to pervert the truth in directions favorable to the images of his readers or hearers. Both history and geography as taught in national schools are devised to give 'perspective' rather than truth: that is to say they present the world as seen from the vantage point of the nation. The national geography is learned in great detail, and the rest of the world is in fuzzy outline; the national history is emphasized and exalted; the history of the rest of the world is neglected or even falsified to the glory of the national image" (Boulding, 1959). What might be thought of as the "natural" forces of group identification are consequently reinforced by the educational practices and material to which students are exposed.

This is not to say that national self-perceptions are fabricated out of pure imagination nor are they deliberately or maliciously contrived. *Some* objective factual data undergird them. Students of national images have as one problem to separate the objective fact from appearances. Because each of us is the product of his own culture and few persons are bi- or tricultural as some are bi- or trilingual, the task of freeing oneself from the biases of upbringing and group identification is exceedingly difficult.

Perhaps an illustration will make this clear. Mr. George F. Kennan, a distinguished diplomat and scholar of the USSR, made this observation (Kennan, 1958):

> From the time of their seizure of power, forty years ago, the Russian Communists have always been characterized by their extraordinary ability to cultivate falsehood as a deliberate weapon of policy. They began by adopting an attitude of complete cynicism about objective truth, denying its value if not its existence, declaring the lie to be no less useful and respectable than the truth if only it served the purposes of the party. Departing from this premise, they have systematically employed it not just as a means of deceiving others and exploiting their credulity, but also as a means of comforting and reassuring themselves. It has seemed to them at all times easier, and in no way improper, to operate a militant political movement on the basis of convenient falsehood than on the basis of awkward truth.

> I think we have to recognize today, particularly on the example of Khrushchev's recent statements and policies, that the effects of this systematic abuse of the human intellect are deep-seated and troublesome. Forty years of intellectual opportunism have wrought a strange corruption of the Communist mind, rendering it incapable of distinguishing sharply between fact and fiction in a single segment of its experience, namely in its relationship to any external competitive power. Let me stress that it is only in this one sector that the Communist mind is thus affected. In other respects, it is extremely shrewd and discerning.

The control of information, however, is not confined to the USSR, as was demonstrated in the outbursts of many newsmen during and after the Cuba crisis late in 1962. The Assistant Secretary of Defense, Mr. Arthur Sylvester, made it clear that the "management" of the news was one of the weapons essential to national security. However, Mr. Arthur Krock, distinguished *New York Times* correspondent, pointed out that "management" of the news was improper as a propaganda mechanism in behalf of the administration in office. He said: "I would make two general judg- ments on the management of the news by . . . the Administration as a whole: 1. A news management policy not only exists but, in the form of *direct and deliberate* action, has been enforced more cynically and boldly than by any previous Administration in a period when the U.S. was not in a war or without visible means of regression from the verge of war. 2. In the form of indirect but equally deliberate action, the policy has been much more effective than direct action in coloring the several facets of public information because it has been employed with subtlety and imagination . . ." (Krock, 1963).

What Mr. Kennan deplored among the Russian diplomats as "a de- liberate weapon of policy" is also employed by the United States in times of crisis. When Mr. Kennan reported that the Communist mind is in- capable of distinguishing between fact and fiction, was he not really projecting our own inability to discern when they are lying and when they are not? And is it any easier for the ordinary citizen in America to deter- mine the truth about his own country's foreign policy and intentions, armed, even as the Russians are not, with a free press? One of the great indoor games of political scientists is to uncover the basic objectives of foreign policies as suggested, but not explicitly revealed, by the various public statements and actual moves.

The Mirror-Image Hypothesis.   We have tried to demonstrate so far that national preceptions of self and others are often distorted. We have indi- cated that such distortions come from one's group identification, supported by nationalistic interpretations of history that are based on stimulus inputs which are ambiguous or even contradictory. Some of the underlying psy- chological forces that help us to understand why these distortions occur include the need to reduce our internal tensions, which arise if we permit ourselves to admit that the opposition may have some merit or may really be like ourselves. To avoid this tension we may erect a perceptual defense that blocks off information contrary to our established perceptions. By accentuating the differences between self and others we justify our group identification and favorable view of our own position.

One final illustration of these mechanisms can be found in the ob- servations of Bronfenbrenner, a Russian-speaking American psychologist who, on repeated visits to the USSR, evolved what he called the mirror- image hypothesis. As he talked informally with Russians in all walks of life, he concluded that by and large, the Russians believe the USA is war-mongering, bent on imposing its system of life on the entire world, including the USSR. They point to American intervention in Russia in 1918, the encirclement of Russia with military bases since the Second World War, the intransigence in Berlin, American interventions in Korea, Cuba, Guatemala, Vietnam, and the offshore islands between Taiwan and mainland China. The U–2 incident they see as a clear case of invasion of their airspace, attempting to force an inspection system over their territory while rejecting their disarmament proposals. They say Americans want to spy, not to disarm. The massive military aid of the United States to underdeveloped countries is, in their view, prima-facia evidence that Americans wish to conquer and control the world by military means.

The American view of the Soviets is almost a mirror duplicate. They say the Soviets are the warmongers. Did they not take over Czechoslovakia, Hungary? Have they not established military governments in East Germany and more generally in all the satellite countries? Did not Mr. Khrushchev boast that he would bury America? Disarmament without inspection is only a device to delude Americans into a position of weakness. To communize the world is the announced objective of the Marxist–Lenin doctrine.

The United States citizen sees the Russian people (as distinct from their rulers) as being duped by their controlled press, prevented from knowing the fruits of the free enterprise system, and uninformed about the machinations of their own government. It is the dictatorial elite that subjugates the masses and controls their thinking. The State is not only the owner but also the high priest. Communism is a religion as well as a political philosophy.

Russian citizens see Americans as reasonably honest people, but controlled (in their view) by a wealthy minority who dictate to the press, operate the politics, control the labor unions, and obviously manage the economy for their greater private profit. They point to the Kennedy, Rockefeller, Morgan, Harriman, and similar families, who are powerful in both political and business affairs. American magazines and newspapers (they say) print only what the advertisers approve, and radio–TV companies broadcast only noncontroversial matters. The appearance of freedom in these mass media is a subtle façade behind which lurks the hand of the government and business. The Soviet people *know* their press is controlled; Americans *think* theirs is not. Americans are therefore the dupes.

The mirror images could be extended to other areas, but enough has been presented to make the point.

There is some supporting evidence for both views; there are also selective factors at work among both the Russians and Americans that obscure the evidence that would at least soften the harshness of the images. The proverbial man from Mars might find neither opponent holding an accurate perception of the other, but instead might discover that a fair appraisal of each lies somewhere between what one believes of himself and what the opposition perceives.

Emotions and Perceptions. Carried beyond some optimal point, increases in the emotional level tend to distort perceptions and restrict one's awareness of alternatives. Up to that point emotional excitement may serve to sensitize the individual to matters he would otherwise ignore. One can be both too lethargic and too excited to assess realistically and accurately the situation in which he finds himself. Postman and Bruner (1948) have shown that under stress an individual confronted with a shifting, ambiguous, or otherwise difficult perceptual task becomes reckless in the meanings he assigns to the situation. Much of the systematic exploration that characterizes the unstressed person in the same situation is short-circuited and responses are triggered off as soon as the stressed person has a minimum of material with which to work.

We find the same phenomena occurring at the national level, although we have less systematic evidence than Postman and Bruner present. There can be no doubt that the Cuban missile crisis of 1962 was a stressful period. Although a full and authentic account of the alternatives considered at that time has not been published, the principal responses considered by the United States appear to have been limited to military actions. At least one opportunity was not seized for dealing with the crisis on the diplomatic level prior to President Kennedy's announcement of the quarantine. Emotional tensions that restrict one's tendency to explore a wide variety of alternatives often crescendo in periods of crisis, when time is a major factor, further restricting the possibility of examining alternatives.

Given this emotional effect on perceptions (sometimes called *tunnel* perception), given also the ethnocentric tendencies to enhance one's view of his own group and degrade the opposition, the net effect in times of major emotional confrontations comes close to being a paranoid pattern of thinking. This kind of thinking first ascribes to others evil designs and plots aimed at destroying the paranoid thinker. The paranoid, operating with some narrow factual basis for his fears, believes he is threatened because he possesses something others covet; his wealth, some mysterious invention, some special prowess. By and large, such a person's beliefs and actions are guided by what he conceives as *possible* attacks on himself rather than the more difficult assessment of what is *probable*. He tends to

(1) exaggerate his own worth, (2) believe that he is vulnerable, and (3) see the surrounding world as hostile. On these three scores, there exists in fact a modicum of truth. But because his perceptions are restricted he tends to ignore the contrary evidence and is unable to estimate the probability that someone may attack him at the precise point where he is vulnerable. What is possible becomes for the frightened person a virtual certainty.

In some quarters the current view of the USSR takes on this color. It is possible that Russian leaders wish to destroy the United States. It is possible that coexistence is a ruse to deceive Americans into lowering their guard. It is possible that the periodic stalling in various negotiations is a deliberate means to wear out patience and force concessions. As long as there is a tunnel perception of the Russians as evil, unscrupulous, cunning, and deceptive, these possibilities are not likely to be cast into probabilities along with other interpretations less threatening. Obviously Americans possess a standard of living envied by others; a position of power and influence challenged mainly by the USSR; a way of life and political system more congenial to Americans than the Russian way. But do Americans really know how strongly either the average Russian or the Russian leaders covet these possessions? Part of the American's perception of the Russian threat may stem from the high values placed on these things, believing that the Russians would want them also.

The influence of high emotion on perceptions not only of the *nature* of the situation but the appropriate *means* for dealing with a situation is restrictive. Heightened emotions also foreshorten one's objectives. Immediate, short-range goals become salient, and long-range objectives assume less relevance. When the USSR sent into orbit the first Sputnik, the United States panicked into a series of premature attempts to duplicate the Russian accomplishment. Under the pressure of public opinion attention was focused on the short-range goal of matching a competitor's performance rather than maintaining an orderly program of development. Under the pressures of the cold war the same sort of foreshortening seems to characterize United States' public reaction to Cuba, the Berlin situation, and other political problems. At the current writing, there is a clamor for the elimination of the Castro regime but virtually no concern for what might follow Castro. The Yalta conference held in February 1945—three months before the surrender of Germany—raised the question of the future of Germany, which was then clearly in retreat and on the verge of surrender. However, Stalin, Roosevelt, and Churchill essentially agreed to wait until after the surrender to decide how Germany was to be ruled, sectioned, and what zones would be assigned to the respective allies. The largest bulk of this conference dealt with short-range military issues (U.S. Dept. of Defense, 1955).

Emotions pitched at a high level consequently encourage a restriction of perceptions, a tendency toward selectively perceiving those elements in the situation that are threatening, a tendency to emphasize the possible rather than assess the probable, and a foreshortening of time perspective.

SOME MEANS OF REDUCING TENSIONS AND IMPROVING TRANSCULTURAL RELATIONS

If we have diagnosed the tension-creating conditions correctly, we should be in a position to recommend corrective measures. It is unrealistic, even if it were desirable, to expect that all international disagreements could be eliminated. We cannot hope that the "lion will lie down with the lamb." But we can expect that the destructiveness of conflict can be sharply reduced. How may we proceed?

Recognition of Perceptual Distortions. First of all, recognizing that perceptions of one's self and opponents are influenced by the conditions just described has a salutary effect. We begin to see evidences of our own distorted views and search more vigorously for valid data, both confirming and disconfirming. We tend to adopt a more tentative attitude toward the opposition and ourselves accept the probability that the responsibilities for discord are often distributed among the parties and not wholly confined to one. If one accepts the possibility that his own judgments may be in error and that another's viewpoint may be more accurate, a climate is established for a mutual search for the elusive truth. This is a very painful process. Emerson made the observation: "God offers to every mind its choice between truth and repose. Take which you please—you can never have both. Between these, as a pendulum, man oscillates ever. He in whom the love of repose predominates will accept the first creed, the first philosophy, the first political party he meets,—most likely his father's. He gets rest, commodity, and reputation but he shuts the door of truth. He in whom the love of truth predominates, will keep himself aloof from all moorings and afloat. He will abstain from dogmatism and recognize all the opposite negations between which, as walls, his being is swung. He submits to the inconvenience of suspense and imperfect opinion, but he is a candidate for truth, as the other is not, and respects the highest law of his being" (Emerson, 1889).

In this quotation we find a recognition of long standing, that dogmatism is easier than doubt, or to put the same thought in more facetious terms, anyone who is not confused by international problems does not understand them.

Development of Superordinate Goals. As people and nations begin to recognize the possibility that their own perceptions may be colored, it becomes easier to believe that one's competitor may have objectives commensurate with one's own. Reference was made earlier to the study by Sherif, in which groups of boys in a summer camp developed from a condition of friendliness to one of mutual hostility after being placed in direct competition. A third phase of that study carried the boys through a period of reconciliation by placing both groups under a requirement to solve a series of problems transcending their private interests. For instance, the water supply of the camp suddenly dried up. (The main supply pipe was deliberately blocked surreptiously by one of the experimenters.) Both groups attacked the problem cooperatively to find the cause and correct it. The significant psychological effect was the reduction of intergroup hostilities that paved the way for additional collaboration on other superordinate goals—goals whose achievement are important to both conflicting groups but which are best accomplished by united efforts.

At the present writing, an agreement in principle has been reached between the USA and USSR to collaborate in a system of weather satellites, making possible world-wide long-range weather forecasting for use in agriculture, shipping, and other areas. The 1957–58 International Geophysical Year, in which a number of countries collaborated in simultaneous observations, served as a trial run on scientific collaboration. Furthermore, the existing international agreement on the study of Antarctica is another example where superordinate goals are working for the mutual benefit of the participants. For such goals to be effective in significantly reducing hostilities, their means of accomplishment and the results attained must redound unambiguously to the benefit of all collaborators. The International Geophysical Year, although of value to scientists, had no obvious benefit to the general public, and the same may be said of the agreement on Antarctica. Hence, although these represent moves toward reduction of international tensions, their effectiveness at the level of the man on the street has been infinitesimal. It is possible that lifting the burden of armament productions, thus releasing economic resources for more direct utilitarian ends, might become a superordinate goal that would hasten not only the process of disarmament but would simultaneously reduce tensions—provided the details of the agreement are such as to minimize mutual suspicions and preserve national security.

A commitment to some goal shared by another group or nation whose attainment requires the collaboration of both parties serves to promote interchanges and negotiations of a noncompetitive kind. Each party may come to accept the help of the other and recognize a mutual dependence. This in fact happened during the Second World War, when the USSR and the Allies joined forces in the defeat of the Axis Powers. When that goal was attained and no substitute goal of comparable salience developed, the coalition fell apart. This historical event suggests that one of the conditions essential for the commitment to superordinate goals is some common need of major proportions impinging on the otherwise competitive groups. This does not mean that the need must arise from threat, although threat to one's existence or survival is clearly a powerful source of need. Neither the USA nor the USSR since the Second World War has so far found a common need of sufficient potency to overshadow their differences. (Perhaps Red China will provide such a need.)

It has been suggested that preliminary to the commitment to superordinate goals, groups in discord might engage in what has been termed *intergroup therapy* (Blake, 1959). This procedure requires that representatives meet to exchange the perceptions that each has of the other and of themselves, the effort being to communicate as accurately and clearly as possible for no other purpose than to clarify both sets of views. As far as possible, the full membership of both groups witnesses this exchange of perceptions. A caucus of the separate groups is then held to develop an understanding of the evident discrepancies in perceptions and to devise appropriate means for reducing these discrepancies. Finally the representatives again meet to help each other correct their invalid perceptions and to consider alternative explanations of their past behavior.

This approach has been relatively unexplored except in small groups but holds some promise as a model for experimentation in situations where more is at stake and the issues are more stubborn. It represents, however, a social invention that might eventually prove useful in a situation that calls for new approaches to important issues.

The Exchange of Persons.   The USA and USSR have engaged for some years in a cultural and educational exchange, bringing to each country artists, teachers, and students from the other country. How effective has this effort been in modifying perception?

Although the number of studies is not large, two general conclusions seem to be repeatedly supported. First, any modification of views about the host country depends in part upon the previous views of the visitor. Persons who visit a foreign country with initial views of a negative sort leave that country more firmly 'convinced of their initial position. But visitors who have initial favorable views of the host country are more favorable when they leave. A study by Kelman and Bailyn (1962) indicated also that changes may occur in the perception of *one's own country* as a consequence of foreign travel. The direction of change was again partly dependent upon initial predispositions and in this case, partly related to a variety of influences, including the area of the United States visited, age, and the kind of living arrangements they experienced. In other words, some people experience a "leveling" between their own and host countries, and others see the contrasts more sharply.

A second general conclusion runs as follows: Those persons who have experienced some "leveling" find themselves in uncomfortable positions when they return home because the prevailing norms of their native groups do not support the newfound perceptions. This is a familiar principle of attitude formation, which states that the individual is strongly influenced to express those views congruent with those of the group in which the individual maintains his primary relationships. Consequently, unless social support is provided for the modified views of returning foreign visitors, the changes in perceptions will not long persist.

Reciprocal Tension Reduction.   The proposal has been made but not sufficiently tested that it may be possible to reduce tensions gradually between nations by a series of planned moves. The idea is to reverse the process, whereby a threatening move by one party provokes a counter-threatening move by the others. Osgood (1962), who has developed the notion, starts with the assumption that negotiations as currently practiced too often fail to lower the tension level; and consequently, unilateral steps are indicated. The downward escalation of tension could be started by one party announcing that it intends to make a move, such as the withdrawal of a token force from Berlin, as a means of reducing tension and at the same time is ready to make other similar moves as soon as the opposition takes a comparable unequivocal step. Such a program leaves control in the hands of each side to determine whether the opposition's move is in fact equivalent to its own. Although some risk might be involved in taking the first step or any subsequent moves, the amount of risk can be controlled by the magnitude of the steps taken. If either side finds the opposition's moves inadequate or of suspicious validity, the subsequent announcement would make this clear to the world and also indicate that because of this impression we (or they) are taking only half a step. Either side can stop the process when it appears that the opposition has not fulfilled its part of the bargain.

Some objections have been raised to the idea on the ground that a tension-reducing move by one party may be accompanied clandestinely by a compensating move somewhere else. For instance, a withdrawal of a token force from Berlin might be accompanied by an economic offensive on one of the neutral nations. Or the closing of missile bases in Turkey might be accomplished at the same time rocket-bearing submarines are added in the Mediterranean. Osgood's idea would require massive intelligence information that would culminate in a global assessment of the tension level in various areas and its various sources. Basically this objection says that the reduction of tensions in one segment of international relations, even if reciprocated, may be neutralized if aggressive moves occur in another segment, especially if the latter are clandestine or subtle.

Another objection is that we have no evidence that the system would in fact work as described. A tension-reducing move if announced in advance might be interpreted by the opposition as weakness and encourage them toward preparations to exploit the "retreat." This might be particularly true after a series of backward steps, leaving one side vulnerable to a lightning strike prepared in secret. Again, the chief means of insuring against such an eventuality is by comprehensive intelligence or some neutral inspection.

In spite of these objections it is worth noting that tension building is a unilateral secretive process in which each party is responding to his perceptions of what the other is doing, based partly upon intelligence reports. On psychological grounds there is reason to believe the process can be reversed, provided adequate safeguards of a political and informational nature are developed.

Simulation of International Relations. At the research level some work is currently developing in applying simulation techniques to the issues of international relations. Simulation is a means of representing the central and critical features of some real-life system of relationships within the confines of a laboratory. Guetzkow (1962) has evolved an international simulation (sometimes called a game) in which three decision makers represent a nation interacting with other similar teams of decision makers. Each team is provided with certain basic rules of operation and are under the requirement that they must satisfy their "constituents" or lose office. Each nation has its individual objectives spelled out in instructions—domination, security, internal growth, and so on. The probability that they will remain in office is determined periodically by formulas developed in advance to reflect the extent that their decisions in concert with the decisions of other teams lead to their objectives. In addition to national goals, and rules of procedure and office holding, each nation is provided with an inventory of resources. Generally the interaction between "nations" takes place through a conference of "external decision makers" or on a bilateral level in which treaties are made, war is declared, alliances developed, and so on. This is but a thumbnail sketch of the arrangements.

The above account may seem no more than a complicated parlor game, but in fact it provides a setting in which a variety of experiments may be carried on in progressively more complex environments. For instance Osgood's graduated tension-reduction procedures might be subjected to examination under a variety of national goal patterns held by nations having differing levels of military and economic resources. Furthermore, it is feasible to have the national teams composed of persons of different national backgrounds behaving as a Greek, Russian, Japanese, and so on. In other words simulation provides an opportunity to test out the usefulness of certain proposals, but more importantly it may provide those observational data that form the basis for conceptualizing the conditions and forces determining the outcome of international intercourse. Although there is a growing body of reports on the theory of simulation itself as a research tool (business games, war games, aircraft simulators) these procedures are still in their infancy but hold great promise as they develop. (Simulation used for training is discussed in Chapter 7 of this book.)

SUMMARY

This chapter has been a brief introduction to the complex but significant issues of international relations to which the psychologist may contribute some understanding. Before a political, military, economic, or other type of decision is reached on matters of international import, some appraisal of the situation is required. In governmental parlance this is called intelligence—itself a psychological term meaning "information" rather than the capacity for problem solving. The meaning, significance, and interpretation of the information is the culmination of perceiving. This chapter has described some of the sources of perceptual distortion, particularly in ambiguous-stimulus situations that characterize international issues. We also reviewed the conditions giving rise to aggressive tendencies—frustration, competitiveness, differing value systems, strategic needs. Finally some tentative suggestions were offered as ways of reducing tensions and of researching some of the problems on a psychological level.

SUGGESTED REFERENCES FOR FURTHER STUDY

Berkowitz, L. (1962). *Aggression: A Social Psychological Analysis*. New York: McGraw-Hill Book Company.

An exhaustive and scholarly review of the psychological literature, significant for anyone who wishes to define researchable problems in the field.

Guetzkow, H. (1962). *Simulation in Social Science: Readings*. Englewood Cliffs, N.J.: Prentice-Hall.

A collection of essays describing a research method that holds promise of straining out significant variables bearing on intergroup relations and negotiations. Some articles are highly technical.

Hall, E. T. (1961). *The Silent Language*. Greenwich, Conn.: Fawcett Publications.

A highly readable theoretical treatment of comparative social anthropology, with numerous fascinating examples of unintended conflicts between cultures.

Kelman, H. C. (ed.) (1965). *International Behavior: A Social-Psychological Analysis*. New York: Holt, Rinehart & Winston.

Articles written especially for the volume by social psychologists dealing with national and cross-national images as well as the effects of actions across national boundaries. The book is research oriented and a fine bibliographical resource.

Kennan, G. F. (1958). *Russia, the Atom and the West*. New York: Harper & Row.

A collection of radio broadcasts by an experienced career diplomat and historian of note. These speeches are especially useful to the psychologist as data from which one may infer psychological assumptions held by a representative of our government who has dealt with the Russians in various high-level capacities.

Klineberg, O. (1964). *The Human Dimension in International Relations*. New York: Holt, Rinehart & Winston.

A sound treatment of the subject written for the non specialist by an author of international experience and renown. Recommended as an over view of psychological aspects of international relations.

Chapter 14
Negotiation

DISPUTES, THAT IN AN EARLIER AGE were settled on a "field of honor" by force of arms, are now often the focus for negotiations. Even though civilization has passed from individual barbarism to unprecedented mass annihilation, nonviolent negotiations often precede the call to arms. The strategies of negotiation, however, are far less understood and consequently less successful than the strategies of combat. Consider, for instance, the time, materiel, and the meticulous care devoted to training for military combat in contrast to the near absence of time spent in understanding, researching, or training in the arts of peacemaking. Armies engage in "exercises," but what diplomats engage in "practice" negotiations? Consider also that after one year of combat, the North Koreans were willing to begin armistice negotiations which required two years of talk to conclude while hostilities continued. It is clear that we knew how to wage that war more effectively than we knew how to stop it. The strange paradox is that we have paid so little systematic attention to the negotiation *process* and so much to the methods of combat, when the former is so obviously more desirable.

What is the psychological nature of the negotiating process? How is it possible to move from disagreement to cooperation? What conditions hinder and help the process? Is it possible to identify stages of progress from conflict to contract? What do we know about the "natural history" of the steps that lead from discord to agreement? Is there "a tide in the affairs of men which, taken at the flood leads on to fortune; omitted, is bound in shallows and in miseries"? The spectacles of extended and repeated negotiations between labor and management, between nations, between pressure groups who would, and those who would not, makes one wonder if

476

there is any system, any order, any formula that characterizes these periodic exacerbations of hostility which, in due course, eventually subside.

It is the thesis of this chapter that the negotiation process can be understood rationally and that certain uniformities can be found in the process independent of the particular issues in dispute. Furthermore, the disputes between unions and managements bear many parallels to disputes between nations, although there are some important dissimilarities that uniquely complicate the latter. We shall therefore, in this chapter, deal with both kinds of negotiations as a strategy to illustrate the psychological concepts common to both.

A GENERALIZED CONCEPT OF THE NEGOTIATION SETTING

McGrath and Julian (1962) proposed that the ultimate outcome of any

Figure 14.1. The Security Council of the United Nations graphically illustrates that behind each nation's spokesman resides not merely expert specialists but a constituency that constrains his personal choices and negotiating moves. (Black Star Photo.)

negotiation depends upon three sets of conditions: (1) the factors operating on the individual negotiators, including partisan forces, strains toward agreement, capacities for creative, and constructive solutions; (2) influences of a neutral moderator (if one is present), including his moderator skills and tactics; (3) the task and situational factors, including the ground rules of the relationship, the interpersonal relations between the parties, the relative power of one party to inflict punishment on or grant rewards to the other, and the complexities of the topic itself. Let us consider each of these three sets of conditions separately.

Factors Operating on the Individual Negotiators. Typically the negotiator is a representative of some constituency whose position he is obliged to present and under whose instructions he must operate. The union spokesman is aware of his membership's commitment to certain positions and must convey the sense of earnestness the members feel, even though he may personally differ with the membership. There is always a possibility of a role conflict between what the negotiator might wish to do and what he is permitted to do either by formal instructions or informal pressures. During the protracted negotiations for an armistice in Korea between 1951 and 1953, this kind of role conflict was a constant source of concern for the United Nations' negotiators. They wished, as reported by Admiral Joy, Senior Delegate and chief negotiator for the UN forces (Joy, 1955), either to hold to certain proposals or to exert certain kinds of pressures on the North Koreans that were not approved by the strategists in Washington. The general tone of Admiral Joy's account of the outcome is one of dissatisfaction. The discrepancy between what the delegates wanted to do and what they were told to do may have accounted in part for their dissatisfaction with the final document. The simple historical fact is that no outbreak of hostilities has occurred since the armistice between North and South Korea, so in this sense the negotiations accomplished their ends. In any event, the conflict between the negotiator and the nations he represented was clearly evident.

McGrath and Julian proposed that a force exists in each negotiator in the direction of gaining an agreement but this is opposite in direction to a force to hold to the initial position taken by the constituents. That is, if a genuine issue exists between the two parties, each is hopeful that his own stand will prevail, but an agreement may not be possible unless one or both parties modify their respective positions.

Both in labor–management negotiations and international disputes, the loyalty of the negotiator to his constituency is usually high, resulting in a very strong tendency to maintain the group's announced position. In other situations, as, for instance, in the case of a lawyer representing a client group, or a delegate from a campus group to a college-wide board, the degree of identification with the constituency may be weaker, resulting in a greater net force toward agreement or a compromise on a *quid pro quo* basis.

A third force may exist in negotiation. This is a force in the direction of some creative, new solution of which neither party has previously thought, which may resolve an impass. This third force does *not* represent merely a compromise between the positions of the contending parties, but instead is orthogonal to the first two forces, one tending toward simple compromise or win–lose, and the other tending toward maintenance of the constituent's initial position. We need to recognize that within the negotiation process it is possible to find agreement at a level of generality either higher or lower than the issues originally presented. This can be illustrated from the disarmament negotiations between the USA and USSR. Although at this writing negotiations have not resulted in a specific plan for disarming, a set of eight principles was accepted in 1961 as the framework for negotiations. To illustrate the level of generality, the first of these principles follows: "The goal of negotiations is to achieve agreement on a program which will ensure that (a) disarmament is general and complete and war is no longer an instrument for settling international problems, and (b) such disarmament is accompanied by the establishment of reliable procedures for the peaceful settlement of disputes and effective arrangements for the maintenance of peace in accordance with the principles of the United Nations Charter" (U.S. Dept. of State, 1961). This and the remaining seven principles represent a level of agreement that evolved out of earlier unsuccessful attempts to be more concrete. They are not compromises in the sense that a border dispute might be settled by halving the difference between two claims.

Not only is it important to recognize that the force toward creative solutions resides primarily in the negotiators, but the need for resolving the disagreement contributes to the possibilities of such a solution. The stronger these needs are, the greater is the possibility of agreement that may in the final form be a combination of compromise and emergent resolutions. It has been suggested that the reason the USSR rather suddenly concluded a peace treaty with Austria and the Western Allies in 1953 was because such an agreement was an aid in releasing troops for use in Eastern Germany. As this instance illustrates, the pressure for agreement may reside in one or another of the negotiating parties, or it may be part of the climate surrounding the total situation. Reasoning from this premise, one might conclude that one possible factor accounting for the failure of disarmament negotiations or any other protracted domestic or international problem is the absence of sufficiently compelling forces requiring a solution. This merely means that a protracted period of disagreement accompanied by efforts to negotiate, however unsuccessful, is preferable in the view of both parties to a compromise settlement or a clear victory for one party. One can see this principle operating in labor strikes. An effort is made to mitigate the usual discomforts of the negotiation period by benefits paid to the strikers, by periodic mass meetings, or even by the free time to engage in some recreation. In the case of Korea or Berlin, the stalemate was preferable to any of the proposed settlements.

The Neutral Moderator. A neutral moderator may be available and involved in intranational issues and to some lesser extent in international disputes. At the latter level the neutral moderator has been useful in negotiations between small powers or between major nations when the issues were not of crucial significance. Unless one conceives of the Secretary General, United Nations, and his assistants as neutral moderators, no one, or no agency is available to perform this function on issues of the highest importance separating the major nations. The absence of an acceptable moderator may partly account for the prolonged discussion over disarmament. What are the useful functions such a moderator may perform, and what conditions influence his effectiveness? In what follows we shall be thinking primarily of intranational disputes, such as labor–management negotiations, although the principles probably apply to international moderators as well.

The moderator represents to some extent those aspects of the social situation within which the issues at dispute are embedded. That is to say, a labor–management negotiation takes place within a community of interests and values which will be affected in some degree by the outcome of the negotiations. The moderator, either by implication or by official appointment, represents such matters as the sense of justice, the broad permissible boundaries of settlement, or the pressure for urgency in the solution. He is primarily a force toward agreement, without the entangling allegiance to a prior position prepared by his constituency. His neutrality is not with respect to procedures or concepts of fair play or what is socially acceptable. Instead, his neutrality pertains to any particular substantive settlement.

Quite clearly the success of a moderator depends upon the way in which he is perceived by the principal negotiators. If one or the other of the contending parties believes the moderator is not neutral but is either covertly or overtly favoring the opposition, the moderator's force toward a settlement is perceived as an ally of the opposition. Furthermore, if he gives the appearance of siding now with one party and later with the other, he runs the risk of generating suspicions in both and losing his value as the "conscience" of the larger social system. This is obviously a difficult tightrope to walk.

The legitimacy of the moderator is a condition established prior to negotiations themselves. How did the moderator get into this position? On some occasions a complicated procedure is established whereby the two contending parties select representatives to pick a third person to be the moderator. This ritual is a method for establishing, not just the neutrality of the moderator, but his legitimacy to perform the functions conferred on him by the parties. Self-appointed moderators are sometimes less successful than those selected, no matter in how complicated a manner, by the contestants themselves. However, one must not confuse the self-appointed moderators with those mediators employed by state or federal agencies to assist, on call, in the settlement of labor–management disputes.

The tactics and procedures employed by the moderator no doubt have important consequences for the success of negotiations. It is possible to list these tactics, as McGrath and Julian have, but it is not possible on the basis of systematic empirical evidence to specify the relative importance of each or the manner in which each affects the negotiation process. This is a task for future research.

McGrath and Julian suggest the following aspects of the moderator's behavior as important (McGrath and Julian, 1962):

(1) The degree to which he attempts to exercise control of the group process and of the content of group interaction, and the extent to which he is successful in such attempts.

(2) The degree of formality or "psychological distance," and the degree of professionalism which he exhibits, in his interaction with group members.

(3) The degree to which he guides the group in a search for bases of agreement, for common ground.

(4) The degree to which he guides the group to explicitly establish their point-to-point differences.

(5) The degree to which he uses the "chair" to prevent or attenuate direct clashes, especially those with an *ad hominum* basis.

Factors in the Task. In addition to the forces residing in the contending parties and the moderator, a number of conditions exist in the task itself which affect the progress and ultimate outcome of negotiations. The first of these is the definition of the issues. In both international and domestic disputes numerous recorded instances show that the contending parties required a long time to discover just where they disagreed! In the New

York City newspaper strike of 1962–63 the printers insisted after 75 days of striking that the issues were A, B, and C. The publishers declared at the same time that on issue A they were in agreement with the printers, whereas B and C were aspects of a fourth issue D! In the Korean armistice negotiations this problem appeared at the outset. The Communists formally proposed as the first two items for discussion (a) establishment of the 38th parallel as the military demarcation line between both sides and establishment of a demilitarized zone, and (b) withdrawal of all armed forces of foreign countries from Korea. The United Nations command at the same time proposed to discuss (a) the location and boundaries of the demilitarized zone across Korea, and (b) the conditions that would ensure against the resumption of hostilities in Korea. Notice that the United Nations topics were more general, leaving open for the negotiation process the possibility of arriving at a specific solution. The Communists, however, wished to discuss the particular solutions before agreeing to some generalized objective (Joy, 1955). This difference may reflect a cultural difference of the same sort that was noticed in the Greeks and mentioned on page 457. Admiral Joy contended, for instance, that only after the armistice was signed and hostilities ceased could the matter of withdrawal of troops be considered. The North Koreans insisted that the withdrawal of troops was a condition of the armistice and had to be accepted rather than some other means of preventing future hostilities. The negotiators were talking at different levels of generality. Ten plenary sessions were required to agree on what to discuss!

The Openness of Negotiation. Woodrow Wilson is credited with the principle of "open covenants, openly arrived at." He was reacting against secret treaties, which had plagued international relations for many decades. However, some danger adheres to advertising one's position to the general public during the course of negotiations. To do so commits the negotiator to a tentative stand from which he cannot retreat without appearing publicly to be weak or vacillating or having taken an untenable initial position. The glare of publicity also tends to inhibit the tentative probings that in subtle and disguised ways say, "If we concede point A, will you concede point B?" In negotiating issues of a semipublic nature, whether at the international or intranational level, the initial positions of the contestants are generally made public, but it is in the process of negotiations themselves, where the public audience is apt to be a hindrance rather than a help. Hence the second condition of the negotiating situation is its degree of publicness.

Douglas, in commenting primarily about labor–management negotiations, expressed the problem this way: "It could be said that the second phase is brought on by the fact that inevitably each side has to pull back from this public show of strength in order (1) to form some estimate of the *real* strength of the other—how far *can* the opponent be safely pushed for concessions before it will turn from negotiating to force a showdown—and (2) to decide how long and how far to continue pressing its own claims—when would it become institutional suicide to get caught in a showdown with the opponent? In other words, it eventually becomes incumbent on each party to begin moving, or to assume a posture conducive to moving toward a modified position which bears some relation to the position assumed by the other side" (Douglas, 1962). If one's public is looking over the shoulder of the negotiators at this stage, such jockeying can be inhibited and be more disturbing than the kibitzer in a bridge game.

Knowledge of Opposing Position. The third condition of the situation affecting the task is the knowledge each party has of the opposition's position on the issue at hand.

Libo (1949) showed that union members attributed to the managements with which they were negotiating positions on bargaining issues that were not the positions the managements actually held. Similarly management's perceptions of the union's positions were also inaccurate. Comparable findings came to light in a study of two neighborhood groups, one organized to build a community fallout shelter and the other brought together as advocates of a "positive" program for peace opposing fallout shelters (Ekman, Cohen, Moos, Raine, Schlesinger, and Stone, 1963). Although on some questions each group accurately judged the position of the other, they were both inaccurate on many more issues in estimating what the other believed, sometimes exaggerating the differences between themselves and the opposition, sometimes underestimating the differences. Both studies give some support to the hypothesis that the issues on which opposing groups are most inaccurate in judging the position of the opposition are those about which there is the greatest sub-rosa hostility. Consequently the opposing sides in a tense negotiation may actually in some instances be fighting false issues and unnecessarily complicating the process. On the other hand, the conventional assumption that both parties generally take into a negotiation session is that it is imprudent to reveal what one really wants or is willing to settle for. In some instances this assumption appears to mitigate against an easy settlement.

Negotiator's Freedom and Authority.   A fourth general condition affecting the outcome is the authority of the negotiators to commit their respective constituents to some agreement. One of the most glaring instances of this was the failure of the United States Senate to ratify the Versailles Treaty, negotiated by President Wilson following the First World War. No matter how much official authority the negotiator possesses, he must always be aware that the settlement must be acceptable to the group he represents. If he is sensitive to those figuratively sitting behind him at the conference table, his concessions and bargaining and tactical moves will be constrained by these unseen influences. When the negotiator's own private beliefs and values are coordinate with those of his constituents, his feeling of constraint from this source is minimal. He can act on his own judgment, with the confident feeling that whatever bargain he makes will be acceptable to those whom he represents. Without this authority of consent the negotiator will find himself not only in a conflict with his counterpart in the negotiation, but also with his constituency. It is therefore helpful if the negotiator is vested with a large amount of authority to conclude agreements and carry the negotiations to a final resolution. Douglas (1962) puts it this way: "In the field one often hears plaintive comments by practitioners that too few of the top echelon in organizations are aware of the impotence which overtakes a conference when negotiators are deprived of the freedom they require if they are to carry out the psychological functions which are integral to [the process]."

At least so far as the United States is concerned, this ideal is not politically feasible on matters of the highest importance to the nation. However, from time to time the President has been given authority, for example, to conclude trade and tariff treaties within certain boundaries and limitations.

We can summarize this section by saying that the negotiation setting involves considerations pertaining to the negotiators, the mediator, and the task or situational factors. The interplay of these separate sources of data is exceedingly complex, and the way in which they mix to produce the final outcome is far from understood. However, given time, care, and penetrating research it is not beyond the realm of possibility that we may be able to discover the formulas that make explicit the interconnections between them.

Let us turn next to a description of the negotiation process as it unfolds over time; first under circumstances where the negotiators are at least unfriendly or even hostile, and second when the parties to the controversy approach the bargaining table with honest differences but some mutual respect if not warm friendship.

NEGOTIATIONS WITH AN ANTAGONIST

Instances of this sort fill the pages of history. One can find union–management examples in which each side conceives of the other as an implacable enemy. Factions (not necessarily political parties) within the body politic may disagree on issues so violently and stubbornly as to fall within this category. Surely on the international level the cold war between Russia and the United States, during which there have been numerous negotiations to find ways of avoiding a hot war, is a prime instance of antagonists attempting to find an area of agreement.

Tacit Agreements.   It has been suggested that even between antagonists it may be possible to reach a tacit agreement without negotiations of a formal sort (Schelling, 1957). For instance, during the Second World War both sides possessed poison gas and bacteriological weapons, but neither side used them. No agreement was ever formally developed to prohibit their use, yet each side refrained. One can surmise that if either antagonist had released poisonous gases or bacteria against the enemy the defenders would have immediately responded in kind. Although this may be thought of as an example of mutual deterrence, nevertheless, mutual deterrence itself, in simple terms, is a tacit agreement of the form "If you don't, I won't."

Tacit agreements characteristically pertain to actions that are unambiguously distinguishable from their alternatives. It would be extremely improbable that a tacit agreement could be developed to prevent *cruel* treatment to prisoners of war, simply because the dividing line between *cruel* and *disciplinary* is ambiguous. One of the significant side lights of the Second World War was the evident breaking of a tacit agreement not to kill prisoners of war. Such an agreement, it is true, is part of the Geneva Convention, but there remains today no effective means for enforcing compliance with the provisions of the Convention. The incident occurred in 1943 when the Germans advancing on Russia discovered the graves of thousands of Polish officers in the Katyn Forest who had evidently been murdered while prisoners of war by the retreating Russians. The hue and cry set up by the discovery signifies not only the importance attached to the tacit agreement but also emphasizes its essential acceptance by nations in violent disagreement on other issues. The psychological point is that the killing of prisoners of war is an act clearly distinguishable from other means of dealing with them, and it is about such unambiguous acts that tacit agreements may be reached. In the same way the release of any poisonous gas in the midst of combat would be an unambiguous act. Neither Russia nor the United States conducted nuclear tests between 1959 and 1961, not because a formal agreement had been negotiated nor because they were incapable of testing. It was merely a tacit agreement that the Russians finally broke, leading the United States to do the same, putting into effect the other side of a tacit agreement "If you do, I will too."

The significance of tacit agreements between antagonists lies in the basis they provide for future negotiated agreements. This may seem paradoxical in the face of the test-ban experience, for when the test moratorium became the subject of formal negotiations over a protracted period, the tacit agreement was broken and did not provide a solid base for establishing more explicitly the conditions of mutual agreement. These conferences were hung up on the subsidiary question of how to provide mutually acceptable guarantees of compliance with the test-ban.

Early Stages.   In the following discussion, drawing heavily upon the work of Harbison and Coleman (1951), the early stages of armed-truce negotiations are discussed. It was pointed out in the previous section that negotiating antagonists have difficulty in establishing an agenda of mutually defined issues. This is the first stage of armed-truce negotiations. The perceptual distortions characteristic of mutually hostile, competitive contestants described in the previous chapter bathe the initial contacts. These perceptions prevent each side from understanding clearly the legitimate needs of the opposition and distinguish these from the objectives of the opposition that may be inimical to the other's own vital interests. We have already referred, earlier in this chapter, to the difficulty of defining the negotiable issues.

However, even before the negotiators meet their antagonists, two kinds of predispositions militate against ultimate success. First, each side views the negotiations as a necessary evil that is likely to fail or succeed only at the cost of losing an advantage either side initially possesses. If the contestants are equally balanced in power, this expectation of failure is especially great. "*They* are intransigent, but we will not sacrifice our position to their demands!" The expectation that negotiations will probably fail is a particularly difficult psychological hurdle, especially after a stalemate has persisted for some time. The negotiator entering a bargaining session with this bias may unwittingly behave in such a manner as to make his expectation come true. This is sometimes called the self-fulfilling prophecy. That is to say, the negotiator does not expect his adversary to move and is not alert to any hints or symptoms foreshadowing points of agreement. His perceptions are narrowed to those evidences that confirm his initial belief, "We can't agree." With respect to his own initiatives, he may fail to restate his position with some modification, believing that it will do no good because "They don't want to reach an agreement." Predisposed to expect failure, the negotiator behaves unwittingly to make his expectation come true. This is in marked contrast, as we shall see later, to the predispositions of negotiators who represent allies.

A second predisposition complicates the movement toward agreement. This is the biased view of what constitutes an equitable resolution (Osgood, 1961). Some experimental evidence suggests that Side A perceives the point of equitable resolution to be such that it réquires Side B to move beyond the point that B perceives as equitable, and vice versa. This is, each side sees itself as willing to reach a fair compromise, but what is seen as fair to both sides by A, is seen as a disadvantage to B, by B. Thus the Russians are willing to tolerate inspection of their disarmament efforts *after* they have occurred, whereas the Americans wish to inspect during the disarming process. The Russians see the American's demands as unfair because they might presumably discover weaknesses that could be exploited during the disarming process. The Americans perceive their inspection demands as fair because each side would have equal opportunity to discover special weaknesses and strengths, and would assure compliance with the agreement. On the other hand, the Russian proposal seems to them eminently fair because neither side will discover any special weaknesses in the other during the disarming process, and both will have the right to inspect armaments retained at the end of the process. In the American view the Russian proposal is unacceptable because they have more military secrets than the United States.

One can see this principle in the following exchange between Admiral Joy of the United Nations Command and General Nam IL, representing the North Koreans, during an early session of the armistice negotiations in 1952 (Joy, 1955).

ADMIRAL JOY: From what you have said this morning it is clear that you don't want an armistice. All you want is a total cease fire so as to permit you to increase your military capability to the extent you desire and at will. Our idea of an armistice is a simple one: that neither side gain a military advantage over the other during the period of the armistice. This is the only basis upon which we can agree. It should be the only basis upon which you should agree if you were sincere in desiring an armistice. As military men, you should recognize that the United Nations Command cannot enter into an armistice with you which does not involve an understanding by both sides to refrain from attempting to gain a military advantage during the suspension of fighting.

GENERAL NAM IL: The question of the military facilities is an internal question, and is not a question to be discussed at the armistice conference. As to the observation question, too, you want to have a freedom of movement in observing in the rear of our side, but that is also an interference in the internal affairs of our side. Outside of the demilitarized zone agreed upon by both sides, you have no right to observe freely in the rear of our side. You said that we, too, could make observation in your rear, but we do not make any such demand and we are not accustomed to doing so. We hope you will clearly understand such stand of ours.

The fact is that inspection has different consequences in the two societies, and each judges these consequences in terms of his own needs for certainty and his own beliefs about the means for meeting those needs. The main point, however, is that the initial concepts each hold of a fair resolution are not identical.

The Middle Stages of Negotiation.   It is not clear whether the processes that lead to an accommodation of viewpoints is best conceived as (1) an exercise in logical persuasion, (2) an application of power and coercion, (3) an exploration of mutually advantageous concessions (*quid pro quo*), (4) a search for a middle-ground compromise, (5) a learning process to understand each side's genuine objectives vis-à-vis some issue, or (6) as a special case of attitude change involving emotional components. Each of these orientations implies quite different strategies in the interactions taking place between the negotiators. It is probably true that in most instances, negotiations between antagonists are characterized by the use of logical persuasion buttressed by power threats, although there may be elements of the other orientations. Serious confusions arise if a negotiator's objective is to change attitudes but uses power, threats, or coercion as his strategy. A host of studies testify to the inappropriateness of force as an effective instrument of attitude change.

The use of power and military action as a means of forcing concessions is well illustrated in the Korean armistice talks that, it will be remembered, took place over a two-year period while hostilities continued, although with somewhat reduced intensity. An initial truce meeting was held on July 10, 1951. After several weeks of fruitless talk the North Koreans began an offensive, and truce meetings were temporarily suspended. In September the United States Eighth Army, having resisted the North Koreans, counterattacked, forcing the North Koreans to a position farther north than they had been at the beginning of their own offensive. The North Koreans then asked to resume the negotiations. It is not possible in this space to recount more than a small segment of the verbal exchanges between the negotiators, but a reading of them shows a frequent appeal to logic and reason by both sides. For instance, in late September the record shows this exchange (Joy, 1955):

ADMIRAL JOY: Yesterday you stated: "Has it occurred to you, that according to your logic, should our army, acknowledged as mighty and superior by the whole world, stop fighting so that your troops will escape the fate of annihilation, are we not entitled to an even greater compensation and to propose a demarcation line and demilitarized zone to the neighborhood of the Naktong River?" Again today you mention your mighty and superior ground forces.

We do not now, nor have we ever disputed the great numerical preponderance of your ground forces. However, in view of your progress northward since February, we ridicule your use of the word "superior." We are quite willing to let the world judge that point.

We also recognize as self-evident the fact that the capabilities of these already numerically greater ground forces, available to you, will begin to increase the day an armistice goes into effect. These same capabilities will continue to materially increase each week the armistice is in effect. It is during this period when our air and naval forces must remain inactive that your ground troops could be rested and re-equipped without interference. They could be positioned at your leisure.

GENERAL NAM IL: We have repeatedly explained the military demarcation line and also the demilitarized zone. We clearly explained that the 38th Parallel should be fixed as the military demarcation line and troops of both sides should withdraw ten kilometers on each side and establish a zone of twenty kilometers as the demilitarized zone.

The 38th Parallel appears clearly on the map. The withdrawal of ten kilometers north and south of the 38th Parallel, that is so clear that one does not have to look it up on a map.

In my statement this morning, I have again made clear the content of our proposal and pointed out that your proposal is unacceptable.

You have deliberately maintained, in order to confuse people, that the military demarcation line and the demilitarized zone you proposed are based on the present battle line and that they are located in the general area of the battle line. You have also deliberately confused the military demarcation line, the southern boundary of the demilitarized zone and the present battle line.

In order to support your proposal of pushing the military demarcation line to the north of the 38th Parallel, deep into our positions, you have persistently emphasized the so-called superiority of your naval and air forces and that, therefore, you must be compensated on the ground.

Yet, today you have presented a new and strange argument that since our army is already superior at present, it will be more so after armistice and, therefore, you should be again compensated for reasons of security. In using these self-contradictory arguments in support of your proposal, do you not feel ridiculous?

In circumstances of the sort illustrated by the Korean armistice talks some theorists have elaborated a number of conditions that tend to make a threat credible to the opposition and thus force him to accept a particular proposal. For instance, if one can make it unquestionably clear that a certain proposal is a "last and final offer" the opposition has the alternative of not concluding the agreement with possible dire consequences triggered by the absence of agreement, or of capitulating. In effect the proposer at this point gives up his freedom of movement in negotiations and his freedom of action as well, leaving it to the opponent to determine whether the strike will take place, or the guns will fire, or the border will be crossed, or finally that the proposed settlement will be accepted.

Another forcing tactic which grows out of the delegate status of the negotiator is to make it clear that the negotiator could not, *even if he wished*, accede to the concessions demanded by the opposition. Sometimes union leaders develop a strong membership expectation for winning a given wage increase, going even to the extreme of suggesting that the negotiators themselves are incompetent unless they reach a certain target. This deliberately reduces their freedom of movement and confronts the management with a stronger opposition than would be the case otherwise. Something like this happened in the New York City newspaper strike of 1963. The union negotiator refused to compromise his demands and demonstrated his limited area of movement when the union rejected a settlement less favorable to themselves than they had been led to expect as possible.

Another possible tactic sometimes found helpful in the course of negotiations is to enlarge the number of people involved in the dispute (Schattschneider, 1960). It has been suggested, for instance, that the weaker of the two antagonists often appeals for support to others not initially concerned. Thus in labor–management issues one or the other side publicizes the dispute in newspaper advertisements or via other mass media. On a somewhat broader scale it has been noted that labor–management disputes were at one time largely private affairs between one union and one company. Especially since 1935 these have come under governmental purview and through this means have involved the public more broadly. In the political arena, disagreements between the executive and legislative branches are often "taken to the people." At the international level and particularly within the United Nations framework, there is a ceaseless wooing of allies on any major dispute. Efforts to enlarge the circle of involved parties lined up in support of the contending negotiators are perhaps means for forcing an agreement by the relative balance of power, rather than a tactic employable within the confines of the negotiating interactions themselves. A countertactic in this same vein is the effort by one party to exploit and widen any rift that may appear among the allies of the opposition. This becomes a means of weakening the power of the opponents.

Schelling (1957) summarized such power negotiations by saying:

"First, they clearly depend not only on incurring a commitment [to a given proportion] but on communicating it persuasively to the other party. Second, it is by no means easy to establish the commitment, nor is it entirely clear to either of the parties concerned just how strong the commitment is. Third, similar activity may be available to the parties on both sides. Fourth, the possibility of commitment, though perhaps available to both sides, is by no means equally available. Fifth, they all run the risk of establishing an immovable position that goes beyond the ability of the other to concede and thereby provoke the likelihood of stalemate or breakdown."

All of these tactics have demonstrated some usefulness in achieving agreements that are to some degree forced from a reluctant victim. None of these gambits change significantly the initial belief systems or attitudes of the party who feels at the end of the negotiations that he was overwhelmed by the power or threats that his opponent was able to exercise. Negotiations by appeals to power have produced agreements that often appear to be temporary truces subject to reconsideration when the power balance has changed. In a psychological sense they are not convincing, although they may be acceptable. A labor leader in the midst of negotiating a contract was asked, "If you get a $2.00 raise this year, what will you ask for next year?" The reply was emphatic and immediate: "Another $2.00!" Attitudes, beliefs, and concepts of what is a fair settlement are rarely modified by agreements reached by the exercise of power alone.

It becomes increasingly clear that negotiating strategies need to be invented that will set as their aim not merely the attainment of an agreement, although this is obviously a minimum objective. The strategies that are needed are those which will result in a change of attitude and a new understanding of the legitimate interests and realistic views of the opposition. Strategies that result in understandings and agreements are exceedingly difficult to apply in an atmosphere of mutual hostility, but perhaps it is not impossible eventually to discover methods for effective interaction under these unfavorable conditions.

NEGOTIATIONS WITH AN ALLY

Differences of opinion requiring negotiations often arise between members of a coalition; between political parties over matters of national foreign policy; between national states bound together in some alliance; between factions within a labor union or within a trade association of companies. Negotiations of this sort have some of the same characteristics already presented but are different in important respects.

These negotiations have the following features:

1. The parties to the conflict enter negotiations with the feeling that a resolution of the difference is not only possible but will prove an asset in the long run.

2. There is a mutual expectation that advantages will accrue to both sides.

3. Both parties may recognize they possess divergent objectives, but they are not in direct opposition.

4. The parties accept and respect each other's zone of responsibility or sovereignty.

5. Each of the parties respects and attempts to accommodate itself to the internal problems of the other.

6. There is an active search for additional areas or issues in which agreements can be reached.

7. Persuasion rather than power is the principal lever employed in the course of the negotiations themselves.

We shall deal briefly with each of these characteristics.

1. One notices in advance of conferences between the United States and its Latin-American or European allies a note of hopefulness and anticipation of success that is in marked contrast with the dogged determination and helplessness that precedes a conference with the Soviet Union. Perhaps in both instances there exists a certain irritation that any conference must be held. It is a diversion from other affairs—a necessary inconvenience. The parties, if they are allies, tend to feel that the task may be difficult yet rewarding in the final outcome. This initial condition, existing before the negotiators meet around the table, predisposes them to search diligently for an accommodation of difference. The self-fulfilling prophecy mechanism is at work, in this instance pointed toward success rather than failure.

2. Related to the above point is the anticipation that each party will come out of the negotiations with something of value and not disadvantage the other. The Alliance for Progress is an example of this kind of agreement, in which Latin-American countries were assured financial aid by the United States if they could rectify certain inefficiencies within their own governmental operations. The Marshall Plan following the Second World War is another and similar example.

In the general model for negotiations presented earlier in this chapter from McGrath and Julian (1962) the negotiators were pictured as having directly opposed initial positions in which Party A wants *a,b,c,X,F,* and Party B wants *F,G,H,X,c,* as shown in Figure 14.2.

The final agreement under these circumstances might come about through mutual concessions with the respective interests balanced somewhere in the vicinity of X.

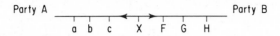

Party A _____ Party B
                 a   b   c   X   F   G   H

Figure 14.2. A diagrammatic representation of the stand of two opponents at the ginning of negotiations.

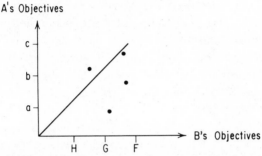

A's Objectives

B's Objectives

Figure 14.3. A diagrammatic representation of the stand of two allies at the be-ning of negotiations.

Now, in negotiations between allies the situation may be represented somewhat as shown in Figure 14.3.

The interests of the two parties are not directly opposed, but they are also not in harmony initially. The final agreement in such a circumstance can be represented by any point between these two lines which will advance the objectives of each party, although it is possible that one may benefit more than another. Solutions that fall on, or close to, the diagonal are obviously those that give equal benefits to both parties and presumably are most sought after and most desirable.

In mature labor–management relations one can find instances in which each party recognizes that their contract should be drawn so that each is less precarious than previously. The company may feel more secure from wildcat strikes, and the union may have gained additional fringe or other benefits. One executive described the situation as follows: "There was no sudden change here. But bit by bit, we found that the union was really doing us a service in bringing to our attention some not very pretty sides of our dealings with our employees. I'm convinced now that we're a better company because the union is here to check up on us. And moreover, we've found that the union officers are a lot easier to get along with since we've stopped bucking theme every time they stirred" (Harbison and Coleman, 1951). Although this quotation does not deal with negotiations directly, it evidences an attitude that both sides may benefit from a relationship periodically renegotiated. Each sees the possibility of assistance from the other.

3. The NATO alliance has had many controversies during its short history, concerning, among other things, the relative military contributions each nation should make to the common defense, some nations wishing to place only token forces at the disposal of the NATO command staff. There have been clearly divergent aims, yet in these disagreements, the objectives were not directly at loggerheads. Sometimes what appears as a difference in objectives is in fact a difference in the preferred means for attaining the same long-range objective. France under DeGaulle, for instance, was desirous of strengthening the European economy against the encroachments of Russia and her allies. DeGaulle believed that end could be achieved best without Great Britain included in the Common Market, a belief not shared by other members of the economic alliance. The fact that the alliance survived this disagreement is evidence that the members were dedicated to a common objective that transcended the difference in means. Negotiable disputes among allies rarely if ever bring major objectives into direct opposition in such a manner that the long-range targets of one party will be preempted by the other. If this does happen the alliance is in danger of dissolution.

An example of the latter sort occurred when the USSR and Nazi Germany broke their nonaggression pact in 1941. In signing this pact Stalin had expected that he would have no opposition from Hitler to expand his influence, if not the borders of the Soviet Union, to the west. Later when Hitler discovered Stalin's objectives were directly counter to his own (Hitler expected to dominate the same areas) the alliance exploded.

A special feature of negotiations between allies is the absence of what game theorists call the zero sum outcome. That is, some games are so structured that one side wins by the amount that the opposition loses. Hence the net sum of winnings and losses is zero. Simple betting games illustrate a zero sum. A and B bet equal amounts on the outcome of a given event, like the toss of a coin. If A wins, then B loses, and the sum of the gain and loss is zero. This was the essential character of the dispute between Hitler and Stalin in 1942. However, in negotiations between allies the win–lose, zero-sum features are absent. This does not mean that one party's judgment may not win out, but in most situations the "winning" solution is more likely to represent the winning of some points for all parties. This kind of a result stems partly from the absence of directly incompatible goals.

4. The parties accept and respect each other's zone of responsibility or sovereignty. Evidence from the field of labor–management relations shows how, under favorable conditions, each party develops an awareness and appreciation for legitimate controls of the other within their respective spheres. This sentiment was well expressed by a corporation executive: "As long as management tries to do everything single handed, it drives the union to search for activities which will emphasize the importance of the union, and consequently give a degree of self-importance to the employees who are the union. As soon as management seeks and accepts the organized cooperation and advice of the employees, particularly through the union which is their organization, it has emphasized its respect for the employees and the union; it has given both of them a constructive opportunity to be important; and it has created the machinery for achieving the 'good of the order' through cooperative planning and action, where collective bargaining cannot be constructively employed" (Harbison and Coleman, 1951). In sum, the attitude expressed recognizes the legitimacy of the union and its right without interference to run its own affairs. Similar views from the union side respecting management's prerogatives are often expressed when the two parties have reached a working rather than a combative relationship.

In the international field, negotiations between allies scrupulously avoid interference with internal affairs of the respective nations. A dispute arose in 1963 between the United States and Canada when a note from the United States was interpreted by the Canadian officials then in power as an effort to influence certain defense policies of Canada that were under debate. The strong protest by the Canadian government provoked an apology from the United States. By contrast, during the same period, however, the United States was openly declaring itself as favoring a new regime in Cuba. These two examples clearly show that a nation is not necessarily consistent in avoiding interference in the domestic affairs of other nations, but instead adapts itself to the nature of the existing relationships.

5. Each of the allied parties respects and attempts to accommodate itself to the internal problems of the other. This point is, of course, closely related to the preceding one, but emphasizes that allies attempt to adjust the issues they raise to the climate of opinion, state of economy, or political winds in their respective countries. The United States wished to negotiate for a full-scale nuclear submarine base in Holy Lock, Scotland, but recognized that a strong, vocal minority within Great Britain opposed the idea and might have embarrassed the government then in

power. Consequently the request was reduced in scale, providing merely for permission to anchor a submarine supply ship in the Lock.

A study conducted by Pruitt (1962) of State Department officers revealed their continuing preoccupation with the effect of United States decisions on the internal affairs of friendly nations. Pruitt confined his interviews to members of one geographic office having primary responsibility for responding to requests for aid and cooperatively developed projects, whether military, economic, or agricultural. Pruitt (1962) paraphrases one of the codirectors of the office as follows: "One of the basic policies of the XYZ Office is to prevent other agencies from irritating too much the countries under our wing, as for instance to stop the Agriculture Department from undercutting the (blank) commodity market in (blank)." Or a little later Pruitt says: "Since the nations assigned to XYZ are sovereign nations which the United States cannot order around, the United States must keep their good will in order to gain cooperation from them on important issues."

In the labor–management area the same sort of concern has been voiced when the relationship has progressed beyond the fighting stage. For instance, a union officer said: "The officials of our company now face severe criticism in the steel industry for signing an agreement which provides for benefits which go beyond the pattern. If our company is to remain solvent in the face of the staggering cost of the benefits which we forced them to give us, it will be necessary to increase production by at least 3 per cent. And if we want to press the company for further gains in the future, then we must remember that the company must be placed in a position to pay for these gains, if we still want our jobs" (Harbison and Coleman, 1951).

6. Each party attempts to explore ways in which it can expand its area of collaboration. The short history of the European Common Market illustrates this point in a gross fashion. In 1949 NATO was established—a military alliance. Then came a series of efforts to form economic alliances, such as custom unions between two or three European nations. The European Common Market itself came into being early in 1958, aiming at a free flow of goods among the members. In 1961 The Organization for Economic Cooperation and Development was established and included most of the countries of Western Europe and the United States. It included subagencies concerned with common support of currencies, exchange of information on the peaceful uses of atomic energy, and so on. This recital only scratches the surface, but emphasizes that among allies agreements may start on a military level and progress outward to include first mutually

advantageous but minor economic arrangements that grow geographically as well as substantively to cover more and more activities.

The progress of labor–management relations follows a similar course. In the early days of collective bargaining, the issue was generally union recognition and union security. In succession, wages, paid holidays, grievance machinery, call-in time, sabbatical leaves, and automation benefits have been the center of discussion. However, it is not so much the salient issues of a period that reveal the expansion of union–management contracts; it is instead the manner in which these issues have been settled. The annual bargaining showdown has been supplemented in many progressive industries by a monthly conference in which each side shares information—the company about its plans for expansion, its market picture, the cost of raw materials or services, and so on—and the union about potential grievance sore spots or suggestions for meeting some of the expected changes in product or procedures. Under favorable circumstances, these monthly meetings serve as channels for two-way communications on a wide variety of matters outside the issues contained in the contract. The formal agreement becomes the center for an amoeba-like progression toward other matters which the contract may eventually engulf.

7. Persuasion rather than power is the principal lever employed in the course of the negotiations. By persuasion we do not mean merely the use of logical argument, although this approach is not eliminated. Persuasion includes all those methods that are not threatening to either party. Pruitt, in the study previously mentioned, evolved a model of negotiations among friendly nations that makes central use of the concepts of *responsiveness* and *fate control*. Responsiveness is the extent to which one of the parties considers the effect of any proposal on the welfare of the other party. Roughly it is the answer to the question "What will happen to my ally if I press for proposal X?" The effect of responsiveness, say, of Party A on negotiations will depend partially upon communicating these considerations to Party B. When B becomes aware that A is responsive to B's welfare there is a greater probability that B will reciprocate by becoming more responsive to A's welfare. Contrariwise, if there should be a reduction in responsiveness by A toward B, the relationships between the two would tend to deteriorate, making it more and more difficult to negotiate later agreements.

Fate control refers to the possibility of one party unilaterally influencing the welfare of the other, either positively or negatively. A nation, for instance, may erect trade barriers discouraging imports from which some other nation derives its major income. Conversely, by encouraging investment in a Latin-American country or by providing agricultural experts for the country, the United States might exercise positive fate control. The greater the fate control of one party over the other, the greater will be the concern of the weaker for maintaining and increasing the responsiveness of the stronger. One strategy for accomplishing this end is to communicate to the stronger the responsiveness of the weaker.

Examples of this mechanism were found in the XYZ office of the State Department. The office seemed to be especially responsive to those countries with which the United States had important trade, military, and political agreements. The State Department officers explained their responsiveness by saying that if these agreements were broken, American interests would be harmed. (They had negative fate control over the United States.) Hence, in order to ensure adherence to the agreements and to keep the door open for additional agreements, the United States expressed its responsiveness with the expectation that the other countries would do likewise.

SOME NEW MODELS FOR NEGOTIATIONS

It is obvious that the conditions, expectations, objectives, and manner in which negotiations take place between hostile opponents and between parties that are allies are quite different. Both require the resolution of disagreements, submerging to some extent the separate sovereign interests of each party. With this framework of considerations, it becomes possible to view the negotiations problem both at the international and intranational levels as one in which we need to discover ways of converting hostile negotiations into the framework of the conditions surrounding the settlement of disputes by allies. Stated in this fashion it is evident that the goal is not the elimination of conflict or disagreement, but instead the goal is to devise means for the management of conflict in such a manner that it does not exacerbate hostilities, throwing the parties to the conflict into the framework of opponents. On the other hand, given the existing condition of hostile parties, is it possible to modify such relationships so that they approximate negotiations between allies?

Deutsch (1964) and Osgood (1962) have proposed sets of conditions that have some hope of achieving just such an end. These suggestions, which have so far not been subjected to experimental test, nevertheless follow from psychotherapeutic theory and practice. In brief, the suggestions are as follows: (1) Prevent the adversary from gaining benefits from his hostile and aggressive behavior. This does not mean necessarily a policy of military deterrence, but it does imply giving emphasis to those measures that neutralize any rewards the adversary might reap from his aggressiveness. The opposition must be taught in small but consistent experiences that aggression does not pay. (2) Simultaneously one side must communicate what Pruitt called responsiveness to the adversary—show convincingly a genuine interest in the public health, education, economic stability, and general cultural welfare of the opposing party. This responsiveness may exclude concern for the maintenance of a particular political ideology or a particular form of government except as these contribute to the enhancement of the common good. (3) The adversary must be given reason to believe that he will gain rather than suffer if he in turn adopts the comparable responsiveness to his opponent's. That is to say, the initiator of these changes must be prepared to give assurances that he is ready to provide concessions or aid if the adversary reduces his tension-creating behavior. This is the counterpart of point (1) emphasizing that rewards should follow those acts that tend to change the orientation of the opponent.

This condensed outline necessarily glosses over the difficult problems of applying these principles. Some occasions may arise (and have arisen) in which it would be impossible to be responsive and deprive the aggressor of his expected rewards. This dilemma illustrates a kind of problem requiring additional analysis and research to determine the conditions under which one principle might take priority over others.

Another suggestion following from the assumption that negotiations often bog down because of honest misunderstandings is that the parties adopt a ground rule that neither will attack the other's position until they fully explore what the opponent really means by his proposal. Lee (1954) presented some experience with a novel parliamentary procedure that required that when an issue appeared to be in danger of reaching a deadlock, the chairman would invoke a rule that no person could state his own opinion about the issue until the proposer had been plied with clarifying questions, such as, "What did you mean when you said——?" "What exactly is the procedure you have in mind?" "Have you considered the effect on——?" After such clarifying questions have been exhausted, the opposition may request information concerning the *uniqueness* of the proposal, how it differs from other proposals, and how one might investigate the proposer's assumptions or predictions. Lee reported that following on the repeated use of this procedure in one organization, cooperation increased in what was previously a discordant group.

A variation of this procedure, suggested and used by a number of writers, requires that before rebuttals can be made to a given proposition the opponents be required to state in their own words the essence of the original proposal and to continue to rephrase the original statement until it satisfies the proposer (Rapoport, 1962). Such a procedure requires much more listening and careful appraisal than is commonly the case in conventional debates, in which each side often tries to subjugate the opposition with the strength of his own logic, making flanking attacks rather than first understanding the main thrust of the opponent. Only *after* the opponent's position is perfectly clear may the rebuttal begin.

These innovations in negotiations have not been given thorough tests even within laboratory settings. They may not be more successful in reaching agreements than conventional debates. However, they flow out of some of the recognized difficulties that now tend to inhibit the negotiation process, and therefore merit at least some consideration and further research.

Before summarizing this chapter it is appropriate to point out that behind the search for effective negotiations is a set of ethical principles we have not examined. Naess (1957) has proposed that a thorough study of the psychological processes and social conditions essential to making these ethical principles effective may be the next most important step for social science, both for the development of its own theoretical framework and for humanitarian ends.

SUMMARY

We have discussed a general model of the negotiation process that attempts to conceptualize the forces in the situation which involves constituents, negotiators, and a neutral moderator, all embedded in a larger context of a culture with its codes and constraints. Given this picture, hostile negotiators approach their task with pessimistic expectations of the outcome, possessing concepts of a fair resolution that are in disagreement, initially unable to agree on the issues to be discussed, and using various forms of power as the principal means for reaching a settlement. Negotiations between allies, on the other hand, appear to be characterized by an initial hopefulness about the outcome, the expectation that both parties will benefit, a mutual respect for the internal affairs of each other, the use of persuasion and responsiveness as levers to reach an agreement, and the consequent efforts to expand the scope of collaborative endeavor. How one moves from a condition of hostility to a condition of tentative collaboration and reduced tension is one of the chief challenges facing behavioral scientists, as well as those who are actively engaged in negotiations at all levels of interaction—intranational as well as international. Some tentative principles have evolved, but their fruitfulness in application has not yet been fully verified. The tasks that lie ahead require the refinement of these tentatively formulated guides to action and the testing of them to determine if the predicted reductions in tension in fact occur.

SUGGESTED REFERENCES FOR FURTHER STUDY

The Journal of Conflict Resolutions.

This bimonthly journal publishes original research and theoretical articles, sometimes in language readily understood by college freshmen. It is a rich source for the most advanced thinking in the field.

Douglas, Ann (1962). *Industrial Peacemaking.* New York: Columbia University Press.

Based upon recordings and notes of several labor–management negotiating meetings, this book provides perhaps the best documentary account of such proceedings. The author provides her own interpretations of the process, which one may check against the lengthy verbatim accounts.

Harbison, F. H., and J. R. Coleman (1951). *Goals and Strategy in Collective Bargaining.* New York: Harpers & Row.

This book is one of the earliest, and remains among the best, systematic treatments of negotiations between labor and management based not only on first-hand data but provocative theoretical propositions.

Joy, C. Turner (1955). *How Communists Negotiate.* New York: Macmillan Company.

A journalistic account of the negotiations between UN and North Korean military representatives written by one who participated in them. Generous portions of the verbatim exchanges are presented. If read as a personal document of the pressures on negotiators and their perceptions, this becomes a highly revealing account.

Osgood, C. E. (1962). *Reciprocal Initiatives.* In James Roosevelt (ed.), *The Liberal Papers* (1962). Garden City, N.Y.: Doubleday & Company.

A highly imaginative proposal designed to reduce international tensions, based on psychological principles, written by a past president of the American Psychological Association.

Schelling, T. C. (1960). *The Strategy of Conflict.* Cambridge, Mass.: Harvard University Press.

A theoretical treatment partly in reference to industrial situations but including international relations as well.

PART FOUR

PSYCHOLOGY APPLIED

TO CRIME

Wiithout delving deeply into the moral implications and overtones, we state what we mean by criminal behavior before we further discuss psychology applied to crime. *Criminal behavior* may be thought of as a breaking of man's law, punishable by society. Man's *law* is the official, sometimes rather stilted, statement of man's understanding of the norms that should be acceptable behavior for members of society. The law mirrors moral norms of our society. The law is a rather arbitrary statement evolving and changing at all times, but reflecting the acceptable morality of society as a group.

Law, reflecting expected behavior of society, changes as the ethical values of society change. Each member of society does not necessarily conform to the rules and regulations or laws in the same manner. As a matter of fact, in modern American society, it is quite acceptable to break some rules but not others. For example, driving on the highway over the lawful speed limit is often discussed and not considered particularly improper by a large segment of the population. On the other hand, if noticed by an authority representing an appropriate governmental agency, speeding is punishable as a crime. Some behavior in opposition to rules or regulations is not at all acceptable to society. For example, embezzling funds is quite unacceptable to most of our society, whereas many people feel that faking expense accounts is acceptable. In fact, some large business organizations condone and seem to encourage cheating behavior on expense accounts by unrealistic policies. They may not allow expenses to be charged for toll roads, but suggest that employees indicate longer driving mileages so that the total reimbursement for miles driven will compensate for the additional cost of driving on a toll road.

It is certainly not strange, therefore, that there is no distinct line between criminal behavior and noncriminal behavior. Criminal behavior, as originally defined, is not the kind of behavior that is reported in statistics. However, reported data gives us some indication of criminal behavior and emphasizes the tremendous importance of crime upon the United States economy. A few crime statistics are cited in Table IV.1.

TABLE IV.1   Total Crime in the United States during 1963 *

	OFFENSES
Murder	8,504
Forcible Rape	16,404
Robbery	100,156
Aggravated Assault	147,757
Burglary	975,879
Larceny ($50 and over)	611,391
Auto Theft	398,990
TOTAL	2,259,081

* J. E. Hoover, *Crime in the United States* (Washington, D.C.: Federal Bureau of Investigation, U. S. Department of Justice, 1964).

In 1963 there were over 2¼ million serious crimes (murder, forcible rape, robbery, and so on, shown in Table IV.1) in the United States. This means that an average of four such crimes occurred each minute during 1963. Admittedly statistics are cold and not too important by themselves, but when one realizes the tremendous amount of energy, money, and human misery expended because of such behavior, one must be concerned with how to handle criminal behavior. The total amount of crime in the United States is increasing faster than the population. During the period 1958 through 1963, crimes increased 40 percent, whereas the population of the United States increased approximately 8 percent.

Of course, the crimes reported are not complete records of the true number of crimes committed. Many crimes are never detected, and crime reports turned in by local police forces to the federal offices do not include questionable convictions or behavior thought to be improper but not bad enough to appear in an official report. In fact, some authorities believe that only 10 percent of all crimes committed result in convictions and thus appear as crime statistics, whereas most of those that do not result in convictions do not appear in the records. (Data presented by the FBI and included in this book concern estimates of crimes reported by local enforcement agencies and so reflect

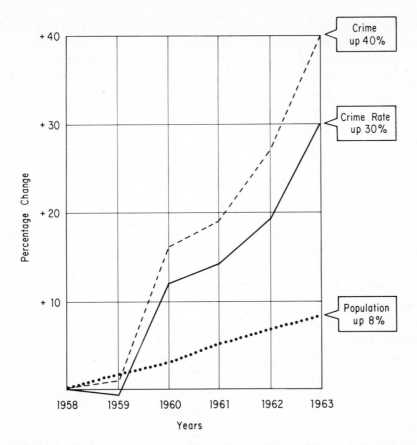

Figure IV.1. Percentage change in crime and population of the United States during the period 1958–1963. Crime indicates the total number of serious crimes (murder, nonnegligent manslaughter, forcible rape, robbery, aggravated assault, burglary, larceny $50 and over, and auto theft) estimated by the Federal Bureau of Investigation. "Crime Rate" indicates the number of offenses per 100,000 population. From J. E. Hoover, *Crime in the United States* (Washington, D.C.: Federal Bureau of Investigation, United States Department of Justice, 1964).

the amount of criminal behavior, not just the convicted cases.) The laws defining crime are constantly under modification and are interpreted by humans (judges). Arrests, convictions, or commitments to prisons are not measures of the amount of crime committed. For example, Sutherland (1939) reported that out of 1,000 consecutive burglaries and robberies of chain grocery stores in Chicago during 1930–31, only two resulted directly in arrest. In 1963, 80 percent of larcenies reported by police did not result in arrests. Many crimes never come to the attention of official investigators. For example, shoplifting in large stores is often not reported to police, but rather, action is taken by the store itself. Thus, we must interpret statistical reports with a good deal of understanding.

Even with problems of analysis of statistical reports, there is overwhelming evidence that there is a large amount of criminal behavior in the United States. Much of this criminal behavior is so antisocial that it is recorded. A great many other acts are of such a level that they do not appear in statistical reports of crime. Antisocial behavior defined as crime can be viewed in a variety of ways. We emphasize the view that criminal behavior is very much the same as any other nonnormal behavior. Thus the criminal is much the same as a mentally ill person.

The reader who does not have a basic understanding of determinism and how behavior may be changed through processes of learning should review other sections of this book. Chapter 1 concerns learning principles, and Chapter 11 describes relationship of behavior and motivation. The material in Chapters 2, 3, and 4 is essential in understanding behavior and mental health problems with which we will be concerned. The assumption through Chapters 15 and 16 is that the human being is not a free agent in any particular situation. A person is not a criminal because he was born to be a criminal. Behavior of a person is the product of environmental and hereditary influences. This means that it is up to society to help an individual have proper experiences so that he will not become a criminal, but instead will generally conform to society's rules in an acceptable manner.

The emphasis in Chapter 15 will be on the use of psychology in detecting criminal behavior and in courtroom functioning of the law system as it involves humans, discussing particularly testimony and jury activity. In Chapter 16, psychology as applied to treating offenders and preventing criminal behavior will be discussed.

Chapter 15

Detection and Conviction

of Criminal Behavior

IN THE UNITED STATES AND OTHER FREE SOCIETIES each man is allowed maximum freedom and protection. This is accomplished by rules and regulations protecting the individual's rights within the group. Although this at first seems incongruous, it actually means that we each give up a certain amount of freedom by obeying rules and regulations that protect other members of society in order to gain the maximum amount of freedom and protection for ourselves. Formalized rules or regulations reflecting the group desires are called laws. Thus criminal behavior becomes the breaking of a rule or regulation called a law.

We must note immediately that laws reflect man's knowledge about the world and his ethical system within this world. As civilizations change, ethics change. Thus laws must change with the passage of time.

Because the norms, or expectations, of society are reflected in laws, these laws are relative or changing, but at the same time absolute. For example, an activity such as slavery or homosexual behavior is always morally wrong, but not always legally wrong. It is up to man in an evolving world to produce laws reflecting current moral ethics. This is often a slow process. Thus the effect is often accomplished by interpretation of laws by judges and other people in authority, rather than in the formulation of new laws.

The fact that crimes are committed in the United States is well known. Each year, the Federal Bureau of Investigation of the United States Department of Justice releases crime statistics for the entire nation. They reported that in 1963 over 2¼ million serious crimes took place. This is a 10-percent increase over 1962 and a 40-percent increase over 1958 (Hoover, 1964). Statistics by themselves must always be questioned, and later in this chapter we discuss some specific points to observe when reading crime reports. However, over 2¼ million serious crimes is an obviously large number, and the increases from 1962 and 1958 are far greater than the yearly 1.5-percent increase in the general population during the same period. Crime, as reported by the police authorities in the United States, is increasing.

But what about criminal behavior that does not show up in statistical reports? Wilson (1951) stated, "One study estimates that the average citizen in one American city, considering himself entirely law-abiding, would unwittingly break sufficient laws to spend over 1,825 years in prison, and to accumulate fines in excess of $2,085,919.55, within one year of orderly living." Obviously then, laws, even though they reflect desirable social norms of the group, are not strictly adhered to by many members of our society, nor can they be, since most individuals simply cannot even know all of the laws.

Lindner (1955) suggested that criminal behavior is not adequately described as simply breaking a rule or regulation, but that different kinds or levels of criminal behavior must be noted. He indicated that behavior called law breaking is a form of legal transgression involving an unintentional action or a circumstance to which a person cannot make a rapid change. A second classification is habitual type offense, and it too is not real criminality, although such offenses take place relatively frequently. They are habits which the transgressor is unable to change in conformance with the law when his old mode of response is no longer legally permissible. Finally real criminals are people involved in acting out unlawful behavior due to internal stress and pathological distortion, so that they can satisfy their own needs or motivations.

Those trained in the law profession have as their duty the understanding of laws pertinent to their activities. Their functions and the function of law is to control behavior. Behavior is also a major interest of psychologists. This and the following chapter will cover many topics of psychology as applied to law. A complete understanding of human behavior and prediction and control of that behavior represents all of psychology and all of law, so naturally, there is a great deal of mutual concern to the two professions.

The topics to be covered in this chapter generally pertain to identifying and evaluating criminal behavior. Although we readily agree that there is no such thing as a criminal type, we will discuss personal and environmental factors related to criminal behavior. In addition, we will discuss methods of detecting deception.

In our system of government a person is guilty of a crime only after proven guilty. It is the duty of the prosecuting attorney to present enough information before a judge or a group of fellow citizens and a judge to absolutely prove that a defendant has committed a crime. The last major segment of this chapter considers the trial of the accused.

IDENTIFICATION OF CRIMINAL BEHAVIOR

Some laymen and professional employees still persist in the notion that criminals are of a particular physiological or anthropometrical makeup. Work done by an Italian military physician in the late nineteenth century (Lombroso, 1911) is probably the basis for attitudes that criminals are of a certain type. Lombroso studied the physiognomy of 5,907 convicts and concluded that the typical criminal had a long lower jaw, flattened nose, a symmetrical cranium, and other physiological characteristics. Such a theory is unfortunately still accepted by many. The work of many other researchers since Lombroso has shown that there are very few physical characteristics of criminals that can be isolated and shown to be different from the general population. Some evidence seems to indicate that physical types are related to particular types of crimes, but even there, the evidence is rather scant. In general, criminals are not criminals because of certain physiological characteristics, but more likely because of psychological and environmental factors.

An individual may exhibit criminal behavior when he is exposed to a criminal influence, when he has a strong motivation to express aggressiveness, or when he has a desire for punishment due to guilt feelings. As yet, specific causes of criminal behavior are not isolated and most likely will not be as long as researchers equate criminal behavior with convicted or arrested individuals. Many sets of criminal behavior occur and do not result in conviction or arrest.

It seems quite evident that criminals develop through an interaction of their personality and psychological characteristics with their environment. Before we can discuss adequately the psychological and environmental factors which seem to predispose an individual to criminal behavior, it is important to understand the shortcomings of crime statistics upon which our estimates of causes of crime are often based.

STATISTICS OF CRIMINAL BEHAVIOR.   In an attempt to get an understanding of the amount of crime in the United States, the Federal Bureau of Investigation annually collects statistics from local law enforcement agencies. Recognizing that good statistics are difficult to collect and analyze, the FBI established specific techniques for collecting the information for the uniform crime reports. Since 1930 the FBI has been collecting the uniform crime reports, and the local agencies have been using very specific techniques of reporting. Even so, variations and report procedures occur because 8,000 jurisdictions report to the FBI. Thus the FBI cautions that criminal acts as indicated in their reports are simply a first means of account of crime in the United States. They state that "Not all crimes come readily to the attention of the police; not all crimes are of sufficient importance to be significant in an index; and not all important crimes occur with enough regularity to be meaningful in index." With these considerations in mind, the FBI reports crime classification in seven categories, as shown in Table IV.1.

All serious crimes increased in 1963 as compared to 1962. The serious crimes are subdivided into crimes of violence (murder, forcible rape, robbery, and aggravated assault) and crimes against property (burglary, larceny of $50 and over, and auto theft). Crimes of violence increased about 5 percent, and crimes against property increased about 10 percent in 1963 as compared to 1962. About 92 percent of the total crimes in 1963 were against property (Hoover, 1964). Figures 15.1a and 15.1b show the trends of crimes in the two subdivisions for the years 1958–1963.

Indexes of crime rates are not absolute measures of crime frequency. The indexes are based on reports of crimes or arrest or commitments to prison and not on the number of people involved or occurrences of crime. Crimes such as stealing from an employer or friend do not show up in statistics if they are never reported to police. Statistics frequently show only major criminal behavior. For example, overtime parking, going through a stop sign, and so on, are illegal but usually not recorded in crime statistics. Reports of total amount of crime are of little use unless compared to another base such as the population at large or the number of people in the environment where crime occurred. For example, it would not be fair to compare the number of vehicle violations in 1920 against 1960 without comparing the total number of vehicles or miles driven. The number of crimes reported does not necessarily reflect amount of criminal behavior, because one crime may involve more than one person. For example, a burglary committed by five people may show up in a police record as one robbery.

Keeping aware of these difficulties in interpreting criminal statistics, we will examine the psychological and environmental factors related to crime rates. These statistics will aid us in evaluating possible causes of criminal behavior.

In earlier chapters of this book the psychologist's concept of behavior as primarily determined by psychological and environmental factors has

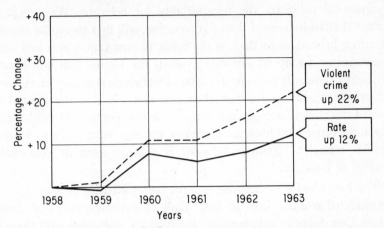

Figure 15.1(a). Percentage of change in violent crime (murder, forcible rape, robbery, and aggravated assault) in the United States during the period 1958–1963. Crime indicates the number of crimes. Rate indicates the number of offenses per 100,000 population. From J. E. Hoover, *Crime in the United States* (Washington, D.C.: Federal Bureau of Investigation, United States Department of Justice, 1964).

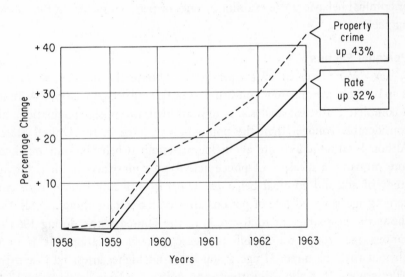

Figure 15.1(b). Percentage change in crimes against property (burglary, larceny $50 and over, and auto theft) in the United States during the period 1958–1963. Crime indicates the number of crimes. Rate indicates the number of offenses per 100,000 population. From J. E. Hoover, *Crime in the United States* (Washington, D.C.: Federal Bureau of Investigation, United States Department of Justice, 1964).

been stated. At times the disparate views of psychologists and attorneys is the result of disagreements concerning free will and determinism. It is not essential to prove that an individual is not a free agent. However, it is important to recognize the responsibility for behavior. We accept the concept that an individual does not have free will in a particular situation but rather behaves as he does as the result of past experiences and innate characteristics. Complete knowledge of all the factors that will create a particular behavior is not now available. Psychology is not an exact science and cannot predict and control behavior precisely. On the other hand, most of our society accepts the concept that a mentally ill person needs help and cannot cure himself. The same concept must be carried over to criminal behavior. Criminal behavior is another form of abnormal or mentally ill behavior.

The individual who responds in a particular situation in a manner that is considered criminal does so as a result of environmental and personal factors. Our discussions of criminal behavior are concerned with these two categories.

By and large, available evidence indicates very little general relationship between environmental or personal factors and criminal behavior. However, different individual factors seem to be related to particular types of criminal behavior. We examine a series of personal factors in the following sections.

Personal Factors

AGE.   Whenever we visit a prison and observe the inmates, we cannot help but note the apparent youthfulness of the inmate population. Without a complete statistical analysis, it appears that the prison populations are considerably younger than the population at large in the United States. Although crime reports are about known criminal behavior and are therefore primarily a measure of police activity, we must accept them for our study of age and criminal behavior. The FBI annually collects data concerning age, sex, and race of persons arrested for certain crimes. Table 15.1 shows the percentage of total arrests in the United States during 1963 by various age groups for all offenses except traffic violations. It is quite obvious that the under-21 age group has a far higher arrest rate than the older groups. It is also disheartening to notice the large percentage (17.4) of total arrests of people under 18 years of age. During the calendar year 1963, arrests of persons under 18 years of age rose 11 percent over the 1961 data whereas the number of arrests for those 18 years and over decreased 0.7 percent in the same period. This upward trend in arrests for young people continued from previous year increases in all crimes except gambling. Particularly large increases in arresting rate were recorded for negligent manslaughter (up 24.8 percent) and embezzlement (up

27.1 percent). For the serious crimes committed in the United States during 1963, juveniles were involved in 46 percent of the total arrests. Figure 15.2 shows the arrest rates by age groups for most serious crimes in the United States during 1963.

TABLE 15.1 Percentages of Total Arrests by Age Groups for Persons in the United States During 1963 *

AGE		PERCENTAGE OF TOTAL ARRESTS	
50 and over		15.5	15.5
Total 40–50		17.7	
	45–49		7.9
	40–44		9.8
Total 30–40		20.1	
	35–39		10.4
	30–34		9.7
Total 21–29		20.0	
	25–29		9.8
	24		2.3
	23		2.4
	22		2.6
	21		2.9
Total under 21		26.7	
	20		3.0
	19		3.1
	18		3.2
	17		3.4
	16		4.0
	15		3.2
Under 15			6.8
Total Arrested		100.0	100.0

* Computed from data in J. E. Hoover, *Crime in the United States* (Washington, D.C.: Federal Bureau of Investigation, U. S. Department of Justice, 1964).

Figure 15.2 shows that a larger proportion of people in the younger age groups are arrested for serious crimes than are members of older groups of the population. Approximately 25 percent of known offenses are cleared by arrests, and about 29 percent of those arrested are eventually found guilty. Thirty-five percent of juveniles arrested are referred to juvenile court and thus do not show up on regular records as guilty or not guilty after arrest. Arresting does not indicate proof of guilt, and arrest rates do not indicate extent of crime, but such statistics do provide us with suitable information to use in comparing one age, sex, or race against another.

Perhaps it is unfair to suggest that the younger age groups are so involved in crime. The data that we are citing concerns those that were suspected or caught. It is conceivable that the person exhibiting criminal behavior at a later age in life has learned how to avoid being caught. Consequently statistics and observation of penal institutions may show a bias in

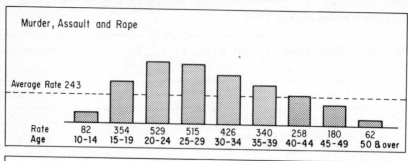

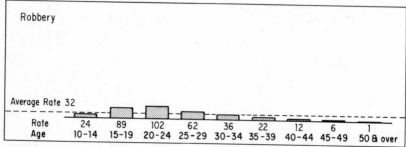

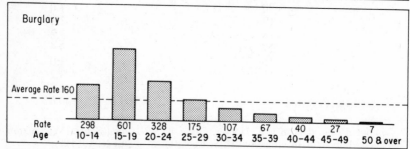

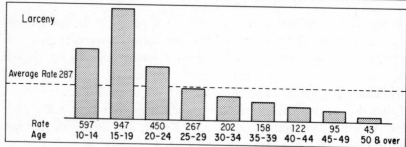

Figure 15.2 Arrest rates by age groups, 1963, for several serious crimes. Rates are per 100,000 population in each age group. For each crime the dotted horizontal line shows the average arrest rate for all age groups. From J. E. Hoover, *Crime in the United States* (Washington, D.C.: Federal Bureau of Investigation, United States Department of Justice, 1964).

the direction of overemphasizing youthfulness in criminal behavior. It is also likely that older people learn to live in their environment without resorting to criminal behavior or that some younger people who have been involved in criminal behavior "go straight" as they grow older.

Perhaps the most important point concerning juvenile delinquents is the known high rate of returning to prison after once serving a term. Recidivism for all criminals as a group is reported to be approximately 60 to 70 percent, meaning that of prisoners once incarcerated, 60 to 70 percent return. (See additional comments concerning recidivism in Chapter 16 of this book.) When a person starts his criminal behavior early in life, he has a great chance of repeating.

Earlier studies have also indicated that recidivism is a characteristic of juvenile delinquents. In fact, most juvenile delinquency guidance programs have had little or no effect on the overall recidivism rate.

Juvenile delinquency has increased at a alarming rate in the United States. Between 1948 and 1960, the juvenile courts experienced a 100-percent increase in referrals. Programs to prevent such behavior did not seem to function adequately, and studies were completed to seek early identification techniques of people who would later become juvenile delinquents. Most studies indicated that home backgrounds and personality development of delinquents and nondelinquents could be differentiated. However, very few studies showed any statistically significant results in terms of predicting juvenile delinquency. For example, Kvaraceus (1962) studied children over a period of three years and found a significant relationship between teachers ratings of behavior and later juvenile delinquency records. Unfortunately he did not report the percentages of students who later became delinquents.

Studies that show juvenile delinquency rates are increasing also indicate that delinquency rates are higher in deteriorated or blighted sections of large cities than in suburban or less blighted urban areas. It seems that juvenile delinquency, and therefore age, is related to criminal behavior, but the relationship is confounded by the cultural system or way of life of the population where these young criminals reside. A particular subsociety may place emphasis on characteristics of behavior that are different from the usually acceptable norms of society and thus foster juvenile delinquency.

On the other hand, it must be remembered that the great bulk of individuals from poorer environments do not go astray. Thus there is something besides the physical and social environment and age of individuals that encourages antisocial behavior.

SEX. The differences in rate of criminal behavior of males and females is absolutely striking. Hoover (1964) reported that the ratio of male to female arrests in the United States during 1963 was about 8 to 1. However, female arrests continued to increase during 1963 at a faster pace than did the male arrests. As might be expected, arrest rates for females were higher than for males in some classifications of criminal behavior, such as commercialized vice, but in most classifications, males far exceeded female arrest rate.

The variance in arrest rate by sex is due to several factors. First of all the physical abilities of males and females are different. Secondly, most girls lead a more restricted life. Even in environments that breed criminal behavior, parents expect the female members of the household to stay nearer home, and they allow them less leniency than males. Finally there is generally more leniency given to females than to males in terms of arrests and convictions. Thus statistics are biased toward an indication of less criminal behavior on the part of women than men.

RACE. Many comments have been made by sophisticated as well as naive observers that one nationality or racial group contributes more than their proportionate share to the crime rate in the United States. Negroes have particularly been blamed for an excessively high criminal behavior. Substantial evidence to support such concepts when other factors such as environment, socioeconomic status, income, age, and so on, are controlled is nonexistent. As a matter of fact, statistics concerning crime must always be carefully considered before drawing conclusions concerning cause-and-effect relations. On the other hand, statistics do provide leads for further investigation.

In a report concerning crime rate in the United States in 1963 (Hoover, 1964), the arrests made by police in some towns and cities are recorded by race. Cities numbering 3,951, with an estimated population of 116,952,000, reported such information. This group reported a total of 4,259,463 arrests during 1963. Of these arrests, 2,943,148 involved white and the remaining nonwhite offenders. In other words, almost 70 percent of arrests for all crimes involved white offenders, whereas 30 percent involved nonwhite offenders. Since it is estimated that the nonwhite population of the United States is about 14 percent of the total, it is obvious that this group contributed to arrest rates more than should be expected. However, again we note that arrest rate can very easily be biased information. In many cities a white person may be reprimanded or ignored by the police for an act that would result in an arrest of a nonwhite. (This is probably not as true of the serious crimes shown in Table 15.2) Nonwhites frequently reside in environmental situations that are more likely to result in antisocial acts and consequent arrests. The role of the nonwhite as an inferior in society such that he does not have proper security and self-respect has been emphasized by many authorities in criminology. Unstable home and family life and exposure to criminal influences result in additional criminal behavior. These factors are more likely to influence a greater proportion of nonwhites than whites.

TABLE 15.2   Percentage of Arrests by Race for Serious Crimes in the United States During 1963 *

| | RACE | | |
CRIME	WHITE %	NONWHITE %	TOTAL %
Murder and Nonnegligent Manslaughter	42.9	57.1	100
Forcible Rape	52.1	47.9	100
Robbery	45.7	54.3	100
Aggravated Assault	43.8	56.2	100
Burglary	68.8	31.2	100
Larceny	69.0	31.0	100
Auto Theft	73.3	26.7	100

*After J. E. Hoover, *Crime in the United States*, Washington, D.C.: (Federal Bureau of Investigation, U. S. Department of Justice, 1964).

Although the overall picture of arrests is probably not a fair indication of the amount of crime of whites versus nonwhites, the classification by offense charged is worthy of note. Table 15.2 shows the percentages of white and nonwhite offenders arrested for serious crimes in 1963. Examination of Table 15.2 reveals a larger percentage of arrests for crimes against a person (murder, assault, forcible rape, and robbery) by nonwhites than for other crimes. Because the overall percentage of nonwhites arrested is about 30 percent it is apparent that a smaller percentage of minor crimes and serious crime against property is committed by this group. Of course, we must also remember that the overall arrest rate for the nonwhites is about twice that of the whites. The type of crime for which an individual is most likely to be arrested varies according to race. This may be the result of other factors that are related to race as well as to type of crime—for example, occupation or accessibility to a particular kind of activity and economic condition that brings about some types of crimes more than others.

INTELLIGENCE.   For years a good many criminologists and psychologists agreed that low intelligence was a major factor contributing to crime. For example, Goddard (1920) stated, "Every investigation of the mentality of criminals, misdemeanants, delinquents, and other antisocial groups has proven beyond the possibility of contradiction that nearly all persons in these classes, and in some cases all, are of low mentality—it is no longer to be denied that the greatest single cause of delinquency and crime is low-grade mentality, much of it within the limits of feeblemindedness."

Such concepts of intelligence as related to crime have long since been outmoded. Many studies have shown that criminals incarcerated for their antisocial activity have intelligence relatively near the general population. Although the studies generally show a prison population average IQ just below the average for the population at large, it is generally conceded that some of the more intelligent criminals are probably not apprehended and that the more intelligent ones are more capable in defending themselves in courtrooms and consequently are not as likely to be convicted and imprisoned.

The author has been particularly interested in the abilities and rehabilitation problems of the inmates of one prison. This is a county prison with a population of approximately 120 men. Although the prison handles all types of criminals, the majority of the inmates are incarcerated for relatively short sentences (under four years) rather than for long terms or life sentences. The Henmon–Nelson Test of Mental Ability was administered to 31 male inmates during the first half of 1964. These men ranged in age from 18 through 41 years. Their average education was 9½ years. Their average (mean) IQ was 91. Considering their ages and level of formal education, it seems that the average prisoner is not below the average non-prisoner in intelligence.

A previously mentioned study by Kvaraceus (1962) evaluated the relationship between intelligence and juvenile delinquency. The correlations ranged from .028 to .217 and were statistically nonsignificant. Kvaraceus indicated, however, a higher relationship between intelligence of boys in special classes and later juvenile delinquency. This was a negative correlation, which seemed to indicate that children with higher intelligence placed in special classes were more likely to become juvenile delinquents than were their duller classmates in the mentally retarded classes. This very likely could reflect the discomfort or conflict on the part of the borderline learners who are placed in special learning centers.

The relationship between intelligence and general criminal behavior is not very firmly established; however, type of crime and intelligence seems to be related. Persons with higher intelligence generally commit crimes requiring more mental ability. (For example, embezzlement and fraud, well-planned robberies, forgery, and counterfeiting.) On the other hand, criminals with lower intelligence are more often involved in such activities as robbery, aggravated assault, and murder. Kahn (1959) reported on a study of two groups, one composed of murderers and the other composed of burglars. Both groups had been admitted to a psychiatric hospital for evaluation of legal sanity. In almost all cases they had pleaded not guilty by reason of insanity. The mean IQ obtained from the Wechsler–Bellevue Intelligence Test for the murderers group was 94.6 and for the burglary group 103.0. The difference between these mean scores was shown to be significant, suggesting that the burglary group functions at a somewhat higher intellectual level than the murderer group.

Variations in intelligence level in relationship to criminal activity are not surprising. Many studies have shown that intelligence is related to various levels of occupation. Consequently antisocial behavior might be expected to vary according to mental ability.

PERSONALITY. The gross personality characteristics of being fairly well balanced or normal personality versus mentally ill or abnormal personality will be discussed in a separate section considering mental stability. In general, the relationship between criminality and measured emotional disorder is not very high. However, certain personality characteristics do seem to be related to criminal behavior.

A review of the available literature concerning personality factors in criminal behavior (Schuessler and Cressey, 1950) indicated that personality traits are distributed in the criminal population in about the same way as in the general population.

Since 1950, studies seem to show that specific characteristics of personality are related to criminal behavior. For example, Panton (1959) reported on the use of a new series of MMPI (Minnesota Multiphasic Personality Inventory) scales to measure male prisoners. He concluded that inmates scored in the direction of inadequacy on those scales designed to measure prejudice, responsibility, dominance, dependency, and ego strength significantly more than did nonprisoners.

In another study using the MMPI, a large group of ninth grade school children were tested and followed up two and four years later. Using a delinquency rating based on records of public and private agencies, the investigators (Hathaway and Monachesi, 1957) found that 33 of the 550 items on the MMPI differentiated significantly between the delinquent and the nondelinquent group. They concluded that a rather youthful exuberance, a love of danger, and a resentment of restrictions go with later juvenile delinquency.

Freedman (1961) reported a study that indicated different personalities in three classes of criminal behavior. Dr. Freedman and his coworkers investigated three classes of deviate behavior: sexual, aggressive, and acquisitive. Sexual behavior was defined as substantially concerned with erotic or genital stimulation, aggressivity had to do with forceful and harmful action directed at another person, and acquisitivity meant the illegal acquisition of property without aggression. They admitted that there couldn't be a clean-cut differentiation in the three kinds of behavior, but they diagnosed behavior in terms of the primary symptoms or characteristics. Dr. Freedman and his coworkers found that "the acquisitive offender is sexually a free-acting poly-focal being. The acquisitive offenders adjusted easily to externally imposed variability of available objects. The interchangeability and relative personal insignificance of his sexual objects as compared to the persistence of his sexual aims is matched by the human objectlessness of his persistently acquisitive aims."

Dr. Freedman continued, ". . . the acquisitive offender is much more typically a subcultural phenomenon, in that there is variance in the values of his entire group and those of the dominant sanctioning community."

The results of Freedman's study showed that the acquisitive offenders are more group-oriented than the sexual and aggressive offenders. The latter two groups offended against society individually, whereas the acquisitives went along with a subculture that was somewhat opposed to the dominant culture. In other words, a group of offenders, the acquisitives, might be identified by their subculture with common personality characteristics, whereas the sexual and aggressive offenders are more individualistic and do not seem to have very many common personality characteristics.

Although several studies have shown positive relationships between personality attributes and particular types of criminal behavior, or criminals versus noncriminals, some studies have questioned such findings. For example, Scodel and Minas (1960) used a "prisoner's dilemma" game with prisoners and college students. The prisoner's dilemma game requires two people to work together toward the solution of a problem. If they do not collaborate, they cannot achieve as good a solution as if they do. The results of the two groups were about the same in that almost all showed no cooperation or collaboration but instead employed definite competitive strategy. Such a study shows that there is little difference between a college group and a prison population in the ideas of cooperativeness and certainly casts some doubt upon the "honor among thieves" concept.

In summary, evidence to date indicates that the personality of the nonconformist or the criminal is not a great deal different from that of the so-called average person. A few personality characteristics, particularly impulsiveness and difficulty in evaluating himself and others, seem to be more common among criminals than noncriminals. As additional evidence is accumulated, it seems likely that personality factors will be valuable means for differentiating potential criminals and noncriminals and types of crime committed.

MENTAL DISORDERS. Earlier chapters of this book discuss mental disorders in detail. Consequently, there is no attempt here to describe the various syndromes of mental abnormalities. However, we must point out that the once generally held concept that criminal behavior is predominantly a particular psychotic condition is somewhat questionable. It is probably realistic to think of all antisocial behavior as abnormal behavior and therefore a type of mental disorder. On the other hand, a true criminal psychosis is probably difficult if not impossible to define. Less than 5 percent of all prisoners are truly insane from a technical standpoint. Thus the classification "criminally insane" represents a rare group, accounting for very little of the crime in the United States.

The idea of criminal insanity developed when the study of psychology and behavior was relatively new and considerably different from today. Psychology and law vary in their concepts concerning prediction and control of behavior. In general law cannot be expected to keep up with all the most recent evidence gathered by psychology; on the other hand, the stability of the traditional systems would be in jeopardy if there was an attempt to change rules and regulations as rapidly as scientific evidence was unearthed. Even so, there are many places where psychology and laws vary to the irritation of people in both fields. Definitions of terms is one area. Admittedly the differentiation between normal and abnormal behavior is difficult to make. In the legal system, a criminal must be mentally healthy to be subject to legal punishment, whereas an insane person is not responsible for his behavior. Psychologists and psychiatrists have repeatedly questioned the concept that a person can be mentally ill and criminally responsible at the same time. If criminal behavior (breaking of moral or ethical codes of conduct or laws of the country) is considered mentally abnormal, it seems illogical to consider such behavior to be that of a legally responsible person.

One of the first legal definitions of insanity came in 1843, when a Scot by the name of McNaghten pleaded innocent of a criminal act on the grounds of insanity. The court acquitted him on the basis of the facts available at that time and that set the precedent for the so-called Mc-Naghten rule, which lasted into the 1950's. According to this rule, it must be clearly proven that a person committing a criminal act was so disturbed at the time of doing the act that he did not know the nature and the quality of the act he was doing, or if he did know it, that he didn't realize that it was wrong. The McNaghten rule has been amended in many of the United States to include an irresistible-impulse clause to account for the possibility of a mental illness where the intellect appears good but emotions are uncontrollable. Although there have been a variety of different rulings, particularly toward more leniency concerning proof of insanity, the principle is still not clearly stated. If anything, the problem of deciding from a legal standpoint what is and is not insanity is becoming more confusing. Many specialists are suggesting that the decision can be made by the same technique that a person is decided guilty or not guilty. In other words, evidence is brought before a jury, and the jury decides whether a person is responsible or not responsible for his actions. Such a technique is a possibility that must be considered.

It is quite true that there is nothing to be gained by suggesting that antisocial conduct of an individual indicates an internal maladjustment and then stating that since a person is psychologically maladjusted he performs an antisocial act. On the other hand, most antisocial behavior must be recognized as a poor adjustment on the part of the individual concerned. Thus the treatment of the offender must be in terms of his personality and psychological makeup rather than just in terms of the crime committed. (Treatment will be discussed in the next chapter of this book.)

An individual with certain personality characteristics that cannot be expressed easily in normal society may learn to contain his urges and behave in a manner agreeable to society, or he may go to a society where his desired behavior is acceptable. For example, homosexual behavior is generally not acceptable in society, but in some subsections of society it is acceptable. In some subsections of society stealing from the employer or taking things from a display case is thought to be "big" or an outstanding activity. The individual that modifies his behavior to fit such a subsection of society is likely to continue such behavior in societies where it is not acceptable. Individuals adjusting their personality to their society or transferring from one subsection to another have difficult changes to make. The abnormal behavior of each person must be treated according to the abnormality rather than the criminal behavior.

MOTIVATION.   All behavior of humans must be considered in the light of motivating causes. Abrahamsen (1946) emphasized this point concerning criminals when he stated that the nature of motivation in criminal behavior does not differ from motivation in any other form of behavior.

Motivation is a condition of seeking to fulfill a need or imbalanced state. (See Chapters 1, 2, 4, and 11 of this book for additional discussions concerning motivation.) All humans are subjected to many different need states at all times. A criminal is no different than any other human in this manner.

The difference between criminal behavior and noncriminal behavior is in the method of satisfying the need situation. Motivation may be just as strong in criminals as in noncriminals. Noncriminals use socially acceptable behavior to fulfill their need states. Criminals have exhibited behavior that is not acceptable to society. The basic physiological changes of the body are important in causing motivation, but learned or derived needs are often of more importance. As discussed in other chapters, most physiological needs are filled relatively easily. The learned needs for status symbols, cooperation with the group, achievement within the group, specialized foods or beverages, are more difficult to fulfill and thus are frequently of importance in criminal behavior. The person who lives in an environment that accepts behavior to fulfill needs, even if it is antisocial, is more likely to be involved in crime than the individual living in a different segment of society. For example, a boy who grows up in an environment that accepts stealing of apples or objects of minor value is more likely to accept the concept of car stealing to go for a joy ride than is the person brought up in an environment that has consistently maintained that "borrowing" without permission is wrong. Abrahamsen (1960) insisted throughout his book that the juvenile delinquent and later the criminal is not born to be a criminal, but has the same basic motivations as the noncriminal. Because of his environment and his inability to fulfill his normal motivational states easily, the juvenile delinquent commits antisocial acts.

All children and adults experience their external environment through their receptor organs. Information is taken within them and is perceived according to past experiences. When the normal child is faced with new situations, he uses his reasoning process to evaluate them and to come up with a solution that is acceptable according to his past experiences. The juvenile delinquent, because of his early experiences, may be unable to integrate the new experiences properly or may respond with antisocial behavior. Such antisocial behavior may not be perceived as such in the perpetrator's own view.

Motivations are not easily determined. They are frequently buried deeply within the individual and even the most intelligent, law-abiding citizen may at times wonder why he does a certain thing. Criminals may find themselves in the same situation, wondering why they have committed a particular act. In fact, they may honestly be unaware or not able to admit to themselves why they do unsocial acts. For example, Sadler (1947) cited a case of a youth who did not want to admit that he stole automobiles to "get even with the old man," whom he subconsciously hated.

Considering motivation for particular criminal behavior, more information is available. It is well accepted that law enforcement agencies usually seek the motivation for a particular crime so that they may unearth the person who committed the act. There is a good deal of scientific evidence and well-founded reasoning behind such activity. When the motivation for a crime is known, police can narrow down the possible suspects. For example, a man and unmarried woman were found dead in bed together. Although the man was shot only once in the chest, the woman had been shot many times and her face badly marked by repeated blows. The man's wife was an obvious suspect, because she might have strong motivation for such an act.

CONCLUDING STATEMENT. Although we have discussed several personal characteristics related to criminal or asocial behavior, we have not professed to cover every possible personal characteristic that might be related to crime. These factors mentioned more often relate to specific types of criminal behavior than to criminal behavior in general. Unfortunately, there is little substantial evidence to differentiate the criminal from the noncriminal, particularly in a predictive manner. Some progress has been made toward understanding where criminals might develop in terms of environment. These factors related to crime are discussed in this next segment of this chapter.

Environmental Factors in Crime

SOCIOECONOMIC STATUS. It is essential to remember that although socioeconomic status and criminality are generally positively related, there are far more noncriminals growing up and living in low socioeconomic environments than there are criminals. Thus, although rates of criminality are generally higher in low socioeconomic environments than in high socioeconomic environments, there are still many, many individuals who live socially acceptable lives in rather poor environmental conditions.

Socioeconomic status refers to a standing within society resulting from the father's occupation, income of the family, education of the individuals in the family, and the neighborhood in which the family resides. Many studies indicate a relationship between socioeconomic status and delinquency or criminal behavior. For example, one study showed that 50 percent of boys investigated in a state training school came from the lower socioeconomic levels and only 4.1 percent from the higher levels (Nye, Short, and Olson, 1958).

Kvaraceus (1959) suggested that the lower socioeconomic background associated with a higher delinquency rate is very possibly only an indication of the real problem. The youth living in a female-based household, where the father is usually absent or rarely involved in the support and raising of the family, encounters more difficulty in personality growth than a child developing in a better socioeconomic home. Thus the youth in the poorer home may think of his father in a negative manner. He may be cautioned, "Don't be a bum like your father," and may develop a negative connotation toward the male adult role. When trying to gain identification, such a child will turn to his street corner gang and identify there rather than with his parents; consequently, in testing his new masculinity, he may turn to forms of norm-violating behavior.

Gardner (1959) also suggested that lower socioeconomic families are frequently broken families and that the economic burden of a child to the mother without the father creates real problems. The mother may eventually identify the child with the absent husband and especially with the bad faults or characteristics that he possessed. The child responds to his mother's behavior by further norm-violating behavior.

The majority of delinquent or criminal behavior comes from the population of deteriorated sections of larger cities. These cities are generally heterogeneous in background, often with lower moral requirements and lacking the facilities and activities for youth found in more favorable neighborhoods. Youth coming from low-income families have less chance of obtaining the initiative for social and economic success. They are often deprived and feel lacking in self-esteem, so that they devise new sets of values. These values are not always acceptable to society at large and thus result in norm-violating behavior. Poor socioeconomic conditions also provide youths with examples of norm-violating behavior by the parents and other respected figures. Consequently youths set up as an idol the more successful members of their subgroup who may be successful because of their norm-violating behavior (Kvaraceus, 1959).

Whether living in the low socioeconomic conditions causes criminal behavior or whether the low socioeconomic conditions and criminal behavior have a common cause is still questionable. Many years ago, at least one author emphasized this point when reviewing available evidence concerning socioeconomic conditions (Berrien, 1944). He stated: "It may be that poor success in the economic struggle and consequent drifting to slum neighborhoods is a reflection of inadequate motivation, lack of intellectual capacity, poor occupational training, or a twisted and distorted emotional life. These same factors in various combinations could conceivably be causative agents in criminal behavior as well." He went on to state that, "It cannot rightly be concluded from this that low economic status is the necessary cause of high criminal rates." Low socioeconomic conditions seem to be related to high criminal rates, and an attempt to upgrade the poorer socioeconomic status of many citizens is at least a step in the direction of reducing known criminal activity.

It seems that the relationships between socioeconomic status and delinquency and crime rate are the reflections of the factors creating low socioeconomic status, such as family breakdown, poor living conditions, impoverished environment, poor educational development, and so on. These factors must be considered in a discussion of crime.

HOME AND FAMILY SITUATION. Two previously cited studies concerning economic conditions are also relevant concerning the family. It is fairly well established that a higher crime rate occurs among children from broken homes than from better adjusted families. When a family disintegrates, for whatever reason, children are often deprived of some of the normal contacts that help them to develop into law-abiding adults. Thus it is entirely possible for a delinquent gang or a group of nonconforming individuals to be especially attractive to a child from a broken home. Robinson (1947) suggested that the broken family resulted in the lack of family protection and was often important in juvenile delinquency. But he also reported that as far as his study was concerned, there were a few cases of juvenile delinquents who had been overprotected during childhood.

Although broken homes seem to be important in creating an environment that is conducive to nonconforming behavior, there are other ways in which home conditions can produce criminal behavior. First, the environment may be such, within a nonbroken home, that the child is forced to seek satisfactions elsewhere. For example, the parents may be overdemanding or overprotective of their children or completely irresponsible in terms of providing training that enables the child to develop normal social behavior. Smith (1955) reported that in a study in Detroit in 1953, 81 percent of the delinquents came from families in which there were no serious quarrels, and 94 percent reported they liked their homes.

The influence of the home is undoubtedly important. The broad classification of broken homes versus unbroken homes is not as crucial as the treatment a child receives in the home. A series of pioneering studies by Sheldon and Eleanor Glueck have investigated the influence upon criminal and noncriminal behavior of different methods of rearing children. After 10 years of investigation, their work has been reported in a variety of sources (Glueck and Glueck, 1950, 1959). They showed that a scale describing parent–child relations as determined by interviews with the parents is a good indicator of future delinquent or nondelinquent behavior. Lack of affection and inconsistency in discipline in the home are related to delinquency.

We emphasize that the legally broken home is not necessarily the most dangerous in terms of creating criminal behavior. An individual from a psychologically broken home, where he does not receive understanding and sympathy, is more likely to do antisocial acts than a person from a well-adjusted home environment. Unfortunately the measurement of psychological breaks in the family seems to be almost impossible. The previously mentioned Glueck and Glueck scale is an attempt to measure this characteristic, but it is not perfect. Thus prediction of delinquent or criminal behavior is difficult if not impossible.

OCCUPATIONAL STATUS. As with many of the other factors related to crime, occupational status seems to be related to the type of the crime more than to criminal or noncriminal behavior. It is rather obvious that crimes of certain types can be perpetrated only by individuals in particular kinds of employment. For example, professional persons most often find themselves in positions where embezzlement, forgery, or fraud or perhaps grand larceny are possible, whereas unskilled or laboring workers find themselves in a position in which embezzlement is almost impossible. However, the latter group are more likely to be involved in vagrancy, abandonment of children, nonsupport, and so on. These differences seem to reflect the differences in criminal opportunities.

In a study of delinquents in one city, Kvaraceus (1945) found a definite relationship between occupation of parents and juvenile delinquency. He found a larger proportion of fathers either working as factory operators or laborers or unemployed among the juvenile delinquents' parents than among the general male population. Correspondingly there were fewer parents in the professions, proprietorships, and clerical or craftsman jobs among the juvenile delinquents' parents than among the gainfully employed workers in general. Thus there does seem to be a relationship between employment of the parent and criminal versus noncriminal behavior. As previously discussed, this is probably an additional factor influencing the relationship between the socioeconomic environment and crime rate.

CLIMATE. Crime rate in various climates is fairly uniform, but there is evidence that the type of criminal activity varies according to environmental conditions of temperature and humidity. Figure 15.3 shows month-by-month variations in crime rate from the 1963 annual average for serious crimes. Inspection of Figure 15.3 reveals that murder, rape, and assault

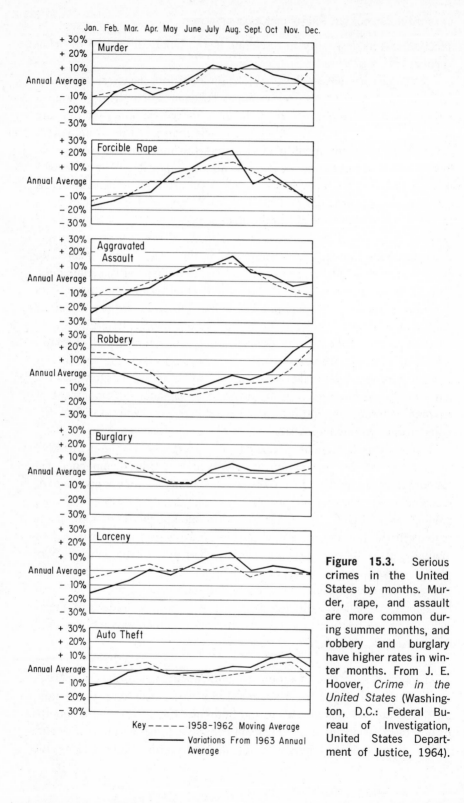

Figure 15.3. Serious crimes in the United States by months. Murder, rape, and assault are more common during summer months, and robbery and burglary have higher rates in winter months. From J. E. Hoover, *Crime in the United States* (Washington, D.C.: Federal Bureau of Investigation, United States Department of Justice, 1964).

occur more frequently under warm weather conditions, and robbery occurs more often during the colder months of the year.

There is a relationship between the kind of crime committed and climatic conditions. The environmental conditions may be the precipitating cause of the particular kind of criminal behavior. In very cold weather, crimes against property are more important for the offender. Crimes against other persons are more likely to occur because of emotionalized conditions more easily aroused in summer months, when the necessities of life, such as food and warmth, are more readily available.

RADIO, TELEVISION, MOVIES, AND THE PRESS. Although a great many comments have been made concerning the disadvantages of television, radio, newspapers, magazines, and movies to the upbringing of American children, little evidence indicates exactly what effect these media have. It is true that attitudes as measured by questionnaires and even behavioral changes can be noted after the presentation of a film or reading of certain materials. On the other hand, who is to say what material a child or a young person should be allowed to read? Even the story of "The Three Bears" can be questioned, because it might be inferred that it teaches a child that it is proper to walk into someone else's home, eat their food or porridge, and sleep in their beds.

Even though we are cognizant of the values of learning in predicting and controlling behavior, most of us do not realize how readily opinions or attitudes of people can be changed. Staats and Staats (1957) described how a meaning response to a word, such as a person's name, could be changed solely by language experience. Presenting nonsense syllables with no apparent emotional connotations to subjects at the same time that emotionally toned words were presented showed that the word meaning could easily be attached to the nonsense syllables. Apparently all that was needed was repeated exposure to the neutral stimulus (the nonsense syllables) at the same time that the emotionally toned words were presented.

Cohen (1964) questioned the work of Staats and Staats. His experimentation essentially replicated their work, but checked on the awareness of the subjects during the learning. He found that such learning could take place, but only for the subjects who were aware that learning was taking place. Thus it seems that attitudes can be changed rather rapidly by learning procedures if a person knows that such learning is to take place. If a person wants to learn something about crime from criminal reporting, he can. Combining names of people with negatively toned words may change a person's attitude toward the names of the people involved, or it may have little or no effect. (The important variable of awareness of the learner is discussed in Chapter 1.)

Individual films, television programs, stories, or radio programs may have an effect upon an individual. When specific details are given about how to commit a particular crime, it is obvious that some people may use such information to commit an antisocial act.

Some reporting may actually enhance criminal activity by glorifying the criminal. Most legitimate public media now recognize the fact that criminals are often seeking publicity by their criminal acts. Thus the reporting is done in such a manner that the individual criminal is shown to poorest advantage. Even a typical Hollywood melodrama inevitably ends up showing retribution for the criminal activity. In summary, we have to repeat that it is possible to influence behavior by mass media. Who is to decide what services media should and should not provide and on what basis such decisions are to be made is highly questionable.

DRUGS AND ALCOHOL. During 1963, 41.2 percent of the total arrests in the United States were for liquor laws violations, charges of driving while intoxicated, and drunkenness charges. Many rules and regulations of society are regularly broken by users of alcohol and drugs. Most of the offenses involving alcohol are less serious charges but occur in large numbers. On the other hand, narcotic drug law violations represented only 0.7 percent of the total arrests during 1963. The most important criminal result of the use of drugs is the behavior of the drug addict brought about by his financial need to purchase the drug. Thus the small percentage of arrests for narcotic drug law violations does not indicate the seriousness of the situation. Various estimates show that 90 to 98 percent of drug addicts are involved in other criminal acts at least partially to support their habit.

The problems of drug addiction are considerably more severe and less socially acceptable than the problems of alcoholism. Thus our discussion primarily concerns drug addiction. First we must define addiction. Bowman (1958) defined addiction as "1. An overpowering desire or need (compulsion) to continue taking the drug and to obtain it by any means; 2. A tendency to increase the dose; 3. A psychic and sometimes a physical dependence on the effects of the drug." The drug addict has progressed to the point where all of his resources are directed toward obtaining the drug.

Usually drug addiction in the United States is to opium and its derivatives (heroin, paregoric, and codeine). Morphine is also derived from opium and with heroin makes up the two most commonly used narcotic drugs in the United States. In addition, cocaine, derived from coca leaves, and marijuana, derived from Indian hemp, are controlled under federal narcotic legislation but are not drug-addicting in the usual sense of producing a physical dependency. The most important characteristic of marijuana and cocaine is that they introduce the user to dependence on a stronger drug for a satisfactory adjustment to life. Likewise, alcohol may also do the same thing. In addition to the drugs just mentioned, the barbituates, such as the bromides, phenobarbital, and benzidrine, can lead to addiction, but these are not ordinarily considered narcotic drugs.

Drug addiction requires repeated dosage on the part of the user. Although there are differences of opinion about how much repeated use is necessary before a person becomes a drug addict, it seems that at least two weeks of daily usage is needed. It is relatively easy to establish the habit, and a tolerance to the use of the drug is rapidly established. Thus the user soon becomes aware of certain desirable physiological reactions after using the drug, but finds that with use, additional quantities must be taken in order to produce the same effects.

The first drug experience is rather temporary and may produce nausea, like the early stage of alcoholic drinking. After the first few dosages, there is usually no nausea and a feeling of goodness or euphoria takes place with the use of the drug. The narcotic drugs are depressants and generally result in a decrease of sexual desire, drowsiness, relief of physical pain, and a general feeling of relaxation and contentment. Many young people get "hooked" into the use of drugs because of an initial trial as a result of a dare or at the suggestion of the neighborhood gang. As the pleasurable effects are experienced they tend to increase the desire to repeat the dosage. After about two weeks of regular dosage, a physical dependence is established. This means that the drug must be consistently received in the body or strong withdrawal symptoms of a physiological nature will take place.

Coleman (1964) described typical withdrawal symptoms: "The first symptoms to be noted are yawning, sneezing, sweating, and anorexia, followed by increased desire for the drug, restlessness, psychic depression and feelings of impending doom, irritability, muscular weakness, and an increased respiration rate. As time passes, these symptoms become more severe; in addition there may be chilliness alternating with vasomotor disturbances of flushing and excessive sweating (this may result in marked pilomotor activity so that the skin of the addict resembles that of a plucked turkey), vomiting, diarrhea, abdominal cramps, pains in the back and extremities, severe headache, marked tremors. The patient refuses food and water, and this, coupled with the vomiting, sweating, and diarrhea, results in dehydration and in weight losses as great as 5 to 15 pounds in a day. Occasionally there may be delirium, hallucinations, and manic activity." The withdrawal symptoms increase in intensity for about 3 or 4 days and then disappear slowly with all acute symptoms usually gone in 5 to 7 days after the last intake of the drugs. Generally restlessness and insomnia may appear with an ordinary physical weakness for 3 or 4 months after the last intake of the drug. Because these withdrawal symptoms are so extreme, a person tends to stay hooked on the habit, and as the tolerance for the drug increases, has to maintain increasingly large dosages just to stay "normal." The drug becomes an indispensable element in the body equilibrium.

The extreme physical dependence upon drugs with the terrible withdrawal symptoms force the addict to purchase a supply continually. In the early 1960's, a drug addict in the United States often needed $60 to $100 worth of drugs per day to maintain a habit. Thus the drug addict is often forced into criminal behavior to obtain enough funds to purchase his needed drug. Perhaps this is far more important in terms of criminal behavior than the actual drug addiction. Because the person addicted to the drug is so busy seeking the drugs and even engaging in illegal behavior in order to obtain financial support for his habit, he rarely has an opportunity to lead a normal life or to develop a vocation.

Why a person turns to drugs seems to be questionable at this time. Many sociologists and psychologists who have studied drug addiction have suggested that psychological problems are the cause of drug addiction. Of course, many people have psychological problems and do not turn to drug addiction. But if a person in need of help tries drugs he may easily become addicted.

Taking the drug away from the person may result in a "cure" in that the person no longer uses the drug. Whether this is really a successful breaking of a habit is quite questionable. There is a general disinterest on the part of society in trying to provide facilities for drug addiction cure and rather unfavorable prognosis for treatment. Ausubel (1958), after discussing drug addiction from a psychological, physiological, and sociological point of view, suggested that many of the researchers in the field did not understand the medical aspects. He suggested that even a 35-percent cure rate would be quite optimistic. Considering that the persons involved in drug addiction have inadequate personalities that are being supported by drugs, Ausubel suggested that it is rather amazing that there is any cure rate at all. He stated that the average relapse rate of "cured" drug addicts is so high that only about 12–15 percent of addicts who receive specialized treatment may be expected to abstain from drug addiction over long periods of time.

Winick (1961) presented a little more optimistic view of drug addict treatment when he wrote that "There are addicts who do not revert to drug use for reasons which are not known because of the lack of adequate research. Only 40 percent of the patients at the hospital at Lexington come back more than once although some have come back for as many as 20 times. Some 14 percent of the patients at Lexington account for 42 percent of the total admissions. Some patients go to Lexington to withdraw so that they can re-establish their addiction at a lower dosage." Winick suggested that most addicts who do revert to the use of drugs seem to have longer and longer periods of abstinence between drug usage. He goes on later to suggest that "The poor results so far obtained with treatment of addicts should not be discouraging, any more than poor results in schizophrenia or cancer research are keeping us from an extensive program of research and treatment in these fields." He felt that the real problem in drug addiction is the lack of public interest in research and understanding of the problems.

Hopes for cures of drug addiction are better than they ever were before. Some researchers find that more and better treatment centers are reducing addiction and that relapse rate is lowered. More public understanding of the problem and additional research and treatment facilities will improve the prognosis for a drug addict and ultimately reduce the problem of drug addiction.

DETECTING DECEPTION

Most criminal behavior is accomplished by people who do not want to be prosecuted or punished for their activity. Therefore evidence proving nonconforming behavior is generally collected from all possible sources including the criminal himself. Whether the individual is telling the truth or not is questionable, so that modern-day criminology uses lie detectors to help estimate whether a person is telling the truth or not. Unfortunately there is no such machine as a "lie detector." There are machines and techniques that allow specialists to estimate whether a person is becoming emotionalized more to some statements than to others. These are the so-called lie detectors.

The "Lie Detector".   The "lie detector" is a machine that records a variety of physiological characteristics that may change during interrogation of a person. It therefore measures physiological changes that take place within an individual with concomitant changes in his emotional state. The use of such a technique is not completely new. Centuries ago, lie-detection measures were attempted. For example, it is reported that King Solomon established the maternity of a child by noting the extreme fear of the actual mother when he threatened to sever the child's body. Torture devices, particularly during the medieval years, were used as methods of forcing true statements. (A carryover of such torture known as the "third degree" is sometimes used by law enforcement employees in an attempt to obtain confessions.)

Modern methods of detecting lies from true statements measure blood pressure, pulse rate or amplitude, electrical conductivity of the skin, and breathing rate. These factors usually vary with the emotional condition of a person. Emotionalized conditions might be expected to change at the same time that a person lies. Thus an estimate of lying behavior is recorded by the measurement of concomitant changes in the body when emotional state changes. It must be recognized that the same changes in emotionalized conditions may take place as the result of a variety of things other than just the lying behavior. For example, a person may generally be upset and may respond to fear of others or factors in the environment. And some individuals simply do not make the same kinds of responses to fear that are made by the average person.

Machines record the physiological changes of the subject. The interrogator and expert evaluate the records of the machine, statements made by the subjects, and their own observations of the subjects to decide when lies were told. (See Figure 15.4.)

BLOOD PRESSURE AND PULSE RATE CHANGES. Many studies have shown that systolic blood pressure changes as a result of innervations from the sympathetic nervous system. This pressure of the blood at the moment when the valves of the heart are open can readily be measured, and changes in the pressure can be automatically recorded. When changes in blood pressure are correlated with the answers obtained during interrogation, an indication of whether a subject lies or tells the truth is obtained. An assumption is made that a person when telling a lie will have a change in innervation of the sympathetic nervous system. Modern apparatus can continuously record heart beat and systolic pressure. However, such records from regular criminal interrogation are difficult to interpret. A suspect who tightens his grip, tenses his legs, or otherwise creates muscular tension can obscure or make difficult the interpretation of the records. Apparently people familiar with lie detectors can bias their responses in such a way that lying and nonlying responses can not be differentiated.

Pulse rate varies for about the same reasons as blood pressure. Thus apparatus for the measurement of pulse rate can show changes that can be interpreted as lying.

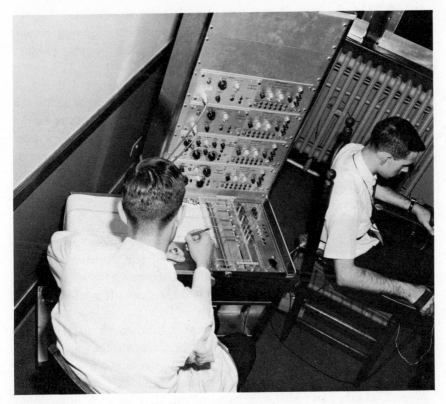

Figure 15.4. A photograph showing operator and subject using a Grass Polygraph or "lie detection" apparatus. (Photograph courtesy of Joseph F. Kubis.)

RESPIRATORY RESPONSES. A pneumograph is an instrument that measures and records breathing rate. The pneumograph consists of a rubber tube, connected around the chest of the suspect, with suitable apparatus to record the inspirations and expirations. The ratio of the time of inspiration and expiration changes with innervation from the nervous system. Although this is not an infallible system for detecting lying, it is another indication. Unusually deep breathing and irregular respiration follow the telling of lies.

PSYCHOGALVANOMIC RESPONSES. The psychogalvanomic responses may be measured in two ways. One method introduces a small amount of electricity to the surface of the skin at one point and measures the amount of that electricity available at another nearby point. Variations in the conductivity of the skin can be noted and are referred to as the psychogalvanomic response. Another method is the measurement of the actual electrical activity on the surface of the skin.

Both psychogalvanomic responses are extremely sensitive and difficult to record and interpret. They represent changes in the organism accompanying changes in the sympathetic nervous system and thus may indicate lying behavior.

BRAIN WAVES. Some minute electrical currents are generated in the brain and may be measured by suitable apparatus. Measurement of the electrical results from the brain shows two wave patterns: (1) a slow rhythmical current, named the Alpha Wave, and (2) a much faster wave, called the Beta Wave, superimposed on the Alpha Wave. The Alpha Wave tends to disappear during states of emotional agitation. Thus measurement of brain waves is another method for estimating lying, but it also involves very sensitive apparatus and difficult interpretation of records.

In addition to previously mentioned techniques, the eye movements of a subject have been measured as estimates of lying behavior. Berrien (1942) reported that judges could differentiate guilty from nonguilty suspects by observing their eye movements during and after interrogation.

USE OF "LIE DETECTORS". Fear, anger, embarrassment, surprise, or strong stimulation from the environment can change any of the physiological measurements just discussed. Thus extraneous factors can corrupt the records of an interrogation. Even with these difficulties, the physiological changes that take place with emotionalized conditions provide information of value in estimating lying behavior. (See Figure 15.5.)

The value of lie detection by the use of polygraphs (lie detectors) is somewhat questionable. Very few courts allow information collected by polygraphs to be presented in court as objective evidence. In some situations, testimony by an expert witness who has read the polygraph recordings and has been present at or has conducted the interrogation of a suspect may be brought into court as evidence. There have been studies indicating that polygraphs can measure lying. One rather elaborate program carried out for the Air Force Systems Command of the United States Air Force was reported by Kubis (1962). He concluded that there is sufficient validity in the experiments that he conducted to warrant confidence in the lie-detecting procedure as an aid to interrogation processes. Although he used a simulated test situation for the experiments, Kubis reported that trained personnel examining data from the lie detector were able to attain significant accuracy in identifying the thief, the lookout, and the innocent suspect. Even so, Kubis concluded that "the intelligent suspect is capable of controlling his reactions to such an extent that he can elude detection in the ordinary lie detection procedure, provided that he has been trained

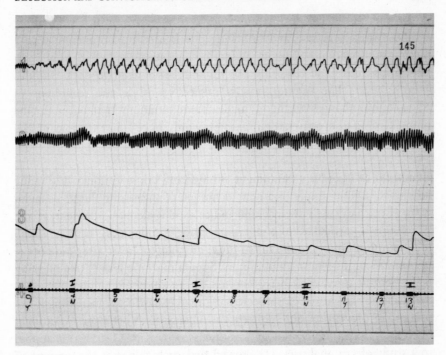

Figure 15.5. A photograph of a section of recording paper from a Grass Polygraph. From top to bottom the chart records respiration pattern (1), pulse rate (2), psychogalvanic skin response (3), and the stimuli marker and time line (4). Large blocks of ink on the time line indicate points at which stimuli (association words) were given to the subject. Significant responses are shown in the pulse rate and psychogalvanic record at I and II. (Photograph courtesy of Joseph F. Kubis.)

in the use of effective countermeasures." He reported that the psychogalvanic response was the most effective measurement of those recorded. He also suggested that the research did not provide sufficient evidence to encourage the development of a computer connected to the lie-detecting apparatus to provide on-the-spot decisions on guilt or innocence of a suspect.

Exactly why there is a change in galvanic skin resistance is not known. A study reported by Johnson and Corah (1963) indicated that there are racial differences in skin resistance. They found that Negro subjects had higher skin resistance than a comparable white population. They suggested that a variety of other factors besides race must be included in the growing list of variables that determine skin resistance. Such variability increases the difficulty in interpreting the results, even though lie detection generally is interested only in variability of resistance rather than actual amount of resistance.

In the lie-detecting situation, the apparatus measuring respiration, psychogalvanic response, and breathing rate is used in conjunction with a special interrogation technique. A series of questions are asked or a word-association technique requiring the response of a word to each stimulus word is used. The interrogation is carried on while the recordings of physiological changes are being made. Thus variations that occur can be pinpointed to the question, answer, or word spoken at the time of the variance of the lie detector records.

New Apparatus. New equipment for fighting crime is constantly being developed. One example of a new technique of measuring illegal behavior is the Breathalyzer. This machine indicates the alcoholic content of the blood and is particularly useful in estimating drunkenness, because symptoms of intoxication are similar to those of epilepsy, heart attack, diabetes, or overdose of insulin or tranquillizers. Such a machine is only one of many new scientific discoveries being applied to the study of criminal behavior. Scientific investigation of suspected criminal behavior is increasingly important in prevention and prosecution of antisocial behavior. Additional fascinating scientific technology was discussed by Kirk (1963) as it applies to a study of criminalistics. He showed that such things as the amount of gold, cobalt, manganese, and other rare minerals in human hair can be measured and used to identify positively the origin of the hair.

COURTROOM PROCEDURES

Now that we have discussed factors in criminal behavior and problems of detecting deception, we turn to proving guilt or innocence. In many countries of the world, including the United States, a suspect is considered innocent until proven guilty. Courts provide a location for presentation of evidence of guilt and innocence and judgment thereof. Courtrooms are generally massive structures with quiet atmospheres. Court proceedings involve a great deal of ritual. The courtrooms and ritual help create the proper atmosphere for a serious investigation of the factors involved in the suspected antisocial act.

Before we further discuss courtroom activity, we must understand some commonly used terminology. There are two general types of court cases. Criminal cases involve prosecution of a person who has broken a rule or regulation of society. The prosecution is on the side of the people and prosecutes the defendant. It is up to the prosecuting attorney to prove the defendant guilty. The defense attorney does everything possible to show his client innocent. In civil cases, a plaintiff is a person who is seeking retribution for an alleged act of another. He asks a judge or jury to decide whether he has been unjustly affected by another person, and if so, to recommend some compensation for the damages incurred. The plaintiff is represented by an attorney who tries to prove by a preponderance of evidence that the plaintiff has been damaged, and the defending attorney tries to show that this was not so. Our discussions are primarily oriented toward criminal cases, although the principles also apply to civil trials.

The purpose of the courts is to protect the liberty and freedom of citizens. Because of this, it is the duty of the prosecutor in a criminal case to prove beyond a reasonable doubt that a defendant has broken a rule or regulation of society. The prosecution must convince a jury or a judge that the defendant is guilty. As Cohen (1961) suggested: "When the defendant appears in the court room, the jurors must consider him innocent, and it is the task of the prosecutor to remove from around the shoulders of the defendant 'beyond a reasonable doubt' this mantle of innocence with which the law has clothed him. 'Presumption of innocence' and 'proof beyond a reasonable doubt' creates psychological factors which favor the defendant. However, other factors inherent in the nature of the trial favor the prosecution."

The suspected criminal and the prosecutor are usually represented by specialists (attorneys). In criminal cases the prosecutor represents the people via a local, state, or federal governmental agency. Thus the trial is the people of the Commonwealth of Pennsylvania versus John Doe; or the United States of America versus John Doe. The prosecutor always stresses this point to show that he is on the side of the people, protecting them from the defendant. The case is usually tried before a well-respected citizen who has been elected or appointed as a judge, and in some cases, a peer group called a jury. The judge has usually been selected because of his education, experience, and knowledge of the law. It is his duty to hear both sides, make a judgment on the guilt or innocence, and pass sentence on the suspect, or in the case of a jury trial, instruct the jury, hear their decision, and then pass sentence.

We will consider psychology and the use of psychological knowledge by attorneys in the courtroom as related to the jury, witnesses, testimony, and judgments of the jury.

The Jury.   In criminal cases, a suspect ordinarily has the right to request a jury or a nonjury trial. If he requests a jury trial, his attorney as well as the prosecuting attorney has the right to select the jurors that will be hearing the facts of the case as presented by the two opposing sides. The choosing and functioning of the jury is an area where psychology is closely involved in legal activity.

The function of a jury is to determine, from the contradictions and assertions of two parties, the truth of the contested issue. The judge can then apply the law to the conclusions reached by the jury and see that the proper sentencing and legal procedures are followed.

Trial by jury originated to supplant a system that was less efficient. In early days the feudal lords or high-placed officials had absolute control over all other citizens. With the passage of time, it became apparent that a group of fellow citizens could do a better and a fairer job of evaluating the behavior of a suspected citizen. The jurors were selected because they knew the individual and the general circumstances involved in the litigation. Such a jury system worked rather well and avoided many of the injustices of the earlier systems.

In modern days the jury system has many shortcomings. For example, modern-day juries must decide which of the facts at issue are to be given the greatest weight. A jury may be asked to decide on a civil case involving liability, or a burglary case, or a homicide. Jurors must evaluate testimonies of all kinds of people from many specialties and varying educational backgrounds. It is impossible to collect jurors who can be competent to interpret all the testimony presented to them. However, this system is in use so we will describe some of the places where psychology comes into the selection of jurors and why this selection is important.

In some jurisdictions the judge questions prospective jurors and selects them for a particular trial. In most situations the prosecuting and defense attorneys have the authority to pass on jurors and therefore select from among an available jury list. The prosecuting and defense attorneys each have the right to waive from duty any person who shows a detrimental view to the proceedings. They each also have a limited number of peremptory challenges which they can use arbitrarily. Thus they may excuse a juror from serving on a particular jury for reason or for no reason at all, if they feel so inclined.

Selecting jurors is difficult because each of the defense and prosecuting sides may question each prospective juror. This questioning is done in an attempt to select jurors who the questioning attorney feels are going to be favorably inclined toward his position, and to prepare them for some of the problems that may arise during the trial.

Apparently there is no experimentally proven best method of selecting jurors. Prospective jurors are often excused on the basis of specific information. For example, a particular religious background or attitude toward a problem may be important during the trial, so an attorney might excuse a prospective juror because of a prejudice that would influence the case. Attorneys during the examination and selection of jurors are creating impressions on the jury that may influence the trial. Thus they have to be very careful about the way they select members to the panel. If they have to excuse a person, they must do so in a manner that will not alienate the other jurors who might tend to identify with the unwanted juror. Most attorneys also like to create a good feeling on the part of the jurors that they do select and so question them in such a manner as to provide a positive attitude at the beginning of the trial. More specific evidence is needed as to exactly what is important in selecting jurors.

Juries decide facts or make decisions on the guilt or innocence on many factors other than the specific evidence presented during the trial. Thus it is important for the attorneys to keep in mind the nationality, educational level, experiences, backgrounds, and so on, of the witnesses, the defendants, the jurors and others when selecting jurors and during the trial. Biases on the part of the jury cannot readily be changed during a trial and are very likely going to be important when the balloting of the jury takes place.

In general, the American citizen is more willing to accept the view that the evidence should be used to decide guilt or innocence than might be expected. The problem is to find jurors who can listen to evidence and decide guilt or innocence according to the facts presented. Prejudices, attitudes, and mental sets color the process of decision and are strongly ensconced in the individual. Prospective jurors do not realize that they have the biases and that the biases may affect their perceptions of the evidence presented. It is up to the attorneys to be "psychologists" when selecting jurors to serve on the panel.

The jury trial ordinarily begins with an opening statement by the prosecutor addressed to the jury. He tries to help the jury understand what is going to happen during the trial. He usually does not engage in an emotional appeal but presents a straightforward picture of the proceedings that will take place to show the jury the kind of crime charged against the defendant. There is a good deal of "psychology" in presentation techniques used, but there is little scientific evidence available as to which of various forms of presentation are best.

After the prosecuting attorney presents his opening statement, the defense attorney has the option of presenting an opening statement or waiting until later. Usually the defense attorney gives his opening statement when presenting his first witness. The "psychological" reasons for this are not well validated, but the reasoning seems logically correct.

Witnesses. In a criminal case, it is the responsibility of the prosecuting attorney to bring in all the witnesses that can present information concerning the events that occurred. When a witness is brought to the witness stand, he ordinarily is sworn in by an oath. This procedure is based on the assumption that a person is a more reliable witness when he has sworn to tell the truth. Although strong oaths including kissing the Bible, and so on, are not as prevalent as they were at one time, there is generally a good deal of emotional appeal to the courtroom situation and the oath taking. Whether or not this increases the veracity of the statements made by the witness is questionable. One study (Burtt, 1951) indicated that in a laboratory situation, subjects that ordinarily gave testimony that was 20–25 percent incorrect gave only 10 percent incorrect testimony when placed under oath. Other laboratory studies are in general agreement with these findings. Unfortunately studies cannot be conducted in the courtroom situation, so objective, practical evidence is not available. Oath taking is apparently conducive to truth telling, especially when a witness has little at stake himself.

There is not much scientific evidence indicating which order of narration of evidence is most valuable for a prosecuting attorney. It is up to the attorney to use his own "psychology" to pick the witnesses and present them in the order that he thinks most valuable to his case. Often the prosecuting attorney picks as the first one a strong witness who he thinks will be able to stand up to strong cross examination by the defense counsel. He then uses the rest of his available witnesses to present the case in what he thinks is an organized manner, generally ending with a strong witness. This procedure is based on the assumption that the testimony of the last witness will be remembered most by the jurors when they adjourn for their deliberations. The order of presenting information has been studied in a laboratory. Such a study (Weld and Roff, 1938) showed that there were shifts in the judgment of guilt or innocence as testimony was presented to a group of "jurors." They also showed that not only the degree to which the jurors were certain of the defendant's guilt varied as the evidence was presented, but different orders of presentation of evidence produced different shifts of judgment of guilty and of a final verdict of the jurors. It does seem that the order of presenting evidence is important. A later study (Weld and Danzig, 1940) showed that the opening and closing statements of the attorneys on both sides were important in the attitudes of the jurors. However, no evidence specifically indicates which material should be presented at a particular time in the sequence to bring about a particular verdict by a jury.

The defense attorney does everything he can to show that the defendant is not as bad as pictured by the prosecuting attorney. Frequently emotional aspects are emphasized rather than the factual presentations of material.

There are a variety of ways in which the defense counsel attempts to develop sympathy for his client. If possible, he tries to raise a doubt in the jurors' minds about the guilt of the defendant and also tries to show that the defendant is a very nice person. The defense attorney may try to show that the prosecuting attorney is being unfair or that the injured party was a bad person in the first place. Humor may be brought into play in an attempt to discredit the opposing attorney's presentation. Although these methods are used, there is apparently little scientific evidence proving one method is better than another or that any of the techniques work.

Cross examination has been mentioned as the only condition where the witness can be tested. Cross examination is the time when an attorney can ask questions of the witness provided by the opposition. In general, it is not appropriate to ask leading questions during direct examination, so that the prosecuting attorney, when presenting his case, must only ask general questions and let the witness present the information. If there are witnesses for the defense, direct examination must be conducted in the same manner. During cross examination, leading questions, trick questions, and attempts to discredit the witness are all legitimate. Thus cross-examination techniques receive a great deal of attention in the training of lawyers. Again, no specific scientific evidence seems to be available to support a particular cross-examination technique. Gair (1961) indicated what the attorney must do during cross examination: "The lawyer must know enough to stop while he is ahead, to let well enough alone. The cross-examiner must constantly sniff the atmosphere for signs of danger. It may be a paradox, but he is at once inwardly apprehensive and outwardly confident. He never cross-examines just to hear once more some evidence which delighted him, either on the witness's direct or on his cross-examination. He may not hear it again. Only too often the witness may rephrase his answer so as to rob it of its original effect. He may guilelessly and with the jury's sympathy explain away his answer." It is fairly apparent that there is no specific way to best cross-examine in all situations.

In the typical courtroom situation, cross examination places a stress upon the witness. The topic of stress has been discussed in some detail by Gerver (1957), who concluded: "In our court system, it would appear that stressful witness behavior results from an interaction of the personal insecurities that the witness brings to the situation and those components of the courtroom situation which function to aggravate these personal insecurities. Ceremony, legal roles and their associated social relationships, public display of private inadequacies, the apparent inflexibility of the rules of evidence seemingly designed to frustrate the witness and limit his contribution, the domination of the proceedings by the lawyers, and that shadowy figure, the judge—all may be perceived by the witness as factors which stimulate and reinforce feelings of insecurity and emotional discomfort." There seems little doubt that the average witness is uneasy in the witness chair and that the stress of the situation may add to the questionable testimony as discussed in the next sections.

Testimony. Psychology as a science has produced a good deal of information concerning the interaction of man with his external environment. Among this data is information concerning how an individual perceives stimulation, interacts with it, and responds. This data is valuable for the courtroom situation. Testimony is the giving of a report by an individual about a specialized situation or series of events that earlier occurred in his presence. Thus the processes of perception, attention, reporting, and memory are involved in testimony.

It is rather unfortunate that relatively little psychological research concerning testimony has appeared since the First World War. Just before 1917, there was a flurry of interest in the problems of the psychology of testimony. From 1918 through 1960 relatively little work concerning this application of psychology appeared in print. Thus we begin our discussion of the factors affecting the accuracy of testimony with material presented by Berrien (1952).

"It is perfectly obvious that accurate testimony in court will depend upon the accuracy with which the initial observations are made. The factors that creep in to distort the original impressions are related, on the one hand, to manifest sensory illusions and defects studied in general psychology. On the other hand, influences not generally recognized also account for some inexact observations.

SENSORY FACTORS—VISION. The courts and the general public are for the most part aware of the common visual defects that may prevent clear observation. Nearsighted persons, when not wearing corrective lenses, cannot be expected to give unimpeachable evidence of events occurring some considerable distance from them, the degree of reliability depending upon the degree of defect. Conversely, farsighted persons have difficulty in making fine discriminations at distances within arm's length. Not often is the farsighted individual handicapped in giving testimony because of his defect, because most events contested in court take place at distances greater than arm's length.

Color blindness, occurring in about 4 percent of the male population and in only about one fourth as many women, is a condition that may distort some testimony without the witness being aware of his limitation.

Some people with moderate degrees of color blindness, in which the reds and greens are distinguished imperfectly, do not discover the fact until adulthood, even though presumably the defect has been present since birth. It is relatively easy to discover even a color weakness by means of the Ishahara test, which consists of a number of cards covered with colored dots. Within the dotted field a pattern of similarly colored dots forms a numeral ordinarily perceptible. The color-blind person either does not see the numeral or does see a pattern, but different from the one normally perceived.

The effect of illumination on visual acuity and also on color vision is an important consideration in evaluating testimony. It is well known that low degrees of illumination decrease visibility, but it is not so well known that the relative brightness of colors changes as illumination decreases. The brightest colors under ordinary daylight are the yellows. As illumination decreases at nightfall or in darkened rooms, the reds and yellows rapidly decrease in brilliance, and the greens and blues become brighter relative to other colors of the spectrum. It is therefore quite possible for a witness in all sincerity to testify apart from all other distorting influences that the accused was wearing a bluish-green jacket and a black skirt when actually the skirt was dark red. 'False' testimony on one color under low degrees of illumination is no reason for striking out testimony concerning other colors.

The problem of illumination entered into a controversy between two taxi companies. The cabs of one company were painted white and the rival cabs were orange. The taxis could readily be distinguished during the day and under ordinary street illumination at night, but in areas flooded with illumination from reddish-orange neon signs the cabs appeared to be the same color. Consequently not only must the degree of illumination be considered but also the quality of colors at night.

It is a well-known fact that we can see better in a darkened room after being in dim light for some time than we can when we step directly from a brightly lighted area. This increase in night vision takes place very rapidly in the first three or four minutes and then more slowly for the next half hour. The red end of the spectrum shows the least improvement in visibility and the violet or blue end shows the greatest improvement (Chapanis, 1947). This suggests that testimony concerning dim red lights at night or in darkened areas is open to more doubt than testimony concerning equally bright (in physical measurements) blue or violet lights. One could also legitimately raise questions about a person's testimony concerning what he saw when he stepped from a brightly lighted room into a darkened street.

Among the illusions that may from time to time distort testimony is the tendency to overestimate vertical and underestimate horizontal distances. Similarly an unbroken line, such as a wire or taut rope, is usually judged shorter than an equal length of rope broken by vertical lines. An empty clothes line would appear shorter than one of equal length with clothes pins on it. 'Unfilled' space (an open lot) is judged smaller than 'filled' space (the same lot with a house on it). Long, perfectly straight lines that intersect with a series of short lines all set at the same oblique angle will appear curved rather than straight.

The visual estimation of speed is often a matter of controversy in cases involving automobile accidents and elsewhere. It has been recognized both by psychologists and the courts that estimation of speed is more inaccurate when motion is directly toward or away from the observer than when it is across his line of vision. This fact is particularly noticeable if one observes an approaching train and compares its apparent speed some distance down the track with the speed as it passes by. An incomplete and unpublished study by some Colgate students, however, found that if the observers were 100 yards to one side of a straight and level road auto speeds were estimated with greater error than if stationed at the roadside. This study also supported the courts' general recognition that practice or experience in estimating speeds improves a witness's competency in giving such testimony.

Still other factors influence estimation of speed. In one study, 29 subjects were asked to judge the rate at which automobiles passed a given point. The cars differed widely, varying from a small four-cylinder car to a large de luxe model. It was clear that the judgments of the observers depended upon the noise the car made, its size, and the rate of the car just preceding (Richardson, 1916).

DISTANCE JUDGMENTS.   When dealing with small distances within reach, people generally overestimate lengths of one to three inches and underestimate distances of four to 40 inches (Brown, Knauft, and Rosenbaum, 1948). For greater distances measured in feet or hundreds of feet no comparable data are available. However, distance judgments of this magnitude depend upon a host of stimulus conditions too numerous to describe at this point. At middle distances—10 to 100 feet—judgments depend heavily upon cues that come from both eyes. The fact that the eyes are separated by about two and one half inches makes it impossible for both eyes to receive exactly the same image. These slight discrepancies in the images are still detectable by special means when viewing objects as far away as a mile. From these disparate images we get cues that aid in estimating distance. Moreover, as objects move from in front of our nose to greater distances, both eyes turn outward, converging less and less. The convergence of the eyes controlled by the extraocular muscles also provides a source of cues for distance judgments. It is apparent, therefore, that one-eyed persons are less apt to be accurate in judging middle distances than people with normal vision in both eyes.

AUDITORY SENSATIONS. The chief difficulty with testimony involving auditory sensations lies in determining the direction from which sound comes. The ability to localize the source of sounds is very easily disturbed by echoes or large reflecting surfaces. For example, a witness was approaching a street intersection surrounding by buildings four to six stories high. As he was walking on the right sidewalk going south, some sixty yards from the intersection he heard a loud report which appeared to come from the intersecting street to the east. Upon investigation, he found the sound source was actually on the west. The false localization was attributed to the sound being reflected from the building on the opposite side of the street from the witness. It is possible to conceive of numerous situations in which testimony may be confused by such false localization.

In the absence of reflecting and echoing surfaces, location of sound sources is ordinarily reasonably accurate except for sound originating in the median plane of the body. By 'median plane' is meant any point which is equidistant from each ear. The confusion in such cases is not in regard to its location to the right or left but rather as to whether the sound came from in front of or behind, above, or below the observer. Gross inaccuracies of this magnitude are rare but do occur, particularly when the sound is unexpected and momentary.

The range of vibrations and frequencies an individual can hear is occasionally of importance in testimony. Generally speaking, as people increase in age they become insensitive to the higher frequencies. From time to time, also, one may meet a witness with a 'tonal island.' Such an individual is insensitive to a range of frequencies but can hear tones that are higher and some that are lower. Ordinary speech makes use of a great variety of vibration frequencies, so that an individual might have a tonal island and be as unaware of it as most people are unaware of the blind spot in each eye. It is conceivable also that a given warning tone might produce just those frequencies to which the individual is deaf. Consequently such an individual's testimony on the sounding of the warning should be considered inaccurate, even though his hearing in other respects might be quite normal.

Background noises also mask sounds that could otherwise be heard. This effect is such that low-frequency noises even at moderately low intensities can blot out enough speech sounds to make a public speaker unintelligible in an open space without a public address system. On the other hand, some people who work in places where. the noise is high in pitch and high in intensity learn to talk 'under the noise' and make themselves understood. High-pitched noise masks principally the high frequencies, but low-pitched noise has a more widespread effect on the total range of sounds (Chapanis, Garner, and Morgan, 1949).

THE CUTANEOUS SENSES. The cutaneous senses include touch, pain, heat, and cold. Ordinarily these play a minor part in testimony. In passing, it may be noted that the effects of contrast and adaptation are also found in other sense impressions that are of somewhat more importance in the cutaneous senses.

Contrast refers to the apparent enhancement of differences in experiences in the same sense field that occur either in rapid succession or simultaneously. Thus a warm object may feel very hot to the hand if the individual has just previously handled something cold.

Adaptation refers to the temporary decrease in sensitivity that comes about either through a gradual change in the stimulating circumstances or through a prolonged exposure to a constant stimulus. For example, one is not ordinarily aware of the pressure of his clothing except when it is first put on. The tub of water may feel hot at first, but as the skin senses become adapted, it becomes just pleasantly warm. Testimony about such experiences ought to be prefaced by statements concerning prior stimulating conditions.

TASTE AND SMELL. Occasionally testimony concerning taste is of legal importance, especially in regard to accusations of poisoning. The principal inaccuracies in this area concern confusion of taste and smell. In reality there are, of course, only four primary tastes: sweet, sour, salt, and bitter. Foods that seem to be primarily fruity or burnt or something other than sweet, sour, salty, or bitter are really smelled rather than tasted. Prior tastes may also distort gustatory observations. Hence it is important when assertions are made about given tastes to know what was eaten or drunk previously."

EXPECTATION. It is a well-documented fact that we perceive what we expect to perceive. The student interested in a particular sports car reports that he sees several such cars around the college campus every day. When other students are questioned, they have never seen such an automobile on the campus. The person who is looking for the particular automobile "sees it." In the same manner, testimony based upon events that have been observed by humans is subjected to the difficulties of expectation on the part of the individual.

The expectation works not only in perceiving what one expects to see but also in remembering and interpreting stimulation from the external environment in terms of expectation. If we expect to see an individual performing a particular function, we are more likely to take semiambiguous stimuli and interpret it as evidence that the person is performing the behavior that we expected. Numerous classroom exercises have demonstrated the influence of attention and expectation on recall. Berrien (1952) reported an experiment in which a student walked into the class late and interrupted the lecture by declaring he had lost some white rats. The student walked slowly across the front of the room, turned around, and went out while carrying on a previously rehearsed conversation with the instructor concerning the loss and the search for the rats. In spite of the fact that the student–actor was well known to the class, the estimate of his weight ranged from 145 to 210 pounds (actual weight 190). Eight of the 43 students in the class said that he wore a maroon-colored sweater (he actually wore a tan double-breasted coat), and the majority declared vehemently that he searched in the corners for rats (he made only one furtive glance toward one of the corners). These reports were based on expectations, because most of the students on the campus at the time did wear maroon sweaters and the searching was expected since he had indicated he was looking for lost rats.

Studies in perception clearly show that perception is strongly influenced by past experience and expectation. When people are shown visual illusions, even though knowing they are not looking at a particular object, they identify the illusion as the object. For example, a trapezoidal-shaped piece of metal painted with various shadings of gray when rotated before American subjects appears to be a window frame oscillating. Even when the group sees the trapezoidal-shaped metal at rest and is given an explanation of the illusion, many members still perceive the object as an oscillating window. On the other hand, when rural Zulu boys were tested with the same illusion, only 45 percent of the group saw the trapezoidal shape as an oscillating window. They had grown up in an environment of huts and enclosures that were round and did not have rectangular windows (Allport and Pettigrew, 1957). Past experience and expectation is so strong that the stimuli received by the receptor cells is always interpreted in light of this expectation.

EMOTION. We again emphasize that the jury system allows for biasing of verdicts in terms of emotion rather than fact. Testimony is accepted from people who present themselves well under such stress situations. Unfortunately evidence, such as the new but well-proven scientific methods of identification as discussed by Kirk (1963), are not admissible as evidence. For example, hair samples can be individualized, positive proof of having fired a gun can be obtained, techniques of biologists show individuality of blood, but such scientific evidence can be introduced only as testimony of experts. The ability of the expert as a witness may overshadow the importance of the scientific fact he is presenting. Thus it is appropriate for all those who will ever serve as jurors to understand the problems of witnesses and to recognize the shortcomings of testimony presented by them.

The hearsay rule in testimony requires that if you do not hear, see, smell, or touch it yourself you cannot testify about it. This rule may encourage the use of witnesses who are poorly prepared to testify. Such witnesses are often emotionalized at the time of the occurrence and are likely to have confused perceptions. For example, customers in a store may have seen part of an armed robbery and might better remember the physical characteristics of a "robber" than would the victim of the robbery. However, the evidence of the victim is usually taken in preference to those of the disinterested observers.

CONCLUDING STATEMENT. The entire problem of collecting testimony, sorting through it, and then coming to a decision needs further investigation. Fishman (1957) suggested many areas where research was needed in the psychology of testimony and concluded with some comments concerning the usefulness of any such research findings. He suggested that lawyers, judges, and jurors are reluctant to utilize and credit the findings of psychological studies. However, he stated: "Over the past half century there have been appreciable changes in the workings of our courts, and we are currently in a period of far more rapid change than is frequently appreciated. Almost all of these changes have been in agreement with the recommendations and findings of psychologists, psychiatrists, social workers, and others. Lawyers prefer to say that these changes have come about due to the common sense or the empirical experience of law practitioners and theorists. The student of sociology of knowledge knows, however, that one generation's common sense often relies quite heavily on the findings and theories of a previous generation of scientists and theorists." There is hope that the future will show more use of scientific evidence concerning testimony and other aspects of psychology applied in the courtroom.

Judgment of the Jury. Just how a jury comes to a conclusion is not known, but there have been forces at work seeking to abolish or change some aspects of the jury system. It is not in the province of this text to discuss possible reforms in the jury procedures, but it is interesting and important to know some of the obvious prejudices and biases that will influence jury decisions. It has been estimated, for example, that the jury system as practiced today is right in 99 percent of the cases, even though it is right for the wrong reason many of the times. By and large, there is a feeling among law enforcement officers and jurists that the use of juries is more reliable in criminal than in civil proceedings, but again there is little supporting scientific evidence.

After remembering that there are prejudices and shortcomings in the selection of jurors, we must also recognize many of the other problems. Generally attorneys use their challenges to select juries that will be most useful for their side of the proceedings. Whether these attempts are successful or not is questionable, but it does appear that a jury can be induced to identify with a particular lawyer's client (Belli, 1956). When juries are actually listening to testimony, there are a variety of obvious flaws in the situation. One of the most obvious is that humans do not have large enough attention spans to attend to all of the details presented during a long trial. Legal language is often filled with redundant terminology at a level that even confuses trained lawyers. Often lawyers seek to impress the jury and end up boring them. Consequently there must be periods of inattention on the part of the jury. There is no known way at this time to handle such inattention.

Recesses in trials play havoc with jurors' understanding of complicated cases. Time for eating and resting is essential, but courts sometimes recess for other reasons, including well-planned "emergencies" of the opposing attorneys. Each time that evidence is presented and a time lag is introduced before new or conflicting evidence is presented, the less-than-perfect memory plagues even the most conscientious jurors. It is unrealistic to expect jurors to keep in mind all of the facts of a case from one day to another, over several days, or even over a few hours.

Bias on the part of individual members of the jury is also a well-known problem. Many television and movie film melodramas have emphasized this topic. The biases of humans are often not recognized even by the person himself and are thus insidious but important in bringing about decisions. For example, in many sections of the United States, there are deep-seated race prejudices that exist in spite of widespread knowledge about equality of races. In some areas cases are decided not in terms of the evidence presented, but in terms of the jury's dominant prejudice in favor of one group or another.

Although evidence concerning such prejudices and influences in the actual courtroom situation is not available, there is data that indicates that people tend to value traits in others that would resemble their own traits (Fensterheim and Tresselt, 1953). Consequently a juror could be expected to side with the plaintiff or defendant who is more nearly like himself. We expect people to behave in a certain manner, and when we see them behave in a manner that is similar to the one that we feel is acceptable, we are more inclined to want to believe what they say. Jurors, witnesses, judges, and prosecuting and defending attorneys all have biases that are important in the courtroom.

Research has also shown that an individual will eventually conform to a group even when he originally thinks it is wrong, if the other members of his group persist in their belief (Asch, 1955). Thus a member of a jury will eventually agree with the other members of his jury in opposition to his original perception of facts presented as testimony. Later the same person may believe what he has agreed to rather than his original perception of the fact. Festinger (1957) has demonstrated that a person who says something he does not believe is in a state of dissonance and must reduce the uncomfortable feeling. Because he cannot change what he has said, he changes what he believes. Thus a juror may agree with others in his group even though he is sure they are wrong, and once he has agreed, will change his belief to fit his statement.

It has been suggested that the psychology of law and criminology is really just general psychology. Thus a knowledge of all psychological mechanisms might be extremely important in court situations. The final decisions made by a jury are the result of a host of factors, including evidence presented by the prosecuting and defense attorneys as well as the atmosphere of the courtroom, temperature on the day of the trial, what each juror had for lunch before attending the trial, the color of the prosecuting attorney's hair, and many, many other details so numerous that they could not be catalogued even if an attempt were made. Thus it would be next to impossible to have each juror know all the pertinent psychological knowledge available. Even if this were done there is still doubt about whether all factors involved in a case could be catalogued anyhow.

At this writing, it seems that jury trials are the best of all known methods for estimating guilt or innocence of individuals. Additional research will point out places where some of the science of psychology will help to improve the legal understanding of human behavior and thus improve trial by jury. In the meantime, we must not get discouraged with the system, for changes do take place and they reflect the knowledge of science collected in past years.

SUMMARY

In this chapter we have discussed many of the factors involved in the detection and background of crime. We have indicated the tremendous extent of criminal behavior in the United States and have recognized the increasing importance of this problem as a larger and larger proportion of the population is involved in activity in opposition to social rules and regulations.

Although no criminal type per se can be found, there is evidence indicating that certain kinds of crime are related to particular age, intellectual, or socioeconomic groups or personality types. At the same time, there are statistics indicating that there is a higher incidence of crime in some times of the year than in others. Generally the kind of crime is related to these factors more than total amount of criminal activity.

A lie detector is a device that records a variety of physiological changes concomitant with emotionalized behavior. Thus the "lie detector" is really an emotion detector and the assumption is made that when a person is emotionalized while answering questions he is more likely to be lying than not.

The second major segment of the chapter concerned courtroom activity and dealt particularly with the jury, witnesses, testimony, and judgments of the jury. Perception, attention, and reporting of events that occur at a previous time were discussed. It was indicated that testimony as presented is frequently biased. The prejudices and biases of judges, attorneys, witnesses, and jurors will be better understood as future research unfolds additional data. There is reason to believe that the jury system, although it has weaknesses, is currently the best available system for establishing guilt or innocence. As new scientific evidence in the field of psychology becomes available it will be used by the courts and the professional courtroom personnel and so improve courts of law.

SUGGESTED REFERENCES FOR FURTHER STUDY

Ausuld, D. P. (1958). *Drug Addiction: Physiological, Psychological, and Sociological Aspects.* New York: Random House.

   Written by an author with firsthand experience as a medical officer, this paperback covers problems, uses, psychological characteristics, social characteristics, treatment, prognosis, and prevention of drug addiction.

Hoover, J. E. (1964). *Crime in the United States, Uniform Crime Report—1963.* Washington, D.C.: Federal Bureau of Investigation, United States Dept. of Justice.

   One issue of a yearly publication by the FBI giving statistical reports of crime in the United States, issued about July or August of each year, covering crime reports for the preceding year.

Toch, H. (ed.) (1961). *Legal and Criminal Psychology*. New York: Holt, Rinehart & Winston.

A coverage of problems of the people who administer laws, special problems of drug addicts, alcoholics, and sex offenders by contributors trained as attorneys, psychologists, sociologists, psychiatrists, and police administrators.

Journal of Criminal Law, Criminology, and Police Science.

Current research and theory concerning crime and police science. Includes abstracts of recent cases and reviews of recent books on criminal law, criminology, and police science.

Journal of Social Issues.

Current research on social issues, including material applicable to criminal behavior and courtroom activity. Specific issues are devoted entirely to a topic; for example, Vol. XIII, No. 2, concerns Witnesses and Testimony at Trials and Hearings.

Chapter 16

Treating Offenders and

Preventing Criminal Behavior

CASE HISTORIES ARE OFTEN VALUABLE as illustrations of a vital point. Table 16.1 presents abbreviated items from one man's life history.

TABLE 16.1 Abbreviated Life History Items of One Man Who Was Convicted and Incarcerated Several Times

DATE	NAME USED	CITY AND STATE	CHARGE	DISPOSITION
1/10/10	Joe Doaks	New York, N.Y.	[Born]	
2/ 5/29	Louis Silver	New York, N.Y.	Petty larceny	6 months' probation
1/29/36	Bill Smith	Chicago, Ill.	Petty larceny	18 months' sentence
11/26/39	Sam Berg	Kansas City, Mo.	Petty larceny	Released
10/21/41	Sam Brown	Flint, Mich.	No peddler's license	$10.00 or 5 days (paid fine)
8/ 7/42	Joe Doaks	Chicago, Ill.	Fraudulent obtaining money	Stricken from record
9/27/42	Joe Doaks	Albany, N.Y.	Grand larceny	Acquitted
3/ 1/43	Sam Brown	Washington, D.C.	Inducted into army	
1/20/46	Sam Brown	Washington, D.C.	Honorable discharge U.S. Army	
8/12/48	Sam Brown	Austin, Texas	Theft U.S. gov't check	Pending
8/20/48	Sam Brown	Austin, Texas	Impersonating Internal Revenue officer	Pending

555

TABLE 16.1—continued

DATE	NAME USED	CITY AND STATE	CHARGE	DISPOSITION
9/22/48	Sam Brown	Philadelphia, Pa.	False representation as U.S. Gov't employee	Pending
12/16/48	Sam Brown	Austin, Texas	Forgery Gov't check	15 months' sentence
6/10/49	Sam Brown	Danbury, Conn.	Forgery Gov't check	15 months' sentence
8/ 4/50	Sam Brown	Baltimore, Md.	Passing bad check	Pending
8/ 4/50	Sam Brown	Baltimore, Md.	False pretenses	Pending
9/30/50	Sam Brown	Baltimore, Md.	False pretenses	Pending
6/15/51	Sam Brown	Baltimore, Md.	Bad check and defrauding hotel	18 months' sentence
3/22/52	Ned Marks	New Orleans, La.	Vagrancy	2 years' sentence
4/ 3/52	Sam Brown	Texarkana, Texas	Passing worthless check	2 years' sentence
10/ 1/53	Sam Brown	Texarkana, Texas	Interstate transportation of stolen property	6 months' sentence
8/30/55	Sam Brown	Columbus, Ohio	Fraudulent conversion of property	2–4 years' sentence
7/15/58	Sam Brown	Boston, Mass.	Interstate transportation of stolen property	6 months' sentence
7/30/58	Sam Brown	New York, N.Y.		
8/ 7/58	Sam Brown	Philadelphia, Pa.		
2/ 4/59	Sam Brown	Danbury, Conn.	National Motor Vehicle Theft Act	6 months' sentence
8/ 6/59	Sam Brown	Akron, Ohio	Passing worthless checks	2–4 years' sentence
12/15/61	Sam Brown	Columbus, Ohio	Fraudulent conversion	2–4 years' sentence

We may feel sorry for Sam Brown (or is it Joe Doaks), or we may feel his life is his own and he deserves whatever he has received. On the other hand, when we think of treatment and rehabilitation, we must wonder about the effectiveness of our penal institutions. Sam is not the tough criminal often portrayed on television and in the movies. He is a soft-spoken fellow nearing 60 years of age, well-mannered, and very cooperative in prison. Yet in repeated discussions Sam still expresses bitter resentment toward society and the prison systems that he has encountered. Upon release, he plans to get a job in another state with some old friends who are involved in "near-illegal" activities. He recognizes his chances of reincarceration if he is picked up with his old associates, but he feels there is no other way for him in this world.

Sam's case may not be typical, but it emphasizes one of the important reasons for the crime rate of the United States. The return of prisoners to prison for a second or subsequent offense is alarmingly high. Although varying for different offenses and different sections of the country, the overall rate of recidivism[1] is often reported as 60 to 70 percent. Although reports vary, and some authorities indicate that the 60-to-70-percent rate is misleading, the fact is that many men who leave prison return for new crimes.

With the current public attitude toward prisons, prisoners, and the understanding of criminal behavior, it seems doubtful that rehabilitation and lowering of crime rate can be accomplished. Society at large must accept the responsibility to treat criminals in a manner in which there is hope for changing behavior, and to provide proper environments for prevention of crime. If society does not care to provide the necessary resources to accomplish these functions, plans for lessening the crime rate are unrealistic.

We assume that the public attitude can and will be changed. Thus we discuss treatment of offenders and prevention of criminal behavior.

TREATMENT OF OFFENDERS

"The generally professed goal of correction is to protect society by preparing men as rapidly and economically as possible to become useful, law-abiding, self-supporting, self-sufficient, independent citizens—men who obey the law because they want to and not because they are afraid not to" (Schnur, 1961). Dr. Schnur hastened to add that although the professed goals of correction are as just stated, these objectives are not being attained. Correction is handicapped by society that does not provide sufficient resources necessary to rehabilitate criminals. In general, members of society simply do not know what they want done with violators of rules and regulations. Treatment procedures are very frequently unrelated to the objective of rehabilitation. The legal processes in many segments of society, the past experience of the law enforcement agents and the prison personnel, the general attitudes of the members of society, all work together to make it difficult if not impossible to rehabilitate criminals. Dr. Schnur (1961)

---

[1] The term *recidivism* is sometimes applied to the repetition or recurrence of criminal conduct. However, we will use the term to refer to those cases in which recurrence of criminal activity leads to readmission to prison.

concluded: "Consequently, confusion and inconsistency, lack of tested knowledge, and vacillation in implementing objectives are all factors which characterize the management of convicted law violators while they are subject to the correctional processes."

Psychological Factors in Rehabilitation. Ideally the treatment of convicted offenders should be such that they will be better qualified as law-abiding citizens after incarceration than before. This means that the eye-for-an-eye or vengeance theory concerning treatment of prisoners simply can no longer be tolerated. Historically convicted criminals have been treated on the theory that they should suffer vengeance for their wrong-doing. In addition, punishment has been provided as a deterrent for criminal behavior on the assumption that punishment of convicted criminals provides examples for others and thus prevents crime. In Chapter 1 of this book, a discussion of learning theory indicated that available evidence generally dispels the belief that punishment can increase desired behavior of an organism. Even so, many law enforcement systems use punishment, even in the form of a death sentence, as just retribution to the lawbreaker and as a deterrent for other potential lawbreakers. A high rate of recidivism persists despite the use of punishment. The techniques of punishment so frequently used have been shown to be ineffective. Isn't it time to emphasize rehabilitation, not punishment?

When To Treat Offenders. To understand the possibilities for rehabilitation we must examine the areas where society provides treatment facilities for convicted offenders. Three commonly used treatment times in the United States are during probation, incarceration, and parole.

PROBATION. Some men convicted of a crime are deemed safe to live in their regular community. They are generally first offenders and those who have a good record before the conviction. It is believed that living at home, under close supervision, with rather stringent requirements concerning activities, will be more advantageous to them than incarceration. In most instances, such men are placed on probation only after the court has secured a presentence investigation and when there is a good prognosis for positive correctional influences.

Although there are great variations from one legal system to another concerning the use of probation, the concept certainly has merit. The probation officer assigned responsibility for the convicted offender should be well qualified and in charge of a relatively light case load. Ideally probation should be a period during which the probationer is observed closely and guided into good behavior. In such a way, a person continues as a participating member of society and the ideal of rehabilitation is attained.

Unfortunately the full possibilities of probation are not always achieved. The case loads of probation officers are often very heavy, so that guidance of probationers is minimal. Often the rules and regulations set up for probationers are so stringent and rigid that life becomes very uncomfortable for the probationer, and his attitudes toward the system become very negative. And some probation officers are not well trained in the field of human behavior. Thus the full impact of the probation system is not often realized.

INCARCERATION. When an individual is convicted of breaking a rule or regulation of society and is deemed unfit to remain in society on probation, he is confined in a correctional institution. The type of confinement is dependent upon a variety of factors, but is usually related to the crime committed and the age and sex of the convicted violator. All too often, factors in the background of the violator are ignored in terms of the kind of incarceration or length of confinement assigned to him by the court. Frequently only the past record of parole and previous conviction is considered. Ideally men should be incarcerated in correctional institutions that can provide a training program that will enhance the possibility of the offender's being a better citizen after his incarceration than before. Unfortunately this is not the situation in most institutions.

Entering a prison is often a traumatic event. Most prisons present massive walls that will confine the prisoner for a segment of his life. When he first enters "the walls" he is searched for concealed contraband, fingerprinted, often photographed and assigned a number, required to complete one or two forms often signing away privileges of communication without censorship, and so on. He is given institutional clothing; his own possessions are filed away. He may then be given a friendly pat on the back with a comment or two concerning his preparation for prison life. All too frequently, the preparation is only a few words by the warden or his deputy suggesting that they are here to help the prisoner, that it is not their fault that he is committed to the institution, and that he should keep his nose clean, his mouth shut, work when asked to, and that cooperation is by far the best policy.

Relatively few institutions have admission or reception centers; some have some diagnostic activity; but such programs usually require considerable time. When diagnostic activity does take place, placement in particular functions or training and rehabilitation programs within the

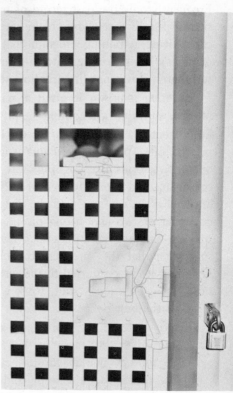

Figures 16.1(a), (b), (c). A series of photographs showing a man entering prison in his own street clothes (opposite), changed to prison clothing and in his cell (lower left), and the final view of the man after the cell door is closed (lower right).

prison takes place at a refined level. It is unfortunate that such programs are in effect in only some federal and state institutions and very rarely in county or local prisons or jails.

In most institutions a prisoner is assigned a living place, often in a cell by himself, at least during the first few days or weeks while he is being evaluated. If the prisoner is fortunate enough to be incarcerated in a correctional institution that can provide some sort of treatment, he will be assigned to a particular function. Usually some religious counseling is available, some education is provided, and a type of work activity or training program is conducted. Again these functions take place in the larger prisons and those operated at federal and state levels far more often than at county or local level.

Rehabilitation programs are usually managed by the person primarily concerned with training or rehabilitation. This often results in friction within the prison staff since the custodial staff, including the warden and his deputies, are primarily responsible for maintaining discipline and order within the institution. Sometimes the treatment or rehabilitation programs seem detrimental to the custodial staff, because extra duties and time may be required of them. Treatment personnel thus may work in an atmosphere that is not especially conducive to their function. The prisoners soon recognize the tensions between treatment and custodial personnel and are prone to show disinterest in rehabilitation programs or to be very cautious concerning such programs, because they do not want to alienate the custodial staff or their fellow prisoners.

When we recall how difficult it is to produce changes in behavior under relatively good conditions in schools and homes we can readily understand that rehabilitation in prisons is necessarily difficult if not impossible.

The average penal institution is a well-established system. If a man becomes less prone to criminal behavior after his prison stay, it is frequently a result of his own doing rather than particular treatment obtained while incarcerated. In many institutions the officials and keepers are political appointees, often of questionable caliber. Many prisons provide practically no activity except some physical play each day. Thus prisoners have much time to sit and talk to others and think and read. During this time, the younger prisoners learn from the old "pros" and often devise many rather fantastic illusions of what the outside world is really like.

The author has been repeatedly amazed at the concepts of prisoners concerning what they will be able to do when they leave prison. Even those who seem to be benefiting by educational programs and are model prisoners sometimes have erroneous concepts of the "outside world." Some believe that when they leave prison with one or two high school courses completed, but no high school diploma, they will be able to get good jobs at above-average income in their community. It is difficult for them to understand that working in a normal fashion takes a good deal of effort, but provides a feeling of self-satisfaction and not just a monetary return.

In some states, particularly in New York and California, there have been some new attempts at rehabilitation in special prisons. In these prisons the emphasis is placed on rehabilitation and psychiatric treatment rather than detention. After sentencing, the patient is sent to a treatment area. He is assigned to a psychiatrist, and various therapeutic techniques are administered. As improvement is noted, he is transferred to a dormitory-style section, with visiting permitted and a more "normal" environmental situation. Thus he is prepared for life in the outside world.

Techniques of treating prisoners are available. Behavioral science knows more than is presently being applied. Unfortunately many institutions pay only lip service to more modern-day concepts concerning rehabilitation. Thus it is not uncommon to hear or read about the great new rehabilitation program in a particular prison or the effectiveness of a new system of handling prisoners. Sometimes such reports are not based on evidence, and very little actual rehabilitation or training is in progress. In such situations the public at large expects that rehabilitation is being accomplished. In other places, the officials in charge are prone to discuss techniques rather than to try them in their own institutions.

For some prisoners a third technique of rehabilitation is used. This technique is parole and is somewhat similar to probation, except that the parolee has already served time in an institution.

PAROLE.   At the time a convicted offender is sentenced, the court ordinarily has the right to order the length of the sentence within limits set by rules and regulations of the state and the crime committed. In some states, a very rigid time schedule is designated for most crimes. Thus the court must adhere to the schedule and assign a man to prison for a particular length of time. In others, the court is allowed to order prisoners to treatment for a variable period of time. In such situations a sentence may be for incarceration for a period not to exceed a maximum nor to be less than a minimum duration. For example, a sentence may be for two to four years. Under such a sentence the prisoner might be eligible for discharge at the end of two years following the specialized conditions for parole. He would be discharged at the end of the maximum sentence of four years with no strings attached.

Parole allows a prisoner to be released into society under special supervised conditions. Each parolee is assigned to a parole officer who is to see that the released violator obeys the rules and regulations of society and the special additional rules enforced upon him by the parole board. In general, the restrictions of the parolee's activity are considerably greater even than for the person on probation. He may be returned to confinement in an institution if he violates any of the parole regulations, and depending upon the state, he may be assigned to a longer sentence than previously, he may be given time off his sentence for the parole time, or he may be restricted from ever having parole again if he is reconvicted. There is no general rule concerning what might happen if a person breaks parole regulations under one jurisdiction as compared to another. However, the general idea of parole is to rehabilitate a person who has been incarcerated by getting him back into society under controlled conditions.

If we consider criminal behavior as similar to mental illness, the individual being treated in a particular specialized situation such as the prison needs special help to adjust to "outside" society. The parole process can provide such an experience. Unfortunately parole officers are frequently overburdened and cannot adequately complete their work. In some jurisdictions the parole regulations are so strict that it is very difficult if not impossible for prisoners to serve out their parole without violations. In most society a person who has served in prison is looked down upon and not treated as a normal citizen. Consequently, although parole is a good technique, it is difficult to use adequately in typical United States society. As more members of society become enlightened concerning prisoners and the purposes of parole, and as there is increased use of indeterminate sentences providing parole as long as the parole officer feels it is needed, parole will gain more value in rehabilitation of criminal behavior.

It is rather interesting to note that some prisoners do not want to go out on parole when eligible. Particularly prisoners who have been given sentences where there is a relatively short time between the minimum and maximum sentences may rather serve the maximum in prison than to go out on parole at the end of the minimum sentence. They feel that their chances of conforming to all of the strict rules and regulations of parole are very slim. Thus they reason that they will be recommitted as parole violators and have even longer incarceration ahead of them. They also feel that if they serve out their complete sentence, they have "paid their debt" to society. Consequently they may want to complete their maximum sentence so that when they are released they are, in their own view, at least as good as regular citizens or maybe a little better since they have paid society and therefore deserve something in return. Unfortunately there is usually not enough competent personnel on the prison staff to change these attitudes of prisoners.

Treatment of Drug Addicts. Specialized treatment for drug addiction has received a great deal of publicity. Although return to the use of drugs is very high, at least one author (Lindesmith, 1957) indicated that contrary to popular beliefs, most drug addicts do want to escape from the habit. He stated that he had never met a person addicted for a year or more who had not tried to kick the habit.

The techniques of getting rid of drug addiction vary, but there are two major concepts of treatment. One consists of completely eliminating the use of the drug by keeping all drugs away from the drug addict even though he may have a physiological dependency. Thus the drug addict is forced to go through withdrawal symptoms as rapidly as possible. A second concept involves the provision of a substitute for the drug or a gradual reduction in the dosage of the drug over a period of time.

Specialized hospitals or wards within hospitals are available for the treatment of drug addiction. Unfortunately the relapse rate is extremely high, and a person once addicted is practically never cured. The ex-drug addict always remembers the experience of the drug and when faced with severe problems may return to the use of the drug.

Treatment of drug addicts is receiving additional publicity and more understanding and sympathy from society at large. Naturally this will help to reduce the numbers of individuals dependent upon drugs for a "normal" feeling in life. As more and more people understand the effect of drugs, the chances of curing drug addiction will greatly improve.

Treatment of Juvenile Delinquents. In general a juvenile delinquent is treated the same as an adult criminal in that parole, probation, and incarceration are all available as techniques. However, specialized institutions and perhaps more liberal views toward behavioral nonconformities are accepted by the courts. Chances for probation are better for a juvenile than for an adult, and more attempts are being made by society to set up treatment and prevention techniques for juvenile delinquents. Admittedly this is a proper direction for reducing crime, since the juvenile delinquents of today are often the criminals of tomorrow.

Most of the treatment or rehabilitation programs for all prisoners, adult or juvenile, have been established in the state and federal institutions for prisoners with relatively long-term sentences. This has actually been a detriment to maximum crime prevention, because the younger criminal is often incarcerated for short sentences. Thus he tends to get little by way of treatment or rehabilitation. Some studies have been completed (London and Myers, 1961) in an attempt to provide information concerning adequate treatment for short-term offenders. After considerable research, the authors concluded that a treatment center for chronic offenders was con-siderably less promising than treatment of the relatively healthy person and for the first offender. These results bear further consideration. Perhaps clinics might be set up in local jails to provide proper treatment for first offenders and relatively healthy people before they become hardened criminals. London and Myers suggested that although most first offenders are healthy, they are in need of guidance and support in their regular environment.

Recently treatment and prevention have been combined. "Predelin-quent" groups have been isolated by some researchers. Attempts have thus been made to prevent delinquent behavior by treating these "pre-delinquents." Kvaraceus (1959) reported that the public schools can become exceptionally valuable as agencies where personnel can spot the potential delinquent and give him a helping hand in his regular cultural milieu. Kvaraceus believes that the delinquent can be prevented somewhat by providing a good community. Such a community is primarily the school and home environment so that programs must be available in these environ-ments. This article emphasized the importance of training techniques to provide "predelinquents" with adequate rather than antisocial adjustment techniques.

Essentially the same position is maintained by a well-known authority in the field of juvenile delinquency, Dr. E. T. Glueck. Glueck (1960) indicated that the common denominator of delinquency seems to be aggressive antisocial behavior and that the task of society is to reeducate families of children found to be vulnerable to delinquency so that the antisocial behavior would not develop into severe enough form to become criminal behavior. Unfortunately the procedures for doing this are not well established. The amount of energy and resources necessary to do such training might at first seem exorbitantly expensive, and consequently society generally is not ready to support preventive treatment.

Although it may seem obvious that treatment must be in terms of the person rather than the crime committed, society at large still doesn't accept such a concept. Most judges, reflecting popular opinion, do not suit the punishment entirely to the criminal. In fact because of the laws, judges often assign punishment according to the crime, tempered with their own "educated guess" of the criminal. Cooper (1961) cited one judge as stating that there is a very definite need to suit the punishment to the offender, not the crime. He stated, "A presentence investigation of high order ought to be a routine aspect of treatment for every first offender before the court. . . ." Many other farsighted judges are considering the same concept and perhaps will lead the way for society to accept the idea of gearing treatment to the person rather than to the crime committed.

New Concepts of Sentencing. In some legal jurisdictions, new laws and interpretations have brought about changes in sentencing. The indeterminate-length sentence, as suggested earlier, has merit for certain areas. If the proper agencies are available, a convicted criminal can be treated until rehabilitated rather than incarcerated or paroled for a certain number of days, weeks, or months without regard to rehabilitation.

A relatively new concept involves the sentencing to a minimum and maximum sentence to be served during nonworking hours or weekends. Such a sentence of 60 to 90 days, for example, might be ordered served from 7:00 A.M. Saturday to 7:00 A.M. Monday for 30 to 45 weeks.

There are many difficulties and problems in implementing a "weekend" incarceration program. The regular routine of the prison is obviously disrupted, prisoners can communicate outside more easily than usual, more checking in and out of sentenced prisoners involves staff personnel in time-consuming activity, more records are necessary, and of course there is a possibility that the sentenced man may not return for his weekend in prison. On the other hand, there are several important advantages. Primarily a home and family may be saved. If a man has a suitable job and is providing support for his family, such a sentence will allow him to continue to do so. The obvious advantage of keeping a family together is supplemented by the saving to the citizens of the community in not having to provide public relief support for a wife and children, and so on, as well as having one more member of the community continue to provide a share of the costs through his taxes. In addition the "weekend prisoner" can lead a more nearly normal life. As he becomes aware of the prison life as well as the "outside" life, he will likely learn that he does not want to spend any additional time in prison. He also will tell others of this and thus will provide a detriment to criminal behavior while still not being as completely biased as a person incarcerated for two or three months at a time. The "weekend prisoner" will also encourage some of the regular prisoners in "going straight" after finishing their sentences.

There are attempts being made to try new methods of handling criminal behavior. As additional techniques are tried and evidence is accumulated, it seems likely that some of the systems will prove to be valuable in reducing crime rate.

Applying Psychological Principles to Correction. At this point we must review some of the comments concerning treatment of criminals in light of the psychological principles of learning discussed in Chapter 1 of this book.

Criminal behavior, like any other behavior, has been learned. Changing criminal behavior should be accomplished by applying the same principles useful in changing any other behavior. Rehabilitation programs, probation, parole, and all other attempts at converting undesirable behavior to more desirable behavior must involve learning. Thus we should reexamine learning theory as explained in Chapter 1.

When we recall the current high rate of recidivism, we realize that the present rehabilitation attempts must not be as adequate as desired. What are some of the characteristics that may lead to the high rate of recidivism? As expressed earlier, except for some new approaches in incarceration procedures, the typical prison provides prisoners with long periods of time with relatively little activity. A great deal of idleness is not only condoned but actually enforced. Keepers and deputies generally do not want to be bothered all the time. Thus prisoners learn to do as little as possible, for the keepers provide reinforcement for such behavior. Any activity that causes additional work for the keepers and deputies is not reinforced and becomes extinguished.

Such an analysis reflects too on the caliber of the keepers, guards, and deputies in many prisons. Unfortunately these positions are often filled for reasons other than the competence of the person to carry out a rehabilitation program for criminals.

Even in prisons where a rehabilitation program is in effect, there are several difficulties in effecting behavior changes of value to prisoners. First, there is a difficult transfer problem from the learning situation in a prison to the situation in the outside world. Society is not ready to establish prisons that are similar to the environment outside of prison. (Perhaps quite legitimately so, since the deterrent effect of the possible incarceration would not be nearly as effective if prison living conditions were the same as living conditions outside of prison.) Thus the stimulus situation in prison is different than the stimulus situation in the outside world. If a prisoner learns to handle a particular type of job or interpersonal relationship with others while in a prison situation, little, if any, of the learned response can be expected to transfer to the situation outside the prison.

Second, it is extremely expensive to provide training facilities and freedom necessary for effective learning in a prison environment. For example, one keeper is usually in charge of many prisoners, and to assure their incarceration, the prisoners must be restricted in their movement and interaction with others.

Third, the length of sentences imposed upon individuals are usually set only as a result of the crime. Individual differences in the ability to learn from a situation are overlooked. Sentences must be more flexible so that individuals who profit from their rehabilitation or learning program may be released or brought back into normal society as rapidly as possible. It is no better to release a man after two years of incarceration if he is not rehabilitated than to keep a man two years if he has been rehabilitated properly in 18 months. Some individuals learn more rapidly than others and this fact must be considered in prison sentences.

Whether or not there is a formal rehabilitation program, the prison environment is certainly not the same as that outside. In the United States, all prisons require segregation of male and female prisoners. Consequently estimates of homosexuality in prison ranging from 30 to 85 percent of the inmates are probably not exaggerated. However, even the lower figure is considerably above the average for the outside world. It seems quite likely that the homosexual behavior is the result of the special environment which forces release of sexual motivation in a homosexual manner. Thus the very nature of the prison environment creates undesirable behavior that is difficult to transfer to the outside.

The problem of homosexual behavior is not very adequately handled in most prisons. Most countries throughout the world do not favor conjugal visits within the prisons. Mexico is the only country making a general exception to this policy.

Conjugal visitations have generally been considered detrimental to the running of prisons for several reasons: (1) the visits seem to emphasize only the physical aspects of sex, (2) married inmates who could enjoy conjugal visits are thought to be the best-adjusted prisoners without such relations, and homosexuals and sex deviates are the ones least likely to benefit from conjugal visits, and (3) wives outside of prison may become pregnant and further increase the problems of the state and the prisoners.

It is somewhat surprising to find that one large facility in the United States allows conjugal visitation as part of its formal rules and regulations. The Parchman Institution of the Mississippi State Penitentiary system has developed an informal conjugal visitation program into official policy that is quite likely to endure. Hopper (1962) stated that the program apparently provides advantages to the entire prison complex. Parchman Institution is set up as a complex of small, community type camps. According to Hopper, this arrangement facilitates conjugal visits in that it affords more freedom of visitation in general. Each camp is somewhat isolated, and visitors go directly to the camp where they wish to visit. There are relatively few inmates in each camp and less than half of them are married, so relatively few wives visit any one camp at one time. The visitation program at Parchman allows a wife to visit her husband every weekend for a short period of time. Hopper stated that the homosexuality problem is only minor at Parchman and that the conjugal visiting has the approval and praise of the staff and inmates of the institution. He concluded that "the experience at Parchman seems to warrant the conclusion that conjugal visiting should be studied not only in comparison with, but in conjunction with, the types of marital relationships and in a variety of institutions. Parchman's experience does not prove that the objections to conjugal visiting are invalid; it suggests, however, that conjugal visiting, at least in some penal situations, cannot be ruled out as a possible adaptation."

It is also important to recognize that society may have other objections to rehabilitation programs. Many writers have suggested that society at large really enjoys having some members incarcerated. It provides the non-criminals with a method of releasing their own feelings of inadequacy or frustration. Even ignoring these hypotheses, we know that society wants crime punished by unpleasant living. Consequently prisons cannot be set up as model societies but must continue to be environments that are less desirable than the normal outside world. Today emphasis is still not upon rehabilitation but on protecting society from the criminal and punishing the criminal for his behavior while providing an example of what might happen to someone else committing the same act.

The use of psychotherapists in prisons has been tried and given a good deal of publicity in many rather isolated situations. By and large, psychotherapy is probably a learning situation, and the principles of learning as discussed in Chapter 1 apply. However, psychotherapy is a more advanced technique and often can accomplish a great deal with some individual criminals. The psychotherapist recognize that offenders frequently do not want to be patients; thus psychotherapy is by no means the answer to all problems. As previously stated, psychotherapeutic techniques are probably advantageous, particularly for first offenders. Such techniques may be extremely valuable for many juvenile delinquents before they get too seriously in trouble with the law.

Our discussions have concerned treatment of offenders. We must remember that the term *offender* refers to a person who has been convicted of a crime. As long as society accepts criminal behavior by some individuals and does not call it crime, we must expect that individuals convicted for the same type of behavior will often feel that rehabilitation programs are ridiculous.

An illustration of special rules for special segments of society was shown in a series of news and editorial articles beginning September 1963.

At a private house party in Southampton, Long Island, following a debutante ball, 125 young men from wealthy homes created several thousand dollars' worth of property damage. At first, the owner of the home and the debutante's stepfather who leased the home as a dormitory for overflow guests refused to prosecute the guilty youths. The youths were released the day after the event on their promises to make good the damages. Many newspaper writers were incensed by the apparent double standards of society that allowed these youths to go without trial or proper penalty for their actions. One writer (Robb, 1963) stated: "When is a delinquent not a delinquent? When is the wanton destruction of property by a gang of young men not a crime?" Robb answered these questions—that it depends upon the individual. Even though $3,000–10,000 worth of damages were inflicted on a home by offenders over 18 years of age and the owner of the house called the police to stop the rioting, there was apparently to be no prosecution. Robb stated, "How can a judge in good conscience, sentence to jail or a correctional institution, an undereducated slum youth who has done $35 worth of damage to a house when he has the Southampton precedent before him?"

Even though the aggrieved parties would not or could not press charges against the youths, the state could prosecute, because damages exceeded $250. Thus in this particular instance, public furor forced the governing bodies to take action. A grand jury invited 27 of the youths to testify. Very few of the youths appeared for the hearing. Later hearings required some of the youths to attend.

Reviewing the follow-up news reports, the whole sequence seems ludicrous. The investigation and trial dragged on through 1964, with charges against one youth dropped at one hearing, several youths acquitted on grounds of insufficient evidence at another trial, charges against others dropped for lack of evidence, and so on. Finally, a little more than one year following the event, the Suffolk County Court dismissed the charges against the last of the youths for insufficient evidence. The case was finally closed. In essence no one was proven guilty of property destruction. Of course, the original rioting and destruction of property had occurred, but no one was legally to blame.

Rehabilitation is difficult enough at any time. Men are incarcerated for crimes that seem as innocent to them as the Southampton event seemed to the youths involved. When such incarcerated men hear how some youths are treated, they lose faith in the entire legal system. Many prisoners feel they were given a bad break in their sentencing. Rehabilitation is even more difficult than usual under such circumstances.

In the United States, as well as most of the civilized world, treatment while incarcerated depends on who you are, what educational and socioeconomic background you come from, and so on. This does not mean to imply that prisons give wealthy prisoners better breaks because they are wealthy. Certainly there are some prison officials, keepers, judges, jurors, and other humans who can be bribed. However, by and large, prison officials try to do a conscientious job. The fact is that doing a good job often results in giving the better-educated prisoner a better situation in prison. The jobs on the prison newspaper, in the library, commissary, and so on, go to those who can best handle them. The person with little or no education gets jobs requiring little ability and learns little from the job or doesn't get a job at all.

We must also be aware that people from better socioeconomic backgrounds and with more education, wealth, and contacts know or learn how to keep from going to prison for some acts that might result in incarceration for another person. By and large, it is the duty of society to provide good rehabilitation programs for the prisoners who have come from lower socioeconomic and educational backgrounds. This emphasis must not be overlooked in designing rehabilitation programs.

PREVENTION

Certainly the topic of prevention of criminal behavior deserves a thorough analysis. Unfortunately only very little good experimental evidence indicating the best method of achieving crime reduction is available. Many of the techniques of treating mental illness discussed in Chapter 4 of this book are valuable for treating criminals. We will not repeat a discussion of these points. Thus we will discuss crime prevention in light of available evidence and with an emphasis on suggesting steps toward improved techniques. We will cover two aspects: (1) the prevention of repetition of criminal behavior by known offenders (we will extend our previous discussions of treatment to cover some additional data concerning developments in correctional procedures), and (2) the prevention of the original criminal behavior (we will reexamine causes of criminal behavior).

Prevention of crime, whether it be the stopping of criminal behavior of a previously convicted offender or a previously law abiding person, depends on the person and society. Thus it is appropriate to consider changing the views of society.

Changing Society.   Society's views toward criminals may be thought of as a prejudice.[2] The problems of prejudices toward minority groups have been

---

[2] Prejudice is a subjective feeling toward another person, persons, or object based on little or insufficient evidence and relatively difficult to modify.

given a great deal of attention. We can draw from this material to suggest means for changing the prejudices of society toward criminals.

In Chapter 15 we considered criminal behavior as breaking rules or regulations of society. We further suggested that unintentional violations or inappropriate habitual transgressions are not normally called criminal behavior. Thus we followed Lindner's (1955) point of view that real criminals are satisfying their own internal needs or motivations. Society must gain some understanding of this type of behavior.

The general public considers a criminal as an undesirable person who cannot become more desirable. In short, most members of society have a stereotype or exaggerated belief associated with the word *criminal*. They believe that anyone branded with the word *criminal* must be expected to have certain traits even though there may be contradictory evidence available.

Since stereotypes aid people in simplifying their thinking and justifying their hostilities about others, they are difficult to modify. But stereotypes do change in time, and there is reason to believe that the common stereotype of a criminal is changing. Thus there is more hope for prevention and rehabilitation programs as the members of society change their views of criminals. Particularly the concepts that criminals are "born bad" and that they are "tough," "unchangeable," and "animals" are giving way.

Social scientists have pointed out tentative laws that are of some use in changing prejudices. The application of such laws to the problem of changing society's view toward criminals opens up new possibilities for prevention of crime. Allport (1954) suggested laws that can influence prejudice and that merit consideration in this discussion. (1) Pyramiding stimulation is an important principle. "While single programs—a film perhaps—show slight effects, several related programs produce effects apparently even greater than could be accounted for in terms of simple summation." (2) Specificity of effect is a principle of importance. What is learned in one context is not necessarily carried over to another as would be expected by generalization effect (discussed in Chapter 1 of this book). (3) People who are not firmly committed to one view or another are easier swayed by mass media and other techniques. (4) Propaganda or other mass media information is more effective when it has no counterpropaganda. This, of course, suggests that pro-tolerance propaganda is needed not just for its positive value, but also to counter the opposite views that might be presented. (5) Messages of mass communication can better effect changes in people if they are geared into the person's existing security systems rather than causing a person anxiety. (6) The prestigeful symbol is well known as an aid in creating changes in beliefs of large numbers of people. Thus an important member of society can speak out in favor of a prison rehabilitation program and have an effect on the beliefs of other members of society.

There are many sources of information about how to change beliefs of people. Advertisers, propagandists, therapists, teachers, and many more use techniques to modify the beliefs of others. The important point is not to argue whether such changes can be accomplished, but to decide on what beliefs concerning criminals are generally in error and then try to change the erroneous beliefs. If society at large will believe that criminals can be rehabilitated, then there will be a greatly improved chance of accomplishing rehabilitation.

Assuming that steps are underway, and will be continued, to educate the public concerning criminal behavior, it becomes feasible to study possible methods of preventing crime.

Rehabilitation and Reducing Recidivism.

The question of whether correctional processes in general use are a success or failure deserves comment. Certainly when a program reduces the repetition rate of known criminals it would seem that the program was more of a success than a failure. On the other hand, just because some individuals are not influenced in the desired manner by a program or process is not proof that the program is necessarily a failure. The high rate of recidivism has often been cited as an indication of the inadequacy of rehabilitation programs. This may be unjustified criticism. The 60-to-70-percent rate of recidivism often reported may well be an artifact of the data collection and reporting techniques.

Rubin (1958) suggested that a rate as high as 60 percent is impossible. He assumed that the average sentence of a prisoner incarcerated for his second or subsequent prison term is for at least four years and that each prisoner could serve several four-year terms before death. If this is so, then the number confined in the United States in state and federal prisons cannot be composed of two thirds of men who have been released previously and reincarcerated. If 60 percent of the men released each year were returned to prison for an average period of four years, the number of men confined at any one time on their second or subsequent prison term alone would be over two and a half times the total number of prisoners released each year. Current statistics show that the number confined in state and federal prisons in the United States is less than two and one half times the number of prisoners released each year.

Simply computing the proportion of inmates in a prison who have served previous terms certainly isn't an indication of the return rate. Most prisoners serve relatively short sentences on the first offense and longer sentences after the first offense. Thus criminals serving their second or third sentence accumulate in prisons to a larger degree than do first offenders.

It is also quite possible that the data often cited simply represents information from some particular prisons. It is fairly well established that some prisons within a system have a higher proportion of two- and three-time losers than do other prisons in the same system.

Considering the available data and the arguments by Rubin, it seems logical to assume that as many as two thirds of prisoners do not return after once being released. Glaser (1964) cited data from one study done by the United States Bureau of Prisons. After five years only 32.6 percent of the prisoners released earlier were sentenced to new terms of imprisonment or returned to prison as parole violators. He also cited data that showed only 51.2 percent of 149,617 inmates of state prisons had compiled prior criminal records.

A study of differential recidivism rates by type of offense was reported by Metuzner and Weil (1963). Two and one half years after release from Massachusetts State Prison, 56 percent of the releasees were returned to prison. Half of the releasees were returned on technical parole violation and half for new offenses. Of the men involved in this study 61 percent had been released on parole, 24 percent on certificate of discharge for finishing sentence, and 15 percent paroled and subsequently discharged from parole during the follow-up period.

Analysis of the returnees showed that the greatest difference in return rate was between sex offenders and all other offenders. The authors prepared a probability-of-return table for inmates classified into six categories. Return rates for prisoners in the various categories were (1) no prior commitments or no prior arrests—22 percent, (2) some prior commitments and either sex offenders or parole violators whose age at last commitment was more than 24—30 percent, (3) no prior commitments but some prior arrests—37 percent, (4) sex offenders or prior violators with prior commitments, age 24 or less at last commitment—61 percent, (5) some prior commitments, offense against person, except sex, or against property or combination of both offenses, white—69 percent, (6) some prior commitments, offense against person, except sex, and offense against property or a combination of both offenses, other than white—86 percent.

In another study using follow-up records Minnesota State Reformatory inmates were checked five years after release. Twenty-one percent of the released inmates had received new felony convictions in the five-year follow-up period. Another 17 percent had been returned to prison for other reasons such as parole violation. Thus a total of 38 percent had returned to prison during the five-year follow-up period (Zuckerman, Barron, and Whittiar, 1953).

A well-done study by Glaser (1964) used 1,015 cases randomly drawn from the population of adult male prisoners released from federal prisons in 1956. This study found that 31 percent of the prisoners released in 1956 were reimprisoned within five years. Glaser also investigated the "failure rate." Thus everyone returned to prison or convicted of a felony type of offense was placed in the failure group. The total failure group was about 35 percent of the releases, since 4 percent of the released prisoners received nonprison sentences for felonylike offenses. Of the remaining 65 percent of releases who were classified as successes, 52 percent had no further criminal record whatsoever; the others had been charged with minor offenses or had been charged but not convicted of more major offenses. Glaser concluded, "In the first two to five years after their release, only about one-third of all the men released from an entire prison system are returned to prison."

Apparently there is not as high a rate of recidivism as has been cited in the past. Perhaps the system of incarceration does decrease the criminal behavior of the once convicted offenders. We shall examine this concept in more detail in the following sections.

THE EFFECTS OF INCARCERATION.   As previously cited, incarceration is often a system for punishing criminal behavior and providing examples for potential criminals. Thus there is little reason to expect that much rehabilitation can be accomplished. On the other hand, there have been attempts in various parts of the United States to improve incarceration as a means of rehabilitating criminals. Notably work in the states of New York, California, Maryland, and Michigan has attempted new techniques and the introduction of more understanding of human behavior to the problem of modifying criminals while they are serving a prison term.

In several special facilities emphasis has been placed on rehabilitation and psychiatric treatment rather than detention and punishment. If a convicted and sentenced criminal seems able to benefit from treatment after testing and introduction into the prison setup, he may be taken to a special treatment wing for the remainder of his sentence. The treatment then is somewhat similar to that given in a mental hospital, with therapeutic techniques being administered under the supervision of a psychiatrist. As marked improvement is noted the prisoner may receive more visitors, live in the dormitory, and be placed in a more comfortable environment rather than one of reprisals and negative reinforcements.

As with prevention of first offenses, it is obvious that there are advantages in expending the greatest rehabilitative efforts on younger convicted criminals. In general they have less strongly entrenched criminal tendencies, are more amenable to changes in behavior, and have a longer life ahead of them as potentially useful citizens. There have been many attempts to improve convicted juveniles and adults. We will discuss a few of the studies concerning each group.

REHABILITATING JUVENILES. As early as 1940 legislation was passed in some states of the United States to provide special methods of treating youthful offenders. The general provisions of the legislative acts created boards, committees, or authorities to handle a juvenile after a court decided guilt. They also established reception centers with diagnostic facilities and special treatment centers. The special legislation for juvenile offenders restricted the court to the judgment of guilt or innocence; then a special authority or committee diagnosed the particular individual and tried to create a program that would best suit his needs. Scott (1961) described some of the program from Michigan when he stated the purposes of the reception-diagnostic center as follows: "1. To provide a thorough evaluation of the offender's personality, background, and experience, and of the nature of the problem behavior 2. To determine which cases require institutional treatment 3. To release other cases directly to the community on probation 4. If an institution is indicated, to select the best one adapted to the offender's possibilities and needs, including the degree of security required 5. To develop a range and variety of institutions and programs sufficiently flexible to provide, insofar as feasible, for the varying needs of offenders 6. To determine the probable date of readiness to return to the community without the limitation of a minimum sentence 7. To separate the younger, less-hardened offender from the older, more-hardened offender. (Obviously calendar age is not the only criterion.)"

The idea of a committee or authority disposing of the guilty offender by setting his sentence has not been agreed upon by most state legislatures. But the concept has been generally accepted under a program whereby the court allows a diagnostic center to recommend a program, and then the court usually imposes the suggested program.

The traditional treatment or rehabilitation for youthful offenders is the same as for the adult offender. Essentially reformatories are by and large the same as regular prisons except for the age of the incarcerated offenders. In some newer attempts at rehabilitation programs, specialized reformatories or technical schools have been established. Such schools are minimum security facilities in which there is an attempt to group together 8 to 10 prisoners or relatively small groups with a leader. One such program is the Michigan Youth Camps.

The camp program in Michigan as described by Scott (1961) involved a group leader working with small groups of 6–8 members in a very free environment. Individuals were allowed to talk as they wished, but were led through training programs to help rehabilitate them to be members of society. The members of the groups were allowed to participate in group therapy sessions, with a good deal of counselor time available for individual consultation. Scott suggested that his personal experience with the program showed that a great many of the problems involved were of an interpersonal nature. What really went on in terms of rehabilitation was the building up of rapport between the counselor and the offender so that attitudes, concepts, and behavior could be changed. Most of the changes that took place were not direct or specified, but instead were indirectly the result of the program. For example, he noticed changes in behavior such as offenders talking about "Mr." instead of "Hey, Teach!" when addressing an instructor.

Scott went on to describe the difficulty of establishing such programs in terms of community relations. It became apparent very early in the programs that the communities where the camps were to be located were not favorably impressed toward such an activity in their immediate environment. With knowledge gained by time and experience, camp programs were set up in such a manner as to directly involve the communities. Thus the individual communities were not just told that the program was going to be there, but members of the community were brought in to work with the personnel in the camps and slowly but surely, volunteer services, lay leaders, interested citizens, and so on, established relationships with the offenders. The camp members were brought into the communities on passes and furloughs so that they were able to more adequately adjust to a real life normal environment when it came time for their release from custody.

Scott emphasized the great importance of the community in the role of crime prevention. He emphasized that future efforts toward lowering crime rate need to be directed toward coordinating all possible services to create proper environments, so that juvenile delinquency will decrease and so that rehabilitated prisoners will be returned to an environment that will be conducive to proper adjustments.

Shelley and Johnson (1961) reported a study of the effectiveness of the counseling service for youthful offenders in the Michigan work camps. Two matched groups of youthful offenders living in minimum security facilities were compared for changes in antisocial scores as measured by the Thematic Apperception Test. The major difference between the two camps was that one had an organized counseling program whereas the other did not, during the period of the study. The data showed a significant difference between the groups in change of antisocial scores. The tests were first administered to prisoners during their first weeks in camp. The second administration was after the prisoners had served six months in camp. The group with the organized counseling program made significantly larger reductions in antisocial scores than did the group in the camp that had no organized counseling program. Follow-up records showed that individuals with the greatest reduction in the antisocial scores had a significantly higher rate of parole success than did those showing little change. Apparently counseling in a correctional camp may have some positive values in reducing antisocial tendencies and improving chances for successful parole.

Work with juveniles has produced positive effects on recidivism. In six years of operation the Pilot Intensive Counseling Organization in California classified over 1,600 youths as amenable or nonamenable to treatment by individual counseling. Half of the youths classified as amenable were given no special counseling (control group), and the other half received individual psychotherapy. Thirty-three months after release, those who received intensive counseling averaged 2¾ months' less time back in prison than did those in the control group.

Even though there have been effective rehabilitation programs in some institutions or work camps, there is a very pessimistic view held by many social workers involved with youthful delinquents. Burks (1964) reported on a two-day workshop concerning Youth Week held in New York City. He reported that the conference in general was optimistic in referring to rehabilitation, training, and antidelinquency programs, yet social workers repeatedly discussed "unreachables."

Burks stated, " 'The unreachables' are those, usually of racial minority groups, who show no interest in reforming their ways or in any kind of training.

Although there were reports of excellent rehabilitation programs, there was also the shadowy feeling expressed by some that the problem might be outgrowing present remedies.

Some of the participating social workers said that a number of existing programs failed for lack of proper emphasis and knowledge.

Many 'unreachable families,' it was noted, cannot identify with, or actively resent, rehabilitation programs that they feel are based on middle-class concepts. More than once Negro social workers pointed out to their white colleagues that 'understanding' and 'respect' are frequently not enough in dealing with delinquents of the lowest rungs of the social order."

Apparently the social workers attending the conference recognized that their colleagues currently being trained are poorly prepared to handle hard-core slum problems. There are thousands of youths brought up in

TREATING OFFENDERS AND PREVENTING CRIMINAL BEHAVIOR **579**

deprived families, clinging to a language and culture that the social workers simply cannot contact. In addition, there are many youths developing in the large population areas of the country that will not be prepared to adequately handle even simple or low-level jobs. Proper attitudes and work habits have to be instilled in the toughest classes, but how to accomplish this is still unknown.

The major effort in rehabilitation of criminals, whether they be juveniles or adults, has been after they are convicted and sentenced for relatively major crimes. There is very little work done with rehabilitation of prisoners in county jails, local jails, or the smaller institutions. Thus it is usually the long-term prisoner convicted for a relatively serious offense that receives some rehabilitative efforts. However, this is not always the case. London and Myers (1961) told of a psychiatric clinic established for youthful offenders confined to a county jail in Connecticut. The experimental clinic was established under a grant from the United States Public Health Service to develop a treatment program which would be effective and could be established in other jails. Significant relationships between the extent and type of psychiatric problems of youthful offenders and their social class, race, and record of recidivism were discovered. The researchers concluded that "the clinic seems more promising to offer definitive treatment for the relatively healthy person and for the first offender. Because these are usually acute cases, they lend themselves to goal-limited therapeutic measures. Most first offenders are healthy but even those who display a mental disorder have a high incidence of stress at the time of arrest, *regardless of diagnosis*. This would tend to support a hypothesis that the first offenders deserve the most careful diagnostic assessment in order to find cases suitable for treatment." The researchers stated that "The jail clinic seems less promising as a treatment center for chronic offenders, especially those with antisocial reactions because they are confined for relatively short sentences. However, careful diagnostic evaluation and planning for treatment after release may be carried out in the clinic for this group."

Apparently this one study indicated that there was hope of working with youthful offenders (age 16–25) at the county or local jail level even though the normal sentence to such jails is for short- rather than long-term incarceration. Unfortunately the type of treatment to use for such youthful offenders is not well established.

ADULT REHABILITATION. The effectiveness of incarceration as a means of reducing criminal behavior has been competently studied and reported by Glaser (1964). An extensive research project supported by the Ford Foundation was specifically designed to study the failure rates of different types of offenders released from prisons. The purpose was to determine the amount of reversion or nonreversion to crime and to determine insofar as possible what practical measures could be used to reduce recidivism. Glaser found from interviews with 250 successful releasees that 52 percent said that they changed from a life of crime during imprisonment. In other words, they were reformed while serving their prison sentence. How the reformation took place was then investigated in some detail by Glaser and his associates.

It was found that in terms of the total rehabilitative effect of the prison when considered in terms of successful post prison life, inmate–inmate relationships were of less importance than inmate–staff relationships. About half of the released prisoners who reported that they changed during imprisonment credited a staff member with being most influential in their reformation. The prison staff members cited most frequently as important in the reformation were the work supervisors. Chaplains, case-workers, volunteer religious workers, and so on, were cited by only a small proportion of the total ex-prisoners who felt that they were reformed while in prison. Glaser concluded "The prison employee who has the greatest reformative influence on an offender is the one who is able to demonstrate sincere and sustained concern for and confidence in the offender's rehabilitation. The prison employee's concern is most effectively manifested by gestures of interest and acts of assistance for the offender which exceed the minimal requirements of the employee's job in the prison." Glaser thought that the minimal impact of caseworkers in the prisons was probably not of importance in the overall view of rehabilitation on prisoners. He found that grouping or isolating prisoners while in prison has an effect on rehabilitation. He suggested that "Promoting the isolation of inmates from each other fosters rehabilitation where the techniques for promoting isolation consists of: a) providing physical arrangements of inmate housing which facilitate an inmate's achievement of privacy when he desires it; b) separating inmates considered criminogenic influences on each other; c) encouraging staff-desired patterns of inmate discrimination in choice of prisoner associates." He further indicated that promoting isolation in inmates is not always good and if the technique is employed to promote the "do your own time" ideology of the prison subculture, isolation becomes a disadvantage rather than an advantage.

Why caseworkers have apparently not been as successful with adult prisoners as with juveniles was also investigated by Glaser. He suggested that "the advancement of treatment goals requires centralization of more authority in the officials who are spokesmen for treatment interests. . . ."

Work in prison has been thought of as a valuable asset for rehabilitation. Certainly lack of things to do in prison would be expected to decrease the probability of successful rehabilitation. Training in specific activities would seem to help a prisoner adjust better when he is released. Glaser (1964) investigated the work situation in federal prisons in some detail. He concluded that ". . . during about the first four months out of prison, prison work experience is used in postrelease employment by only about a quarter of those releasees who by then have some postrelease jobs of one week or more. . . ." He further suggested "that in about one-tenth of inmate postrelease jobs there are benefits from new learning acquired in prison work, in about three or four percent of these jobs there are benefits from the preservation of old skills through practice in prison, and in about five or six percent of the postrelease jobs the prison provided useful physical or psychological conditioning."

Some of the data collected by Glaser and his associates showing the

TABLE 16.2 Percentages of Prison Releasees Returned or Successful by Type of First Postrelease Job, and for Jobs Requiring Training, by Type of Prison Training or Work Experience *

	FIRST POSTRELEASE JOB LASTING ONE WEEK OR MORE	
	RETURNED VIOLATORS %	SUCCESSES %
A. Type of Post Release Job		
Unskilled job—no training required	59	61
Some training required	21 †	34 †
No postrelease job of one week or more	20 †	5 †
B. Used no prison training or experience	56	47
C. Used prison training or experience	9 ‡	18 ‡
D. Major source of prison aid in jobs requiring training:		
Prison vocational training	19	19
Prison industry experience	2	10
Prison maintenance experience	12	13
Prison clerical experience	6	1
Prison school training	5	8
Other prison training or experience		2

* From *The Effectiveness of a Prison and Parole System* by Daniel Glaser, copyright © 1964, by The Bobbs-Merrill Company, Inc., reprinted by permission of the publisher.

† Differences this large or larger could occur by chance alone, in samples of this size, less than once in 1,000 times.

‡ Differences this large or larger could occur by chance alone, in samples of this size, less than once in 500 times.

comparison of failures and successes of released prisoners compared to the type of prison training or work experience and use of that training on post release jobs is shown in Table 16.2. There are small but significant differences between success and failure rates outside of prison for releasees using prison training or experience on their first post release job. In Table 16.3 more of Glaser's data is presented showing that the failure rates for releasees of federal prisons varies according to the type of work assignment while in prison. Obviously the unskilled or semiskilled jobs in prison are no more closely related to failure outside of prison than are the more complicated or higher level jobs in prison. Apparently there is little relationship between type of work in prison and recidivism rate, but the prison jobs with highest influence in the prison (orderly, officer's clerk, and so on) seem to be held by prisoners who have highest "failure rate" after release.

TABLE 16.3 Failure Rates After Five Years from Release for Releasees by Last Prison Work Assignment of Three or More Months *

LAST ASSIGNMENT	FAILURE RATE %	NO. OF CASES
Food service	39	178
Typing and bookkeeping	40	50
Orderly, runner, or officer's clerk	44	107
Skilled work (other than above)	35	105
Semiskilled work (other than above)	28	186
Unskilled work (other than above)	35	239
Other, or no information	31	150
Total cases	35 †	1015

* From *The Effectiveness of a Prison and Parole System* by Daniel Glaser, copyright © 1964, by The Bobbs-Merrill Company, Inc., reprinted by permission of the publisher.
† Differences as great as those between the failure rates for the separate work assignments and that of the total cases would occur by chance alone in samples of this size less than once in 50 times (by Chi Square test).

Again citing Glaser (1964), the effectiveness of prison education systems in reducing recidivism is somewhat disappointing. Glaser suggested the following qualified conclusion: "For most inmates, prison education is statistically associated with above average postrelease success only when the education is extensive and occurs in the course of prolonged confinement. For most prisoners, especially for those with extensive prior felony records, the usual duration and type of involvement in prison education is associated with higher than average postrelease failure rates; while a small amount of education in prison frequently impairs postrelease prospects of inmates indirectly, by inspiring them with unrealistic aspirations, or by the education's being pursued instead of alternative prison programs which could provide more useful preparation for postrelease life." This may seem a rather harsh and discouraging view of prison education. However, it is based on a good deal of research and makes good sense logically when we consider the difficulties of trying to educate prisoners in most prisons. (This same problem has been referred to in earlier sections of this and the preceding chapter.)

The effect of incarceration is governed not only by the factors just discussed but also by the institution's feeling about what it should do. In most prisons, treatment programs are considered secondary to the running of a smooth organization with as little upheaval and effort as possible. What limited treatment resources are available are often provided only after other institutional assignments have been completed. As indicated in earlier sections of this and the preceding chapter, there is a strong feeling among many prison personnel that the rehabilitation efforts place additional load on the custodial personnel and that it is unfair and unfortunate for them that such programs are in effect. The rehabilitative effort is frequently carried out by people of the same status as the custodial staff or is forgotten completely in many institutions.

Some evidence that the attitudes of custodial and treatment personnel differ and that it influences prisoners' attitudes was collected by Rabin and Hess (1965). They administered a questionnaire covering origins of criminality, prison politics, treatment methods, and other aspects of penal philosophy to prison personnel and inmates and compared the returned forms. Custodial and administrative personnel had no differences in attitudes as measured by their questionnaires. However, there were some differences of opinion between custodial or administrative staff vs. treatment personnel and marked differences between inmates and custodial or administrative personnel. There were relatively few differences between inmates and treatment personnel opinions, yet both groups differed considerably from the custodial and administrative personnel.

Even when some rehabilitative effort is carried out in the prison there is only a slim hope that this effort will have lasting effects on releasees. Schnur (1961) emphasized this point of view when he asked, "Just how much can society expect from the correctional processes?" He went on to suggest that the correctional processes can often be held accountable for the lack of rehabilitation of prisoners, but that other factors are also important. He stated: "It would not be realistic to blame them for all the failures even if the correctional processes were perfectly implemented. After all, the releases from such a perfect program re-enter an imperfect society that made criminals out of them originally. These influences are still in vicious operation. Part of the price for the freedom of the strong to enjoy their vices is paid by the crimes committed by the weak. A man released who is highly resistant to crime can often be expected only to resist so much of the crime-inciting conditions. His success or failure is affected by the weakness and strengths of the social conditions into which he is released. A less resistant man released into conditions with more strengths than weaknesses may be more successful than the strongly resistant released into very weakening conditions. The fact is that success or failure of correctional clients is to be explained by both the correctional process and the experiences in the release situation.

"Some sectors of our society expect the correctional process to immunize a man from a criminal career for the rest of his life, no matter how contagious the social situation is. They feel the ineffectuality of the correctional processes is documented whenever a one-time client commits a new crime, no matter how many years separate him from the correctional process. This is expecting more of correctional treatment than is expected of medical treatment. Physicians are not called quacks for every recurrent attack of illness.

"As long as society refuses to remove the legal impediments to effective treatment, hesitates to implement contemporary knowledge, neglects to provide for the discovery of additional knowledge, and fails to control adequately the social and economic conditions productive of criminal behavior, accountability for recurrent crime (recidivism) must be shared by society with the correctional processes."

POSTPRISON ENVIRONMENT.   As has been repeatedly emphasized, the prisoner incarcerated for a criminal act serves his term because he violated a rule or regulation of society. He violated this rule or regulation because something within him interacted with his environment. One well-accepted concept concerning effective rehabilitation is to train a person to handle himself adequately in the world at large. Unfortunately most prisoners return to the same environment from which they originally entered prison. In other words, they go right back to the environment in which it was easy for them to commit a crime, but society expects them to have learned something in prison that will make them law-abiding citizens.

It seems obvious that society must attempt to change the environment as well as the individual, so that the interaction will result in acceptable behavior instead of criminal behavior.

What does the prisoner find upon release from his incarceration? Can he be expected to go to a nonprison environment and find wonderful economic opportunities and possibilities for a good life? The question, of course, must be answered almost categorically, no. Very few prisoners leave their period of incarceration to return to a rosy, economic future. Most will have more difficulty in finding positions, adequate compensation, and a decent standard of living than they had before they entered prison in the first place.

Previously we pointed out that prisoners often gain unrealistic views of the outside world while they are serving their term in prison. Often they believe that they will be able to earn a far better income and maintain a higher standard of living than can be realistically achieved. The reasons for these have been discussed earlier, but the fact remains that this is going to make things more difficult for them when they do reenter society. Glaser (1964) in his study found what kind of jobs prisoners expect upon release from prison. Table 16.4 shows the results of a survey of prisoners and releasees from federal prisons. The expectations are quite unrealistic. Forty-two percent of new prisoners and 54 percent of releasees, four months out, expect to have professional or business positions five years after release from prison. Other studies have shown the same unrealistic view to be common in prisoners.

On the other hand, when most prisoners are released they have little resources available at the time of release and find that the postrelease jobs are generally low-level, with relatively small income. Many do not find any employment. Glaser found that only one half of the releasees of federal prisons work from 80 to 100 percent of the time during the second month out of prison, and that this proportion only rises to two thirds in the third month out of prison.

Releasees upon leaving prison generally have low economic income capability. They have expenditure expectations that are quite high. This combination leads to an easy return to criminal behavior. A valuable type of educational program within a prison might well be directed toward helping prisoners understand their possibilities in the "outside world" and helping them to achieve more realistic expectations of the future.

Successfulness of obtaining and staying on a postrelease job is directly related to successfulness in staying out of prison. The type of postrelease employment obtained is most often not just the result of a prison record, but rather a lack of extensive or skilled work experience or ability. Thus it is imperative while in prison to get some training of value immediately after release or to gain experience as soon after release as possible.

Glaser (1964) also studied the social world of the ex-prisoner and indicated that: "Over 90% of the men released from prison returned to communities in which they previously resided. This means that they generally returned to an area where their criminal reputation is known, that it also generally means that they returned to the area where they can receive as-

TABLE 16.4 Type of Job Wanted or Expected by Prisoners and Releasees at Various Intervals After Release from Prison *

TYPE OF EMPLOYMENT	TIME OF INTERVIEW	WANTED AT RELEASE (IF IN PRISON) OR NOW (IF 4 MOS. OUT)	EXPECTED AT RELEASE	EXPECTED ABOUT ONE YEAR AFTER RELEASE	EXPECTED ABOUT FIVE YEARS AFTER RELEASE
Profession, semi- professional, business manager, or owner †	Prison entry	20	10	21	42
	Near release	16	8	20	47
	Four months out	15	—	14	54
Craftsmen, foremen, skilled workers ‡	Prison entry	31	23	29	26
	Near release	26	17	25	26
	Four months out	19	—	11	14
Service workers **	Prison entry	14	14	12	8
	Near release	11	13	10	6
	Four months out	18	—	20	14
Operatives ††	Prison entry	19	27	24	15
	Near release	31	29	30	13
	Four months out	30	—	37	10
Unskilled heavy labor, farm labor or mental service work ‡‡	Prison entry	16	26	14	9
	Near release	16	34	16	8
	Four months out	18	—	18	7
Nonspecific responses, "don't know," etc.	Prison entry	7	12	16	19
	Near release	9	15	20	26
	Four months out	4	—	27	40

* From *The Effectiveness of a Prison and Parole System* by Daniel Glaser, copyright © 1964, by The Bobbs-Merrill Company, Inc., reprinted by permission of the publisher. Examples of types of employment.

† Manager or owner of business, including garage, restaurant, or farm; any work for which a college education or special vocational schooling beyond high school is required (stenographer, IBM clerk, bookkeeper, embalmer, medical technician, licensed barber, etc.).

‡ Carpenter, plumber, machinist, electrician, painter, crane or heavy-equipment operator, long-distance or heavy truck driver.

** Milkman, restaurant cook, waiter, salesman, gas-station attendant, cab driver.

†† Semi- or unskilled factory machine-tender, shipping or stock clerk, unskilled office worker, packing-house laborer, local truck driver, etc.

‡‡ Dock worker, coal miner, railroad section hand, construction common labor, farm laborer or sharecropper owning neither land nor equipment, garbage collector, janitor, dishwasher.

sistance from kin." Glaser showed, somewhat contrary to general expectations concerning environmental influences on criminal behavior, that there is a higher than average postrelease failure rate for ex-prisoners who go to a community other than their preincarceration residence. He does show, however, that the most unfavorable postrelease environment is one in which the ex-prisoner lives alone.

There is no doubt that postprison environment has an influence upon the release. Remedies for postrelease problems must include action in the communities as well as work with the releasee both before and after release. Glaser suggested some remedies for post release problems as follows:

N1. Major advances in the contribution of prisons to the solution of inmate postrelease problems, with a relatively small percentage increase in total prison costs, could be achieved merely by systematic extension of programs already successfully initiated. Notable among these expandable programs are:
   a. compulsory inmate savings of some prison earnings to meet postrelease expenses, supplemented by gratuities or loans where necessary;
   b. graduation of the disbursement of such funds, through parole supervision offices;
   c. facilitation of inmate communication with law-abiding outside persons, through reduction of censorship of correspondence and of impediments to visiting;
   d. involvement of outside organizations in inmate organizations, and vice versa, through service and hobby clubs, personal development and mutual therapy groups, churches, and other types of voluntary organizations;
   e. communication of parole supervision staff with inmates prior to the inmate's release (in correspondence, in prerelease classes, and in initial parole interviews at the prisons);
   f. operation of loan funds as flexible financial aid effective for some releasees, administered through parole supervision agencies in a manner based on the experience of the states that have operated these funds for decades.
N2. Routinization of these programs, so they will be more consistently operated and developed, requires their administration by persons who continually receive feedback indicating the consequences of these programs; this means that their operation at the prisons should be, at least in part, a regular responsibility of parole supervision staff.
N3. Selective employment of parolees and of prison dischargees by government agencies, and augmentation of their eligibility for unemployment insurance, can reduce the net social and economic costs to the public from recidivism and reimprisonment.
N4. This half-century's most promising correctional development for alleviating postrelease problems of prisoners consists of the counseling

centers in metropolitan areas to which prisoners scheduled for release are transferred some months before their release date, and from which they regularly go forth to enter the job market and to develop correctionally acceptable postprison social relationships, before they are released on a regular parole or on any other traditional types of release from prison.

Residential centers for the community guidance and graduated release of convicted persons are a logical extension of a changing conception of the state's responsibility in dealing with felons. This is a change from the classic objective of completely depriving a man of his freedom for a period which ends abruptly when he has "paid for his crime," to the objective of both removing and restoring freedom on a gradual basis, in a manner which will most facilitate the felon's achievement of a noncriminal life. Parole and probation were earlier steps in this direction, but they were handicapped through the inability of staff to be in contact with their clients' lives in the free community as much as occurs with the new types of institution. However, we have found that parole and probation vary tremendously in these and other respects, both in actual administration and in the standards that officials seek to attain.

Preventing New Crime. Although it has been pointed out in this and the preceding chapter of this book that the prevention of new crime is difficult if not impossible there is some hope that preventive techniques can lessen crime rate. In Chapter 15 we concluded that, by and large, individual characteristics were not related to criminal versus noncriminal behavior but were related to specific types of criminal behavior. There was considerably more evidence available to indicate that environmental factors are related to criminal versus noncriminal behavior. Thus in the following discussions we will consider characteristics of the environment which might be controlled to lower the amount of criminal behavior.

Preventing new crime may be approached from two directions. (1) The global approach is concerned with improving the entire social milieu and environmental conditions. (2) The individual approach attempts to isolate potential criminals before they become criminals. We will discuss characteristics of the environment under the above two mentioned categories as well as the feasibility of selecting predelinquents.

GLOBAL APPROACH. In the earlier parts of this chapter and in Chapter 15 we reviewed many characteristics of the environment that seemed to be related to criminal versus noncriminal behavior. It appears that more criminals are developed in certain environments than in others. However, we must constantly bear in mind that even in the delinquency or criminally prone environments only a very small proportion of the total population resort to criminal activity.

In the early 1920's several investigators found that a tendency for crime and delinquency was unevenly distributed throughout the various geographic areas they studied. Extensive research in Chicago showed that certain areas produced a larger number of criminal cases than did other areas of the city. This led to the conclusion that social environment had something to do with the development of delinquency and criminal behavior. This thinking has been expanded into the concept of a "delinquent subculture." The concept of a subculture related to deviant behavior leads to consideration of a global approach as a means of lowering overall crime rate. However, there are people who challenge the general theory. Many experts suggest that delinquency rates vary because of the treatment by police and the courts and that the environment doesn't create the situation as much as the individuals who might be involved in criminal behavior gravitate to a particular environment. It is also conceivable that many delinquent or criminal activities will go unnoted from some subcultures of society, whereas the same activities will be recorded in police records if they take place in other societies. Of course, the more serious offenses are generally reported regardless of the subcultures in which they take place.

Forman (1963) was concerned with the problem of whether a general subsection of society may be largely involved in criminal behavior. If so, he wondered how such an environment could affect some of its members but not all. Forman suggested that it is possible that there simply aren't enough people from one subculture in a particular neighborhood to make a global approach to crime prevention reasonable. Some experts have previously suggested that only 10 to 15 percent of a culture might be involved in crime. Forman obtained data to show that in some high-rate-delinquency areas more than 33 percent of all the boys in the area within the age range which might logically be considered juveniles, were delinquent. In other words, the high rate areas may contain a subculture making up one third of the total population.

If we can assume that there is some retardation of delinquents in schools, Forman showed that in a room of 30 students of a high-delinquency-rate area, about six of the students would be delinquents. If these six delinquents were evenly distributed throughout the room, every student in the room would be within arm reach of a delinquent. Forman thus concluded that within this context the delinquent subculture theory seems quite tenable. He stated, "A concentration of this magnitude of delinquents would seem to provide a sufficient number of individuals in close contact with each other to maintain and pass on the attitudes, knowledge, skills, etc., making up a delinquent sub-culture and a large enough group so that it could offer substantial rewards to those who conformed to it and punish those who did not."

The concept of a global approach has been popular for many years. Dudycha (1957) expressed generally accepted views that social factors are important in the development of criminal behavior. Particular areas of the country such as transition areas on the fringes of commercial and industrial sections of the cities are conducive areas for the development of delinquency. He suggested that displacement of residential areas by commerce or by population movements are important. Even so, Dudycha emphasized that there is no real prevention program that can work by handling an entire area or environment because such an approach must by necessity include so many nondelinquents that it becomes unwieldy as a program. He suggested the best technique seems to be a psychological approach where particular individual problems are studied and courses of action are tailored to an individual's needs.

Even though it is difficult to consider treating an entire environment following the global approach, there have been attempts to do so. How successful these programs have been was reviewed by Witmer and Tufts (1954). They concluded that the effectiveness of most environmental measures directed specifically to reduction of delinquency had not been adequately determined. For example, curfew laws, laws forbidding the sale of liquor to minors, particular plans of school curriculum or changes of school environment, have been tried but good studies of the effectiveness of these were not known to the authors. Witmer and Tufts concluded that there was no definite evidence of the value of local self-help enterprises in the high-delinquency-rate areas. Although many people working on such projects feel that there was a definite decline in delinquency rates as the lower socioeconomic or slum areas were improved, objective data to support such feelings was not reported.

Witmer and Tufts also evaluated the increased use of recreational programs in delinquent areas. By and large, there was a reduction in delinquency rate, but such a reduction might have been the result of a selection process. The children who obtained supervised recreation might have been less prone to delinquency anyhow.

In summary, we must conclude that theoretically the global approach has some merit. However, most data concerning the success of delinquency prevention programs does not favor the global approach.

INDIVIDUAL APPROACH. The available objective evidence concerning prevention of crime indicates that the best procedure is identification of the potential delinquent or criminal followed by intensive care or treatment.

In Chapter 15 we discussed some aspects of identifying criminals. In Chapters 1, 2, and 3 we considered modifying behavior and some of the problems of mental health. We will not repeat these points at this time, but we will consider some of the recent information concerning diagnosis or prognosis of delinquents' or criminals' behavior.

Two researchers, Sheldon and Eleanor Glueck, are well known for their work in predicting delinquent behavior. After intensive study of many delinquents and nondelinquents, the Gluecks developed a table for predicting delinquency. We will consider this prediction technique in some detail.

Before considering prediction techniques or the use of interviews or scales, it is important to heed a point brought out by Kvaraceus (1959a). One of the best, if not the best, single indicator of possible future delinquency is past behavior. Kvaraceus pointed out that in the United States it usually takes at least five or six delinquent acts before the community begins to take a delinquent seriously. He stated: "Few youngsters turn delinquent overnight. Most of them take about ten years to develop into a full-fledged delinquent. During this incubation period, they give off many signs and signals of their future difficulties—if we would only catch the cue or take the hint." Many cases of delinquent behavior are not disposed of officially by petition or formal hearings in the courts. If these cases are watched more carefully in the future, there is a good possibility that pre-delinquents may be kept from becoming delinquents or criminals.

THE GLUECK SOCIAL PREDICTION TABLE. The Gluecks studied many juveniles and found that five social factors reflecting parent–child relationships differentiated the true juvenile delinquents from the nondelinquents with whom the delinquents had been matched case by case for age, ethnic derivation, general intelligence, and residence in underprivileged urban areas. The five factors that differentiated delinquents from nondelinquents were (1) discipline of boy by father, (2) supervision of boy by mother, (3) affection of father for boy, (4) affection of mother for boy, and (5) family cohesiveness. Other factors were investigated, but these five worked best in discriminating true juvenile delinquents from nonjuvenile delinquents before entering school. These factors were used for a prediction table, although they were selected by studying juveniles who were known to be delinquents or nondelinquents. This method of estimating validity of the scale may not provide predictive validity. However, the scale did have concurrent validity. (See Chapter 6 of this book for details on techniques of estimating validity.)

Eleanor Glueck (1962) recognized that the five factor prediction table was constructed retrospectively on one group of persistent juvenile offenders and their matched nonoffenders. She had hoped that it would predict delinquency of young children before overt symptoms of delinquentlike behavior were shown. Dr. Glueck hoped that the scale could be improved and sharpened to identify delinquents before the onset of evidences of delinquentlike behavior. She suggested that three factors, supervision of boy by mother, discipline of boy by mother, and rearing by affectionless parent substitutes could be used instead of the original five-factor table. She reported an analysis of data with these three factors showing that a fair or suitable supervision of boy by mother resulted in a delinquency score of 29.7; unsuitable supervision of boy by mother, a delinquency score of 83.2. On the factor of discipline of boy by mother, firm but kindly, gave a delinquency score of 6.1; lax, overstrict, or erratic, a delinquency score of 73.7. Children reared by a parent substitute had a delinquency score of 79.3; those reared by parents, a score of 38.0. Dr. Glueck concluded that the Social Prediction Table was valuable and had concurrent validity. She also recognized that other factors related to personality make-up and primary associations must be investigated. She suggested that additional data was being gathered by others concerning this topic.

Prigmore (1963) reported a study concerning the Social Prediction Table. Using different judges or raters, he obtained various ratings of the same individuals to the extent that he questioned the reliability of the scale. Prigmore used southern-educated Negroes, northern-educated Negroes, southern-educated white and northern educated-white social workers to rate 60 cases. The education and experience for all raters were somewhat the same, because they were all social workers. Prigmore concluded that the Glueck scale might have to be restricted to a particular reference group, or else a clear-cut system of categories must be established. He said, "The Glueck scale cannot be used by raters from different cultural backgrounds if reliable ratings are to be obtained." Prigmore further investigated the reliability of the Glueck factors themselves and thought that they were open to question. He said: "The Glueck factors are complex, highly inferential variables for which adequate external criteria are only partially available. It is to be noted from the findings that corporal punishment by father or lack of it is such a clear-cut external criterion for parental discipline that the factor showed less variability. But the other factors, particularly the extremely complex factors on affection, lack such clear-cut criterion." He went on to explain that a predictive instrument that is unreliable cannot be valid. Therefore, because of the lack of reliability, the validity of the Glueck scale for prediction of delinquency is dubious. (Prigmore's work was carried out before the previously mentioned article by Eleanor Glueck had been reported. In effect, Eleanor Glueck had conceded the lack of reliability of ratings on some of the factors and had suggested the three new factors mentioned in the preceding paragraphs.)

Eleanor Glueck (1963) reported a further analysis of the Glueck Social Prediction Table to allow for the problem of raters having difficulty with some of the original five factors. In many homes, discipline of the boy by the father is not very likely because the father is not a part of the family. She showed that a second three-factor table consisting of (1) supervision of boy by the mother, (2) discipline of boy by mother, and (3) rearing by parent substitute, was a valuable means of estimating predelinquents. Further, she indicated that by dropping the rearing-by-parent-substitutes factor and substituting a family-cohesiveness factor, the identification of delinquents was improved. Dr. Glueck defined cohesiveness of a family as a "we" feeling among members of the immediate family as evident by *group interests*, and so on.

At this writing complete data on the use of the Glueck Table as a predictor of delinquency has not become available. The New York City Youth Board and the Commissioners Youth Council of Washington, D.C. are making experimental use of the new three-factor prediction table. Dr. Glueck indicated that the results are more than promising and "it looks very much as if the newest three-factor table can now be recommended for general use." The three-factor table she refers to include (1) supervision of boy by mother, with suitable supervision giving a delinquency score of 9.9, fair supervision, 57.5, unsuitable supervision, 83.2; (2) discipline of the boy by the mother, firmly but kindly yielding a delinquency score of 6.1, erratically, 52.3, over strictly, 73.3, and laxly, 82.9; (3) cohesiveness of family, with marked cohesiveness of the family yielding a 20.6 delinquency score, some cohesiveness, 61.3, and none, 96.9.

Many people have pointed out that the dialogue concerning the Glueck scale will continue until long-range validation studies have either proven or disproven its value. However, Voss (1963) reported some data on predictive validity of the scale. He indicated that retrospective investigations did not establish validity for the Glueck Social Prediction Table. Voss stated: "The table was constructed on the basis of equal numbers of delinquents and nondelinquents, and is inefficient as a prognostic device when only a small percentage become delinquent. A reasonable approximation of the actual delinquency rate must be used in the construction of a prediction table. Otherwise, the labeling of every boy in the sample as a nondelinquent delivers a higher degree of predictive accuracy." He concluded his statement of his work in analysis of validation studies completed so far as follows:

"The validity of the Glueck's Prediction Instrument is still in doubt, and only an amazing reversal of the current results in the Youth Board investigation will validate the Glueck Social Prediction Table."

Other scales have been devised. In general we do not now have the ability to predict delinquency accurately. Several studies have shown specific factors related to delinquent behavior. By and large these studies show concurrent validity rather than an ability to predict future delinquency.

One study that did show evidence of predictive validity was reported by Shelley and Toch (1962). They showed that readiness to perceive violence is related to a tendency to behave violently. They stated, "What can be affirmed with confidence, in other words, is that psychological dispositions related to the tendency to perceive violent pictures seemed to increase the likelihood of troublesome behavior." Although their work considered short-term predictions, they felt that long-term prediction might be possible.

In conclusion we must remember that at present we may not be able to accurately predict who will or will not become a delinquent or a criminal. However, society at large is becoming more adjusted to the concept that there are special problems in handling people who are delinquents or who may become delinquents. The true delinquent does not become a delinquent overnight. More specialists trained in understanding juvenile behavior and how to handle the problems of juvenile delinquency can help in the prediction and, therefore, the prevention of the true juvenile delinquents.

Most of the states in the United States are currently involved in the plans for comprehensive mental health programs, as mentioned in Chapters 2 and 3 of this book. These programs will involve new approaches and efforts to keep more people mentally healthy. One of the prime targets of such a program will be the setting up of programs and centers for the immediate care of problem children and adults. If these centers can be adequately staffed and personnel who work with juvenile delinquents and criminals can be adequately trained, there is hope that juvenile delinquency and crime rate may be lowered by working with people before they become too deeply involved in criminal behavior.

SUMMARY

Once a person has been convicted of breaking a rule or regulation of society he is usually provided special treatment by society. Frequently the treatment consists of incarceration, so that the criminal is no longer in contact with society at large. Often the treatment includes special programs to help the convicted criminal become a better-adjusted member of society.

Most of the population of the world is still not certain how much emphasis should be placed on rehabilitating criminals as compared to locking them in institutions so that society will not be bothered with them.

There are three major times when convicted criminals are treated; during probation, incarceration, or parole. Persons convicted of breaking society's rules may be sentenced to a probation period rather than incarceration. During a probation period, the convicted person lives in his regular environment under close supervision. The full possibilities of such programs are rarely realized due to the case loads on the probation officers and others, but such programs may be extremely valuable in reducing repetitive criminal behavior.

Incarceration is the most common treatment provided convicted criminals. When a convicted person is deemed unfit to remain in general society, he is sentenced to a prison, jail, work camp, juvenile home, or elsewhere. Within the institution he may receive rather elaborate training and counseling to help him prepare for a better life as a law-abiding citizen, or he may be locked up in an environment that provides little or no training or counseling. Often the type of incarceration is determined only by the available facilities or the judge's decision. In some situations diagnostic centers determine the needs of the prisoners and develop programs for them. The efficacy of incarceration in preventing repetition of criminal behavior is not known. However, behavioral science knows more about how to change human behavior than is currently being put to large-scale use in prisons.

Most convicted persons receive sentences requiring a minimum and maximum incarceration period. If they serve their minimum sentences as good prisoners they are often eligible for parole. The parole period, like probation, is served in general society under strict supervision and regulations. As with probation, lack of adequate personnel and facilities frequently hamper the effectiveness of the parole period. However, the system has merit as a means of helping prisoners adjust upon their return into general society.

Specialized treatment programs for drug addicts and juvenile delinquents are being expanded. The latter deserves special attention, because the juvenile delinquent of today often becomes the criminal of tomorrow.

New concepts in sentencing criminals include "weekend" prison service. Such techniques provide members of society with a means of venting their vengeance on prisoners, providing an example to others and still allowing a convicted person to maintain himself and his family.

Modifying behavior of individuals by techniques discussed in earlier chapters is considerably more difficult in prison. However, the same psychological principles apply in prison and outside. Criminal behavior can be reduced through the application of known psychological principles both to the changing of the criminal and to the changing of society.

Society in general has not decided that criminals can be converted to law-abiding citizens, nor even if they want to spend the necessary funds or energy to try to effect such changes. Such views can, and are, being changed. Many of the known techniques of changing prejudices might be adapted to speed the modification of society's views toward criminals.

The effectiveness of rehabilitation programs for incarcerated criminals is questionable. The rate of recidivism is high (although probably not the 60–70 percent often cited). Rehabilitation programs are most effective with juvenile offenders. Several special programs with youths have shown promise as means of reducing recidivism. So far, the major rehabilitative efforts for juveniles and adults have been with criminals sentenced for relatively long terms and generally in state or federal prisons. There is a real need to provide the proper type of treatment for first offenders who often have short sentences in county or local jails. Prisoners need a more realistic understanding of the general society in which they will reside after release and more realistic standards or expectations for their own performances.

Preventing new crime has been approached from two directions, a global approach and an individual one. In general the global approach of treating an entire geographical area by slum clearance, housing redevelopment, and so on, has not proven effective in reducing crime. The individual approach of intensive treatment of the predelinquent is apparently more successful. Unfortunately, there are few, if any, well-validated tests or scales for selecting predelinquents. However, juveniles don't become delinquents overnight. Several delinquent acts usually occur before society takes a delinquent seriously. Thus youngsters who might become delinquents can be identified, and proper programs might be established to lessen the probability of future criminal behavior.

SUGGESTED REFERENCES FOR FURTHER STUDY

Abrahamsen, D. (1960). *The Psychology of Crime.* New York: Columbia University Press.

A book covering many aspects of crime, particularly criminal behavior as a psychological disorder and therefore amenable to the same kind of treatment and interpretations as mental illness.

Dudycha, G. J. (ed.) (1959). *Psychology for Law Enforcement Officers.* Springfield, Ill.: Charles C. Thomas.

A book edited by a person working in the field of psychology applied to law. Nine other authors contribute in their own specialty areas. Topics covered include a general view of psychology, selection and placement of policemen, lie detection, human relations, leadership, and group control (specifically handling of highway traffic and traffic control), psychology and the court, mental abnormalities and crime, juvenile delinquency, adult criminal behavior, alcoholic behavior, drug addiction, the work of the courts, and parole boards in action.

Glaser, D. (1964). *The Effectiveness of a Prison and Parole System.* Indianapolis, Ind.: Bobbs-Merrill Co.

This book reports the findings of a large research effort plus a review of available knowledge in the fields of prisoner return after release, the effects of imprisonment, and the postrelease experience. There are also a series of implications and set of conclusions or suggestions for improvement of prison and rehabilitation programs.

References—
Author Index[*]

A.S.H.R.A.E. (1960). *Heating, Ventilating, Air Conditioning Guide*. New York: American Society of Heating, Refrigeration and Air-Conditioning Engineers. [282]

Abrahamsen, D. (1946). "Motivation of Crime," *J. Nerv. Ment. Disease*, **103**, 549–570. [522]

——— (1960). *The Psychology of Crime*. New York: Columbia University Press. [523]

Adams, H. F. (1916). *Advertising and Its Mental Laws*. New York: Macmillan. [275]

Adams, S. *See* Weston and Adams (1935).

Allport, G. W. (1954). *The Nature of Prejudice*. Cambridge, Mass.: Addison-Wesley. [572]

——— (1961). *Pattern and Growth in Personality*. New York: Holt, Rinehart. [104]

Allport, G. W., and T. F. Pettigrew (1957). "Cultural Influence on the Perception of Movement: The Trapezoidal Illusion Among the Zulus," *J. Abnorm. Soc. Psychol.*, **55**, 104–133. [549]

American Psychiatric Association (1952). *Diagnostic and Statistical Manual of Mental Disorders*. Washington, D.C.: American Psychiatric Association. [72, 126]

American Psychological Association (1954). *Technical Recommendations for Psychological Tests and Diagnostic Techniques*. Washington, D.C.: American Psychological Association. [206, 208]

Amrine, M. (1963). "Psychology in the News," *Amer. Psychol.*, **18**, 322. [226]

---

[*] The pages on which citations appear are listed in brackets.

Anastasi, Anne (1961). *Psychological Testing* (2d ed.), New York: Macmillan. [129, 132]

Anderson, W. J. R., D. Baird, and A. M. Thomson (1958). "Epidemiology of Still Births and Infant Deaths Due to Congenital Malformation," *The Lancet*, **1**, 1304–1306. [94].

Angoff, W. H.   *See* Berrien and Angoff (1960).

Anonymous (1938). "Rest Periods—Experiments Conducted at the Tennessee Valley Authorities Office," *Mgmt. Rev.*, **27**, 153. [288]

Arey, L. B., *et al.* (1935). "The Numerical and Topographical Relation of Taste Buds to Human Circumvallate Papillae Throughout the Life Span," *Anat. Rec.*, **64**, 9–95. [159]

Argyris, C. (1953). "Some Characteristics of Successful Executives." *Personnel J.*, **32**, 50–55. [365]

————— (1961). *Personnel Administration: Present and Future*. Ann Arbor, Mich.: Bureau of Industrial Relations, University of Mich. [391]

Arnold, J. D. (1961). "Six Guides to Help You Get Across," *Mgmt. Methods*, **19**, 55–57. [351]

As, D.   *See* French, Israel, and As (1960).

Asch, S. E. (1955). "Opinion and Social Pressure," *Scientific American*, **193**, 5, 31–35. [552]

Ausubel, D. P. (1958). *Drug Addiction: Physiological, Psychological, and Sociological Aspects*. New York: Random House. [532]

Bach, G. R. (1963). "A Theory of Intimate Aggression," *Psychol. Rep.*, **12**, 449–450. [459]

Bailey, A. W.   *See* Sweeney, Bailey, and Dowd (1957).

Bailyn, L.   *See* Kelman and Bailyn (1962).

Baird, D.   *See* Anderson, Baird, and Thomson (1958).

Bales, R. F. (1954). "In Conference," *Harvard Business Review*, **32**, 2, 44–51. [353]

Bandura, A., Dorothea Ross, and Sheila Ross (1963). "Imitation of Film-Mediated Aggressive Models," *J. Abnorm. Soc Psychol.*, **66**, 3–11. [61]

Bandura, A., and R. H. Walters (1963). *Social Learning and Personality Development*. New York: Holt, Rinehart. [138]

Barkin, S. (1961). *The Decline of the Labor Movement*. Santa Barbara, Calif.: Center for the Study of Democratic Institutions. [372]

Barron, A. J.   *See* Zuckerman, Barron, and Whittier (1953).

Barry, C. E. (1959). "Executive Responsibility Can Be Taught in the Classroom," *Personnel J.*, **38**, 172–174. [251, 256]

Barton, W. A. (1930). *Outlining As a Study Procedure*. New York: Teachers College, Columbia University. [33]

Basowitz, H.   *See* Korchin and Basowitz (1957).

Bassett, G. A. (1962). "The Screening Process: Selection or Rejection?" *Personnel*, **39**, 4, 31–37. [230]

Battle, M. (1949). "Effect of Birth on Mentality," *Amer. J. Obstet. Gynec.*, **58**, 110–136. [94]

Bauer, W. W.   *See* Jenkins, Shacter, and Bauer (1953).

Baxter, B., A. A. Taaffe, and J. F. Hughes (1953). "A Trainee Evaluation Study," *Personnel Psychol.*, **6**, 402–417. [391]

Beal, V. A. *See* Burke, Beal, Kirkwood, and Stuart (1943).

Becker, W. C. (1964). "Consequences of Different Kinds of Parental Discipline," in M. L. Hoffman and Lois Hoffman (eds.), *Review of Child Development Research*, Vol. 1. New York: Russell Sage Foundation. [106, 107]

Beers, C. (1948). A *Mind That Found Itself*, (7th ed.). Garden City, N.Y.: Doubleday. [43]

Belli, M. (1956). *Ready for the Plaintiff*. New York. Holt, Rinehart. [551]

Bender, Lauretta (1938). "A Visual Motor Gestalt Test and Its Clinical Use," *Amer. Orthopsychiat. Assoc. Res. Monogr.*, No. 3. [130]

Berelson, B., P. Lazarsfeld, and W. N. McPhee (1954). *Voting*. Chicago: University of Chicago Press. [461, 462]

Berkowitz, L. (1962). *Aggression: A Social Psychological Analysis*. New York: McGraw-Hill. [456]

Berniger, J. *See* Fleishman and Berniger (1960).

Berrien, F. K. (1942). "Ocular Stability in Deception," *J. Appl. Psychol.*, **26**, 55–63. [536]

———— (1944). *Practical Psychology*. New York. Macmillan. [525]

———— (1952). *Practical Psychology*. (Revised ed.) New York: Macmillan. [155, 544, 549]

Berrien, F. K., and W. H. Angoff (1960). "The Sensitivity of An Employee Attitude Questionnaire," *Personnel Psychol.*, **13**, 317–327. [398]

Berry, P. C. (1961). "Effect of Colored Illumination on Perceived Temperature," *J. Appl. Psychol.*, **45**, 248–250. [281]

Birch, J. W. *See* Sloan and Birch (1955).

Birren, J. E., R. C. Casperson, and J. Botwinick (1950). "Age Changes in Pupil Size," *J. Gerontol.*, **5**, 216–221. [157]

Birren, J. E., and D. F. Morrison (1961). "Analysis of the WAIS Sub-tests in Relation to Age and Education," *J. Gerontol.*, **16**, 363–369. [162, 164]

Birren, J. E., K. F. Riegel, and D. F. Morrison (1962). "Age Differences in Response Speed As a Function of Controlled Variations of Stimulus Condition: Evidence of a General Speed Factor," *Gerontologia*, **6**, 1–18. [160]

Birren, J. E. and Shock, N. W. (1950). "Age Changes in Rate and Level of Visual Dark Adaptation," *Appl. Psychol.*, **2**, 407–411. [157]

Blain, Isabel (1959). "Practice and Knack: Some Comments on Learning and Training in Industry," *Ergonomics*, **2**, 167–170. [256]

Blake, R. R. (1959). "Psychology and the Crisis of Statesmanship," *Amer. Psychologist*, **14**, 87–94. [471]

Blake, R. R., and J. S. Mouten (1964). *Toward Achieving Organizational Excellence*. Washington, D.C.: National Training Laboratories, Report 2. [253]

Bloom, W. (1961). "Shift Work and the Sleep–Wakefulness Cycle," *Personnel*, **38**, 24–31. [286]

Blum, M. L. *See* Mintz and Blum (1949).

Blum, M. L. (1956). *Industrial Psychology and Its Social Foundations*. New York: Harper. [395]

Boice, M. L., M. A. Tinker, and D. G. Patterson (1948). "Color Vision and Age," *Amer. J. Psychol.*, **61**, 520–526. [156]

Botwinick, J. *See* Birren, Casperson, and Botwinick (1950).

Boulding, K. (1959). "National Images and International Systems," *J. Conflict Resolut.*, **3**, 122. [464]

Bowman, K. A. (1958). "Some Problems of Addiction," in Hoch and Zubin (eds.), *Problems of Addiction and Habituation*. New York: Grune and Stratten. [530]

Brantner, J. P. *See* Good and Brantner (1961).

Brayfield, A. H., and H. F. Rothe (1951). "An Index of Job Satisfaction." *J. Appl. Psychol.*, **35**, 5, 307–311. [397, 398]

Brayfield, A. H., and W. H. Crockett (1955). "Employee Attitudes and Employee Performance," *Psychol. Bull.*, **52**, 396–424. [392, 395]

Brayfield, A. H., R. V. Wells, and M. W. Strate (1957). "Interrelationships Among Measures of Job Satisfaction and General Satisfaction," *J. Appl. Psychol.*, **41**, 201–205. [391]

Bridges, Katherine (1932). "Emotional Development in Early Infancy," *Child Develp.*, **3**, 324–341. [97]

Brill, H., and R. E. Patton (1959). "Analysis of Population Reduction in New York State Mental Hospitals During the First Four Years of Large-Scale Therapy with Psychotropic Drugs," *Amer. J. Psychiat.*, **116**, 495–509. [141]

Broadbent, D. E., and E. A. J. Little (1960). "Effects of Noise Reduction in a Work Situation," *Occup. Psychol.*, **39**, 133–140. [276]

Bronfenbrenner, U. (1961). "Some Familial Antecedents of Responsibility and Leadership in Adolescents," in L. Petrullo and B. M. Bass (eds.), *Leadership and Interpersonal Behavior*. Springfield, Ill.: Charles C. Thomas. [107]

Brooks, P. R. (1962). "Bleaching the Blue Collar," *Dun's Review and Modern Industry*, No. 1. [390]

Brouha, L. (1954). "Fatigue-Measuring and Reducing It," *Advanc. Mgmt.*, **19**, 9–19. [399]

Brown, I. D. *See* Gibbs and Brown (1955).

Brown, J. A. C. (1954). *The Social Psychology of Industry*. Baltimore, Md.: Penguin Books. [385, 386, 392, 398, 401]

Brown, J. M., and C. M. Weiser (1958). "Prediction of Productive Success from the Application Blank," Unpublished research report, Lafayette College. [212]

Brown, J. S., E. B. Knauft, and G. Rosenbaum (1948). "The Accuracy of Positioning Reactions As a Function of Their Direction and Extent," *Amer. J. Psychol.*, **61**, 167–182. [546]

Brown, J. S., and A. T. Slater-Hammel (1949). "Discrete Movements in the Horizontal Plane As a Function of Their Length and Direction." *J. Exp. Psychol.*, **39**, 84–95. [318]

Bruner, J. *See* Postman and Bruner (1948).

Bruner, J., and C. Goodman (1947). "Value and Need As Organizing Factors in Perception," *J. Abnorm. Soc. Psychol.*, **42**, 33–44. [461]

Bunker, D. R. (1963). *The Effect of Laboratory Education upon Individual Behavior*. Washington, D.C.: National Training Laboratories, Report 4. [253]

Burgess, E. W., (1954). "Social Relations, Activities, and Personal Adjustment," *Amer. J. Sociol.*, **59**, 352–360. [184]

Burke, Barbara S., V. A. Beal, S. B. Kirkwood, and H. C. Stuart, (1943). "Nutrition Studies During Pregnancy," *Amer. J. Obstet. Gynec.*, **46**, 38–52. [94]

Burks, E. C. (1964). Editorial in *The New York Times*, December 6, 1964. [578]

Buros, O. K. (1959). *The Fifth Mental Measurements Yearbook*. Highland Park, N.J.: Gryphon.

———— (1961). *Tests in Print*. Highland Park, N.J.: Gryphon. [220, 225]

Burtt, H. E. (1951). *Legal Psychology*. Englewood Cliffs, N.J.: Prentice-Hall. [542]

Campbell, D. C., and B. V. Tyler (1957). "The Construct Validity of Work-Group Morale Measures," *J. Appl. Psychol.*, **41**, 91–92. [395]

Cannon, W. B. (1960). *The Wisdom of the Body*. New York: Norton. [67]

Cantril, H. *See* Hastorf and Cantril (1954).

Carlucci, C., and W. J. E. Crissy (1961). "The Readability of Employee Handbooks," in E. A. Fleishman (ed.), *Studies in Personnel and Industrial Psychology*. Homewood, Ill.: Dorsey. [350]

Carp, F. N., B. N. Vitola, and F. L. McLanathan (1963). "Human Relations Knowledge and Social Distance in Supervisors," *J. Appl. Psychol.*, **47**, 78–80. [366]

Carzo, R., Jr. (1961). "Organizational Realities," *Business Horizons*, Spring. [345]

Casperson, R. C. *See* Birren, Casperson, and Botwinick (1950).

Caudill, W. (1958). *The Psychiatric Hospital As a Small Society*. Cambridge, Mass.: Harvard University Press. [142]

Chapanis, A. (1947). "The Dark Adaptation of the Color Anomalous Measured with Lights of Different Hues," *J. Gen. Physiol.*, **30**, 423–437. [545]

————. *See* Morgan, Chapanis, Cook, and Land (1963).

———— (1963). "Engineering Psychology," in P. R. Farnsworth, O. McNemar, and Q. McNemar (eds.), *Annual Review of Psychology*. Palo Alto, Calif.: Annual Reviews, Inc., [328]

———— (1964). "Knowledge of Performance As an Incentive in Repetitive, Monotonous Tasks, *J. Appl. Psychol.*, **38**, 4, 253–267. [394]

Chapanis, A., W. R. Garner, and C. T. Morgan (1949). *Applied Experimental Psychology*. New York: Wiley. [331, 332, 548]

Chisman, J. A., and J. R. Simon (1961). "Protection Against Impulse-Type Industrial Noise by Utilizing the Acoustic Reflex," *J. Appl. Psychol.*, **45**, 6, 402–407. [278]

Clark, R. E. (1961). "The Limiting Hand Skin Temperature for Unaffected Manual Performance in the Cold," *J. Appl. Psychol.*, **45**, 3, 193–195. [280]

Clark, R. E., and C. E. Jones (1962). "Manual Performance During Cold Exposure As a Function of Practice Level and the Thermal Conditions of Training," *J. Appl. Psychol.*, **46**, 276–280. [281]

Clausen, J. A., and Judith R. Williams (1963). "Sociological Correlates of Child Behavior," in H. W. Stevenson (ed.), "Child Psychology," *Yearb. Nat. Soc. Stud. Edu.*, **62**, Part I. [84]

Clegg, W. C. (1959–60). "The Effectiveness of Practice in Simulated Situations As Training for Actual Use of a Skill," *Ontario J. Educ.*, **2**. [257]

Cohen, A.   *See* Fine, Cohen, and Crist (1960).

Cohen, B. H. (1964). "The Role of Awareness in Meaning Established by Classical Conditioning," *J. Exp. Psychol.*, **67**, 373–378. [529]

Cohen, L.   *See* Ekman, Cohen, Moos, Raine, Schlesinger, and Stone (1963).

Cohen, J. S. (1961). "Trial Tactics in Criminal Cases," in H. Toch (ed.), *Legal and Criminal Psychology*. New York: Holt, Rinehart. [539]

Cole, Luella (1959). *Psychology of Adolescence* (5th ed.). New York: Holt, Rinehart. [111]

Coleman, J. C. (1956). *Abnormal Psychology and Modern Life* (2d ed.). Chicago: Scott, Foresman. [43, 63]

——— (1960). *Personality Dynamics and Effective Behavior*. Chicago: Scott, Foresman. [53, 58]

——— (1964). *Abnormal Psychology and Modern Life* (3d ed.). Chicago: Scott, Foresman. [531]

Coleman, J. R.   *See* Harbison and Coleman (1951).

Colquhoun, W. P. (1959). "The Effects of a Short Rest-Pause on Inspection Efficiency," *Ergonomics*, **2**, 367–372. [289]

Conger, J. J.   *See* Mussen, Conger, and Kagan (1963).

Connor, N. B.   *See* Jenkins and Connor (1949).

Cook, J. S.   *See* Morgan, Chapanis, Cook, and Lund (1963).

Cook, T. W. (1937). "Whole Versus Part Learning the Spider Maze," *J. Exp. Psychol.*, **20**, 477–494. [20]

Cooper, I. B. (1961). "Can We Prevent the Second Step in Crime?" *Bull. Menninger Clin.*, **25**, 152–163. [565]

Copley, F. B. (1923). *Frederick W. Taylor*, Vol. II. New York: Harper. [322]

Corah, N. L.   *See* Johnson and Corah (1963).

Cowdry, E. V. (1940). "We Grow Old," *Scient. Monthly*, **50**. 54. [175]

Crawford, P. L. (1960). "Hazard Exposure Differentiation Necessary for the Identification of the Accident-Prone Employee," *J. Appl. Psychol.*, **44**, 192–194. [404]

Cressey, D. R.   *See* Schuessler and Cressey (1950).

Crissy, W. J. E.   *See* Carlucci and Crissey (1961).

Crist, B.   *See* Fine, Cohen, and Crist (1960).

Crites, J. O. (1962). "Parental Identification in Relation to Vocational Interest Development," *J. Educ. Psychol.*, **53**, 262–270. [105]

Crockett, W. H.   *See* Brayfield and Crockett (1955).

Cronbach, L. J. (1963). *Educational Psychology* (2d ed.). New York: Harcourt, Brace & World. [92]

Crowder, N. A. (1959). "Automatic Tutoring by Means of Intrinsic Programming," in E. H. Galanter (ed.), *Automatic Teaching: The State of the Art*. New York: Wiley. [16]

Crutchfield, R. S.   *See* Krech and Crutchfield (1948).

Culbert, S. S., and M. I. Posner (1960). "Human Habituation to an Acoustical Energy Distribution Spectrum," *J. Appl. Psychol.*, **44**, 4, 263–267. [275]

Cumming, E., and I. McCaffrey (1960). "Some Conditions Associated with Morale Among the Aging," paper read at American Psychopathology Association, New York. [186]

Dahlstrom, W. G., and G. S. Welsh (1960). *An MMPI Handbook*. Minneapolis: University of Minnesota Press. [131]

Danzig, E. R. *See* Weld and Danzig (1940).

David, P.R., and L. H. Snyder (1962). "Some Interrelationships Between Psychology and Genetics," in S. Koch (ed.). *Psychology: A Study of a Science*, Vol. 4. New York: McGraw-Hill. [77]

Davis, K. (1953). "Management Communication and the Grapevine," *Harvard Business Review*, **31**, 5, 43–50. [352, 353, 396]

Dealey, W. L. *See* Dvorak, Merrick, Dealey, and Ford (1936).

Dearborn, D. C., and H. A. Simon (1961). "Selective Perception: The Departmental Identifications of Executives," in E. A. Fleishman (ed.), *Studies in Personnel and Industrial Psychology*. Homewood, Ill.: Dorsey. [349]

Demming, J. A., and S. L. Pressey (1957). "Tests 'Indigenous' to the Adult and Older Years," *J. Counsel. Psychol.*, **4**, 144–148. [162]

Denny, E. C. *See* Nelson and Denny (1960).

Deutsch, M. (1949). "The Effects of Cooperation and Competition upon Group Process," *Hum. Relat.*, **2**, 129–152, 199–231. [454]

——— (1964). "On Producing Change in an Adversary," in R. Fisher (ed.), *The Craigville Papers on Handling International Conflict*. New York: Basic Books. [498]

Dickson, W. J. *See* Roethlisberger and Dickson (1939).

Dill, W. R. (1961). "Management Games for Training Decision Makers," in E. A. Fleishman (ed.) *Studies in Personnel and Industrial Psychology*. Homewood, Ill.: Dorsey. [251]

Dollard, J., L. Doob, N. Miller, D. Mower, and R. Sears (1939). *Frustration and Aggression*. New Haven: Yale University Press. [454]

Dollard, J., and N. E. Miller (1950). *Personality and Psychotherapy*. New York McGraw-Hill. [100]

Donnison, C. P. (1943). Quoted by O. Klinebert in *Mental Health in Later Maturity*. Public Health Reports Supplement No. 168, 86. [156]

Doob, L. *See* Dollard, Doob, Miller, Mower, and Sears (1939).

Douglas, A. (1962). *Industrial Peacemaking*. New York: Columbia University Press. [483, 484]

Dowd, J. F. *See* Sweeney, Bailey, and Dowd (1957).

Dudycha, G. J. (ed.) (1955). *Psychology for Law Enforcement Officers*. Springfield, Ill.: Charles C. Thomas. [590]

Dvorak, A., N. I. Merrick, W. L. Dealey, and G. C. Ford (1936). *Typewriting Behavior*. New York: American Book. [323]

Ebaugh, F. G. *See* Strecker, Ebaugh, and Ewalt (1947).

Ebbinghaus, H. (1885). *Memory*. Translated by H. A. Ruger and C. E. Bussenius. New York: Teachers College, Columbia University Press. [17]

Ebbs, J. H., F. F. Tisdall, and W. A. Scott (1942). "The Influence of Prenatal Diet on the Mother and Child," *Millbank Memorial Fund Quart.*, **20**. 35–36. [94]

Ekman, P., L. Cohen, R. Moos, W. Raine, M. Schlesinger, and G. Stone (1963). "Divergent Reactions to the Threat of War," *Science*, **139**, 88–94. [483]

Emerson, R. (1889). *Essays, First Series*. Boston: Houghton Mifflin. [469]

English, Ava C. *See* English and English (1958).

English, H. B., and Ava C. English (1958). A *Comprehensive Dictionary of Psychological and Psychoanalytical Terms.* New York: Longmans, Green. [123]

Enzer, N. *See* Simonson, Kearns, and Enzer (1944).

Ericksen, S. C. (1942). "Variability in Attack in Massed and Distributed Practice," *J. Exp. Psychol.*, **31**, 339–345. [18]

Erikson, E. (1963). *Childhood and Society* (2d ed.). New York: Norton. [98, 110]

Ewalt, J. R. *See* Strecker, Ebaugh, and Ewalt (1947).

Eysenck, H. J. (1952). "The Effects of Psychotherapy: An Evaluation," *J. Consult. Psychol.*, **16**, 319–324. [138]

———— (1961). "The Effects of Psychotherapy," in H. J. Eysenck (ed.), *Handbook of Abnormal Psychology.* New York: Basic Books. [139]

———— (ed.) (1959). *Behaviour Therapy and the Neuroses.* London: Pergamon.

Farmer, E. (1923). "Time and Motion Study," *Industrial Fatigue Research Board Report*, Report No.14. [326]

Faushel, D. *See* Kutner, Faushel, Togo, and Langner. (1956) [176]

Fensterheim, H., and M. E. Tresselt (1953). "The Influence of Value Systems on the Perception of Peaple," *J. Abnorm. Soc. Psychol.*, **48**, 93–98. [552]

Ferster, C. B., and B. F. Skinner (1957). *Schedules of Reinforcement.* New York: Appleton-Century. [10]

Festinger L. (1957). A *Theory of Cognitive Dissonance.* Evanston, Ill.: Row, Peterson. [552]

Fine, B. J., A. Cohen, and B. Crist (1960). "Effect of Exposure to High Humidity and High and Moderate Ambient Temperature on Anagrams Solution and Auditory Discrimination," *Psychol. Rep.*, **7**, 171–181. [281]

Fishman, J. A. (1957). "Some Current Research Needs in the Psychology of Testimony," *J. Soc. Issues*, **13**, 260–67. [550]

Flack, A. (1949). "Make Your Plant a Safe, Pleasant Place to Work," *Factory Management and Maintenance*, **101**, November. [283]

Flanagan, J. C. (1949). "A New Approach to Evaluating Personnel," *Personnel J.*, **26**, 35–42. [198]

————. *See* Glaser, Schwarz, and Flanagan (1958).

Fleishman, E. A. *See* Harris and Fleishman (1955).

Fleishman, E. A., J. Berniger (1960). "One Way To Reduce Office Turnover," *Personnel*, **37**, 63–69. [215]

Ford, G. C. *See* Dvorak, Merrick, Dealey, and Ford (1936).

Ford, D. H., and H. B. Urban (1963). *Systems of Psychotherapy.* New York: Wiley. [133]

Forman, R. E. (1963). "Delinquency Rates and Opportunities for Subculture Transmission," *J. Criminal Law, Criminology and Police Science*, **54**, 3, 317–321. [589]

Fox, F. (1937). "Family Life and Relationships As Affected by the Presence of the Aged," *Mental Hygiene in Old Age.* New York: Family Welfare Association of America. [180]

Fox, J. M. (1957). "What It Takes To Be a Manager," *Advanc. Mgmt.*, **22**, June. [366]

Freedman, L. Z. (1961). "Sexual, Aggressive and Acquisitive Deviates," *J. Nerv. Ment. Disease*, **132**, 1. [519, 520]

French, J. R. P., I. T. Ross, S. Kirby, J. R. Nelson, and P. Smyth (1958). "Employee Participation in a Program of Industrial Change," *Personnel*, **35**, 16–29. [359]

French, J. R. P., J. Israel, and D. As (1960). "An Experiment on Participation in a Norwegian Factory: Interpersonal Dimensions of Decision-Making," *Human Relations*, **13**, 3–19. [359]

Freud, S. (1905). *Three Essays on the Theory of Sexuality* (Standard ed., 1953). London: Hogarth. [87]

Funkenstein, D. H. (1955). "The Physiology of Fear and Anger," *Scient. American*, **192**, 5, 74–80. [68]

Gair, H. A. (1961). "Trial Tactics in Civil Cases," in H. Toch (ed.), *Legal and Criminal Psychology*. New York: Holt, Rinehart. [543]

Galanter, E. H. (ed.) (1959). *Automatic Teaching, the State of the Art*. New York: Wiley. [14, 38]

Gardner, G. E. (1959). "Separation of the Parents and the Emotional Life of the Child," in S. Glueck (ed.), *The Problem of Delinquency*. Boston: Houghton Mifflin. [525]

Garfield, S. L. (1957). *Introductory Clinical Psychology*. New York: Macmillan. [129]

Garmezy, N. *See* Kimble and Garmezy (1963).

Garner, W. R. *See* Chapanis, Garner, and Morgan (1949).

Garvey, W. D. *See* Taylor and Garvey (1959).

Gates, A. I. *See* Harrell, Woodyard, and Gates (1955).

Gebhard, J. W. *See* Mowbray and Gebhard (1961).

Gebhard, P. H. *See* Kinsey, Pomeroy, Martin, and Gebhard (1953).

——— (1961). *Lighting for Profit in Industry*. Report LS–176. [273]

Gerver, I. (1957). "The Social Psychology of Witness Behavior with Special Reference to the Criminal Courts," *J. Soc. Issues*, **13**, 2, 23–29. [543]

Gibbs, C. B., and I. D. Brown (1955). "Increased Production from the Information Incentive in a Repetitive Task," *Med. Res. Council, Appl. Psychol. Res. Unit, Great Britain*, No. 230. [393]

Gilbert, J. G. (1936). "Senescent Efficiency and Employability," *J. Appl. Psychol.*, **20**, 266–272. [178]

——— (1941). "Memory Loss in Senescence," *J. of Abnor. and Soc. Psychol.*, **36**, 73–86.

——— (1952). *Understanding Old Age*. New York: Ronald. [162]

——— (1957). "Age Changes in Color Matching," *J. Gerontol.*, **12**, 210–215.

Gillerman, S. W. (1963). "Personnel Testing: What the Critics Overlook," *Personnel*, **40**, 3, 18–26. [224]

Gilmer, B. H. (1961). "Toward Cutaneous Electro-Pulse Communication," *J. Psychol.*, **52**, 211–222. [247, 248, 331]

Glaser, D. (1964). *The Effectiveness of a Prison and Parol System*. Indianapolis, Ind.: Bobbs-Merrill. [574, 575, 579, 580, 581, 582, 585, 586, 587]

Glaser, R., P. A. Schwarz, and J. C. Flanagan (1958). "The Contribution of

Interview and Situational Performance Procedures to the Selection of Supervisory Personnel," *J. Appl. Psychol.*, **42**, 69–73. [366]

Glaser, R. *See* Lumsdaine and Glaser (1960).

Glueck, Eleanor T. *See* Glueck and Glueck (1950).

——— . *See* Glueck and Glueck (1959).

——— (1960). "Efforts To Identify Delinquents," *Fed. Probation.*, 24(2), 49–56. *Int. J. Loc. Psychiat.*, **6**, 206–217. [565]

——— (1962). "Toward Improving the Identification of Delinquents," *J. of Criminal Law, Criminology and Police Science*, **53**, 2, 164–170. [591, 592]

——— (1963). "Toward Further Improving the Identification of Delinquents," *J. of Criminal Law, Criminology and Police Science*, **54**, 2, 178–180. [593]

Glueck, S., and Eleanor T. Glueck (1950). *Unraveling Juvenile Delinquency.* Cambridge, Mass.: Harvard University Press.

——— (1959). *Predicting Delinquency and Crime.* Cambridge, Mass.: Harvard University Press. [526]

Goddard, H. H. (1920). *Human Efficiency and Levels of Intelligence.* Princeton, N.J.: Princeton University Press. [518]

Goldfarb, W. (1943). "The Effects of Early Institutional Care on Adolescent Personality," *J. Exp. Educ.*, **12**, 106–129. [88]

Goldstein, K., and M. Scheerer (1941). "Abstract and Concrete Behavior; An Experimental Study with Special Texts," *Psychol. Monogr.*, **53**, 2. [130]

Goodell, H. *See* Hardy, Wolff, and Goodell (1943).

Goodman, C. *See* Bruner and Goodman (1947).

Greenwood, M., and H. M. Woods (1919). "The Incidence of Industrial Accidents upon Individuals with Specific Reference to Multiple Accidents," *Industrial Fatigue Research Board*, Report 4, London, England. [403]

Grether, W. F. (1948). "Factors in the Design of Clock Dials Which Affect Speed and Accuracy of Reading in the 2400-Hour Time System," *J. Appl. Psychol.*, **32**, 159–169. [329]

——— (1949). "Instrument Reading. I. The Design of Long-Scale Indicators for Speed and Accuracy of Quantitative Reading," *J. Appl. Psychol.*, **33**, 4. [328]

Gross, M. L. (1962). The Brain Watchers. New York: Random House. [221]

Grossberg, J. M. (1964). "Behavior Therapy: A Review," *Psychol. Bull.*, **62**, 2, 73–88. [138]

Guetzkow, H. (1962). *Simulation in Social Sciences: Readings.* Englewood Cliffs, N.J.: Prentice-Hall. [473]

Hadley, J. M. (1958). *Clinical and Counseling Psychology.* New York: Knopf. [129]

Hall, E. T. (1961). *The Silent Language.* Greenwich, Conn.: Fawcett Publications. [457]

Hall, G. S. (1922). *Senescence.* New York: Appleton-Century. [174]

Harbison, F. H., and J. R. Coleman (1951). *Goals and Strategy in Collective Bargaining.* New York: Harper. [486, 494, 495, 496]

Hardy, J. D., H. G. Wolff, and H. Goddel (1943). "The Pain Threshold in Man," *Amer. J. Psychiat.*, **99**, 744–751. [159]

Harper, R. A. (1959). *Psychoanalysis and Psychotherapy: 36 Systems.* Englewood Cliffs, N.J.: Prentice-Hall. [133, 135]

Harrell, Ruth F., Ella Woodyard, and A. I. Gates (1955). *The Effects of Mothers' Diets on the Intelligence of Offspring.* New York: Teachers College. [94, 95]

Harris, E. F., and E. A. Fleishman (1955). "Human Relations Training and the Stability of Leadership Patterns," *J. Appl. Psychol.*, **39**, 20–25. [245]

Hastrof, A. H., and H. Cantril (1954). "They Saw a Game: A Case Study," *J. Abnorm. Soc. Psychol.*, **49**, 129–134. [454]

Hathaway, S. R., and J. C. McKinley (1951). *Minnesota Multiphasic Personality Inventory* (rev. ed.). New York: Psychological Corp. [130]

Hathaway, S. R., and E. D. Monachesi (1957). "The Personalities of Pre-delinquent Boys," *J. Criminal Law, Criminology and Police Science*, **48**, 149–163. [519]

Havighurst, R. J. (1953). *Human Development and Education.* New York: Longmans, Green. [87, 111]

——— (1961). "Successful Aging." *Gerontologist*, **1**, 8–13. [185, 186]

Hebb, D. O. (1955). "Drives and the CNS (Conceptional Nervous System)," *Psychol. Rev.*, **62**, 243–253. [4, 275]

Helton, R. (1939). "Old People: A Rising National Problem," *Harper's Magazine*, **179**, 454. [176]

Henderson, H. L. (1958). *The Relationship Between Interests of Fathers and Sons and Sons' Identification with Fathers.* Unpublished doctoral dissertation, Columbia University. [105]

Henry, G. W.   *See* Zilboorg and Henry (1941).

Henry, H. (1958). *Motivation Research: Its Practice and Uses for Advertising, Marketing, and Other Business Purposes.* New York: Frederick Ungar. [431]

Hersey, R. (1955). *Zest for Work.* New York: Harper. [385]

Hess, J. H.   *See* Rabin and Hess (1965).

Hilgard, E. R. (1963). "Motivation in Learning Theory," in S. Koch (ed.), *Psychology: A Study of a Science*, Vol. 5. New York: McGraw-Hill. [38]

Hobbs, N. (1963). "Statement on Mental Illness and Retardation," *Amer. Psychol.*, **18**, 295–299. [44]

Hoch, P. (1959). "Drug Therapy," in S. Arieti (ed.), *American Handbook of Psychiatry*, Vol. 2. New York: Basic Books. [142]

Hoffman, B. (1962). *The Tyranny of Testing.* New York: McGraw-Hill [221]

Hoffman, L. R.   *See* Mann and Hoffman (1960).

———.   *See* Maier, Hoffman, and Lansky (1960).

Holland, J. G., and B. F. Skinner (1961). *The Analysis of Behavior.* New York: McGraw-Hill. [16, 38]

Holsti, O. R. (1962). "The Belief System and National Images: A Case Study," *J. Conflict Resolut.*, **6**, 244–252. [463]

Hoover, J. E. (1964). *Crime in the United States, Uniform Crime Reports in 1962.* Washington, D.C.: Federal Bureau of Investigation, United States Dept. of Justice. [504, 505, 507, 510, 511, 513, 514, 516, 517, 528]

Hopper, C. B. (1962). "The Conjugal Visits at Mississippi State Penitentiary," *J. Criminal Law, Criminology and Police Science*, **53**, 3, 340–343. [568]

Horrocks, J. E. (1964). *Assessment of Behavior.* Columbus, Ohio: Charles E. Merrill. [129]

Hovland, C. I. (1951). "Human Learning and Retention," in S. S. Stevens (ed.), *Handbook of Experimental Psychology*. New York: Wiley. [20]

Hughes, J. F. *See* Baxter, Taaffe, and Hughes (1953).

Hunsicker, P. A. (1955). *Arm Strength at Selected Degrees of Elbow Flexion*, *WADC–TR 54–548*. Wright Air Development Center, Wright-Patterson Airforce Base, Ohio: Aero Medical Laboratory. [334]

Hutchins, Robert M. (1963). *A Conversation on Education*. Santa Barbara, Calif.: Fund for the Republic, Inc. [310]

Ingenohl, I. (1957). "Personality Tests—Just What Are They Talking About?" *Advanc. Mgmt.*, **22**, 8, 16–24. [227]

Inhelder, B., and J. Piaget (1958). *The Growth of Logical Thinking from Childhood to Adolescence*. New York: Basic Books. [86]

Israel, J. *See* French, Israel, and As (1960).

Jackson, J. N. (1959). "The Organization and Its Communications Problems," *J. Commun.*, **9**, 158–167. [348]

Jahoda, Marie (1958). *Current Conceptions of Positive Mental Health*. New York: Basic Books. [44]

Jenkins, Gladys G., Helen Shacter, and W. W. Bauer (1953). *These Are Your Children* (Expanded ed.). Chicago: Scott, Foresman. [87]

Jenkins, W. L., and N. B. Connor (1948). *Optimal Design Factors for Making Settings on a Linear Scale*. Unpublished manuscript, Lehigh University. [335, 336]

Jennings, E. E. (1954). "Elements of Democratic Supervision," *Advanc. Mgmt.*, **19**, 19–22. [363]

Jerison, H. J. (1959). "Effects of Noise on Human Performance," *J. Appl. Psychol.*, **42**, 2, 96–101. [276]

Johnson, L. C., and N. L. Corah (1963). "Racial Differences in Skin Resistance," *Science*, **139**, 3556, 766–767. [537]

Johnson, W. F. *See* Shelley and Johnson (1961).

Joint Commission on Mental Illness and Health (1961). *Action for Mental Health*. New York: Basic Books. [44, 147, 149]

Jones, C. E. *See* Clark and Jones (1962).

Jordan, N. (1963). "Allocation of Functions Between Man and Machines in Automated Systems," *J. Appl. Psychol.*, **47**, 3, 161–165. [321]

Joy, C. T. (1955). *How Communists Negotiate*. New York: Macmillan. [478, 482, 487, 488]

Judy, C. J. (1958). "Field Training Versus Technical School Training for Mechanics Maintaining a New Weapon System," *J. Appl. Psychol.*, **42**, 6, 384–388. [244]

Julian, J. W. *See* McGrath and Julian (1962).

Kagan, J. (1962). "The Choice of Models: A Developmental Analysis of Conflict and Continuity in Human Behavior." Paper read at Amer. Coll. Pers. Assoc., Chicago, April, 1962. [104]

———. *See* Mussen, Conger, and Kagan (1963).

Kahn, M. W. (1959). "A Comparison of Personality, Intelligence, and Social History of Two Criminal Group." *J. Soc. Psychol.*, **49**, 33–40. [519]

Kallejian, V. *See* Tannenbaum, Kallejian, and Weschler (1954).

Kallman, F. J. (1959). "The Genetics of Mental Illness," in S. Arieti (ed.), *American Handbook of Psychiatry*. New York: Basic Books. [77]

Kaponya, P. R. (1962). "Salaries for All Workers." *Harvard Bus. Rev.*, **40**, 3, 49–57. [390]

Kaplan, O. J., Jr., (1945). *Mental Disorders in Later Life*. Calif.: Stanford University Press. [161]

Kardiner, A. (1937). "Psychological Factors in Old Age," in *Mental Hygiene in Old Age*. New York: Family Welfare Association of America. [176]

Karlin, J. E. (1961). "Human Factors Evaluation of a New Telephone Numerical Dialing System," in E. A. Fleishman, (ed.), *Studies in Personnel and Industrial Psychology*. Homewood, Ill.: Dorsey. [329]

Katz, B.   *See* Thorpe and Katz (1948).

Kearns, W. M.   *See* Simonson, Kearns, and Enzer (1944).

Keister, M. R., and R. Updegraff (1937). "A Study of Children's Reactions to Failure and an Experimental Attempt To Modify Them," *Child Developm.*, **8**, 241–248. [60]

Kelman, H., and L. Bailyn (1962). "Effects of Cross-Cultural Experience on National Images: A Study of Scandinavian Students in America," *J. Conflict Resolut.*, **6**, 319–334. [472]

Kennan, G. (1958). *Russia, the Atom and the West*. New York: Harper. [464]

Kennedy, J. F. (1963). "Message from the President of the United States Relative to Mental Illness and Mental Retardation." *H. R. Document No. 58*, 88th Congress, 1st Session. [40]

Kerr, W. A. (1950). "Accident Proneness in Factory Departments," *J. Appl. Psychol.*, **34**, 167–170. [308]

———— (1957). "Complementary Theories of Safety Psychology," *J. Soc. Psychol.*, **45**, 3–9. [404]

————.   *See* Sherman, Kerr, and Kosinar (1957).

Kidd, J. S. (1959). "Summary of Research Methods, Operator Characteristics, and System Design Specifications Based on the Study of a Simulated Radar Air Traffic Control System." *USAF WADC Tech Rep.* #59–236. [276]

Kilpatrick, F. P. (ed.) (1961). *Explorations in Transactional Psychology*. New York: University Press. [461]

Kimble, G. A., and N. Garmezy (1963). *Principles of General Psychology* (2d ed.) New York: Ronald. [60]

Kinsey, A. C., W. B. Pomeroy, and C. E. Martin (1948). *Sexual Behavior in the Human Male*. Philadelphia: Saunders. [169]

Kinsey, A. C., W. B. Pomeroy, C. C. Martin, and P. H. Gebhard (1953). *Sexual Behavior in the Human Female*. Philadelphia: Saunders. [169]

Kirby, S.   *See* French, Ross, Kirby, Nelson, and Smyth (1958).

Kirk, P. L. (1963). "Criminalists," *Science*, **140**, 3565, 367–370. [538, 550]

Kirkwood, S.   *See* Burke, Beal, Kirkwood, and Stuart (1943).

Kling, J. W., J. P. Williams, and H. Schlosberg (1959). "Patterns of Skin Conductants During Rotary Pursuit," *Perceptual and Motor Skills*, **9**, 303–312. [288]

Knouft, E. B.   *See* Brown, Knouft, and Rosenbaum (1948).

Kohlberg, L. (1963). "Moral Development and Identification," in H. W.

Stevenson (ed.), *Child psychology. Yearb. Nat. Soc. Stud. Educ.*, 62, Part I. [105]

Kolb, L. C. *See* Noyes and Kolb (1963).

Kopstein, F. F., and I. J. Shillentad (1962). *"A Survey of Auto-Instructional Devices."* Wright-Patterson Air Force Base, Ohio: Aeronautical Systems Division, Air Force Systems Command, United States Air Force. [14]

Korchin, S. J., and H. Basowitz (1957). "Age and Differences in Verbal Learning," *J. Abnorm. Soc. Psychol.*, 54, 64–69. [166]

Kosinar, W. *See* Sherman, Kerr, and Kosinar (1957).

Kossoris, M. D. (1944). *Studies of the Effects of Long Working Hours.* United States Dept. of Labor, Bureau of Labor Statistics, Bull. No. 7, Part 2, 3. [285]

Kotkov, B., and B. Murawski (1952). "A Rorschach Study of the Personality Structure of Obese Women." *J. Clin. Psychol.*, 8, 391–396. [433]

Krech, D., and R. S. Crutchfield (1948). *Theory and Problems of Social Psychology.* New York: McGraw-Hill. [362]

Krock, A. (1963). "Mr. Kennedy's Management of the News," *Fortune*, 67, 3, 82. [465]

Kubis, J. F. (1962). *Studies in Lie Detection, Computer Feasibility Consideration.* Griffen Air Force Base, New York: Rome Air Development Center, Air Force Systems Command, United States Air Force. [536]

Kuder, G. F. *See* Richardson and Kuder (1933).

———. *See* Richardson and Kuder (1939).

Kuhlen, R. G. (1963). "Needs, Perceived Need Satisfaction, Opportunities and Satisfaction with Occupation," *J. Appl. Psychol.*, 47, 1, 56–64. [392]

Kutner, B., D. Faushel, A. M. Togo, and T. S. Langner (1956). *Five Hundred over Sixty.* New York: Russell Sage Foundation. [176]

Kvaraceus, W. C. (1945). *Juvenile Delinquency and the School.* Yonkers-on-Hudson, New York: World Book. [527]

——— (1959). *Delinquent Behavior—Principles and Practices.* Washington D.C.: National Education Association of the United States. [524, 525, 565]

——— (1959a). "Meeting the Serious Behavioral Problems in Junior High Schools," *Bulletin of the Nat. Assoc. of Secondary-School Principals*, 43, 246, 1–7. [591]

——— (1962). "Forecasting delinquency," *Exceptional Children*, 27, 8, 429–435. [515, 518]

Lagemann, J. K. (1954). "Job Enlargement Boosts Production," *Nation's Business*, Dec. [236]

Landis, A. T. (1942). "What Is the Happiest Period in Life?" *Sociol. Soc. Res.*, 55, 643–645. [179]

Landsberger, H. A. (1958). *Hawthorne Revisited.* Ithaca, N.Y.: Cornell University Press. [288]

Langdon, J. N. *See* Wyatt, Langdon, and Stock (1937).

Lange, F. (1951). "Untersuchungen zur normalen Verteilung des Lichtsinns in der Netzhaut und ihrer Altersabhängigkeit," *Arch. Ophth.*, 153, 93–104. [156]

Langner, T. S. *See* Kutner, Faushel, Togo, and Langner (1956).

Lansky, L. M. *See* Maier, Hoffman, and Lansky (1960).

Lawshe, C. H. (1945). "Studies in Job Evaluation No. 2: The Adequacy of Abbreviated Point Ratings for Hourly Paid Jobs in Three Industrial Plants," *J. Appl. Psychol.*, **29**, 177–184. [303]

Lawshe, C. H., and G. A. Satler (1944). "Studies in Job Evaluation No. 1: Factor Analyses of Point Ratings for Hourly Paid Jobs in Three Industrial Plants," *J. Appl. Psychol.*, **28**, 189–198. [303]

Lawshe, C. H., and R. F. Wilson (1946). "Studies in Job Evaluation No. 5: An Analysis of the Factor Comparison System As It Functions in a Paper Mill," *J. Appl. Psychol.*, **30**, 426–434. [303]

Lawshe, C. H., and A. A. Maleski (1946). "Studies in Job Evaluation No. 3: An Analysis of Point Ratings for Salary Paid Jobs in an Industrial Plant," *J. Appl. Psychol.*, **30**, 117–128. [303]

Lazarsfeld, P. *See* Berelson, Lazarsfeld, and McPhee (1954).

Lazarus, A. A. (1958). "New Methods of Psychotherapy: A Case Study," *South African Med. J.*, **33**, 660–663. [138]

Leavitt, H. J., and R. A. H. Mueller (1951). "Some Effects of Feedback on Communication," *Human Relations*, **4**, 401–410. [354]

Lee, I. (1954). "Procedure for 'Coercing' Agreement," *Harvard Bus. Rev.*, **32**, 39–45. [499]

Lehman, H. C. (1936). "The Creative Years," *Scient. Monthly*, **43**, 151–162. [170, 171, 172]

——— (1941). "The Creative Years," *Scientific Monthly*, **52**, 450–461. [170, 171, 172]

——— (1947). "The Age of Eminent Leaders Then and Now," *Amer. J. Sociol.*, **52**, 342–356. [173]

Lem, C. *See* Smith and Lem (1953).

Lemkau, P. V. (1959). "Mental Hygiene," in S. Arieti (ed.), *American Handbook of Psychiatry*, Vol. 2. New York: Basic Books. [43]

Levinson, D. J. *See* Greenblatt, Levinson, and Williams (1957).

Levy, D. M. (1943). *Material Overprotection*. New York: Columbia University Press. [102]

Lewin, K. (1935). *A Dynamic Theory of Personality*. New York: McGraw-Hill. [57, 58]

Lewin, K., R. Lippitt, and R. K. White (1939). "Patterns of Aggressive Behavior in Experimentally Created Social Climates," *J. Soc. Psychol.*, **10**, 271–301. [362]

Libo, L. M. (1949). *Attitude Prediction in Labor Relations—A Test of Understanding*. Stanford University, Stanford School of Business, Industrial Relations Series, No. 10. [483]

Likert, R. (1954). *Motivation Research As a Means of Gaining New Understanding of the Consumer*. In J. D. Scott (ed.), Ann Arbor, Michigan: Bureau of Business Research, School of Business Administration, University of Michigan, Michigan Business Papers, No. 30, 1-17. [426]

Lillienfield, A. M. *See* Pasamanick and Lillienfield (1955).

Lindesmith, A. R. (1955). "The Psychology of the Drug Addict," in G. Dudycha (ed.), *Psychology for Law Enforcement Officers*. Springfield, Ill.: Charles C Thomas. [564]

Lindner, H. (1955). "The Psychology of the Adult Criminal," in G. Dudycha (ed.), *Psychology for Law Enforcement Officers*. Springfield, Ill.: Charles C Thomas. [508, 572]

Lippitt, R.　*See* Lewin, Lippitt, and White (1939).

Lippmann, W. (1922). *Public Opinion*. New York: Macmillan. [460]

Little, E. A. J.　*See* Broadbent and Little (1960).

Litwack, L. (1962). *The American Labor Movement*. Englewood Cliffs, N.J.: Prentice-Hall. [371]

Lombroso, C. (1911). *Crime, Its Causes and Remedies*. Boston: Horton. [509]

London, N. J., and J. K. Myers (1961). "Young Offenders," *Arch. Gen. Psychiat.*, **4**, 274–282. [564, 579]

Lovaas, O. I. (1961). "Interaction Between Verbal and Nonverbal Behavior," *Child Developm.*, **32**, 37–44. [61]

Lowell, A. (1923). *Public Opinion in War and Peace*. Cambridge: Harvard University Press. [460]

Luborsky, L. (1954). "A Note on Eysenck's Article 'The Effects of Psychotherapy: An Evaluation,' " *Brit. J. Psychol.*, **65**, 129–131. [139]

Lumsdaine, A. A., and R. Glaser (eds.) (1960). *Teaching Machines and Programmed Learning: A Source Book*. Washington, D.C.: N.E.A. Department of Audio-Visual Instruction. [14, 38]

Lund, N. W.　*See* Morgan, Chapanis, Cook, and Lund (1963).

Lysaught, J. P., and C. M. William (1963). *A Guide to Programmed Instruction*. New York: Wiley. [14, 39]

McBain, W. N. (1961). "Noise, the 'Arousal Hypothesis,' and Monotonous Work," *J. Appl. Psychol.*, **45**, 5, 309–318. [275]

McCaffery, I.　*See* Cumming and McCaffrey (1960).

McCaldwell, Betty, and R. Watson (1952). "An Evaluation of Psychologic Effects of Sex Hormone Administration in Aged Women," *J. Gerontol.*, **7**, 228–244. [167]

McCord, J.　*See* McCord, McCord, and Zola (1959).

McCord, W., J. McCord, and I. K. Zola (1959). *Origins of Crime*. New York: Columbia University Press. [107]

McDermid, C. D. (1960). "How Money Motivates Men," *Business Horizons*, Winter. [388, 389]

McGehee, W., and E. D. Owen (1940). "Authorized and Unathorized Rest Pauses in Clerical Work," *J. Appl. Psychol.*, **24**, 605–614. [288]

McGrath, J. E., and J. W. Julian (1962). *Negotiation and Conflict: An Experimental Study*. Urbana, Ill.: United States Public Health Grant M–1774, University of Illinois, Tech. Report 16. [477, 478, 481, 492]

McGuigan, F. J. (1960). "Variation of Whole–Part Methods of Learning," *J. Educ. Psychol.*, **51**, 213–216. [20]

McKinley, J. C.　*See* Hathaway and McKinley (1951).

McLanathan, F. L.　*See* Carp, Vitola, and McLanathan (1963).

McMurry, R. N. (1947). "Validating the Patterned Interview," *Personnel*, **23**, 4, 2–11. [216]

McPhee, W. H.　*See* Berelson, Lazarsfeld, and McPhee (1954).

Machir, D. F., and D. L. Russell (1963). "Rater Reliability and Prediction of Diagnoses with the Wittenborn Psychiatric Rating Scales," *J. Consult. Psychol.*, **27**, 6, 546. [128]

Mahler, W. R., and W. H. Monroe (1952). *How Industry Determines the Need for and Effectiveness of Training.* Contract report to Personnel Research Section, Adjutant General's Office. New York: The Psychological Corporation. [234, 235]

Maier, N. R. F., and L. F. Zerfoss (1952). "MRP: A Technique for Training Large Groups of Supervisors and Its Potential Use in Social Research," *Human Relation,* **5,** 177–186. [251]

Maier, N. R. F., L. R. Hoffman, and L. M. Lansky (1960). "Human Relations Training As Manifested in an Interview Situation," *Personnel Psychol.,* **13,** 11–30. [245]

Maleski, A. A. *See* Lawshe and Maleski (1946).

Mandell, M. M. (1956). "The Conduct of the Individual Interview," Chapter IV from *Employment Interviewing,* Personnel Method Series No. 5. Washington, D.C.: United States Civil Service Commission. [219]

Mann, F. C., and L. R. Hoffmann (1960). *Automation and the Worker: A Study of Social Change in Power Plants.* New York: Holt [359]

Mann, I., and F. W. Sharpley (1947). "The Normal Visual (Rod) Field of the Dark Adapted Eye," *J. Physiol.,* **106,** 301–304. [156]

Maritz, J. S. (1950). "On the Validity of Inferences Drawn from the Fitting of Poisson and Negative Binominal Distributions to Observed Accident Data," *Psychol. Bull.,* **47,** 434–443. [404]

Martin, C. E. *See* Kinsey, Pomeroy, and Martin (1948).

———. *See* Kinsey, Pomeroy, Martin, and Gebhard (1953).

Maslow, A. H. (1943). "A Theory of Human Motivation," *Psychol. Rev.,* **50,** 370–396. [56, 387]

Maxwell, J. M. (1962). *Centers for Older People: Guide for Programs and Facilities.* New York City, National Council on Aging. [183]

Mellenbruch, P. L. (1961). "So This Is Modern Training?" Parts I and II, *Personnel J.,* **39,** 309–310. 356–358. [233]

Mellinger, G. (1956). "Interpersonal Trust As a Factor in Communication," *J. Abnorm. Soc. Psychol.,* **52,** 304–309. [347]

Mental Retardation Facilities and Community Mental Health Centers Construction Act of 1963. Public Law 88–164, 88th Congress, S. 1576, October 31, 1963. [45]

Merrick, N. I. *See* Dvorak, Merrick, Dealey, and Ford (1936).

Merrill, M. A. *See* Terman and Merrill (1960).

Metzner, R., and G. Weil (1963). "Predicting Recidivism: Base-Rates from Massachusetts Correctional Institution, Concord," *J. of Criminal Law, Criminology and Police Science,* **54,** 3, 307–316. [574]

Miller, J. G. (1955). "Toward a General Theory for the Behavioral Sciences," *Amer. Psychologist,* **10,** 513–531. [52]

Miller, J. I. (1962). Quoted in *The Corporation and the Union.* Interview by D. McDonald with J. I. Miller and W. P. Reuther. Santa Barbara, Calif.: Center for the Study of Democratic Institutions. [373]

Miller, N. E. *See* Dollard, Doob, Miller, Mower, and Sears (1939).

———. *See* Dollard and Miller (1950).

Minos, J. S. *See* Scodel and Minos (1960).

Mintz, A., and M. L. Blum (1949). "Reexamination of the Accident Proneness Concept," *J. Appl. Psych.*, **33**, 196–198. [403]

Monachesi, E. D. *See* Hathaway and Monachesi (1957).

Monroe, W. H. *See* Mahler and Monroe (1952).

Moore, J. W. *See* Smith and Moore (1962).

Moos, R. *See* Ekman, Cohen, Moos, Raine, Schlessinger, and Stone (1963).

Morgan, C. M. (1937). "Attitudes and Adjustments of Recipients of Old Age Assistance in Upstate and Metropolitan New York," *Arch. Psychol.*, **214**, 16–71. [179, 181, 185]

Morgan, C. T., A. Chapanis, J. S. Cook, and N. W. Lund (1963). *Human Engineering Guide to Equipment Design*. New York: McGraw-Hill. [162, 164]

Morgan, C. T. *See* Chapanis, Garner, and Morgan (1949).

Morrison, D. F. *See* Birren and Morrison (1961).

————. *See* Birren, Riegel, and Morrison (1962).

Morton, H. C. (1955). "Putting Words to Work," *Dun's Review and Modern Industry*, September. [355]

Mouten, J. S. *See* Blake and Mouten (1964).

Mowbray, G. H., and J. W. Gebhard (1961). "Man's Senses As Informational Channels," in H. W. Sinaiko (ed.), *Selected Papers on Human Factors in the Design and Use of Control Systems*. New York: Dover. [317]

Mower, D. *See* Dollard, Doob, Miller, Mower, and Sears (1939).

Mowrer, O. H. (1950). "Identification: A Link Between Learning Theory and Psychotherapy," in *Learning Theory and Personality Dynamics*. New York: Ronald. [4, 104]

Mueller, R. A. H. *See* Leavitt and Mueller (1951).

Murawski, B. *See* Kotkov and Murawski (1952).

Murphy, D. P. (1947). *Congenital Malformations* (2d ed.). Philadelphia: Lippincott. [95]

Murray, H. A. (1943). *Thematic Apperception Test*. Cambridge, Mass.: Harvard University Press. [131]

Murrell, K. F. H. (1962). "Industrial Aspects of Aging," *Ergonomics*, **5**, 147–152. [179]

Mussen, P. H., J. J. Conger, and J. Kagan (1963). *Child Development and Personality* (2d ed.). New York: Harper. [101]

Myers, J. K. *See* London and Myers (1961).

Naess, Arne (1957). "A Systematization of Gandhian Ethics of Conflict Resolution," *J. Conflict Resolut.*, **1**, 140–155. [500]

National Association for Mental Health (1963). *Facts About Mental Illness*. New York. [40]

National Safety Council (1962). *Accident Facts*. Chicago: National Safety Council No. 021.62. [306, 307]

———— (1963). Preliminary condensed edition of *Accident Facts*. Chicago: National Safety Council, February. [305]

Needler, M. (1960). "Hitler's Antisemitism: A Political Appraisal," *Publ. Opin. Quart.*, **24**, 665–669. [455]

Nelson, J. R. *See* French, Ross, Kirby, Nelson, and Smyth (1958).

Nelson, M. J., and E. C. Denny (1960). Revision by J. I. Brown, *Examiner's*

Manual: The Nelson-Denny Reading Test. Boston: Houghton Mifflin. [30, 222]

New York Times, Aug. 7, 1955, p. 7. [463]

NICB (1954). "Personnel Practices in Factory and Office," in *Studies in Personnel Policy No. 145.* New York: National Industrial Conference Board. [238, 240, 242]

———— (1957). "Executive Development Courses in Universities (revised)," in *Studies in Personnel Policy, No. 160.* New York: National Industrial Conference Board. [249, 254, 255]

———— (1958). "Statements of Personnel Policy," in *Studies in Personnel Policy No. 169.* New York: National Industrial Conference Board. [246]

———— (1960). *Studies in Personnel Policy No. 180. Personnel Procedure Manuals.* New York: National Industrial Conference Board. [210]

Nixon, R. E. (1962). *The Art of Growing.* New York: Random House. [87]

Noyes, A. P., and L. C. Kolb (1963). *Modern Clinical Psychiatry* (6th ed.). Philadelphia: Saunders. [76, 139, 140]

Nye, F. I., J. F. Short, and V. J. Olson (1958). "Socioeconomic Status and Delinquent Behavior," *Amer. J. Soc.,* **63,** 381–399. [524]

Odiorne, G. S. (1962). "Management Style Change for the 60's," *Michigan Business Review,* November. Ann Arbor, Mich.: University of Michigan Graduate School. [364]

Ohmann, O. A. (1941). "A Report of Research in the Selection of Salesmen at the Tresco Manufacturing Company," *J. Appl. Psychol.,* **15,** 18–19. [215]

Olson, V. J. *See* Nye, Short, and Olson (1958).

Orlansky, H. (1949). "Infant Care and Personality," *Psychol. Bull.,* **46,** 1, 1–48. [98]

Orlansky, J. (1949). "Psychological Aspects of Stick and Rudder Controls in Aircraft," *Aeronautical Engineering Rev.,* **8,** 1. [334]

Osgood, C. E. (1961). *Graduated Reciprocation in Tension-Reduction.* Urbana, Ill.: University of Illinois, Institute of Communications Research, 23–25. [487]

———— (1962). "Graduated Unilateral Initiatives for Peace," in Q. Wright, W. M. Evan, M. Deutsch (eds.), *Preventing World War III: Some Proposals.* New York: Simon and Schuster. [472, 498]

Owen, E. D. *See* McGehee and Owen (1940).

Owens, W. A., Jr. (1953). "Age and Mental Abilities: A Longitudinal Study," *Genet. Psychol. Monogr.,* **48,** 3–54. [163]

Packard, V. (1957). *The Hidden Persuaders.* New York: David McKay. [434]

Panton, J. H. (1959). "The Response of Prison Inmates to Seven New MMPI Scales," *J. Clin. Psychol.,* **15,** 2, 196–197. [519]

Papanicolaou, G. N. *See* Ripley, Shorr, and Papanicolaou (1940).

Pasamanick, B., and A. M. Lillienfield (1955). "Association of Maternal and Fetal Factors with Development of Mental Deficiency. I. Abnormalities in the Prenatal and Paranatal Periods," *J. Amer. Med. Assoc.,* **159,** 155–160. [94]

Patterson, D. G. *See* Boice, Tinker, and Patterson (1948).

Patton, R. E. *See* Brill and Patton (1959).

Peterman, J. N. (1940). "The 'program analyzer': A New Technique in Studying Liked and Disliked Items in Radio Programs," *J. Appl. Psychol.*, **24**, 728–741. [424]

Pettigrew, T. F.   *See* Allport and Pettigrew (1957).

Piaget, J. (1932). *The Moral Judgment of the Child.* New York: Harcourt, Brace. [87]

———.   *See* Inhelder and Piaget (1958).

Pickering, E. J. (1959). "An Experimental Investigation of Doppler Training," *U.S.N. Bur. Naval Personnel Tech. Bull.* No. 59–29. [257]

Poffenberger, A. T. (1932). *Psychology in Advertising.* New York: McGraw-Hill. [417]

Politz, A. (1956–57). "Motivation Research from a Research Viewpoint," *Public Opinion Quarterly*, **20**, 4, 663–673. [437]

Pomeroy, W. B.   *See* Kinsey, Pomeroy, and Martin (1948).

———.   *See* Kinsey, Pomeroy, Martin, and Gebhard (1953).

Porter, L. W. (1963). "Job Attitudes in Management: II. Perceived Importance of Needs As a Function of Job Level," *J. Appl. Psychol.*, **47**, 141–148. [367]

Posner, M. I.   *See* Culbert and Posner (1960).

Postman, L., and J. Bruner (1948). "Perception Under Stress," *Psychol. Rev.*, **55**, 314–323. [467]

Presbrey, F. (1929). *The History and Development of Advertising.* Garden City, N.Y.: Doubleday. [415]

Pressey, S. L. (1926). "A Simple Apparatus Which Gives Tests and Scores—and Teaches," *Sch. Soc.*, **23**, 373–376. [15]

———.   *See* Demming and Pressey (1957).

——— (1957). "Potentials of Age: An Exploratory Field Study," *Genet. Psychol. Monogr.*, **56**, 159–205. [153, 162]

Prigmore, C. S. (1963). "An Analysis of Rater Reliability on the Glueck Scale for the Prediction of Juvenile Delinquency," *J. of Criminal Law, Criminology and Police Science*, **54**, 1, 30–41. [592]

Pruitt, D. G. (1962). "Responsiveness Between Nations," *J. Conflict Resolut.*, **6**, 5–18, [496]

Quinn, J. R. (1963). "Sure-Fire Ways To Stunt Your Subordinate's Growth," *Personnel*, **40**, 1, 44–48. [360]

Rabin, A. I., and J. H. Hess (1965). "Attitudes of Prison Personnel and Inmates to Crime and Punishment." Unpublished paper. [583]

Raine, W.   *See* Ekman, Cohen, Moos, Raine, Schlesinger, and Stone (1963). [483]

Rapoport, A. (1962). "Rules for Debate," in Q. Wright, W. Evan, M. Deutsch (eds.), *Preventing World War III: Some Proposals.* New York: Simon and Schuster. [500]

Record, R. G.   *See* Smith and Record (1955).

Reves, E. (1946). *The Anatomy of Peace.* New York: Harper. [463]

Ribble, Margeret (1943). *The Rights of Infants: Early Psychological Needs and Their Satisfactions.* New York: Columbia University Press. [98]

Richardson, F. E. (1916). "Estimations of Speed of Automobiles," *Psychol. Bull.*, **13**, 72–73. [546]

Richardson, M. W., and G. F. Kuder (1933). "Making a Rating Scale that Measures," *Personnel J.*, **12**, 36–40 [193]

——— (1939). "The Calculation of Test Reliability Coefficients Based upon the Method of Rational Equivalence," *J. Educ. Psychol.*, **30**, 681–687. [206, 207]

Riegel, K. F.   *See* Birren, Riegel, and Morrison (1962).

Ripley, H. S., E. Shorr, and G. N. Papanicolaou (1940). "Effect of Treatment of Depression in Menopause with Estrogen Hormone," *Amer. J. Psychiat.*, **96**, 905–914. [168]

Riley, R.   *See* Wallin and Riley (1950).

Robb, Inez (1963). Editorial in the *Easton Express*, Easton, Pa., Easton Publishing Co.

Roberts, J. W. (1959). "Sound Approach to Efficiency," *Personnel J.*, **38**, 6–8. [284]

Robinson, R. (1947. "Beneath the Surface," *Survey*, **83**, 41–52. [526]

Roethlisberger, F. J.   *See* Rogers and Roethlisberger (1952). [348, 351]

Roethlisberger, F. J., and W. J. Dickson (1939). *Management and the Worker —An Account of a Research Program Conducted by the Western Electric Company, Hawthorne Works, Chicago.* Cambridge, Mass.: Harvard University Press. [341, 356]

Roff, M.   *See* Weld and Roff (1938).

Rogers, C. R. (1942). *Counseling and Psychotherapy.* Boston: Houghton Mifflin. [135]

——— (1951). *Client-centered Therapy.* Boston: Houghton Mifflin. [135]

——— (1962). "The Interpersonal Relationship: The Core of Guidance," *Harvard Educ. Rev.*, **32**, 4, 416–429. [135]

Rogers, C. R., and F. J. Roethlisberger (1952). "Barriers and Gateways to Communication," *Harvard Bus. Rev.*, **30**, 4, 46–53. [348, 351]

Rorschach, H. (1942). *Psychodiagnostics: A Diagnostic Test Based on Perception* (trans. by P. Lemkau and B. Kronenburg). Berne: Hans Huber; New York: Grune & Stratton. [131]

Rosenbaum, G.   *See* Brown, Knauft, and Rosenbaum (1948).

Rosenzweig, S. (1938). "Frustration As an Experimental Problem. VI. General Outline of Frustration," *Charac. & Pers.*, **7**, 151–160. [57, 60]

——— (1954). "A Trans-valuation of Psychotherapy—A Reply to Hans Eysenck," *J. Abnorm. Soc., Psychol.*, **49**, 298–304. [139]

Ross, Dorothea.   *See* Bandura, Ross, and Ross (1963).

Ross, I. T.   *See* French, Ross, Kirby, Nelson, and Smyth (1958).

Ross, Sheila.   *See* Bandura, Ross, and Ross (1963).

Rothe, H. F. (1960). "Does Higher Pay Bring Higher Productivity?" *Personnel*, **37**, 20–38. [389]

Rothe, H. F.   *See* Brayfield and Rothe (1951).

Roussel, F.   *See* Weekers and Roussel (1946).

Rubin, S. (1958). "Recidivism and Recidivism Statistics," *National Probation and Parole Assoc. J.*, **4**, 3, 236. [573]

Ruch, F. L. (1934). "Differentiative Effects of Age upon Human Learning," *J. Genet. Psychol.*, **11**, 261–286. [165]

Russell, D. L. (1953). *A Comparison of Rating, Test, and Sociometric Meas-*

ures of Personality Measurement. Unpublished Ph.D. thesis, University of Minnesota. [51]

———— . *See* Machir and Russell (1963).

Sadler, W. S. (1947). *Mental Mischief and Emotional Conflict.* St. Louis: C. V. Mosby Co. [523]

Satler, G. A. *See* Lawshe and Satler (1944).

Sayles, L. (1962). "On-the-Job Communication: Why Isn't It Easier? *Supervisory Management,* **7,** 2–6, 12–15. [346]

Schaffer, H. R. (1958). "Objective Observations of Personality Development in Early Infancy," *Brit. J. Med. Psychol.,* **31,** 174–183. [98]

Schattschneider, E. E. (1960). *The Semi-sovereign People.* New York: Holt, Rinehart. [490]

Scheer, W. E. (1959). "Let's Be Practical About Training Supervisors," *Personnel J.,* **38,** 15–18. [245]

Scheerer, M. *See* Goldstein and Scheerer (1941).

Schelling, T. C. (1957). "Bargaining, Communication and Limited War," *J. Conflict Resolut.,* **1,** 19–36. [485, 490]

Schlesinger, M. *See* Ekman, Cohen, Moos, Raine, Schlesinger, and Stone (1963).

Schlosberg, H. (1941). "A Comparison of Five Shaving Creams by the Method of Constant Stimuli," *J. Appl. Psychol.,* **25,** 401–407. [421]

———— . *See* Kling, Williams, and Schlosberg (1959).

Schnur, A. C. (1961). "Current Practice in Correction: A Critique," in H. Toch (ed.), *Legal and Criminal Psychology.* New York: Holt, Rinehart. [557, 583]

Schuessler, K. F., and D. R. Cressey (1950). "Personality Characteristics of Criminals," *Amer. J. Sociol.,* **55,** 476–484. [519]

Schwarz, P. A. *See* Glaser, Schwarz, and Flanagan (1958).

Scodel, A., and J. S. Minos (1960). "The Behavior of Prisoners in a 'Prisoners Dilemma' Game," *J. Psychol.,* **50,** 133–138. [520]

Scolley, R. W. (1957). "Personal History Data As a Predictor of Success," *Personnel Psychol.,* **10,** 23–26. [215]

Scott, C. R. (1963). Personal communications. [97, 98, 102, 364]

Scott, J. P. (1957). "Comment," in H. D. Kruse (ed.), *Integrating the Approaches to Mental Disease.* New York: Hoeber-Harper. [50]

———— (1963). "The Process of Primary Socialization in Canine and Human Infants," *Monogr. Soc. Res. Child Develpm.,* **28** (Whole No. 85), 47. [96, 97, 102]

Scott, R. H. (1961). "The Youthful Offender: An Illustration of New Developments in Correction," in H. Toch (ed.), *Legal and Criminal Psychology.* New York: Holt, Rinehart. [576]

Scott, W. A. *See* Ebbs, Tisdall, and Scott (1942).

Scott, W. D. (1913). *The Psychology of Advertising.* Boston: Small, Maynard, and Company. [417, 418]

Scriven, L. E. (1958). "Rationality and Irrationality in Motivation Research," in R. Ferber and H. G. Wales, *Motivation and Market Behavior.* Homewood, Ill.: Richard D. Irwin. [435]

Searle, L. B., and F. V. Taylor (1948). "Studies of Tracking Behavior. I. Rate and Time Characteristics of Simple Corrective Movements," *J. Exp. Psychol.*, **38**, 615–631. [335]

Sears, R. *See* Dollard, Doob, Miller, Mower, and Sears (1939).

Selye, H. (1956). *The Stress of Life*. New York: McGraw-Hill. [67, 69, 80]

Seymour, W. D. (1959). "Training Operatives in Industry," *Ergonomics*, **2**, 143–147. [257]

Shacter, Helen. *See* Jenkins, Shacter, and Bauer (1953).

Sharpley, F. W. *See* Mann and Sharpley (1947).

Shelley, E. L. V., and W. F. Johnson (1961). "Evaluating an Organized Counseling Service for Youthful Offenders," *J. of Counseling Psychol.*, **8**, 4, 351–354. [577]

Shelley, E. L. V., and H. H. Toch (1962). "The Perception of Violence As an Indicator of Adjustments in Institutionalized Offenders." *J. of Criminal Law, Criminology and Police Science*, **53**, 4, 463–469. [594]

Sheppe, W. M. *See* Stevenson and Sheppe (1959).

Sherif, Carolyn. *See* Sherif and Sherif (1953).

Sherif, M., and Carolyn Sherif (1953). *Groups in Harmony and Tension*. New York: Harper. [453]

Sherman, P. A., W. Kerr, and W. Kosinar (1957). "A Study of Accidents in One Hundred Forty-seven Factories," *Personnel Psychol.*, **10**, 43–51. [307]

Shields, J., and E. Slater (1961). "Heredity and Psychological Abnormality," in H. J. Eysenck (ed.), *Handbook of Abnormal Psychology*. New York: Basic Books. [78]

Shillentad, I. J. *See* Kopstein and Shillentad (1962).

Shorr, E. *See* Ripley, Shorr, and Papanicolaou (1940).

Short, J. F. *See* Nye, Short, and Olson (1958).

Shock, N. W. *See* Birren and Shock (1950).

Silverman, R. E. (1959). "The Comparative Effectiveness of Animated and Static Transparencies," *J. Appl. Psychol.*, **43**, 16–20. [257]

Simmons, L. W. (1946). "Attitudes Towards Aging and the Aged: Primitive Societies," *J. Gerontol.*, **1**, 83. [177]

Simon, H. A. *See* Dearborn and Simon (1961).

Simon, J. R. *See* Chisman and Simon (1961).

Simonson, E. (1947). "Physical Fitness and Work Capacity of Older Men," *Gereatrics*, **2**, 110–119. [168, 335]

Simonson, E., W. M. Kearns, and N. Enzer (1944). "Effect of Methyltestosterone Treatment on Muscular Performance and the Central Nervous System of Older Men," *J. Clin. Endocrin.*, **4**, 528–534. [158]

Skinner, B. F. (1938). *The Behavior of Organisms. An Experimental Analysis*. New York: Appleton-Century. [4]

——— (1954). "The Science of Learning and the Art of Teaching," *Harv. Educ. Rev.*, **24**, 86–97. [15]

———. *See* Ferster and Skinner (1957).

———. *See* Holland and Skinner (1961).

Slater, E. *See* Shields and Slater (1961).

Slater-Hammel, A. T. *See* Brown and Slater-Hammel (1949).

Sleight, R. B. (1948). "The Effect of Instrument Dial Shape on Legibility," *J. Appl. Psychol.*, **32**, 170–188. [317]

Sloan, W., and J. W. Birch (1955). "A Rationale for Degrees of Retardation," *Amer. J. Ment. Defic.*, **60**, 258–264. [74]

Smith, A., and R. G. Record (1955). "Fertility and Reproductive History of Mothers of Mongoloid Defectives," *Brit. J. Prev. & Soc. Med.*, **9**, 51–55. [95]

Smith, G. H. (1954). *Motivation Research in Advertising and Marketing.* New York: McGraw-Hill. [433, 434]

Smith, H. C. (1947). "Music in Relation to Employee Attitudes, Work Production and Industrial Accidents," *Appl. Psychology Monogr.*, **14.** [284]

Smith, M. B. (1961). " 'Mental Health' Reconsidered: A Special Case of the Problem of Values in Psychology," *Amer. Psychologist*, **16**, 299–306. [45]

Smith, M. W. (1952). "Evidences of Potentialities of Older Workers in a Manufacturing Company," *Personnel Psychol.*, **5**, 11–18. [179]

Smith, Patricia C. (1953). "The Curve of Output As a Criterion of Boredom," *J. Appl. Psychol.*, **37**, 2, 69–74. [288, 292]

—————— (1955). "The Prediction of Individual Differences in Susceptibility in Industrial Monotony," *J. Appl. Psychol.*, **39**, 5, 322–339. [293]

Smith, Patricia C., and C. Lem (1955). "Positive Aspects of Motivation in Repetitive Work: Effects of Lot Size upon Spacing of Voluntary Work Stoppages," *J. Appl. Psychol.*, **39**, 330–333. [293, 294]

Smith, P. M. (1955). "Broken Homes and Juvenile Delinquency," *Sociology and Social Res.*, **39**, 307–311. [526]

Smith, W. I., and J. W. Moore (1962). *Programmed Learning: Theory and Research.* Princeton, N.J.: D. Van Nostrand. [14]

Smyth, P. *See* French, Ross, Kirby, Nelson, and Smyth (1958).

Snow, C. P. (1961). *Science and Government.* Cambridge: Harvard University Press. [449]

Snyder, L. H. *See* David and Snyder (1962).

Sontag, L. W. (1944). "War and Fetal Maternal Relationship," *Marriage Fam. Liv.*, **6**, 1–5. [94, 96]

Sorenson, H. (1930). "Adult Ages As a Factor in Learning," *J. Educ. Psychol.*, **21**, 451–459. [165]

—————— (1933). "Mental Ability over a Wide Range of Adult Ages," *J. Appl. Psychol.*, **17**, 729–741. [165]

Spitz, R. A. (1945). "Hospitalism: An Inquiry into the Genesis of Psychiatric Conditions in Early Childhood. Part I," *Psychoanal. Stud. Child*, **1**, 53–74; **2**, 113–117. [98]

Staats, A. W. *See* Staats and Staats (1957).

Staats, C. K., and A. W. Staats (1957). "Meaning Established by Classical Conditioning," *J. Exp. Psychol.*, **54**, 74–80. [529]

Steelways (1963). American Iron and Steel Institute, **19**, 2, 10–13. [304]

—————— (1964). American Iron and Steel Institute, **20**, 5. [199]

Steimel, R. J. (1960). "Childhood Experiences and Masculinity-Femininity Scores," *J. Counsel. Psychol.*, **7**, 212–217. [105]

Stessin, L. (1959). "Is the Arbitrator Your Friend?" *Supervisory Management Magazine*, **4**, 9–16. [375]

Stevenson, I., and W. M. Sheppe, Jr. (1959). "The Psychiatric Examination," in S. Arieti (ed.), *American Handbook of Psychiatry*, Vol. I. New York: Basic Books. [128]

Stewart, L. H. (1959). "Mother–Son Identification and Vocational Interest," *Genet. Psychol. Monogr.*, **60**, 31–63. [105]

Stieglitz, H. (1962). "Optimizing Span of Control," *National Industrial Conference Board, Management Record*, **24**, September. [346]

Stock, F. G. See Wyatt, Langdon, and Stock (1937).

Stone, G. See Ekman, Cohen, Moos, Raine, Schlesinger, and Stone (1963).

Stott, D. H. (1959). "Evidence for Prenatal Impairment of Temperament in Mentally Retarded Children," *Vita Humana*, **2**, 125–148. [94]

Strate, M. W. See Brayfield, Wells, and Strate (1957).

Strecker, E. A., F. G. Ebaugh, and J. R. Ewalt (1947). *Practical Clinical Psychiatry*. Philadelphia: Blakiston. [128]

Stryker, P. (1959). "The Rarest Man in Business," *Fortune Magazine*, **59**, 5, 119. [363]

Stuart, H. C. See Burke, Beal, Kirkwood, and Stuart (1943).

Sundberg, N. D., and Leona E. Tyler (1962). *Clinical Psychology: An Introduction to Research and Practice*. New York: Appleton-Century. [85, 124, 125, 128, 133]

Sutherland, E. H. (1939). *Principles of Criminology*. Philadelphia: Lippincott. [505]

Sweeney, J. S., A. W. Bailey, and J. F. Dowd (1957). "Comparative Evaluation of Three Approaches to Helicopter Instrumentation for Hovering Flight," *U. S. N. Research Laboratory Report*, 4954. [316]

Symonds, P. M. (1946). *The Dynamics of Human Adjustment*. New York: Appleton-Century. [60]

Taaffe, A. A. See Baxter, Taaffe, and Hughes (1953).

Tarjan, G. (1961). "Studies of Organic Etiologic Factors," in G. Caplan (ed.), *Prevention of Mental Disorders in Children*. New York: Basic Books. [92]

Taylor, F. V. See Searle & and Taylor (1948).

———— (1960). "Four Basic Ideas in Engineering Psychology," *Amer. Psychologist*, **15**, 643–649. [316, 318, 319]

Taylor, F. V., and W. D. Garvey (1959). "The Limitations of a 'Procrustean' Approach to the Optimization of Man-Machine Systems," *Ergonomics*, **2**, 187–194 [257]

Taylor, F. W. (1911). *The Principles of Scientific Management*. New York: Harper. [289]

Terman, L. M., and M. A. Merrill (1960). *Stanford–Binet Intelligence Scale: Manual for 3rd Rev.*, Form L–M Boston: Houghton Mifflin. [129]

Thomson, A. M. See Anderson, Baird, and Thomson (1958).

Thorndike, E. L. (1928). *Adult Learning*. New York: Macmillan. [164]

Thorpe, L. P., and B. Katz (1948). *The Psychology of Abnormal Behavior*. New York: Ronald. [69]

Thumin, F. J. (1962). "What Psychologists Should Know About Marketing and Advertising Research," *J. Psychol.*, **53**, 329–347. [415]

Tinker, M. A. (1947). "Illumination Standards for Effective and Easy Seeing," *Psychol. Bull.*, **44**, 435–450. [268]

————. See Boice, Tinker, and Patterson (1948).

Tisdall, F. F.   *See* Ebbs, Tisdall, and Scott (1942).

Toch, H. H.   *See* Shelley and Toch (1962).

Togo, A. M.   *See* Kutner, Faushel, Togo, and Langner (1956).

Tompkins, W. T., and D. G. Wiehl (1954). "Deprivation and Stress in Pregnancy and Child Bearing," in I. Galdston (ed.), *Beyond the Germ Theory.* New York: Health Education Council. [94]

Tresselt, M. E.   *See* Fensterheim and Tresselt (1953).

Tufts, Edith.   *See* Witmer and Tufts (1954).

Tyler, B. V.   *See* Campbell and Tyler (1957).

Tyler, Leona E.   *See* Sundberg and Tyler (1962).

Underwood, B. J. (1961). "Ten Years of Massed Practice on Distributed Practice," *Psychol. Rev.,* **68,** 229–247. [17, 18]

Uhrbrock, R. S. (1961). "Music on the Job: Its Influence on Worker Morale and Production," *Personnel Psychol.,* **14,** 9, 9–38. [324]

United States Department of Defense (1955). *Foreign Relations of the United States: The Conferences at Malta and Yalta, 1945.* [469]

United States Department of Labor (1939). *Dictionary of Occupational Titles, Part I and Supplements, Part II and IV.* Washington, D.C.: United States Government Printing Office. [200]

United States Department of State (1961). "United States and Soviet Union Agree on Statement of Principles for Disarmament Negotiations," *United States Department of State Bulletin,* **45,** 589–596. [479]

Updegraff, R.   *See* Keister and Updegraff (1937).

Urban, H. B.   *See* Ford and Urban (1963).

Vernon, H. M. (1926). *Survey of Industrial Relations.* His Majesty's Stationery Office, 174. [285]

——— (1937). *Accidents and Their Prevention.* New York: Macmillan. [307]

Viteles, M. S. (1932). *Industrial Psychology.* New York: Norton. [281]

Vitola, B. N.   *See* Carp, Vitola, and McLanathan (1963).

Voss, H. L. (1963). "The Predictive Efficiency of the Glueck Social Prediction Table," *J. of Criminal Law, Criminology and Police Science,* **54,** 4, 421–430. [593]

Vroom, V. H. (1959). "Some Personality Determinants of the Effects of Participation," *J. Abnorm. Soc. Psychol.,* **59,** 322–327. [359]

Wallin, R., and R. Riley (1950). "Reactions of Mothers to Pregnancy and Adjustment of Offspring in Infancy," *Amer. J. Orthopsychiat.,* **20,** 616–622. [94, 96]

Walters, R. H.   *See* Bandura, and Walters (1963).

Watson, G. (1939). "Work satisfaction," in G. W. Hartmann and T. Newcomb (eds.), *Industrial conflict.* New York: Cordon. [292]

Watson, J. B. (1932). Foreword in H. C. Link (ed.), *The New Psychology of Selling and Advertising.* New York: Macmillan. [419]

Watson, R.   *See* McCaldwell and Watson (1952).

Watson, R. I. (1959). *Psychology of the Child.* New York: Wiley. [99]

Wechsler, D. (1949). *Wechsler Intelligence Scale for Children.* New York: The Psychological Corporation. [129]

——— (1955). *Manual for the Wechsler Adult Intelligence Scale.* New York: The Psychological Corporation. [129]

Weekers, R., and F. Roussel (1946). "Introduction à l'étude de la fréquencée de fusion en clinique," *Ophthalmologica*, **112**, 305–319. [158]

Weil, G. *See* Metzner and Weil (1963).

Weinland, J. D. (1930). "How Successful College Students Study," *J. Educ. Psychol.*, **21**, 521–526. [12]

Weiser, C. M. *See* Brown and Weiser (1958).

Weiss, A. D. (1959). "Sensory Functions," in J. E. Birren (ed.), *Handbook of Aging and the Individual*. Chicago: University of Chicago Press. [158, 159]

Weld, H. P., and M. Roff (1938). "A Study of the Formation of Opinion Based upon Legal Evidence," *Amer. J. Psychol.*, **51**, 607–629. [542]

Weld, H. P., and E. R. Danzig (1940). "A Study of the Way in Which a Verdict Is Reached by a Jury," *Amer. J. Psychol.*, **53**, 518–536. [542]

Welford, A. T. (1950). *Skill and Age*. London: Oxford University Press.

———— (1959). In J. E. Birren (ed.), *Handbook of Aging and the Individual*. Chicago: Chicago University Press. [160]

Wells, R. V. *See* Brayfield, Wells, and Strate (1957).

Welsh, G. S. *See* Dahlstrom and Welsh (1960).

Werner, H. (1948). *Comparative Psychology of Mental Development* (Rev. ed.). Chicago: Follett. [87]

Weschler, I. R. *See* Tannenbaum, Kallejian, and Weschler (1954).

Weston, H. C., and S. Adams (1935). *The Performance of Weavers Under Varying Conditions of Noise*. Great Britain: Industrial Health Research Board, Rep. 70. [275]

White, R. K. *See* Lewin, Lippitt, and White (1939).

Whittier, H. B. *See* Zuckerman, Barron, and Whittier (1953).

Whyte, W. H. J. (1956). *The Organization Man*. New York: Simon and Shuster. [342]

Whyte, W. S. (1952). "Economic Incentive and Human Relations," *Harvard Bus. Rev.*, **30**, 73–79. [393]

Wiehl, D. G. *See* Tompkins and Wiehl (1954).

Wiesner, J. B. (1962). "Strengthening the Behavioral Sciences," *Science*, **136**, 233–241. University of Chicago Press. [450]

Williams, C. M. *See* Lysdaught and Williams (1963).

Williams, J. P. *See* Kling, Williams, and Schlosberg (1959).

Williams, Judith R. *See* Clausen and Williams (1963).

Williams, R. H. (1953). *Psychiatric Rehabilitation in the Hospital*. Public Health Reports, 68. Revised 1955, Public Health Reports, Reprint No. 3223. [146]

———— . *See* Greenblatt, Levinson, and Williams (1957).

———— (ed.) (1962). *The Prevention of Disability in Mental Disorders*. Mental Health Monograph 1, Washington, D.C.: United States Department Health, Education, and Welfare. Public Service Publication No. 924. [142]

Williams, R. M., Jr. (1947). *The Reduction of Intergroup Tensions*. Soc. Sci. Res. Council Bull., No. 57. New York: Social Science Research Council. [452]

Willing, J. Z. (1962). "The Round-table Interview—A Method of Selecting Trainees," *Personnel*, **39**, 2, 26–32. [219]

Wilson, D. P. (1951). *My Six Convicts.* New York: Holt, Rinehart. [508]

Wilson, R. F. *See* Lawshe and Wilson (1946).

Winick, C. (1961). "The Drug Addict and His Treatment," in H. Toch (ed.), *Legal and Criminal Psychology.* New York: Holt, Rinehart. [532]

Witmer, Helen L., and Edith Tufts (1954). *The Effectiveness of Delinquency Prevention Programs.* Washington, D.C.: United States Department of Health, Education, and Welfare. Children's Bureau Publication No. 350. [590]

Wittenborn, J. R. (1955). *Psychiatric Rating Scales.* New York: The Psychological Corporation. [130]

Wolff, H. G. *See* Hardy, Wolff, and Goodell (1943).

———. *See* Wolf and Wolff (1946).

Wolf, S., and H. G. Wolff (1946). "Psychosomatic Aspects of Peptic Ulcers," *Scope,* **2,** 4–9. [71]

Wolpe, J. (1958). *Psychotherapy by Reciprocal Inhibition.* Stanford: Stanford University Press. [138]

Wood, W. F. (1947). "A New Method for Reading the Employment Questionnaire," *J. Appl. Psychol.,* **31,** 9–17. [211]

Woods, H. M. *See* Greenwood and Woods (1919).

Woodson, W. E. (1954). *Human Engineering Guide for Equipment Designers.* Berkeley: University of Calif. Press. [271]

Woodyard, Ella. *See* Harrell, Woodyard, and Gates (1955).

Wyatt, S. (1929–30). "Fatigue and Worker Efficiency," *Personnel J.,* **8,** 161–171. [291]

Wyatt, S., J. N. Langdon, and F. G. L. Stock (1937). *Fatigue and Boredom in Repetitive Work.* Great Britain: Industrial Health Research Board, Report 77. [291]

Zerfoss, L. F. *See* Maier and Zerfoss (1952).

Zilboorg, G., and G. W. Henry (1941). *A History of Medical Psychology.* New York: Norton. [42]

Zola, I. K. *See* McCord, McCord, and Zola (1959).

Zuckerman, S. B., A. J. Barron, and H. B. Whittier (1953). "A Follow-up Study of Minnesota State Reformatory Inmates," *J. of Criminal Law, Criminology and Police Science,* **43,** 5, 622–636. [575]

Subject Index

Prenatal
　care, 114, 118
　factors influencing adjustment, 95,
　　　96
　factors in mental illness, 78, 93
　factors, table, 94
　influences, 79, 82
Prevention
　of crime, 571-94
　of mental illness, 40-41, 49, 51, 52,
　　　80-81, 85, 89-92, 96, 114,
　　　117-19, 123, 143
　see also Rehabilitation
Probation, 558-59
Problem-centered approach, 418
Problem-solving, *see* Coping
Product testing, 439
Production, factors affecting, 264-305
　atmospheric conditions, 279-83
　　adverse conditions, 282-83
　hours of work, 284-86
　illumination, 264-73
　music, 283-84
　nature of the task, 290-95
　noise, 273-79
　　adaptation, 274
　　habituation, 274-75
　　performance decrement resulting
　　　from, 275-76
　　protection against, 276-79
　pay, 295-96
　　fringe benefits, 304
　　job evaluation, 296-304
　　profit sharing, 304
　rest pauses, 287-90
　time of day, 286-87
Profit sharing, 304
Programed learning, 14
Projection, 63, 65, 82
　assimilative, 63, 66
　disowning, 63, 65
　see also Adjustment reactions
Projective method of testing, 64; *see
　　　also* Assessment; Blacky pic-
　　　tures; Rorschach; Tests;
　　　Thematic Apperception Test
Psychiatric aides, 144
Psychiatrist, 80, 117, 123, 127, 133,
　　　150
Psychoanalysis, 50; *see also* Freud; Psy-
　　　chotherapy
Psychodrama, *see* Psychotherapy

Psychological differences measure-
　　　ment, 202-203
Psychologist
　clinical, 117, 123, 127, 128, 133
　counseling, 117, 123
　school, 117
Psychology, 3
Psychoneurosis, 42, 70-71, 74, 82, 117
Psychosis, 70, 71, 74, 82, 117
　functional, 73-74
　involutional, 77
Psychosomatic disorders, 43, 71, 72, 78
Psychotherapy, 50, 80, 117-18, 123,
　　　124
　aims, 132
　client-centered, 135-36
　criticisms of, 138-39
　eclectic, 136
　group, 43, 117, 133, 136, 143
　individual, 117
　play therapy, 136-37
　in prisons, 569, 579
　psychoanalysis, 135
　psychodrama, 136
　types, 133
　see also Psychoanalysis
　see also Therapy
　see also Treatment
Publicity, 415
Punishment, 100-102, 105-107, 109
Purdue Peg Board, 228

Qualitative symbolic display, 328
Quality, 273-74
Quantitative symbolic displays, 330-31
Questionnaire construction, 427
Questionnaires, 418
Quickening, 336-37

Radio Research: Program analyzer,
　　　421
Ranking method of job evaluation,
　　　298; *see also* Job evaluation
Rank-order rating technique, 193-94;
　　see also Rating techniques
Rapport, 217-18
Rater bias, 193
Rating, *see* Mental status rating
Rating, scale, 130
Rating techniques, 192-98, 418
　critical incident technique, 198
　descriptive phrases, 193
　forced choice, 197-98
　forced distribution, 195